D1238126

HENRY JAMES: THE CRITICAL HERITAGE

THE CRITICAL HERITAGE SERIES

GENERAL EDITOR: B. C. SOUTHAM, M.A., B.LITT. (OXON.)
Formerly Department of English, Westfield College, University of London

Volumes in the series include

JANE AUSTEN   B. C. Southam

BYRON   Andrew Rutherford,
                 University of Aberdeen

DICKENS   Philip Collins,
                 University of Leicester

HENRY FIELDING   R. Paulson,
                 The Johns Hopkins University, Baltimore
                 and Thomas Lakewood,
                 University of Washington

HENRY JAMES   Roger Gard,
                 Queen Mary College, London

TENNYSON   J. D. Jump,
                 University of Manchester

THACKERAY   Geoffrey Tillotson and Donald Hawes,
                 Birkbeck College, London

TROLLOPE   Donald Smalley,
                 University of Illinois

HENRY JAMES

THE CRITICAL HERITAGE

Edited by

ROGER GARD

Queen Mary College, University of London

LONDON: ROUTLEDGE & KEGAN PAUL

NEW YORK: BARNES & NOBLE INC

Published 1968
in Great Britain
by Routledge & Kegan Paul Limited
and in the United States of America
by Barnes & Noble Inc.

© Roger Gard 1968

SBN 7100 6068 8

Printed in Great Britain
by W & J Mackay & Co Ltd, Chatham

General Editor's Preface

The reception given to a writer by his contemporaries and near-contemporaries is evidence of considerable value to the student of literature. On one side, we learn a great deal about the state of criticism at large and in particular about the development of critical attitudes towards a single writer; at the same time, through private comments in letters, journals or marginalia, we gain an insight upon the tastes and literary thought of individual readers of the period. Evidence of this kind helps us to understand the writer's historical situation, the nature of his immediate reading-public, and his response to these pressures.

The separate volumes in *The Critical Heritage Series* present a record of this early criticism. Clearly, for many of the highly-productive and lengthily-reviewed nineteenth and twentieth-century writers, there exists an enormous body of material; and in these cases the volume editors have made a selection of the most important views, significant for their intrinsic critical worth or for their representative quality.

For writers of the eighteenth century and earlier, the materials are much scarcer and the historical period has been extended, sometimes far beyond the writer's lifetime, in order to show the inception and growth of critical views which were initially slow to appear.

In each volume the documents are headed by an Introduction, discussing the material assembled and relating the early stages of the author's reception to what we have come to identify as the critical tradition. The volumes will make available much material which would otherwise be difficult of access and it is hoped that the modern reader will be thereby helped towards an informed understanding of the ways in which literature has been read and judged.

B.C.S.

to

NORMAN CALLAN

Contents

ACKNOWLEDGEMENTS   *page* xx

INTRODUCTION   I

NOTE ON THE ARRANGEMENT OF HEADNOTES ETC.   19

1 W. D. HOWELLS on the young James, December 1866   21
2 W. D. HOWELLS on James's public, August 1867   21
3 James on his ambition as an American writer, September 1867   22
4 WILLIAM JAMES on the early stories, March 1868   24
5 WILLIAM JAMES on the early stories, April 1868   26
6 James on not pandering to the multitude, August 1872   27
7 WILLIAM JAMES on the early style, November 1872   28

'The Madonna of the Future' (1873)

8 W. D. HOWELLS, letter, March 1873   29

9 James on criticism, March 1873   30

A Passionate Pilgrim, and Other Tales (1875)

10 Unsigned review, *Atlantic Monthly*, April 1875   31

Roderick Hudson (1875)

11 Unsigned review, *Atlantic*, February 1876   35
12 Unsigned review, *North American Review*, April 1876   39

The American (1877)

13 James on the ending of the novel, March 1877   43
14 GEORGE SAINTSBURY, review, *Academy*, July 1877   45
15 Unsigned review, *Scribner's Monthly*, July 1877   47

The Europeans (1878)

16 R. H. HUTTON, review, *Spectator*, October, 1878   49

CONTENTS

17 Unsigned review, *Athenaeum*, October 1878   *page* 53
18 W. E. HENLEY, review, *Academy*, October 1878   54

The Europeans and Daisy Miller (1878)

19 RICHARD GRANT WHITE, review, *North American*,
    January 1879   56

The Europeans

20 Unsigned review, *Scribner's Monthly*, January 1879   62
21 Unsigned review, *Appleton's Journal*, January 1879   63
22 Unsigned review, *Eclectic Magazine*, January 1879   65
23 CONSTANCE FENIMORE WOOLSON, review, *Atlantic*,
    January 1879   66
24 Editor's Literary Record, *Harper's New Monthly
    Magazine*, January 1879   70
25 Unsigned review, *Atlantic*, February 1879   71

26 W. D. HOWELLS on the *Daisy Miller* scandal,
    June 1879   74

Roderick Hudson (English edition 1879)

27 R. H. HUTTON, review, *Spectator*, July 1879   75
28 Unsigned review, *British Quarterly Review*,
    October 1879   78

29 James on his progress in England, May 1879   79

'An International Episode' (1878)

30 Unsigned review, *Blackwood's Magazine*, July 1879   80

Confidence (1879)

31 Unsigned review, *Spectator*, January 1880   83

32 James on the American public, February 1880   87
33 James on the decline of letters, February 1881   87

Washington Square (1880)

34 R. H. HUTTON, review, *Spectator*, February 1881   88
35 Unsigned review, *Literary World*, January 1881   91
36 Unsigned review, *Atlantic*, May 1881   92

CONTENTS

The Portrait of a Lady (1881)

37 Unsigned review, *Spectator*, November 1881   *page* 93

38 Unsigned review, *Athenaeum*, November 1881   97

39 Unsigned review, *Saturday Review*, December 1881   98

40 Unsigned review, *Blackwood's Magazine*, March 1882   101

41 Unsigned review, *Literary World*, December 1881   105

42 Unsigned review, *Critic*, December 1881   107

43 H. E. SCUDDER, from a review, *Atlantic*,
   January 1882   109

44 H. A. HUNTINGTON, from a review, *Dial*,
   January 1882   111

45 Unsigned review, *Nation*, February 1882   113

46 Unsigned review, *Lippincott's Magazine*,
   February 1882   118

47 MRS. HENRY ADAMS, letter, December 1881   120

48 HENRY ADAMS, letter, January 1882   120

49 A *Literary World* contributor's protest against the
   American reception of James, January 1882   121

50 PROFESSOR JOHN NICHOL on James as a minor
   novelist, 1882   124

51 W. D. HOWELLS on James as *the* modern
   novelist, *Century*, November 1882   126

52 An indignant rejoinder to Howells from the
   Quarterly Review, January 1883   135

53 JOHN HAY on James as the prey of patriotism,
   December 1882   139

54 JULIAN HAWTHORNE on James as the non-heroic
   realist, *Princeton Review*, January 1884   140

55 James on the desperate state of Anglo-Saxon
   letters, February 1884   142

56 EDGAR FAWCETT on *The Portrait of a Lady*,
   Princeton Review, July 1884   144

'A New England Winter' (1884)

57 W. D. HOWELLS, letter, August 1884   148

58 James on the state of criticism, September 1884   149

Tales of Three Cities (1884)

59   'M.L.H.' from a review, *Literary World*,
       September 1884   *page* 150
60   Unsigned review, *Nation*, November 1884   152
61   WILLIAM MORTON PAYNE, from a review, *Dial*,
       December 1884   153

The Author of 'Beltraffio', etc. (1885)

62   Unsigned review, *Critic*, May 1885   154

63   GERTRUDE ATHERTON on the Henry James
       craze [1932]   155
64   MARK TWAIN on other modern novelists, July 1885   156

The Princess Casamassima (Serialisation 1885)

65   MRS. ROBERT LOUIS STEVENSON, letter, August or
       September, 1885   157

The Bostonians (1886)

66   James explains his difficulties and disappointments,
       October 1885   158
67   WILLIAM JAMES on re-reading *The Bostonians*,
       May 1886   159
68   James on the faults of *The Bostonians*, June 1886   161
69   R. H. HUTTON, review, *Spectator*, March 1886   162
70   Unsigned review, *Nation*, May 1886   164
71   Unsigned review, *Literary World*, June 1886   165
72   H. E. SCUDDER, from a review, *Atlantic*, June 1886   166

73   HENRY SIDGWICK on Howells and James,
       August 1886   169
74   GEORGE MOORE on James's Limitations, 1886   170

The Princess Casamassima (1886)

75   JULIA WEDGWOOD, from a review, *Contemporary
       Review*, December 1886   173
76   R. H. HUTTON, review, *Spectator*, January 1887   175
77   'H.B.' from 'London Letter', *Critic*, December 1886   179
78   Unsigned review, *Nation*, February 1887   180

79   James on his evil days, January 1888   182
80   James on criticism, July 1888   184

CONTENTS

The Reverberator (1888)

81 R. H. HUTTON, review, *Spectator*, August 1888   *page* 185

81a THOMAS HARDY on James's small perfection,
      July 1888   186
82 ROBERT BUCHANAN on James as a 'superfine young'
      critic, March 1889   187
83 WILLIAM WATSON on James as an anaemic novelist,
      October 1889   190

A London Life (1889)

84 Unsigned review, *Spectator*, August 1889   192

The Tragic Muse (1890)

85 WILLIAM JAMES, letter, June 1890   193
86 James on his public, July 1890   194
87 Unsigned review, *Athenaeum*, July 1890   195
88 Unsigned review, *Saturday*, August 1890   197
89 Unsigned review, *Scots Observer*, August 1890   198
90 Unsigned review, *Graphic*, August 1890   200
91 GEORGE SAINTSBURY, review, *Academy*, August 1890   201
92 Unsigned review, *Murray's Magazine*, September 1890   203
93 Unsigned review, *Spectator*, September 1890   204
94 Unsigned review, *Dublin Review*, October 1890   206
95 Unsigned note, *Critic*, May 1890   207
96 Unsigned review, *Literary World*, July 1890   208
97 Unsigned review, *Dial*, August 1890   209
98 W. D. HOWELLS, from the 'Editor's Study', *Harper's*,
      September 1890   210
99 H. E. SCUDDER, review, *Atlantic*, September 1890   213
100 Unsigned review, *Nation*, December 1890   218
101 W. D. HOWELLS on the reception of *The Tragic
      Muse*, September 1890   220

102 Unsigned article, 'Mr Henry James', *Murray's*,
      November 1891   221

103 ANDREW LANG's parodistic allusion to *Daisy
      Miller*, 1892   234

xiii

The Lesson of the Master (1892)

104   Unsigned review, *Nation*, April 1892   *page* 237

105   VERNON LEE's ambiguous portrait of James in
           'Lady Tal', *Vanitas*, 1892   238

The Wheel of Time (1893) and *The Private Life* (1893)

106   Unsigned review, *Nation*, November 1893   243

107   FRANK HARRIS on 'Max' and senseless abortions of
           mediocrity [1924]   245
108   NORMAN HAPGOOD on James's refinement and
           limitations, 1898   246
109   James on his evil days and his future, January 1895   254
110   LENA MILMAN's tribute in *The Yellow Book*,
           October 1895   256
111   EDWIN ARLINGTON ROBINSON on James's
           surprising genius, February 1896   258

Embarrassments (1896)

112   Unsigned review, *Spectator*, August 1896   259

The Other House (1896)

113   Unsigned review, *Saturday*, October 1896   261
114   Unsigned review, *Critic*, November 1896   263

115   STOPFORD BROOKE on James's style, August 1897   263
116   D. C. MURRAY on his listless contemporary, 1897   264

The Spoils of Poynton (1897)

117   Unsigned review, *Academy*, February 1897   266
118   Unsigned review, *Bookman*, May 1897   267
119   JOSEPH CONRAD, letter, 1897   268

What Maisie Knew (1897)

120 Unsigned review, *Academy*, (Fiction Supplement)
  October 1897 *page* 269
121 Unsigned review, *Spectator*, October 1897 270
122 Unsigned review, *Literary World*, December 1897 272

In the Cage (1898) and *The Two Magics* (1898)

123 Unsigned review, *Athenaeum*, October 1898 274
124 Unsigned review, *Critic*, December 1898 276

'The Turn of the Screw' (1898)

125 OSCAR WILDE, letter, 1899 277

126 HENRY HARLAND on James's wonderful
  temperament, November 1898 278
127 JOSEPH CONRAD's defence of James as the most
  civilized of writers, February 1899 279
128 James on his detachment from the public, May 1899 281

The Awkward Age (1899)

129 Unsigned review, *Spectator*, May 1899 282
130 Unsigned review, *Literature*, May 1899 283
131 Unsigned review, *Saturday*, May 1899 285
132 Unsigned review, *Academy*, May 1899 286
133 Unsigned review, *Athenaeum*, May 1899 289
134 WILLIAM MORTON PAYNE, review, *Dial*, July 1899 291
135 Unsigned review, *Bookman* (America) July 1899 292
136 Unsigned review, *Literary World*, July 1899 294
137 Unsigned review, *Critic*, August 1899 295
138 Unsigned review, *Nation*, August 1899 298
139 Unsigned review, *Sewanee Review*, January 1900 299

140 DESMOND MACCARTHY on James's isolation [1931] 300
141 EDMUND GOSSE on *The Awkward Age* and the
  emergence of James's 'little clan' [1922] 302
142 A. C. BENSON on James's pessimistic view of English
  Art [1926] 303

CONTENTS

143 James on the condition of criticism and his own
     style, January 1900   *page* 304
144 WILLIAM ROTHENSTEIN on James as Grand
     Old Man [1932]   305

The Sacred Fount (1901)

145 Unsigned review, *Spectator*, March 1901   306
146 CORNELIA ATWOOD PRATT, from a review,
     Critic, April 1901   307
147 HARRY THURSTON PECK, from a review, *Bookman*
     (America), July 1901   308
148 OWEN SEAMAN's parody of *The Sacred Fount*, 1902   309

The Wings of the Dove (1902)

149 WILLIAM JAMES on the perverse success of *The
     Wings of the Dove*, October 1902   317
150 James on the inevitability of his later style,
     November 1902   318
151 Unsigned review, *Times Literary Supplement*,
     September 1902   319
152 Unsigned review, *Saturday*, January 1903   322
153 James on Howells's praise for *The Wings of the Dove*,
     on his indifference to the public, and on *The
     Sacred Fount*, December 1902   324
154 J. P. MOWBRAY on *The Wings of the Dove*, and
     James's effeminacy, November 1902   326
155 HARRIET WATERS PRESTON on *The Wings of
     the Dove*, January 1903   332

156 F. M. COLBY on James's bloodless perversity,
     June 1902   335
157 F. M. COLBY on James's slight improvement in
     The Wings of the Dove, November 1902   339
158 EDITH WHARTON on the later James and his
     sensitivity [1934]   342
159 The *Edinburgh Review* on James's achievements,
     January 1903   345
160 OLIVER ELTON on *The Wings of the Dove*, and the
     greatness of James, October 1903   349

The Ambassadors (1903)

161 FREDERICK TABER COOPER, from a review,
Bookman (America) January 1904 *page* 359

162 GERTRUDE ATHERTON on discovering later James
[1932] 361

163 Gertrude Atherton's fictional tribute in *The Bell in the Fog*, 1904 363

164 SYDNEY WATERLOW on James as the subtlest and
strongest modern writer, November 1904 365

165 ARNOLD BENNETT on not finishing *The Ambassadors*,
January 1905 373

The Golden Bowl (1904)

166 Unsigned review, *Times Literary Supplement*,
February 1905 374

167 Unsigned review, *Academy*, February 1905 376

168 Unsigned review, *Illustrated London News*,
February 1905 378

169 Unsigned review, *Graphic*, March 1905 379

170 Unsigned review, *Athenaeum*, March 1905 380

171 Unsigned review, *Saturday*, March 1905 381

172 Unsigned review, *Nation*, January 1905 385

173 CLAUDE BRAGDON, from a review, *Critic*,
January 1905 389

174 Unsigned review, *Bookman* (America), January, 1905 391

175 WILLIAM JAMES on the perverse success of *The
Golden Bowl* and the desirability of an easier
'fourth manner', October 1905 392

176 James on his intellectual separation from his brother,
and the latter's crudity as a literary critic,
November 1905 393

177 W. C. BROWNELL on James's position in literature,
Atlantic, April 1905 395

178 SIR ALMERIC FITZROY on the hermit of Rye,
January 1906 429

179 WILLIAM JAMES on the greatness of *The
American Scene* and the rumness of the late
style, May 1907 430

CONTENTS

180   H. G. DWIGHT on American hostility to James,
          and its probable causes, May and July 1907   *page* 432
181   W. A. GILL on James's similarity to Marivaux,
          October 1907   450
182   JOHN BAILEY on *The Portrait of a Lady*, July 1908   463
183   HUGH WALPOLE'S fictional reminiscence of the
          later James and his reputation in 'Mr Oddy' [1933]   464
184   W. D. HOWELLS on the 'wonder' of *The Tragic
          Muse*, December 1909   478
185   W. D. HOWELLS on the greatness of *The
          Bostonians*, February 1910   479
186   VERNON LEE on the handling of words in
          The Ambassadors, June 1910   480

The Finer Grain (1910)

187   ARNOLD BENNETT on James's tedious perfection,
          October 1910   488

188   CLARA F. MCINTYRE on James's late style in the
          light of his revisions for the New York
          edition, 1912   491
189   M. STURGE GRETTON on James's later development
          in the light of the Prefaces to the New York
          edition, January 1912   503
190   MURIEL DRAPER on James's cultured admirers [1929]   513
191   THEODORA BOSANQUET on James and his
          readers [1924]   515
192   H. G. WELLS'S attack and parody in *Boon*, 1915   517
193   James on *Boon*, July 1915   527
194   James on Well's apology for *Boon*, July 1915   529
195   James on the New York edition, on *The
          Bostonians*, and on the destruction of the
          'plates' of his novels, August 1915   531
196   ANTHONY HOPE on James as man and writer,
          February 1916   533
197   MRS HUMPHRY WARD on James as a great man
          and a great master, 1918   534
198   HENRY NEWBOLT on James's amusing lack of
          talent, April 1920   538

CONTENTS

199   W. D. HOWELLS on American unkindness to James,
        May 1920   *page* 539

APPENDIX I THE CHIEF OMISSIONS FROM THIS
COLLECTION   540

APPENDIX II JAMES'S SALES   545

INDEX   559

I wish to thank the following for permission to reprint copyright extracts or complete items from the sources listed below:

George Allen and Unwin Ltd. for Amy Cruse, *After the Victorians*; *The Atlantic Monthly* for articles by W. C. Brownell, W. A. Gill, W. D. Howells, H. W. Preston, H. E. Scudder, and C. F. Woolson; The Belknap Press of Harvard University for *Mark Twain—Howells Letters 1872–1910*, ed. H. N. Smith and W. M. Gibson; The Bodley Head Ltd. for Vernon Lee, *Vanitas*; Cassell & Co. Ltd. for Edmund Gosse, *Aspects and Impressions*; Constable and Co. Ltd. for *Letters of Henry Adams 1858–1891*, ed. W. C. Ford, and Edith Wharton, *A Backward Glance*; the copyright owners of George Moore for George Moore, *Confessions of a Young Man*; Curtis Brown Ltd. for Gertrude Atherton, *Adventures of a Novelist*, and Almeric Fitzroy, *Memoirs of Sir Almeric Fitzroy*; Doubleday and Co. Inc. and the owner of the copyright for *The Journals of Arnold Bennett*, ed. Newman Flower; Duke University Press for Virginia Harlow, *Thomas Sergeant Perry: A Biography and Letters to Perry from William, Henry, and Garth Wilkinson James*; The Executors of H. G. Wells for H. G. Wells, *Boon*; John Grigg, Esq. for articles by William Watson in the *National Review* and Vernon Lee in the *English Review*; Harper & Row, Inc. for an article by W. D. Howells in *Harper's New Monthly Magazine*; Rupert Hart-Davis, Esq. for Hugh Walpole, 'Mr. Oddy' in *All Soul's Night*; Harvard University Press for *Untriangulated Stars: The Letters of Edwin Arlington Robinson to Harry de Forest Smith*, ed. Denham Sutcliffe; William Heinemann Ltd. for G. Jean Aubry, *Joseph Conrad, Life and Letters*; the heirs of Mildred Howells for *Life in Letters of William Dean Howells*, ed. Mildred Howells; The Hogarth Press Ltd. for Theodora Bosanquet, *Henry James at Work*; Houghton Mifflin Company for *Letters of Henry Adams 1858–1891*, ed. W. C. Ford; John James, Esq. for letters by William and Henry James which were published for the first time in F. O. Matthiessen, *The James Family*; MacGibbon & Kee Ltd. for Desmond MacCarthy, *Portraits*; Macmillan & Co. Ltd. for Gertrude Atherton,

The Bell in the Fog and F. E. Hardy, *The Early Life of Thomas Hardy 1840–1891* (reprinted in 1962 in *The Life of Thomas Hardy 1840–1928*); The Master and Fellows of Magdalene College, Cambridge for *The Diary of Arthur Christopher Benson*, ed. Percy Lubbock: Methuen & Co. Ltd. for E. V. Lucas, *The Colvins and their Friends*; The Modern Language Association of America for an article by Clara F. McIntyre in *Publications of the Modern Language Association of America*; John Murray Ltd. for *John Bailey 1864–1931. Letters and Diaries edited by his Wife*, and *Life and Letters of Stopford Brooke*, ed. L. P. Jacks; The *New Statesman* for an article by S. P. Waterlow; the owner of the copyright for *The Later Life and Letters of Sir Henry Newbolt*, ed. Margaret Newbolt; *Punch* for a parody by Owen Seaman; *The Quarterly Review* for an article by Oliver Elton; Arthur Leonard Ross, Esq. for Frank Harris, *Contemporary Portraits, Series IV*; Sir John Rothenstein and Michael Rothenstein, Esq. for William Rothenstein, *Men and Memories*; and George L. Saintsbury, Esq. for articles in the *Academy* by George Saintsbury; and Robert H. Tener for generously making available the results of his work on R. H. Hutton and the *Spectator*.

I would further like to thank Macmillan & Co. Ltd. for their kind permission to publish some details of the sales of James and others from their records; and finally—less formal but certainly not less important debts—Dr. F. R. Leavis, Dr. M. K. Tanner, Mr. Morris Shapira, Mr. J. M. Newton, and my wife for various kinds of help at various times.

R.G.

Introduction

The purpose of this book is to enable the student of James to read and judge for himself the contemporary response to the novels, and to gauge its probable effects on the novelist's remarkable development. That there is a need for fairly exhaustive documentation of this subject is largely due to the tendency we all have to distort when we generalize. There is a widespread, and correct, general notion that James's relations with his public were not happy. He himself repeatedly tells us as much. But the details are not well known. It is, for example, surely regrettable that rival authorities can offer widely differing accounts of his whole career. Thus the American scholar G. H. Ford characterizes the reception as consisting of 'much early misunderstanding, the growth of a fit audience, though few, and a gradual recognition'; but Sidney Colvin, an acquaintance of James's and much nearer to events, wrote in 1924 that 'the early tales and novels . . . (were) received with keen appreciation by at least the critical portion of the public, and the work of his latter years with relative and at last almost complete neglect'. Neither of these is really right, though neither completely wrong. And they are typical.

But the problem in trying to substitute an accurate picture is one of selection. By the latter half of the nineteenth century a vast amount of periodical comment on literature was being produced—probably even more than there is today. In reviewing this for publication nothing would have been easier than to choose the relatively small number of outstanding articles and to let them stand for the rest. But this would, I think, have been misleading. It would not, for example, have given the reader a sense of what James was referring to when he wrote in 1891 in the essay 'Criticism': 'The bewildered spirit may ask itself, without speedy answer, What is the function in the life of man of such a periodicity of platitude and irrelevance? Such a spirit will wonder how the life of man survives it, and above all, what is much more important, how literature resists it . . .' Without a detailed presentation of the evidence we would have little feeling for *why* he wrote these sentences (and many more like them) and no means of judging whether or not his pessimism was justified.

So I have tried, within the limits of space allowed and with as much regard as possible to the intrinsic interest of the material, to make a reasonably comprehensive selection—some of the low points as well as most of the high ones. I have tried particularly to give a sense of the *texture* of feeling about James in his lifetime by the use of comment (often fragmentary comment) from as wide a range of sources as possible. This, together with the chronological order in which the excerpts are arranged, has no doubt led to some sacrifice of symmetry and drama in the collection; but it is, nevertheless, the only way in which we can now recapture a sense of James's historical situation.

The period covered is from James's earliest years as a writer up until his death in 1916. A few of the items I have reprinted appeared a little later than this, but they follow up responses within the period.

The material can be classified as follows:

1. Reviews of and articles on James in periodicals and books (but not in newspapers).
2. Letters by, to, and about him, remarks in diaries, etc.
3. Memoirs of those who knew him.
4. Allusions to him in fiction or parody.

The first of these is by far the largest class. All of them include responses from both England and America. All but the last have been stringently selected from a mass of material, including, for instance, sixty-four periodicals of which only thirty-eight are quoted. Nearly all concern the novels and stories but not the plays, biography, criticism, or travel writing.

Five of the novels, taken as summing up stages in James's career, are singled out for special treatment. For them I have given a relatively full picture of contemporary response by reprinting most of the available material. They are *The Europeans* (1878), *The Portrait of a Lady* (1881), *The Tragic Muse* (1890), *The Awkward Age* (1899), and *The Golden Bowl* (1904). For the other works I have included only what seemed of interest either:

1. As good criticism.
2. As coming from a significant source.
3. As representative of a significant section of opinion.

I would note particularly that I have omitted a great deal of the abusive or off hand reviewing which James received throughout his career, and especially before 1900.

Appendix II contains some information about the sales of the novels and stories.

There have had to be further important omissions, of two kinds:

1. To reduce the chosen material to manageable size I have cut parts of many items. This is regrettable on principle, though the majority of reviews cannot be said to have lost very much. I would urge the reader to pursue the more interesting fragments, such as those from Vernon Lee's incisive little story 'Lady Tal'. Full references are given in the headnotes to each selection.

2. Some leading documents are excluded altogether. This is because they are too long to reprint, are intrinsically unsuitable, or—most important—are easily available elsewhere. Thus *The Tragic Muse* is— very obviously—both too long, and easily available; LeRoy Phillips's 1906 *Bibliography* of James is not easily available but is clearly unsuitable; Max Beerbohm's two parodies are suitable and of reasonable length but have been recently reprinted—and so on. Leaving out some of these has been painful because no history of James's reception is really complete without them. But I have supplied a detailed list with comments in Appendix I, and I believe that there is no really important item which could not be obtained in a library of even moderate size. For the moment I would like to stress that by far the *most* important are undoubtedly James's own fiction, criticism, and notebooks (see 1–3 in Appendix I).

II

The collection of much of the evidence in one volume should, then, supply what has previously been lacking in materials for the reader's own first-hand judgement of James's reception. But such a mass of detail has dangers as well as advantages, and I wish to devote the remainder of this Introduction to suggesting the general shape and tendency of his relationship with the public as it emerges through the documents. And, since this relationship cannot intelligently be seen apart from its significance for the situation of other artists and for the development of James's own work, my discussion will inevitably entail the raising of some broader issues.

EARLIEST YEARS (NOS. 1–12)

James was first known as a writer of short stories. For ten years after the publication of what may be his first attempt, 'A Tragedy of Error' of 1864, his work appeared regularly in the *Atlantic Monthly* and the *Galaxy*. But the readers of these periodicals, the witnesses of his slow development into a major writer, were both few and local. James made no sudden impact on literature, and no international reputation. His audience was close to him and familiar—the educated class of Boston and New York. And accordingly he relied at first for criticism on a lively circle of family and friends, the recipients of 'Harry's latest'. Even the occasional reference to his work in the pages of the periodicals where it appeared, or in the *Nation*, tended to strike rather a familial note: 'a very charming love story . . . written with grace and spirit' says the *Nation* of 'A Landscape Painter' (1866).

But all this was changed by the publication in 1875 of his first two books of fiction: *A Passionate Pilgrim, and Other Tales* (No. 10) and *Roderick Hudson* (Nos. 11–12 and 27–28). The latter, in particular, demanded a more public, sustained, and formal attention than anything he had previously written. It laid the foundation for an international reputation. And it is the point at which reviews become our main evidence for the quality of contemporary response to James. Reviews are valuable to *us* because they provide concrete evidence of the requirements, the competence and seriousness, of the audience they address. In direct relation to their reader they probably mirror some of his difficulties and limitations, especially over new art. They allow us to assess, at several different cultural levels, the climate of opinion that a writer has had to face. But it would obviously be simple-minded to suppose that at any period the conditions under which they are commonly produced will encourage profound understanding and criticism of new art, especially when the art is a difficult and subtle one. In this period the reviewer's prime object tended to be simply descriptive: to inform the public, not to reform the author. The tone of the 'Great Reviews' whereby the latter is addressed, admonished, and corrected (which often seems much more than a rhetorical convention) was still used by some critics, and powerfully at times, but even so comments were usually in much more general terms than would be helpful to a writer. On the other hand reviews might indirectly affect him by moulding opinion for or against him; and above all they might be expected to distinguish, in general terms at least, the important writers of the age from the others.

CHARACTERISTICS OF JAMES'S RECEPTION IN HIS EARLY MATURITY (NOS. 13–50)

It is this work of discrimination that the reviews of the early novels failed, I think, to accomplish decisively. *The American* (1877) (Nos. 13–

15), *The Europeans* (Nos. 16–25), *Daisy Miller* (1878) (Nos. 19 and 26), and *Washington Square* (1880) (Nos. 34–36) all had a fair proportion of favourable comment. They established James in both England and America as a novelist to be considered, as the refined, 'artistic', and very clever exponent of the 'International Contrast'. *Daisy Miller* in particular, considered as a portrait of the American Girl in all her topical and amusing frightfulness, provided an international talking point and a short-lived addition to the language (on a trip in 1889 E. L. Godkin, editor of the *Nation* and typical of cultured America embarrassed by its compatriots, wrote home that he had seen 'Daisy Miller from Milwaukee with her sister and mother . . . at the next table'). Finally many of the reviews of *The Portrait of a Lady* (Nos. 37–46) have a respectful tone, and the implication that they are dealing with something larger and more important than usual. But all this—superficially a steady rise to fame, and even at times giving James himself the impression of a flourishing reputation and an expanding public—is perhaps somewhat deceptive. In the light of what happened later we have to ask how much readers, even when well disposed, really understood. How firmly did they differentiate James from other 'art' novelists of the period?

Of course some critics, notably and consistently W. D. Howells (see especially No. 51), did this. But what of the average educated reader? In looking at the documents we soon get the impression that even the best periodicals—those of which we could confidently say that they have declined since that time, like the *Spectator*—were hampered by requirements and expectations which are not consonant with the freedom necessary for an art to develop in harmony with its audience. We quickly learn to recognize a certain set of critical terms, used alike by hostile and favourable reviewers, which have the effect of shutting out from consideration many of James's most individual and valuable achievements. There must be a story in the mysterious sense in which there are not stories in James. The method must not be over 'analytic'. There must not be pessimism—which often seems to mean that there must be the assumption that right succeeds in the world, and a happy ending for preference. There must be nothing 'unpleasant' in the English sense of that word. There must be no 'flat-tones'—that which tends against clear-cut characters and exciting action. National pride must not be seriously assaulted. The ending should be final, with no irritating loose ends or disturbing inconclusiveness. And above all, hitting right the centre of James's art, the reader must be able to place his sympathy, quickly and for good, with certain characters, and not have them subjected to any dramatic interplay which would produce change or qualification in his attitudes.

Not all of these requirements can be dismissed easily. But what is puzzling now is to find them constantly, and quite often aggressively, made of an author who was not at all obviously provoking. It is true that 'agnosticism', or the abstention from *overt* moral judgement on his characters which is typical of him, may have seemed new and shocking (just as it later had a mild appeal for the aesthetic young men of the 1890's). But James was not a revolutionary. He is extremely reticent on Controversial Subjects like religion or sexual relations. At that period he was not even especially taxing to read. Yet he was frequently considered disturbingly modern by his contemporaries in a way that is now very difficult to understand.

We might consult here, as an example, Richard Grant White's review of *The Europeans* in the *North American Review* (No. 19). Both critic and periodical were of the highest standing. The leading general points made were present, before and after, in the work of both more and less intelligent contemporaries. They account in considerable degree for the majority view of James as much less than a great writer. And because of their predominance it would obviously be rash to dismiss them without careful consideration. They are certainly not perverse. Yet can we feel them to be other than misunderstandings? For example, one of Grant White's leading observations is the following:

The author of *The Europeans* styles it upon his title-page a sketch, probably recognizing himself, by that word, its absence of plot, and confessing that in writing it he did not propose to himself to interest his readers strongly in the fate of his personages. And indeed the sayings and doings of these shadowy people are not such as to trouble us much as to what becomes of them. Their sayings are many and their doings few.

Now it is true that in comparison with many previous novels—and certainly with the great Victorian classics—the plot of *The Europeans* is slight. But it is not uniquely so, not enough to justify the word 'absence' (compare the plots of Jane Austen). And supposing that the defender of the book were to admit this point and to argue that the main interest is deliberately thrown on the interplay of representative characters, with no great or stirring events to distract the attention, then the situation would be even worse, for the ensuing complaint is that the people are 'shadowy' and 'bloodless' puppets, incapable of emotion. This is very puzzling because it leaves us with the problem as to why it is that many modern readers *naturally* find the best characters in this novel, and in the rest of early James, both lively and credible. They are highly articulate in many cases. They are made to seem representative figures, and therefore have carefully selected characteristics. They are part of a structure in which most details (though not every detail, as some over-inspired modern critics would have us believe) contribute to the overall meaning. But all this does not now seem to make them coldly 'intellectual' or 'analytic' creations. It is not simply that we disagree with the judgements and descriptions of early James by Grant White and most of his contemporaries, but that in an odd way they scarcely seem to apply to our reading of the novels. They do not challenge, as a good modern hostile critic might, but seem instead to be talking of some other, thinner, experience. And the exigencies of reviewing conditions do not altogether account for this (but compare No. 23).

The reception of the early novels is therefore particularly interesting because of its mixture of growing acceptance and respect with a way of talking which implies only limited understanding; and it leads us directly into the central problem posed by the development of James's reputation, both before his death and after it. Was he, and is he, so difficult and specialized an artist that we could not expect him to appeal to the majority of educated readers? Obviously, as he himself early recognized, he was never 'a free-going and light-paced enough writer to please the multitude'. But does this also involve that only a very few in any generation will be able and willing to understand him? I think we can answer this by external observation as well as by discussing the novels (for which there is no space here). But to do so we have to glance at more recent developments. The description most often given of the fluctuation of reputation is that an artist is accepted and appreciated in his lifetime, though often only at the end of it and after a struggle; then disproportionately scorned shortly after his death; and then, if he is considerable, elevated to a more or less permanent position once the immediate reaction is past. An obvious example is Tennyson, or, on a much larger scale, Wagner. This pattern is very rough, but it does describe a large number of cases. It does not, however, describe that of James. He was never read at all widely in his lifetime (see, especially, Appendix II); and he is perhaps symptomatically modern in having emerged as a writer for a relatively large public some twenty or thirty years after his death. But emerged he has. The changed pattern must be at least partly due to the absolutely unprecedented increase in this

7

century of 'professional' students of literature. But James's recent, and seemingly permanent, popularity does show that, although the later novels are still considered difficult, he is not of his nature inaccessible to a reasonably wide public (witness many recent paperback publications). And we must therefore assume that his failure to find a satisfactory audience of any magnitude in his own time was something to do with that audience, and not simply the fault of his obscurity.

Do we then have to fall back on some such idea as that of a 'change of sensibility' between then and now? I think we do. But even so the phrase is something of a *pis aller*, and only provides a general heading under which can be grouped more or less useful particular observations. For example, one of the simplest meanings contained in the word 'sensibility' is that of 'having a taste for'—and here, I think, we are on relatively easy ground. We can see that there was no pre-existing general demand for the type of fiction James wrote, whereas there was a demand for a quite different type of novel. The *Blackwood's* notice of *The Portrait of a Lady* (No. 40), for instance, was fairly typical in thinking that the book was tremendously clever, but not at all real; it is to be recommended to one who has 'leisure for the kind of reading which is delightful for its own sake in complete independence of its subject'. It is significant that this review was preceded by an enthusiastic account of J. H. Shorthouse's *John Inglesant*—a novel which was an immense success *because* of its subject. Mr. Gladstone was photographed with it on his knee, and among its other admirers were Ruskin, Huxley, and Lord Acton. What mattered about it (and *a fortiori* about Mrs. Humphry Ward's *Robert Elsmere* of 1888) was its dramatization of religious problems and not, given a sympathetic and competent exposition, the permanent depth of its treatment. And while this reflects credit on the seriousness of the late Victorian public in a certain sense, it also suggests reasons for the lack of ready sympathy with James's work. The genuine importance of *his* subjects is not to be divined without a previous willing application of imagination; his books are not *manifestly* serious and worth the application of serious men. Thus we find that many who did like his work saw it chiefly as delightful and highly-wrought trifling, while others, granting it more power, thought the novels morally uncommitted and therefore suspect (No. 40 is actually a mixture of both these attitudes). The same cast of mind tended to reject Flaubert, Zola, and Ibsen in a different and more obvious way. But nowadays our taste or appetite for novels no longer demands clear-cut moral and social credentials. Rather the contrary.

Other implications of 'sensibility' are, however, much more complicated. Instead of asking the relatively simple question whether James's first readers had a predisposition to *like* the kind of novel he wrote, the word as used by criticism asks whether they had the emotional readiness to *understand* them easily in any but the most superficial way. Were they, in other words, at all attuned to be responsive to the characteristic strengths of feeling, insight, and wit which make him a great novelist for many modern readers? We have seen that Richard Grant White was not, and it is my impression that he was typical. But it is also my impression that this was not the 'fault' of James's contemporaries—which is the reason for introducing a stop-gap like 'change of sensibility'. He was difficult to understand even when the subject of serious and intelligent reading. There were of course exceptions, or partial exceptions, to this—in the case of *The Europeans* W. E. Henley's *Academy* review stands out (No. 18)—but the general truth does present us with a problem to which I shall have to return later.

THE EARLY 1880's AND JAMES'S RESPONSE TO CRITICISM (NOS. 51–63)

How conscious was James of the extent to which he was understood? In his *Selected Letters* (see Appendix I) Leon Edel says that his 'usual rule was to ignore reviews and reviewers'; but it is also clear from many remarks and actions throughout his career that he was acutely aware of what his public thought of him. Probably his remark to T. S. Perry in 1914 that 'I never "see many notices", but the general sense of the press . . . is blown in upon me by the wandering airs' is nearest to the truth. And we should of course remember that some comments must always have been more influential than others. In the case of public appraisal a judgement from the *Atlantic* would obviously carry more weight than one from the *Graphic*, for instance; and in private the remarks of William James, or in a different and less involuntary way, Robert Louis Stevenson, were especially important to him. We can never know just how much encouragement, advice, and criticism he received from his very large circle of friends and acquaintance in the Anglo-Saxon and French literary worlds, nor how influential this was. But whatever the channels through which he gained his impressions of outside opinion it is fairly clear that the full implications of the reception of the early books were only very occasionally apparent to him at the time—and *The Portrait of a Lady* did mark a high point. It must account in large measure for the confidence, and even playfulness, which marks many of his comments on the reading public in the early 1880's. But after it, with some sympathetic exceptions like Edgar Fawcett's admiring article in the *Princeton Review* (No. 56), a change gradually set in which eventually provoked a reaction in James. People began to be bored by his work (a comparison of Nos. 49 and 59 provides a neat example of this). It is true that in 1882 W. D. Howells's crusading article on his friend in the *Century* (No. 51) caused fairly widespread disapproval, and something like apoplexy in the *Quarterly* reviewer (No. 52). But the main new feature of these years was a growing feeling among reviewers and others that James was repeating himself, that he had little new to offer (for example Nos. 59 and 61). Readers still professed to be shocked by his 'pessimism' and evident affiliations with the French school, but their tone was increasingly one of indifference and satiety with a series of limited effects (for example No. 62).

It is against this background that we should see one of the most famous of James's critical utterances, 'The Art of Fiction' of 1884. This is, I think, part of the evidence that he was fast becoming fully, as opposed to sporadically, aware of the tendencies shown by his reviewers in the last few years. It is of course likely, although not inevitable, that knowledge of the context out of which critical writings come will enrich our sense of their purpose, of what they meant to the writer, if not of what they ought to mean to us. But in this case especially I find that such knowledge deepens our response, for the essay sums up so finely James's sense of his situation after the first elation of his appearance before an international public had faded. Most readers will already feel that it testifies to the need felt by James to infuse seriousness and intelligence and liberality into the discussion of the novel. But the reader of this collection will also be able to see, when he returns to the essay, that it is a specific, although for the most part covert, reply to contemporary criticism and indifference. James had his reviewers in mind. This is most directly indicated by his teasing of the *Pall Mall Gazette* reviewer (Andrew Lang) for his 'no story' stricture on 'certain tales in which "Bostonian nymphs" appear to have "rejected English Dukes for psychological reasons" '. But it goes much further than this. To take one example: a common objection to the novels appears in refined form in the *Lippincott's* review of *The Portrait of a Lady* thus:

Mr. James's reluctance, or rather his positive refusal, to complete a book in the ordinary sense of the word is a curious trait, and one which piques study. In the matter of detail his books are finished to the last degree, but he cannot bring himself to the vulgarity of a regular dénouement, and he lacks the poetic force to substitute for it a suggestive or picturesque climax. (No. 46).

This, together with other common objections discussed above, is surely dealt with, wittily and firmly, in the following:

. . . another would say that [a novel's being good] depends on a 'happy ending', on a distribution at the last of prizes, pensions, husbands, wives, babies, millions, appended paragraphs, and cheerful remarks. Another still would say that it means being full of incident and movement, so that we shall wish to jump ahead, to see who was the mysterious stranger, and if the stolen will was ever found, and shall not be distracted by any tiresome analysis or 'description'. But they would all agree that the 'artistic' idea would spoil some of their fun. One would hold it accountable for all the description, another would see it revealed in the absence of sympathy. Its hostility to a happy ending would be evident, and it might even in some cases render any ending at all impossible. The 'ending' of a novel is, for many persons, like that of a good dinner, a course of desserts and ices, and the artist in fiction is regarded as a sort of meddlesome doctor who forbids agreeable aftertastes.

The reader will be able to recognize many more such correspondences for himself. Placed in the context of what had been written about him the essay is a poignant monument to James's conviction that 'Art lives upon discussion, upon experiment, upon curiosity, upon variety of attempt, upon the exchange of views and the comparison of standpoints . . . Discussion, suggestion, formulation, these things are fertilizing when they are frank and sincere.' A monument because of its permanent value as a contribution (almost a foundation) to discussion: poignant because James was responding so eagerly and generously to critical work so markedly below him in urbanity and intellectual strength. He was suggesting an interest in the serious art of the novel which his own reviewers infrequently supplied.

1885–1895 (NOS. 64–108)

The next, and in many ways the most painful, part of James's career confirmed in nearly every way the tendencies of his early maturity. In 1886 he published (in volume form) the two novels which he had been preparing in the relatively quiescent years following *The Portrait of a Lady*, *The Bostonians* and *The Princess Casamassima*. These could almost be seen as an answer to the current implications that he had nothing fresh to say, that he was merely the exquisite exponent of limited and sometimes dubious themes. Neither of them concerns the contrast and interplay of American and European civilization; both are large and inclusive with many characters and a great variety of life. Yet both sold very badly, and *The Bostonians* was particularly ill-received in America (Nos. 70–72—of which No. 71 is by far the most typical). If the late boredom was successfully dissipated, its successor in some quarters was distaste. On the other hand the obviously exciting and topical theme of the *Princess* pleased a number of reviewers (Nos. 75–78), and there was a slight upward trend in the tone of comment on the smaller productions of the later 1880's (Nos. 81 and 84). But this was qualified by an increased stress on James's cynical modernity which it is difficult to understand today—'this is the novel of a writer who thinks all the world aimless, and loves to exaggerate that aimlessness' said the *Spectator* of the *Princess* (No. 76)—and it did not extend to the major work of these years, a novel significantly about the relation between art and 'the world', *The Tragic Muse* of 1890. This, both in sales and in many of its British reviews, was the nadir of James's career as a novelist (Nos. 87–100). Its reception forced on him the full consciousness of how little interest there was in his work. And it had immediate consequences in determining him to devote himself (1890–5) to writing plays for the commercial theatre. It is ironical that only a little while after he had embarked on this, his fiction received one of the most sympathetic, vigorous, and discriminating treatments ever to appear in his lifetime: an anonymous article in *Murray's Magazine* for 1891 (No. 102). This is remarkable for its assumption that James is among the greatest writers (only Howells at this date had expressed a similar view) and for its stress on his vigour and power; and in this and other ways it curiously resembles much modern critical writing.

James's uncharacteristic and ultimately disastrous venture into the theatre is outside the scope of the documents reprinted below; it is in any case a tale fairly often told. The main problem posed by it in the present context—and granted that he had nothing very fine to give to the drama—is *why* he persisted in it after indifferent success. The two most usual explanations, that he was fascinated by the technical rigours of dramatic presentation and that he needed money, seem to me only partially adequate. It is certainly true that when he later recalled these years it was usually, and significantly, in a context of some great problem of 'doing', of technique—but by that time he had, after all, decisively returned to the novel. And money, much as he himself stressed it in his own defence—'Don't be hard on me . . . I have had to try to make somehow or other the money I don't make by literature' he wrote to Stevenson in 1891—was never a real *necessity* for him. Unless it was seen as some kind of symbol of success it is surely too shallow a motive to be the complete explanation of the deflection from his life's main purpose of a dedicated writer who was never in danger of living anything but the life of a gentleman.

There are, however, hints of another motive. One occurs in a letter to Stevenson written after the opening of *The American* at Southport (January 1891) where James professes himself to be still blushing at a success 'pronounced—really pronounced'; another in a letter to William James where he speaks of the 'demand' for his plays: 'Which I—and others for me—judge (still very sanely and sensibly) to be *certain* to be made upon me from the moment I have a *London*, as distinguished from a provincial success. . . . I feel at last as if I had found my *real* form . . .' The point seems to be that these predictions, artistically and with regard to popularity, were not particularly sane and sensible. They were rather fevered. James's tone betrays it, as did such things as the elated scorn with which he treated William Archer's advice on the theatre, at Southport. He was *too* excited by his success there—by all other accounts a very moderate one. Edmund Gosse says of the slight London failure of *The American*, 'James was now cast down as unreasonably as he had been uplifted . . . we endeavoured to persuade him that, on the whole, he was not justified (in continuing in the theatre) but he swept our arguments aside'. Surely the reasons for this, as for his almost euphoric persistence, were that James turned to the theatre in the hope, not only of money, but of a tangible response to his work. The extreme elation at Southport would be the result, literally, of the physical conditions of the theatre: a visible audience, audible applause. His respect for his productions was, at least, ambiguous; the financial motive was not imperative; but the desire for positive response was born of his whole recent experience.

If this was so the reception of *Guy Domville* in January 1895—audible disapprobation—must have been a decisive blow for more than just his theatrical ambition.

JAMES'S AUDIENCE IN THE LATER YEARS (NOS. 109-99)

But if a lack of enthusiasm in the general reader compelled him to seek a more satisfactory response elsewhere, it was in these very years that James's fiction gained a public which was to stay with him for the rest of his life. While writing plays he also wrote short stories—many of them significantly and bitterly about the relations of artists to their audiences. ᐟCritics had often in the past preferred his shorter work because there 'analysis' and a lack of story seemed less unacceptable than in the novel. But in the reviews of these stories we encounter for the first time with any consistency a happy and *positive* sense that James is and should be the concern of the sensitive minority, the artist of the few (for example No. 110).ᐟAfter the events of 1890 and 1895 he could in any case never again think of himself as even potentially a novelist with a wide appeal—although the serialization of *The Other House* in the *Illustrated London News* in 1896 does seem to have been a last flicker of his desire for popularity. And in fact as the years passed he became more and more the 'Master' of a select literary *élite*—related to the emergent Bloomsbury Group but including such powerful independent figures as most of the members of which were Edith Wharton but including well bred, wealthy, and fairly talented (see, for example Nos. 126, 140–141, and 190). Much of the situation might be most economically and poignantly suggested to the reader by his consulting the relevant parts of the biography of one of James's younger disciples, Rupert Hart-Davis's *Hugh Walpole* (1952). Consider, for example, the pathos of the great novelist's suggestion that the young Walpole should address him as 'Très-Cher Maître or My very dear Master'. The whole development was a strange Edwardian fate for the eager and decisive young American aristocrat of the 1870's; but, as the reader of the later parts of this collection will see, it was the most sympathetic response he ever received from more than a few friends or isolated admirers. It gave him some kind of stable public—someone to write for—and in many ways an extremely attractive one.

Many years later Hugh Walpole wrote an appealing, though rather indulgent, story, 'Mr. Oddy' (No. 183), which takes us back to this period. It shows a disciple's devotion; but, significantly, it also concerns the callow contempt which James's eventual elevation as a grand old man earned him among progressive intellectuals in the years before 1914. For the development within the cultured minority was not, of course, without its consequences in the world outside. In the public sphere James became something of an upper-order celebrity, a distinguished figure on the sources of whose distinction it was not necessary to be too definite. His visit to America in 1904, for example, caused a stir and interest which his novels (since *Daisy Miller* at any rate) had never shown signs of doing. In 1915 his naturalization, a protest against the reluctance of the United States to enter the War, produced a minor furore. At the very last he received the Order of Merit. And there were parallel developments in the wider literary world. Gradually more and more reviewers found it natural to compliment James rather than to rebuke him. It is true that *The Awkward Age* received rather hostile treatment in England (Nos. 129–33), but it is after all one of the most difficult of the novels, and we should set against its reception the surprising tolerance and respect with which James's later manner very quickly came to be treated. Even the severe *Spectator*, for example, was reasonably deferential to *The Sacred Fount* (No. 145) despite not liking it at all; and many other reviews of that extreme work (not reprinted below) accepted its oddities as a matter of course. *The Wings of the Dove* (Nos. 149–55) aroused hostility and even accusations of perversity from ordinary reviewers, but in 1903 the stamp of respectability was set on James's oeuvre by a long article in the *Edinburgh Review* (No. 159). And finally the reviews (Nos. 166–74) and sales of *The Golden Bowl* even seemed to promise a real extension of interest in his work.

It would be wrong to give the impression that everything in these developments was purely conventional. Some really perceptive criticism was published on James after 1900, certainly more than there had been before. In particular his English admirers developed a passionate admiration of the late novels which produced such fine essays as those by Oliver Elton (No. 160) and Sydney Waterlow (No. 164). And in America the best work, like the *Nation* review of *The Golden Bowl* (No. 172) or the essays of W. C. Brownell (No. 177) and H. G. Dwight (No. 180), seems sometimes more valuable because it savours less of a cult. By the end of his life, too, James had become the subject of some respectable, academic, interest, represented below by W. A. Gill's parallel with Marivaux (No. 181) and by Clara McIntyre's criticisms of the revisions of his novels in *PMLA* (No. 188).

However, all this granted, the final reception of James gives us little ground for pleased contemplation. He was, for one thing, still the object of brutal attack—H. G. Wells's *Boon* (No. 192) being only a slightly more refined and expanded version of George Moore's conversational *mot* 'Henry James—the eunuch!'. And, more importantly there seems to have been only a minimum of interest among other influential minds. D. H. Lawrence's remark (in a letter of 1915) that 'subtle conventional design was his aim' differs in this respect only in courtesy from Arnold Bennett's off hand review of *The Finer Grain*

(No. 187). And although Hardy's attitude to the 'Polonius . . . of novelists' had softened a little since his reading of *The Reverberator* (No. 81a), an entry in his journal for 1915 scarcely implies a ready sympathy: 'It is remarkable that a writer who has no grain of poetry, or humour, or spontaneity in his productions, can yet be a good novelist. Meredith has some poetry, and yet I can read James when I cannot look at Meredith.' Correspondingly it seems unlikely that James was understood more by the wider public than he had been. How essentially different was the routine compliment after 1900 from the routine complaint of earlier years? If we compare, for example, J. P. Mowbray's treatment of *The Wings of the Dove* (No. 154) with Richard Grant White's review of *The Europeans* discussed above, we encounter a very similar kind of puzzle. All the great forces and feelings of life, says Mowbray, were stopped while reading the novel 'in a pallid inquisitorial equilibrium'. And we have to wonder how such an obviously clever and articulate man, unsympathetic as he is (and reiterating the old complaint about the lack of a story), could possibly fail to perceive at all the force of the passions, of more than one kind, which animate Kate Croy or Mrs. Lowder or Lord Mark. This is not a matter of 'judgement', but of the most ordinary and basic recognition of what is done in the novel —the kind of thing that I believe a modern reader would immediately perceive even if he disliked it thoroughly. And, of course, Mowbray was not alone in his reading, but only unusual in being hostile. Because of his distinction as a critic W. C. Brownell provides an even more pointed example (in No. 177).

Now, if we did not know James's earlier history this and similar failures would—and indeed to many people do—seem fairly easily explicable. The difficulty and novelty of the later books might well baffle contemporaries, especially since there was no powerful and accepted notion of James's greatness to make them persevere. But with the whole of the reception before us we can see that this is not an adequate account: there was, broadly, a constant level of understanding, though not of approval, throughout his career, and seemingly irrespective of the changes in his work.

Above all, in spite of the intelligence and good will of many reviewers, at no stage of his life do we find that decisive critical demonstration of James's importance which would have established him as a great writer for his contemporaries.

It seems possible that the ways evolved by some authors of dramatizing their deepest insights are precisely those elements in their work which it takes *most* time, and perhaps imitation, to perceive. For, when we have done full justice to all the complaints of James's first audience, we still have a body of work which the admirers of George Eliot or (for obscurity and idiosyncrasy) Meredith should, one would have thought, have been able to read with ease and profit. Only a very few of them did this, and so I think we have to discount relatively super-ficial considerations like overt subject matter or—the most popular candidate—James's technical difficulty, and to return to the idea of 'sensibility', the readiness to feel with an author in his most important perceptions. James may have been caught between a period which found its major writers more or less readable, and one in which the highbrow-lowbrow distinction simplified the situation—James Joyce would not even have been mentioned (except as a subject of scandal) in some of the periodicals which reviewed James. But we cannot therefore rest with the over-simple conclusion that the literary culture of the time was extraordinarily stupid or even perverse (an opinion to which James himself often understandably inclined). There was no lack of stupidity and perversity, especially in the new flood of journalism, but it is also clear that many of the men who proved inadequate to James were of very high ability and attainment elsewhere. We have to accept that, whatever the mechanics of the process, the general sensibility of educated readers has changed in James's favour; and that it has taken decades (and imitators and critics) for this to happen.

JAMES'S RESPONSE TO HIS NEW AUDIENCE

The increasing honour in which he was held after the late 1890s did have its inevitable effect on James's attitudes. He became outwardly more serene, and more like the benign and rambling 'hermit of Rye' of countless anecdotes. The bitterness and disappointment with the public which had been so near the surface in the late 1880's and early 1890's became much less sharp and lost its personal immediacy. And his art went its own strange way unhampered by the desire to appeal to a wide audience. We find him often actually saying that he will retire to his own conceptions, and write to please himself and possibly the 'few' who could read him intelligently (for example No. 128). To Howells, speaking in 1902 of the 'childishness of publics', he remarked 'it is (has been) in my mind long since discounted, and my work definitely insists upon being independent of such phantasms, and on unfolding itself wholly from its own "innards" ' (No. 153). He deliberately made the general public matter less to him than it had done. He cultivated detachment with success, as is most beautifully shown in his calm and witty response—so different from earlier responses—to William James's criticisms of *The Golden Bowl* (No. 176).

Even so, much of the new serenity was superficial. As de la Mare said a little later 'A select group, representative of civilization, had . . . protested its devotion, but how far can one write for a select group?'. It can be seen even from the few letters quoted in this collection that James had no illusions as to how much he was read and understood. If anything his real sense of isolation grew as he got older. Consider the most poignant letter to Gosse, written a few months before his death, where he calmly records that some of the 'plates' for printing his novels must be destroyed—for ever as it must have seemed to him (No. 195). In view of the enthusiasm of some of his later critics the extent of James's disenchantment may strike some readers as excessive. But we should remember that it was only after twenty-five years of unremitting search for a public that he could find even muted satisfaction in a highly specialized art and in the admiration of a small circle.

I must now leave readers to judge of James's reception for themselves.

NOTE ON THE ARRANGEMENT OF HEADNOTES ETC.

The following abbreviations are used in the headnotes and elsewhere:

LJ   *The Letters of Henry James*, ed. Percy Lubbock, 1920.
LH   *Life in Letters of William Dean Howells*, ed. Mildred Howells, 1928.
JF   *The James Family*, by F. O. Matthiessen, New York, 1947.
LP   *Thomas Sergeant Perry*, by Virginia Harlow, Durham N.C., 1950.
SL   *Selected Letters of Henry James*, ed. Leon Edel, 1956.
BHJ   *A Bibliography of Henry James*, by Leon Edel and Dan H. Laurence, 1957.

I have referred to William James and Henry James by their initials, finding that the convenience outweighs the rather over-familiar tone.

I have not usually identified the authors of unsigned reviews or articles, because (*a*) this is very rarely of importance, and (*b*), one of the interests of the collection is in reading James's reception as it appeared at the time. There are a few exceptions to this where the identity of the critic is of particular interest or importance.

I have given brief descriptions of those authors who are named (other than the famous ones) where these help to evoke the intellectual climate around James. Similarly I have identified the people or events referred to in the extracts when these are obscure and help or enhance understanding.

I have only mentioned where a letter was sent from, or a diary written, if it has some special relevance.

Periodicals are referred to by a short title after their first appearance. When only part of a review or article is reprinted I have given page references to the whole.

I have corrected obvious typographical errors, *but have left misspellings etc. of the names of James's novels or characters as they are*, since these often have some significance.

Generally the material is arranged chronologically, which means that some comments on a book are printed after the main body of reviews, and a few before. But there are important exceptions: I have grouped separately the English and American reviews of each work because the place of publication here seems more important than the precise date; and I have printed memoirs, anecdotes, fictional reminiscences, etc. in the contexts to which they seem to refer rather than in order of publication.

1. W. D. Howells on the young James

1866

Howells to E. C. Stedman, December 1866 (LH, i, 116).
Howells (1873–1920), the American novelist, editor, and critic,
was James's loyal friend and supporter from their first association
in Cambridge, Mass., in the early 1860s. Stedman (1833–1908) was
a stockbroker, a poet, and an influential critic and anthologist.

Talking of talks: young Henry James and I had a famous one last evening, two or three hours long, in which we settled the true principles of
literary art. He is a very earnest fellow, and I think extremely gifted—
gifted enough to do better than any one has yet done toward making us
a real American novel.

2. W. D. Howells on James's public

1867

Howells to C. E. Norton, August 1867 (LH, i, 117–18).
Norton (1827–1908), the great Boston scholar and 'apostle of culture' to America, was first associated with HJ in the early 1860s.

I see the Jameses rather frequently. They are all in town. Harry James
has written us another story, which I think admirable; but I do not feel
sure of the public any longer, since the *Nation* could not see the merit of
Poor Richard. It appeared to me that there was remarkable strength in
the last scenes of that story; and I cannot doubt that James has every
element of success in fiction. But I suspect that he must in a great degree
create his audience. In the meantime I rather despise existing readers.

3. James on his ambition as an American writer

1867

HJ to T. S. Perry, September 1867 (LP, 284–5).
Perry (1845–1928) was a Boston literary scholar and teacher, and a friend of James from boyhood. The missing (illegible) word about a third of the way through the passage is surely 'alone' or something similar.

I should think that by the time you get home you will have become tolerably well saturated with the French language & spirit; and if you contrive to do as much by the German, you will be a pretty wise man. There will remain the classical & the English. On the 1st I say nothing. *That* you will take care of; and I suppose you will study Latin & Greek by the aid of German & *vice-versa*. But the English literature & spirit is a thing which we tacitly assume that we know much more of than we actually do. Don't you think so? Our vast literature and literary history is to most of us an unexplored field—especially when we compare it to what the French is to the French.—Deep in the timorous recesses of my being is a vague desire to do for our dear old English letters and writers *something* of what Ste. Beuve & the best French critics have done for theirs. For one of my calibre it is an arrogant hope. *Aussi* I don't talk about it.—To enter upon any such career I should hold it invaluable to spend two or three years on English soil—face to face with the English landscape, English monuments and English men and women. —At the thought of a study of this kind, on a serious scale, and of possibly having the health and time to pursue it, my eyes fill with heavenly tears and my heart throbs with a divine courage.—But men don't accomplish valuable results . . . , dear Sarge, and there will be nothing so useful to me as the thought of having companions and a laborer with whom I may exchange feelings and ideas. It is by this constant exchange & comparison, by the wear and tear of living & talking & observing that works of art shape themselves into completeness; and as artists and workers we owe most to those who bring to us most of human life.—When I say that I should like to do as

22

Ste. Beuve has done, I don't mean that I should like to imitate him, or reproduce him in English: but only that I should like to acquire something of his intelligence & his patience and vigour. One feels—I feel at least, that he is a man of the past, of a dead generation; and that we young Americans are (without cant) men of the future. I feel that my only chance for success as a critic is to let all the breezes of the west blow through me at their will. We are Americans born—*il faut en prendre son parti.* I look upon it as a great blessing; and I think that to be an American is an excellent preparation for culture. We have exquisite qualities as a race, and it seems to me that we are ahead of the European races in the fact that more than either of them we can deal freely with forms of civilization not our own, can pick and choose & assimilate and in short (aesthetically &c) claim our property wherever we find it. To have no national stamp has hitherto been a regret & a drawback, but I think it not unlikely that American writers may yet indicate that a vast intellectual fusion and synthesis of the various National tendencies of the world is the condition of more important achievements than any we have seen. We must of course have something of our own—something distinctive & homogeneous—& I take it that we shall find it in our moral consciousness, our unprecedented spiritual lightness and vigour. In this sense at least we shall have a national *cachet.*—I expect nothing great during your lifetime or mine perhaps; but my instincts quite agree with yours in looking to see something original and beautiful disengage itself from our ceaseless fermentation and turmoil. You see I am willing to leave it a matter of instinct. God speed the day.

4. William James on the early stories

1868

WJ to HJ, March 1868 (JF, 316–7).
Matthiessen tells us that the stories immediately under review are
'The Story of a Masterpiece' and 'The Romance of Certain Old
Clothes' (1868).

Both stories show a certain neatness and airy grace of touch which is
characteristic of your productions (I suppose you want to hear in
an unvarnished manner what is exactly the impression they make on
me). And both show a greater suppleness and freedom of movement in
the composition; although the first was unsympathetic to me from
being one of those male *vs.* female subjects you have so often treated,
and besides there was something cold about it, a want of heartiness
or unction. It seems to me that a story must have rare picturesque
elements of some sort, or much action, to compensate for the absence
of heartiness, and the elements of yours were those of everyday life. It
can also escape by the exceeding 'keen'ness of its analysis and thoroughness of its treatment, as in some of Balzac's (but even there the result is
disagreeable, if valuable); but in yours the moral action was very lightly
touched, and rather indicated than exhibited. I fancy this rather dainty
and disdainful treatment of yours comes from a wholesome dread of
being sloppy and gushing and over-abounding in power of expression,
like the most of your rivals in the *Atlantic* . . . and that is excellent,
in fact it is the instinct of truth against humbug and twaddle, and when
it governs the treatment of a rich material it produces first class works.
But the material in your stories (except 'Poor Richard') has been *thin*
(and even in P. R., relatively to its length), so that they give a certain
impression of the author clinging to his gentlemanliness though all else
be lost, and dying happy provided it be *sans déroger*. That, to be sure, is
expressed rather violently, but . . . I feel something of a . . . want
of blood in your stories, as if you did not fully fit them, and I tell you
so because I think the same thing would strike you if you read them as
the work of another. . . . if you see what I mean perhaps it may put

you on the track of some useful discovery about yourself, which is my excuse for talking to you thus unreservedly. So far I think 'Poor Richard' the best of your stories because there is warmth in the material, and I should have read it and enjoyed it very much indeed had I met it anywhere. The story of 'Old Clothes' is in a different tone from any of yours, seems to have been written with the mind more unbent and careless, is very pleasantly done, but is, as the *Nation* said, 'trifling' for you.

5. William James on the early stories

WJ to HJ, April 1868 (JF, 318).

I have got your last *Atlantic* story ('Extraordinary Case'), and read it with much satisfaction. It makes me think I may have partly mis-understood your aim heretofore, and that one of the objects you had had in view has been to give an impression like that we often get of people in life: Their orbits come out of space and lay themselves for a short time along of ours, and then off they whirl again into the un-known, leaving us with little more than an impression of their reality and a feeling of baffled curiosity as to the mystery of the beginning and end of their being, and of the intimate character of that segment of it which we have seen. Am I right in guessing that you had a conscious intention of this sort here? . . . You seem to acknowledge that you can't exhaust any character's feelings or thoughts by an articulate dis-playing of them. You shrink from the attempt to drag them all reeking and dripping and raw upon the stage, which most writers make and fail in. You expressly restrict yourself, accordingly, to showing a few external acts and speeches, and by the magic of your art making the reader *feel* back of these the existence of a body of being of which these are casual features. You wish to suggest a mysterious fulness which you do not lead your reader through. It seems to me this is a very legitimate method, and has a great effect when it succeeds. . . . Only it must succeed. The gushing system is better to fail in, since that admits of a warmth of feeling and generosity of intention that may reconcile the reader. . . . . Your style grows easier, firmer and more concise as you go on writing. The tendency to return on an idea and over-refine it, becomes obsolete,—you hit it the first lick now. The face of the whole story is bright and sparkling, no dead places, and on the whole the scepticism and, as some people would say, impudence im-plied in your giving a story which is no story at all, is not only a rather *gentlemanly* thing, but has a deep justification in nature, for we know the beginning and end of nothing. Still, while granting your success here, I must say that I think the thorough and passionate conception of a story is the highest, as of course you think yourself.

6. James on not pandering to the multitude

1872

HJ to WJ, August 1872 (JF, 320–1).
HJ was replying to the criticism that his travel sketches were too
literary for 'newspaporial purposes'. Note the very early recognition that he could not pretend to be a really popular writer.

Your criticism of my *Nation* letters was welcome and just: their tendency is certainly to over-refinement. Howells wrote to me to the
same effect and you are both right. But I am not afraid of not being able
on the whole, and in so far as this is deeply desirable, to work it off
with practice. Beyond a certain point, this would not be desirable I
think—for me at least, who must give up the ambition of ever being
a free-going and light-paced enough writer to please the multitude. The
multitude, I am more and more convinced, has absolutely no taste—
none at least that a thinking man is bound to defer to. To write for the
few who have is doubtless to lose money—but I am not afraid of
starving. . . . All writing not really leavened with thought of some sort
or other is terribly unprofitable, and to try and work one's material
closely is the only way to form a manner on which one can keep afloat
—without intellectual bankruptcy at least. I have a mortal horror of
seeming to write thin—and if I ever feel my pen beginning to scratch,
shall consider that my death-knell has rung.

7. William James on the early style

1872

WJ to HJ, November 1872 (JF, 321).

I send you today the last *Nation* with your letter about Chambery, etc.,—a very delightful light bit of work, and perhaps the best of all for commercial newspaporial purposes. I must, however, still protest against your constant use of French phrases. There is an order of taste, and certainly a respectable one, to which they are simply maddening. I have said nothing to you about 'Guest's Confession' which I read and enjoyed, admiring its cleverness though not loving it exactly. I noted at the time a couple of blemishes, one of the French phrase *les indifférents* at the end of one of [the] sentences which suddenly chills one's very marrow. The other the expression: 'to whom I had dedicated a sentiment'. . . . Of the people who experience a personal dislike, so to speak, of your stories, the most I think will be repelled by the element which gets expression in these two phrases, something cold, thin-blooded and priggish suddenly popping in and freezing the genial current. And I think that is the principal defect you have now to guard against. In flexibility, ease, and light power of style you clearly continue to gain—'Guest's Confession' and this last letter in the *Nation* are proofs of it; but I think you should fight shy of that note of literary reminiscence in the midst of what ought to be pure imagination absorbed in the object, which keeps every now and then betraying itself, as in these French phrases. I criticize you so much as perhaps to seem a mere caviler, but I think it ought to be of use to you to have any detailed criticism from even a wrong judge, and you don't get much from anyone else. I meanwhile say nothing of the great delight which all your pieces give me by their insight into the shades of being, and their exquisite diction and sense of beauty.

8. 'The Madonna of the Future'

1873

W. D. Howells to HJ, March 1873 (LH, i, 175–6).
Dennett was the critic of the *Nation*.

I've been burning to tell you how much I like your 'Madonna,' and to report the undissenting voice of acclaim with which it has been hailed. Ever so many people have spoken of it, the Delphic Dennett alone remaining mum. Truly it has been a success, and justly, for it is a bravely solid and excellent piece of work. All like the well-managed pathos of it, the dissertations on pictures, the tragic, most poetical central fact, and I hope that many feel with me its unity and completeness. Every figure in it is a real character, and has some business there. The sole blemish on it to my mind is the insistence on the cats and monkeys philosophy. I don't think you ought to have let that *artista* appear a second time, and, I confess, to have the cats and monkeys for a refrain at the close, marred the fine harmony of what went before, till I managed to forget them.

9. James on criticism

1873

HJ to C. E. Norton, March 1873 (SL, 72).
For Norton see No. 2.

I do . . . believe in criticism, more than that hyperbolical speech of mine would seem to suggest. What I meant to express was my sense of its being, latterly, vastly over-done. There is such a flood of precepts and so few examples—so much preaching, advising, rebuking and re-viling, and so little *doing*: so many gentlemen sitting down to dispose in half an hour of what a few have spent months and years in producing. A single positive attempt, even with great faults, is worth generally most of the comments and amendments to it.

A PASSIONATE PILGRIM,
AND OTHER TALES

1875

---

10. Unsigned review, *Atlantic Monthly*

April 1875, xxxv, 490–5

This may be by Howells.

Mr. Henry James, Jr., has so long been a writer of magazine stories, that most readers will realize with surprise the fact that he now presents them for the first time in book form. He has already made his public. Since his earliest appearance in *The Atlantic* people have strongly liked and disliked his writing; but those who know his stories, whether they like them or not, have constantly increased in number, and it has therefore been a winning game with him. He has not had to struggle with indifference, that subtlest enemy of literary reputations. The strongly characteristic qualities of his work, and its instantly recognizable traits, made it at once a question for every one whether it was an offense or a pleasure. To ourselves it has been a very great pleasure, the highest pleasure that a new, decided, and earnest talent can give; and we have no complaint against this collection of stories graver than that it does not offer the author's whole range. We have read them all again and again, and they remain to us a marvel of delightful workmanship. In richness of expression and splendor of literary performance, we may compare him with the greatest, and find none greater than he; as a piece of mere diction, for example, 'The Romance of Certain Old Clothes' in this volume is unsurpassed. No writer has a style more distinctly his own than Mr. James, and few have the abundance and felicity of his vocabulary; the precision with which he fits the word to the thought is exquisite; his phrase is generous and ample. Something

31

A Passionate Pilgrim

of an old-time stateliness distinguishes his style, and in a certain weight
of manner he is like the writers of an age when literature was a far
politer thing than it is now. In a reverent ideal of work, too, he is to
be rated with the first. His aim is high; he respects his material; he is
full of his theme; the latter-day sins of flippancy, slovenliness, and
insincerity are immeasurably far from him. . . . The tales are all freshly
and vigorously conceived, and each is very striking in a very different
way, while undoubtedly 'A Passionate Pilgrim' is the best of all. In this
Mr. James has seized upon what seems a very common motive, in a
hero with a claim to an English estate, but the character of the hero
idealizes the situation; the sordid illusion of the ordinary American
heir to English property becomes in him a poetic passion, and we are
made to feel an instant tenderness for the gentle visionary who fancies
himself to have been misborn in our hurried, eager world, but who owes
to his American birth the very rapture he feels in gray England. The
character is painted with the finest sense of its charm and its deficiency,
and the story that grows out of it is very touching. Our readers will
remember how, in the company of the supposed narrator, Clement
Searle goes down from London to the lovely old country-place to which
he has relinquished all notion of pretending, but which he fondly
longs to see; and they will never have forgotten the tragedy of his
reception and expulsion by his English cousin. The proprietary Searle
stands for that intense English sense of property which the mere
dream of the American has unpardonably outraged, and which in his
case wreaks itself in an atrocious piece of savagery. He is imagined with
an extraordinary sort of vividness which leaves the redness of his
complexion like a stain on the memory; and yet we believe we realize
better the dullish kindness, the timid sweetness of the not-at-once
handsome sister who falls in love with the poor American cousin.
The atmosphere of the story, which is at first that of a novel, changes to
the finer air of romance during the scenes at Lockley Park, and you
gladly accede to all the romantic conditions, for the sake of otherwise
unattainable effects. It is good and true that Searle should not be shocked
out of his unrequited affection for England by his cousin's brutality,
but should die at Oxford, as he does, in ardent loyalty to his ideal; and
it is one of the fortunate inspirations of the tale to confront him there
with that decayed and reprobate Englishman in whom abides a longing
for the New World as hopeless and unfounded as his own passion for
the Old. The character of Miss Searle is drawn with peculiar sweetness
and firmness; there is a strange charm in the generous devotion masked

32

by her trepidations and proprieties, and the desired poignant touch is given when at the end she comes only in time to stand by Searle's death-bed. Throughout the story there are great breadths of deliciously sympathetic description. At Oxford the author lights his page with all the rich and mellow picturesqueness of the ancient university town, but we do not know that he is happier there than in his sketches of Lockley Park and Hampton Court, or his study of the old London inn. Everywhere he conveys to you the rapture of his own seeing. . . .

In imaginative strength it surpasses the other principal story of the book. In 'Madame de Mauves' the spring of the whole action is the idea of an American girl who will have none but a French nobleman for her husband. It is not a vulgar adoration of rank in her, but a young girl's belief that ancient lineage, circumstances of the highest civilization, and opportunities of the greatest refinement, must result in the noblest type of character. Grant the premises, and the effect of her emergence into the cruel daylight of facts is unquestionably tremendous: M. le Baron de Mauves is frankly unfaithful to his American wife, and, finding her too dismal in her despair, advises her to take a lover. A difficulty with so French a situation is that only a French writer can carry due conviction of it to the reader. M. de Mauves, indeed, justifies himself to the reader's sense of likelihood with great consistency, and he is an extremely suggestive conjecture. Of course, he utterly misconceives his wife's character and that of all her race, and perceives little and understands nothing not of his own tradition. . . . here is something from the baron that is delicious:

'I remember that, not long after our marriage, Madame de Mauves undertook to read me one day a certain Wordsworth,—a poet highly esteemed, it appears, *chez vous*. It seemed to me that she took me by the nape of the neck and forced my head for half an hour over a basin of *soupe aux choux*, and that one ought to ventilate the drawing-room before any one called.'

The baron's sister, in her candid promotion of an intrigue between Madame de Mauves and Longmore, we cannot quite account for even by the fact that she hated them both. But Madame de Mauves is the strength of the story, and if Mr. James has not always painted the kind of women that women like to meet in fiction, he has richly atoned in her lovely nature for all default. She is the finally successful expression of an ideal of woman which has always been a homage, perhaps not to all kinds of women, but certainly to the sex. We are thinking of the heroine of 'Poor Richard', of Miss Guest in 'Guest's Confession', of

Gabrielle de Bergerac in the story of that name, and other gravely sweet girls of this author's imagining. Madame de Mauves is of the same race, and she is the finest,—as truly American as she is womanly; and in a peculiar fragrance of character, in her purity, her courage, her inflexible high-mindedness, wholly of our civilization and almost of our climate, so different are her virtues from the virtues of the women of any other nation. . . . It is indeed a marvelous first book in which the author can invite his critic to the same sort of reflection that criticism bestows upon the claims of the great reputations; but one cannot dismiss this volume with less and not slight it. Like it or not, you must own that here is something positive, original, individual, the result of long and studious effort in a well-considered line, and mounting in its own way to great achievement. We have a reproachful sense of leaving the immense suggestiveness of the book scarcely touched, and we must ask the reader to supply our default from the stories themselves. He may be assured that nothing more novel in our literature has yet fallen in his way; and we are certain that he will not close the book without a lively sense of its force. We can promise him, also, his own perplexities about it, among which may be a whimsical doubt whether Mr. James has not too habitually addressed himself less to men and women in their mere humanity, than to a certain kind of cultivated people, who, well as they are in some ways, and indispensable as their appreciation is, are often a little narrow in their sympathies and poverty-stricken in the simple emotions; who are so, or try to be so, which is quite as bad, or worse.

RODERICK HUDSON

1875

---

11. Unsigned review, *Atlantic*

February 1876, xxxvii, 237–8

HJ was pleased by this, and wrote to Howells, 'Why didn't
you tell me the name of the author of the very charming notice
of RH in the last *Atlantic*. . . . I don't recognise you, and I don't
suspect Mrs. Wister. Was it Lathrop? If so please assure him of my
gratitude.' (SL, 96). For Mrs. Wister see No. 12. G. P. Lathrop
(1851–98) was Hawthorne's son-in-law, and a poet and critic. HJ
seems later to have conceived a much lower opinion of him: he
wrote to Perry in 1880 that 'Poor little Lathrop ought to be . . .
and put to bed, & forbidden the use of pen & ink'. (LP, 306.)

In re-reading Mr. James's novel, we have been curiously impressed
with the after-wave of strongly agreeable sensation which must inevitably follow the study of such a story, when it has suffered the de-
lays of serial issue and attained its normal identity as a volume. We
think that even those who most admired the work while it was appearing in *The Atlantic* will be surprised to find how much still remains in
its pages to impress, attract, and satisfy them; how much also which
deserves renewed and careful consideration. It is of course precisely
this quality of endurance in a book, this possibility of often-recurring
pleasure in it, which determines the position of an author; and in
classing Mr. James—as we must now naturally begin to do—this alone
allows us to accord him a high place among the keenest literary artists in
English and American fields; indeed, it is difficult to see how so excellent
a piece of writing should fail to attract the attention of the better reading public for many years to come. The texture of Mr. James's language has a certain indestructibleness about it, a clear sparkle which

35

betokens crystalline organization. He gives us the large outlines and broad surfaces of a fresco, along with a finish which we discover to be that of a mosaic: there is no mere illusion of style, but a given space is filled with a given number of polished and colored words that have their full effect. Yet there is one reason, as it seems to us, why Roderick Hudson will not keep so firm a hold on the memory of readers as we could wish for it; and this is its manifest and at times even offensive want of compression.

The plot of the book is one which would easily have admitted of greater conciseness; and this, by the way, is one of the reasons why the novel gains so much by being read in book form. But grant Mr. James his chosen area, and it must be admitted that he conducts the movement of his narrative with great discretion and skill. There is no obvious mystery, no ostentatious covering up of tracks, yet the suspense excited is extremely acute and continues up to the catastrophe, which after all comes upon us with no strain, and appears the most natural thing in the world. At first the reader is led to suspect that Rowland's sentiment for Cecilia is to prove an important element; but this is thrown aside as soon as it has served its purpose of masking the affair of Roderick with Mary Garland. The next important supposition is that Christina is to unseat Miss Garland from her place in the young sculptor's heart, and that Roderick and she are somehow to come out of the *mêlée* hand in hand; but this in turn is lightly abandoned just as we have seen our way most clearly to the outcome, and the theme of Rowland's bravely subdued attachment to Mary, which has up to this point been carried along in the bass, rises to a controlling position, and forms the closing strain of the whole. All this is very simple but excellent art. And we must also give unqualified praise to the boldly broken ending of the story, which so completely lends it the air of a detached piece of life, without injuring its individual completeness.

Undoubtedly the main triumph of the book, so far as the representation of persons is concerned, is in the picture of Christina Light—whose name, it should be said in passing, is an inspiration of aptness in its application to the character, and of curious suggestiveness in general. Her total avoidance of conventional demeanor is carried out with remarkable grace, and she is everywhere the prism from which the other persons get their most brilliant refraction. Very fine is the indication of those internal struggles of her singular nature, throughout, and to our mind nothing in the book is more moving than her scene with Rowland, in the tenth chapter. Rowland, although in his passive position an equal interest would be out of place, has struck us as on the whole needlessly monotonous. But on the other hand Roderick is perhaps the most abundantly vigorous creature Mr. James has yet introduced to us. We have before spoken of the sometimes undue violence of his characters, and it would seem that in the case of Roderick the author had chosen to wreak his utmost impulse toward this sort of thing. Roderick is an epitome of emotional extravagance in certain directions. But the result is very picturesque, and frequently highly entertaining. Nothing more appropriately eccentric could have been devised, either than his conduct on hearing that Christina has broken her engagement with Prince Casamassima, when in the extremity of his delight he writes to his mother and his *fiancée* that they are not to see him for a week, and then arranges himself in a white dressing-gown on his divan, with roses and violets scattered about the floor of his studio and a white rose in his hand, to give himself up to his rapture. The final circumstance of Roderick's death, too, is managed with much fitness. 'He had fallen from a great height, but he was singularly little disfigured. The rain had spent its torrents upon him, and his clothes and hair were as wet as if the billows of the ocean had flung him upon the strand. An attempt to move him would show some hideous fracture, some horrible physical dishonor; but what Rowland saw on first looking at him was only a strangely serene expression of life. The eyes were dead, but in a short time, when Rowland had closed them, the whole face seemed to awake. The rain had washed away all blood; it was as if Violence, having done her work, had stolen away in shame. Roderick's face might have shamed her; it looked admirably handsome.' Yet it is noticeable how little this result plays upon one's sympathies. There is a certain chilliness in the aesthetic perfection of the event which represses any grief the reader might feel at its sombreness. Possibly it is desirable to have it so in such a case; but to us it seems not desirable, and we may here suggest that this coldness is probably connected with the excessive activity alluded to above, which is a thing in some danger of becoming a substitute for deeper imaginings, more truly effective by reason of their repose. There is the same want of pathos about Mary Garland, however, who is the acme of quietude, and for the rest an admirable study upon which Mr. James is to be congratulated.

One great merit remains always prominent in reading this novel, and that is its singularly perfect evenness of execution. There are no bare spots. All the details are treated with an equal dignity and completeness. Some of the portraits of persons in a few words are exceptionally good, as this of the Cavaliere: 'He was a grotesque-looking personage and might have passed for a gentleman of the old school, reduced by adversity to playing cicerone to foreigners of distinction. . . . He had a little black eye, which glittered like a diamond and rolled about like a ball of quicksilver, and a white mustache cut short and stiff, like a worn-out brush.' Furthermore, the book is noteworthy as a success in giving general interest to a theme which at first seems to require too much detail, namely, the history of a developing genius. Though it is largely by virtue of his affinity with the French school of fiction that Mr. James has been able to do this, the circumstance is so much in his favor; for he still amply justifies his position as a unique and versatile writer of acute power and great brilliancy in performance.

12. From an unsigned review, *North American Review*

April 1876, cxxii, 420–5

This is probably by the Mrs. Wister mentioned in No. 11. She was a daughter of Fanny Kemble (see No. 13), and an acquaintance of HJ.

If the authorship of *Roderick Hudson* were a secret, we think few people would guess it to be a first novel. It has little of the freshness and none of the crudeness of most such attempts. Its merits and its interest are not such as usually gush from a new-found spring of talent, while its faults are not those of youth and inexperience. Yet the reading public would be puzzled on whom to fix it. Anonymous productions of so much ability are immediately assigned to half a dozen well-known writers, with more or less plausibility; the book in question reminds us of no other; Mr. James has imitated nobody; the only novelist to whose temper of mind there is the least affinity is Thackeray, and few writers resemble one another less. Therefore, to begin with, if *Roderick Hudson* is not what can be called an original work of genius, it is entirely peculiar. As far as one can describe a book in a single phrase, this one is a study of character. There is no plot, strictly speaking; the slight framework which supports the personages being the career of a young village genius who is taken by a munificent acquaintance from the purgatory of a law-office in his native Northampton to study sculpture in Rome. The story follows him, and three or four others whose common tie is in him, through the hopes and fears, the promise and disappointment, of his course. These three or four are, first, Rowland Mallet, the hero's friend and patron; Mary Garland, his cousin and betrothed; Christina Light, his fate: there are several other characters of less importance who are quite as carefully and minutely drawn. There is too much of this minuteness, too much detail. It was not necessary to our comprehension of Rowland Mallet that we should be told all about his father and mother, his grandfather and grandmother, as he inherited nothing from them, except, perhaps, from the

39

last his Dutch coloring and phlegm; but that stolid quality in him becomes an amiable longanimity, not always maintained without struggle; so that we must set down as works of supererogation those two delightful portraits of the silent sea-captain with his weather eye always to windward, and the good housewife who sought consolation for her lost Holland in having the front pavement scrubbed and scoured. And why, as the cousin Cecilia had no part to play in the book, is she so conspicuous a figure; and why, since she is so nice a woman, does the author of her being like her and let us like her so little? With her, the Cavaliere Giacosa, and one or two more, it looks as if Mr. James had had these admirable studies in his sketch-book and could not resist transferring them to his canvas, although they have as little to do as lay-figures, or at best the *deus ex machina*. There are no lay-figures in Mr. James's compositions; the perfect finish of each part is like nothing but some performances we once saw given by the leading actors of the Théatre Français in London, during the Commune, when Bressant and Delaunay appeared as walking gentlemen, and Got, the manager, merely brought in a letter on a salver. There is in this elaboration a trace of the influence of M. Tourguénieff, of whom Mr. James is an admirer and student, but the effect is very different from that of M. Tourguénieff's simply grouped supernumeraries.

The central figure, of course, is Roderick Hudson, and we foresee that the undiscriminating will fancy a resemblance between him and Hawthorne's Donatello, but it is scarcely skin-deep. The irresponsibility of the Faun is his greatest attraction, it is Roderick Hudson's most intolerable vice. The character of the hero strikes us as the great failure of the book; the conception is capital and is consistently carried out; but in working it up there occur traits of selfishness and shamelessness which, although natural in themselves, make the relations of others to him unnatural. His personal charm is not felt by us, while his detestable egotism is; we are repelled, and the friendship of Rowland, the constancy of Mary, and even the idolatry of his mother, seem like infatuation. This is a cardinal error, for it leaves the reader outside the sympathies of the whole circle; he has no hold on the electric chain which binds them together. It is due in great part to this, no doubt, that their wonderfully told vicissitudes of feeling leave us cold; it is not that they are unlike real people; they are most real and living, but we do not identify ourselves with them; we never for a moment cease to be spectators; we are intellectually interested, but as unmoved as one may suppose the medical class of a modern master of vivisection to be. Rowland is not meant for the hero, and, like him as we must, we cannot concentrate our sympathies on the second fiddle; at the same time we are very grateful for such a delightful, possible character, if he be not impossibly good; one almost loses patience sometimes with his patience. . . . the conversations are often too prolonged, and the author endows all his personages with his own turn for analyzing, in consequence of which they all occasionally talk alike, blurring for the moment their individuality. The effect of this perpetual analysis is fatiguing; the book never ceases to interest, but it taxes the attention like metaphysics. There are signs that it occasionally wearied the author; while such pains and care are bestowed upon his characters, his style is sometimes slipshod. He says, 'deceased brother' for 'dead brother', and uses other equally objectionable expressions; how else did he come to write such a sentence as the following? 'She herself was a superior musician, and singers found it a privilege to perform to her accompaniment.' On the same ground we account for his putting the same word into everybody's mouth, 'hideous' for instance, which Christina, Rowland, and Roderick all use at different times in a moral sense, yet which is not a common word so applied. This, however, is allied to an old fault of Mr. James's, which is the repetition of one striking word or phrase until it loses its force; the word 'formidable' is unusual and impressive, but it occurs so often in the latter part of the present book that any other would express as much; there is so much about 'passion' and 'passionateness' that at length the fervid sound falls coldly on the ear of the unimpassioned reader. . . .

Looking at the book as a whole, it is like a marvellous mosaic, whose countless minute pieces are fitted with so much skill and ingenuity that a real picture is presented, but with an absence of richness and relief, of all that is vivid and salient; there is a pervading lowness of tone, and flatness of tint. This should not be the impression left by a novel of remarkable talent; we think, however, that it is not the result of a failure to produce the desired effect, but of a mistaken aim. The method, too, is a mistaken one; no aggregate of small particles, however cunningly put together, will produce the effect of honest cutting and shaping from the piece; it may be *marqueterie*, or a Chinese puzzle, but it will not be art. Moreover, such work has the disagreeable property of making criticism seem like picking to pieces.

From these strictures the last two chapters must be excepted. The story has the immense merit of rising to a climax at the end; there is more breadth and movement in the final twenty-five pages than in all the rest of the book. We have heard it objected, that Mr. James has resorted to a hackneyed expedient for getting rid of a troublesome hero; but there is nothing hackneyed in his way of using it. The effect falls short of what it might have been, because author and reader are still left looking on, curious, speculative, philosophical; we stand apart and watch the working of Rowland's anguish, and note the 'magnificent movement' of Mary Garland's despair. But the close of *Roderick Hudson* is beautiful, powerful, tragical; it is intense, yet not overstrained; all it lacks is to have been told with more human feeling.

THE AMERICAN

1877

13. James on the ending of *The American*

HJ to W. D. Howells, March 1877 (JF, 500–1).
Howells had criticized the ending of the novel. Mrs. (Fanny)
Kemble (1809–93) was one of the famous theatrical family,
celebrated for her Shakespearean readings, and an intelligent
and friendly critic of the early HJ.

I am supposed to be busily scribbling for lucre this morning, but I must
write you three lines of acknowledgment of your welcome long letter.
Its most interesting portion was naturally your stricture on the close of
my tale, which I accept with saintly meekness. These are matters which
one feels about as one may, or as one can. I quite understand that as an
editor you should go in for 'cheerful endings'; but I am sorry that as a
private reader you are not struck with the inevitability of the *American*
dénouement. I fancied that most folks would feel that Mme. de Cintré
couldn't, when the finish came, marry Mr. N; and what the few persons
who have spoken to me of the tale have expressed to me (e.g. Mrs.
Kemble t'other day) was the fear that I should really put the marriage
through. *Voyons;* it would have been impossible: they would have been
an impossible couple, with an impossible problem before them. For
instance—to speak very materially—where could they have lived? It
was all very well for Newman to talk of giving her the whole world
to choose from: but Asia and Africa being counted out, what would
Europe and America have offered? Mme de C. couldn't have lived in
New York, depend upon it; and Newman, after his marriage (or
rather *she*, after it) couldn't have dwelt in France. There would have
been nothing left but a farm out West. No, the interest of the subject
was, for me, (without my being at all a pessimist) its exemplification of
one of those insuperable difficulties which present themselves in people's

43

lives and from which the only issue is by forfeiture—by losing something. It was cruelly hard for poor N. to lose, certainly: but *que diable allait-il faire dans cette galère?* We are each the product of circumstances and there are tall stone walls which fatally divide us. I have written my story from Newman's side of the wall, and I understand so well how Mme. de Cintré couldn't really scramble over from *her* side! If I had represented her as doing so I should have made a prettier ending, certainly; but I should have felt as if I were throwing a rather vulgar sop to readers who don't really know the world and who don't measure the merit of a novel by its correspondence to the same. Such readers assuredly have a right to their entertainment, but I don't believe it is in me to give them, in a satisfactory way, what they require.—I don't think that 'tragedies' have the presumption against them as much as you appear to; and I see no logical reason why they shouldn't be as *long* as comedies. In the drama they are usually allowed to be longer— *non é vero?*—But whether the *Atlantic* ought to print unlimited tragedy is another question—which you are doubtless quite right in regarding as you do. Of course you couldn't have, for the present, another evaporated marriage from me! I suspect it is the tragedies in life that arrest my attention more than the other things and say more to my imagination.

14. George Saintsbury, review, *Academy*

July 1877, xii, 33

George Saintsbury (1845–1933) was a literary historian and reviewer who later (1895) became Professor of English at Edinburgh. In 1879 HJ wrote to Perry that 'I never saw Saintsbury, who seems so much and so strangely to interest you. I believe he is a schoolmaster' (LP, 303). Lady Kew is the worldly and cynical grandmother of the heroine of Thackeray's *The Newcomes*.

We have but one thing against Mr. James, and we wish we could say as much for most of the novelists whose work comes before us. He has read Balzac, if it be possible, just a little too much; has read him until he has fallen into the one sin of his great master, the tendency to bestow refined dissection and analysis on characters which are not of sufficient intrinsic interest to deserve such treatment. No doubt this is a fault which savours of virtue; but still it is a fault, and a fault which renders it extremely difficult to fix one's attention on *The American* until the excellence of Mr. James's manipulation fairly forces one for very shame to interest oneself in his story. The hero and heroine are the chief stumbling-blocks. He is a typical Yankee who, after serving with distinction in the civil war, has set to work at making a fortune, and has made it by the help of things in general—washtubs, soap, and oil being more particularly specified. He comes naturally to Paris to spend the fortune, and to look out for something exceedingly superior in wives. Unfortunately for himself, he has proposed to him a certain Countess de Cintré, an angel in herself, but appertaining to a by no means angelic family, who represent in race and character the stiffest types both of English and French nobility. They, of course, cannot away with the washtubs, even though transmuted into dollars, and by working on Mdme. de Cintré's filial ideas they at last succeed in getting the match broken off. There are several minor characters who are decidedly better than the principals. Such are the old Marquise, who bears, however, a rather perilous likeness to Lady Kew; her younger son, a capital fellow and a partisan of the ill-treated Yankee; a match-making and platonically flirtatious American matron, and others. Also we have a ghastly family secret, a fatal duel, and a retirement to a convent; so that Mr. James has been by no means stingy of what some people will regard as the solids of his feast. But we wish we could like his chief figures. The portrait of his countryman must of course be taken as accurate, and is evidently sympathetic. But if not only the *naïf* consciousness and avowal of being as good as anybody else, but also the inability to understand how the anybody else may possibly differ from him on this point, be taken from life, the defect of repulsion strikes us as a serious one. There is, moreover, something exceedingly jarring to our possibly effete nerves in the idea of a man who seriously entertains the idea of revenging himself for a personal slight by making use of a family secret which he has surreptitiously got hold of. It is true he does not do it, but he threatens to do so, and tries to make profit of the threat. After this we cannot help feeling on the side of his enemies, scoundrels as they are. And the lady, though her temperament and French ideas of duty explain her conduct not insufficiently, is far too shadowy and colourless. The book is an odd one, for, though we cannot call it a good book, there is no doubt whatever that it is worth a score of the books which we are wont truly enough in a sense to call good.

15. From an unsigned review, *Scribner's Monthly*

July 1877, xiv, 406–7

Those who have faith in the growth of literature according to seed and soil, have long cherished the hope—deferred from season to season—that the 'great'-ness which characterizes so many American things would soon develop itself in fiction. A great American novel has seemed to many a confident and hopeful patriot to be heralded with the incoming of each new writer. Mr. James early showed qualities which justified the turning of expectant gaze in his direction. The 'Passionate Pilgrim', 'A Modern Madonna,' and 'The Last of the Valerii,' showed some qualities which might well grow to greatness. It is true that in 'Madame De Mauves' and in *Roderick Hudson*, expectation received a warning; but Mr. James had given such unmistakable evidence of originality and delicacy, and of skillful *technique*, that when the first chapters of *The American* made their appearance we were justified in looking for a novel thoroughly American in character and sufficiently good to satisfy our national literary longing. It was evident that the movement of the story was to be on foreign soil,—where its author is so much at home,—and that but one of its important characters was to be of our own people, but this one character was so thoroughly of the best typical American sort as to afford a safe basis for the highest hopes that might be built upon it. Big, rich, frank, simple-hearted, straightforward, and triumphantly successful, he satisfied us entirely by his genuine and hearty manliness, and he seemed to carry in his very blood a genius for success in any direction toward which his modest strength might be turned. . . . Up to the time of Valentin's death, we had gained such faith in his stability and in his straightforward determination to attempt only what was right, and to follow up his attempt to crowning success, that it would have seemed the most natural thing in the world for him not only to marry Madame de Cintré, but to become the guiding head of the whole house of Bellegarde, gaining a controlling respect within the circle of the *haute noblesse* of which that house was a centre. . . .

For many chapters after the fatal duel there is nothing in the movement of the story to disturb our faith in its hero. He followed the clue that Valentin had given him, and came into full possession of the tragic secret of the Bellegardes. Madame de Cintré quailing before her fiendish mother, and her stone-hearted older brother, cowered away into her Carmelite novitiate. A strong, clean-souled, upright, and resolute American, whose inmost life she had stirred with an admiring and satisfying love, held the power to overcome their stern will, and to bring her back to such happiness as, under their hard heel, she never could have known. Up to this point Mr. James had the full sympathy of his readers. Thenceforth, save for a waning hope that at the last moment he might still not betray our trust, the successive steps of the story grow more and more disheartening, and we finally close the volume, conscious victims of misplaced confidence. . . .

It is the best compliment we can pay to Mr. James's writing to say that he gave us such a living interest in his hero, that we are made angry by his own failure to comprehend the character he had created. Can it be that we owe such a fiasco in some degree to the fact that the author has been unconsciously twisted out of his own individuality by the strong influence of Tourguéneff's example? Tourguéneff, however, would justify so miserable an ending; he is remorseless, but he does not shock nor disappoint.

THE EUROPEANS

1878

16. From an unsigned review, *Spectator*

October 1878, li, 1334–6

This and later *Spectator* reviews of HJ have recently been identi-fied by Robert H. Tener as the work of the distinguished editor R. H. Hutton (1826–97). *Spectator* standards certainly seem to decline after his increasing ill-health and personal troubles in the late 1880's.

It is pleasant to see the promise of a new figure in English,—or perhaps, we should rather say, in Anglo-American,—literature, and there appears to be the promise of a new figure in Mr. Henry James. We have recently noticed the unusual ability of his critical essays. In this slight novel,— or 'sketch,' as he accurately enough terms it, for it is, indeed, of very slender materials,—there is evidence enough of a genuine and brilliant creative power of the dramatic kind. We cannot exactly compliment him on the plot. In the first place, the little there is of it is essentially disagreeable, as it turns in great measure on the ambiguous position of a woman who has made a morganatic marriage with one of the younger branches of a petty German house, a marriage which the reigning prince,—the scene is laid thirty years ago,—is anxious to dis-solve. The lady herself, the daughter of an American family, though born and bred in Europe, evidently would not object, if she saw her way to any more brilliant position as the consequence of assenting to its dissolution; and during the period covered by the 'sketch' she is paying a flying visit to her relations in the neighbourhood of Boston, to ascertain what prospect she might open for herself among her Massachusetts relations, if she were to acquiesce in the dissolution of her marriage. This is an unpleasant subject. . . . We must not be

49

supposed to mean that there is any indelicacy in the manner in which Mr. Henry James treats the subject. The Baroness Münster, false at heart and only conventionally brilliant, is not intended to be an attractive figure, and might, indeed, with but a little alteration in the setting, have been painted expressly to show how despicable conventional charm and total insincerity may be. But what is disagreeable is the light way in which a rather rigorous Massachusetts society take her position. It rather appears to add to her fascination for one of them that she is living in doubt whether she shall dissolve her marriage with another man or not, and that the doubt appears to depend on whether or not she can see a clear prospect of substituting a more satisfactory tie for the one concerning which she is hesitating. Even the ladies of this rigorous Puritan set seem to take much the same view. . . . Our next objection is purely literary, that there is hardly any plot at all. The story is of the very thinnest,—perhaps sufficient, but barely sufficient, for threading together some admirably dramatic and highly humorous conversation, wherein European manners are skilfully contrasted with the thin and refined provincialism of Boston society. It is hardly a story. But none the less very few, even of really good three-volume novels, contain indications of so much dramatic ability as the exceedingly slight novelette contained in these two thin, widely-spaced, and largely printed volumes. We judge from it, as we have already said, that Mr. Henry James may make a considerable figure in Anglo-American literature.

But we do not ground this opinion on the picture of Baroness Münster, the morganatic wife, herself. She is indeed very cleverly sketched in the opening conversation with her brother, but she never again comes up to the brilliancy which we are, in that scene, led to expect from her, and the effect of which on her Yankee relatives we are promising ourselves the amusement of observing. After the opening of the sketch, she does not in the least justify her reputation. She tells fibs, and distributes rather common-place compliments, but except where she undertakes the worldly education of young Mr. Wentworth, we hardly recognise again even her strength of mind; and even in that scene there is a certain want of finesse,—a plumpness of speech—which is hardly suitable to the character and the occasion. What makes the book so striking is not the sketch of the Baroness Münster, but that of her light-hearted, happy, almost frivolous, and almost French, brother, Felix Young, and the exquisitely painted contrast between his character and that of the shy, rather melancholy, washed-out Puritans,—whose

Puritanism has been diluted into Unitarianism,—with whom he claims relationship, and into whose good graces he smiles his way. When this young gentleman applies for the hand of Mr. Wentworth's daughter, Gertrude, and apologies for his poverty, the anxious Bostonian, who has been hoping to marry her to a young Unitarian minister, and who receives his suit rather coldly, remarks, by way of apology for his coldness, 'It's not your want of means.' 'Now it's delightful of you to say that,' replies Felix; 'only don't say it's my want of character, because I have a character, I assure you I have; a small one, a little slip of a thing, but still something tangible.' And that 'little slip of a thing' is precisely what is painted, and painted with exquisite humour, in every conversation in which Felix takes part,—while those in which he does not take part are, relatively speaking, of no account. It is the character of a thoroughly sweet-tempered Bohemian,—a vagabond but innocent sort of amateur, who is incapable of shyness, or modesty, or *mauvaise honte*, or ill-temper, or ingratitude, or want of tact, and whose radiant audacity in carrying his point, when he has one to carry, is quite superb. The way in which this easy, happy, lively nature is painted, a nature so completely fused with the usually irritable and insatiable artistic temper, as to make quite a new species of character, would be in itself sufficient for a literary success; but contrasted, as Mr. Henry James contrasts it, with the anxious embarrassments and sad ethical fatigue of the Puritan temperament, the effect is a picture full of those fine touches which make you laugh heartily even when alone, —and not with the laughter of mere amusement, but rather with the laughter which comes of finding your own perceptions suddenly widened by the skill of your author. . . . The contrast between Charlotte's shyness and Felix's incapacity for shyness, or any approach to shyness, between Mr. Wentworth's slow, anxious temperament and Felix's swift, light, fluent happiness, is most effective; and when two other figures come on the scene, first, Mr. Brand, the solemn young minister, who had aspired to be Gertrude's husband, but who is beginning to aspire to be Charlotte's instead,—and then Gertrude herself, who had gained a great reputation with her family for 'peculiarity,'— which meant restlessness in that rather narrow world, and an imagination which longed for a fuller life,—the grave little comedy is almost perfect. We must say, however, that no figure is really quite adequate, except those of Felix Young and Charlotte Wentworth. The slowness and inherited gravity of Mr. Wentworth, admirably as these qualities are conceived, are just a little exaggerated, and pushed almost to the point of extravagance; and Gertrude remains something of a problem to the reader, no less than to her own family.

But the character of Felix Young, born of American blood, but on French soil, educated a Bohemian, by profession a strolling sort of artist, incapable of earnestness, and yet incapable of real levity, preferring to attach himself to stronger natures, and yet keeping a perfectly elastic independence of his own, is a picture so original, and so admirably worked out, that it alone may not improbably give to this little book a permanent, if a modest place, in English literature. We only wish the main situation of the sketch were open to less serious criticism. We see with sincere pain, even though the treatment be quite delicate, that American literature is following in the track of American State-law on the subject of marriage.

17. From an unsigned review, *Athenaeum*

October 1878, 2658, 431

Though it is nowadays not a novelty for the heroine of a story to be otherwise than perfectly beautiful, it may be doubted whether it be politic to follow Miss Brontë and to make her positively plain, and perhaps it is not easy to take a very romantic interest in a young person who 'was tall and pale, thin and a little awkward; her hair was fair and perfectly straight; her eyes were dark, and they had the singularity of seeming at once dull and restless' . . . the author has hardly employed the materials at his service to the best advantage, and . . . even a 'sketch' could have borne somewhat more development of plot and character. The tale is, however, on the whole, pleasantly written, and, like the rest of the accomplished author's books, it is defaced by remarkably few of what we commonly think Americanisms.

18. W. E. Henley, review, *Academy*

October 1878, xiv, 354

W. E. Henley (1849–1903) was a poet and critic. Earlier in 1878 he had written to HJ for advice about Turgenev; and it was in the essay on that writer in *French Poets and Novelists* (1878) that HJ had said 'When fiction is written in this fashion, we believe as we read'.

If Mr. Henry James's new novel could only be regarded as the harbinger of a whole noise of such fowl, the pleased critic would look forward to the coming season very cheerfully. As it is, and with every reason to believe that *The Europeans* is alone in the world, he is glad to welcome it for its own sake. It is an extremely clever book, and a book withal that is readable from first line to last. It is scarcely so touching as *Daisy Miller*, which is out and away the best thing of its kind in recent English; but it is a piece of work so capable and original, so vigorous, and to a certain point so telling, as to be worthy of equal praise and study. Mr. James, who would seem to be an exponent of the refined, eclectic realism of Turgénieff, has produced in it a novel remarkable for complete absence of intrigue, of didactics, of descriptiveness. There is not any plot in *The Europeans*; there are scarcely any landscapes or interiors; and such good things in the way of phrase or generalisation as occur in it are quite inseparable from their context, and would seem commonplace outside of it. And yet it is not possible to read *The Europeans* without the admiration of absorption. It has all the qualities of a rare etching: of an etching, that is to say, the beauty of which is a beauty of line, and depends in no measure on a property of tone or an arrangement of masses. The effect of the whole thing is that of something colourless and cold, but so subtle and right, so skilful and strong, as to force the attention first and afterwards the respect of those who consider it. Mr. James has a sufficient contempt for prettiness and obviousness. His form is ascetic even to uncomeliness; he has nothing whatever to say that is not absolutely essential; and he suppresses all signs of his own personality with such austerity as could scarcely have been believed to be within the compass of a modern novelist. His purpose has been, not at all to write a book, and still less to write a story, but to show off the spiritual machinery of some six or eight men and women all of whom are interesting from a certain human point of view, but none of whom are in any degree heroic, or even extraordinary; and to do this with as much art and as little apparent excuse for it as could possibly be imagined. In this aim he has been altogether successful.

His people are so completely apprehended and so intelligently conveyed that, as he himself has written of the greatest of living novelists, 'you believe as you read'. All are handled with equal acuteness and with equal sympathy, so that the reader's intelligence of one and all is for the nonce as perfect as the writer's. The book is, in fact, a remarkable book: in its merits as in its shortcomings. As it stands, it is perhaps the purest of realism ever done. And there seems every reason to believe that, if Mr. James could, or would, endow such work as in it he approves himself capable of with the interest of a high tragic passion, he might be not only one of the ablest but also one of the most renowned novelists of his epoch.

THE EUROPEANS AND
DAISY MILLER

1878

---

19. Richard Grant White, review,
North American

January 1879, cxxviii, 101–6

Richard Grant White (1821–85) was an eminent literary and musical critic, and editor of Shakespeare. The Marquis of Brotherton and Dean Lovelace are characters from Trollope's *Is He Popenjoy?*, reviewed earlier in the article. Later Mrs. Hodgson Burnett's *That Lass o'Lowries* is hailed as 'Of all recent fiction, the flower and crown', marking, like *Jane Eyre* and *Adam Bede*, 'the advent of a new writer of original power'.

From the long-practiced British novelist let us turn to a young American, Mr. Henry James, Jr., who, although he is the author of several books, including now four novels, is, compared with Mr. Trollope, almost a tyro. But, although one of the younger writers of the day, Mr. James is no timid experimenter, doubtful of his powers, ignorant of the field upon which he has entered, and uncertain of his aims. We do not know a living writer, except Matthew Arnold, who produces upon his readers a greater impression of self-knowledge, of self-restraint, or of perpetual self-consciousness, nor one whose work shows more evidence of fastidious taste, cautious proceeding, and careful elaboration. Indeed, in his mental traits and literary workmanship, Mr. James does not belong to the English school (English and American being in literature but one), but rather to the French. His cast of thought is French; he has the French nicety of taste, the French reserve of

56

manner, dexterity of hand, and fineness of finish; what wit he has is French, and he is French in the paleness and paucity of his humor. He seems to have Balzac before him as his model; and the best thing he has yet produced is 'Madame de Maulves,' a sketch which appeared in the *Galaxy* magazine, and which Balzac himself need not have been ashamed to own.

Mr. James's latest work in fiction of any importance is *The Europeans*, which is intended, of course, as a companion piece to *The American*. The author of *The Europeans* styles it upon his title-page a sketch, probably recognizing himself, by that word, its absence of plot, and confessing that in writing it he did not propose to himself to interest his readers strongly in the fate of his personages. And indeed the sayings and doings of these shadowy people are not such as to trouble us much as to what becomes of them. Their sayings are many and their doings few. The Europeans are two European-born Americans of very Bohemian type and tendency: a youngish woman, Eugenia Young, who as the morganatic wife of a German prince has received the title of Baroness Munster, and her brother, a clever draughtsman, half amateur, half professional, who is engaged in furnishing sketches to an illustrated journal in Europe. To put the matter plainly, the Baroness Munster is an adventuress, nothing more nor less. As an adventuress she became a morganatic wife of the brother of a petty German grand duke (it was thirty years ago), and now as an adventuress she comes to America to try her fortune in finding some rich American to take her in some fashion—as a wife preferable of course—off her German prince's hands. In the first place it is difficult to see why these people are called 'the Europeans.' They are in a certain sense indeed the product of the conditions of society upon the continent of Europe, as the Marquis of Brotherton and Dean Lovelace are the product of the conditions of society in England. But they are not, like the Marquis and the Dean, indigenous products of that society, integral parts of it; they are waifs and strays—Europeanized Americans of a not very admirable sort. It was a little fretting to see Mr. Newman set forth as 'the American' by Mr. James; that personage being hardly, we think, what Mr. James himself would like to have accepted as a fair representative of the social product of his country. But Mr. James's Europeans have really no claim whatever to the style and title which he bestows upon them; being simply cosmopolite Bohemians of European origin; folk which the real people of no country would acknowledge as being of themselves, not to say take pride in owning.

These adventurers find their New England kinsfolk living in one of the suburbs of Boston, and are kindly received by them and placed in a pretty cottage near their own house. There the Baroness and her brother remain week after week, month after month, visiting the big house, doing nothing, suffering nothing, getting into no trouble and therefore getting out of none, making no material for a story even of the slightest kind, but revealing their own characters and drawing out those of their cousins, young and old. These cousins are a father, Mr. Wentworth, and two daughters, Charlotte and Gertrude, who seem to be presented as types of New England people of their condition. And what character they have, it may be acknowledged, is New-England-ish. Their common trait seems to be a pale, intellectual asceticism; but besides this they have very little character at all. Their coldly moral view of life is admirably described by Mr. James. As he makes Felix say to Gertrude, who is falling in love with him, she and her family 'take a painful view of life'. This is also indicated reflexively by Gertrude, who, going from the bare neatness and respectability of New England to the Baroness's drawing-room in the little cottage, which the latter has decked and softened with curtains and colored drapery (some of it rather dingy), looks at it, and then ' "What is life, indeed, without curtains?" she secretly asked herself; and she appeared to herself to have been leading hitherto an existence singularly garish, and totally devoid of festoons.' These Yankee girls have none of the conventional reserves to which Felix has been accustomed; and the effect upon him is thus delicately suggested: 'He had known fortunately many virtuous gentle-women, but it now appeared to him that in his relations with them (especially when they were unmarried) he had been looking at pictures under a glass. He perceived at present what a nuisance the glass had been—how it perverted and interfered, how it caught the reflection of other objects and kept you walking from side to side.' These traits of character and others like them, on both sides, are touched by Mr. James with a dainty and skillful hand.

Although Mr. James's Wentworths may be recognized as possible New England people, they can not be accepted as fair representatives, mentally or physically, of their class. His description of the young ladies personally is puzzling. Gertrude, whose slumbering love for the vanities of the world is aroused by the Baroness's festoons, and who finally captivates Felix, is described as being 'tall and pale, thin and a little awkward; her hair was fair and perfectly straight; her eyes were dark, and they had the singularity of seeming at once dull and restless—

differing herein, as you see, fatally from the ideal fine eyes, which we always imagine to be both brilliant and tranquil.' Her sister Charlotte 'was also thin and pale; but she was older than the other; she was shorter, and she had dark smooth hair.' And yet these most unattractive young ladies are afterward referred to more than once as beautiful. The truth seems to be that Mr. James, clever literary artist as he is, is not strong in imagination. His personages do not exist, even for himself, as living, independent, 'self-contained' human beings. They act and speak only as he wishes them to act and speak from time to time. He has no personal respect for them. How could it be otherwise? How could he treat them with any deference when they plainly have no existence for him out of the range of his own consciousness? He calls *The Europeans* a sketch; and indeed its effect is very sketch-like as well as very French. It brings to mind some of those very clever things of which so many are done by French painters: a mere outline, with a dot or a line suggestive of light and shade set here and there, and then filled with color very faintly washed in; the whole thing indicative of the great skill that comes from careful training, but nevertheless a very shadowy hint of humanity, demonstrative rather of great half-exercised powers on the part of the artist than of the solid and vital personality of the subject. The author seems to be making his sketches, just as Felix did his, to send them to his illustrated paper. Hence it is, probably, that while they are touched off so cleverly they are so unsatisfactory. And yet this lack of individuality and vital force in their personages is the great defect of all Mr. James's novels. His men and women, although they talk exceedingly well, are bloodless, and remind one of the 'vox et præterea nihil' of his youth. This shadowy, bloodless effect is not at all the consequence of the particular type of New England personage depicted in *The Europeans*; for, besides that it is manifest in the peopling of all of Mr. James's novels, let the Wentworths, any or all of them, be compared with Madame Launay in Trollope's recent *Lady of Launay*, which is a mere sketch no longer then Mr. James's own *Daisy Miller*. It consists chiefly of a pair of every-day lovers, and of an old lady who is ready to sacrifice everything and everybody, herself included, upon what she regards as the altar of duty. The lovers have the virtue of constancy; the old lady, Madame Launay, that of inexorable firmness. She is ill, she is almost bed-ridden, she becomes a shadow; but there is more strength, more individuality in this attenuated old woman than in a regiment of Mr. Wentworths. There is one scene in this little sketch in which Philip Launay faces his mother and wins a victory over her, partly by his boldness in assaulting her fortress of will, and partly by the treachery of love within the walls, in which that young man outweighs a ton of such men as are in *The Europeans*, although one of them, Mr. Brand, is an enormous specimen of muscular Christianity, and the other is the sinfully positive and joyous Felix Young. This is the question in regard to Mr. James's ultimate success as a novel-writer—whether he will be able to bring before us living personages in whose fate we take an interest. As to his literary skill there is no question. The impression which Felix, always gay, always a little aggressive in his fullness of animal spirits, makes upon the shy and shrinking Charlotte, is illustrated—we might say illuminated—with a little flash of wit of which the most brilliant French writer might be proud: 'Poor Charlotte could have given no account of the matter that would not have seemed unjust both to herself and to her foreign kinsman; she could only have said—or rather she never would have said it—that she did not like so much gentlemen's society at once.'

The moral pedantry and the chilly unemotional life characteristic of a not inconsiderable part of New England society in past generations are delicately exposed all through the book. These might have depressed a much less sybaritic person than the Bohemian Baroness. As the story, if story it must be called, draws to a close, these motives find happy expression in the view taken by Mr. Wentworth of the love affairs of Gertrude, who was with his approval to have been given to Mr. Brand, the big young minister, but who with that gentleman's consent transfers herself to Felix. When the change was made known to him, 'Where are our moral grounds?' demanded Mr. Wentworth, who had always thought that Mr. Brand would be 'just the thing for a younger daughter with a peculiar temperament.' And soon after, when he is urged to consent to the marriage, he again reverts to his cherished view of her case: ' "I have always thought,' he began slowly, 'that Gertrude's character required a special line of development." ' This brings to mind Mr. Howells's humorous presentation of the same trait of character in his charming *Lady of the Aroostook*, yet incomplete. When the Rev. Mr. Goodlow's advice is asked in regard to the unfortunate circumstance of Lydia Blood's being the only woman on board that vessel, and her making the voyage to 'Try-East' in company with five men, exclusive of the crew, he replies, 'I think Lydia's influence upon those around her will be beneficial, whatever her situation in life may be.'

But merely remarking that Mr. James commits an error of fact and of time in making people of the position of the Wentworths, living in the suburbs of Boston, so ignorant as they are represented to be in regard to European social life and art and literature only thirty years ago, say 1845, we turn to his *Daisy Miller*. This he calls a study; and probably it is, as surely it might have been, a study from nature. Daisy Miller is a beauty, and, without being exactly a fool, is ignorant and devoid of all mental tone or character. She dresses elegantly, has 'the tournure of a princess,' and is yet irredeemably vulgar in her talk and her conduct. She shocks all Europeans and all well-bred Americans by the terms on which she is with the courier of her party, and by making chance acquaintances with men and flirting with them. She has a grand affair of this kind in Rome, which, after excluding her from the society of more reserved American women, ends in her going to see the Coliseum by moonlight with her Roman cavalier, who is not a gentleman, and taking there the fever of the country and dying. In *Daisy Miller* Mr. James has undertaken to give a characteristic portrait of a certain sort of American young woman, who is unfortunately too common. She has no breeding, little character, a headstrong will, in effect no mother, and with all this has personal attractions and a command of money which are very rare in Europe, even among people of rank. As she flares through Paris, and flits from place to place over the continent, attended but not controlled by her parents, she is the wonder and horror of all decorous people, American and European. Mr. James's portrait is very faithful. He has succeeded to admiration in the difficult task of representing the manner in which such people as Mrs. and Miss Miller talk; the difficulty being caused by the extremely characterless nature of their conversation, which is never coarse, or very vulgar, or even very foolish. It is simply inane and low-bred, and is marked by certain slight perversions of language; for example, 'going around,' instead of 'going about,' of which one phrase, by the way, Mr. James makes rather too much. It is perhaps well that he has made this study, which may have some corrective effect, and which should show European critics of American manners and customs the light in which the Daisy Millers are regarded by Americans themselves. But the probability is that, on the contrary, Daisy Miller will become the accepted type and her name the *sobriquet* in European journalism of the American young woman of the period.

THE EUROPEANS

20. From an unsigned review, *Scribner's Monthly*

January 1879, xvii, 447

We feel that here are the elements for something worth reading without intermission to the end. The unfolding is slow, but irritation at the slowness is rather pleasant than otherwise. Yet, after all is over, we become aware that something more was expected than the tame return to Europe of Eugenia, and the equally tame marriage of Felix with Gertrude Wentworth. It may be urged that Mr. James is highly consistent. The Baroness really could not be expected to stand the dullness of life in the suburbs of Boston. Robert Acton, whom she attracts, could not be expected to love her enough to keep her away from the fascinations of Europe, nor to excuse sufficiently the numerous small untruths of which, first and last, she is guilty. Nevertheless, the story lacks a strong satisfactory close. It has weakness at the end, as so many of this charming writer's stories have. It will neither please the main bulk of novel-readers, nor the fastidious few who demand to be stirred by an author. But its audience will be found in a highly respectable and well-read class, which may be termed the 'upper middle cultured;' for they will be delighted throughout with its air of gentlemanliness, excellent diction, and fastidious turns of thought, while they will not miss the want of life and incident. On every page there is something to show how earnest and observant a literary artist Mr. James is. It is not his fault, if he does not strike a ringing note. Meanwhile, it is saying a great deal that he steadily improves in his style and methods. In certain points, he takes the lead among American writers; with such a foundation, there is no reason why he should not achieve far higher laurels.

21. Unsigned review, *Appleton's Journal*

January 1879, NS vi, 94–5

Readers of Mr. James's *The Americans* will naturally expect to find in *The Europeans* a companion or complement to that subtile and elaborate study; but in the latter Mr. James has experimented in another field and aimed at quite different literary effects. *The Europeans* is truly described as 'a sketch'—events and persons being outlined rather than analyzed, and large dependence being placed by the author on the cooperation of the reader's imagination with his own. Yet, in spite of its slightness, *The Europeans* will be generally admitted, we think to contain Mr. James's best and most artistic work. The picture of the Wentworths, as a typical American family, is an unmistakable achievement of genius, and is sufficient of itself to lift the story into the domain of genuine creative art. The art with which it is painted is very delicate and unobtrusive, but its effectiveness and power and imaginative truth are proved by the persistency and clearness with which it arises in the mind after the book is laid aside and mere details have sunk into hazy indistinctness. The family as a whole, indeed, is a greater conception than any individual member of it. Charlotte is the only one whose portrait is painted at full length, and this is chiefly owing to the essential commonplaceness and simplicity of her character, which, however, is not without a certain reposeful charm of its own. Gertrude, who is in a sense the heroine, baffles the reader to the end quite as much as she puzzles her relatives and friends; and the austere personality of Mr. Wentworth is hinted at rather than portrayed. The family, as we have said, dominates and subordinates its constituent factors; and it would be difficult to conceive a finer and truthfuler picture of that high-minded simplicity, that serene fidelity to a somewhat ascetic conception of duty, that physical and moral cleanliness, and that virginal purity, which characterize American life at its best, and which dwarf into insignificance its comparative deficiencies on the side of grace, and amenity, and social complaisance.

Very great skill is expended upon the figure and character of the Baroness—greater, we think, than is justified by the part which she plays in the story—but she never quite succeeds in pleasing, and after one or two experiments, as it were, is gradually relegated to the background. It is as if the author shrunk from following her character along its natural and logical pathway; and though at the beginning she promises to take the part of leading lady in the drama, she proves on trial incongruous with her surroundings, and is speedily assigned to a subordinate and not very interesting *rôle*. Equally skillful in execution and much happier as a conception is the character of her brother, Felix Young—American by parentage, European by birth and nurture, and Bohemian by profession and practice. He is the apostle, exponent, type, and exemplar of happiness as a creed and as a standard of conduct; and his influence upon the story is similar to that of a joyous smile upon a beautiful human face. The contrast between European and American life on their moral side, as exemplified in the Baroness, is only hinted at by the author; and we have reason to be grateful for the protest which Felix Young embodies against the ascetic ideals, the hyperpuritanic standards, the strained conscientiousness, and the distrust of everything that takes the semblance of pleasure for pleasure's sake, which make American life, in spite of a certain austere nobleness and purity, the most colorless, joyless, physically wearing and mentally exhausting, in the world.

We have already referred to the delicacy and refinement of Mr. James's art, and we return to the point only to remark that it is almost too subtilely delicate for its purpose. The reader has to be constantly on the alert, must meditate over passages in order to secure their full flavor, and even when the story is finished must go over it again to catch those delicate *nuances* which constitute its atmosphere and tone. The model of the workmanship is to be sought, not in English or American, but in French fiction; and not less conclusively than his essays on French novelists, *The Europeans* demonstrates that Mr. James's studies in this field have been profound and fruitful.

22. Unsigned review, *Eclectic Magazine*

January 1879, xxix, 123

In our notice of Mr. James's *The American* at the time of its appearance we praised it for the minute elaboration of its character-studies, for the vivid realism of its portraiture, for the versatility of resource which it exhibited on the part of the author, and for the opulence and amplitude of its style. *The Europeans* deserves even higher praise, but on quite different grounds. It is described by the author as 'a sketch', and such it is in comparison with either *The American* or *Roderick Hudson*. Details are well-nigh ignored, accessories are glanced at instead of being emphasized and obtruded upon the attention, painstaking elaboration of minor points is carefully avoided, and the characters, their surroundings, their individual traits, and the social background against which they are projected, are all painted in bold, distinct, rapid, and luminous outlines. At the same time, there is no lack of definiteness in the design or of finish in the execution. On the contrary, the story is remarkably artistic in construction, and the refinement of method and polish of style are almost too obvious. The essential difference between this and Mr. James's previous novels is that he has substituted the dramatic for the analytical method, and portrays persons and character by showing them in action rather than by a subtle analysis of motives. The gain is great both in vividness and in brilliance; and *The Europeans* will be generally accepted, we think, as Mr. James's most artistic, most satisfactory and most characteristic work. It would claim a permanent place in our literature, if for nothing else, for the exquisite picture of a typical American family and home which it contains—a picture so true, so real, so vivid, and yet so gracious and pleasing that it causes the reader to feel a sort of conscious pride in being an American. Yet the portraits of the two Europeans are quite as skilful and effective, and only a degree less pleasing.

If we go on, however, we shall reveal more of the story than we ought; so we will content ourselves with recommending it to all who can appreciate thoroughly artistic, refined, and finished work.

23. Constance Fenimore Woolson, review, *Atlantic*

January 1879, xliii, 106–8

Constance Fenimore Woolson (1840–90) was an American 'regional' novelist and friend of HJ on whom he very kindly included an essay in *Partial Portraits* (1888). These comments are part of 'The Contributors Club' and precede the regular *Atlantic* review of *The Europeans* (see below, No. 25).

Mr. Henry James's *Europeans* is, to me, his best work, so far; always excepting two or three of his short stories. For his peculiar style of mere hints as to such commonplace things as reasons, motives, and causes seems to me better adapted to a short story, which is necessarily a sketch or condensation, than to the broader limits of a novel, where we are accustomed to more explanation and detail. It is true that Charles Reade, also, seldom tells us what his characters mean, intend, or think, but only what they say or do; leaving us, as James does, to study them as we study our living neighbors, who carry no windows in their breasts. But the difference here is that Reade's characters always do such tremendous things, and so incessantly, that their mere bodily activity sufficiently defines their mental processes; whereas Mr. James, as far as possible, has *his* people do nothing at all.

What atmosphere could possibly have been contrived more quiet than the wide, cool Wentworth homestead, and its little cottage opposite, from which, as scene, the story scarcely wavers, save for that one glimpse of the Acton mansion, emphasized and slightly colored by its 'delightful chinoiseries.' The two Europeans arrive, and, after one sharply drawn picture of their dislike for the Boston horse-cars, they depart to this Wentworth home, and stay there through to the end of the tale. No one does anything; a drive for Madame Münster and a drifting about in a skiff for Gertrude are about all the action allowed. So quiet is the story in this respect that when, in the eleventh chapter, the baroness goes to see Mrs. Acton, and goes on foot, the description of her 'charming undulating step' as she walked along the road is a kind of relief to us, and mentally we all go with her, glad of the exercise and movement and fresh air. Mr. James has advanced in his art; in *this* story of his there is absolutely no action at all. What is there, then? There is contrast of character, and conversation.

I suppose it will be allowed without question that we are all far more interested in the baroness than in the other characters. Felix is, to me, a failure, in spite of his felicitous name; or rather he is a shadow, making no definite impression of any kind,—like Mirah in *Daniel Deronda.* His 'intense smiling' does not save him; does not give him body, any more than the brilliant rainbow gives body to the spray at Niagara Falls. Gertrude is not a failure; but she is not sufficiently explained. Minute details concerning her are given, such as for instance, that 'her stiff silk dress made a sound upon the carpet' as she walked about the room; yet she remains from first to last like a tune which the composer has as yet but briefly jotted down. *He* knows it; but *we* do not. There is no mystery about it, however; it is only that he has not written it fully out,—that is all. Mr. Wentworth is excellent throughout; we see him, we are acquainted with him, sitting there 'with his legs crossed, lifting his dry pure countenance from the Boston Advertiser.' There is no indistinctness in the outline; he is a figure clearly and carefully finished; some of James's finest art has been given to him. Clifford and Lizzie are good, the latter an amusingly accurate picture of a certain type of very young American girl,—pretty, coolly self-possessed, endowed with a ready, unappalled, and slightly-stinging native wit; a small personage whose prominence and even presence amaze and secretly annoy the baroness, who is not accustomed to consider and defer to the opinions of 'little girls' in her graceful and victorious progress through society.

Mr. Brand is the good, slow, serious, clean young man, with large feet and a liking for substantial slices of the excellent home-made cake of well-regulated households, whom many of us know. There is an unregenerate way (which Mr. James shares) of looking at these young men, which sees only their ludicrous points. Light-natured fellows like Felix (or what we suppose Felix is intended to be) are always laughing at them. Even when poor Brand gives up the girl he loves, and stiffens his resolution by offering, in his official capacity, to unite her to his rival, a ludicrous hue is thrown over the action, and we all unite in an amused smile over the young minister and his efforts, which, judged soberly, is unfair. The 'Brands' always seem to me to belong to a soberer age;

they are relics of plainer and more earnest times, and out of place in this American nineteenth century, where everything is taken lightly, and where ridicule is by far the most potent influence. During the war, the Brands had a chance: they marched to the war with tremendous earnestness; nobody minded their big feet on the plain of battle; their slowness was mighty, like a sledge-hammer. Their strong convictions fired the assault; they headed the colored regiments; they made, by their motives and beliefs, even small actions grand. The whole nation was in earnest then; the Brands found their place. But now they are left to themselves again, and are a good deal like mastodons, living by mistake in a later age, objects of amusement to the lighter-footed modern animals, and unable to help it.

The baroness is, however, *the* character. She is the 'European,'—the contrast; she is the story.

In the first description of her personal appearance, I do not think Mr. James was quite fair; he followed Tourguéneff, and pictured the irregularities of her features and personal deficiencies so minutely that I, for one, have never been able to forget it, or to think of her as in the least handsome. Now the baroness *was* handsome; she was an extremely charming woman. We have all met women of that sort; I mean women who had irregular features, but who yet, by their coloring, their grace, or some one single and wonderfully great beauty, kept us from noticing when with them whether their noses were classical, or their mouths large or small. If in real life this is a truth, it should be a truth doubly remembered and guarded in books, where necessarily the warmth of the personal presence is lost. Mr. James might have stated that her face was irregular, judged by rule, but he should have dwelt upon what beauties she *did* have, so that they would make a vivid impression; just as, in real life, they would have domineered vividly over her lacks, if she had entered the room where we were sitting. She is *his* creation; *we* don't know her. He should have answered for her in this respect, and started us fairly.

What was the baroness's fault? The moral of the story?—if there is any. Acton was deeply in love with her; yet he would not quite marry her.

According to my solution, the fault was (and the moral) that she lied; and, in our raw American atmosphere, delicate and congenial lying has not yet been comprehended as one of the fine arts. This is my idea of what Mr. James means.

George Eliot says, in speaking of Gwendolen's mood early one morning, 'It was not that she was out of temper; but that the world was not equal to the demands of her fine organism.' So likewise it was not that the baroness spoke untruths; but the American world was not equal to the accomplishments of her fine organism, or the habits bred in older and more finished society on the other side of the Atlantic.

Mr. James's delightful style is even more delightful than usual in this story. Mr. Wentworth's 'thin, unresponsive glance;' Mr. Brand, 'stiffly and softly' following; the 'well-ordered consciousness' of the Wentworth household; Clifford Wentworth's 'softly growling tone,' indicative, however, merely of 'a vaguely humorous intention' (how good that is!); and, best of all, the last visit of the baroness to Mrs. Acton, and the conversation between the two women, Madame Münster at last giving up in despair, as she perceives that all her delicate little points of language and tone are thrown away, and feeling 'that she would *never* know what such a woman as that meant,'—these are perfect, and make us, for a while, impatient with less artistic stories.

One peculiarity of style I have noticed, namely, the large number of what seem to me 'stage directions.' Thus, fourteen times in three consecutive pages, taken at random from those containing conversation, it is particularly noted down that they 'looked at' each other. As 'Gertrude looked at her a moment, and then, "Yes, Charlotte," she said simply;' 'Gertrude looked at Lizzie Acton, and then looked away;' 'She looked down at him a moment, and then shook her head.' They 'look at' each other 'a moment,' and 'then' speak, uncountable numbers of times. Generally, in print, *cela va sans dire*. I don't mean, that this is a fault at all; but certainly it is a characteristic peculiarity.

24. From the Editor's Literary Record, *Harper's New Monthly Magazine*

January 1879, lviii, 309

Auld Lang Syne is by 'the author of *The Wreck of the Grosvenor*'; I have included the beginning of its notice to suggest the kind of context in which HJ was often reviewed at this time.

Mr. James discriminates judiciously when he styles *The Europeans* a sketch rather than a novel. It is, indeed, a series of brilliant sketches, held together by a slight thread of continuity, but lacking the intimate fusion of parts essential to narrative or dramatic unity. Mr. James describes street scenes, houses, gardens, and country sights and sounds better than he does human characters, apparently because the former are conscientious copies from a model, while his men and women are fictions of the intellect merely, whom he makes known to us by description and assertion instead of by the natural unfolding of their dispositions and characters through the medium of their thinkings and sayings and doings. Interesting studies, therefore, as his portraitures in *The Europeans* unquestionably are, and although his actors are cleverly conceived and placed in lights and situations ingeniously contrived to afford entertainment, they do not seem sufficiently real to rouse our sympathies and to give the semblance of probability to fiction.

The reader of *Auld Lang Syne* will pay it the involuntary compliment of wishing it twice as long as it is. There is not a dry or tedious page in it; its characters are strongly contrasted or harmoniously blended; and its incidents are exciting and dramatic without being sensational. . . .

25. From an unsigned review, *Atlantic*

February 1879, xliii, 167–9

W. H. Mallock (1849–1923) was an English satirist, now best remembered for his Peacockian novel *The New Republic* (1877).

To read Mr. Henry James, Jr., is to experience a light but continuous gratification of mind. It is to be intellectually *tickled*, provided one is capable of such an exercise. It is to take a pleasure so simple and facile that it seems only one step removed from physical content in the lavish cleverness of an almost incessantly witty writer,—a pleasure enhanced, no doubt, by a lurking sense that one must be a little clever one's self in order to keep pace with such dazzling mental agility. To people who have read a good deal of French, and read it because they liked it,— and why else should an Englishman or an American ever advance in that literature beyond the absurd Racine of his school-days?—the writing of Mr. James has the additional interest of offering the best of proof that the English language approaches the French much more nearly than is usually supposed, in its capacity for what may be called *current* epigram. Occasionally, also, Mr. James comes strikingly near to showing that our 'sober speech' might, under proper cultivation, blossom as richly as that of the lively Gaul, into what Mr. Mallock calls 'that perfect flower of modern civilization, the innuendo.' But to do our countryman justice, he is too truly refined to indulge more than sparingly in this exotic species of literary ornament. The clean turns and crisp graces of his style are such as peculiarly befit an essayist, and some of his critical sketches are extremely admirable; but he is too freaky and irresponsible to be always a safe guide, even in matters of bookish opinion, and it is as a novelist only that we propose to consider him.

Within the last three years, Mr. James has written two noteworthy stories, both of which appeared first in these pages. One and the same purpose animates them, and that is to illustrate the different types of character and manners produced by European and American civilization; or, more strictly speaking, by European civilization and American semi-barbarism. On this one point our author keeps all his bright faculties intently focused, and studies the human specimens, which he has first carefully selected, with the methodical minuteness and ecstatic patience of a microscopist . . . [a summary of *The American* and *The Europeans*].

It will be perceived at a glance that all these plans—they cannot be called plots—afford abundant opportunities for humor of situation, every one of which, it need hardly be said, Mr. James brilliantly improves. Newman, before the old Marquise de Bellegarde, replying to her slow and pompous explanations of the uncompromising pride of the race he dared seek to come among by the cheerful assurance that *he* wasn't proud, and didn't mind them; Felix expatiating to his blameless uncle, sitting reluctantly for his portrait, on the ravishing novelty of 'calling on twenty young ladies and going out to walk with them,' sitting in the evening on the piazza and listening to the crickets, and going to bed at ten o'clock; Mr. Brand making a pale, intrepid confession of Unitarianism to the heathen strangers who had never heard of that form of faith; and the Rev. Benjamin Babcock taking a small bag of hominy with him to all the principal Continental hotels, and passing sleepless nights because he cannot make Newman feel, as he does, the overwhelming 'seriousness of art and life,'—all these are spectacles that minister a malign delight. It is in single scenes, detached portraits, and episodes like those of Valentin's duel and Newman's summer tour with Mr. Babcock, that Mr. James is at his very best. The habit of his mind is so irresistibly analytic that he must needs concentrate himself in succession upon each separate detail of his subject. His romance is a series of situations imperfectly vivified by action. There is a scene in *The American*,—a stormy night in the Rue de l'Université, when Madame de Cintré goes to the piano and plays,—and there are a dozen idle scenes in the more languid *Europeans*, which have absolutely no connection with the thread of the story. In like manner his portraits are a succession of uncolored features, and his philosophy is a succession of admirably quotable aphorisms. Here probably we have the reason suggested why we can hear Mr. James's characters so much better than we can see them. In the nature of things only one word can be spoken at a time, and Mr. James is an acute listener and an alert reporter; so that his conversations, except when he endeavors to put into the mouths of his creatures some of his own over-subtle considerations, are exquisitely real and just. But over and above all the items of aspect, whether in places or people, there is a physiognomy, a *look*, and this is what Mr. James never imparts. He tells us clearly, and with an almost anxious emphasis, that Claire de Cintré had a 'long, fair face;' that Gertrude Wentworth had 'sweet dull eyes;' that his delightful and deplorable Valentin de Bellegarde had 'a round head high above the ears,' and 'a crop of short silky hair;' and that the Wentworth mansion in Watertown had white wooden pilasters in front, supporting a pediment with one large central window and two small ones. And we listen as if we were blindfolded, and credit our informant certainly, but do not see at all.

It is a question whether Mr. James himself sees. He is so *spirituel*, and his conceptions are so subtle, that he has not *sense* enough (the term is used metaphysically and with entire respect) to give them form, still less flesh. And so, although a most entertaining chronicler, he escapes being an artist, for an artist must *portray*.

The American is perhaps the finest fragment in modern fiction, but it is only a fragment. *The Europeans* is much less fine, but equally unfinished. His narratives are so fine-spun and so deficient in incident, so unpicturesque as a whole and weak in the way of sensuous imagery, that they are specially ill fitted for serial publication. His flavor is too delicate to be suspended and superseded for a month. But he never wrote anything which was not well worth a connected reperusal. . . .

26. W. D. Howells on the *Daisy Miller* scandal

1879

Howells to J. R. Lowell, June 1879 (LH, i, 271).
Lowell (1819–91) was a distinguished American poet, critic, and diplomat.

Harry James waked up all the women with his *Daisy Miller*, the intention of which they misconceived, and there has been a vast discussion in which nobody felt very deeply, and everybody talked very loudly. The thing went so far that society almost divided itself in Daisy Millerites and anti-Daisy Millerites. I was glad of it, for I hoped that in making James so thoroughly known, it would call attention in a wide degree to the beautiful work he had been doing so long for very few readers and still fewer lovers. Besides, I felt that he had got his best touch in that little study. His art is an honor to us and his patriotism—which was duly questioned—is of the wholesome kind that doesn't blink our little foibles.

RODERICK HUDSON
English Edition

1879

27. From an unsigned review, *Spectator*

July 1879, lii, 854–5

By R. H. Hutton. Like many *Spectator* reviews this makes effect-ive use of extensive quotation, which has been omitted here for reasons of space.

We learn in a prefatory note that *Roderick Hudson* was originally pub-lished in Boston in 1875, and hence we suppose that it is not a later work than *The American*, *The Europeans*, and 'An International Episode', but an earlier one. We are glad of this, as it is certainly in some respects inferior to them. Like all Mr. Henry James writes, it is skilful and subtle, and also somewhat dreary in its total effect upon the mind. But it certainly contains less vivacity and more dreariness than the books we have referred to. Mr. Henry James is never tired of contrasting the complexity of the Old World with the simplicity of the New. We hardly know which he prefers. Apparently he prefers the Old World intellectually, and the New morally . . . the whole novel may be said to be a study of the effect produced by Roman art and manners on different types of American character. First, and perhaps foremost, there is Mrs. Light, the American adventuress, who had deserted her father, betrayed her husband, and eventually taken to spurious piety, and to superstitions of the fortune-telling kind, in addition to the great work of her life, the making a of great match for her beautiful daughter. Nothing in the book is better done, perhaps nothing quite so well done, as the curious mixture of frantic superstition and frantic but purely Yankee worldliness in Mrs. Light, when she finds her daughter determined to reject an extraordinarily wealthy Neapolitan Prince, Prince Casamassima, who is anxious to marry her. . . .

The hero, Roderick Hudson, is certainly not equally well, though much more elaborately painted. Mr. Henry James's object has been to draw a man of thoroughly original, but of what may be called a *thin* vein, of genius, a man with too little genius to find a resource in his genius from the fermentation of his griefs and passions, a man who needs to guard carefully the tranquillity of his heart, in order to extract any perennial spring of suggestion from his head. He is a restless egotist, who is blind to almost everything in others which has no special significance for himself; but yet a brilliant egotist, whose interest for himself is so great, that by means of that which interests him in himself, he can interpret powerfully a good deal in other people. The picture is powerful in itself, and to a certain extent, natural. Only what we doubt is this,—whether any man of genius so great as Roderick Hudson's, ever could be so long and so completely diverted from the natural themes of that genius by an unhappy passion. If we know anything of the true artist, we should say that when the first edge of bitterness due to personal disappointments was once dulled, the imagination of the sculptor, instead of being dried up, would be quickened by the new insight it had gained into the meaning of certain lines of expression written on the countenance. Roderick Hudson must be quite a new type of artist, if, with the power and orginality attributed to him, his imagination was simply dried up by his unreturned passion for Christina Light. His selfishness and egotism are not, perhaps, over-done. But his artistic sterility under pain and disappointment surely is. Surely nothing has greater effect in stimulating the imagination than mental pain of which the first keenness is past.

But probably the cleverest sketch in this dismal little group is poor Mrs. Hudson, the motherly little wren of a woman, who is, as Mr. James says, in relation to her influence in society, quite 'imponderable,' and who nevertheless manages to make her son's friend and patron so very miserable, by her quaint assumption of a right to reproach him— to hold him responsible—for her son's derelictions of duty and defects of character. . . . But making all allowance for these admirable pictures, and for many graphic passages describing Rome and Italian scenery, we cannot but say that, on the whole, this is a dismal story. Indeed, Mr. Henry James delights in dismal stories. He thinks, apparently, that it is flying somehow in the face of his own genius to let any story fall out happily. But still, in most of them though he insists on making you dismal in the end, he contrives to amuse you very much in the interval. But in this book he makes you dismal almost from beginning to end. He makes it so very evident that Roderick is to go to the bad, that Mary Garland will not desert him, and will never return Rowland's love, that Rowland Mallet will not desert Roderick, and that Mrs. Hudson will be a burden on all, that there is hardly a ray of sunshine through the story. Even Christina Light is a dismal beauty. You cannot enjoy her picturesque, grand ways, because you feel that an inward dreariness is at the bottom of them all, and so there is no set-off against the dreariness of the main story. Why is Mr. Henry James, with all his great talents, so deeply persuaded of the pessimism of human destiny? Is it that he thinks it the destiny of all New Englanders, not only 'to suffer and be strong,' but to suffer the more from making acquaintance with the main stream of civilisation, and be all the stronger for thus suffering the more? Certainly he has never published anything of which it has not been the chief idea that evil comes from the Old World, against which the New World fights desperately a losing battle, or at least a battle in which it loses happiness, at the expense of a sort of dismal aureole of moral glory.

28. From an unsigned review,
British Quarterly Review

October 1879, lxx, 529–30

This, although in many ways an admiring review, exhibits with particular clarity some of the preconceptions of the time.

Roderick Hudson, originally published in Boston in 1875, is full of the subtle but somewhat morbid analysis that is so prominent a characteristic of Mr. James's genius. He seems very emphatically to dissent from his hero's theory that ugliness is treason to art, and that if artistic things are not positively beautiful they are to be set down as failures. Without maintaining what in such an absolute form would be a paradox, we may maintain that the province of art is to create ideals, and that ideals are necessarily beautiful, each in its domain. Whereas for ideals Mr. James substitutes types, which he exaggerates; and as his choice seems instinctively to be of defect and disorder, the almost uniform impression of his novels is painful. He does not incite by great examples; he warns by shocking beacons, and this, we say again, for the hundredth time, is not the true conception of the poem or the novel any more than of the picture or the statue. Where processes of development are exhibited almost uniformly the evil element overcomes the good, not the good the evil. . . . Not a single character throughout the story produces satisfaction. It is as cynical and as pessimist as *The American* reviewed in our last number. Christina and her husband disappear into infinite possibilities, nay, certainties of misery, if not of shame. Her mother is left to the bitter reaping of her worldliness. Roderick's mother to the misery of weak reproaches and senile sorrow. Roderick's own tragic fate is the great moral of the story. The book is unrelieved in its melancholy failures, masterly as are the penetration and power with which these are analyzed. It is the pessimism of life. Heraclitus is its presiding genius. It is Ecclesiastes in a story.

29. James on his progress in England

1879

HJ to Perry, May 1879 (LP, 302).
The 'little novel' was *Confidence*.

. . . I scratch along on this crowded highway of London life & shall probably do so for an indefinite period. I have got a good deal of fame & hope some day to get a little money. I have had, I think, more success with the dull British public in a few months than with that of my native land in all these long years that I have been scribbling to it. This fact of course helps me to be comfortable & contented here. I am just finishing another little novel which is to appear (alas!) in the dreadful *Scribner's*, but which I strongly urge you not to read until it is republished.

30. 'An International Episode'

1878

From an unsigned survey of James's recent work *Blackwood's Magazine*, July 1879, cxx, 100–7.
The reviewer has just discussed France's treatment of Newman in *The American*.

. . . England treats with less cruelty the American woman whom Mr. James presents to us, with a touch of indulgence for the mother country, as the representative of the New World in London. We find Miss Bessie Alden first at home in the multitudinous life of an American watering-place, where the whole population sits out in breezy verandas (called piazzas in native phraseology) within sight of the sea, in white dresses, and talks. To this society arrive two Englishmen, Lord Lambeth and Mr. Percy Beaumont, who are made very much of by the pretty wife and beautiful sister of the New York man of business, to whom they have been introduced. Bessie Alden, the sister, is a Boston young lady, not accustomed to the gaiety of the New-Yorkers, and much impressed by her first encounter with an Englishman. The picture is very pretty and charming. The girl looks at the handsome, somewhat dull, very ignorant, and perfectly good-tempered and good-mannered Englishman with a little awe. To her he is a type of that cultivated and beautiful Old World full of associations, full of poetry, about which she has been reading all her days, and to see which is, as she says, the dream of her life. . . . It is, however, when his gay and elegant and beautifully-dressed and pretty-mannered Americans come to London that Mr. James's intention becomes apparent. We are doubtful whether his indictment is most against the British aristocracy for not rushing to throw itself at the feet of Mrs. Westgate and Miss Alden, or against Mrs. Westgate for expecting this rush. Both are involved in the pretty and lively talk of the lady, who, conscious of having taken so many Englishmen to her heart in America, is delicately and gaily bitter as to the absence of all return on their part when she appears in their kingdom. Lord Lambeth is most anxious to return their civilities, and devotes himself to their service; but he cannot make his duchess-mother equally eager, and the whole brilliant little episode collapses in the inferred refusal by Bessie of her noble lover, which is caused, we are not sure whether by her indifference to himself, or by her indignant perception of the manner in which her proud innocence is regarded by all around him. Thus it all comes to nothing once more; and the pretty Americans go forth 'to spread their conquests further,' into the gayer French world, where they apparently expect a better reception, but where, as Mr. James has already shown us, still more tragic and in-comprehensible hostilities lurk.

Thus we are made to see the generous open-heartedness of American society, and the mean jealousy and unresponsiveness of our own. But do not let us say our own—for Mrs. Westgate is charmingly *naïve* in her determination to see no society worthy of her which does not include all the dukes and duchesess, personages whom most of us scarcely take into account at all as indispensable to enjoyment.

I don't want any superior second-rate society, (said this charming woman); I want the society I have been accustomed to. The first time I came to London I went out to dine. After dinner, in the drawing-room I had some conversation with an old lady. . . . I forget what she talked about; but she presently said, in allusion to something we were discussing, 'Oh, you know the aristocracy do so-and-so—but in one's own class of life it is very different.' In one's own class of life! What is a poor unprotected American woman to do in a country where she is liable to have that sort of thing said to her?

This is perhaps the most delicate and refined snobbishness that was ever put upon record, and Mr. James evidently knows the ways of thinking of his people. . . . These ladies take all the conventionalities of society *au grand sérieux*. They are wounded by the fact that Her Grace must walk before them out of a room; yet they feel themselves not in the society to which they have been accustomed when they are not with the duchesses. The picture is very amusing and characteristic, and full of candour. Miss Alden, however, who is from Boston, is very desirous of carrying with her into the best society another class not always found there—'the eminent people—the authors and artists—the clever people'. 'We hold them in great honour; *they go to the best dinner-parties,*' she says, with delightful simplicity. The young Bostonian is not less conscious of her superiority to 'the distinguished people' than is the Marquis of Lambeth; but her sense of her power to do them honour is much more lively. Altogether there have been few things more piquant in recent literature than this contrast and contact of the Old World and the New. The American in France had much the worse of the conflict. The *Americaine* in England carries off the honours, though they are somewhat barren.

CONFIDENCE

1879

31. From an unsigned review, *Spectator*

January 1880, liii, 48–9

The reader will notice, among so much that is incisive and genu-inely challenging in this review, an unwillingness to discriminate between *Confidence* (surely by far the weakest of the novels) and HJ's previous work. This is typical of the period, when even the best minds obviously found it difficult or impossible to respond fully and naturally to HJ's art, and particularly to its deeper emotional effects.

It cannot be said of any one of Mr. James's stories, 'This is his best,' or, 'This is his worst;' because no one of them is all one thing; like human beings, they are partly good, and partly not so good; they have their phases of exceeding strength and veracity, and also phases which are neither strong nor veracious. It does not concern us to give an explana-tion of this fact; it is to be found, of course, in the character or literary views of the writer himself; but we may observe that it seems to indicate either an actual lack of experience in certain directions, or else a con-stitutional reserve which prevents Mr. James from writing up to the experience he has. The experience we refer to is not of the ways of the world, with which Mr. James has every sign of being politely familiar; nor of men and women in their every-day aspect; still less of literary ways and means, of which he may be pronounced, in his own line, almost a master. The experience we mean is experience of passion. If Mr. James be not incapable of describing passion, at all events he has still to show that he is capable of it. During the last fifteen years, more or less, he has been writing stories of remarkable subtlety, charm, and literary finish; he has introduced us to many characters who seemed to have in them capacities for the highest passion,—as witness Christina Light, in the novel called *Roderick Hudson*; and yet he has never allowed them to bring those capacities to the proof. He uniformly evades the situation; but the evasion is managed with so much ingenuity and plausibility, that although we may be disappointed, or even irritated, we are deprived of the right of giving those emotions satisfactory expression. We feel more or less vaguely, that we have been unfairly dealt with, but we are unable to show exactly how the unfairness comes about. . . .

Beyond this complaint—which, to be sure, goes rather deep—we have little to say of Mr. James's novels that is not complimentary. He does not much trouble himself to contrive intricate plots, or to imagine strange situations; but he cuts a slice out of life almost at haphazard, and then goes about to reveal and analyse its constituent parts. This method, when well applied, is very telling, though open to some obvious disadvantages, For, while the human element in fiction has ever the stronger interest, few human lives are so completely rounded as to give opportunity for an artistic *dénouement*. The story ends, but it leaves the reader still with something to wish for. Something in the way of incident and circumstance is useful to fill up the gap. However, Mr. James is never dull; his power of felicitous statement, taken by itself, would ensure him against that; and his occasional wit, his frequent touches of arch irony, and his unfailing thoughtfulness and purity of diction, are all so much to the good. He always puts his reader in a good humour, and makes him feel as if he were moving in the most cultivated society. The interest of his stories lies, as we have said, in the characters; we are introduced to them, and we generally see them distinctly enough, but we do not know them until later on, if at all; and we can never be sure what they will do next. This is what happens in real life; it is piquant and stimulating, and if it be not the very best plan to work upon in fiction (as to which point we are not at present prepared to give an opinion), it has, at all events, the authorisation of so eminent a master as Tourguéneff. What is more to the purpose, it evidently suits Mr. James, whose creed, so far as it may be guessed from his writings, seems to be a refined and elevated sort of materialism, insomuch that he objects to believe in anything that he has not objectively seen or known; and although endowed with a strength of superficial imagination which has seldom been surpassed, he shrinks from setting down in black and white anything for which his imagination is his only warrant. This is a most commendable principle, though there are doubtless limits to the extent to which it should be followed; Shakespeare, for example, could hardly have written some scenes of *Lear* from his actual knowledge; but, grasping as he did the very core of human nature, he was able to construct thence any conceivable human situation. We do not want Mr. James to write another *Lear*, but we do wish, in reference to his present book, that he had been pleased in the *dénouement*, to trust a little more to what imagination would say might have happened, and a little less to what his personal experience of life had to propound on the matter. In *Confidence* as in nearly all of Mr. James's novels, there is a point at which the reader could lay down the book and say. 'This is one of the finest stories ever written.' But the reader goes on, and he is disappointed. All the elements of a masterly conclusion are here, but the opportunity is not taken advantage of. The heroine, Angela Vivian, in one of Mr. James's best and largest feminine conceptions, which is saying a great deal, for his women are always better than his men, and his men are far above the ordinary fiction-level. Angela's character is steadily and luminously developed, without one false note or insufficient phrase, up to the 197th page of the second volume. Thenceforward she, and all the rest of the *dramatis personae* with her, become—to our comprehension, at least—incomprehensible. Gordon Wright, the last person in the world to do such a thing, abruptly puts on the mask of a scoundrel and a 'cad.' Bernard Longueville, the accomplished and clever man of the world, assumes the guise of a poltroon and an ass. And Angela, the noble, proud, and tender woman, whose mixture of simple honesty and inscrutable reserve has rendered her thus far a heroine for every reader to fall in love with,— Angela lapses into a theatric tone and attitude, and for the sake of creating a dramatic surprise utters and proposes absurdities which Blanche herself might have shrunk from. The effect altogether, is as if the whole party, after having led a logical and respectable existence in a reasonable world, had suddenly grouped themselves before the foot-lights of some obscure, provincial stage, and begun to enact a piece of melodramatic claptrap. What could Mr. James have been thinking of?

The only suggestion we can make in answer to this question is, that he desired to avoid the true artistic conclusion demanded by his premises; and the reason of this desire was a reluctance to undertake the description of a passionate situation. It was a situation the right treatment of which would have raised Mr. James's reputation as a novelist to a place among the highest. Bernard Longueville was not the man tamely to submit to a gross insult levelled at the woman to whom he was betrothed, nor was Angela the woman either to be so insulted, or, in the very heat of the moment, composedly to execute a knowing little manœuvre of insight, and, at the same time, to devise a far-fetched and improbable scheme of reconciliation. She would have set the wrong right, no doubt, as a heroine should; but it would have been by some grand dilation of the spirit, overawing and paralysing the baser soul. As for Bernard, unless we are greatly mistaken, he would have beckoned Gordon out of the room, and would then have promptly and relentlessly kicked him downstairs. Men who are in love and engaged to be married have a strong sense of possession, which will make a champion of the veriest craven, upon occasion given. The result of Mr. James's reticence—to call it by no severer name—is this: that he loses all belief in his own characters, and that they consequently lose their lifelikeness; that the remaining situations are tamely described through the medium of Angela's letters, and that the novel ends prematurely and stagnantly.

32. James on the American public

1880

HJ to Perry, February 1880 (LP, 305).
HJ's remarks about the thinness of American culture in *Hawthorne*
had given a great deal of offence.

The hubbub produced by my poor little *Hawthorne* is most ridiculous;
my father has sent me a great many notices, each one more abusive &
more abject than the others. The vulgarity, ignorance, rabid vanity &
general idiocy of them all is truly incredible. But I hold it a great piece
of good fortune to have stirred up such a clatter. The whole episode
projects a lurid light upon the state of American 'culture', & furnishes
me with a hundred wonderful examples, where, before, I had only
more or less vague impressions. Whatever might have been my own
evidence for calling American taste 'provincial', my successors at least
will have no excuse for not doing it.

33. James on the decline of letters

1881

HJ to Perry, February 1881 (LP, 309).

You say that literature is going down in the U.S.A. I quite agree with
you—the stuff that is sent me seems to me written by eunuchs &
sempstresses. But I think it is the same every where—in France & in
England. I suspect the age of letters is waning, for our time. It is the age
of Panama Canals, of Sarah Bernhardt, of Western wheat-raising, of
merely material expansion. Art, form, may return, but I doubt that I
shall live to see them—I don't believe they are eternal, as the poets say.
All the same, I shall try to make them live a little longer!—Yes, I know
Matt. Arnold very well & like him much. I was pleased to hear that
he told a friend of mine the other day that 'Henry James is a de-ah!'

WASHINGTON SQUARE

1880

34. From an unsigned review, *Spectator*

February 1881, liv, 185–6

By R. H. Hutton. The 'second and third pieces' mentioned are 'The Pension Beaurepas' and 'A Bundle of Letters' which were published with *Washington Square*.

Mr. Henry James is always more or less embarrassed by what he very likely regards as the artificial necessity of making a whole. He finds that life very seldom makes a whole. If you may trust him as your guide, even human passion is not commonly dramatic. It ends oftener in a ravelled thread than in a true *dénouement*. And whether that be true or false, it interests him much more to paint the various aimless ways in which human beings get almost involuntarily into a sort of entanglement with each other, than to paint the course of a series of events which show the natural development of strong character, and the natural resultant of the encounter between conflicting purposes and complicated circumstances. If, indeed, you may believe Mr. Henry James, the result of such encounters is much more frequently indeterminate than not. In his pictures, most passions fade away; most influences fail of their characteristic effect; most comedies are spoiled; most tragedies break down before the tragic crisis; most catastrophes, as the Irishman would say, never come off; while that which fulfils its function most completely in the world is the power, inherent in most of us, to spoil or hamper the life of other people, an agency the conspicuous success of which almost all Mr. James's writings commemorate.

There has never been a more adequate illustration of this tendency of Mr. Henry James's than the dismal tale entitled *Washington Square*, in which there is no agreeable character, only one likeable character,—

we mean the plain, mute, tenacious heroine, of whom we are told that 'she knew she was obstinate, and it gave her a certain joy,'—no very detestable character, nothing but common-place affectionateness, common-place and even vulgar selfishness, somewhat more than common-place cruelty and cynicism, very common-place insincerity, and very common-place misery. Mr. Henry James seems to take quite a pleasure in making us study this leaden-coloured group of emotions, and take home to our hearts that life, even among well-to-do New Yorkers who have something like culture, and care to study Europe, is like that. . . . The story is marvellously clever. To our minds, nothing more unique in the presenting of human nature than Dr. Sloper's cold-hearted experiments on his daughter's nature, and utter failure to do anything except rob her of her admiration for him, has ever been given us; nor is Mrs. Penniman's silly love of intrigue, and her brother's scornful treatment of it, less admirably drawn. Catherine's dumb, slow, tenacious nature, too,—which, in spite of its occasionally rather needless and meaningless lapses into falsehood, affords us the only glimpse of anything tolerable in the tale, is a fine study of its sort. But why is the whole painted against that blank, leaden sky, not merely of absolute hopelessness, but absolute indifference to hope? Why are we made to feel that there was nothing elastic in Catherine which rose against her troubles, nothing that found for her a gain in loss, nothing that strengthened and sweetened her nature, and made the permanent and sole companionship of such a silly and insincere old woman as Mrs. Penniman an impossibility to her? Why is the dismal experience of so dead and dull a weight of sorrow left just where it is, with nothing to indicate why it did not sour Catherine? or how, in spite of her double loss of hope abroad and hope at home, she contrived still to live in tolerable content with herself and the world, and not to feel either crushed or bitter? Mr. Henry James strikes us as in nothing less humane than in the indifference with which he treats his characters, after he has brought them through such melancholy shifts in their lot as he generally provides for them. He seems not to care himself about the fate of such 'residuum' of the character he has created as remains after he has treated it with the various materials mingled in the alembic of his fiction. . . . He has no interest in the moral equities of life, and cares no more in this tale, for instance, to estimate what Catherine Sloper has gained and lost by her dreary love-story, and the estrangement from her father which it involved, than he cares what may result to the proprietresses of the two *pensions* in his second and third pieces, from the departure of their various guests. It is impossible to give effectual illustrations from *Washington Square* of the sort of genius shown in it. There is no doubt that it is genius, and genius of the most marked order, genius for painting character, and genius for conceiving unalloyed dismalness of effect, without tragedy and without comedy. If you desire a consummately clever study of perfect dreariness, you have it in *Washington Square*.

35. From an unsigned review, *Literary World*

January 1881, xii, 10

The *Literary World* was a prominent Boston publication, and extremely moralistic. The following is offered as an early example.

If any of our more penetrating readers can say what Mr. Henry James's last story amounts to, we shall be happy to publish the estimate. Doubtless the writing of it occupied this literary saunterer so many hours, and the printing of it took up so many pages in *Harper's Magazine,* where, we believe, it first appeared. What more? Of course it is a clever bit of psychological anatomy. . . .

The truest thing we can say of *Washington Square* is that it is a piece of literary dilettanteism. It does not give Mr. Henry James, Jr., credit for being even an earnest trifler.

36. From an unsigned review, *Atlantic*

May 1881, xlvii, 709–10

Certainly, if one presents to himself the high problems of life for solution, he may be pardoned a little impatience over the elaborate nonentities who occupy the pages of *Washington Square*. . . . Mr. James appears to have set himself the task of portraying the mental features of a dull woman capable of a species of dumb devotion to a man who easily assumes the place of an ideal being in the somewhat arid waste of her life. That she is capable of steadfastness, and, after she is jilted, of self-respect, are the results which he extracts from his observation, and he has succeeded in making these evident. He has sketched also a silly aunt, who busies herself as stage manager of all the romantic scenes; and he has given us the character of a father who, from first to last, looks upon his daughter with scarely a spark of paternal feeling. That the book is witty and sometimes ingenious is almost its sole excuse for being, but the wit is expended by the author in his own reflections, and rarely emanates from the characters and situations. Does he not indeed feel a certain contempt for his heroine? At least, he fails to give the reader any stronger interest in her behavior than one of curiosity. We should have been glad to be allowed to pity her, even if we could not greatly admire her, but in the passages which treat of her suffering at the hands of her father and lover, the author introduces so effectively his own wit and ingenuity that he withdraws our sympathy from her, and enlists our admiration only for his own cunning.

THE PORTRAIT OF A LADY

1881

37. From an unsigned review, *Spectator*

November 1881, liv, 1504–6

By R. H. Hutton.

If Mr. Henry James had called this book 'The Portrait of Two Gentle-men,' we might have admitted the aptness of the description, for the real power of the book consists in the wonderful pictures given of Ralph Touchett and Mr. Osmond, which have rarely been equalled in fiction for the skill and delicacy of the painting. But as for Isabel Archer—or Mrs. Osmond, as she afterwards becomes—who is the lady of whom the portrait is taken, we venture to say that the reader never sees her, or realises what she is, from the beginning of the book to the close. She is the one lady of whom no portrait is given, though she is studied till the reader is weary of the study. We have a very admirable portrait of Mrs. Touchett, a brilliant one of the Countess Gemini, a very clever one of Madame Merle, a most finished and attractive one of poor little Pansy Osmond, a very humorous one of Henrietta Stackpole; but of Isabel Archer one has no portrait at all, but only an interminable and laborious effort to paint one, an effort which is entirely in vain. One knows that she is pretty, that she loves freedom, that she loves experience, that she has endless day-dreams, that she is compassionate to the helpless, that she is grateful for goodness, and proud, not to say defiant, towards those who are not good to her; but beyond that, one knows nothing about her. Apparently, she has no faith whatever, no fixed standard even of inward life and motive, though she is always chasing ideals with no particular substance, or even uniformity, in them. Why she is so much fascinated by a man so utterly destitute of anything that is large in mind or heart, as Mr.

Osmond, so made up, indeed, of fastidious selfishness,—unless it be for the artistic deference of his manner towards her, it is impossible to say. He says of himself, 'No, I am not conventional, I am convention itself;' and, indeed, after one great breach of convention, sedulously concealed, he appears to have accepted convention, as distinguished from any of the moral or spiritual grounds of convention, as the whole aim of his life. So far as the reader has been prepared by the very elaborate studies of Isabel which precede the acquaintance with Mr. Osmond, one would have said that such a character as his could not have had any true fascination for her, and it remains one of the problems of the story why it ever had such a fascination,—a problem that it is all the more difficult to solve, since the reader, though fully understanding the rather feline character of Mr. Osmond's love of convention, is never really let into the confidence of his wife. It is this which, together with Mr. Henry James's very agnostic view of Art, spoils the book. The effect of the picture as a whole is this,—that while all the subsidiary painting is most lucid and delicate, the central figure remains shrouded in mist. Where the strongest light and the most definite impression should be, there is nothing but haze, nothing but a laborious riddle. Nevertheless, Mr. Henry James shows something more than his habitual skill,—and how great that is, in our opinion, we have often had occasion to state,—in the wonderful picture of Mr. Osmond's temporary transfiguration during the few scenes in which he is presented to us as a suitor for Isabel. There one does, at least for a moment, understand that there might be some illusion about him,—not an illusion as to largeness of character, for he has not even a shadow of it, but as to the reverence and sweetness of his nature, of which he has really nothing but the outside, and yet so good an outside of it, that it is difficult for a moment to doubt that there is not something more behind. Let us contrast the subtlety of the painting of Osmond, when he is making his own offer, with the mode in which he throws cold water on poor little Rosier, when the latter comes to him in the vain hope of being permitted to marry Pansy. We give first the close of the interview in which Osmond makes his offer to Isabel:

[quotes Ch. xxix from ' "Go everywhere," he said at last, in a low, kind voice . . .' to ' "There are so many things we might talk about".']

It would be difficult, we think, to surpass the delicacy and subtlety of that painting, so far as regards Mr. Osmond. The sudden brightness of manner, the artistic deference, the studied frankness, the tone of pure disinterestedness, are all such as a man of this kind, with a sincere love for the refined externals of life, and no heart behind it, would be able to assume, without feeling his assumption in the least degree hypocritical or false. Now, let us see him as he receives and discountenances the lover of his daughter, whom he desires to reserve for a much wealthier match:

[quotes Ch. xxxvii from 'Rosier, coming in unannounced . . .' to ' "I have nothing that I wish to match".']

That gives sufficient indication of Mr. Osmond's two manners, the refined, reverential manner, by which he wins favour with Isabel; and the curt, contemptuous manner, with which he expresses his scorn for what he regards as beneath him, when he has no object to gain by concealing it. In scene after scene this character is developed, and always with some fresh touch of fastidious insolence or intense though petty pride, which makes of it a wonderful, and yet most repulsive, artistic achievement. As a set-off against this disagreeable picture is that of Ralph Touchett, the humorous, Anglo-American invalid,—who throughout the book is dying slowly of consumption,—and who shuffles about with his hands in his pockets and a shrewd eye always fixed on the life about him, eliciting all its characteristic features, in love with Isabel himself, though without ever thinking of sacrificing her, and indeed generously forgetting his own future in the desire to add to his cousin Isabel's happiness. Ralph Touchett is a very powerful picture, and a fine pendant to that of Osmond, the delicately-enamelled idolator of his own tastes and dignity, for whom Ralph's improvident generosity to his cousin unfortunately set a trap, by endowing her with wealth to which she had no claim, and which proves to her a pure misfortune. Such are the two leading characters of the book,—as powerfully drawn as Isabel's is feebly and faintly drawn,—companion pictures of niggardness of soul, on the one side, and magnanimity, of an unpretending type, on the other. Besides these, there are, as we have said, plenty of side-figures, many of them exhibiting Mr. Henry James's best insight and highest humour. As regards the latter quality, the relation of Henrietta Stackpole and Captain Bantling are painted with a finer humour than anything we remember in our author's work.

But the cloven foot of Mr. Henry James's agnosticism,—as artist no less than as thinker,—is shown at the close of his tale, with even more nakedness than he has ever shown it yet. That he always likes to end his tales with a failure of anything like the old poetic justice, we all know. That perplexing relations should ravel themselves, rather then unravel themselves, and end, so far as there is an ending at all, in something worse than they began in, is one of Mr. Henry James's canons of art. The tendency of life, he holds, is to result in a general failure of the moral and spiritual hopes it raises. If you let your story land itself in a wreck, or fade away into a blank and pallid apathy,—that is true art to this author. But never before has he closed a novel by setting up quite so cynical a sign-post into the abyss, as he sets up at the close of this book. He ends his *Portrait of a Lady*, if we do not wholly misinterpret the rather covert, not to say almost cowardly, hints of his last page, by calmly indicating that this ideal lady of his, whose belief in purity has done so much to alienate her from her husband, in that it had made him smart under her contempt for his estimates of the world, saw a 'straight path' to a liaison with her rejected lover. And worse still, it is apparently intended that this is the course sanctioned both by her high-minded friend, Miss Stackpole, and by the dying cousin whose misfortune it had been to endow her with wealth that proved fatal to her happiness. The close of *The Portrait of a Lady* throws a strange light on the results to be expected from pure agnosticism in its relation to Art. Mr. Henry James long ago rejected the idea that real life is intelligible and significant, even as far as this—that the artistic presentation of it ought to satisfy the mind and heart, as the greater dramatists and novelists have always endeavoured to satisfy the mind and heart. But he has never till now ventured to indicate that the natural end of a noble nature, after it has wrecked itself by a great mistake, is ignoble surrender to selfish passion. Yet it is quite true that pure agnosticism is most likely to lead hither. Isabel is painted as trusting to nothing to keep her right in life but vague, generous aspirations, without compass and without clue; and for such a one, it is natural enough that, at the last pinch, all morality should seem nothing but convention, and the 'straight path' a mere descent to selfish indulgence. We can hardly speak too highly of the skill and genius shown in many parts of *The Portrait of a Lady*. We can hardly speak too depreciatingly of the painting of that portrait itself, or of the moral collapse into which the original of the portrait is made to fall. After all, even if it had been provided that Isabel should have attained her ideal, the result we certainly expected, we should not have cared much for a young lady made up of such extremely vague aspirations. As it is, we are filled with wonder that agnostic Art should have got so far as to place a great blot in the centre of a carefully-painted picture, without seeing that agnostic Art has, as Art, committed suicide in so doing.

38. From an unsigned review, *Athenaeum*

November 1881, 2822, 699

It is impossible not to feel that Mr. James has at last contrived to write a dull book. *The Portrait of a Lady* is of enormous length, being printed much more closely than is usual with three-volume novels; and a large part of it is made up of page after page of narrative and description, in which the author goes on refining and distinguishing, as if unable to hit on the exact terms necessary to produce the desired effect. . . . There is no doubt that reticence is a virtue in a novelist, but it may be carried too far, and this Mr. James, from a feeling, probably, of repugnance for the gushing and sensational, seems to have done. He should remember that much of human life cannot be painted in 'tertiary' tints, and that if he wishes to be a master in the art of portraying it he must furnish his box with some stronger colours, and lay them on boldly.

It is marked by the same merits and the same defects which are to be noticed in nearly all that he has written. There is the same minute and accurate observation, the same adroitness in keeping the reader's curiosity, if not always his interest, alive to the end, the same ingenious analysis of superficial feeling and motive. But in *The Portrait of a Lady*, as in so much that Mr. James has written, we cannot help remarking the care which the writer takes not to go down, if he can possibly avoid it, below the surface of his characters and of the situations in which he places them. And in those cases where he cannot escape doing so, he seems at once to lose hold of the characters whose outward and superficial qualities he depicts with so much ability. The real nature of his characters, which should appear most clearly in serious and critical situations, sees at such times to have no connexion with what he has told us of their past history. Mr. James devises a plot skilfully, and leads us up to a crisis where all our expectation is awake; but when the moment for action comes, he evades the catastrophe altogether, either —which is his most common method—by making his actors do nothing at all, or by making them do something which seems to be prompted by no reasonable motive. In either case he frustrates the curiosity of the reader, and leaves him with the sense that the plot, however ingenious, breaks down at the critical moment. Mr. James has certainly many of the qualities of a fine novelist; but his reluctance to go below the surface, or to grasp a character as a whole, renders his short sketches and little episodes more successful than his longer works. . . . What Isabel's charm is we can hardly make out. She is young, pretty, imaginative, and apparently has the faculty of striking her company as a girl of much depth and strength of character. She is, in truth, a rather selfish and heartless young lady, who acts as if the world were arranged in order to satisfy the claims of her imagination. She succeeds, however, in the course of the story in making three men deeply in love with her, and in making a fourth marry her; not however, by in any way intentionally drawing them on, but simply by the impression her personality makes upon them. Where the charm lies the reader cannot easily discover, and he is in no way helped in his endeavours by any explanations of the writer. The first of Isabel's victims is a young American Caspar Goodwood, whom, it appears, she had encouraged in his suit before she left her native country. The next two are Lord Warburton and Ralph Touchett, the former of whom declares himself after he has known her a few days, and who, notwithstanding that he is a young English patrician of the most wholesome and eligible sort, is rejected, on the ground, apparently, that the lot he offers her is too circumscribed, and does not promise enough of the unforeseen for her imagination to feed upon. The third lover, Ralph Touchett, makes Isabel no offer of marriage, which his state of health puts out of the question; but gives her to understand what his feelings towards her are, and follows her career partly with the chivalrous devotion of a lover whom circumstances forbid to seek to be more than a friend, and partly with the speculative curiosity of an active mind condemned by physical weakness to play the passive part of a spectator of the life of others. We are given to understand that Isabel is one of the striking complex, and problematic natures which repay such a study; but the reader can hardly help feeling that the chief point of interest in her is that we cannot quite tell what she will do next. However, her lack of defined motive passes with all her admirers as a sign of depth and originality. . . . The character of Osmond—a selfish, heartless, accomplished, and still ineffective man, reminding one in a good many points of George Eliot's Grandcourt—is one of the most successful in the book. In the teeth of the remonstrances of her aunt, Mrs. Touchett, and of her still faithful lovers, Ralph Touchett and Caspar Goodwood, Isabel, after once refusing Osmond, marries him at last. As to Isabel's change of mind, and the means Osmond takes to bring it about, we are left altogether in the dark. A year or so is supposed to elapse after the refusal, and we are then re-introduced to Isabel as an engaged woman. Surely if the portrait of Isabel's character is to be a living one, we ought to see something of the mental processes which decide her to take the gravest step of her life. Casper Goodwood, a powerful, energetic, positive, commanding nature, is rejected; Lord Warburton, a generous, manly, attractive, and every way eligible suitor, is rejected; Ralph Touchett, different from both, but quite as noticeable in his way, is hardly ever thought of as a man to be loved. The trains of feeling and association which lead a good and clever woman to prefer to types like these a person of Osmond's stamp, and the illusions she must create for herself before she can do so, are precisely the subjects on which a skilful analyst of human nature should be able to throw some light; but it is just here that Mr. James leaves us most in the dark. We can only wonder that a situation should be devised so cunningly on purpose, as it almost seems, to be made no use of. . . . As we said before, till the time for action comes Mr. James's men and women are admirable imitations of human beings; but the moment the hour arrives for decision and deeds, they reveal themselves as mere *simulacra*. And this defect, which is characteristic of most of Mr. James's works, is nowhere more conspicuous than in his latest book.

40. From an unsigned review, *Blackwood's Magazine*

March 1882, cxxxi, 374–82

This gentleman's [James's] work in the world seems to be a peculiar one. It is to record and set fully before us the predominance of the great American race, and the manner in which it has overrun and conquered the Old World. . . . Mr. James shows us his countrymen in the attitude of conquerors, dominating, not intruding, upon the foreign world about them. . . .

[quotations from and comments of HJ's picture of the American colony in Paris in *Portrait of a Lady*]

We linger upon these sketches of the dominant race, of which all readers have come to appreciate the importance through Mr. James's very popular works, because it is more easy to enjoy studies so fine and so keen, cut with the precision of an old gem, than to find our way, as we should like, through the maze of delicate analysis and psychological study, tempered with a number of brilliant social sketches, which makes up in three very large volumes *The Portrait of a Lady*. The one thing which the book is not, is what it calls itself. There are several portraits of subordinate ladies—of Mrs. Touchett and Miss Stackpole, for example, both of which are admirable pictures; but of the heroine, upon whom the greatest pains have been expended, and to whom endless space is afforded for the setting forth of her characteristics, we have no portrait, nor, even with the enormous amount of material supplied by Mr. James, do we find it easy to put together anything which will serve to supply the defect. . . .

There is but little vicissitude . . . in her career; she comes to 'Europe' with something of the intention which Mr. James illustrated with, we think, a great deal more power, though less of the extremely refined and cultivated skill of which he is now master, in *The Americans*, the first work by which he was known in England; that is, to get everything she can out of her life and its opportunities,—all the sensation, the information, the variety of experience which it is possible it can convey. There is this difference between the young and visionary girl and the mature man, that whereas Mr. James's first hero wanted practical satisfaction for his desires, and to get possession of all that was best, including, as the most indispensable article of all, the fairest and most costly flower of womanhood which was to be found or purchased anyhow,—Isabel prefers not to have anything but the sense of having —the wealth of spiritual possession. For this reason she likes to retain a hold upon the lovers whom she will not marry. The English lord with all his fine qualities—and it cannot be said that our American author and heroine do not do full justice to these qualities with a refined sense of the admirableness of the position, and the importance which attaches to so curious and desirable a specimen of humanity—gives her the most agreeable consciousness of power, though all his advantages do not tempt her to marry him, and she is sorry for vexing him—almost as sorry as she is agreeably excited by the incident altogether. Indeed it would appear that this accompaniment of homage is natural to the young American woman, and that she would feel herself to be treated unfairly if at least one English lord, besides innumerable other candidates of different descriptions, did not attest her power. This is very different from the more vulgar development of the American young woman, who is bent on securing a title for herself. Mr. James's young ladies never do this. . . .

It was inevitable that such a heroine should end unhappily—even if it were not inevitable that all Mr. James's books should break off with a sharp cut of arbitrary conclusion, leaving all the questions they so skilfully raise unsolved. . . . We confess to being quite unable to understand how it is that Isabel falls into Osmond's toils, unless it is because so elaborate and self-conscious a personality recoils instinctively, even though full of an abstract admiration for truth, from the downright and veracious, and finds in the complications of an elaborately conventional mind something that has the air of being larger and richer than the true. The reader is never for a moment taken in by the superiority of this most carefully dressed and posed figure, whose being altogether is mysterious, and of whom, notwithstanding the author's elaborate descriptions, we never penetrate the *fin mot*. . . . and the almost immediate failure of their after relations is confusing and unaccountable. Something of the same curious failure we remember to have found in *Daniel Deronda*, where Gwendolen and her husband, after their elaborate drawing together, fly asunder the moment they are married, with a suddenness and bitterness—brutality on the man's part, and misery on the woman's—for which we find no adequate motive, since there was neither passion between them to die out, nor motive enough beforehand to force a union which was to end so abruptly. . . .

[a description of Goodwood's final wooing of Isabel]

She does not yield, it is needless to say: our author could not have so far forgotten himself. But when this impetuous lover, by no means despairing of success, finds that she has returned to her home, he is consoled by her friend Miss Stackpole, with the significant words—the last in the book—'Look here, Mr. Goodwood,' she said; 'just you wait!' . . . . What [does James] mean, we wonder? Isabel, so far as she has any body at all, is as free from fleshly stain as the purest imagination could desire. Is it only that in her search after experience her author felt it necessary that she should taste also the excitement of an unlawful passion? or is it his mind to preach that the world being so hollow and miserable, and devoid of hope, the best thing we can do is to eat and drink, for to-morrow we die? Anyhow, it is a most equivocal if not debasing conclusion, and brings us up sharp with a discord instead of the symphony of harmonising chords with which it has been the habit of art to accompany the end of every story. As a rule Mr. James rejects symphonies, and attempts no harmonising conclusions. He leaves us usually tantalized, half angry with an end which is left to our imagination. But this is not a way of leaving matters to the imagination which we can at all consent to take from his hand. . . .

In following out the chief thread of this elaborate work, we have in reality neglected the best of it, which is to be found in the characters which are secondary. . . .

The book altogether is one of the most remarkable specimens of literary skill which the critic could lay his hand upon. It is far too long, infinitely ponderous, and pulled out of all proportion by the elaboration of every detail; but there is scarcely a page in it that is not worked out with the utmost skill and refinement, or which the reader will pass over without leaving something to regret—that is, if he has leisure for the kind of reading which is delightful for its own sake in complete independence of its subject. The conversation in it is an art by itself. To give an appearance of actualness and spontaneity to an artificial production so careful, refined, and elaborate, must have required a prodigious effort. We have heard it characterised very cleverly as resembling one of those games in which one of the party has to go out while the others task their ingenuity in devising how to puzzle him. When he returns with his mind on the full strain, the ingenious succession of questions and answers which are struck out by a party accustomed to the art may approach, if it is very well done, the perfection of the endless pages in which Mr. James carries on his word-fence with the most curious *vraisemblance* and air of being real. But nothing so elaborate ever could be real, and the dazzle sometimes fatigues, though the effect is one which cannot be contemplated without admiration.

41. From an unsigned review, *Literary World*

December 1881, xii, 473–4

This is a book that piques both mental analysis and conscience in a very curious fashion. The root fact about it is that it is a representative society novel of the nineteenth century, and as such exposes very grave social drifts and problems. It is a book of conventional life with some highly unconventional people in it, yet fastidiously clean in its morals and situations. In parts it runs to metaphysics, like George Eliot's novels, to the delay of the plot; yet its style is as clear as crystal and as sharp cut. Put by the side of a novel of Sir Walter Scott's, the style is epigram itself; not stately, picturesque, or poetical, but strong, incisive, and prompt, as the business temper of the age. Full of love scenes and motives, more or less complex, we hardly remember a book of so little sentiment, at least of the effusive and old-fashioned kind. It might almost be called a cruel book in its dissection of character and exposure of the nerves and sinews of human actions. It is not a book to inspire, but to instruct and warn. It is curiously free from any disposition to preach morals or religion, and yet in the antitheses of the social life unfolded it is a well-bred but tremendous homily in behalf of something better. Except for a certain twilight of virtue, due possibly to a Christendom yet extant, this book might have been written among or for cultured heathen. This strikes us as a curious sign in literature; perhaps a prophecy. Mr. James is a realistic painter of landscapes with a minuteness in portraiture which reminds us of DeFoe. His analyses are often exquisitely keen and neat; but any sort of enthusiasm is markedly absent from his book. . . .

[a discussion as to whether Isabel will eventually leave Osmond for Goodwood]

This, in the book, at least, she does not do, yet the story closes with a neatly arranged puzzle as to whether she will or will not do it some other time. The question of her unrevealed future has, in Mr. James's handling, two very distinct sides to it, and the true answer must depend on what a woman with Isabel Osmond's curious make-up will be prone to do. For our own part we judge she will. This puzzle, we presume, is already at work in the minds of many lady readers. What she ought to do depends, of course, on the standard by which her judges will measure duty. . . .

As a representative book this *Portrait of a Lady* is worth study. It is of a new epoch and has its own virtues. The minor notes of the age, we might almost call them notes of despair, run through its pages. If it be not an unhealthy book, it is at least non-healthy. There is no sea air in it, and its sunshine shows through mists. One bright baby in a happy mother's arms would have more. We hear in this book a semi-wail, as it were, of the latter Roman empire. If life be a fine art, society, as here shown, works in marble. We are so old-fashioned as to say 'Let us work in soul.' The boulevards have their charm, but so have the wild hills and the sea.

Our old English writers loved to tell of gentle milkmaids and girls that tended flocks. Mr. James and men like him prefer the product of the salon and the casino. *Chacun à son goût*. This book in some respects is not so much 'the portrait of a lady' as of the age.

42. From an unsigned review, *Critic*

December 1881, i, 333-4

All lovers of the analytical method in novel-writing will find in *The Portrait of a Lady* the perfection of this form. There is not a single character in the book to whom we grow enthusiastically attached, not one whom we approve of steadily. They are the best when they are left half drawn. . . . There is one general trait which all the characters have in common. They are all excessively witty and caustic. They bite, and snap, and criticise each other—that is, they bite and snap politely. Mr. James's idea of dialogue seems to be that it is only meant to afford the personages an opportunity to develop each other's character. When he is tired of minute analysis himself, or thinks his reader may be weary of it, he varies the form only, and sets the personages to doing it for him. Each gentleman takes his turn in criticizing the young lady. Each lady seems bent on some inquisitorial proceeding—all in a polished, refined way, of course, but persistently. The author has no skill in making action tell the story. It must be done by the analytical method, or not at all. And the characters develop themselves, not to the reader alone, but to each other. The action is nowhere abundant, but the analysis is protracted—not tiresome, or dull, or unilluminated—but still protracted through scores on scores of pages. It is only in description that the author lets a word do the work of a page, and here he shows great skill. His touches, while without the illumination which a spiritual imagination might supply, are happy, neat, and very effective. He presents what scenery he needs, but seems to be easily overcome with ennui, as if some editorial function had brought him acquainted with many young ladies' journals, or as if reading many books of travel had made him mad. . . . He seems able to deal with but one thing at a time. When we have finished Lord Warburton, as we think, pretty effectually, then we may take up Madame Merle. When she is labeled and ticketed we may have Mr. Osmond. When Mr. Osmond is well under way and has lost our sympathy, we may start afresh with his daughter; and as Lord Warburton by this time shows signs of life, we may stop long enough to knock him on the head—ah, that was a harsh word, and we take it back; we will only stretch him on the table. We say little of the nationality of the characters, because they seem to us to represent national peculiarities only in a gross way. Most of the persons are American, but so alienated that the type is confused. In Henrietta Stackpole we recognize very clearly the American girl turned journalist, and a certain freedom of motion and social forwardness in all is pretty distinctively American. But all the persons are on their travels. We recognize the girls in American social life, but they are second-rate. In good society in any of our large cities they would be considered peculiar. Still with all his limitations, we are disposed to place Mr. James among our keenest and most vigorous character painters.

43. H. E. Scudder, from an unsigned review, *Atlantic*

January 1882, xlix, 126–30

H. E. Scudder (1838–1902) later became editor of the *Atlantic*.

A person hearing the narrative might be pardoned if he failed to see the making of a great novel in it, but only when one has recited it does he become aware how each step in the fatal series is a movement in the direction of destiny. By a fine concentration of attention upon the heroine, Mr. James impresses us with her importance, and the other characters, involved as they are with her life, fall back into secondary positions. It is much to have seized and held firmly so elusive a conception, and our admiration is increased when reflection shows that, individual as Isabel is in the painting, one may fairly take her as representative of womanly life today. The fine purpose of her freedom, the resolution with which she seeks to be the maker of her destiny, the subtle weakness into which all this betrays her, the apparent helplessness of her ultimate position, and the conjectured escape only through patient forbearance,—what are all these, if not attributes of womanly life expended under current conditions?

The consistency of the work is observable under another aspect. Mr. James's method is sufficiently well known, and since he has made it his own the critic may better accept it and measure it than complain of it. What renders it distinct from say, Thackeray's method, with which it has been compared, or from George Eliot's, is the limitation of the favorite generalizations and analyses. If the reader will attend, he will see that these take place quite exclusively within the boundaries of the story and characters. That is to say, when the people in the book stop acting or speaking, it is to give to the novelist an opportunity, not to indulge in general reflections, having application to all sorts and conditions of men, of whom his *dramatis personæ* are but a part,—he has no desire to share humanity with them,—but to make acute reflections upon these particular people, and to explain more thoroughly than

The Portrait of a Lady

their words and acts can the motives which lie behind. We may, on general grounds, doubt the self-confidence or power of a novelist who feels this part of his performance to be essential, but there can be no doubt that Mr. James's method is a part of that concentration of mind which results in a singular consistency.

Yet all this carries an intimation of what is curiously noticeable in his work. It is consistent, but the consistency is with itself. Within the boundaries of the novel the logic of character and events is close and firm. We say this after due reflection upon the latest pages. There can be little doubt that the novelist suffers more in the reader's judgment from a false or ineffective scene at the close of his story than he gains from many felicitous strokes in the earlier development of plot or character. The impatient, undiscriminating objection, It does not end well, although it may incense the writer, is an ill-formulated expression of the feeling that the creation lacks the final, triumphant touch which gives life . . . we can understand the hesitation which a reader might feel before the somewhat ambiguous passage of Isabel's last interview with Goodwood. The passage, however, admits of a generous construction, and we prefer to take it, and to see in the scene the author's intention of giving a final touch to his delineation of Goodwood's iron but untempered will, Isabel's vanishing dream of happiness, and her acceptance of the destiny which she had unwittingly chosen. . . .

To return to our point. This self-consistency is a separate thing from any consistency with the world of reality. The characters, the situations, the incidents, are all true to the law of their own being, but that law runs parallel with the law which governs life, instead of being identical with it. In Andersen's quaint story of the 'Emperor's New Clothes', a little child discovers the unreality of the gossamer dress, and his voice breaks in upon the illusion from the outer world. Something of the same separation from the story, of the same unconscious naturalness of feeling, prompts the criticism that, though these people walk, and sit, and talk, and behave, they are yet in an illusionary world of their own. . . .

The perfection of Mr. James's art is in its intellectual order, and the precision with which he marshals all incidents and characters; we have hinted at its weakness when we have referred the reader's pleasure to an intellectual glow rather than to a personal warmth of feeling. The imagination which rules governs a somewhat cold world, and gives forth light rather than heat.

44. H. A. Huntington, from a review, *Dial*

January 1882, ii, 214–5

I am not certain of the biography of this reviewer but, since the *Dial* was a Chicago publication, it seems likely that he was a public figure of that city, a Civil War hero and a writer, who lived from 1840 to 1907.

Mr. James is emphatically a painter of drawing-room life—the sort of life for the delineation of which he sought many years ago to demonstrate the incapacity of George Eliot. More or less a product of the art enlightenment of the past ten years, he has come to look at humanity through stained glass. He is apt to miss the intrinsic in his worship of the luxurious or conventional accidents of life,—to 'give to dust that is a little gilt, more laud than gilt o'er-dusted.' We can hardly fancy him dealing with the genteelest indigence. At the outset, Isabel Archer gives some bright promise of poverty, but it is never fulfilled. She has only to hold up her apron, and seventy thousand pounds drop into it. . . . If Osmond had been even a fraudulent reformer, with some pretence of worthy ambition, we might pardon her infatuation; but to throw herself away upon a man who owes his sole consequence to the paternity of Madame Merle's child, is something not to be forgiven. This we take to be the weak spot in an immensely clever story. It is asking too much that we should believe that a woman of Isabel's intellectual force could be taken in by so transparent a cheat. Burke once said that the Misellas, Lorimas, Properantias, and Rhodoclias of the great lexicographer were all Johnsons in petticoats. Far be it from us to liken the airy and graceful creations of Mr. James to the uncouth figures of *The Rambler*, but we fear that Isabel Archer is only Mr. James in domino. If popular opinion be not at fault, Osmond is the sort of man to attract a female James.

Like all of Mr. James's stories, *The Portrait of a Lady* runs so smoothly that one almost longs for a jolt—something to indicate where the rails join, and destroy the illusion of the canal. Like all of them, not a character in it has a touch of religious sentiment—not even Pansy, or

III

the casual nun who hurries across the scene. Otherwise it marks a decided advance on the part of its author. He has, however, not yet overcome his inability to write what may be called a fifth act. A lamer conclusion to a brilliantly written story could ill be conceived.

45. Unsigned review, *Nation*

February 1882, xxxiv, 102–3

Mr. James's novel, which caused each number of the *Atlantic Monthly*, to be awaited with impatience last year, gains in its complete presentation, and, like most novels of any pretensions, is most readable when read consecutively. Unlike most novels, however, whose fate (and the fortune of whose authors) it is to appear serially, the reason for this does not consist in the condensation which the reader is thus enabled to make in spite of the author, but in the fact that it is a work of art of which the whole is equal to no fewer than all of its parts, and of which there is a certain 'tendency,' to lose which is to miss one of the main features of the book. In other words, *The Portrait of a Lady* is an important work, the most important Mr. James has thus far written, and worthy of far more than mere perusal—worthy of study, one is inclined to say. It is in fact a little too important—to express by a paradox the chief criticism to be made upon it—or, at all events, the only impression left by it which is not altogether agreeable. For the first two or three hundred pages one is beguiled by a kind of entertainment always of a high order—the dissection of an interesting character by a clever and scrupulous demonstrator. After that, though it would be misleading to say that the interest flags—the interest being throughout the book remarkable for its evenness—the feeling supervenes that to be still entertained argues a happy aptitude for most serious and 'intellectual' delectation. Most persons will recall some experience of the same sensation in first becoming acquainted with undisguisedly philosophical writings—such as the writings of Emerson or Burke. To others it may be indicated by saying that it is just the sensation Carlyle missed in finding the works of George Eliot 'dool—just dool.' In America, it is well known, we do not find George Eliot dull, and it is upon our appetite for this sort of provender that Mr. James doubtless relies, and undoubtedly does well to rely. Nevertheless, it is possible to feel what Carlyle meant without agreeing with it; and though maintaining firmly the absorbing interest of *The Portrait of a Lady*, we are ready to admit that once or twice we have laid aside the book for a season, with the exhilatation which Mr. Howells has somewhere observed to be coincident with giving up a difficult task. One of the happiest of the many happy remarks made in *The Portrait of a Lady* is in Miss Stackpole's characterization of her *fiancé*; 'He's as clear as glass; there's no mystery about him. He is not intellectual, but he appreciates intellect. On the other hand, he doesn't exaggerate its claims. *I sometimes think we do in the United States.*' The person of whom this is said naturally cuts a smaller figure in the novel than the more complex organizations, in dealing with which Mr. James is most at home; and it is the inference from this circumstance that we have in mind. For not only are the simpler though perennial elements of human nature in general eschewed by Mr. James, but his true distinction—that is to say, his strength and weakness also—consists in his attempt to dispense with all the ordinary machinery of the novelist except the study of subtle shades of character. In other words, his masterpiece, as *The Portrait of a Lady* must be called, is not only outside of the category of the old romance of which *Tom Jones*, for example, may stand as the type, but also dispenses with the dramatic movement and passionate interest upon which the later novelists, from Thackeray to Thomas Hardy, have relied. In a sense, and to a certain extent, Turgeneff may be said to be Mr. James's master, but even a sketch or a study by Turgeneff is turbulence itself beside the elaborate placidity of these 519 pages. This involves the necessity of the utmost care in presenting the material, and accordingly we have that squaring of the elbows and minute painstaking which not only result inevitably in occasional lumbering movements, but which lend the work an air of seeming more important than any book whatever could possibly be; so that it is perhaps fortunate for its popularity (which, by the way, we believe is extraordinary) that we exaggerate the claims of intellect occasionally in the United States.

Even this measure of fault-finding however, seems a little ungracious, not to say hypercritical, in view of the distinguished success of Mr. James's experiment in applying the development theory to novel-writing, so to speak. We have ourselves followed the succession of his stories since *Roderick Hudson* appeared with mingled interest and regret, because he has seemed to be getting further and further away from very safe ground, where he was very strong, and into the uncertainties of an unfamiliar region of which it was impossible to tell whether its novelty or its real merit gave it its interest. The elemental characters and dramatic situations of the novel just mentioned were strongly handled, and the work being, comparatively speaking, a youthful one, its promise seemed even greater than its actual qualities. But, almost as if he had been an amateur dipping into another branch of effort after having demonstrated his ability in one, Mr. James immediately abandoned the field of imaginative romance as it is generally understood. He at once made clear his faculty for his new choice, and the field he entered on with *The American*, and continued with the shorter stories illustrative of American types, became immediately popular. *Daisy Miller* may almost be said to mark an era in the mental progress of many persons who exaggerate the claims of intellect occasionally; it is wearisome to recall the 'discussions' it occasioned in drawing rooms and in print. There was, to be sure, a Chauvinist view, so to speak, taken of this and its associated sketches, by persons who omitted to perceive that Mr. James had not only made the current mechanical speculations about 'the coming American novel' an anachronism, but had also displayed his patriotism and the national genius by inventing a new variety of literature. But naturally Mr. James might be expected to heed rather those of his readers who appreciated and enjoyed his motives and rejoiced in his discovery of romantic sociology. And this seemed his real danger; for though to these readers this reading conveyed a peculiarly refined pleasure, on account both of its novelty and the cleverness of its execution there was no certainty that this pleasure was not a rather temporary mood, and likely to pass away after the novelty had worn off. Instead, however, of avoiding this danger by a return to the perennially interesting material with which he first dealt, Mr. James has conquered it, *vi et armis*, by a persistence that at one time seemed a little wilful. No one can now pretend, whatever his own literary likes and dislikes may be, that romantic sociology, exploited as Mr. James has shown it capable of being, is not a thoroughly serious field of literature, whose interest is permanent and dignified.

The Portrait of a Lady is a modest title, though an apt one. The portrait of the lady in question is indeed the theme of the book, and it is elaborated with a minuteness so great that when finally one begins to find it confusing it becomes evident that the ordinary point of view must be changed, and the last detail awaited—as in a professedly scientific work—before the whole can appear. Miss Isabel Archer is an orphan to whom her aunt gives an opportunity of seeing the world, and to whom her aunt's husband leaves a large fortune, at the instance of his son, who is unselfishly and romantically interested to see what his cousin will make of her life when nothing prevents her from doing as she wishes. The reader at once assumes the position of this young man and with more or less (less in our own case, we confess) sympathy, watches the progress of the drama which he has set going. At the climax the heroine discovers that she has wrecked her life most miserably. The spiritual transition from the Isabel Archer of Albany to the Mrs. Osmond of Rome is of course accomplished in part by natural disposition and in part by the influence of the numerous characters which surround her. The way in which this influence is exhibited is a marked feature of the book. If George Eliot was the first to make of this important moral phenomenon a distinct study, Mr. James has here, in our opinion quite surpassed her. Any one can judge by comparing the reciprocal effect upon the development of each other's characters of the Lydgates in *Middlemarch* with that of the Osmonds here. The other characters are treated with a microscopy hardly inferior. Osmond himself is one of the most palpable of those figures in fiction which are to be called subtle. Madame Merle, his former mistress, mother of his child, who makes the marriage between him and his poverty and Isabel and her wealth, and who, up to the climax of the book, is Isabel's ideal, is, if anything, even better done. There is something almost uncanny in the perfection with which these secretive natures are turned inside out for the reader's inspection. As for the heroine, the American girl *par excellence*, it seems as if, scientifically speaking, Mr. James had said the last word on this subject; at any rate till the model herself is still further developed. For example 'She never looked so charming as when, in the genial heat of discussion, she received a crushing blow full in the face and brushed it away as a feather.' There are pages as good.

It has long been evident that Mr. James's powers of observation are not only remarkably keen, but sleepless as well. But *The Portrait of a Lady* would not be what it is if it did not possess a *fonds* of moral seriousness, in addition to and underlying its extraordinary interest of purely intellectual curiosity. There is a specific lesson for the American girl in the first place; there are others, more general, which accompany every imaginative work of large importance. That these are nowhere distinctly stated is now nothing new in fiction even of a distinctly moral purpose. But Mr. James has carried suggestiveness in this regard further than any rival novelist, and though, unless one has ears to hear, it is entirely possible to miss the undertone of his book, to an appreciative sense there is something exquisite in the refinement with which it is conveyed. Refinement in this respect cannot be carried too far. In strictly literary matters Mr. James's fastidiousness may be objected to, perhaps, if one chooses; he has carried the method of the essayist into the domain of romance: its light touch, its reliance on suggestiviness, its weakness for indirect statement, its flattering presupposition of the reader's perceptiveness, its low tones, its polish. Upon occasion, where the circumstances really seem to warrant a little fervor, you only get from the author of *The Portrait of a Lady* irreproachability. Objection to this may easily be carried too far, however; and those who do thus carry it too far, and argue that no people ever spoke and acted with the elegance and precision of the personages here portrayed, must of necessity pay the penalty of ultra-literalness and miss the secret of Mr. James's success. To characterize this secret with adequate fulness would require far more than the space at our disposal; but it may be sufficiently indicated by calling it the imaginative treatment of reality. In this unquestionably lies Mr. James's truly original excellence. *The Portrait of a Lady* is the most eminent example we have thus far had of realistic art in fiction *à outrance*, because its substance is thoroughly, and at times profoundly, real, and at the same time its presentation is imaginative. On the one hand, wilfulness and fantasticality are avoided, and on the other, prose and flatness. One may even go further, and say that the book succeeds in the difficult problem of combining a scientific value with romantic interest and artistic merit.

46. From an unsigned review, *Lippincott's Magazine*

February 1882, xxix, 213–5.

HJ was not born in Boston.

The fortunes of Isabel Archer exact a closer attention and approach perceptibly nearer to the reader's sympathies than any of Mr. James's former themes, while the critical interest which he never fails to excite must be keener than ever in presence of what is in every way—in length, scope, and finish—his most important work. In characterizing it so unreservedly as his *chef-d'œuvre*, we do not mean to imply that *The Portrait of a Lady* exhibits a new development of power, or that it contrasts in any way with its predecessors. Mr. James is not a writer who advances by bounds or strides. His literary career has been throughout a steadily progressive one, but it has been a quiet progression, consisting in refinement and selection. A somewhat finer diction, a little closer analysis, a more careful attention to detail,—these are the slender stakes which mark his course. . . .

The Portrait of a Lady is at once finer and closer in workmanship than anything Mr. James had before done . . . Here are more than five hundred closely-printed pages, on which every line is apparently studied, every word happily chosen. . . .

The same untiring vigilance which distinguishes the style we find in the thought of the book. The analysis of character and motive, which fills so large a part in Mr. James's writings, is here conducted with all the accuracy and completeness of a mathematical demonstration. The reader is not confronted at once with the intricacies of the problem or fatigued by its length: he is led by logical process from one point to another, his interest being riveted all through by the detail. Each conclusion is clearly marked, all possible aids are given to the memory, and when at last the demonstrator breaks off in the abrupt way which has startled all his readers, it is with the air of saying, 'I have furnished all the points and shown you how to proceed. Find the answer for yourselves.'

Mr. James's reluctance, or rather his positive refusal, to complete a book in the ordinary sense of the word is a curious trait, and one which piques study. In the matter of detail his books are finished to the last degree but, he cannot bring himself to the vulgarity of a regular *dénouement*, and he lacks the poetic force to substitute for it a suggestive or picturesque climax. Everything in one of Mr. James's books seems to be leading to a simple and satisfactory end, but coming near the goal he sees a crowd there and turns aside in disgust. There is no time to change his destination, but he will not go out at the common turnstile, happen what may.

The same causes which make Mr. James's *dénouements* so unsatisfactory both from a popular and an artistic point of view are traceable in his delineations of character, giving to his figures that delicacy of aspect, that absence of weight and reality, which is characteristic of them. These causes are, first his instinctive avoidance of commonplace, and, secondly, a peculiarity of organization, which comes perhaps from his having had the misfortune to be born in Boston, a locality in which it is not infrequent. We allude to the habit of looking at an object by reflection and under cross-lights,—of divining and comprehending instead of seeing it. Now, divination, it is well known, can often transcend actual vision, penetrating into finer chinks and crevices: still as a substitute for straightforward sight it has its inconveniences. The process is certainly seen at its best in the portrait of Miss Archer, which in all other respects than that of reality is a brilliant success. It is original, consistent in every particular, full of distinction, and painted with wonderful delicacy and precision. Mr. James has drawn from an actual though rare type of American girlhood. He has taken it at its highest development and selected all its finer qualities. He has studied every little nerve and fibre, all the intuitions and reasonings which belong to it: as an exercise in mental anatomy the delineation is perfect. The warmth of intellectual interest, the absense of any religious motive, combined with the clearest moral sense, make Isabel a character belonging to the time perhaps rather than the country, but one which is found here at an earlier age than elsewhere. To make Isabel become Caspar Goodwood's mistress at the end would be to destroy the entire texture of her character, and we cannot believe that Mr. James intended to point to that as the solution. A sweeter nature than hers might be one more susceptible of corruption. Isabel was aloof from it rather than above it, and if moral support failed her she was certain to be saved by that other instinct with which the author has endowed her,—the dread of vulgarity.

47. Mrs. Henry Adams to her father

December 1881

The Letters of Mrs. Henry Adams 1865–83, ed. Ward Thoron, 1937, 306. Mrs. Adams (1843–85) was, like her husband (see No. 48) a member of the extensive American leisured society which included the James family. HJ had known her since at least 1870. The Appletons were a Boston family. 'Sir Walter' is, of course, Scott.

At the same minute came *Portrait of a Lady*, which the author kindly sent me. It's very nice, and charming things in it, but I'm ageing fast and prefer what Sir Walter called the 'big bow-wow style.' I shall suggest to Mr. James to name his next novel 'Ann Eliza.' It's not that he 'bites off more than he can chaw,' as T. G. Appleton said of Nathan, but he chaws more than he bites off.

48. Henry Adams to Charles Milnes Gaskell

January 1882

Letters of Henry Adams 1858–91, ed. W. C. Ford, 1930, 333. Adams (1838–1918), the American aristocrat and historian, was long acquainted with HJ. Gaskell (1842–1919) was a Yorkshire landowner and public figure.

Henry James has been in Washington for a month, very homesick for London and for all the soft embraces of the old world. He returns to your hemisphere in May next. I frankly own that I broke down on *The Portrait of a Lady*, but some of my friends, of whose judgment I think highly, admire it warmly, and find it deeply interesting. I hope you may be of their opinion.

49. A *Literary World* contributor's protest against the American reception of James

1882

Contributor's letter, *Literary World*, January 1882, xiii, 10–11. Signed 'M.L.H.' and written from Newburgh, N.Y. (and not, as Lyon. N. Richardson has it in the Bibliography of *The Question of Henry James*, the work of M. L. H. Newburgh).

It seems rather absurd to set about seriously defending a writer of novels from the charge of unpatriotic sentiment. We do not usually look on novels as vehicles of expression for opinions and feelings of this sort. But for some reason Mr. Henry James, Jr., has been seriously accused of this serious fault of lack of patriotism, and I cannot refrain from saying a word in the interest of common sense. Mr. James will doubtless be able to sustain the attack upon him, serene in the possession of a clear conscience, and what most distresses my truly patriotic mind is the obtuseness my countrymen—or some of them—are showing on the subject. As I have no personal acquaintance whatever with Mr. James, he may be, for aught I know, a snob and an American unworthy of his privileges; but one thing is clear to me, that he cannot be proved such from his books. The *Pall Mall Gazette* (I think) says of him that he flatters the English; and there are journals here at home which say that in his American portraits this writer does great injustice to our noble race, and thereby casts upon himself great discredit. General and sweeping charges of this sort are the easiest things in the world to invent, but the indictment to be damaging must be more specific. Let the *Pall Mall Gazette* point out where and how the author has flattered the English—at the expense of Americans as implied. Is it in the sketch of that Honorable snob, Percy Beaumont, or the elegant-mannered Lord Lambeth? Is the refined and brilliant Captain Lovelock a type of which Britons are justly proud? Can any critic mention the name of more than a single Englishman whose portrait he has made attractive? That manly pleasant fellow, Lord Warburton, is the only Englishman for whose acquaintance I thank Mr. James.

That there is much in the English landscape and in the English life which Mr. James enjoys is plain, but if that be an error or a fault it is one that hundreds of Americans share with him. Out of the eight novels of this writer four must be counted out as having no pertinence to this important dispute. Let us examine the rest for a moment. In *The American* no contrast of English and American types is presented, but the central figure of Newman could only have been drawn by a countryman who had studied with a thorough appreciation his admirable and truly national characteristics. In *The Europeans*, 'A Bundle of Letters' and 'The Pension Beaurepas' one and the same attempt is made, to exhibit the wholesome simplicity, the fresh, instinctive, native virtue, of the American types in contrast with the sophistication, conventionality, and lower moral ideas and standards of the European. And that these qualities are represented as co-existing with other less desirable and admirable characteristics—with the narrow-mindedness of a Puritan family and the vulgarity of *nouveaux riches* tourists,—merely proves the fidelity of Mr. James's observation, and gives to his creations the stamp of genuine reality. The failure of the Wentworth family to comprehend the Baroness Eugenia is a testimony to their single-minded purity of thought; and the ineffectual endeavor of Miss Aurora Church to conduct herself like one American-born though European-bred brings into relief the sincerity and straightforwardness as well as the plebeian breeding of Miss Sophie Ruck. The fact that this purity and sincerity of nature are attributed to persons whom we recognize as 'common,' low-placed in the social scale, is what makes Mr. James's compliment to his countrymen the more significant: these virtues, he implies, are everyday virtues among us Americans; we take them as matter-of-course, unaware how precious they are and how far from being the current coin of social life in other countries.

Amanda, in *A Bundle of Letters*, and Henrietta Stackpole, are exemplifications of this same thing. With the exception of this last-named, none of the characters in Mr. James's last novel are in any special sense typical Americans. Osmond might be of any nationality; there is a something in Isabel which points to her American origin; yet the author does not mean to lay any stress upon it; it is rather as an individual than as a type of national character she is brought before us. This fine novel has met with a curiously cold reception, even from those English whom the author has so basely flattered. Mr. James doubtless is resigned to knowing his books to be 'caviare to the general,' and may console himself for the condemnation of many reviewers with the conviction that his fit audience still exist and admire his work as much as ever, though it does not voice itself in print. Yet for their own sakes it is a pity that Americans should show themselves so blind to the service of exquisite justice this author has done them. One recalls here the homely old proverb about the dog with a bad name. Some one, in a fit of most incomprehensible indignation, threw a bad name at Mr. James about a year ago, and the unintelligent, as their way is, have picked it up and used it.

50. Professor John Nichol on James
as a minor novelist

1882

John Nicol, from *American Literature: An Historical Sketch 1620–1880*, 1882, 389–97.
This is the first 'academic' treatment of HJ, Nichol (1833–94) being Professor of English at Glasgow University. Clifford Pyncheon and Tito Melema are characters in Nathaniel Hawthorne's *The House of the Seven Gables* and George Eliot's *Romola* respectively. For Julian Hawthorne, whose works Nichol has just been assessing, see below No. 54.

The just popularity of Mr. Henry James is due in great measure to the deftness of his workmanship, the skilful manner in which he interweaves his quick and keen impressions of America, England, Italy, and France; and to the fact that he is in essential sympathy with the better average of the world. His style, defaced at starting by pedantry, has, in his later work, become more precise and clear. In his pages light and shade are pleasantly interlaced: his satire is sometimes sharp but never savage; his morality always reliable, *i.e.* orthodox without being obtrusively conventional; for he brings his actors under the influence of temptation, while we feel assured they will always make their escape from it. Without vanity, he seems on good terms with himself; and makes friends by a genial seriousness. He is frequently commonplace, tiresomely diffuse in dealing with trifles, or reporting imaginary gossip; but he is seldom absurd. Mr. James has somewhat the same relation to Nathaniel Hawthorne that Mr. Anthony Trollope has to Thackeray. His works are not those of a recluse, who has lived in remote corners, and heard strange people, in and about them, discourse of strange matters. They are the sometimes brilliant essays of a versatile man of affairs; a favourite, we should imagine, of the society of which, at home and abroad, he has taken shrewd, but seldom cynical, notes. His numerous novels and sketches, though apparently thrown off with an almost fatal facility, are infected by excess of analysis. He applies the same chemistry

to minor eccentricities that his predecessors in his own country,—and perhaps his more frequent models—Balzac and Turgénieff in Europe, have
applied to the deeper and graver anomalies of character. Of his longer
and more celebrated works, *The Europeans* exhibits this and other defects
in their most pronounced form. The principal character, the Baroness
Eugenia Münster,—the run-away Morganatic wife of Prince Silber-
stadt Schreckenstein,—is a disagreeable fortune-huntress, who ought to
have got into more trouble. Her brother, Felix (who, with his sister,
quarters himself on his cousins, in the coolest way), is a very feeble
Clifford Pyncheon, or Tito Melema; Wentworth, a stupid and stiff
New Englander; Brand, an uninteresting curate; and Robert Acton
insufficiently real. Charlotte and Gertrude are shadowy; and the whole
story, despite its graphic opening, is improbable, with the unredeemed
improbability of common life. . . .

Mr. James never pierces to the same deeps as Julian Hawthorne; but
he walks over the surface with a far securer tread. His novels are like
excellent *vers de société*, contrasted with imitations of Browning or of
Blake. His work leaves us with the impression of vast versatility, sharp
sight, perfect propriety, and an indefinite cleverness, often aiming, like
the artists of his own frequent satire, at something higher than it
generally hits.

[the following note is added to an ensuing discussion of the American
Girl as she appears in the novels of Howells and HJ]

'Isabel,' in Mr. James's recent *Portrait of a Lady*—a tiresome book—
is one of the most salient representatives of the type we are describing;
but, after scorning the love of the one really fine character, Roger
Touchett, and formally rejecting that of two amiable devotees (including the customary lord), she is exceptionally unfortunate in her final
choice. It is, however, a testimony to Mr. James's realism that he makes
us entertain towards her, as to other mere creations of his brain, *e.g.*
Henrietta Stackpole, a strong personal dislike.

51. W. D. Howells on James as *the* modern novelist

1882

W. D. Howells, 'Henry James Jr.,' *Century Illustrated Monthly Magazine*, November 1882, iii, 25–9.

(The *Century* had evolved out of *Scribner's* in 1881.) As will be seen, the claims made here caused considerable resentment, often of a nationalistic kind, and a lot of rather irrelevant talk about 'the new school of fiction'. Even Professor Nichol (see above No. 50) felt impelled to add another footnote to his book (452–3) in which he describes the article as the culmination of 'the abuse of "mutual admiration" ', dismisses 'the almost heartlessly conceited "Isabel" in the almost intolerably analytic *Portrait of a Lady*', and warns Americans that 'As the wit of the best American humorists is a shadow to the genius of *Chuzzlewit*; so all their living novelists, working together, might despair to approach *The Newcomes*; and, despite the superfine squeamishness of New England, *Tom Jones* is likely to survive *Roderick Hudson*, and *Daisy Miller* to predecease *Clarissa Harlowe*.'

The events of Mr. James's life—as we agree to understand events—may be told in a very few words. His race is Irish on his father's side and Scotch on his mother's, to which mingled strains the generalizer may attribute, if he likes, that union of vivid expression and dispassionate analysis which has characterized his work from the first. There are none of those early struggles with poverty, which render the lives of so many distinguished Americans monotonous reading, to record in his case: the cabin hearth-fire did not light him to the youthful pursuit of literature; he had from the start all those advantages which, when they go too far, become limitations.

He was born in New York city in the year 1843, and his first lessons in life and letters were the best which the metropolis—so small in the perspective diminishing to that date—could afford. In his twelfth year his family went abroad, and after some stay in England made a long sojourn in France and Switzerland. They returned to America in 1860, placing themselves at Newport, and for a year or two Mr. James was at the Harvard Law School, where, perhaps, he did not study a great deal of law. His father removed from Newport to Cambridge in 1866, and there Mr. James remained till he went abroad three years later, for the residence in England and Italy which, with infrequent visits home, has continued ever since.

It was during these three years of his Cambridge life that I became acquainted with his work. He had already printed a tale—'The Story of a Year'—in the *Atlantic Monthly*, when I was asked to be Mr. Fields's assistant in the management, and it was my fortune to read Mr. James's second contribution in manuscript. 'Would you take it?' asked my chief. 'Yes, and all the stories you can get from the writer.' One is much securer of one's judgment at twenty-nine than, say, at forty-five; but if this was a mistake of mine I am not yet old enough to regret it. The story was called 'Poor Richard,' and it dealt with the conscience of a man very much in love with a woman who loved his rival. He told this rival a lie, which sent him away to his death on the field,—in that day nearly every fictitious personage had something to do with the war,—but Poor Richard's lie did not win him his love. It still seems to me that the situation was strongly and finely felt. One's pity went, as it should, with the liar; but the whole story had a pathos which lingers in my mind equally with a sense of the new literary qualities which gave me such delight in it. I admired, as we must in all that Mr. James has written, the finished workmanship in which there is no loss of vigor; the luminous and uncommon use of words, the originality of phrase, the whole clear and beautiful style, which I confess I weakly liked the better for the occasional gallicisms remaining from an inveterate habit of French. Those who know the writings of Mr. Henry James will recognize the inherited felicity of diction which is so striking in the writings of Mr. Henry James, Jr. The son's diction is not so racy as the father's; it lacks its daring, but it is as fortunate and graphic; and I cannot give it greater praise than this, though it has, when he will, a splendor and state which is wholly its own.

Mr. James is now so universally recognized that I shall seem to be making an unwarrantable claim when I express my belief that the popularity of his stories was once largely confined to Mr. Fields's assistant. They had characteristics which forbade any editor to refuse them; and there are no anecdotes of thrice-rejected manuscripts finally printed to tell of him; his work was at once successful with all the magazines. But with the readers of *The Atlantic*, of *Harper's*, of *Lippincott's*, of *The Galaxy*, of *The Century*, it was another affair. The flavor was so strange, that, with rare exceptions, they had to 'learn to like' it. Probably few writers have in the same degree compelled the liking of their readers. He was reluctantly accepted, partly through a mistake as to his attitude—through the confusion of his point of view with his private opinion—in the reader's mind. This confusion caused the tears of rage which bedewed our continent in behalf of the 'average American girl' supposed to be satirized in Daisy Miller, and prevented the perception of the fact that, so far as the average American girl was studied at all in Daisy Miller, her indestructible innocence, her invulnerable new-worldliness, had never been so delicately appreciated. It was so plain that Mr. James disliked her vulgar conditions, that the very people to whom he revealed her essential sweetness and light were furious that he should have seemed not to see what existed through him. In other words, they would have liked him better if he had been a worse artist—if he had been a little more confidential.

But that artistic impartiality which puzzled so many in the treatment of Daisy Miller is one of the qualities most valuable in the eyes of those who care how things are done, and I am not sure that it is not Mr. James's most characteristic quality. As 'frost performs the effect of fire', this impartiality comes at last to the same result as sympathy. We may be quite sure that Mr. James does not like the peculiar phase of our civilization typified in Henrietta Stackpole; but he treats her with such exquisite justice that he lets *us* like her. It is an extreme case, but I confidently allege it in proof.

His impartiality is part of the reserve with which he works in most respects, and which at first glance makes us say that he is wanting in humor. But I feel pretty certain that Mr. James has not been able to disinherit himself to this degree. We Americans are terribly in earnest about making ourselves, individually and collectively; but I fancy that our prevailing mood in the face of all problems is that of an abiding faith which can afford to be funny. He has himself indicated that we have, as a nation, as a people, our joke, and every one of us is in the joke more or less. We may, some of us, dislike it extremely, disapprove it wholly, and even abhor it, but we are in the joke all the same, and no one of us is safe from becoming the great American humorist at any given moment. The danger is not apparent in Mr. James's case, and I confess that I read him with a relief in the comparative immunity that he affords from the national facetiousness. Many of his people are humorously imagined, or rather humorously *seen*, like Daisy Miller's mother, but these do not give a dominant color; the business in hand is commonly serious, and the droll people are subordinated. They abound, nevertheless, and many of them are perfectly new finds, like Mr. Tristram in *The American*, the bill-paying father in the 'Pension Beaurepas,' the anxiously Europeanizing mother in the same story, the amusing little Madame de Belgarde, Henrietta Stackpole, and even Newman himself. But though Mr. James portrays the humorous in character, he is decidedly not on humorous terms with his reader; he ignores rather than recognizes the fact that they are both in the joke.

If we take him at all we must take him on his own ground, for clearly he will not come to ours. We must make concessions to him, not in this respect only, but in several others, chief among which is the motive for reading fiction. By example, at least, he teaches that it is the pursuit and not the end which should give us pleasure; for he often prefers to leave us to our own conjectures in regard to the fate of the people in whom he has interested us. There is no question, of course, but he could tell the story of Isabel in *The Portrait of a Lady* to the end, yet he does not tell it. We must agree, then, to take what seems a fragment instead of a whole, and to find, when we can, a name for this new kind in fiction. Evidently it is the character, not the fate, of his people which occupies him; when he has fully developed their character he leaves them to what destiny the reader pleases.

The analytic tendency seems to have increased with him as his work has gone on. Some of the earlier tales were very dramatic: 'A Passionate Pilgrim,' which I should rank above all his other short stories, and for certain rich poetical qualities, above everything else that he has done, is eminently dramatic. But I do not find much that I should call dramatic in *The Portrait of a Lady*, while I do find in it an amount of analysis which I should call superabundance if it were not all such good literature. The novelist's main business is to possess his reader with a due conception of his characters and the situations in which they find themselves. If he does more or less than this he equally fails. I have sometimes thought that Mr. James's danger was to do more, but when I have been ready to declare this excess an error of his method I have hesitated. Could anything be superfluous that had given me so much pleasure as I read? Certainly from only one point of view, and this a rather narrow, technical one. It seems to me that an enlightened criticism will recognize in Mr. James's fiction a metaphysical genius working to æsthetic results, and will not be disposed to deny it any method it chooses to employ. No other novelist, except George Eliot, has dealt so largely in analysis of motive, has so fully explained and commented upon the springs of action in the persons of the drama, both before and after the facts. These novelists are more alike than any others in their processes, but with George Eliot an ethical purpose is dominant, and with Mr. James an artistic purpose. I do not know just how it should be stated of two such noble and generous types of character as Dorothea and Isabel Archer, but I think that we sympathize with the former in grand aims that chiefly concern others, and with the latter in beautiful dreams that primarily concern herself. Both are unselfish and devoted women, sublimely true to a mistaken ideal in their marriages; but, though they come to this common martyrdom, the original difference in them remains. Isabel has her great weaknesses, as Dorothea had, but these seem to me, on the whole, the most nobly imagined and the most nobly intentioned women in modern fiction; and I think Isabel is the more subtly divined of the two. If we speak of mere characterization, we must not fail to acknowledge the perfection of Gilbert Osmond. It was a profound stroke to make him an American by birth. No European could realize so fully in his own life the ideal of a European *dilettante* in all the meaning of that cheapened word; as no European could so deeply and tenderly feel the sweetness and loveliness of the English past as the sick American, Searle, in 'The Passionate Pilgrim.'

What is called the international novel is popularly dated from the publication of *Daisy Miller*, though *Roderick Hudson* and *The American* had gone before; but it really began in the beautiful story which I have just named. Mr. James, who invented this species in fiction, first contrasted in the 'Passionate Pilgrim' the New World and Old World moods, ideals, and prejudices, and he did it there with a richness of poetic effect which he has since never equalled. I own that I regret the loss of the poetry, but you cannot ask a man to keep on being a poet for you; it is hardly for him to choose; yet I compare rather discontentedly in my own mind such impassioned creations as Searle and the painter in 'The Madonna of the Future', with *Daisy Miller*, of whose slight, thin personality I also feel the indefinable charm, and of the tragedy of whose innocence I recognize the delicate pathos. Looking back to those early stories, where Mr. James stood at the dividing ways of the novel and the romance, I am sometimes sorry that he declared even superficially for the former. His best efforts seem to me those of romance; his best types have an ideal development, like Isabel and Claire Belgarde and Bessy Alden and poor Daisy and even Newman. But, doubtless, he has chosen wisely; perhaps the romance is an outworn form, and would not lend itself to the reproduction of even the ideality of modern life. I myself waver somewhat in my preference—if it is a preference—when I think of such people as Lord Warburton and the Touchetts, whom I take to be all decidedly of this world. The first of these especially interested me as a probable type of the English nobleman, who amiably accepts the existing situation with all its possibilities of political and social change, and insists not at all upon the surviving feudalities, but means to be a manly and simple gentleman in any event. An American is not able to pronounce as to the verity of the type; I only know that it seems probable and that it is charming. It makes one wish that it were in Mr. James's way to paint in some story the present phase of change in England. A titled personage is still mainly an inconceivable being to us; he is like a goblin or a fairy in a storybook. How does he comport himself in the face of all the changes and modifications that have taken place and that still impend? We can hardly imagine a lord taking his nobility seriously; it is some hint of the conditional frame of Lord Warburton's mind that makes him imaginable and delightful to us.

It is not my purpose here to review any of Mr. James's books; I like better to speak of his people than of the conduct of his novels, and I wish to recognize the fineness with which he has touched-in the pretty primness of Osmond's daughter and the mild devotedness of Mr. Rosier. A masterly hand is as often manifest in the treatment of such subordinate figures as in that of the principal persons, and Mr. James does them unerringly. This is felt in the more important character of Valentin Belgarde, a fascinating character in spite of its defects,— perhaps on account of them—and a sort of French Lord Warburton, but wittier, and not so good. 'These are my ideas,' says his sister-in-law, at the end of a number of inanities. 'Ah, you call them ideas!' he returns, which is delicious and makes you love him. He, too, has his moments of misgiving, apparently in regard to his nobility, and his acceptance of Newman on the basis of something like 'manhood suffrage' is very charming. It is of course difficult for a remote plebeian to verify the pictures of legitimist society in *The American*, but there is the probable suggestion in them of conditions and principles, and want of principles, of which we get glimpses in our travels abroad; at any rate, they reveal another and not impossible world, and it is fine to have Newman discover that the opinions and criticisms of our world are so absolutely valueless in that sphere that his knowledge of the infamous crime of the mother and brother of his betrothed will have no effect whatever upon them in their own circle if he explodes it there. This seems like aristocracy indeed! and one admires, almost respects, its survival in our day. But I always regretted that Newman's discovery seemed the precursor of his magnanimous resolution not to avenge himself; it weakened the effect of this, with which it had really nothing to do. Upon the whole, however, Newman is an adequate and satisfying representative of Americanism, with his generous matrimonial ambition, his vast good-nature, and his thorough good sense and right feeling. We must be very hard to please if we are not pleased with him. He is not the 'cultivated American' who redeems us from time to time in the eyes of Europe; but he is unquestionably more national, and it is observable that his unaffected fellow-countrymen and women fare very well at Mr. James's hands always; it is the Europeanizing sort like the critical little Bostonian in the 'Bundle of Letters,' the ladies shocked at Daisy Miller, the mother in the 'Pension Beaurepas' who goes about trying to be of the 'native' world everywhere, Madame Merle and Gilbert Osmond, Miss Light and her mother, who have reason to complain, if any one has. Doubtless Mr. James does not mean to satirize such Americans, but it is interesting to note how they strike such a keen observer. We are certainly not allowed to like them, and the other sort find somehow a place in our affections along with his good Europeans. It is a little odd, by the way, that in all the printed talk about Mr. James —and there has been no end of it—his power of engaging your preference for certain of his people has been so little commented on. Perhaps it is because he makes no obvious appeal for them; but one likes such men as Lord Warburton, Newman, Valentin, the artistic brother in *The Europeans*, and Ralph Touchett, and such women as Isabel, Claire Belgarde, Mrs. Tristram, and certain others, with a thoroughness that is one of the best testimonies to their vitality. This comes about through their own qualities, and is not affected by insinuation or by downright *petting,* such as we find in Dickens nearly always and in Thackeray too often.

The art of fiction has, in fact, become a finer art in our day than it was with Dickens and Thackeray. We could not suffer the confidential attitude of the latter now, nor the mannerism of the former, any more than we could endure the prolixity of Richardson or the coarseness of Fielding. These great men are of the past—they and their methods and

interests; even Trollope and Reade are not of the present. The new
school derives from Hawthorne and George Eliot rather than any
others; but it studies human nature much more in its wonted aspects,
and finds its ethical and dramatic examples in the operation of lighter
but not really less vital motives. The moving accident is certainly not
its trade; and it prefers to avoid all manner of dire catastrophes. It is
largely influenced by French fiction in form; but it is the realism of
Daudet rather than the realism of Zola that prevails with it, and it has
a soul of its own which is above the business of recording the rather
brutish pursuit of a woman by a man, which seems to be the chief end
of the French novelist. This school, which is so largely of the future as
well as the present, finds its chief exemplar in Mr. James; it is he who is
shaping and directing American fiction, at least. It is the ambition of
the younger contributors to write like him; he has his following more
distinctly recognizable than that of any other English-writing novelist.
Whether he will so far control this following as to decide the nature of
the novel with us remains to be seen. Will the reader be content to
accept a novel which is an analytic study rather than a story, which is
apt to leave him arbiter of the destiny of the author's creations? Will he
find his account in the unflagging interest of their development? Mr.
James's growing popularity seems to suggest that this may be the case;
but the work of Mr. James's imitators will have much to do with the
final result.

In the meantime it is not surprising that he has his imitators. Whatever exceptions we take to his methods or his results, we cannot deny
him a very great literary genius. To me there is a perpetual delight in
his way of saying things, and I cannot wonder that younger men try to
catch the trick of it. The disappointing thing for them is that it is not a
trick, but an inherent virtue. His style is, upon the whole, better than
that of any other novelist I know; it is always easy, without being
trivial, and it is often stately, without being stiff; it gives a charm to
everything he writes; and he has written so much and in such various
directions, that we should be judging him very incompletely if we considered him only as a novelist. His book of European sketches must
rank him with the most enlightened and agreeable travelers; and it
might be fitly supplemented from his uncollected papers with a volume
of American sketches. In his essays on modern French writers he
indicates his critical range and grasp; but he scarcely does more, as
his criticisms in the *The Atlantic* and *The Nation* and elsewhere could
abundantly testify.

There are indeed those who insist that criticism is his true vocation, and are impatient of his devotion to fiction; but I suspect that these admirers are mistaken. A novelist he is not, after the old fashion, or after any fashion but his own; yet since he has finally made his public in his own way of story-telling—or call it character-painting if you prefer,—it must be conceded that he has chosen best for himself and his readers in choosing the form of fiction for what he has to say. It is, after all, what a writer has to say rather than what he has to tell that we care for nowadays. In one manner or other the stories were all told long ago; and now we want merely to know what the novelist thinks about persons and situations. Mr. James gratifies this philosophic desire. If he sometimes forbears to tell us what he thinks of the last state of his people, it is perhaps because that does not interest him, and a large-minded criticism might well insist that it was childish to demand that it must interest him.

I am not sure that my criticism is sufficiently large-minded for this. I own that I like a finished story; but then also I like those which Mr. James seems not to finish. This is probably the position of most of his readers, who cannot very logically account for either preference. We can only make sure that we have here an annalist, or analyst, as we choose, who fascinates us from his first page to his last, whose narrative or whose comment may enter into any minuteness of detail without fatiguing us, and can only truly grieve us when it ceases.

52. From an indignant rejoinder to Howells in the *Quarterly Review*

January 1883, clv, 212-7

For a more reasonable English reaction to Howells see Arthur Tilley's article referred to in Appendix I (section 9). The present extracts are from a long review article on American fiction which contains much praise of some authors, e.g. Bret Harte and George Cable; they begin at the end of an enthusiastic treatment of Mrs. Hodgson Burnett's *Louisiana*. The previous *Century* 'notice' of Howells was by T. S. Perry.

. . . and yet for one reader who has admired *Louisiana,* a hundred have read *Daisy Miller*, with its artificial mannerisms and its tawdry smartness, and have fancied that they were being initiated into the secrets of American life and character. . . . Mr. Henry James has done scant justice to his countrywomen; perhaps he has studied them less than he has studied the women of Europe. In the truly 'first-class notice' (with a pretty portrait attached) which Mr. Howells has liberally devoted to Mr. James—Mr. Howells having received a similar notice, also with a pretty portrait, a few months previously—we are told that Mr. James's 'race is Irish on his father's side, and Scotch on his mother's;' that much of his early life was spent in Europe; that he was at Harvard a few years, and then 'took up his residence in England and Italy which, with infrequent visits home, has continued ever since.' It would therefore appear that the studies of Americans which Mr. James presents to us are made chiefly from a distance, and there are not a few Americans, proud of their own descent from the old stock, who would be inclined to receive with much coldness the credentials of his 'race'. . . . This may have something to do with the singularity of the 'types' which supply Mr. James with his American portraits. The women are all flirts, so far as they are anything; the men are very like the conventional American of the stage. Daisy Miller goes about Rome at all hours with an enamoured Italian, and refuses to heed the remonstrance of her mother and her friends, and all the while—as we are led to suppose—she is really in love with some one else. The hero of *The American*—which is perhaps the best of Mr. James's books—is a man who does all sorts of impossible things; indeed, every situation in the book is impossible. . . . The plot, in fact, is simply chaotic—a wild caricature of real life; but Mr. James contrived to make his story interesting. Since the production of this work, he appears to have been guided by the principle which is expressed in Mr. Howells's panegyric; 'Will the reader be content to accept a novel which is an analytic study rather than a story?' The answer to this question, from nine readers out of ten, will be emphatically No: on that point neither Mr. Howells nor Mr. James need be in doubt for a single moment. When once the general reader is made to understand that he is not to go to these gentlemen for entertainment, even of the tamest kind, but only for philosophic instruction and dawdling sentimentality, their occupation will be gone . . . Mr. James, in his latest completed work—*The Portrait of a Lady*—carries out unflinchingly the theories of his school. There is no story. The book is one of the longest of recent times—767 closely-printed pages; and there is not a single interesting incident in it from beginning to end. No one can possibly care, for a single moment, what becomes of any of the characters. If an earthquake swallowed them all up in the middle of the second volume, the reader would only be tempted to thank the fates for a good deliverance. Three volumes of 'analysis' in small type is somewhat trying, even to the most sternly cultivated æstheticism. The characters are described at enormous length by Mr. James; then they describe themselves; then they are described by the other characters. Between them all, it would be strange if their 'points' were not sufficiently brought out. But nothing can relieve their inborn tediousness. Mr. James's descriptive writing is not remarkable for either grace or power, and his conversations are not brilliant. True Mr. Howells assures us that Mr. James's style 'is, upon the whole, *better than that of any other novelist*;' but some of us may perhaps hope for pardon if we prefer Scott, Thackeray, or George Eliot. It is evident that the Trans-atlantic æsthetic reformers will not run the risk of placing too low an estimate upon the services which they are rendering to literature. And then the theory is laid down, that the silly old custom of finishing a novel should be discarded. There is to be no beginning, no middle, and no end. It is like a lucky-bag at a bazaar—you thrust your hand in anywhere and take out anything you can find. As Mr. Howells says, the reader must be left 'arbiter of the destiny of the author's creations.'

The novelist provides the characters, and everybody is left free to dispose of them according to his own taste. Thus, in *The Portrait of a Lady*, the fate of all the personages in the book is left unsettled. . . .

We have said that Mr. James's conversations, though long, are never brilliant. Open his pages where one may, and it will be found that the men and women are prosing on in the same hum-drum fashion, and with apparently only one definite object in view—that of providing as many pages as possible of 'printed matter.' In a serial story, running, say, for twelve or eighteen months, this is a very important consideration. Mr. James has made himself, by practice, proficient in what may be called the tea-pot style of conversation:—

'I wonder if he will have some tea. The English are so fond of tea.'
'Never mind that; I have something particular to say to you.'
'Don't speak so loud or everybody will hear us,' said Pansy.
'They won't hear us if you continue to look that way: as if your only thought in life was the wish that the kettle would boil.'
'It has just been filled; the servants never know!' the young girl exclaimed with a little sigh.
'Do you know what your father said to me just now? That you didn't mean what you said a week ago.'
'I don't mean everything I say. How can a young girl do that? But I mean what I say to you. . . .'
Pansy raised the lid of the teapot, gazing into this vessel for a moment; then she dropped six words into its aromatic depths. 'I love you just as much.'
—*The Portrait of a Lady*, ii. 235, 236.

What sort of a cup of tea these six words made after they were dropped into the pot the author does not explain; but then he does not explain anything. The *dramatis personæ* wander about like babes in a wood. So, at least, it must seem to the ordinary reader, but we now know, from the information vouchsafed by Mr. Howells, that all this barren wilderness of conversation is intended as a mental exercise—it is an 'analytic study.' That Mr. James himself has studied before propounding his analysis must be taken for granted. But it is sometimes rather difficult to conjecture *where* he has studied for his characters, whether American or English—unless, perhaps, in the theatre, at a comic performance. . . .

Now no one is disposed to deny either to Mr. James or to Mr. Howells any reasonable degree of credit which they may choose to demand for this kind of work; the reception of their novels in this country is sufficient proof of that. But what we are not prepared to concede is the extraordinary claim which has recently been put forward by one of them, and not disavowed by the other, to be accounted superior to Dickens and Thackeray. . . .

Whatever may be the differences of opinion as to the value of the new 'school,' it must be acknowledged on all sides that a novelist enjoys an immense advantage in being a contributor to an illustrated magazine, which is ready not only to publish his works, but to issue elaborate articles on their merits—accompanied, as we have said, by that most affecting of souvenirs, a 'portrait of the author,' duly softened and idealized. The art of puffery gets 'finer' every day, whatever we may think about the art of novel-writing. Literary men are only just beginning to learn how to use it with effect.

53. John Hay on James as the prey of patriotism

1882

John Hay to W. D. Howells, December 1882. (*The Life and Letters of John Hay*, ed. W. R. Thayer, 1915, i, 411.)
Hay (1838–1905) was a poet, historian, and statesman; as a young man he was Lincoln's private secretary, and from 1898 until his death the American Secretary of State. It seems likely that in the third sentence below 'no' has been omitted before 'forgiveness'.

By the way, how James is catching it for his 'Point of View'! In vain I say to the Howling Patriot: 'The point of view is clearly and avowedly the point of view of a corrupted mother and daughter, spoiled by Europe; of a filthy, immoral Frenchman; of a dull, well-meaning Englishman!' But they respond: 'Miss Sturdy is James himself'; and as she says children are uproarious in America, and women's voices are higher than their manners, there is forgiveness for the writer. The worst thing in our time about American taste is the way it treats James. I believe he would not be read in America at all if it were not for his European vogue. If he lived in Cambridge he could write what he likes, but because he finds London more agreeable, he is the prey of all the patriotisms. Of all vices I hold patriotism the worst when it meddles with matters of taste.

54. Julian Hawthorne on James as a non-heroic realist

1884

Julian Hawthorne, from 'Agnosticism in American Fiction', *Princeton Review*, January 1884, xiii, 1–15.

Hawthorne (1846–1934) the son of Nathaniel, was a novelist himself. The 'two men' of the first sentence are, of course, HJ and Howells. HJ was acquainted with Hawthorne throughout his early life, and wrote some pleasant, but slightly patronizing, reviews of him in the *Nation* and the *Atlantic* (reprinted by Albert Mordell in *Literary Reviews and Essays by Henry James*, New York, 1957). The two men were not, apparently, conscious rivals, and Hawthorne always spoke of HJ 'glowingly and affectionately'.

We are thus brought face to face with the two men with whom every critic of American novelists has to reckon; who represent what is carefullest and newest in American fiction; and it remains to inquire how far their work has been moulded by the skeptical or radical spirit of which Turguénieff is the chief exemplar.

The author of *Daisy Miller* had been writing for several years before the bearings of his course could be confidently calculated. Some of his earlier tales,—as, for example, 'The Madonna of the Future,'—while keeping near reality on one side, are on the other eminently fanciful and ideal. He seemed to feel the attraction of fairyland, but to lack resolution to swallow it whole; so instead of idealizing both persons and plot, as Hawthorne had ventured to do, he tried to persuade real persons to work out an ideal destiny. But the tact, delicacy, and reticence with which these attempts were made did not blind him to the essential incongruity; either realism or idealism had to go, and step by step he dismissed the latter, until at length Turguénieff's current caught him. By this time, however, his culture had become too wide and his independent views too confirmed to admit of his yielding unconditionally to the great Russian. Especially his critical familiarity with

French literature operated to broaden, if at the same time to render less trenchant, his method and expression. His characters are drawn with fastidious care, and closely follow the tones and fashions of real life. Each utterance is so exactly like what it ought to be, that the reader feels the same sort of pleased surprise as is afforded by a phonograph which repeats, with all the accidental pauses and inflections, the speech spoken into it. Yet the words come through a medium; they are not quite spontaneous; these figures have not the sad, human inevitableness of Turguénieff's people. The reason seems to be (leaving the difference between the genius of the two writers out of account) that the American, unlike the Russian, recognizes no tragic importance in the situation. To the latter, the vision of life is so ominous that his voice waxes sonorous and terrible, his eyes, made keen by foreboding, see the leading elements of the conflict, and them only; he is no idle singer of an empty day, but he speaks because speech springs out of him. To his mind the foundations of human welfare are in jeopardy, and it is full time to decide what means may avert the danger. But the American does not think any cataclysm is impending, or if any there be, nobody can help it. The subjects that best repay attention are the minor ones of civilization, culture, behavior; how to avoid certain vulgarities and follies, how to inculcate certain principles: and to illustrate these points heroic types are not needed. . . .

There are two kinds of reserve—the reserve which feels that its message is too mighty for it, and the reserve which feels that it is too mighty for its message. Our new school of writers is reserved, but its reserve does not strike one as being of the former kind.

And yet Mr. James and Mr. Howells have done more than all the rest of us to make our literature respectable during the last ten years.

55. James on the desperate state of Anglo-Saxon letters

1884

HJ to W. D. Howells, February 1884, from Paris. (LJ, i, 104–5.) I have been unable to find out whose success it was that sickened HJ. For Miss Woolson see above, No. 23.

. . . ask Osgood to show you also the sheets of another thing I lately sent him—'A New England Winter.' It is not very good—on the contrary; but it will perhaps seem to you to put into form a certain impression of Boston.—What you tell me of the success of——'s last novel sickens and almost paralyses me. It seems to me (the book) so contemptibly bad and ignoble that the idea of people reading it in such numbers makes one return upon one's self and ask what is the use of trying to write anything decent or serious for a public so absolutely idiotic. It must be totally wasted. I would rather have produced the basest experiment in the 'naturalism' that is being practised here than such a piece of sixpenny humbug. Work so shamelessly bad seems to me to dishonour the novelist's art to a degree that is absolutely not to be forgiven; just as its success dishonours the people for whom one supposes one's self to write. Excuse my ferocities, which (more discreetly and philosophically) I think you must share; and don't mention it, please, to any one, as it will be set down to green-eyed jealousy. . . . I have been seeing something of Daudet, Goncourt, and Zola; and there is nothing more interesting to me now than the effort and experiment of this little group, with its truly infernal intelligence of art, form, manner—its intense artistic life. They do the only kind of work, to-day, that I respect; and in spite of their ferocious pessimism and their handling of unclean things, they are at least serious and honest. The floods of tepid soap and water which under the name of novels are being vomited forth in England, seem to me, by contrast, to do little honour to our race. I say this to you, because I regard you as the great American naturalist. I don't think you go far enough, and you are haunted with romantic phantoms and a tendency to factitious glosses; but you are in the right path, and I wish you repeated triumphs there —beginning with your Americo-Venetian—though I slightly fear, from what you tell me, that he will have a certain 'gloss.' It isn't for me to reproach you with that, however, the said gloss being a constant defect of *my* characters; they have too much of it—too damnably much. But I am a failure!—comparatively. Read Zola's last thing: *La Joie de Vivre*. This title of course has a desperate irony: but the work is admirably solid and serious. . . . Addio—stia bene. I wish you could send me anything *you* have in the way of advance-sheets. It is rather hard that as you are the only English novelist I read (except Miss Woolson), I should not have more comfort with you.

56. Edgar Fawcett on *The Portrait of a Lady*

1884

Princeton Review, July 1884, xiv, 68–86.
Fawcett (1847–1904) was an American novelist. I have printed here the closing pages of a thorough survey of 'Henry James's Novels'.

Chronologically speaking, we should not have left until the last a novel of Mr. James's which we have reserved for final treatment. He has published no small amount of fiction since he wrote *The Portrait of a Lady,* and yet this deserves a last place on the list of his novels. Into this work, as it seems to us, Mr. James has poured his soul, and given the world something that it will not soon let die. Four magnificent volumes now stand recorded to his credit as an author. These are: *The Passionate Pilgrim and Other Tales, Roderick Hudson, The American,* and *The Portrait of a Lady.* Much of his intermediate writing is fine and admirable. But it would have given him a secondary place in letters, while these four books just mentioned lift him to a primary, we were about to add a supreme, place in letters. If he should never put pen to paper again, his fame is secure and permanent through those four books alone. And after the most careful consideration of each, it appears to us that *The Portrait of a Lady* is paramount over the rest. It is the longest thing that he has written, but it is also the most majestic and unassailable. Its heroine is a character whose misfortunes are the imperative catastrophes resultant from her own ideal strivings. Unlike Roderick Hudson, Isabel Archer does not recklessly sow the seed of her own future torments. She makes a pitiable error, but she makes it in all womanly faith and sincerity. She is a beautiful, talented, exceptionally lovable girl, and suddenly, at a period when she desires more than ever before to wrest a fecund and splendid victory from the usual aridity of life—to ennoble herself by subjugating herself—to live a power for good and to die somehow perpetuating such a power—at this very period, we say, she is lifted from the inertia of longing to the possibility of achievement. A fortune is left her, in a most unexpected manner; vistas of new purpose are opened to her; the prospect is dazzling at first; she hardly knows what she shall do with these charming, golden opportunities. She does what nearly every woman of her personal graces would do under the same conditions. Out of four suitors (if poor, consumptive Ralph Touchett may be called a suitor) she selects a man whom she marries, believing him a paragon of wisdom, virtue, taste, refinement, notability. He is poor, and it is a comfort for her to feel him so. For this reason he and she shall be yoked, all the more, in exercise of noble end. Her love, which is a reverence, becomes a horror of disappointed discovery. The whole novel is a sort of monumental comment upon the dread uncertainties of matrimony. Isabel's husband, whom she believed of a spirit equally lofty and amiable, turns out a frigid self-worshipper, a creature whose blood is ichor, whose creed is an adoration of *les usages*, whose honor is a brittle veneer of decorum, beneath which beats a heart as formally regular as the strokes of a well-regulated clock. He has married her with very much the same motive as that which might prompt him to buy a new bit of antique *bric-à-brac* at slight cost from a shrewd dealer. He is a virtuoso, a collector, a person who puts immense value upon all exterior things, and he considers life, happiness, matrimony, womanhood, principle, even divinity itself as an exceedingly exterior thing. Isabel's amazement, her grief, her dismay, her passionate mutiny, and her final bitter resignation, constitute the chief substance of this remarkable book. But much more than this goes to make the book, as a thousand turrets, traceries, illuminations and sculptures go to make a great result in architecture. It is a book with a very solid earth beneath it and very luminous and profound sky above it. It is rich in passages of quotable description, and no less rich in characters of piercing vividness. It contains more than one 'portait of a lady,' as it contains more than one portrait of a man. Madame Merle, the perfectly equipped woman of the world, the charmer, the *intrigante*, the soft-voiced, soft-moving diplomatist, and yet (as we feel more than we are really told) the force for ill, the adulteress, and the arch-hypocrite—Madame Merle, we say, is incomparably depicted. Again, the dying Ralph Touchett, with his mixture of the cynic and the humanitarian, with his love for Isabel alike so exquisitely concealed and revealed, with his patience, his outbursts of regret, his poetry of feeling, his inalienable dignity and manhood, is an astonishingly striking conception. He exists, to our knowledge, nowhere else in any pages of fiction. He is the high-tide mark of what Mr. James can do with a human individuality, and he represents what Mr. James likes most to do with one. We all must recognize him if we have lived and thought. As the author first presents him to us, we involuntarily recall having seen some one who looked just like him. This may not be true, but the sensation of having met Ralph Touchett before is none the less insistent, and proves how marvellous is Mr. James's faculty for hitting off with a few airy or rough touches the physical 'points' of his fellow-creatures. 'Tall lean, loosely and feebly put together,' runs the description of Ralph Touchett, 'he had an ugly, sickly, witty and charming face, furnished, but by no means decorated, with a straggling mustache and whisker. He looked clever and ill—a combination by no means felicitous; and he wore a brown velvet jacket. He carried his hands in his pockets, and there was something in the way he did it that showed the habit was inveterate. His gait had a shambling, wandering quality; he was not very firm on his legs.' We get to love this poor dying consumptive very dearly before he dies. He has a great warm heart behind those wasting lungs. He is a philosopher, but he is also through and through a man.

But, after all, tho he and Isabel are the two triumphs of the book, they are merely the crown of a perfect edifice; all the rest of the structure is of a correspondent excellence. The demure little Pansy, with her unswerving propriety, her devout, filial faith, her enormous sense of rule and law and obedience, is a picture of puritanic simplicity whose tints should last for other generations than ours. So, too, Lord Warburton, as regards crisp and potent yet harmonious and secure character-painting. He is the Liberal English peer to a fault,—with mind enough to understand that his position is absurd, yet with inherited pride enough to preserve an unblemished caste. Quotation, in *The Portrait of a Lady*, is a dangerous temptation. Every page offers abundant chance for it, filled as every page is with epigram, thought, knowledge of the world, glancing play of humor, and sportive resilience of fancy.

Mr. James, as we understand, is still in middle life. His career has thus far been enviably brilliant. He has secured heed, place and note in England; he is honorably known throughout Germany and France. In his own country he has stimulated eager debate, caused sides to be formed for and against him, won his lovers and his haters after the manner of all literary men who have ever risen high above mediocrity. He has attained much—how much this article has been of meagre worth if it has not already somewhat plainly shown. He has put his stamp upon the literature of his age; he has employed a bewitching, resonant, cultivated style in which to express, not merely himself, but the best of himself—not merely his ideas, but his most careful, solid and durable ideas. That he will give us, in the future years which supposably still await him work of even a stouter fibre against oblivion than any which he has yet produced, is far from improbable. Toward that result his admirers—and we venture to assert that they are a more numerous tho more modest *clientèle* than some current newspapers would rather maliciously have us believe—entertain strong and obvious reasons for hope. Fame has rarely crowned so young a writer with bays of so fine a verdure. But he has won them, when all is said, very honestly. He bears the palm because he merits it. Let him merit new honors and these are sure to reward him. As it is, there is little doubt that he deserves to-day to be called the first of English-writing novelists.

57. W. D. Howells on 'A New England Winter'

1884

W. D. Howells to HJ, August 1884 (LH, i, 366–7). Compare Nos. 59–61.

I am just back from a visit of a few days at Campobello, which is so far off that I feel as if I had been to Europe. It is a fashionable resort, in spite of its remoteness, and I saw many well-dressed and well-read girls there who were all disposed more or less to talk to you, and of your latest story, 'A New England Winter'. Generally speaking I should say that its prime effect had been to imbue the female Boston mind with a firm resolve to walk on the domestic roof at the first opportunity. The maiden aunt gives universal satisfaction, especially in her rage with her nephew when he blows her a five-fingered kiss. I myself having the vice of always liking you, ought perhaps to be excluded from the stand, but I must bear my witness to the excellence particularly of some of the bits of painting. In just such a glare of savage sunshine I made my way through Washington street in such a horse-car as you portray, the day I read your advance sheets. Besides that, I keenly enjoyed these fine touches by which you suggest a more artistically difficult and evasive Boston than I ever get at. The fashionableness which is so unlike the fashionableness of other towns—no one touches that but you; and you contrive also to indicate its contiguity, in its most ethereal intangibility, to something that is very plain and deeply practical. It is a great triumph which Pauline Mesh embodies. The study pleases me throughout: the mother with her struggles—herculean struggles—with such shadowy problems; the son with the sincere Europeanism of an inalienable, wholly uninspired American. As for the vehicle, it is delicious.

58. James on the state of criticism

1884

HJ to Perry, September 1884 (LP, 317). HJ is replying to Perry's note of praise for the 'The Art of Fiction'. Later, of course, R. L. Stevenson responded to the essay in 'A Humble Remonstrance' (December 1884).

I thank you for all its appreciation & its friendly feeling which makes me feel that I didn't write my few remarks in *Longman* in vain. But it is the only thing that does make me feel so,—for my poor article has not attracted the smallest attention here & I haven't heard, or seen, an allusion to it. There is almost no care for literary discussion here,— questions of form, of principle, the 'serious' idea of the novel appeals apparently to no one, & they don't understand you when you speak of them.

TALES OF THREE CITIES

1884

59. 'M.L.H.' from a review, *Literary World*

September 1884, xv, 308–9

Compare No. 49.

It is a sad experience to find that a writer who has always delighted us
hitherto has no longer the same power to please. I am sure that others
of Mr. James's admirers besides me must have undergone this experience lately. . . . That a good many persons did not agree with us in
our estimate of this author mattered little to us his admirers, and it did
not affect our enjoyment of his writings that dull readers failed to see
the point of their satire, and rabid American 'patriotism' thought it
detected snobbishness on every page. But what worse charge can be
brought against an author than that he is dull? and if the accusation be
true what excuse can be made? In the 'Impressions of a Cousin', a great
falling-off became apparent. . . .

'Lady Barbarina' has affected still more strongly our respect for the
author's powers. The style is here again notable for its self-consciousness,
and, in spite of long-drawn sentences full of clauses, for a disjointed
jerkiness which may be the result of carelessness or of too much care;
while as to the matter of the sketch—' 'tis naught,' that is all one can
say of it. If there is a point to it, I for one have grown too obtuse to
perceive it.

What is to be said of the latest of these magazine tales, 'A New
England Winter'? We can hardly suppose it written simply for the sake
of inserting a few paragraphs descriptive of the unpleasantness of the
Boston climate and the discomfort experienced by the Boston citizen
who makes use of the horse-car to convey him about his business. . . .
But if the author's purpose in writing 'A New England Winter' be not

to abuse New England and its people, what in reality is it? Florimond Daintry, his mother and his aunt, his cousin Pauline, and his more-removed cousin Rachel, have not character enough between them to make an account of their private thoughts, their speech and actions, so interesting that we should give a couple of hours to hearing it, nor is there enough piquancy in the mere situation to make up for the lack of character and incident. Life is too short, we must decide, to read even Mr. James's stories, if they are to be hereafter no more entertaining than these.

60. From an unsigned review, *Nation*

November 1884, xxxix, 442

The *Tales of Three Cities*, now gathered together from the *Century*, show Mr. James at his best. It is a pity that they will perhaps be fully appreciated only by an inner circle of readers. It can hardly be expected in these days of abundant sunflower decorations, of chromos (in books as well as pictures), that the labor of the cunning worker in ivory, or of the lapidary, will find wide recognition.

61. William Morton Payne, from a review, *Dial*

December 1884, v, 206–7

Payne (1858–1919) was a teacher, translator, and critic, who became associate editor of the *Dial* in 1892.

. . . it is becoming painfully evident that Mr. James has written himself out as far as the international novel is concerned, and probably as far as any kind of novel-writing is concerned. These stories of American millionaires and English lords and ladies become less and less interesting, more and more diluted, with every turn of Mr. James's literary kaleidoscope. Probably it is because his style is so intrinsically good within its narrow limits that a new story by him is sure to find many readers, who are willing to forget that it tells them nothing new for the sake of the delightful manner in which the old things are re-said. But style and invention are both becoming old stories already with most of his readers, who are sure to drop off one by one if he cannot hit upon some fresh literary device by which to renew his bond with them. Mr. James certainly does more at times than merely to point out the real faults of American life and character. His representation of Jackson Lemon in one of these stories as a typical American gentleman, is a piece of gratuitous vulgarity which it is difficult to pardon. . . . Every new volume of stories by Mr. James deepens the impression that he is a much better writer of books of literary criticism and travel than of any other kind of fiction.

THE AUTHOR OF
'BELTRAFFIO' ETC.

1885

62. From an unsigned review, *Critic*

May 1885, NS iii, 206–7

For once we must confess ourselves thoroughly 'put out' with Mr. Henry James, and yet—how thankful one ought to be that he has printed all his disagreeable stories in a single volume! Accustomed as we have been to delicate flavors, to refined delineation, to savory and ingenious talk from his pen, we opened *The Author of Beltraffio* with pleasant anticipations which, we must say at once, have been grievously disappointed. Why does Mr. Henry James print so much? Wherefore such literary incontinence, that seems absolutely incapable of restraining itself and pours forth good, bad, and indifferent with equal impartiality and equal abundance? . . .

'The Author of Beltraffio' is a painful and repulsive story, followed by several others hardly less painful and repulsive. Shine on putrescence as genius may, it cannot glorify it. . . . In 'Georgina's Reasons'—another flower in these *fleurs du mal*—we have a story even more abominable; the story of an ungirlish girl who deliberately gets herself into all sorts of difficulties by her disingenuous concealments and conduct towards her parents, and who ends by committing bigamy for no assignable reason. Mr. James is walking on ground perilously like prurience in this story, and strikes in it, and in the rest of this volume, a note of distinct degeneration. . . . We beg to remind Mr. Henry James of the *alter ego*—the former delightful self—and pray him not to write himself to death; not to fritter his gentility and gentle skill away, and not to patch his tunic with the cast-off purple patches of a fast-decaying Frenchy school, however great the temptation.

63. Gertrude Atherton on the Henry James craze

[1932]

Gertrude Atherton, from *Adventures of a Novelist*, 1932, 107 and 116. Mrs. Atherton (1857–1948) was at the time an aspiring writer. The passages are impossible to date with precision, but she seems to be recalling the mid-1880's or earlier.

It was during the following summer that I had my first introduction to Henry James. The Selbys, who lived on the neighbouring estate, returned from one of their frequent visits to Europe. The girls, Annie and Jeannie—the last a beauty, who some years later married Faxon—had 'caught the Henry James craze,' and had all his books to date. I became an immediate convert. Howells's star was also in the ascendant, but he made all life seem commonplace, and I detested him. I think it a pity he ever lived, for he was a blight on American letters. He founded the school of the commonplace, and to any young writer who hated the commonplace as I did, the Howells tradition was an almost insurmountable obstacle on his upward path. Those who followed in his footsteps were reasonably sure of success, not only because the critics, largely of his own ilk, decreed that realism (littleism would have been a better word) was the fashion, but because the majority of fiction readers were necessarily commonplace and enjoyed reading about their own kind. James, even in his first manner, was too aristocratic, too lofty and detached, to command as large a following as Howells, but that following was an ardent one. And mostly among women. I remember an irritated male calling us 'Henry James fools.'

* * *

Helen encouraged me in the belief that my book must find a haven at last—when we were not quarrelling over Henry James. We were both in love with him! As he looked dark in his pictures I maintained that I had the best hope of winning his affections—did we ever meet! —as I was a blonde and she a brunette. Then she came down one day with a copy of *Roderick Hudson* in her hand, and pointed triumphantly to a line in which the heroine was almost gloatingly described as having 'a mass of dusky hair over a low forehead.' I gave up.

64. Mark Twain on other modern novelists

1885

Mark Twain to W. D. Howells, July 1885. (*Mark Twain-Howells Letters 1872–1910*, ed. H. N. Smith and W. M. Gibson, Cambridge, Mass., 1960, 534.)
This was written after the seventh instalment of the serial publication of *The Bostonians* had appeared.

I can't stand George Eliot, & Hawthorne & those people; I see what they are at, a hundred years before they get to it, & they just tire me to death. And as for the *Bostonians*, I would rather be damned to John Bunyan's heaven than read that.

THE PRINCESS CASAMASSIMA

Serialization 1885

---

65. Mrs. Robert Louis Stevenson to Sidney Colvin

August or September 1885. (E. V. Lucas, *The Colvins and their Friends*, 1928, 161.)
Mrs. Stevenson was an American who had married Stevenson in 1880. Colvin (1845–1927) was a critic and scholar who became Slade Professor of Fine Art at Cambridge, Director of the Fitzwilliam Museum, and keeper of prints and drawings at the British Museum.

I have been reading the beginning of Henry James's new novel. Most excellent, I think it, and altogether a new departure,—not but that I have always liked his other work: but this is different, with the thrill of life, the beating of the pulse that you miss in the others.

THE BOSTONIANS

1886

66. James explains his difficulties and disappointments

HJ to WJ, letter, October 1885 (JF, 327).

WJ had criticized the serial version of *The Bostonians* for containing in Miss Birdseye a portrait of Miss Peabody, Nathaniel Hawthorne's sister-in-law. HJ rebutted the charge, saying among other things that 'the story is, I think, the best fiction I have written'. (The exchange is too well known to need reprinting here.) Then WJ added what Matthiessen describes as 'more relevant criticism', and HJ replied as follows.

I concur absolutely in all you say, and am more conscious than any reader of the redundancy of the book in the way of descriptive psychology, etc. There is far too much of the sort of thing you animadvert upon, though there is in the public mind at the same time a truly ignoble levity and puerility and aversion to any attempt on the part of a novelist to establish his people solidly. All the same, I have overdone it—for reasons I won't take time to explain. It would have been much less the case if I had ever seen a proof of *The Bostonians*; but not a page had I before me till the magazine was out. It is the same with the *Princess Casamassima*, though that story will be found probably less tedious, owing to my having made to myself all the reflections your letter contains, several months ago, and never ceased to make them since. The *Princess* will, I trust, appear more 'popular'. I fear *The Bostonians* will be, as a finished work, a fiasco, as not a word, echo or comment on the serial (save your remarks) have come to me (since the row about the first number) from any quarter whatever. The deathly silence seems to indicate that it has fallen flat. I hoped much of it, and shall be disappointed—having got no money for it, I hoped for a little glory.

67. William James on re-reading *The Bostonians*

1886

WJ to HJ, May 1886 (JF, 328–9).
Written after WJ had read *The Bostonians* in book form.

I seize my pen the first leisure moment I have had for a week to tell you that I have read *The Bostonians* in the full flamingness of its bulk, and consider it an exquisite production. My growling letter was written to you before the end of Book I had appeared . . . and the suspense of narrative in that region, to let the relation of Olive and Verena grow, was enlarged by the vacant months between the numbers of the magazine, so that it seemed to me so slow a thing had ne'er been writ. Never again shall I attack one of your novels in the magazine. I've only read one number of *The Princess Casamassima*—though I hear all the people about me saying it is the best thing you've done yet. To return to *The Bostonians*; the last two books are simply sweet. There isn't a hair wrong in Verena, you've made her neither too little nor too much —but absolutely *liebenswürdig*. It would have been so easy to spoil her picture by some little excess or false note. Her moral situation, between Woman's rights and Ransom, is of course deep, and her discovery of the truth on the Central Park day, etc., inimitably given. Ransom's character, which at first did not become alive to me, does so, handsomely, at last. . . . I hear very little said of the book, and I imagine it is being less read than its predecessors. The truth about it, combining what I said in my previous letter with what I have just written, seems to be this, that it is superlatively well done, provided one admits that method of doing such a thing at all. Really the *datum* seems to me to belong rather of the region of fancy, but the treatment to that of the most elaborate realism. One can easily imagine the story cut out and made into a bright, short, sparkling thing of a hundred pages, which would have been an absolute success. But you have worked it up by dint of descriptions and psychologic commentaries into near 500— charmingly done for those who have the leisure and the peculiar mood to enjoy that amount of miniature work—but perilously near to turning away the great majority of readers who crave more matter and less art. I can truly say, however, that as I have lain on my back after dinner each day for ten days past reading it to myself, my enjoyment has been complete. I imagine that the inhabitants of other parts of the country have read it more than natives of these parts. They have bought it for the sake of the information. The way you have touched off the bits of American nature, Central Park, the Cape, etc., is exquisitely true and calls up just the feeling. Knowing you had done such a good thing makes the meekness of your reply to me last summer all the more wonderful.

68. James on the faults of *The Bostonians*

1886

HJ to WJ, June 1886 (JF, 329).
A reply to No. 67.

Thank you for your letter . . . on the subject of *The Bostonians*. Everything you said in it gratified me extremely—and very superfluous was your retraction of what you wrote before (last autumn while the thing was going on in the magazine and before you had more than dipped into it). I myself subscribe just as much to those strictures now as I did then—and find 'em very just. All the middle part is too diffuse and insistent—far too describing and explaining and expatiating. The whole thing is too long and dawdling. This came from the fact (partly) that I had the sense of knowing terribly little about the kind of life I had attempted to describe—and felt a constant pressure to make the picture substantial by thinking it out—pencilling and 'shading'. I was afraid of the reproach (having *seen* so little of the whole business treated of,) of being superficial and cheap—and in short I should have been much more rapid, and had a lighter hand, with a subject concerned with people and things of a nature more near to my experience. Let me also say that if I have displeased people, as I hear, by calling the book *The Bostonians*—this was done wholly without invidious intention. I hadn't a dream of generalizing—but thought the title simple and handy, and meant only to designate Olive and Verena by it, as they appeared to the mind of Ransom, the southerner and outsider looking at them from New York. I didn't even *mean* it to cover Miss Birdseye and the others, though it might very well. I shall write another: *The Other Bostonians*. However, this only by the way, for after one of my productions is finished and cast upon the waters it has, for me, quite sunk beneath the surface—I cease to care for it and transfer my interest to the one I am next trying to float.

69. From an unsigned review, *Spectator*

March 1886, lix, 388–9

By R. H. Hutton.

The Bostonians consists chiefly of a truly wonderful sketch of the depth of passion which has been embodied in the agitation of woman's wrongs and woman's rights,—a depth of passion which it is hardly possible for us in England to associate with anything short of religious fervour. Miss Olive Chancellor is the central figure of this agitation. . . . It is hardly possible to speak with too much admiration of this powerful sketch of a refined, passionate, reserved woman, loathing the vulgar side of publicity, and yet so eager for what she thinks the great reform of the age, that she is launched into the vulgarities of the trading Yankee philanthropist against her will, and in spite of the most lively sensation of horror and reluctance. Her consuming desire for a friendship that should amount to a passion, her steadfast and self-forgetting devotion when she finds such a friendship, her deep and fierce jealousy when it is threatened by her friend's liability to a stronger passion, and the tragic collapse both of the tie and of the great mission on which the two friends had embarked, beneath the blighting influence of this stronger love, are painted with a force and originality such as even Mr. Henry James has never before exhibited in an equal degree. . . .

We could not give any adequate illustration of the cultivated fanatic and of her eloquent friend in any one extract, and must refer our readers to the book itself for the very powerful study of this pair of characters. But we must say that Mr. Henry James has fallen so deeply in love with his own study, that he is tempted to dwell on it and almost maunder over it, till it bores his readers; and it is not till we get to the second half of the third volume that the picture of the struggle between the fanatic friend and the imperious lover, for the heart of Verena Tarrant, rises to the highest point of interest and power. The close of the book is singularly effective, though, as usual, Mr. Henry James snuffs out the light of his story with a disagreeable sort of snap in his last sentence. He has apparently almost repented himself of having thrown so much true feeling into the death-scene of Miss Birdseye, and he makes up for it by breaking-off, with perhaps even more than his usual *brusquerie*, the love-story of Verena Tarrant. On the whole, though we can truly say that we have never read any work of Mr. Henry James which had in it so much that was new and original, we must also say that we have never read any tale of his that had in it so much of long-winded reiteration and long-drawn-out disquisition. Perhaps that, too, is in its way a reflection of the thin, long-drawn elaborateness of Bostonian modes of thought.

70. Unsigned review, *Nation*

May 1886, xlii, 407–8

The Bostonians is a novel which invites elaborate criticism by its own elaboration. It is apparently designed to bring out a number of contrasts—the contrast between the ladies who are filled with the enthusiasm of the woman's-rights movement, and the ladies who are not filled with anything of the kind; between the somewhat antique 'chivalrous' young Southern man and the brusque, progressive Northern young woman, with a redundancy of ideas; between Boston and, as logicians would say, all that is not-Boston in the world. These contrasts are pushed far, and bring out remorselessly much that is peculiar to the civilization of the day. Every American reader will find in the book some reflection of his or her mind; and as for the Bostonians, they have already given plain notice to the world that, in their opinion, the volume is libellous—not as being an absolutely false, but as a distorted picture. Everybody has heard the story of the New York wag who approved his tedious friend's determination to lecture in Boston, on the ground that he 'always had hated the Bostonians.' Something of this feeling is prevalent in many places outside of New England, and while we are not willing to say that Mr. James panders to it, it must be admitted that the reader gets the impression that, were the novelist to permit himself such emotions, he would confess to a dislike of many of the things which, in New York, are thought to be particularly Bostonian. But Mr. James very wisely eschews likes and dislikes. An observer and critic by nature and training, he would spoil his best effects did he permit himself to become identified with the puppets whom he so cleverly exhibits. In *The Bostonians* he is by no means at his best. The story drags in places, and the conversations betray that want of naturalness into which the author's passion for a sort of dramatic repartee leads him. Nevertheless, the criticism and analysis and observation are so good that we cannot refrain from admiration even when we do not always enjoy it. We cannot help feeling that we are in the hands of one of the first of American novelists.

71. From an unsigned review, *Literary World*

June 1886, xvii, 198

Frank Stockton (1834–1902) was a successful writer of comic fantasies. This review is more typical of the American reception of *The Bostonians* than that in the *Nation* or the *Atlantic*.

The magnitude of Mr. James's last work was never so apparent as now, when it comes in a bulky volume of about four hundred and fifty pages. But justice demands the statement that in this gay attire of cardinal and flame color—was it meant to relieve the internal somberness?—the tediousness is more endurable; nay, if one had time it might be a positive pleasure to go over this interminable story afresh. On a further consideration, and a second looking along the pages, it seems possible to accept the apathetic Basil as representing some (hitherto unknown) type of the Southern gentleman, though, as a hero, he is no better than the average hero of the woman novelists who evolve that personage from their own consciousness instead of from actual life. . . . To say that the *finale* of the Verena experiment is worthy of Frank Stockton, must be taken as complimentary by the author of *The Bostonians*. Mr. James is probably thought by the English fairly to represent some phases of American life in his careful and highly elaborated novels; but we protest that the advanced women and their men associates, as typified by the Tarrants and others, have an atrociously exaggerated importance attached to them. The types, the class, the cause, are not worth the space they occupy; and the author has made a lamentable misuse of his keen analytic powers in reporting Olive's states of feeling and the slow dragging of the reform; it is like bringing heavy artillery to bear on shadows.

72. H. E. Scudder, from a review, *Atlantic*

June 1886, lvii, 851-3

The three novelists under review are HJ, Howells, and F. Marion Crawford. The 'Laphams and Coreys' are characters in Howells's *The Rise of Silas Lapham*. Scudder (see No. 43) commences by rejoicing that the three write for their reader's entertainment and 'so rarely ask us to listen to their opinion on any of the topics which we go to them to escape.'

It might be supposed, at first glance, that Mr. James in his latest novel was not going to let us off, but intended to drag us with him into the labyrinth of the woman question. Nothing could be more unjust. Mr. James, with the quick instinct of an artist, saw his opportunity in the strange contrasts presented by a phase of Boston life which is usually taken too seriously for purposes of fiction. We do not remember any more striking illustration of Mr. James's general self-expatriation. He comes back, as it were, to scenes once familiar to him, bringing with him habits of thought and observation which make him seize upon just those features of life which would arrest the attention of an Englishman or Frenchman. The subtle distinctions between the Laphams and Coreys are nothing to him, but he is caught by the queer variety of humanitarianism which with many people outside of Boston is the peculiar attribute of that much suffering city. He remembers, we will suppose, the older form, the abolition sentiment which prevailed in his youth, and now is curious about the later development, which he takes to be a medley of woman's rights, spiritualism, inspirationism, and the mind cure. He notices a disposition on the part of what a clever wit called Boston Proper to break away from its orbit and get entangled in this nebulous mass, and so he takes for his main figure a woman who is young and old by turns, according to the need of the novelist, a Bostonian of the straiter sect, who has yet, by the very force of her inherited rigidity of conscience, martyred herself, and cast in her lot with a set of reformers who are much the worse for wear. Olive

Chancellor's high-bred disdain of her seedy associates is mingled with lofty devotion to the cause which they misrepresent, and the composition in character is extremely truthful and skillfully shown. What renders it even more fine as a personal portrait is the admixture of passionate, womanly appropriation of the girl whom she looks upon as the young priestess of the new church of womanhood; and the manner in which the woman is always getting the better of the doctrinaire strikes us as showing more completely than anything else in the book how thoroughly Mr. James has possessed himself of this character.

The second lady of this drama is Verena Tarrant, who was constructed for the purposes of the story, and is, we may say, a purely imaginary being. Mr. James may have had an indefinite image of the Priscilla of Hawthorne's *The Blithedale Romance* floating in his mind when he built this impossible Verena. Impossible, we say, because, while Hawthorne manages to invest Priscilla with a delicacy of nature in spite of her surroundings, Mr. James, in his analysis of Verena, makes her refined, beautiful, spiritual in her power, and in a hundred ways, when he is not analyzing her, succeeds in betraying a cheap imitation of spiritual beauty. That Olive Chancellor, with a cataract over her inner eye, should fail to perceive the innate vulgarity of the girl is not surprising, but it is too much to ask of us that we should make Basil Ransom stone blind also.

Basil Ransom, however, is in certain ways equally remote from the life which he is supposed to represent. It was a clever notion to bring the antipathetic element from the South, and in a few features this hero of the story has a little likeness to an actual Mississippian; but we cannot resist the conviction that Mr. James has never been in Mississippi, as the phrase goes, and trusts to luck that his readers have not been there, either. . . .

The character, however, on which Mr. James has plainly expended the most careful and, we are tempted to say, loving descriptive art is that of Miss Birdseye. At first one fears that the author does not appreciate her, but one ends by seeing that Mr. James knew the pathetic nobility of the figure, and admired it, even while he was apparently amusing himself and his readers. It is not art alone that can do this,— something of personal tenderness must go into the process; and this character is the one redeeming feature of the book, if one is considering the humane aspects. The other persons are either ignoble, like the Tarrants and Mrs. Luna, or they are repellent for other reasons; but Miss

Birdseye one falls in love with, quite to the exclusion of the proper heroine.

When we say that most of the characters are repellent, we are simply recording the effect which they produce upon the reader by reason of the attitude which the author of their being takes toward them. He does not love them. Why should he ask more of us? But since he is extremely interested in them, and seems never wearied of setting them in every possible light, we also accede to this interest, and if we have time enough strike up an extraordinary intimacy with all parties. It is when this interest leads Mr. James to push his characters too near the brink of nature that we step back and decline to follow. For instance, the details of the first interview between Olive and Verena in Olive's house carry these young women to dangerous lengths, and we hesitate about accepting the relation between them as either natural or reasonable. So far does this go that in the author's exhaustive reflections upon the subject directly afterward we feel as if another step only were needed to introduce a caricature by Mr. James upon himself. All this is still more apparent in the final scene of the book, which ought to have been the climax; instead of which, by its noise and confusion, and its almost indecent exposure of Miss Chancellor's mind, this scene allows the story just to tumble down at the end. . . . It is when we stop and take the book as a whole that we forget how fine the web is spun, and remember only the strong conception which underlies the book; the freshness of the material used; the amazing cleverness of separate passages; the consummate success shown in so dangerous a scene as the death of Miss Birdseye, where the reticence of art is splendidly displayed; and, in fine the prodigal wealth scattered through all the pages. There is sorry waste, and one's last thought about the work is a somewhat melancholy one, but we all have a lurking affection for prodigals.

73. Henry Sidgwick on Howells and James

1886

Henry Sidgwick from his Journal, August 1886. (A.S. and E.M.S., *Henry Sidgwick. A Memoir*, 1910, 454.)
Sidgwick (1838–1900) was a utilitarian philosopher, a great figure in late nineteenth century Cambridge (and thus English) culture, and a decisive influence on the start of University education for women.

I have been reading Howells's *Lemuel Barker*, as far as it has gone. Certainly it is good. I think the short and simple amours of the lower middle classes, depicted with this *de haut en bas* prosaic realism, may bore me soon, but I have not been bored so far. It is interesting to compare Howells's (superior) Bostonians with James's. There is the same *fond* of moral earnestness and introspective scrupulosity in both types; but in James it is unmitigatedly serious and naively wearisome; in Howells it is veiled and tempered—in well-bred persons—by a surface of vivacious self-critical humour and mutually critical banter. Probably Boston includes both sorts, but Howells's sort are more readable.

George Moore, from *Confessions of a Young Man*, 1886, Ch. XII.
Confessions is an autobiographical novel which makes a great
virtue of being lively and outspoken. I quote here from the final
version of 1916, but the reader should note that the book was
revised in 1904 and 1916, and that on each occasion the comments
on HJ were made a little sharper. For 'Mr. Lang' see No. 80.

The first book that came under my hand was *A Portrait of a Lady*, by
Henry James. I will admit that an artist may be great and limited; by
one word he may light up an abyss of soul; but there must be this one
magical and unique word. Shakespeare gives us the word, Balzac,
sometimes, after pages of vain striving, gives us the word, Tourgueneff
gives it always; but Henry James only flutters about it; his whole book
is one long flutter near to the one magical and unique word, but the
word is not spoken; and for want of the word his characters are never
resolved out of the haze of nebulæ. We are on a bowing acquaintance
with them; they pass us in the street, they stop and speak; we know
how they are dressed, and we watch the colour of their eyes. The
crowd of well-dressed people, in *A Portrait of a Lady*, comes back to me
precisely as an accurate memory of a fashionable soirée—the staircase
with its ascending figures, the hostess smiling, the host at a little distance with his back turned; some one calls him. He wheels round, and
I see his white kid gloves. The air is sugar-sweet with the odour of the
gardenias; there is brilliant light here, there is shadow in the further
rooms, the women's feet pass to and fro beneath the stiff skirts, I call
for my hat and coat, I light a cigar, I stroll up Piccadilly . . . saying
to myself, 'a very pleasant evening, I have seen a good many people I
knew, I have observed an attitude, and an earnestness of manner that
proved that a heart was beating . . . somewhere.'

Mr. James might say, 'If I have done this, I have done a great deal,'
and I would answer, 'No doubt you're a man of talent, cultivation, and
not at all of the common herd, and to please you I'll place you in the

very front rank, not only of novelists but of men of letters.' But a man of genius, Oh, no!

I've read nothing of Henry James's that didn't suggest a scholar; so there shall be none of the old taunts—why does he not write complicated stories? Why does he always avoid decisive action? In his stories a woman never leaves the house with her lover, nor does a man ever kill another man or himself. Why is nothing ever accomplished? In real life murder, adultery, and suicide are of common occurrence; but Mr. James's people live in a calm, sad, and very polite twilight of volition. Suicide or adultery has happened before the story begins, suicide or adultery happens some years after the characters have left the stage, but in front of the reader nothing happens. The suppression or maintenance of story in a novel is a matter of personal taste; some prefer character-drawing to adventures, some adventures to character-drawing; that we cannot have both at once I take to be a self-evident proposition; so when Mr. Lang says, 'I like adventures,' I say, 'Oh, do you?' as I might to a man who says 'I like sherry,' and no doubt when I say I like character-drawing, Mr. Lang says, 'Oh, do you?' as he might to a man who says, 'I like port.' But Mr. James and I are agreed on essentials; we are more interested in human portraiture than with searches made for buried treasure according to scripts left behind by ancient mariners. But for human portraiture models are necessary, and the drawing-room presents few accents and angles, conformity to its prejudices and conventions having worn all away. Ladies and gentlemen are as round as the pebbles on the beach, presenting only smooth surfaces. Is there really much to say about people who live in stately houses and eat and drink their fill every day of the year? The lady, it is true, may have a lover, but the pen finds scanty pasturage in the fact; and in James's novels the lady only considers the question on the last page, and the gentleman looks at her questioningly.

In connection with Henry James the name of W. D. Howells is often mentioned, and I bought some three or four of his novels and finding them overflowing with girls in white dresses, languid mammas, mild witticisms, and young men, some cynical, some a little over-shadowed by love (in a word, a Tom Robertson comedy faintly spiced with American), I said: 'Henry James went to France and read Tourgueneff. W. D. Howells stayed at home and read Henry James.'

Henry James's mind is of a higher cast and temper; I have no doubt at one time of his life Henry James said, I will write the moral history of America, as Tourgueneff wrote the moral history of Russia—he borrowed at first hand, understanding what he was borrowing. W. D. Howells borrowed at second hand, and without understanding what he was borrowing. Altogether Mr. James's instincts are more scholarly, and I often regret his concessions to the prudery of the age, and cannot but feel that his concessions, for I suppose I must call them concessions, are to a certain extent self-imposed. He would answer me somewhat in this fashion—regretfully, perhaps: 'It is true that I live in an age not very favourable to artistic production, but the art of an age is the spirit of that age; if I violate the prejudices of the age I shall miss its spirit, and an art that is not redolent of the spirit of its age is an artificial flower, perfumeless, or perfumed with the scent of flowers that bloomed three hundred years ago.' To carry the analysis one step further, we will answer the apology that we conceive Mr. James would make to us were we to address him in a question of this sort: 'Why don't you turn your hand to a girl who gets thirty shillings a week and thinks she would be very happy if she could get thirty-five.' 'The woman of leisure,' he would answer, 'lives in a deeper intellectual mood than the work-girl whose ambition is an extra five shillings a week.' The interviewer in us would like to ask Henry James why he never married; but it would be vain to ask, so much does he write like a man to whom all action is repugnant. He confesses himself on every page, as we all do. On every page James is a prude and Howells is the happy father of a numerous family; the sun is shining, the girls and boys are playing on the lawn, they come trooping in to high tea, and there is dancing in the evening.

THE PRINCESS CASAMASSIMA

1886

75. Julia Wedgwood, from a review, *Contemporary Review*

December 1886, i, 899–901

Julia Wedgwood (d. 1913) was a descendant of Josiah Wedgwood, the niece of Darwin, and herself author of several books including the *Life of John Wesley* (1870). She has been reviewing W. H. Mallock's *The Old Order Changes* and J. H. Shorthouse's *Sir Percival* and the 'considerations' referred to at the beginning of the extract are those of Christian belief in relation to atheism and socialism. *Landon Deecroft* by Laon Ramsey is subtitled 'A Socialistic Novel'.

If these considerations take too stern an aspect to be appropriate in a review of fiction, the reader will find it a welcome change to turn to the last work of Mr. Henry James. He at least cannot be accused of trying to make a single reader wiser or better by his writings. He copies more or less the world as it is, and recognizes the existence of philanthropic endeavour as a taste of the day; but he is far too dainty an artist to allow himself to be 'earnest' about that or anything else. There is in him a vein of sympathy with patient, struggling, genteel poverty, and the American respect for women; but except for these indications of human feeling, we can promise the frivolous reader whom we have warned against Mr. Mallock and Mr. Shorthouse, that he may peruse *The Princess Casamassima* from beginning to end without perceiving a glimmer of a conviction or a moral standard. . . . Mr. James is always witty, and, wit, we freely allow, is one of the rarest gifts of literature, and one of the most conservative; but surely it ought to have something to conserve. A meal of spices is as little palatable as whole-some. However, what we are now concerned to urge is that spice used to disguise the flavour of tainted meat is worse than wasted. There is so little meat here that perhaps the reader will feel disgust as much out of place as approbation, but the moral effect of fiction depends not on what it narrates, but what it suggests. The Italian-American lady, whose portrait Mr. James draws so elaborately, may be intended by him to be a person of spotless character; but the account of her inter-course with the hero has recalled to our mind that of a fine lady in London with Tom Jones, and the coarseness of Fielding seems to us much nearer purity than the suggestive decorum of Mr. James. . . .

Princess Casamassima is a study of the new Socialism, a picture of the seething revolutionary energy and feverish destructiveness which has, to many in our day, taken the place of the Christianity they have abandoned. Such a feeling is a subject as legitimate for the artist as it is a problem obligatory on the moralist. Perhaps a true picture of that strange volcanic manifestation of our time, with its lurid background, might be the most valuable contribution that an artist could make to the student. But the picture of such a subject in the dainty stippling touch of Mr. James—a study where the tastes of a vulgar shop girl claim impartial interest with the reconstruction of Society, and where a languid but wakeful curiosity is the atmosphere through which we regard life, death, man, woman, and the empty space where God has vanished—for whom has such a picture any value? If marriage has lost its sanctity, if reverence for human life is to be regarded as an obsolete superstition, then let us enter at least into a dramatic sympathy with those who attack the old order of which these things are a part. It is not difficult, for the moment, to take their point of view. Our civilization is not so triumphant a success but what we can sympathize with those who, intent on the gulf between what it professes and what it is, desire to sweep it into nothingness. For our own part we can take up with positive refreshment after the *Princess Casamassima* such a work as *Landon Deecroft*, an artless and to our mind pathetic effort to express, in the form of a narrative, the writer's belief that Society has only to abolish religion and interest on money, and also to make wages a share of capital, in order to bring heaven to earth. Hatred is not so remote from reverence as dilettantism is.

76. From an unsigned review, *Spectator*

January 1887, lx, 14–16

By R. H. Hutton

. . . if it is a novel, it is one of a very unique kind. It has hardly any incident, unless the tendency of the whole network of circumstance and character to the tragedy with which the third volume abruptly closes, may be regarded as in itself constituting a single massive incident. But strange and unsatisfactory as the book is from every point of view but one, Mr. Henry James has never shown his extraordinary subtlety and strength to greater advantage. One reason of this is that what he loves best to draw, and draws with most success, because there is something in him which this kind of fiction best expresses, is character adrift from all its natural moorings,—character not fitting kindly to its circumstances. And since this story concerning the aspirations of the Nihilists enables him to present us with a whole group of characters which are thus adrift, men who, however well they may discharge their ordinary duties, are deeply convinced that instead of discharging them, they ought to be turning society upside down, and to be despisers of the modest routine by which they earn their bread, it gives him just the sort of field of which he is prepared to make the best use. . . . Miss Pynsent is one of Mr. Henry James's foils to the Nihilists of his picture. And for that purpose her character is very happily chosen. She 'could not embrace the state of mind of people who didn't apologise, though she vaguely envied and admired it, she herself spending much of her time in making excuses for obnoxious acts she had not committed.' Again, Millicent Henning, the vulgar beauty who in her childhood dirties the little Hyacinth's face, as he himself had shrewdly conjectured, by kissing him against his will, and whose vitality and beauty, in spite of her coarse hands, her execrable taste, her restlessness and chattering, her wonderful stories, her bad grammar, her insatiable thirst, and her grotesque opinions, become indispensable to Hyacinth, is a still more admirable foil to the Nihilists of Mr. Henry James's fiction; indeed, no portrait could easily be more vigorous.

Hyacinth Robinson himself is intended to represent the struggle between the inherited feelings of an aristocratic father with all kinds of refined tastes and insights, and the light rebellious nature of his French mother, the combination having resulted in his case in a singularly fine artistic faculty, which ultimately renders him at heart very disloyal to the destructive work in which, in his raw enthusiasm for the revolutionary party, he had hastily embarked. . . . But except that Hyacinth Robinson learns to love the great products of the artistic spirit in all ages with a genuine ardour, and that he recognises how little of clear method or principle the revolutionaries have in their destructive designs, his mind is as much adrift as to the true ideal of human life as the minds of all the other persons, not slaves of convention, painted in this book; nor is there one gleam of light that tends to make him think one course rather than another right or wrong. He evidently thinks the Conservatives and the Destructives alike the mere victims of prejudice; and if he learns to dislike the attack on civilisation, it is only because he feels more and more deeply that there is nothing proposed by the revolutionists which could be set up in its place. With the Princess Casamassima herself it is not much better. The glamour of her beauty is admirably described by Mr. James, and her love of emotion for the sake of emotion, too. But as for her principles, she has none except a principle of revolt against things as they are. She believes herself to be so horrified at the miseries of the poor that she would prefer an earthquake of the most destructive character to leaving things as they are; but neither she nor any of her friends pretends to have the smallest notion of the reconstructive principles which are to restore order when once the existing order receives its death-blow.

Even Lady Aurora, the only really noble character in the book, the plain, *gauche*, shy, ill-dressed, noble-minded spinster who devotes herself to alleviating the misery of the poor, partly because she finds the conventional life of the aristocracy so extremely dull and wearisome, but still more from innate goodness, has a kindness for the revolutionary party only because she is half in love with one of the pillars of that party, and has the deepest possible belief that if no one else sees his way, he does. Yet, so far as Mr. Henry James permits us to judge of his characters, no one of them is more completely adrift, no one of them knows less what he intends to do by way of revolutionising society, or how it can be so done as to substitute a more tolerable system for the existing system of *laissez faire*, than this same hero of the revolutionary party, Paul Muniment. He is extremely well described so far as his exterior

nature goes. His good-humoured contempt for the vapouring demo-
crats, his advice to the rich and the powerful to enjoy themselves while
they can, and not to be so weak as to come half-way to meet those who
wish to overturn the existing system, his perfect consciousness of the
selfishness and weakness of his comrades, his complete willingness to
lead an old friend into imminent peril of his neck without any evidence
that the gain to the cause of revolution which will result from the
assassination ordered, will be great, his candour in letting the Princess
Casamassima know that while he admires her beauty, he avails himself of her friendship chiefly for the money she can give to the cause,
and the complacency with which he recommends her to go back to her
jealous Italian husband the moment he finds that these supplies of money
will be stopped, make up a remarkably vivid picture of a half-educated,
strong, passionless, self-reliant, and apparently selfish man. But that of
which Mr. James does not contrive to give us even the faintest notion,
and which yet would be necessary to complete the picture, is the ground
on which Paul Muniment had persuaded himself that it was worth the
while of any strong, sane man to upset all existing institutions, if he
could. The bare chance that he himself and the abler leaders of the
anarchists might be able to build up something stable in the place of
what they intended to upset, would certainly not be a sufficient ground
to such a man as Muniment. He is described as a man who knows his
own mind, and who would not willingly go into captivity to any one.
He sees vividly the weakness of the frothy revolutionary party. He is
not represented as having any unmeasured faith in the strong and disinterested doctrinaires of the party. He is just such a man, if we understand Mr. James's sketch aright, as would leave political dreams alone,
and make his way up the ladder by steady thrift and industry. The great
blot on the novel is that the novelist does not contrive even to hint
which side of the man it was that made him a revolutionist; hardly even
to make us feel quite sure that he is one at all except in appearance. Mr.
James does not show us either the strong point in the policy of the party
of action which had laid hold of Muniment, or the weak point in
Muniment which laid him open to the seductions of an anarchical
theory destitute of any strong point. In Mr. James's novel as it stands,
Muniment is almost unintelligible,—hard, clear, confident, capable, yet
in alliance with men who are dreamers of dangerous, sanguinary, and
impracticable dreams. All his other characters might be what they are in
real life. Paul Muniment, while one of the most lifelike in mere appearance, is,—at least without the exhibition of links which Mr. Henry

James has suppressed,—out of place and out of relation to the Nihilism of the story. . . . With all its extraordinary interest, this sort of novel is the novel of a writer who thinks all the world aimless, and loves to exaggerate that aimlessness in his own descriptions of it. The world is not an easy matter to understand; but we can at least see more of a clue and a plan in the world as it is, than in Mr. Henry James's pictures of it, in which the tangles are made more conspicuous than they are in real life, and the helplessness much more universal.

77. 'H.B.', from 'London Letter', *Critic*

December 1886, NS vi, 252–3

'Bulwer' is Sir Edward (later Baron) Bulwer-Lytton (1803–73), the dandy, statesman, and author of society and historical novels and plays.

Mr. Henry James has published *The Princess Cassamassima*, and marked a new stage of development and a new departure in art. I like it much, though, as is natural in 'le Bulwer de nos jours' (it reminds me of the Bulwer of *Night and Morning*), it is overweighted with analysis and conversation. It is a surprise, indeed, in more ways than one. Who, for instance, would ever have believed that the author of *Daisy Miller* would ever condescend to make a real story? Who would ever have anticipated that he could do it so well? . . . I was horribly tired—and so were many others—of the feeble emotions and the futile creatures that formed the staple of Mr. James's art. I had greeted Miss Miller with enthusiasm; but in *The Portrait of a Lady* I found such poppy and mandragora as were merely irresistible. 'O change beyond report!' Here is a genuine romance, with conspirators, and harlots, and stabbings, and jails, and low-lived men and women who drop their h's, and real incidents, and strong emotions, and everything 'in a concatenation accordingly.' I cannot congratulate the author too heartily on his escape into fiction, nor advise too strongly that he should be encouraged on all hands, in the way which authors love, to go on in his new path, and leave forever behind him the land of ghosts and shadows in which he has sojourned so long.

The Princess Casamassima disturbs the conviction that Mr. James is the chief apostle of that restricted realism which ignores extraordinary events and unusual characters, and denies the influence of the apparently accidental on the general current of life, and of exceptional individuals on the history of humanity. It fits an empirical yet generally accepted definition of realistic fiction about as neatly as does 'Aladdin and the Wonderful Lamp'. One hardly stretches a point in drawing a parallel of improbability between the adventures of Aladdin with his Princess and the adventures of Hyacinth, bookbinder of Soho, with his Princess, the 'most wonderful woman in Europe.' Let it not be supposed that Mr. James has gone over to romance and magic; he has only selected people whom very few of us are likely ever to know, placed them in circumstances best suited to develop them, and dispassionately told the whole truth about them. His persistent desire to see the truth and his marvellous ability for telling it, whether the case under consideration be special or typical, prove that he has become a 'realist' in the only significant or, indeed, intelligent sense of the word. Though, as a rule, the value of a study of types is, of course, greater than that of exceptions, the exceptional, if well chosen, almost certainly gives the author the best chance to show his greatest strength. In this series of studies of exceptions Mr. James shows a versatility and power hardly hinted at in his former work. Such complex and high-strung natures as Hyacinth and the Princess call out reserves of keenness and intellectual refinement unexpected even in him; and in the score of uncommon people temporarily united by common interest in a great question, his wit and sarcasm are agreeably tempered by a tenderness and even intensity of feeling which he has hitherto carefully repressed. The gain to the reader in interest is enormous, for, if a novelist will not give us a dramatic plot or thrilling scenes and will leave off just when he has prepared us for a splendid finish, we are more than compensated for emotional disappointment by the intellectual pleasure of thought directed towards aims and objects not circumscribed by personal desire or local predisposition and habit. Throughout the novel we are carried far away from the average man and his motives in the ordinary conditions of life, but we are not invited to step outside of humanity; on the contrary, our understanding of humanity and sympathy with it are very materially extended and stimulated.

The Princess is an enigma, brilliant and inscrutable. All her frank and illogical talk, all her eccentric behavior, all the author's analysis, fail to make her comprehensible, but they accomplish his intention to portray a woman beyond shadow of doubt dazzlingly incomprehensible. . . . The Princess, as nearly as we can get at her, is a monument of sincere insincerity, and it was well for poor little Hyacinth, who long supplied her imagination with a concrete representative of her caprice, that the end came before he wholly realized the truth.

Little Hyacinth, born in a slum, bred on a poor dressmaker's charity, doomed to bear the burden of a parentage doubtful in all but its shame, is the great figure of the book. His organization is most sensitive and exquisite, and in him all the author's intellectual subtlety and distinction find expression. . . . At his worst, Hyacinth is never sordid or grudging or snobbish; at his best he is aflame with nobility, not heroic, romantic, and impossible, but entirely consistent with modern sentiment and the aspiration that is permissible or possible to us. Always, in his enthusiasms and dejection, in the light, ironical mood which is most frequent, Hyacinth is indefinably sad. . . .

It is rash to venture any conclusions about the author's personal attitude towards the Socialistic movement which agitates and colors the lives of his characters. He may be accused of using a serious movement simply for literary purposes, of scoffing at its intensity, playing with its passion, treating it often as frivolously as if it were a question of woman's-dress reform. But there is an undertone of earnestness suggesting that he, like Hyacinth after his eyes began to open, sees most clearly, at the bottom of the cry about elevating the people, the ulcer of envy, the passion of a party hanging together for the purpose of despoiling another to its advantage.

It is hardly fair to leave this novel without a word about its literary manner and style. There is, of course, very little plot, and that little is immaterial. There is a mass of what, from a hasty reading, may be stigmatized as super-subtle analyses, ultra-refined phrases, fine-spun nothings. But a careful reading—and for the dimmest appreciation that is necessary—will pretty surely acquit the author of such sins, and compel the recognition that, putting aside his skill as a novelist, he has written a book remarkable for the precision, elegance, and distinction of its style.

79. James on his evil days

1888

HJ to W. D. Howells, January 1888 (LJ, i, 136–7).

I have entered upon evil days—but this is for your most private ear. It sounds portentous, but it only means that I am still staggering a good deal under the mysterious and (to me) inexplicable injury wrought—apparently—upon my situation by my two last novels, the *Bostonians* and the *Princess*, from which I expected so much and derived so little. They have reduced the desire, and the demand, for my productions to zero—as I judge from the fact that though I have for a good while past been writing a number of good short things, I remain irremediably unpublished. Editors keep them back, for months and years, as if they were ashamed of them, and I am condemned apparently to eternal silence. You must be so widely versed in all the reasons of things (of this sort, to-day) in the U.S. that if I could discourse with you awhile by the fireside I should endeavour to draw from you some secret to break the spell. However, I don't despair, for I think I am now really in better form than I have ever been in my life, and I propose yet to do many things. Very likely too, some day, all my buried prose will kick off its various tombstones at once. Therefore don't betray me till I myself have given up. That won't be for a long time yet. If we could have that rich conversation I should speak to you too of your monthly polemics in *Harper* and tell you (I think I should go as far as that) of certain parts of the business in which I am less with you than in others. It seems to me that on occasions you mix things up that don't go together, sometimes make mistakes of proportion, and in general incline to insist more upon the restrictions and limitations, the *a priori* formulas and interdictions, of our common art, than upon that priceless freedom which is to me the thing that makes it worth practising. But at this distance, my dear Howells, such things are too delicate and complicated—they won't stand so long a journey. Therefore I won't attempt them—but only say how much I am struck with your energy, ingenuity and courage, and your delightful interest in the charming questions. I don't care how much you dispute about them if you will only re-member that a grain of example is worth a ton of precept, and that with the imbecility of babyish critics the serious writer need absolutely not concern himself. I am surprised, sometimes, at the things you notice and seem to care about. One should move in a diviner air. . . . I even confess that since the *Bostonians*, I find myself holding the 'critical world' at large in a singular contempt. I go so far as to think that the literary sense is a distinctly waning quality.

80. James on criticism

1888

HJ to Robert Louis Stevenson, July 1888 (LJ, i, 139).
Stevenson shared HJ's passion for fiction as a high art and his interest in its technical problems—their friendship stemmed from HJ's 'The Art of Fiction' of 1884 and Stevenson's reply to it (reprinted in Janet Adam Smith, see Appendix I, section 2). The novel HJ had just begun became *The Tragic Muse*. 'Lang' (who wrote for the *Daily News*) was Andrew Lang (1844–1912) the journalist, historian, and expert on myth and folklore (see Nos. 74 and 103).

I have just begun a novel which is to run through the *Atlantic* from January 1st and which I aspire to finish by the end of this year. In reality I suppose I shall not be fully delivered of it before the middle of next. After that, with God's help, I propose, for a longish period, to do nothing but short lengths. I want to leave a multitude of pictures of my time, projecting my small circular frame upon as many different spots as possible and going in for number as well as quality, so that the number may constitute a total having a certain value as observation and testimony. But there isn't so much as a creature here even to whisper such an intention to. Nothing lifts its hand in these islands save black-guard party politics. Criticism is of an abject density and puerility—it doesn't exist—it writes the intellect of our race too low. Lang, in the D.N., every morning, and I believe in a hundred other places, uses his beautiful thin facility to write everything down to the lowest level of Philistine twaddle—the view of the old lady round the corner or the clever person at the dinner party.

THE REVERBERATOR

1888

---

81. From an unsigned review, *Spectator*

August 1888, lxi, 1066–7

By R. H. Hutton

In *The American* there was a great breadth of life and passion; in *The Reverberator* there is but one phase of life, and no touch even of passion. The skill is as great as ever, but the difference in the delineation of American character is the difference between a study of life which is full and even massive, and a study of life which has either shrunk into a phase of vulgar professionalism or has never expanded beyond that neutral stage in which the higher interests are all completely undeveloped. And so, too, with regard to the study of French life. . . . However, we must not quarrel with our literary food when it is so exquisite in kind as Mr. Henry James provides. And certainly it would be well-nigh impossible to succeed more completely in what he has attempted than Mr. Henry James has succeeded here. . . . Half the power of the picture depends on the skill with which the thick-skinned impenetrability of the special correspondent's nature is delineated, and the complete innocence with which his American friends, Mr. Dosson and his two daughters, regard this enterprise of his, which they look upon purely in the light of a bold commercial speculation of the most legitimate kind. Probably nobody ever attempted before to paint a creature at once so amiable, so shrewd, and so vacant-minded as Mr. Dosson. Of him it is impossible to say that he is vulgar, because he is completely destitute of the kind of pretentiousness which chiefly constitutes vulgarity, and yet it is equally impossible to say that he is a gentleman, because he is equally destitute of the refinements of perception and feeling which constitute a gentleman. He is simply an affectionate father with a keen eye for investments, and no intellectual interest of his own of any sort or kind, but entirely wanting in any feeling of inferiority to those who rank higher in society than he does, and in any pride or self-inflation as regards his own wealth. Nothing could better explain the neutral character of the people amongst whom the *Reverberator* is popular, than Mr. Dosson's admiration for George Flack, and his perfect incompetence to understand the enormities of which these purveyors of private gossip to the public, are guilty. . . .

But, after all, the story is, as we have said, one of the thinnest performances which was ever marked throughout by real genius. Nothing slighter can well be imagined.

81a. Hardy on James's small perfection

1888

Thomas Hardy, from his journal, July 1888. (F. E. Hardy, *The Early Life of Thomas Hardy 1840–1891*, 1928, 277.)

Reading H. James's *Reverberator*. After this kind of work one feels inclined to be purposely careless in detail. The great novels of the future will certainly not concern themselves with the minutiae of manners. . . . James's subjects are those one could be interested in at moments when there is nothing larger to think of.

82. Robert Buchanan on James as a 'superfine young' critic

1889

Robert Buchanan, from 'The modern young man as critic', *Universal Review*, March 1889, iii, 355–9.

This article is a protest against modern cleverness, emasculation, and vulgarity, of which it classifies five types. HJ, the 'superfine young man', is an example of the first. The other four are: The Detrimental Young Man (Paul Bourget), The Olfactory Young Man (Maupassant), The Young Man in a Cheap Literary Suit (William Archer), and the Bank Holiday Young Man (George Moore). Buchanan (1841–1901, and two years older than HJ) was a prolific and combative poet and novelist who is perhaps best remembered for his pungent attack on the pre-Raphaelites, 'The Fleshly School of Poetry' (1871). He was also one of the subjects of Matthew Arnold's irony in Ch. VI of *Culture and Anarchy*.

Taking the types in their intellectual and natural order, for I propose to work down the scale from the highest note to the lowest, I can find no better example of the Superfine Young Man than Mr. Henry James, well known as the author of several minor novels and numerous minor criticisms. Highly finished, perfectly machined, icily regular, thoroughly representative, Mr. James is the educated young or youngish American whom we have all met in society; the well-dressed person who knows everybody, who has read everything, who has been everywhere, who is nebulously conscious of every astral and mundane influence, but who, as a matter of fact, is most at home on the Boulevards, and whose religion includes as its chief article the well-known humorous formula—that good Americans, when they die, go to Paris. No one can dispute Mr. James's cleverness; he is very clever. He is, moreover, well-spoken, agreeable, good-tempered, tolerant. He can even upon occasion affect, and seem to feel, enthusiasm; can talk of Tourgenieff as 'lovable,' of Daudet as 'adorable.' For the first quarter of an hour of our conversation with him we are largely impressed with his variety, his catholicity;

after that comes a certain indescribable sense of vagueness, of super-ficiality, of indifferentism; finally, if we must give the thing a name, a forlorn feeling of vacuity, of silliness. With a sigh we discover it: this young man, with all his information, with all his variety and catholicity, with all his wonderful knowledge of things *caviare* to the general, is, *au fond*, a fatuous young man. Startled at first by our discovery, we turn away from him; then, returning to him, under dishallucination, we per-ceive that he does not really know so much, even superficially, as we imagined, that his easy air of omniscience is a mere cloak to cover com-plete intellectual indetermination. For him and his, great literature has really no existence. He is secretly indifferent about all the gods, dead and living. He takes us into his confidence, welcomes us into his study; and we find that the faces on the walls are those, not of a pantheon, but of the comic newspaper and the circulating library. He appears to recognise the modern Sybil in George Eliot; and why indeed should he not take that triumphant Talent seriously, when the inspiration of his childhood was the picture gallery in *Punch*, when he sees a profound social satirist in Mr. du Maurier, and when he can fall prone before the masterpieces of that hard-bound genius *in posse*, Mr. Robert Louis Stevenson? These, then, are the glorious discoveries of the young man's omniscience— George Eliot, Alphonse Daudet, Flaubert, du Maurier, Mr. Punch, and the author of *Treasure Island*. With these, one is bound to say, he is, like all well-bred Americans, thoroughly at home. He says charming things concerning them. He finds more than one of them (adopting that hideous French phrase) 'adorable.' He becomes the little prophet of the little masters, and he publishes a little book about them—a book full of the agreeable art of conversation, such as we listen to in a hundred drawing-rooms. Nor is it at all out of keeping with this elegant young man's character that his talk about his literary ideals is, when it is most admiring, most patronising. He keeps in reserve a latent scepticism even concerning the *dii minores* of his microscopic religion; nay, he suggests to us that his remarks concerning them are merely lightly thrown-out illustrations of his own superabundant sympathy—that, if you really put him to it, he *would* read Shakespeare with appreciation, and *could* share the boy's enthusiasm about Byron. . . . It matters little whether he is pattering to us about George Eliot, or about 'his friend' Tourgenieff, or about Alphonse Daudet, or about the caricatures in *Punch*, or about the Art of Fiction—the effect is invariably the same. No sooner is one opinion advanced than it is qualified with another; scarcely is one view taken when another is substituted; an endless succession of personal pronouns—'*I* think,' '*I* will admit,' '*I* consider,' '*I* suspect,' &c.—covers a total absence of critical personality. The young man's very religion is 'qualified.' His mind is bewildered by its dreadful catholicity. He has not a spark of hate in him, because (with all his admirations and 'adorations') he has not a spark of love.

83. William Watson on James as an anaemic novelist

1889

William Watson, from 'Fiction—plethoric and anaemic', *National Review*, October 1889, xiv, 169–70.

The article also complains about a decline in modern standards, and says that since George Eliot (now absurdly despised in the 'wretched gabble' of silly critics) fiction has become either 'plethoric' or 'anaemic'. Robert Buchanan is, curiously enough, the example given of the first type. His stories are 'produced in response to this vulgar clamour for "movement" of any sort, no matter how spasmodic, and "action" at any cost, no matter what sacrifice of nature and the verities. The incidents are like a series of jerks and jolts. It is narrative in a state of perpetual precipitation. etc.' Watson (1858–1935) was a patriotic poet, much admired by Gladstone, and often inspired by current events. He tended to lament the decline of Empire and of Poetry.

Yes, plethoric fiction. But how about the opposite variety? For, alas, we suffer from both extremes, and of the two morbid conditions, the over-sanguine and the anæmic, it is hard to say which is the worse or the more inveterate. Plethora may, to some extent, be treated by bloodletting. Anæmia is not so easy to put right. Who that has read the novels of Mr. James and Mr. Howells can fail to observe how attenuation and depletion are becoming features of modern literature? Emaciated fiction has had a successful run, and to some extent, one cannot deny, has deserved it; for pale and fragile as the creature is, the merest slip of a thing, with consumption written legibly on her super-refined features and in the hollows of her languid eyes, she has come to us exquisitely dressed in the most perfect taste, recommended by the most faultless manners, in short, with everything that culture and millinery could do to make her attractive. How is it that in the presence of all these charms we feel a vague want, an aching void, as the sweet hymnist has it? How is it that in the middle of an emaciated novel—if it can be said to have a middle, for it mostly seems one long beginning and ever-deferred end —instead of feeling happy, for instance, in one of Mr. James's æsthetic drawing-rooms, among those most superior people to whom he introduces us so gracefully, we find ourselves looking out of window and thinking wistfully of the substantial literary entertainment of our youth, when novelists, like genial hosts, gave us broad hospitality and hearty English fare? The reason is, emaciation as a literary trait cannot permanently satisfy. No doubt Mr. Henry James has admitted us to the privilege of hearing the conversation of most cultivated people, who have been everywhere, met everybody, and absorbed the universe generally, but somehow, in our heart of hearts, we could not help thinking that even a little downright vulgarity would be refreshing as a change. These people have evidently imbibed the best modern ideas, and have the most perfect *ton*. Their vocabulary, too, is irreproachable. But, positively, we should like to hear some Billingsgate for variety. These people have clearly the most cosmopolitan minds, and are a walking rebuke to our insularity; but, horrible to tell, in the midst of their cleverest talk, and they talk very cleverly, we actually find ourselves guilty of inattention. Our minds are wandering. Perhaps we are saying to ourselves, Oh, for a ride across country after the hounds with Squire Western! Ay, or a chat about Homer with Parson Adams, over a pot of ale.

A LONDON LIFE

1889

84. From an unsigned review, *Spectator*

August 1889, lxiii, 211–3

The subject is intensely disagreeable; the catastrophe imminent from the first pages, and concerning two very disagreeable persons in whom it is impossible to feel an interest, offers none of the morbid excitement sometimes attendant upon such situations; fortunately, the author is far from having any intention of the kind. The characters, with one slight exception, are for the most part repellent, and certainly most unloveable. The whole atmosphere of the book, from beginning to end, is full of a cold, calculating, and helpless selfishness which depresses us to the last degree, and seems without a redeeming point. But there is undoubted power, we fear to say truth, in the story as a picture of a certain phase of modern social life, and to make a story worth reading nowadays, beauty of character and incident do not seem indispensable. Upon Mr. Henry James's characters and the aim of his books, we always feel that we have a perfect right to put our own interpretations, a right fully recognised by the author. We know that he has had certain peculiar advantages over us, but of these he gives us the benefit as far as he can, and laying before us, bit by bit, traits and characteristics and incidents which have come under his notice, invites our solution of the problem along with his own. This dim groping in the minds and sayings and doings of his personages for an explanation of their characters and actions, which seems to place author and readers on a common level of inquiry, tends to give an air of intense reality to Mr. Henry James's books; but we have generally found it aggravating, especially at the end of a tale, when, to gain a clear idea of what the author means, we would often dispense with our share in the responsibility for following up the clue.

THE TRAGIC MUSE

1890

85. WJ to HJ

June 1890 (JF, 332–3)

At last you've done it and no mistake. *The Tragic Muse* caps the climax. It is a most original, wonderful, delightful and admirable production. It must make you feel jolly to have so masterfully and effortlessly answered the accusation that you could do nothing but the international and cosmopolitan business; for cosmopolitan as the whole atmosphere of the book is, yet the people and setting are most easily and naturally English, and the perfect air of good society which reigns through the book is one of its most salient characteristics. It leaves a good taste in one's mouth, everyone in it is human and good, and although the final winding up is, as usual with you, rather a losing of the story in the sand, yet that is the way in which things lose themselves in real life. The only thing I positively find to object to in the book is the length of the chapter on Mr. Nash's portrait, which is a little too much in the Hawthornian allegorizing vein for you.

I have nothing to say in detail. The whole thing hangs together most intimately and well; and it is truly a spectacle for rejoicing to see that by the sort of practice a man gives himself he attains the plenitude and richness which you have at last got. Your sentences are straighter and simpler than before, and your felicities of observation are on every page. . . . The whole thing is an exquisite mirage which remains afloat in the air of one's mind. I imagine that that sort of thing is extremely educative to a certain 'section' of the community. As for the question of the size of your public, I tremble. The work is too refined, too elaborate and minute, and requires to be read with too much leisure to appeal to any but the select few. But you mustn't mind that. It will *always* have its audience. No reason, however, for not doing less elaborate things for wider audiences; which I hope ere long to have direct testimony that you have done.

86. James on his public

1890

HJ to WJ, July 1890. (LJ, i, 173.)
A reply to No. 85. Alice was their sister, whereas 'your Alice' was WJ's wife.

I had from you some ten days ago a most delightful letter written just after the heroic perusal of my interminable novel—which, according to your request, I sent off almost too precipitately to Alice, so that I haven't it here to refer to. But I don't need to 'refer' to it, inasmuch as it has plunged me into a glow of satisfaction which is far, as yet, from having faded. I can only thank you tenderly for seeing so much good in the clumsy thing—as I thanked your Alice, who wrote me a most lovely letter, a week or two ago. I have no illusions of any kind about the book, and least of all about its circulation and 'popularity.' From these things I am quite divorced and never was happier than since the dissolution has been consecrated by (what seems to me) the highest authorities. One must go one's way and know what one's about and have a general plan and a private religion—in short have made up one's mind as to *ce qui en est* with a public the draggling after which simply leads one in the gutter. One has always a 'public' enough if one has an audible vibration—even if it should only come from one's self. I shall never make my fortune—nor anything like it; but—I know what I shall do; and it won't be bad.

The handling is ill assured and tentative, as well as too heavily laboured for the issues and interests at stake, which are slight, not to say trivial, in essence, or postponed and attenuated to the merest nothingness. Mr. James still shows himself fond of working round a situation, of circling and wheeling about it, but always receding without even carrying away the barriers, yet returning to it again and again from another direction or from another vantage, but never, so to speak, vaulting it triumphantly. The story, if we may say so, is for the most part negative —a history of occurrences that do not occur, unions that perpetually hang fire, passions that come to nothing, aspirations—political and intellectual—that have no fruition, with other episodes of a clever but barren quality. There is, too, more French than one cares for in an English novel. Mr. James, as we know, has lately had much to say about the canons of art in general, and of the drama in particular. The part relating to it and the theatrical *débuts* of the young person of Jewish antecedents is, perhaps, more interesting and better presented than the rest. There is also a good deal about painting, mostly of the contemporary and actual chatter of the studios, but given with an air of some gravity and conviction—the sort of talk that is so much with us just now; the 'art for art's sake' point of view, which the British public is struggling to grasp. There are three or four personages (male and female), society people mostly, and the actress, with her mother, who has some of Mr. James's familiar but good touches. In Lady Agnes and her surroundings we have a picture that is characteristic of life as it is in London drawing-rooms, or at any rate in Mr. James's conception of them, which perhaps comes to much the same thing. There is the suspicion of a male snob somewhere about—we will not say where, but he is present. It is the actress who has the most body—and soul, too— who is, in fact, the most human of the party. She has some force, and, above all, some directness, which is not given to the others. All more or less produce the feeling of people playing at a game called life, the deeper issues and the more significant moves of which Mr. James may manage to suggest with some cleverness, but which one shrewdly suspects he could not really 'tackle' if he would. One young man is burdened with the feeling 'of that complexity of things of which the sense had lately increased with him, and to which it was owing that any thread one might take hold of would probably lead one to something discomfortable'; also with 'an acute mistrust of the superficiality of performance into which the desire to justify himself might hurry him.' There is a good deal of this sort of thing about the story, of course interspersed with many and sundry good things. Altogether those who know Mr. James's writing well are principally struck by the sense of flatness and absence of relief, and the undeniable cleverness of what is, however, after all, much more like studio work than work that is the result of direct contact with nature.

88. From an unsigned review, *Saturday*

August 1890, lxx, 141

The Tragic Muse will have a special interest for Mr. Henry James's English readers, as in it for the first time he shakes himself free of the toils imposed by his nationality, and gives to the world a novel which does not contain even one American. Not one *soi-disant* American, that is; for it must be confessed that Miriam Rooth, the Tragic Muse herself, and her friend, Gabriel Nash, are much more like certain types of Americans with whom fiction has made us familiar (does not Miriam even talk of 'once in a while'?) than any known form of English development. . . . One of the best scenes in the book is the early one where Miriam, accompanied by her adoring mother, proceeds to give recitations to an old French actress, with the irrepressible Gabriel Nash and two other young Englishmen, Dormer and Sherringham by name, for audience. The impartiality of the Frenchwoman's attitude towards the apparently stolid and hopeless performer, her practical questions and suggestions, and the determination with which she declines to be led from the point by the maternal garrulity of Mrs. Rooth, are admirably rendered, and, as far as we are aware, are a new 'note' in fiction. . . . In the picture of Biddy Dormer as the best type of English girl Mr. James has achieved a triumphant success. It is not an easy thing to convey on paper the charm of a young girl (in the English, not the American, sense of the term) who is modest, yet not shy or silly; able to take care of herself when necessary, but always preferring to be looked after by somebody else. We feel all the fascination of Biddy and are even prepared to forgive her her horrible name. The other characters are less true to nature and less agreeable to contemplate. Biddy's mother, Lady Agnes Dormer, mother likewise of Nick and Grace, is intended to be a good, narrow-minded, hardworking Englishwoman; but she is likewise intended to be a lady, and surely it is not the custom of ladies to talk so very plainly as Lady Agnes does about the desirability of Nick proposing to his rich cousin Mrs. Dallow, or to allow eligible suitors to see as clearly into their hearts as she allows Peter Sherringham to see into hers? However, every one is so odd on this same question of love affairs, that perhaps Lady Agnes may only have accommodated herself to the prevailing spirit. . . . Gabriel Nash is a superfluous figure altogether, and only serves the purpose of perpetually admiring Miriam, and exclaiming 'Isn't she wonderful?'

August 1890, iv, 282–3

. . . Length is the dominant characteristic of the romance. The number of pages is by no means excessive; and though there is a good deal in each, the number of words is probably not greater than in many a commonplace three-volume novel. But the stodginess of it! the complacent reeling off of paragraph after paragraph pages long, made up of sentences like this: 'Imitation is a fortunate homage only in proportion as it is delicate, and there was an indefinable something in Nash's doctrine that would have been discredited by exaggeration or by zeal'! Of course the author occasionally permits the characters to speak to each other, but when they do they are as fluent, as refined, as circuitous, and as cryptic, if not quite as long-winded, as Mr. James himself.

There was a vulgar girl called Miriam Rooth, who wanted to be an actress, and became one, and immediately had an extravagantly brilliant success, and is left at the end of the story playing Juliet in a blaze of popularity, and married to a fool who was also an actor. There was Nick Dormer, whose friends made him a member of Parliament, and who, after thinking and talking over the question as if he had all eternity to do it in and nothing else to do in eternity, abandoned politics for portrait-painting. There was Mrs. Dallow, a rich young widow, who loves Nick and whom Nick sometimes wanted to marry, and first she would and then she wouldn't and then she was inclined to think perhaps after all she should (at which stage we leave her, thankful to be permitted to do so on any terms). There was Mrs. Dallow's brother Peter, a secretary of embassy and presently minister to a Central American republic, who had a most consuming passion for Miriam, and when she married the actor promptly consoled himself as well as he could with Nick's sister—the only person in the book who is at all pleasant or natural. Then there is one Nash, a partly crazy little philosopher given to uttering paradoxes, whom Nick thought extremely amusing and whom Nick's friends thought rather offensive, whose philosophy was that no one should ever do anything except lounge and gratify his sense of the beautiful. And that is all: at least, none of the four or five other personages is of any importance.

The events, therefore, are one successful parliamentary candidature, one resignation of a seat, the commencement of three portraits (none of them ever finished) and the painting and exhibition of a fourth (in the valedictory paragraphs), one marriage, (about) six offers of marriage (four of them Peter to Miriam), two resulting engagements (Nick and Peter), one subsequent breach of promise (Nick—at least he was the victim of it), three successful dramatic productions (Miriam), and one change of vocation (Nick). About which episodes they all talk on, and on, and on, and on, especially Mr. Henry James. None of them, except occasionally the crushed Nash, says anything that seems to have been really worth the trouble of printing, and the impression one gathers from the whole is that Mr. James is a nightingale or some other bird of a poetic character who 'does but yarn because he must', or, to put it another way, because he enjoys yarning. The practical conclusion arrived at and acted upon by Mr. Dormer, that a man with a considerable taste and some ability for portrait-painting, and no taste at all for parliamentary life, will probably enjoy himself more as a fairly good portrait-painter than as a Liberal member of Parliament, will command general assent, but cannot honestly be hailed as an important discovery.

Mr. James writes much better grammar and uses many fewer strained and fantastic locutions than his compatriot Mr. Howells, but he is nearly as dull . . . and much longer. He ambles equably through his unending paragraphs, but there is nothing violent about him, only a few little sloppy inaccuracies. Several of the chief characters have lived more or less in Paris, and introduce French tags into their talk with exasperating frequency. Otherwise there is nothing about them that can be called offensive except their existence; and they need not exist for any one who does not want them.

90. Unsigned review, *Graphic*

August 1890, xlii, 175

One of the characters in Mr. Henry James's *The Tragic Muse* is considered—and with justice—by some of his acquaintances as an impertinent ass. He does not repel the accusation; but, by way of set-off, pleads—with no sort of justice whatever—that at any rate he is not dreary. If according to his doctrine, dreariness is the note of pertinence and wisdom, then is *The Tragic Muse* the flower and quintessence of both qualities. *The Tragic Muse* is perhaps—it would be rash to be positive on such a point—the very dreariest production which has issued even from the pen of Mr. Henry James; and there are three long volumes of it, instead of his normal and comparatively less unmerciful two. Of course it has a purpose; and it seems to be the energy of genius in overcoming circumstances, in the will of its possessor, as exemplified under very different conditions in Nicholas Dormer and Miriam Rooth. The stars in their courses are fighting to make Nicholas nothing less than Prime Minister, but they cannot prevent his turning professional portrait painter; and Miriam, under equally adverse conditions, gives the novel its title. We may be wrong in our view of Mr. James's intention—it is not his method to be lucid, and the sham cleverness of his conversations and illusive profundity of his analyses are more exasperating than ever.

91. George Saintsbury, review, *Academy*

August 1890, xxxviii, 148

For *'marivaudage'* see No. 181 below.

We have sufficient respect for Mr. Henry James to review him frankly
—the greatest compliment that can be paid to a novelist. And therefore,
we shall say at once that, to our thinking, *The Idiot Asylum* would have
been a better title for his new book than *The Tragic Muse*. Such a company of, by their own showing, imbeciles in word and deed has rarely
been got together by a writer of great talent. We remember long ago
an innocent critic-without-knowing-it who, casting in despair a book
aside, exclaimed: 'I can't make out why anybody does anything!' A
similar lamb of the flock might with justice make a similar remark on
The Tragic Muse. There are about two people in it—Peter Sherringham,
the diplomatist, and his sister, Julia Dallow, a wealthy widow—who,
though the former is besotted with a mindless actress, and the latter
with a backboneless coxcomb, are alive and human, it being indeed
extremely human and alive to be so besotted. But the actress and the
coxcomb and his mother, the correct Lady Agnes, and his sisters (one
pretty and *sympathique*, the other plain and dense), and his friend Mr.
Gabriel Nash, who is a kind of caricature of a long series of other
caricatures, and the rest of them, are such things as nightmares are made
of. They come, like the language that they talk, of constant imitation
and re-imitation, not of real life or of anything like real life, but of
thrice and thirty times redistilled literary decoctions of life. As for the
language just mentioned, Mr. James, who was always clever at a
wonderful kind of American *marivaudage*, has this time 'seen himself'
at his very best hitherto, and gone we hardly know how much better.
Somebody 'smiles like a man whose urbanity is a solvent.' Somebody
else had 'a nose which achieved a high free curve.' A third 'acquitted
herself in a manner which offered no element of interest;' but a fourth
'remained conscious that something surmounted and survived her
failure—something that would perhaps be *worth taking hold of*.' Fancy
'taking hold' of 'something' which 'surmounts and survives' a 'failure'

which is also an 'acquittal without an element of interest!' It is all very well for smart undergraduates and governesses who have read Mr. Meredith without the ghost of an understanding, and Mr. Stevenson with a keen relish for exactly the things which are not good in him, to attempt distinction by this sort of thing. But Mr. Henry James really might give us something a little more like English sense and a good deal less like French-American rigmarole. We cannot honestly say that there is much in the story or the characters of *The Tragic Muse* to redeem this fatal fault; but even if there were, it would probably still be fatal.

92. From an unsigned review, *Murray's Magazine*

September 1890, viii, 431–2

It is not all easy to judge a novel of Mr. Henry James's, because it always seems to need a special standard of criticism. When we hear that a lady 'supremely syllabled' a very ordinary remark, we feel inclined to speak slightingly of the writer's intellect; but then, lo and behold! we come across some suggestive epithet, some delicately-turned phrase which we feel to be worthy of the author of *Daisy Miller* and *The Portrait of a Lady* . . . only the consummate skill with which the characters are made to grow before our eyes could bring us to the end without more than a half-supressed yawn. For, indeed, the story is very long drawn out, and perhaps Miriam Rooth, interesting as she is, would have been rather more interesting if her interviews with Peter, her wavering lover, had been somewhat curtailed. It is she who most engages our affection; but Nick Dormer, the M.P. turned painter, is a very clever piece of portraiture. In Gabriel Nash's extravagant æstheticism there is an element of caricature which detracts from its life-likeness, and Mrs. Dallow is rather shadowy and eludes our grasp as she eluded Nick's. For the comfort of those who fail to appreciate a story without an end, we may mention that in this book at least Mr. James so far condescends to the popular level as to give us a very clear hint of the way in which his *dramatis personæ* finally solve the problem set before them.

93. Unsigned review, *Spectator*

September 1890, lxv, 409–10

It is interesting to find Whistler still being used as an example of the especially difficult or refined artist—he had been rejected by the Paris Salon as early as 1859.

When any person acquires a taste for an article of diet which is not attractive to the unsophisticated palate—say, caviare or truffles—he will notice, should he be in the habit of examining his sensations, that his pleasure is derived from the very quality of flavour which in the first instance most strongly repelled him. In this respect, there is an exact correspondence between taste dietic and taste artistic or literary. For example, there is probably no known instance of the 'natural mind' having been drawn by instinctive admiration to the pictures of Mr. Whistler or the books of Mr. Henry James; for to the natural mind the former are meaningless, and the latter dull. When, however, a certain educational process has been gone through, the cultured person who has been subjected to it finds not merely that he has gained a new pleasure, but that the new pleasure consists in exquisite appreciation of the quality that he once called meaninglessness or dullness. What to the outsider is the marring defect, is to him the making virtue of the master's work, and therefore the more prominently it betrays itself, the warmer will be his enthusiasm. This being so, it seems highly probable that the little company of superior persons who regard the novels of Mr. Henry James as specially admirable and enjoyable works of art, will attach a peculiar value to his latest book, *The Tragic Muse*, which is, we think, stronger than any of its predecessors in those Jamesian peculiarities by which they are charmed and the profane crowd repelled. Though the book is a very long one, there is even less of that vulgar element known as 'the story' than usual; indeed, were the narrative summarised, it would be seen that Mr. James has all but realised that noble but perhaps unattainable ideal,—a novel without any story at all. Even that surely less vulgar kind of interest which is secured by the lively and lifelike presentation of character, is minimised to the utmost, for Mr. James cannot be said to *present* his men and women at all: what he does present is a thin solution of talk, in which they are, so to speak, dissolved, and from which we have to extract them by a mental process of precipitation. Considering that the flow of talk is perpetual, and that all the people in the book are fond of talking about themselves, it is absolutely astonishing how much Mr. James manages to write without giving a single revealing hint. The secret of this density of the conversational medium, which makes his characters appear like men and women seen through a mist, is to be found in his persistent refusal to employ the method of characteristic selection. Open a novel of Jane Austen at any page (and we name her because she, like Mr. James, is a realist who loves the commonplace) and you cannot read a couple of pages without forming a fairly clear idea of the situation and of the attitudes of the actors, because the talk, both in its matter and in its tone, is not merely talk which would have been natural at any time, but talk which would have been inevitable at that special time to those special talkers. In *The Tragic Muse*, on the contrary, the chatter hardly ever bears any recognisable impress of character of a situation; it is external, automatic talk *pour passer le temps*, that is heard in the club smoking-room, or in a drawing-room while afternoon tea is being handed round, or in a railway-carriage during a long journey, when a common boredom inspires a mechanical sociability. We do not learn to know people in these places, because only the outer shell of their nature is in evidence; and we do not learn to know the people in Mr. James's novel, for the same reason. 'That's the delightful thing about art,' says Mr. Gabriel Nash, 'that there is always more to learn and more to do; one can polish and polish, and refine.' Well, that is true; but there must be something to which these processes can be applied, and it is this something that we miss in *The Tragic Muse*. If Mr. James had made Miriam Rooth and Peter Sherring-ham and Nick Dormer sufficiently substantial to bear it, he might have polished and refined them at pleasure: as it is, so far from possessing substance, they have hardly recognisable outline.

94. Unsigned review, *Dublin Review*

October 1890, 3rd Series xxiv, 466–7

The *Tragic Muse* of the title-page is an underbred girl with a strong vocation for the stage, and an unlimited supply of the pushing egotism which so often accompanies that and other forms of genius. Beauty is at first her only apparent qualification for her profession, but being a heroine she develops the remaining ones in process of time, and become a famous actress, whose success, however, fails to interest the reader in any degree. The other characters are almost equally out of the range of sympathy. The hero, 'Nick' Dormer, is a contemptible creature with æsthetic proclivities, who throws up a promising parliamentary career to potter over an easel, and alienates by his half-hearted courtship, the beautiful and wealthy woman who is willing to bestow her heart and fortune on him. The book is, as a matter of course, rich in clever satire of minute points of character, but shows total inability to grasp or present any one as a whole. Mr. James's artistic vision is microscopic, and consists entirely of analysis of detail without the synthetic power of combining the magnified minutæ on which our whole attention is concentrated. He is consequently best as a satirist, or in the lighter sketches, where a caricature likeness of character will suffice. On a large canvas his vagueness becomes blottesque rather than suggestive, and the attempt to fill in his outlines only make them more unreal. In the present work the story is of the slenderest, and stagnates through three closely printed volumes of prolix conversations, varied by tedious dissection of motive in common-place characters. The author's sarcastic vein finds a butt in the portraiture of the professional æsthete, Gabriel Nash, whose artistic epicureanism is scarcely an exaggeration of the inanities idulged in by this modern type of humanity.

95. From an unsigned note, *Critic*

May 1890, NS xiii, 250

This is an item from a 'Boston Letter'. For 'Mr. Lowell' see No. 26.

Henry James's *Tragic Muse*, which has been running as a serial in *The Atlantic*, will attract fresh interest on its publication in book form, and readers who lack the power of concentration which is necessary for the enjoyment of 'continued' stories will have the opportunity of taking it leisurely. . . . I hear that Mr. Lowell thinks it the most notable thing that James has done. The freshness of the story lies in the fact that it delineates a kind of society woman that has almost formed itself into a class—the stage-struck sort.

96. From an unsigned review, *Literary World*

July 1890, xxi, 231–2

Suggestive, provoking, agreeable, notwithstanding his fashionable slang and his society manner of saying the best thing he can think of at the moment, Mr. James tends inevitably toward disillusion. His tragic Muse is no Muse at all. She is his own discovery, a creature too artificial for sex, with finesse for life-blood, beauty as an adornment, variety and dash for personal graces, and unbounded persistence at the bottom of all. Here is an immense fund of highly developed cleverness invested for our benefit; shall we be most grateful for the entertainment it affords, or secretly vexed with the observer who cares only for the unimportant, and exaggerates in his work all the defects of the photograph?

There is something paradoxical in a success which leaves our real sympathies untouched. We perceive a curiously brilliant surface, but we are not in the least dazzled. Real pathos, real power, strike their roots deeper. What a wide difference, too, between finish and style! Style is something quite above workmanship, even of the best; it is an emanation of personality. Clever writers abound, but where is the great novelist?

97. Unsigned review, *Dial*

August 1890, xi, 92–3

The Tragic Muse has been so long with us, in the pages of the *Atlantic Monthly*, that its portentous volume, extending, in book form, to 882 pages, is not a matter for surprise. The reader who engages upon its perusal will, however, do so advisedly, for he knows by this time the limitations and the excellences of the author's art. On the whole, he will not be disappointed, for the novel takes a high rank among Mr. James's works. If second to anything, it is only to *The Princess Casamassima*, and it is far superior to either *The Bostonians* or *The Portrait of a Lady*. Of course, there is no story worth mentioning; there are merely half a dozen men and women engaged in protracted conversations that lead to nothing in particular, and they are mostly of rather vulgar types. And their relations are nearly as unsettled at the end of the 882 pages as they were at the beginning. But they are all distinctly individual, and the product of a very delicate art. We might wish that art exercised upon more attractive material, but such a wish is well-nigh hopeless with reference to any work by Mr. James. The heroine is a young woman of dubious origin and strong artistic instincts, making her way upon the stage by force of sheer persistence and obtuse disregard of obstacles that would have blocked the path of a more sensitive aspirant. The dramatic motive thus playing a large part in the story, an opportunity is offered the author to indulge in various bits of dramatic criticism which constitute almost the most delightful feature of the novel. We say almost, because one of the characters claims the first place in our regard. Mr. Gabriel Nash, apostle of candor and exponent of the fine art of living, is so genially conceived a creation that the book is more than worth reading for his sake alone. And it need not all be read for that purpose, for it is very easy to pass over the pages of monotonous analysis that interrupt the narrative from time to time. A chapter lost here and there makes little difference; the chances are that nothing essential to the understanding of the story will have happened.

98. W. D. Howells, from the 'Editor's Study' *Harper's*

September 1890, lxxxi, 639–41

Howells reprinted much of this in his *Criticism and Fiction* (1891). HJ later wrote, a trifle ironically, of his friend, 'He hates a "story" . . .'.

The fatuity of the story as a story is something that must early impress the story-teller who does not live in the stone age of fiction and criticism. To spin a yarn for the yarn's sake, that is an ideal worthy of a nineteenth-century Englishman, doting in forgetfulness of the English masters and grovelling in ignorance of the Continental masters; but wholly impossible to an American of Mr. Henry James's modernity. To him it must seem like the lies swapped between men after the ladies have left the table and they are sinking deeper and deeper into their cups and growing dimmer and dimmer behind their cigars. To such a mind as his the story could never have value except as a means; it could not exist for him as an end; it could be used only illustratively; it could be the frame, not possibly the picture. But in the meantime the kind of thing he wished to do, and began to do, and has always done, amidst a stupid clamor, which still lasts, that it was not a story (of *course*, it was not a story!) had to be called a novel; and the wretched victim of the novel-habit (only a little less intellectually degraded than the still more miserable slave of the theatre-habit), who wished neither to perceive nor to reflect, but only to be acted upon by plot and incident, was lost in an endless trouble about it. Here was a thing called a novel, written with extraordinary charm; interesting by the vigor and vivacity with which phases and situations and persons were handled in it; inviting him to the intimacy of characters divined with creative insight; making him witness of motives and emotions and experiences of the finest import; and then suddenly requiring him to be man enough to cope with the question itself; not solving it for him by a marriage or a murder, and not spoon-victualling him with a moral minced small and then thinned with milk and water, and familiarly flavored with sentimentality or religiosity. We can imagine the sort of shame with which such a writer, so original and so clear-sighted, may sometimes have been tempted by the outcry of the nurslings of fable, to give them of the diet on which they had been pampered to imbecility; or to call together his characters for a sort of round-up in the last chapter.

The round-up was once the necessary close of every novel, as it is of every season on a Western cattle ranch; and each personage was summoned to be distinctly branded with his appropriate destiny, so that the reader need be in no doubt about him evermore. The formality received its most typical observance in *The Vicar of Wakefield*, perhaps, where the modern lover of that loveliest prospect of eighteenth-century life is amused by the conscientiousness with which fate is distributed, and vice punished and virtue rewarded. It is most distinctly honored in the breach in that charming prospect of nineteenth-century life, *The Tragic Muse*, a novel which marks the farthest departure from the old ideal of the novel. No one is obviously led to the altar; no one is relaxed to the secular arm and burnt at the stake. Vice is disposed of with a gay shrug; virtue is rewarded by innuendo. All this leaves us pleasantly thinking of all that has happened before, and asking, Was Gabriel Nash vice? Was Mrs. Dallow virtue? Or was neither either? In the nineteenth century, especially now toward the close of it, one is never quite sure about vice and virtue: they fade wonderfully into and out of each other; they mix, and seem to stay mixed, at least around the edges.

Mr. James owns that he is himself puzzled by the extreme actuality of his facts; fate is still in solution, destiny is not precipitated; the people are still going uncertainly on as we find people going on in the world about us all the time. But that does not prevent our being satisfied with the study of each as we find it in the atelier of a master. Why in the world should it? What can it possibly matter that Nick Dormer and Mrs. Dormer are not certainly married, or that Biddy Dormer and Sherringham certainly are? The marriage or the non-marriage cannot throw any new light on their characters; and the question never was what they were going to do, but what they were. This is the question that is most sufficiently if not distinctly answered. They never wholly emerge from the background which is a condition of their form and color; and it is childish, it is Central African, to demand that they shall do so. It is still more Central African to demand such a thing in the case of such a wonderful creature as Gabriel Nash, whose very essence is elusiveness; the lightest, slightest, airiest film of personality whose insubstantiality was ever caught by art; and yet so strictly of his time, his country, his kind. He is one sort of modern Englishman; you are as sure of that as you are of the histrionic type, the histrionic character, realized in the magnificent full-length of Miriam Rooth. *There* is mastery for you! There is the woman of the theatre, destined to the stage from her cradle: touched by family, by society, by love, by friendship, but never swayed for a moment from her destiny, such as it is, the tinsel glory of triumphing for a hundred nights in the same part. An honest creature, most thoroughly honest in heart and act, and most herself, when her whole nature is straining toward the realization of some one else; vulgar, sublime; ready to make any sacrifice for her art, to 'toil terribly,' to suffer everything for it, but perfectly aware of its limitations at its best, while she provisionally contents herself with its second best, she is by all odds so much more perfectly presented in *The Tragic Muse* than any other like woman in fiction, that she seems the only woman of the kind ever presented in fiction . . . we find nothing caricatured or overcharged, nothing feebly touched or falsely stated. As for the literature, what grace, what strength! The style is a sweetness on the tongue, a music in the ear. The whole picture of life is a vision of London aspects such as no Englishman has yet been able to give: so fine, so broad, so absolute, so freed from all necessities of reserve or falsity.

99. H. E. Scudder, unsigned review, *Atlantic*

September 1890, lxvi, 419–22

For Scudder see No. 43.

Mr. James has achieved a kind of success in his latest novel which goes far to illustrate a great canon of the art of fiction. The mind of his readers may be taken to reflect his mind, and we make the assertion with confidence that if, after reading the novel as it has been appearing in *The Atlantic*, with delight in the brilliancy of the group of portraits which it presents, they now take up the two comely volumes in which the serial is gathered, their attention will be held by what may be called the spiritual plot of the tale. That which first commands admiration may not have been first in the author's mind, but it was first in the order of presentation. The artistic defect in novels of a purpose is that the function of the novel as a reproduction of life is blurred by the function of the tract. On the other hand, the artistic defect in the novel without a purpose lies in a superficial dexterity which supposes life itself to be shallow and incapable of anything more than a surface gleam. It is in the nice portrayal of surfaces, by which an undercurrent of moving life is now revealed, now concealed, that the highest art is disclosed. Sometimes this undercurrent is made manifest by the steady movement of the characters toward some final catastrophe; sometimes it is brought to light in the relation of the characters to each other as illustrative of a single large theme, and in such cases neither tragedy nor comedy is necessarily resultant; the issue may be in the decision of each person, the definite fixing of the place of each in some microcosm.

It is this latter class of novels, where the judgment of the persons delineated is not emphasized and made unmistakable by a rude confirmation of external circumstance, that is winning the regard of the most thoughtful and most penetrating writers. And is it not characteristic of a view of life at once profound and bright that the creator of fictitious forms should be indifferent to *coups de théâtre*, and should care most for those human judgments which seem best to reflect divine judgment? For the lightning does not strike the blasphemer, vengeance does not fall swiftly upon the parricide, hell does not open before the betrayer of innocence. It is a finer power which discerns the crumbling of the interior defenses of the human citadel, and discloses the ruin by glimpses through the fair exterior. Surely the art of the novelist is acquiring a wider range when to the novel of adventure, the novel of dramatic completeness, the novel of character, is added the novel which gives us a picture of human life as it passes before the spectator, who might himself be a part of it, and at the same time offers an interpretation of that life, and attempts something like a generalization of the sub-order to which it belongs.

This at any rate, is what we conceive Mr. James has done for us in *The Tragic Muse*. As we have intimated, after we have admired the brilliancy of the figures which compose the group constantly before the sight, we become even more interested in the revelation of those characters to the mind by the patient and apparently inexhaustible art of the novelist, showing them by the aid of a few incidents only, but of innumerable expressions in situation and converse. The simple theme on which Mr. James plays with endless variations is profound enough to justify all the labor which he has expended in illustrating it. We are tempted to say, in the light of his great success, that it is the only adequate mode by which the theme could be treated in fiction. For the relations of man to art admit and of demand such subtlety of thought that the fine shades of these relations can only be distinguished by the most painstaking setting forth of delicate workings of this thought in action and speech. Thus, as one recalls the wealth of phrase in which this masterly work abounds, he will admit that it is the lavishness of true art, not the prodigality of a spend-thrift in words. Follow as one will the lines of movement in the novel, they all lead to the few fundamental, authoritative principles which form the ground-work of the novel. To the careless reader there is a waste of material in determining the question whether or not Nick Dormer is to marry Julia, whether Peter Sherringham is to marry Biddy or Miriam. He may be amused by the suspense in which he is kept, and entertained indefinitely by the spirited dialogue, but, judging the novel by its issue, he would have his own applause if he demanded, Is the game worth the candle?

The triumph of the novelist, in our judgment, lies in the fact that he can hold the careless reader to the close, cajoling him with the notion that he is in for the matrimonial hunt of the conventional novel, while at the same time he slowly opens to the student of life a singularly interesting relation of the progress of human souls, each moving toward its determination by choice and the gravitation of nature, and presenting constantly fresh examples of the problems of which they are themselves only now and then distinctly conscious. Perhaps the subtlest of these disclosures is in the delicately suggested nature of the attitude which Miriam Rooth holds at the last toward Nick Dormer. The real stanchness of this artist's fidelity to his art is seen in the sincerity of his dealings with Julia Dallow, and his absolute immobility under the tentative advances of Miriam. Indeed, the reader comes to have a sense of compassion for the tragedienne which is nowhere directly solicited by the author. He reads between the lines, not because the author has written a story faintly there, but because he has described the persons so truthfully, so completely, that, given the persons and stiuations, this unexpressed relation is inevitable. Here is an artist brave with no heroics, but through the simple honesty of his nature. He is the rock toward which Miriam turns, uncompromising in fidelity to her art, as instanced by her penetrating disclosure of Sherringham's nature, but also conscious of her own feminine dependency. It was a stroke of genius, and not the *pis aller* of a novelist intent upon pairing off his characters, which made her contemptuously tuck Basil Dashwood under her arm at the last.

Mr. James, to the thinking of many, gave himself space enough for the explication of his theme, but it is clear that he limited himself deliberately by recognizing in his study of the relations of art to life only two forms of art, the pictorial and the histrionic. He needed two because he needed both Nick Dormer and Miriam Rooth; and some of his happiest interpretations of the entire theme are in the glimpses which he gives of Nick Dormer's attitude toward portrait-painting. Once, at least, also, he throws in a fine illustration from the art of writing when Gabriel Nash says:—

Life consists of the personal experiments of each of us, and the point of an experiment is that it shall succeed. What we contribute is our treatment of the material, our rendering of the text, our style. A sense of the qualities of a style is so rare that many persons should doubtless be forgiven for not being able to read, or at all events to enjoy us. But is that a reason for giving it up, for not being, in this other sphere, if one possibly can, a Macaulay, a Ruskin, a Renan? Ah, we must write our best; it's the great thing we can do in the world, on the right side. One has one's form, *que diable*, and a mighty good thing that one has. I'm not afraid of putting life into mine, without unduly squeezing it. I'm not afraid of putting in honor and courage and charity, without spoiling them; on the contrary, I'll only do them good. People may not read you at sight, may not like you, but there's a chance they'll come round; and the only way to court the chance is to keep it up—always to keep it up. That's what I do, my dear fellow, if you don't think I've perseverance. If someone likes it here and there, if you give a little impression of solidity, that's your reward; besides, of course, the pleasure for yourself.

Nash is a writer, though the fact is lightly stated, and Mr. James has not worked him as a *littérateur*. It is sometimes hard to say just what he meant to make of the figure, whose personality is faintly sketched, and who seems scarcely more than a stalking-horse of clever approaches to the main game; his taking off is the most effective part. The great character of the book is the title character, and the art which is most elaborately analyzed is the histrionic. The actual development of the perfected artist out of the crude shape in which we first discover Miss Rooth is not given. Instead we have the much more interesting study of Miss Rooth in her earlier phase, and then, presto! change! the Miss Rooth who blazes forth. For the author's interest and the reader's is not in how to make a great artist out of unpromising material, but how, when the artist is made, everything looks to her. There are few more deft touches in this clever book than the genuine surprise which all enjoy, Sherringham, Dormer, Madame Carré, and the reader, when the cocoon is broken and the brilliant butterfly emerges.

It is a striking illustration of Mr. James's power of handling his material that from first to last Miriam Rooth is always seen *en face*. That is to say, though their author indulges in analysis of his other characters, he gives the reader only a front view of his heroine. When she appears she is on exhibition. We see her reflected occasionally in the faces of her audience, but we are not helped to a more intimate knowledge through the private advices of her creator. The brilliancy of the effect is greatly enhanced by this means, and the sort of theatrical show which goes on is wonderfully effective as a mode of carrying off the study which Mr. James is constantly making of the tragedian's art, as seen in the attitude toward it of the tragedian himself, or, as in this case, herself. He seems to ask himself, How would a girl having this genius for the stage regard herself, the stage, the play, the critic, the audience; how even would she look upon marriage, so universally regarded as the crown of a woman's life. But inasmuch as this artistic life is led in the glare of publicity, he preserves the illusion by making Miss Rooth ask all these questions, as it were, in public. There are no concealments, and there is no evasion. The persistency with which histrionic art in its personal aspect is pursued, without any wearisome, impersonal discussion, is most admirable. The unfolding of this theme is the unfolding of the story. Not for a moment does the reader find himself in any eddies of conversation; he is always in the current. It would be easy to quote passage after passage in illustration of the wit, the insight, the broad sense, which mark the development of this interior plot of the story, but we should only be printing over again what already has been printed in these pages. We can only advise students of literature and art who wish to see how a fine theme may be presented with a technique which, at first blush, would seem inconsistent with breadth of handling, but on closer scrutiny proves to be the facile instrument of a master workman who is thinking of the soul of his art, to read *The Tragic Muse*.

100. Unsigned review, *Nation*

December 1890, li, 505–6

If Mr. James were, like his only English rival in the art of fiction, Mr. Stevenson, naturally impelled to write chiefly stories of adventure he would get more applause than he does for his beautiful manner and exquisite style. Many instinctive censors of literature believe that Stevenson's stories are all action, therefore great; that James's stories are all rest, therefore fine-spun inanity. This sort of comment leads one to suppose that people who are not continually rolling down stairs must not consider the charge of torpidity an aspersion, and that nothing ever is accomplished in life by less violent methods. Most of the people in *The Tragic Muse* are exceedingly careful of their steps, and yet they achieve a good deal. Nicholas Dormer gives up fine political prospects and a great marriage for the sake of a beggarly art; Peter Sherringham, after much vacillation, is ready to fling over diplomacy and the star of an ambassador for love of the Tragic Muse; the Tragic Muse herself, Miriam Rooth, never dreams of giving up anything, but holds fast to her one idea, much to her worldly advantage. It is true that the two men and most of the subordinate characters are less interesting for what they do than for what they think, for mental activity preliminary and subsequent to physical. Mr. James is, in fact, guilty of selecting complex creatures—creatures who are centuries away from savage simplicity—and of devoting his greatest energy to the exhibition of the storehouse of their complexities, the mind. He finds an infinite variety of mind, and its tricks are vastly more surprising and entertaining than a conjurer's tricks, which we see but do not in the least understand. There is the dull, ponderous, pre-judiced mind of Lady Agnes; the naïve mind of her daughter Biddy, its ingenuousness crossed by inherited worldliness; the worldly mind of Mrs. Dallow, with innumerable shades, refinements, and even contra-dictions of worldliness; the mind of Peter Sherringham, her brother, very like hers, but the contradictions heightened by greater possibility of passion; the mind of Nicholas Dormer, slow like his mother's, but much less under control, capable of no end of fantastic flights; last, the mind of Gabriel Nash, serenely philosophical, but nebulous, unreliable, elusive.

Nash is nothing but a mind, a sort of incarnation of wisdom gathered through observation, the sharpness and justice of which have never been impaired by feeling. The other minds are only parts of substantial beings—far the most important parts, most subtle and intricate, altogether most worthy of one whose avowed profession is the complete representation of men and women. But Mr. James realizes that approximately primitive people, people who do more and better than they think, are still to be found in the world, often making great bustle and exciting wild curiosity. The Tragic Muse is one of these. Of mixed race, with a not distant Jewish strain, vagabond from her birth, beautiful, polyglot, and poor, she turns instinctively to the stage, where her natural advantages can be most brilliantly utilized and the disadvantages of circumstance most speedily conquered. Enormously vain, with imperturbable self-assurance, showy, hard, not ungenerous, capable of assuming every emotion and incapable of feeling any not connected with public applause and the receipts of the box-office—such is the Tragic Muse, by far the most brilliant and faithful representation of the successful modern actress that has ever been achieved in English fiction.

101. W. D. Howells on the reception of *The Tragic Muse*

1890

Howells to HJ, September 1890 (LH, ii, 7).
This optimism was not justified by the sales of the book.

I'm glad to say that *The Tragic Muse* is almost the tutelary deity of our reading public, as I hope the publishers' returns will persuade you to believe. It's a pity they don't publish fifty cent editions of your books, as I now have the Harpers do simultaneously with the bound editions of mine. You ought to be got into the hands of the people.

102. From an unsigned article, 'Mr Henry James', *Murray's*

November 1891, x, 641–54

This article is surely one of the critical oases in HJ's reception. In sympathy and intelligent penetration it outclasses most of what even the most favourable critics had so far written. Only a few opening sentences, on HJ's plays, have been omitted here.

In speaking of the work of Mr. Henry James, the first, the imperative thing to be said about it is that it is the work of an artist, and of one with a complete and exhaustive knowledge of his art and its resources. Whilst no writer is more vividly modern, Mr. James is, in a sense, an artist as an ancient Greek was an artist; he represses systematically, that is to say, his own personality in view of the work on which he is engaged. By the public, and—shall we say?—by the English public in particular this supreme quality of workmanship is one of the qualities least esteemed and least appreciated. The generous public hates the Augur's mask; it likes to peep and see the human countenance behind, to shake hands, so to speak, with the wearer, and congratulate him on having a soul like its own. Mr. James never, or by inference only, allows us the smallest peep; his reserve is impenetrable; he invariably treats his characters and his plots with the impartiality of the workman who apprehends that the truth of a thing, and not his own colouring of it, is what, before all, is needed.

We so far share the feeling, whilst absolutely disclaiming any share in the opinion of the public, on this point, as to find a particular pleasure in those *impressions de voyage*, those little sketches of travel collected under the various titles—*A Little Tour in France, Portraits of Places, Foreign Parts*—in which the writer, in the easiest, simplest, most genial manner imaginable, lets us into the secret of his personal impressions, his fine artistic discriminations, his good inns and his bad inns, his chance comrades, his satisfactions and disillusions. It is the charm of individuality that pervades these charming pages, and which, by the happiest instinct, the author has known how to convey without a touch of obtrusive egotism of fatiguing iteration of detail. It needs indeed but a glance over a hundred dreary and futile *impressions de voyage*, to borrow again that convenient term, to understand the rare and consummate skill that goes to the composition of these little articles in which, without any uneasy self-consciousness or self-assertion, the writer takes us into his confidence, shows us what is best worth seeing and the best way to see it, quotes his guide-book with a humorous guilelessness, and makes himself, in short, through his books, the most delightful travelling-companion in the world.

In putting forward these little volumes first, however, we are not doing Mr. James's work, and what we may imagine to be his own estimate of it, the injustice to rank them amongst his foremost productions. The field of literature that he has traversed is wide; both as critic and essayist he has gained particular distinction, no less than by the charming papers just mentioned. But it is as a novelist that he has found a foremost place among modern writers; it is his unique and delightful gift of fiction that, above all, claims consideration in treating of his work.

I.

Every writer of original excellence has one or more distinct lines along which his genius developes itself, and with which he becomes, as it were, identified. Mr. James, as we shall endeavour to show, has that larger outlook on the vast human comedy that distinguishes the great masters of fiction; but his earliest stories have a certain character in common that intimately connects them with what for convenience has been termed, the International novel. Mr. James, in fact, might not unreasonably claim to be the inventor of that particular form of romance; and though it would be manifestly unjust to consider him exclusively or even principally in relation to it, since much of his most masterly as well as his most delicate work does not touch on the International question—that is to say, the interfusing influences of America and Europe—at all; yet there is no doubt that it was his earlier productions, *The American*, *The Europeans*, *Daisy Miller*, 'An International Episode,' and half-a-dozen other tales on the same line, that won for him in the first instance much of the wide reputation he enjoys. Mr. James must at some time have studied his countrymen and countrywomen with extraordinary minuteness and detachment of vision. To him might be applied what Sainte-Beuve somewhere says of La Bruyère: 'En jugeant de si près les hommes et les choses de son pays, il paraît désintéressé comme le serait un étranger, et déjà un homme de l'avenir.' This disinterested view has, we believe, brought Mr. James into some discredit with a certain section of his compatriots; the fresh perception and keen insight he has brought to the contemplation of his country and theirs has not always pleased them. They are probably apparent to the English mind, which, contrasting its knowledge of America now with what it was some twenty or thirty years ago, perceives how largely, among other causes, Mr. James has contributed to that knowledge; how clear a light, and how favourable a light, has been thrown upon the subject by his interpretations. This is the more valuable that there can be no suspicion of the author's impartiality; that if, as is the fact, there is in the course of his stories hardly a contest between an American and a European in which the American does not show the finer of the two, it is, we are persuaded, because, given the characters and the circumstances, the American must of necessity show the finer of the two. Nothing, indeed, could be more impossible than to treat Mr. James as even remotely a partisan; nothing could be further removed from his method, from the large and even glance he turns on one character and another. When he convinces us, it is through his presentment of the truth of things, never through the expression of his personal bias. He himself tells us somewhere that it is his constant habit to tip the balance; and, if he had not told us, we might have divined it from his work. It is probably a natural quality that he has cultivated to a degree that makes it impossible for him in contemplating a subject seriously to look at it from one point only; he turns it in his hands, so to speak, as one turns a globe, considering it from every side. This habit of mind is, of course, one of the finest and most essential that a writer can bring to his work; and if it occasionally exhibits the defect of its quality in carrying disinterestedness to the verge of coldness, it has the supreme merit of leaving the reader's judgment free, of never affronting him by undue insistence on one point to the hindrance of another.

It results naturally from the perfection to which Mr. James has brought this particular method of observation, that the men and women of his tales should have, both physically and mentally, an air of solidity and reality only occasionally attained to in the same degree; he sees them impartially, he depicts them unerringly, with an extreme delicacy and distinction; they are set in clear and open daylight, in a perspective as wide, in an atmosphere as free as those of the two continents of which he treats. His characters are types and yet individual; they belong at once to the universe and to their own epoch; they have, in short, that combination of the general and the particular that is indispensable to the complete vitality of a creature of the imagination; and they stand out in a relief that is the bolder, perhaps, that they are, as a rule, provided with little more scenery for their surrounding than is requisite to indicate the local colouring of the story. To Mr. James, we gather from his novels as a whole, life presents itself not pictorially, as a number of pictures, that is, in which human action displays itself against the vast scenic background of the world, not dramatically, as a succession of scenes culminating in a logical catastrophe (though both these points of view are necessarily included in his scheme of work), but primarily as a series of problems, moral, social, or psychological, to be worked out and solved. An involved situation, a moral dilemma, the giant and complex grasp of society in its widest sense, upon the individual—these and such as these are the problems to the tracing out and solution of which he brings an extreme fineness and subtlety, subtle and fine as the workings of the human mind hardly conscious of its own movement from point to point. It may be said at once, that in exercising his admirable gift of psychological insight and imagination, Mr. James frequently resupposes great attention on the part of his readers, and an intelligence of reception hardly less than his own intelligence of representation. He is one of the finest of analysts; but nevertheless he not seldom reaches a point where he ceases to analyse and simply suggests with a delicacy conveying the flattering assumption that the reader has keenness and imagination enough of his own to follow up the writer's suggestion with as much certainty as when, a hand being seen at a window, it may be inferred that a human being stands behind it. As a fact, we believe that Mr. James flatters his public too much. The average reader has neither brains nor imaginations to follow out a suggestion; he yawns at psychology; he is apt to resent explanation and non-explanation alike. He loves a good downright legend: 'This is a wood', 'This is a barn-door,' which he who runs may read; he loves an obvious plot, an honest mystery, a conclusion that rounds off everything. All that is a point of view already over-discussed perhaps, and for which there will doubtless be always much to be said; we only refer to it now, because whilst the lovers of Mr. James's stories find a charm beyond that of any other, in his method, at once delicate and powerful, it may probably always forbid his volumes the honour of the railway bookstall, or the seventy thousandth copy of the cheap edition.

In using the word 'powerful,' it must be understood in the wide sense in which it is applicable to Mr. James's work. There is a usual and perfectly legitimate sense in which it is employed, as expressing a certain movement of passion or energy on the writer's part, through which certain scenes stand out from the remainder of the work, and move the reader in his turn to an emotion that for ever remains in his memory. Such scenes as these are rare with Mr. James; it is perhaps an excess of the artistic sense of detachment, that occasionally compels him, when we should expect him to be most emotional, to be most restrained. His power is of another kind altogether; it arises from a profound knowledge of what he is writing about, from what seems sometimes an almost exhaustive knowledge of human nature; his anatomy is perfect; every hidden bone and muscle is in its place. His surface (to change the metaphor) may be level, but it never rings hollow; its foundations are deep as those of the life of which he treats; the result is that impression of sustained power that is met with only in the great masters, that is *the* distinguishing mark of the great masters. Others may charm us—and claim our eternal gratitude for the charm—by their imagination, their genius even; but somewhere or other there is a gap in the carpentry, and through the chink the light of disillusion shines. With Mr. James, we tread solidly and look at his presentment of life without a misgiving. it is the first in quality, it is the most essential boon a writer can give us.

We might refer in this connection, and as being among the most perfect presentments of his art, to two of Mr. James's earlier and less well-known stories—'Madame de Mauves', and *Washington Square*. The first of these is a story of no great length, with hardly any plot; one of those subtle problems of character and situation in which the author takes pleasure, and ended finally by an epigram, as his stories occasionally find themselves ending, after a fashion somewhat disconcerting to the reader. It is, in brief, the story of a young American girl married to a French *roué*, M. de Mauves, with whom one of her own countrymen falls passionately in love. The point of the story lies in the fashion in which this passion is treated by the husband, the lover, and Madame de Mauves herself; and one has only in reading it to consider what might be made of this apparently hackneyed theme by a superficial, a commonplace, or a vulgar writer to appreciate the delicate originality and powerful handling Mr. James has brought to its treatment. The whole story is in low relief, without a salient incident; its strength lies in the sense that the roots of the faintly-blooming flowers of the little drama reach down to the deepest springs of human action;

that the underlying strata of life presupposed by the surface are familiar
to the writer as the surface itself. The other story, *Washington Square*,
is much longer, but its *motif*, given in abstract form, is hardly more
novel than that of 'Madame de Mauves.' The scene is chiefly laid in
New York, and it is the history of a young girl, who accredited with
the prospect of inheriting a large fortune at her father's death, is pursued by a needy adventurer, with whom she falls blindly in love. The
father, as in duty bound, opposes the marriage; the young girl, after
many struggles, consents at last to put her lover to the test; he disappears
and the girl lives and dies an old maid. That is all the plot; but this little
history, that for sustained and masterly treatment may be compared to
Eugénie Grandet (which for the rest it does not in the least resemble),
holds the reader's interest from beginning to end. It has not the special
charm of Balzac's masterpiece; the heroine, Catherine, a difficult
character to draw, and drawn with extraordinary skill, is represented
as a dull girl of limited intelligence and fixed ideas, who wins our
sympathy indeed, but appeals much less to the imagination than the
immortal Eugénie; as the house in Washington Square yields in romantic suggestion to that of the old and faded mansion with the broken
stair that we have each of us inhabited in turn. But in historical accuracy
and broad grasp of the foundations of life, there is no work with which
the American novel can be so fitly mated as with that of the great
French master.

II.

These are only two of various masterpieces that Mr. James has
given to the world. He has written about a dozen novels, and a considerable number of short stories; and his treatment of the two forms
of narrative is sufficiently distinct to demand that they should be considered somewhat apart.

It is a commonplace of literature that the short story, brought to so
much perfection by the French, has never flourished in England. Half-
a-dozen causes might be assigned for the fact; but it is probably chiefly
due to the inferior sense of art as art, possessed by the English as compared with the French. The short story is above all a matter of form, of
proportion; and the English sense of form, in respect of literature, is
apt to be conspicuously wanting. There are exceptions, of course, and
notable ones; but we speak of the rule. Mr. James, whose particular
genius and method of work touches that of the French on more sides

than one, is nowhere more French than in this; he satisfies our sense of form, of truth of proportion beyond any other writer in the English language that we could name. His shorter stories are of a length varying from a few pages to nine or ten chapters; but in the best of them, of whatever length, and that includes a large proportion, the form is perfect. It would be hard to find a flaw in the construction of *Daisy Miller*, 'The Madonna of the Future,' 'Four Meetings,' 'The Pension Beaurepas,' and 'Benvolio'; or, to come down later, in 'The Siege of London,' 'The Author of Beltraffio,' 'The Aspern Papers,' 'The Solution,' and a dozen other that might be named. These delightful stories have, of course, a hundred other claims on our admiration; wit, humour, pathos, a charming gaiety, acute observation of life and character; but it is the faultless skill with which they are framed, that above all, perhaps, 'places' them as consummate works of art. The short story, properly treated as such, deals with a single idea, an isolated situation— a rule from which Mr. James never swerves; but much of the singular perfection of his short stories lies in the fact that while the idea, the situation is exhibited, developed and worked out to its legitimate conclusion within the compass of the few pages, more or less, that he allows himself, it is in fact no more isolated than it is possible for any situation in real life to be; it stands with its just relation to the universe exactly indicated, bound to the common life by the million threads that unite common humanity. This is, of course, only to say that when the author sits down to write a short story, he knows his business; but that particular knowledge is so rare among us, that some insistence on it in this case may be permitted. In longer novels, his method is of necessity somewhat different. Like all the greater novelists, Mr. James is interested not merely in the telling of a story, properly so called, in the working out of a situation, the conduct of a love-affair, the development of a plot, but with the entire moving drama of life, the great human comedy, in which situations take their place as mere incidents. In *The Portrait of a Lady*, in *The Bostonians*, *The Princess Casamassima*, *The Tragic Muse*, and in a less degree *The Europeans*, *The American*, *The Reverberator*, we feel less that the curtain has risen on a comedy of manners or of plot, than on a vast section of society, and of society considered with especial reference to some of its more modern developments. In his earlier as in some of his later work, Mr. James, as we have seen, selected the wide field of the opposing and harmonizing influences of America and Europe; in *The Bostonians*, he touches the question of Women's Rights; in *The Princess Casamassima*, we are with the

Socialists; whilst his most recent book, *The Tragic Muse*, sets before us the curious relations that the latest whirligig has brought round between art, and society in its conventional sense. As a novelist, Mr. James is necessarily concerned with the manifestation of any particular phase with which he is dealing, through the experience of individuals; but it is obvious that for this a large canvas, a complex scheme is needed, in which perfection of form has in some degree to yield to the exigencies of the spectacle of the huge haphazard activities, the apparently crude fatalities of human existence. There are readers who will always prefer Mr. James's shorter stories, their delicate manipulation, their exquisite style, and perfect proportion; there are others who will find a deeper interest in the larger issues brought before them in his longer narratives. The question is not one that need trouble us; it is the privilege of an artist to affect men's minds in very various ways, and there is no danger that Mr. James's admirers will quarrel among themselves.

A novelist's presentment of life, or more justly, perhaps, his choice, his selection out of life, is one thing; the way in which he personally looks at life and appreciates it, is obviously another. A distinction has always to be sought between a writer's mental attitude and the results given to the world; and to disengage the man from the artist, the artist from the man, must not unfrequently present itself as a problem a little resembling that of Shylock's pound of flesh. With some writers, indeed, the task is sufficiently easy; it may simply be abandoned. The author puts, as it is called, his whole soul into his work; the shaping artist plays a secondary part; the result may be brilliant, charming, passionate, sentimental or the reverse; but it at least presents no particular problem; the author and his work are one. To others, again, the picturesque, the emotional, the moral or the sensational side of existence may appeal so strongly, that an irresistible impulse leads them inevitably to reveal their idiosyncrasy through their presentation of life. With a writer so impersonal as Mr. James, the case is different, the problem more complicated. He has to be considered primarily in his artistic capacity; it is his supreme distinction that he invariably includes and excludes as an artist, not as a man; and his work lends itself to negative deductions, as it were, rather than to positive ones. To speak, for instance, of his writing as ironical, is on the surface to state an untenable proposition; he is genial (one might rather say), he is good-humoured, he is indifferent, he is at moments extraordinarily tender; it would, we believe, be impossible to find from beginning to end of his works one cruel or sarcastic word. It is only by degrees we come to a perception of the profound irony implied by that attitude of good-humoured neutrality, of genial indifference. His books, on the whole, strike one as optimistic; a certain kindly view of the events and accidents of life pervades them; they deal by preference with the saner rather than with the more morbid side of humanity; but they create finally a sense of aloofness on the part of the writer that seems to imply a profound disenchantment, what we have ventured to call a profound irony lurking at the root of his conception of life, a sense of the singular sadness, futility and vanity on the whole, of the beings whom he observes and depicts as they cross and recross the stage of the world. As might be expected, this is less apparent in his earlier than in his later work; it is nowhere more apparent than in his latest novel, *The Tragic Muse*. In that remarkable book, modern to a degree that makes all other novels seem for the moment old-fashioned and out-of-date, by comparison, what is termed the general and the particular is carried to the last point; the central figure and the central motive, that is to say, being a woman of an artistic type common to all time, brought into contact with the newest modes and developments of culture and society. The theme is one that lends itself with particular felicity to the author's especial genius for unimpassioned observation; it is developed with the mature strength of a splendid and virile talent; but the final impression it creates is of something a little hard, perhaps, a little too irresponsible.

The impression, we must immediately add, arises in great measure from the fact that the scheme of the story does not happen to include any of those characters that Mr. James knows how to treat with a particular kindness, with a genial warmth even, springing from a larger sympathy with human nature than the most discriminating observation can supply. It is entirely characteristic of the author, that it is not, as a rule, in the delineation of his principal heroes and heroines that we discover this kindly and sympathetic note, but in that of his humbler characters. There is no commoner or cheaper device of the inferior novelist than to seize upon one or another weak or absurd side of a human being and hold it up to scorn; to pillory a character for some physical or mental defect, to paint the smaller vices with an air of being above the human race, in colours as false as the follies that are described. Mr. James not only (it need not be said) has nothing to do with vulgarities such as these, not only he never laughs at, but always with his characters; he does much more. In his treatment of the old, the poor, the humble, the disgraced by fortune, such as come into all work that

embraces wide fields of human action, there is a tenderness equalled by
no other writer that we can recall. We feel disposed to insist upon this
quality because it is the most personal, perhaps the only personal note
he allows to modify the rigour of disinterested observation. Sometimes,
in fact, he dramatises it, so to speak, by leaving the story to be narrated
by an imaginary person, as where he deals with the disillusioned painter
in 'The Madonna of the Future;' with Mr. Ruck, the ruined American
father, in 'The Pension Beaurepas;' or Caroline Spencer, in 'Four
Meetings.' Elsewhere, however, those humbler individuals who have
the honour to hold (as we judge) an especial place in the author's
regard, take their place among the other characters in an impersonal
narrative; we need only mention Madame Grandoni, in *Roderick
Hudson*; Miss Birdseye, in *The Bostonians*; the old violinist, Lady
Aurora, Miss Pynsent, in *Princess Casamassima*, to illustrate our meaning.
And in connection with this point may be mentioned the particular
power of pathos shown by Mr. James on the very rare occasions—not
half-a-dozen perhaps in the whole course of his books—that he cares
to exercise it; that pathos which, in its entire freedom from self-
consciousness, from the implied invitation, 'Come, let us weep, for
this is a melancholy occasion,' is among the rarer gifts of the novelist.
Few people, we should think, could read unmoved the death of Miss
Birdseye, which in simple and suggestive beauty recalls the description
of the passage of Christiana across the river of death in the *Pilgrim's
Progress*; or that other chapter in *The Princess Casamassima*, where the
tenderly humorous enhances the pathetic, as the devoted little dressmaker comforts herself on her deathbed with the illusions of her adopted
son's greatness; or again, in altogether another key, the scenes darken-
ing to the tragic close of the same novel. These passages, of an absolute simplicity, show how far Mr. James's genius can, with his rare
permission, carry him in that direction; though the very rarity of the
occasions on which he indulges it, enhances perhaps its final value.

III.

This, indeed, may be said in general of what is emotional and of what
is descriptive in Mr. James's novels. No one can describe better than he
can; but he has apparently decided, and we think on the whole justly,
that novels are not the proper vehicle for descriptions of scenery as
such, and we seldom come across more than is requisite for the mere

mise en scène. We say justly, on the whole; because whilst accepting the theory as true, it is possible to recall novelists who indulge in a richer decoration for their characters than Mr. James does, and with whom we find no ground for quarrel on that score. In the same way with the emotional; Mr. James for the most part avoids it, travels round it, gets at his effects without it; and considering the floods of futile words, the pages of sentiment that do duty for passion and feeling, we are again disposed to say that he is right. Nevertheless, emotion is a great weapon in the hand of a master; Mr. James, as he proves in passages here and there, wields it with as much mastery as any one; there are moments when we find ourselves wishing he would wield it a little oftener.

A novelist, however, is obviously what the grace of heaven and his own wit make him. Mr. James may be only sometimes descriptive and occasionally emotional; but he is witty, he is humorous, he is epigrammatic; he is learned—consummately learned in human nature. He is, in brief, pre-eminently the novelist of character and observation. Of the ordinary resources of the story-teller, indeed, Mr. James is apt to avail himself but sparingly. Of love-making proper, for instance, there is but little in his volumes. There are lovers, of course, and marriages, —often unhappy ones; but these are not the main business on hand. That lies in tracing through delicate and minute observation of the surface, the hidden sources that determine action. His imagination, which may be held to be wanting in richness in certain directions, is of extraordinary strength in the conception of these springs of motive and of conduct, of the action and interaction of the human mind. In the same way, the brilliant procession of heroines that passes through his pages, seem to be there less to illustrate a charming side of life, than because no picture of life, charming or the reverse, is complete without them. A good deal might be said about Mr. James's treatment of women. One's first impression (and even one's last impression, perhaps) is that he treats them coldly; that in his moments of keenest insight into their motives and sentiments, he still views them, as it were, from outside, and at a distance. This, of course, may simply be taken as part of his disinterested treatment in general; but the impression of coldness remains, even with the fresh memory of the tenderness of touch that goes to the delineation of Miss Birdseye and Miss Pynsent, of the genial mood in which he gives us Olive Chancellor and the incomparable Henrietta Stackpole, and the mingled humour and gentleness of his presentment of Pansy Osmond, that peerless little flower among

jeunes filles. For whilst other authors often leave on our mind a sense
of their affection, their sympathy with, their admiration for their
heroines, of their endowing them with delightful qualities for private
ends of friendship, Mr. James stands aloof from all that. His women,
good and bad, pass before him, and he views each in turn with a careful
and impartial eye; he cares, he gives us to believe, no more for Isabel
Archer or Madame de Cintré than for Madame Merle, or Mademoiselle
Noémie. The method has its advantages; the reader is never torn in
two by the antagonism between his own preferences and those forced
upon him by the author; he could never hate the worst of Mr. James's
women, and he has one or two very bad ones, as he hates the virtuous
Laura Bell. And yet there are moments when we feel that he might
maintain a rather less distant attitude. We feel it, because we feel that
the author's position towards certain of his heroes is, without any
detriment to the attitude of 'detachment', of a somewhat warmer
character; we are sure that he is on terms of the friendliest intimacy
with Ralph Touchett and Lord Warburton, with Nick Dormer, and
even with poor little Hyacinth Robinson.

For the rest, we can feel nothing but gratitude for the long and
varied succession of portraits that Mr. James hangs before our eyes;
his portraiture is always true and brilliant; he seizes the salient points
with unerring skill, and there are faces and figures in his books that live
in our memory as part of the more intimate experience of life. We can
imagine certain of his women, in the future, forming part of the furniture of the nineteenth century, as in another art the women of Lely
and of Reynolds furnish for us the court of Charles II, and the social
life of George III. It is needless to say that none of these portraits are
made to order; more than that, Mr. James, as we have intimated, shows
no special predilection for one type over another; that is the good side
of the rather melancholy indifference of which we were accusing him
just now. One of his earliest successes associated him with a certain
exceptional type of the American girl; but admirably as he depicts her,
we cannot perceive that he scores successes less admirable, in his
delineation of types who have little in common with Daisy Miller.
Nevertheless, his heroines being almost exclusively of one nationality
—with the exception of the charming Biddy Dormer, English, and
English again to her very finger-tips, he has given us no heroine of
importance who is not American—one or two characteristics appear in
almost all; though varying so much in colour and degree in one and
another, that we hardly know how to define them otherwise than as the

breath of New England animating its daughters. This is vague, but not more vague perhaps than the impalpable spirit that Mr. James has caught with so certain an instinct and communicated so delicately to every woman, young or old, who hails from the Transatlantic shores in his novels. It is companion to that hardly less vague, but no less certain breath of what we may venture to term the American tradition that flutters through Mr. James's volumes; a breath too little deliberate, too little conscious of itself to be named Puritanism, but associated with a certain conception of the American character that no one has illustrated more happily than Mr. James himself. It might, we say again, be hard to define; it might be difficult to put one's finger on a passage and say: 'it is here or there'; it may be summed up finally, perhaps, in the impression left by the volumes, as a whole, that the good and evil of the world indifferent to the author as an artist, are not indifferent to him as a man. To quote his own words: 'There is one point where the moral sense and the artistic sense lie very near together; that is, in the light of the very obvious truth that the deepest quality of a work of art will always be the quality of the mind of the producer.' It is in this sense that we seem to distinguish throughout Mr. James's work the faint aroma of the Puritan tradition.

103. Andrew Lang's parodistic allusion to *Daisy Miller*

1892

Andrew Lang, from *Old Friends, Essays in Epistolary Parody*, 1892, 25–9.
This is one of a series of grotesque pairings, some of which—Lovelace from *Clarissa* being assailed by a booby called Tom Jones, or Catherine Morland from *Northanger Abbey* on a visit to Mr. Rochester and Jane Eyre—are considerably more amusing. The joke here is, admittedly, mostly at the expense of Ouida, but it does show that Daisy Miller was still a well known name. Ouida was the pseudonym of Marie Louise de la Ramée (1839–1908) the popular novelist of romanticized high life.

From the Hon. Cecil Bertie to the Lady Guinevere

Mr. Cecil Tremayne, who served 'Under Two Flags,' an officer in Her Majesty's Guards, describes to the Lady Guinevere the circumstances of his encounter with Miss Annie P. (or Daisy) Miller. The incident has been omitted by Ouida and Mr. Henry James.

You ask me, Camarada, what I think of the little American *donzella*, Daisy Miller? *Hesterna Rosæ*, I may cry with the blind old bard of Tusculum; or shall we say, *Hesterna Margaritæ?* Yesterday's Daisy, yesterday's Rose, were it of Pæstum, who values it today? *Mais où sont les neiges d'automne?* However, yesterday—the day before yesterday, rather—Miss Annie P. Miller was well enough.

We were smoking at the club windows on the Ponte Vecchio; Marmalada, Giovanelli of the Bersaglieri, young Ponto of the K.O.B.'s, and myself—men who never give a thought save to the gold embroidery of their *pantoufles* or the exquisite ebon laquer of their Russia leather cricket-shoes. Suddenly we heard a clatter in the streets. The riderless chargers of the Bersaglieri were racing down the Santo Croce, and just turning, with a swing and shriek of clattering spurs, into the Maremma. In the midst of the street, under our very window, was a little thing like a butterfly, with *yeux de pervenche*. You remember, Camarada, Voltaire's love of the *pervenche;* we have plucked it, have we not? in his garden of Les Charmettes. *Nous n'irons plus aux bois! Basta!*

But to return. There she stood, terror-stricken, petrified, like her who of old turned her back on Zoar and beheld the incandescent hurricane of hail smite the City of the Plain! She was dressed in white muslin, *joli comme un cœur*, with a myriad frills and flounces and knots of pale-coloured ribbon. Open-eyed, open-mouthed, she stared at the tide of foaming steeds, like a maiden martyr gazing at the on-rushing waves of ocean! 'Caramba!' said Marmalada, 'voilà une jeune fille pas trop bien gardée!' Giovanelli turned pale, and, muttering *Corpo di Bacco,* quaffed a *carafon* of green Chartreuse, holding at least a quart, which stood by him in its native pewter. Young Ponto merely muttered, 'Egad!' I leaped through the open window and landed at her feet.

The racing steeds were within ten yards of us. Calmly I cast my eye over their points. Far the fleetest, though he did not hold the lead, was Marmalada's charger, the Atys filly, by Celerima out of Sac de Nuit. With one wave of my arm I had placed her on his crupper, and, with the same action, swung myself into the saddle. Then, in a flash and thunder of flying horses, we swept like tawny lightning down the Pincian. The last words I heard from the club window, through the heliotrope-scented air, were 'Thirty to one on Atys, half only if declared.' They were wagering on our lives; the slang of the paddock was on their lips.

Onward, downward, we sped, the fair stranger lifeless in my arms. Past scarlet cardinals in mufti, past brilliant ἑταῖραι like those who swayed the City of the Violet Crown; past *pifferari* dancing in front of many an albergo; through the Ghetto with its marmorine palaces, over the Fountain of Trevi, across the Cascine, down the streets of the Vatican we flew among yells of 'Owners up,' 'The chestnut wins, hard held,' from the excited *bourgeoisie*. Heaven and earth swam before my eyes as we reached the Pons Sublicia, and heard the tawny waters of Tiber swaying to the sea.

The Pons Sublicia was up!

With an oath of despair, for life is sweet, I rammed my persuaders into Atys, caught him by the head, and sent him straight at the flooded Tiber!

'Va-t-en donc, espèce de type!' said the girl on my saddle-bow, finding her tongue at last. Fear, or girlish modesty, had hitherto kept her silent.

Then Atys rose on his fetlocks! Despite his double burden, the good steed meant to have it. He deemed, perchance, he was with the Quorn or the Baron's. He rose; he sprang. The deep yellow water, cold in the moon's rays, with the farthest bank but a chill grey line in the mist, lay beneath us! A moment that seemed an eternity! Then we landed on the far-off further bank, and for the first time I could take a pull at his head. I turned him on the river's brim, and leaped him back again.

The runaway was now as tame as a driven deer in Richmond Park.

Well, Camarada, the adventure is over. She was grateful, of course. These *pervenche* eyes were suffused with a dewy radiance.

'You can't call,' she said, 'for you haven't been introduced, and Mrs. Walker says we must be more exclusive. I'm dying to be exclusive; but I'm very much obliged to you, and so will mother be. Let's see. I'll be at the Colosseum to-morrow night, about ten. I'm bound to see the Colosseum, by moonlight. Good-bye;' and she shook her pale parasol at me, and fluttered away.

Ah, Camarada, shall I be there? *Que sçais-je?* Well, 'tis time to go to the dance at the Holy Father's. Adieu, Carissima—Tout à vous,

CIS.

THE LESSON OF THE MASTER

1892

104. Unsigned review, *Nation*

April 1892, liv, 326

It is indispensable that a good story-teller, even as a good judge, should preserve strict impartiality, that he should have the knack of keeping out of the quarrel. To stand apart and watch the fight (or even the small scrimmages) of life, and then to tell, neither approving nor condemning—that is the lofty and lonely function of the modern artist in fiction. To attain this height he must not become a monster incapable of emotion or sympathy, but he must feel *for* all the participants in the conflict and not *with* any. He is a spectacle of pure intellect and artistic sensibility dominating commoner if not inferior qualities. For all who enjoy this interesting and singular spectacle, Mr. James's book will be a source of pure delight. Only in one instance does he appear to discard his impenetrable mask and to speak his own mind. The 'Master' seems to express the author's convictions about the tribute which literature exacts from one who has espoused the profession of letters and would be worthy of his calling. The Master's denunciation of himself as a worshipper of false gods, and of his confrères who work for money (not to live on but to riot on), certainly has an admonishing ring. The story of 'The Pupil' illustrates an impersonality proof against all temptation. The pathos of the situation is so subtle and so profound, the induce-ment to exclaim, 'Now behold the sorrow of this! Reflect on the pity of that!' is so strong, that the author's self-restraint appears marvellous. Yet he makes no faintest deviation from his dispassionate calm, and the result is that the reader, by the aid of his own unguided beholding and reflecting, is gradually consumed with pity, and, at the catastrophe, has a moment very near to personal anguish.

105. From Vernon Lee's ambiguous portrait of James in 'Lady Tal', *Vanitas*

1892

These are short excerpts from a very interesting story, the subjects of which are obviously HJ and perhaps Vernon Lee herself in the title role. HJ wrote in 1893 to WJ (who was about to meet her): 'I hope you won't throw yourself into her arms. . . . My reasons are several, and too complicated some of them to go into; but one of them is that she has lately, as I am told . . . directed a kind of satire of a flagrant and markedly "saucy" kind at me!! . . . a particularly impudent and blackguardly sort of thing to do to a friend and one who has treated her with such particular considera-tion as I have. For God's sake don't betray that I have *spoken* to you of the matter or betrayed the faintest knowledge of it: I haven't read these tales and never mean to. They are, moreover, the others, excessively, to my sense, brutal and bad.' 'Vernon Lee' was, of course, the pseudonym of Violet Paget (1856–1935), the bluestocking, novelist, and critic, and part of HJ's resentment was no doubt due to his having been painstakingly kind to her on her entry into literary life.

The church of the Salute, with its cupolas, and volutes, stared in at the long windows, white, luminous, spectral. A white carpet of moonlight stretched to where they were sitting, with only one lamp lit, for fear of mosquitoes. All the remoter parts of the vast drawing-room were deep in gloom; you were somehow conscious of the paintings and stuccos of the walls and vaulted ceilings without seeing them. From the canal rose plash of oar, gondolier's cry, and distant guitar twang and quaver of song; and from the balconies came a murmur of voices and women's laughter. The heavy scent of some flower, vague, white, southern, mingled with the cigarette smoke in that hot evening air, which seemed, by contrast to the Venetian day, almost cool.

As Jervase Marion lolled back (that lolling of his always struck one as out of keeping with his well-adjusted speech, his precise mind, the something conventional about him) on the ottoman in the shadow, he was conscious of a queer feeling, as if, instead of having arrived from London only two hours ago, he had never ceased to be here at Venice, and under Miss Vanderwerf's hospitable stuccoed roof. All those years of work, of success, of experience (or was it not rather of study?) of others, bringing with them a certain heaviness, baldness, and scepticism, had become almost a dream, and this present moment and the similar moment twelve years ago remaining as the only reality. Except his hostess, whose round, unchangeable face, the face of a world-wise, kind but somewhat frivolous baby, was lit up faintly by the regular puffs of her cigarette, all the people in the room were strangers to Marion: yet he knew them so well, he had known them so long.

There was the old peeress, her head tied up in a white pocket-handkerchief, and lolling from side to side with narcoticised benevo-lence, who, as it was getting on towards other people's bedtime, was gradually beginning to wake up from the day's slumber, and to murmur eighteenth-century witticisms and Blessingtonian anecdotes. There was the American Senator, seated with postage-stamp profile and the attitude of a bronze statesman, against the moonlight, one hand in his waistcoat, the other incessantly raised to his ear as in a stately 'Beg pardon?' There was the depressed Venetian naval officer who always made the little joke about not being ill when offered tea; the Roumanian Princess who cultivated the reputation of saying spiteful things cleverly, and wore all her pearls for fear of their tarnishing; the English cosmopolitan who was one day on the Bosphorus and the next in Bond Street, and was wise about singing and acting; the well turned out, subdued, Parisian-American æsthete talking with an English accent about modern pictures and ladies' dresses; and the awkward, enthusiastic English æsthete, who considered Ruskin a ranter and creaked over the marble floors with dusty, seven-mile boots. There was a solitary spinster fresh from higher efforts of some sort, unconscious that no one in Venice appreciated her classic profile, and that every one in Venice stared at her mediæval dress and collar of coins from the British Museum. There was the usual bevy of tight-waisted Anglo-Italian girls ready to play the guitar and sing, and the usual supply of shy, young artists from the three-franc pensions, wandering round the room, candle in hand, with the niece of the house, looking with shy intentness at every picture and sketch and bronze statuette and china bowl and lacquer box.

The smoke of the cigarettes mingled with the heavy scent of the flowers; the plash of oar and snatch of song rose from the canal; the murmur and laughter entered from the balcony. The old peeress lolled out her Blessingtonian anecdotes; the Senator raised his hand to his ear and said 'Beg pardon?' the Roumanian Princess laughed shrilly at her own malignant sayings; the hostess's face was periodically illumined by her cigarette and the hostess's voice periodically burst into a child-like: 'Why, you don't mean it!' The young men and women flirted in undertones about Symonds, Whistler, Tolstoy, and the way of rowing gondolas, with an occasional chord struck on the piano, an occasional string twanged on the guitar. The Salute, with its cupolas and volutes, loomed spectral in at the windows; the moonlight spread in a soft, shining carpet to their feet.

Jervase Marion knew it all so well, so well, this half-fashionable, half-artistic Anglo-American idleness of Venice, with its poetic setting and its prosaic reality. He would have known it, he felt, intimately, even if he had never seen it before; known it so as to be able to make each of these people say in print what they did really say. There is something in being a psychological novelist, and something in being a cosmopolitan American, something in being an inmate of the world of Henry James and a kind of Henry James, of a lesser magnitude, yourself: one has the pleasure of understanding so much, one loses the pleasure of misunderstanding so much more.

A singing boat came under the windows of Palazzo Bragadin, and as much of the company as could squeezed on to the cushioned gothic balconies, much to the annoyance of such as were flirting outside, and to the satisfaction of such as were flirting within. Marion—who, much to poor Miss Vanderwerf's disgust, had asked to be introduced to no one as yet, but to be allowed to realise that evening, as he daintily put it, that Venice was the same and he a good bit changed—Marion leaned upon the parapet of a comparatively empty balcony and looked down at the canal. The moonbeams were weaving a strange, intricate pattern, like some old Persian tissue, in the dark water; further off the yellow and red lanterns of the singing boat were surrounded by black gondolas, each with its crimson, unsteady prow-light; and beyond, mysterious in the moonlight, rose the tower and cupola of St George, the rigging of ships, and stretched a shimmering band of lagoon.

He had come to give himself a complete holiday here, after the grind of furnishing a three-volume novel for Blackwood (Why did he write so much? he asked himself; he had enough of his own, and to spare, for a dainty but frugal bachelor); and already vague notions of new stories began to arrive in his mind. He determined to make a note of them and dismiss them for the time. He had determined to be idle; and he was a very methodical man, valuing above everything (even above his consciousness of being a man of the world) his steady health, steady, slightly depressed spirits, and steady, monotonous, but not unmanly nor unenjoyable routine of existence.

[However Marion soon becomes uncharacteristically involved in instructing Lady Tal (Atalanta) in 'the art of the novelist'.]

. . . he had, not without considerable self-contempt, surrendered himself to the demon of character study. This passion for investigating into the feelings and motives of his neighbours was at once the joy, the pride, and the bane and humiliation of Marion's placid life. He was aware that he had, for years and years, cultivated this tendency to the utmost; and he was fully convinced that to study other folks and embody his studies in the most lucid form was the one mission of his life, and a mission in nowise inferior to that of any other highly gifted class of creatures. Indeed, if Jervase Marion, ever since his earliest manhood, had given way to a tendency to withdraw from all personal concerns, from all emotion or action, it was mainly because he conceived that this shrinkingness of nature (which foolish persons called egoism) was the necessary complement to his power of intellectual analysis; and that any departure from the position of dispassioned spectator of the world's follies and miseries would mean also a departure from his real duty as a novelist. To be brought into contact with people more closely than was necessary or advantageous for their intellectual comprehension; to think about them, feel about them, mistress, wife, son, or daughter, the bare thought of such a thing jarred upon Marion's nerves. So, the better to study, the better to be solitary, he had expatriated himself, leaving brothers, sisters (now his mother was dead), friends of childhood, all those things which invade a man's consciousness without any psychological profit; he had condemned himself to live in a world of acquaintances, of indifference; and, for sole diversion, he permitted himself, every now and then, to come abroad to places where he had not even acquaintances, where he could look at faces which had no associations for him, and speculate upon the character of total strangers. Only, being a methodical man, and much concerned for his bodily and intellectual health, he occasionally thought fit to suspend even this contact with mankind, and to spend six weeks, as he had intended spending those six weeks at Venice, in the contemplation of only bricks and mortar.

And now, that demon of psychological study had got the better of his determination. Marion understood it all now from the beginning: that astonishing feebleness of his towards Lady Atalanta, that extraordinary submission to this imperious and audacious young aristocrat's orders. The explanation was simple, though curious. He had divined in Lady Atalanta a very interesting psychological problem, considerably before he had been able to formulate the fact to himself: his novelist's intuition, like the scent of a dog, had set him on the track even before he knew the nature of the game, or the desire to pursue. Before even beginning to think about Lady Atalanta, he had begun to watch her; he was watching her now consciously; indeed all his existence was engrossed in such watching, so that the hours he spent away from her company, or the company of her novel, were so many gaps in his life.

Jervase Marion, as a result both of that shrinkingness of nature, and of a very delicate artistic instinct, had an aversion of such coarse methods of study as consist in sitting down in front of a human being and staring, in a metaphorical sense, at him or her. He was not a man of theories (their cut-and-driedness offending his subtlety); but had he been forced to formulate his ideas, he would have said that in order to perceive the real values (in pictorial language) of any individual, you must beware of isolating him or her; you must merely look attentively at the moving ocean of human faces, watching for the one face more particularly interesting than the rest, and catching glimpses of its fleeting expression, and of the expression of its neighbours as it appears and reappears. Perhaps, however, Marion's other reason against the sit-down-and-stare or walk-round-and-pray system of psychological study was really the stronger one in his nature, the more so that he would probably not have admitted its superior validity. This other reason was a kind of moral scruple against getting to know the secret mechanism of a soul, especially if such knowledge involved an appearance of intimacy with a person in whom he could never take more than a merely abstract, artistic interest. It was a mean taking advantage of superior strength, or the raising of expectations which could not be fulfilled; for Marion, although the most benevolent and serviceable of mortals, did not give his heart, perhaps because he had none to give, to anybody.

This scruple had occurred to Marion almost as soon as he discovered himself to be studying Lady Tal; and it occurred to him once or twice afterwards. But he despatched it satisfactorily.

THE WHEEL OF TIME

1893

and *THE PRIVATE LIFE*

1893

106. From an unsigned review, *Nation*

November 1893, lvii, 416–7

In the essay on Gustave Flaubert included in Mr. James's volume, *Essays in London and Elsewhere*, when referring to the few people who understand what Flaubert tried for, the author says, 'it is only when a reader is also a writer and a tolerably tormented one that he particularly cares.' This is an example of the personal note occasionally struck in the volume, and echoes like a response to the sound of many voices clamoring criticism of Mr. James. No writer of fiction has suffered more from the people who won't or can't understand what he is trying for, while none has more consistently directed his energy towards one issue—the perfection of form and expression. Public obtuseness is probably more real than affected, for there is nothing of which the average Anglo-Saxon has less intuitive appreciation than of literary form apart from subject, except, it may be, of the resources of his own language. One may deplore such defective perception, but can hardly regard it as a valid excuse for angry rejection of every effort at education. . . .

With a clear notion of what Mr. James is trying for, and with thankful recognition of the effort, we get from his two latest volumes of fiction the impression of form without substance, of fine-spun elusive phantoms with no claim on emotional regard, and rather irritating to the intelligence. One has no objection to the fine quality of the garment clothing figures mostly artificial or trivial, but a resentful sense of waste. There are times, too, when the garment fails to please or satisfy, when the phrase is so subtle or so elliptical that lucidity is missed. Such failure is especially noticeable in the conversations, where the reader has often to rely on the descriptive sentence, 'he said with a laugh,' or 'she answered gravely,' for a cue to the mental attitude of the characters and an adjustment of his own. Close attachment to refinement of expression is also detracting from Mr. James's creative force. Finish of phrase is not, for instance, characteristic of the British matron, no matter how exalted her station. This somewhat heavy, worldly, and inane personage makes a frequent appearance in these stories, but we cannot think that she ever appeared elsewhere with such polished and vivacious sentences at her tongue's end. It may please Mr. James to toy with this ponderous figure, but the reality recedes from view in proportion to the elaboration of his presentment.

Failure to give the sense of life is of course the irretrievable fault in fiction. We do not mean to burden Mr. James with the imputation of a positive failure in the essential of his art, but only to indicate a possible result from an obvious cause. By the perfection of his rendering of an episode, a situation, a state of the mind or soul, he has achieved unique distinction in English letters; but to take a place in what he calls the great tradition, his exquisite method must be applied to subjects that are well in the range of common experience, and that appeal with some passion to intelligence and emotion.

107. Frank Harris on 'Max' and senseless abortions of mediocrity

[1924]

Frank Harris, from *Contemporary Portraits*, Series IV, 1924, 127–8. This is part of a section devoted to Max Beerbohm. It is difficult to be sure to what period Harris is referring, but since he first met Beerbohm when the latter was an undergraduate (early 1890's), and since he refers in another account of the same conversation in his memoirs (see Appendix I, Section 10) to having subsequently read *The Turn of the Screw*, it seems that it would be some time in the mid-1890's. Harris (1855–1931) was, of course, the Irish editor, critic, story writer, and adventurer, who made a considerable impact on English literary life by his editorship of the *Evening News* and the *Fortnightly Review* in the 1880's and 1890's.

Now and then he went astray with the many 'incapable of perfectness,' as Bacon said, and worshipped some false god. Just as Shaw tries to find something to admire in Mark Twain, so Max, I remember, was resolved to speak of Henry James with reverence.

When I derided *Daisy Miller* and the other senseless abortions of mediocrity, Max retreated at once to his last line of defence: 'James builds up his sentences,' he said, 'and arranges his word-bricks with patient artistry'; finally adding: 'James writes like no one else, and surely that alone lends supreme distinction to style.' But I would not have it: 'No one writes prose like Martin Tupper,' I continued, 'or like Swinburne, and assuredly no one wants to: there is no distinction in bad work, and that it's laboured is an additional offence.' Smilingly, with the tinge of pity that suited his youth, Max recognised the obstinacy of my mental astigmatism.

108. Norman Hapgood on James's refinement and limitations

1898

Norman Hapgood, from *Literary Statesmen and Others*, 1898, 193–208. This essay was written in 1894, and was clearly specifically prompted by *Essays in London and Elsewhere*. Hapgood (1868–1937) was an American publicist, editor, and reformer, who at this time was contemplating the reform of literary criticism. His idea about the possible effects of HJ on an American audience seems to me well worth considering. Commenting on the book in *Literature* (May 1898, ii, 593–4), HJ reported 'a considerable warming of the heart' but also that 'he strikes me, as yet, rather as feeling for his perceptions—hunting for his intelligence'.

The ironical attitude, according to Mr. Henry James, is the attitude of the artist; an opinion which may well be startling until one learns that the artist is one thing and the poet its opposite. With irony, in his own sense, Mr. James is impregnated. The unusual shadings given to words, the complicated and facile syntax, the broken sentences in dialogue, that suggest a shrug, the frequent French, the irrelevant parentheses, the completions that are so close to repetitions,—all these have the airiness of irresponsibility about them. Mr. James does not crash into the heart of a thought with a noun. He hovers about it, pricks it here, with delicacy, then there, so near that sometimes here and there seem like one point. The fineness of his distinctions, their abundance, and the apparent ease with which they are dropped, contribute much to our sense of the futility of the world he is describing; partly because the world is so blind to all this, partly because at first these delicate touches seem to create a world all surface, a soap-bubble, as it were, in which familiar things are refracted into shapes at once fantastic and persuasive. Imagine a young American, crude, matter-of-fact, and rather bored by his crudities and literalness, meeting for the first time this spirit. Suppose him just enough irritated at and balked by the rigid world he knows to be ready to attack it, but weaponless.

Roderick Hudson falls into his hand. He settles back on his lounge before he has read ten lines, with the excitement of feeling that he has found the needed secret and that it is a long and full one. He has read Emerson before, and has sneered at the plastic arts. Before he has read a week he longs to see the Madonna of the Chair, because Henry James has mixed it in with his universe by some flitting adjective. He longs to see Florence and Rome, because Christina and Rowland yawned and talked and influenced and came to nothing there. His whole thought takes a back-ground that he believed foreign to it. There is a world that laughs at the limitations and rigidity that annoyed him—that is gay, intellectual, unproselyting; that is, the attractive people are all this, and the Philistines are simply funny and unimportant. He knows now more clearly what he wants to see and be. He wants to see people whose divisions of the world are not hampering, and he wants to be an ironical and unprejudiced observer. His Emerson goes on to the shelf, marked abstract and provincial. Instead he buys photographs of Italian paintings, studies atlases, plans a trip to Europe, and reads Mérimée and Turgenieff.

For Mr. James is not all the fascinating and cultivated satirist. There are forms built of the mass of apparently surface touches that are adequate expressions of the deepest and most lasting experiences. Though the author was in each sentence of the book, we realize at the end of the thick volume that he was not all there. The detail was deliciously redolent of a certain point of view; the whole that gradually appears is deeply typical of life, with much of its mystery. To quote one of the author's stories: 'He lived once more into his story and was drawn down, as by a siren's hand, to where, in the dim under-world of fiction, the great, glazed tank of art, strange, silent subjects float. He recognized his motive and surrendered to his talent.'

Of course there are intelligent readers for whom Mr. James's work seems almost frivolous. Those who are literal, inelastic, limited to set classifications and distinctions, find him remote, unreal, indefinite, inconclusive. They say that by nature he is a psychologist or a critic, no novelist; that in a kind of expression where he would be forced to speak his meaning he would be valuable. What they call the meaning they want put directly and explicitly. A world which is not obviously sifted for them, which is all one lump of vague reality, the end of which is to create with any methods, be they more usually seen in the essay, the novel, or any other form, the impression corresponding to that the actual world makes on us, with its solidity, its complexity, its irrationality,—such a piece of expression is meaningless to them. And to other minds, more vital and less ingenuous, it is meaningless too. Though in its most general features the world they see is the one Mr. James paints, they do not like his details, they do not enjoy the flavor of his mind, and they therefore cannot go through the many pages to get the general plan. The author himself believes that his novels were felt by Ivan Turgenieff to be hardly food for men. The elaboration, the thousand slight touches that make the general effect, bore such men. The work seems to them embroidery. They want more directness, simplicity, force. Turgenieff has an awful fatalism of his own, but it is too simple and too strenuous to come within our definition of irony. In the slang of the day, Mr. James is too 'elegant' to come near to the man whom he calls the poet, as he does Turgenieff. But to his friends reason dressed in banter is more amiable, law is lighter when it speaks in the tones of irresponsibility. One who sees his matter as clearly as his manner can hardly fail to feel that he is distinguished by range as surely as by precision, by endurance as surely as by acuteness; that his insight is as extensive as it is fine, and his art is equal to its expression. This is not to deny that the variety of persons, scenes, or situations which he handles is rather slight. It is to assert, however, that with the illustrations he does use he sets forth adequately, completely, some essential springs of the mind. Though his people and his scenes have not the profusion of contrast that life has, that some artists have, the relations are there in their proper proportions, only in a shorter scale.

A limitation in means similar to this lack of exuberance is an inability to paint vividly the physical world. One understands—feels—the surroundings, but he hardly sees them. The most striking of his descriptions have something the air of feats. It is difficult to illustrate a negative, but here is a sentence in which the picturesque is tried for:

There is a certain evening that I count as virtually a first impression—the end of a wet, black Sunday, twenty years ago, about the first of March. There had been an earlier vision, but it had turned gray, like faded ink, and the occasion I speak of was a fresh beginning.

Perhaps the following description of the first appearance of Christina Light will show how he just misses the visual:

A pair of extraordinary dark blue eyes, a mass of dusky hair over a low forehead, a blooming oval of perfect purity, a flexible lip just touched with disdain, the step and carriage of a tired princess,—these were the general features of his vision.

The clothing of the personages and their physique seem described with effort, and so do the landscape, the room, or whatever the setting may be. The author is not to a large degree a man for whom the visible world exists, in the sense of Gautier's famous phrase. Its interest is adjective mostly: the interest of its effect on persons first, and, second, an interest of suggestion. It is rich in analogy. Mr. James feels its importance, and he usually gives its effect adequately, but sometimes one feels that his work is weakened by rather more than is necessary of direct description of the environment; one is disappointed at the unconvincing touch. For, to the reader who is best fitted to appreciate Mr. James, this literal setting is not necessary. The atmosphere is created without it; it comes from what the personages do and say, and from the author's manner of talking about them. The environment is a great bully with some of the best literary workmen of recent times. It is a very important element of art, but it doesn't need to be labelled. In the main Mr. James is free from this exaggeration. He has a rare, distinguished genius, and it is the genius of an artist, but the artist is a psychologist. The idea is what gives life to his work; the personal, the abstract idea; though this idea does not exist apart from its embodiment, and is described, necessarily, when it is most adequately described, in terms of its external expression,—it is the side of final interest. 'A psychological reason is, to my imagination, an object adorably pictorial,' says Mr. James; and the reverse is as true: when a pictorial object interests him, his interest is delightfully psychological. One who feels this inseparability of form and idea in Mr. James is rather supported by the discovery that his father was a logician at once acute and picturesque, and that his brother is a studied psychologist who connects the ordinary matter of his science with the mixed stream of life with uncommon subtlety and with uncommon definiteness, seeming at once psychologist and logician, scientist and poet. One is pleased also to read that at the age of seven Mr. Henry James lay on the hearth rug and studied *Punch*, and that he longed to know the life suggested by the pictures. There is nothing told us of the child's love for the lines and colors of nature. It is beauty that is a human expression that interests him; that is information about human character. There is no truancy in the mind. It sticks to the fact from the beginning. There are no fables and fairy stories for it, no fancy, no forms that are not fact; and, on the other hand, the young psychologist is an artist, and all his facts have form. Later he has said that he can imagine no object in weaving together imaginary events except the representation of life. The child's mind was as loyal to the same object.

To explain what is meant by saying that, while everything is expression, everything is also form to Mr. James, may after one has denied him any remarkable eye for line and color, be rather difficult. Of the truth of the proposition, however, there can be little doubt. He says somewhere that the most definite thing about an emotion is its surface. The metaphor is at once baffling and convincing, as his metaphors are likely to be. The thing I wish to emphasize is that it is his perception of the shapes of the moral world that gives him his distinguished value. In this bit, for instance, there is a fair visual image, slight, however, compared to the picturesqueness one feels.

I always left him in a state of 'intimate' excitement, with a feeling that all sorts of valuable things had been suggested to me; the condition in which a man swings his cane as he walks, leaps lightly over gutters, and then stops, for no reason at all, to look, with an air of being struck, into a shop-window where he sees nothing.

These powers and these limitations sometimes lead one to wonder why Mr. James is not more a critic and less a novelist. As a matter of fact, most of his power is in his fiction, and the greater part in his long novels. He needs time for a multitude of his light touches to give to his picture a convincing simplicity. The best short stories, plays, and essays have been made in bolder, shorter strokes. In the drama, he not only misses the living touch, but loses his own charm. His dialogue in becoming shorter becomes stiff, instead of becoming intense. Directness and simplicity of feeling are outside of Mr. James's power of representation. There is a scene in *The Tragic Muse* in which Julia takes Nick's head in her hands and kisses it. It makes the reader close his teeth, as at a false note. He feels that the airy world, so parallel to the real world, so representative of it, is shattered when such material is forced into it. The comedy of his universe is 'the smile of the soul,' as Beyle said of French wit, and his tragedy is the sigh of the soul. The laugh and the throb are not in his scale; and the smile of the body and the sigh of the body are not there, either. His art, a firm and rounded representation of life, is no direct presentation of it, no copy. His dialogue may improve in plausibility and flexibility, but not so much that one cannot feel that he is describing a world that his imagination never saw; that he has seen the astral bodies of people and seen them static, in certain relations, to be described by him in long paragraphs of his own delicate observations, saying comparatively little themselves—speaking only for confirmation, as it were; that this fairy world of his, containing in it the essence of the interest of life for many, will not for any be visible to the outer eye, with fleshly bodies and tangible clothes, furniture, relations of actual space.

In criticism he is less successful than in fiction, for reasons other than this inability to give the direct blow. He repeats, sometimes grossly. A number of times he says without variation that, however flat his joke, du Maurier's picture has its unfailing charm; even the language scarcely changes. It may be that part of this iteration is due to sympathy, to the desire to make the length of his comment equal his interest, a desire which, when his attitude toward his subject is very simple, is disastrous. Much could be learned by comparing this essay with Mérimée's criticism of his friends, where the critic is as brief as he is when he carves his stories. Mr. James has no power of sacrifice. Effort, effort, always effort, he says, is the secret of success for all ambitious workers in the field of art. It is a secret that sometimes leads him astray, for he neglects other conflicting secrets; he fails to rest and he fails to throw away duplicates. 'You cannot,' he says to the young writer, 'take too many notes.' Without quibbling over the metaphor, one may believe it possible to take notes too constantly and with too much strain, and certainly possible to use too many of one's notes.

Another quality, which is one of the merits of the stories,—delicacy, —becomes aggressive and turns into a defect, squeamishness, in some of the essays. 'Be generous and delicate,' Mr. James says to the young writer, 'and then, in the vulgar phrase, go in!' That parenthetical apology for colloquialism occurs rather too often. It begins to savor of literalness. We should like to have rather more taken for granted. We feel too insistent an air of distance, of fine breeding, even of condescension. We like to see one artist strictly bounded by the delicacy of his tastes; but we wish the critic to know that it may be another artist's strength to be crude or naked. The instinct of privacy, for instance, is something upon which Mr. James's taste absolutely insists. He cannot talk long enough or severely enough about the publication by M. Edmond de Goncourt of an account of his brother's mental wreck, and of the nervous disease of both of them, or of the publication of Flaubert's letters, and he interjects his respect for privacy on all occasions. It is safe to say he does not feel imaginatively Balzac's racy and unquotable illustration of his ideal of openness. This queasiness might be parodied by the story of a man who could not believe that athletes are sincerely without any feeling of shame when they run, bare to the knee, through the city streets. The critic must not insist too solemnly on his view of etiquette, if the world is to listen to him.

The one fault of the essays still to be mentioned is comparatively trifling, and, like the others, akin to a virtue, to the originality of Mr. James's choice of words,—a virtue particularly apt in a writer whose end is exact and fine discrimination; for in words, as in objects, familiarity dulls our vision, and of two words expressing a shade with equal accuracy the rarer is the one that Mr. James always chooses. It is one of his methods of sharpening his reader's mind and keeping fresh his attention. His fault is that he narrows his vocabulary by overworking his fresh and apt words. He not only sacrifices variety of phrase; he sometimes lets a word try for an idea that a more familiar term would hit more precisely. What essay can you read through without finding 'mitigated,' 'casual,' 'inveterate,' and other adjectives that have driven all rivals from the field and gained themselves a factotum air? They are delicious at first, and finally flat.

Perhaps, after all, however, this last word is unfair. It may be that the weaknesses of this inclusive, subtle, contemporary spirit are rooted in its strength. If so, it would be silly to object. It may be that what looks like queasiness of taste to an outsider is a part of the elegance, and that what looks like flippancy is only the more radical manifestation of the subtlety. It is, of course, only appreciation that we seek, and if in the world of a writer whom we are studying certain details which do not please us are an organic part of that world there is no more to be said. In this case, fortunately, it is of small importance whether these particular characteristics be spots on a bright art or features of it, for they are so slight that they are scarcely visible in a general view of the work that Mr. James has done,—a work of equal value to the detached student of life and to the sympathizer with special human progress. Standing alike in the world of art and in the world of sympathy, he has been the interpreter of each to the other with equal fairness if not with equal love. The breadth of the impression of life that can be got from his books is due to this broad stand, covering two points of view as far apart as any: the standpoint of the man to whom life is a thing to be lived, with emotion and prejudice, and the standpoint of the man to whom it is a lot of lines and shades that can be combined into attractive and representative surfaces. The literal attitude is to Mr. James apparently the more pathetic, and the artistic or symbolic one the more distinguished. He himself is intimate with both, and in his novels the two natures, each in many grades, are kept face to face, and each is shown as it seems to itself and as it seems to the other. Therefore to us Anglo-Saxons he has been an education that we needed, for the artistic attitude (in the present sense of the unmoral, form-loving attitude) is particularly hard for us to see. Closely allied to this conflict is the contrast between culture and primitiveness which he has painted so carefully and so often in his groups of Americans and Europeans. To these two great pictorial ideas Mr. James has given his best work, and in doing the best he could for art has done what was most fit and timely for the needs of some of his countrymen. Giving to them their own eloquence and coherence, he helps them see with some comprehension the people to whom they are fantastic. They know whom he likes to be with, but they trust his impartiality none the less, for they feel that he does not like too strongly to be with any one. His artistic friends, his cultivated friends, he sees in their limits too, although not so clearly as he sees his Daisy Millers and his Millicent Hennings. If he patronizes Emerson and lauds Mrs. Humphry Ward we can forgive him, as we can if his essay on London has more infatuation than power. We forgive him because he has written *The Tragic Muse*, *The Princess Cassimassima*, and *The American*; because, although in his essays he has told what his limitations of sympathy are, he has in his novels spoken more impersonally. Whether his novels can live, whether the world will take him thinned and spread out into so many volumes, may well be doubted, for he does not justify himself page by page and word by word; and one seldom rereads him. But he has been a marked man of his time and has done a good work in it.

109. James on his evil days and his future
1895

HJ to W. D. Howells, January 1895 (LJ, i, 236–8).
In the event *The Sacred Fount*, *The Wings of the Dove*, *The Golden Bowl*, and *The Outcry* failed to find berths in magazines.

You put your finger sympathetically on the place and spoke of what I wanted you to speak of. I *have* felt, for a long time past, that I have fallen upon evil days—every sign or symbol of one's being in the least *wanted*, anywhere or by any one, having so utterly failed. A new generation, that I know not, and mainly prize not, has taken universal possession. The sense of being utterly out of it weighed me down, and I asked myself what the future would be. All these melancholies were qualified indeed by one redeeming reflection—the sense of how little, for a good while past (for reasons very logical, but accidental and temporary,) I had been producing. I *did* say to myself 'Produce again —produce; produce better than ever, and all will yet be well;' and there was sustenance in that so far as it went. But it has meant much more to me since *you* have said it—for it *is*, practically, what you admirably say. It is exactly, moreover, what I meant to admirably do—and have meant, all along, about this time to get into the motion of. The whole thing, however, represents a great change in my life, inasmuch as what is clear is that periodical publication is practically closed to me—I'm the last hand that the magazines, in this country or in the U.S., seem to want. I won't afflict you with the now accumulated (during all these past years) evidence on which this induction rests—and I have spoken of it to no creature till, at this late day, I speak of it to you. . . . All this, I needn't say, is for your segretissimo ear. What it means is that 'production' for me, as aforesaid, means production of the little *book*, pure and simple—independent of any antecedent appearance; and, truth to tell, now that I wholly *see* that, and have at last accepted it, I am, incongruously, not at all sorry. I am indeed very serene. I have always hated the magazine form, magazine conditions and manners, and much of the magazine company. I hate the hurried little subordinate part that one plays in the catchpenny picture-book—and the negation of all literature that the insolence of the picture-book imposes. The money-difference will be great—but not so great after a bit as at first; and the other differences will be so all to the good that even from the economic point of view they will tend to make up for that and perhaps finally even completely do so. It is about the distinctness of one's *book-position* that you have so substantially reassured me; and I mean to do far better work than ever I have done before. I have, potentially, improved immensely and am bursting with ideas and subjects—though the act of composition is with me more and more slow, painful and difficult. I shall never again write a *long* novel; but I hope to write six immortal short ones—and some tales of the same quality.

Lena Milman, from 'A Few Notes upon Mr. James', *Yellow Book*,
October 1895, vii, 71–83.
It will be noticed that in this tribute from the 'aesthetic' minority
the *descriptions* of HJ's art are very similar to those by ordinary
critics, while the *judgements* differ radically.

To think of form as characteristic of emptiness, as though all spheres
were bubbles, is an æsthetic heresy bequeathed to us by the Puritans who,
as surely as they added to our national muscle, bereft us of a certain
sensibility of touch. In their eyes, art was a mere concession to the
bauble-loving folly of the crowd, and beauty itself was anathema to
the wise few unless it clothed some grave moral teaching, which could
not otherwise be made acceptable to the foolish many. . . .

The contempt for the short story prevalent in England, but unknown
elsewhere, is surely as traceable to Puritan influence as the mutilation of
the Mary Altar at Ely, and of the shrine of Saint Thomas; for, insisting,
as it has become our English bent to do, upon some serious side-purpose
in art, we are not content with a beautiful suggestion, with a sketch be
it never so masterly; the narrative must illustrate a principle, the picture,
a fact. It is not yet ours to realise how the most exquisite in life are just
those passing emotions, those elusive impressions which it behoves the
artist to go seeking, over them so cunningly to cast his net of words or
colour as to preserve the rapture of that emotion, that impression, for the
delight of mankind for ever. We are too apt to regard the short story
as the cartoon for a possible novel, whereas any elaboration of it is as
thankless a process as the development of a fresco from an easel-painting. The treatment, the pigment, the medium, the palette are other
from the very beginning. The rugged outline, which adds vigour to
the fresco, could not be tolerated on canvas, the gem-like tones of the
easel-painting would look blurred if transferred to the wall. Mr. James's
pictures must be on the line; sky them, and it is not worth while to
crane our necks for the modicum of pleasure they can afford. He has

indeed written several books in the form of novels, but his method is too analytical, and we enjoy the stories much in the way we enjoy travelling over a picture with a microscope. We can detect no fault of technique; on the contrary, each movement of the glass reveals some new beauty, some wonder of skill; but we are conscious all the while that, as a whole, the work is a failure. . . .

With a delightful style, a facile invention, a wide culture, what writer could be better equipped than Mr. James?

Alas, that he must write for a generation upon whom two at least of these qualities are as though they were not! Alas, that it should be the concurrence of illiterate opinion, (an opinion often then most illiterate when most elegantly uttered,) that constitutes popularity! . . . There are certain elementary emotions, there are certain melodramatic situations, of which they never tire; and a writer who prefers to tell of subtle emotions, of bloodless situations, whose reputation, moreover, does not chiefly rest upon one of those respectable monuments of British industry, novels in three volumes, will never see his works stacked high upon the bookstalls. If, like Mr. James, he is further hampered by a tender literary conscience, which makes him reverent and temperate in the use of words, which hinders him from writing even daintily of things foul, it will go even harder with him, since he cannot hope for a place on that index which has made so many reputations in the marring. . .

111. Edwin Arlington Robinson on James's surprising genius

1896

Edwin Arlington Robinson to Harry De Forest Smith, February 1896. (*Untriangulated Stars. Letters of E. A. Robinson to H. De Forest Smith*, ed. D. Sutcliffe, New Haven, 1947, 239.) Robinson (1869–1935) was the later famous New England poet, at this time obscure and unpublished.

Three or four days ago, I took the liberty to borrow Henry James's *The Lesson of the Master* and have read it to find that H. J. is a genius. No smaller word will do it for the man, who produced such work as this. Did you read it? If you didn't, you must. If there is any more of his stuff out there let me know, and I shall try to read it, though I must take a rest for a time.

EMBARRASSMENTS

1896

---

112. Unsigned review, *Spectator*

August 1896, lxxvii, 273

Whatever measure of success has been achieved by Mr. Henry James in his new volume of stories is entirely independent of their literary form, which we confess to finding simply atrocious. Setting aside the constant use of slang—*e.g.*, 'It was bang upon this completeness all the same that the turn arrived,' &c.—there is hardly a page undisfigured by some gross sloveliness or obscurity of expression. 'The effect of my visit to Bridges,' we read on p. 7, 'was to turn me out for more profundity.' On p. 75 the narrator—he is an artist—observes,—'It was an effect of these things that from the very first, with every one listening, I could mention that my main business with her would be just to have a go at her head, and to arrange in that view for an early sitting.' Worse still, on p. 159, we find the following sentence:—'Pretty pink Maud, so lovely then, before her troubles, that dusky Jane was gratefully conscious of all she made up for, Maud Stannace, very literary too, very languishing and extremely bullied by her mother, had yielded, invidiously as it might have struck me, to Ray Limbert's suit, which Mrs. Stannace was not the woman to stomach.' Really these stories are often *Embarrassments* in a sense other than that intended by their author. Happily the matter, though of extreme tenuity of texture, is a great improvement on the manner. 'The Figure in the Carpet' strikes us chiefly in the light of a satire on the extravagances of modern literary hero-worship, but we have an uneasy consciousness that this may not be the aim of the writer. Embarrassment No. 2 is a decidedly clever and rather pathetic study of a girl consumed by an idolatrous worship of her own beauty. The *dénouement*, though dramatic and touching, is marred by its inherent improbability. No person who was stone-blind could contrive to impose upon a shrewd observer in the way that Flora succeeds in doing. The third story, though too full of literary and journalistic 'shop,' is by a far the best in the collection. Here Mr. James gives us an acute and sympathetic sketch of a writer of genius, entrusted with an esoteric mandate, driven by stress of circumstances to coin his brains, striving deliberately and desperately to write down to the level of the gross public, but failing again and again in the attempt. As his friend says of him, 'When he went abroad to gather garlic he came home with heliotrope.' The last tale is a brief but tantalising excursion into the domain of the quasi-super-natural. One rises from the perusal of these stories with a ready recognition of the ability of their author, mingled with dismay at the elaborate futility of most of the subjects he has chosen and the strange amalgam of slipshod colloquialism and preciosity of which his style is compounded. The finicking ways of the narrator, in conclusion, are a constant source of irritation. The man who alludes to his male acquaintances as 'poor dear' is bad enough in real life; he is detestable in fiction.

THE OTHER HOUSE

1896

113. From an unsigned review, *Saturday*

October 1896, lxxxii, 474–5

Within the past few years Mr. Henry James has produced a number of relatively short stories, each having for its central figure a novelist, which taken together exhibit, as perhaps no other work of his does, all the choicest qualities of his art. It is to be hoped that in some future edition of the author's writings it may be found possible to bring them all together in a single volume. Thus combined, they would present a study of contemporary bookmaking such as no other language but our own contains. It is never quite fair to identify a novelist with any given point of view in his work; but it is impossible to ignore the note of pained contempt for the kind of fiction the crowd runs after nowadays which is sounded in all these tales. . . .

We hasten to deprecate any direct application of what we have quoted to the case of this new novel by Mr. Henry James. During all the twenty years and more of his writing life, the author has produced nothing which makes more incessant demands upon those peculiar faculties of perception and swift yet delicate analysis that he has himself developed in his admirers. None the less, *The Other House* is clearly the product of a determination on the part of the writer to open a new vein—to assume, in the words of the poor hero of 'The Next Time,' a 'second manner.' The change has no reference, it is true, to what are imagined to be the tastes of the circulating libraries, although, oddly enough, it happens that the book furnishes one of the few exceptions of the year to the new rule of single-volume novels. It may be put down instead to the increasing hold which the idea of writing for the stage has fastened upon Mr. James's fancy.

The Other House is conceived in a purely dramatic spirit, and worked

261

out with a scrupulous regard for the conventions and limitations of the theatre. . . .

The most obvious drawback to this method of construction is that it sacrifices almost entirely that side of Mr. James's art in which he is most nearly without rivals; there is room for very little of the daintily whimsical commentary upon his characters, their looks and thoughts and motives and amiable absurdities, which he knows how to make so delightful. When he is not putting dialogue into the mouths of these characters, he is engaged almost wholly in providing that necessary description of their movements, their smiles and sighs and general stage-business, which in the theatre the spectator would see with his own eyes. One cannot escape the feeling that this latter is work which other and much lesser men do with more facility than Mr. James. The cultivated indirection of his style, so charming when it has a subject to match, gets in his way when it is merely a question of supplying the physical links in a chain of earnest and momentous dramatic dialogue.

At the risk of seeming captious, we have dwelt upon this less welcome aspect of *The Other House*, for the reasons that whatever Mr. Henry James does is of importance to literature, and that any display of his craftsmanship employed under new conditions, or upon novel materials, must be of great interest to other writers. The means by which he arrives at his final effect are open, it seems to us, to a good deal of criticism. As has been said, men who are not to be compared with him, artistically, would handle the merely conventional machinery of narration with much more simplicity and effectiveness than he has been able to command. The reader preserves an annoying sense of this almost to the end of the book. But one admits, on the other hand, that when this end is reached, the grim force and power of it are truly re-markable.

114. From an unsigned review, *Critic*

November 1896, xxvi, 355

The appearance of a new book by Mr. Henry James is always an event to the connoisseur of letters. It cannot be stated too explicitly or published too widely that *The Other House* is an event of the first order. In a small way it is a revolution. Mr. James has done something new. His name has been for long a synonym for cleverness and conscious skill, but on laying down this volume the reader is forced to confess that henceforward, if the writer so wills, it is also a synonym for power. The book has grip. Up to this time Mr. James's grip has apparently been nothing more than an exquisite sense of touch.

115. Stopford Brooke on James's style

1897

Stopford Brooke to Mrs. Crackanthorpe, August 1897 (*Life and Letters of Stopford Brooke*, ed. L. P. Jacks, 1917, ii, 528–9).
Brooke (1832–1916) was a divine and man of letters whose best work, *A Primer of English Literature* (1876), received notable praise and criticism from Matthew Arnold.

. . . he has now arrived at so involved and tormented a style that I find the greatest difficulty in discovering what he means. I read and read again and again his sentences, and it is like listening to a language I do not know. I read his last novel but one, and I was in the same helpless condition. I believe this style is the fine flower of modern culture at present, and that not to appreciate it is to be in the outer darkness, but I prefer outer darkness.

116. D. C. Murray on his listless contemporary

1897

D. C. Murray, from *My Contemporaries in Fiction*, 1897, 160–4.
Murray (1847–1907) was a British journalist and writer of novels.

Mr. Henry James is a gentleman who has taken a little more culture than is good for the fibre of his character. He is certainly a man of many attainments and of very considerable native faculty, but he staggers under the weight of his own excellences. The weakness is common enough in itself, but it is not common in combination with such powers as Mr. James possesses. He is vastly the superior of the common run of men, but he makes his own knowledge of that fact too clear. It is a little difficult to see why so worshipful a person should take the trouble to write at all, but it is open to the reader to conjecture that he would not be at so much pains unless he were pushed by a compulsory sense of his own high merits. He feels that it would be a shame if such a man should be wasted. I cannot say that I have ever received from him any supreme enlightenment as to the workings of that complex organ, the human heart, but I understand quite definitely that Mr. James knows all about it, and could show many things if he were only interested enough to make an effort. He is the apostle of a well-bred boredom. He knows all about society, and *bric-à-brac*, and pictures, and music, and natural landscape, and foreign cities, and if he could feel a spice of interest in any earthly thing he could be charming. But his listless, easy air—of gentlemanly-giftedness fatigued—provokes and bores. He is like a man who suppresses a yawn to tell a story. He is a blend of genuine power and native priggery, and his faults are the more annoying because of the virtues they obscure and spoil. He is big enough to know better.

It is likely enough that to Mr. James the fact of having been bred in the United States has proved a disadvantage. To the robuster type of man of letters, to the Dickens or Kipling kind of man, it would be impossible to wish better luck than to be born into that bubbling potfull of things. But Mr. James's over-accentuated refinement of mind has received the very impetus of which it stood least in need. He has grown into a humorous disdain of vulgar emotions, partly because he found them so rich about him. . . . It is both curious and instructive to notice how the too-cultured sensitiveness of a man of genius has blinded him to the greatest truth in the human life about him. Born into the one country where romance is still a constant factor in the lives of men, he conceives romance to be dead. With stories worthy of a great writer's handling transacting themselves on every hand, he is the first elucidator of the principle that a story-teller's business is to have no story. The vision of the sheet which was let down from Heaven to Peter was seen in vain so far as he is concerned, but the story of that dream holds an eternal truth for the real artist. Mr. James is not the only man whose best-nursed and most valued part has proved to be destructive. With a little more strength he might have kept all his delicacies, and have been a man to thank God for. As it is, he is the victim of an intellectual foppery.

THE SPOILS OF POYNTON

1897

117. From an unsigned review, *Academy*

February 1897, li, 256

Mr. Henry James writes for the few, and belongs to the very few. It is, indeed, almost a pity that so many dunces have been banged, bullied, and frightened into saying that they like the work of Mr. Henry James, but that he is really too subtle. It is a pity, because, in the first place, no dunce ever liked the work of Mr. Henry James; and, in the second place, because the trouble with Mr. Henry James is, that he is not subtle enough. For instance, he seems to have feared at times that his style wanted warmth, geniality, spontaniety; and, thus fearing, he gives us an occasional 'didn't' for 'did not.' This is not subtle, and it misses its effect. His heroes and heroines, again, take that course of action which best satisfies good taste and feeling. But, though rejected, the other course is considered. They deliberate. They choose. They are painfully anxious to have the good approval of everybody. Their most spirited action is discounted by nervousness and long self-communion. We find ourselves liking them less than we ought to like them; they are all right, but they have to take so much trouble to be all right. Mr. Henry James is subtle enough to work out the difficult sum correctly; but not subtle enough to rub out the working on his slate, and leave only the effective answer. His characters are not marionettes; they do live, and move, and have their being, but they know all the time that Mr. Henry James is looking; they are not sufficiently disengaged and projected. . . . There is much that is good in the delineation of Owen and Fleda, but they do not convince as Mrs. Gareth convinces. The story contains at least two strong dramatic situations: the humour is delightful; the style is Mr. Henry James. If it disappoints, it is for want of a little more warmth and humanity, because the reader cries out for someone who shall be admirable without being nervous and hesitating, and never finds that person.

118. From an unsigned review, *Bookman*

May 1897, xii, 42–3

One almost maligns the worth of *The Spoils of Poynton* in mentioning the frivolous structure on which it supports nearly three hundred pages. A woman of supreme good taste, with a genius for making a house a haven of harmony, finds herself face to face with the ugly fact that her son is about to marry an arch-Philistine, for whom she must give way. She is a woman of spirit and will, and the situation is intolerable. . . . The result is that decorous farce, in which Mr. James is unsurpassable. The vigorous shoving onslaught of the Philistine family, the brave holding out of the bold marauder, are a joy to witness. We back the Philistines all through; for the marauder has but a poor ally in Fleda. She is not even an ally in the marauding, only in artistic appreciation, and in a secret adoration of the stupid and charming young man: and the strength from these is undermined by a terribly active conscience and a sense of refinement which inconveniently goes far beyond the æsthetic region, and pervades her whole being. The Philistines rollick into victory, of course; and after all one cannot feel a very keen regret for the stupid Owen's fate. . . .

Perhaps another would have left it all comedy, and he would probably have been right. But Mr. James's human sympathies, if rather shy, are unconquerably strong. And here comes in his individual power, that in a story, the fun of which makes our eyes glisten, and with whose finer heroine we almost lose patience for a subtle virtue and refinement so much beyond the needs of the case, our last thought is still with her. Her little tragedy, in this setting, comes perilously near to spoiling the story; and yet, after all, we do not resent its stopping our fun, for it gives permanence and the element of the substantial to the graceful, trivial farce.

119. Joseph Conrad to Edward Garnett

1897

Quoted in, Amy Cruse, *After the Victorians*, 1938, 154.
Garnett (1868–1907) was a critic and author, and member of a
distinguished intellectual family.

But I imagine with pain the man in the street trying to read it. And my
common humanity revolts at the evoked image of his suffering. One
could almost see the globular lobes of his brain painfully revolving, and
crushing and mangling the delicate thing. As to his exasperation, it is a
thing impossible to imagine and too horried to contemplate.

WHAT MAISIE KNEW

1897

120. From an unsigned review, *Academy* (Fiction Supplement)

October 1897, lii, 89

I have read this book with amazement and delight: with amazement at its supreme delicacy; with delight that its author, in spite of such discouragement as may come from lack of popular acclaim, retains an unswerving allegiance, to a literary conscience that forbids him to leave a slipshod phrase, or a single word out of its appointed place. As admirers of Mr. James foresee—and Mr. James has a devoted band of admirers, who follow every line that he writes—the bare outline of the story is of the simplest. . . . But to state the plot of one of Mr. James's books is to state next to nothing. He deals not in events, but in events as they mirror themselves in the thoughts, the fleeting impulses, of his characters. By a rare psychological intuition, he lays bare the under side of his story. And in this book the whole sordid drama of petty jealousy, rancour, wantonness, and vacillation plays itself out for the amusement of Maisie. You follow the story through the mind of Maisie; you see and hear only what Maisie saw and heard; and yet, such is the combined humour and pathos of the presentment, you know so much more than Maisie could possibly know, though Maisie had her childish moral arithmetic, whereby she could put two and two together. . . . Certainly there is no living writer who has achieved the feat which Mr. James has here achieved, in analysing and purifying the baser passions of our nature by passing them through the pure mind of a little child.

121. From an unsigned review, *Spectator*

October 1897, lxxix, 603

Against the moral subversiveness of *What Maisie Knew* and Hardy's *Jude* this review puts Mrs. Oliphant's 'acute yet sympathetic insight into the workings of the human heart'; the 'deeply interesting . . . thrilling' *The Pomp of the Lavilettes* by Gilbert Parker; and the 'brilliantly written' *A Fair Deceiver* by George Paston.

In *What Maisie Knew* Mr. Henry James presents the unedifying spectacle of a man of great talent and subtlety, whose sympathies are obviously on the side of the angels, toiling with unflagging persistence and desperate attention to detail over the portraiture of half a dozen as unlovely and squalid souls—spite of their fashionable surroundings and showy exteriors—as it has been our misfortune to encounter in the range of modern fiction. It reminds us of nothing so much as a beautifully dressed child making an elaborate mud-pie in the gutter. The mud-pie is a regular work of art, and the child continues to keep its own hands and dress unsoiled. But when all is said and done, the result is only a mud-pie and nothing more. Maisie is the only child of thoroughly disreputable parents, who have just been divorced at the opening of the tale. According to the arrangement, Maisie spends her time alternately with her father and mother. Governesses are provided, and her father marrries the younger, handsomer, and incomparably more worthless of the two. The mother also marries again, her second husband being a feeble, invertebrate creature called Sir Claude. Then Maisie, who all the time is tossed about like a shuttlecock between this disreputable quartet, is the innocent means of bringing her new stepmother and stepfather together, with results that can be easily imagined from their antecedents. Mr. James, it is true, refrains from the crowning feat of making the father and mother marry each other again. That would have exposed him to the charge of attempting to enter into rivalry with the hideous finale of *Jude the Obscure*. But it could not have rendered the book more disagreeable than it is. The elaborate ingenuity with which this wretched little child is hemmed round with undesirable relatives in our opinion entirely robs the figure of its intended pathos. Maisie escapes in the end, thanks chiefly to the dogged determination of the ugly governess, and to the gradual emergence in the child of a moral sense. There are a great many passages in the book which are evidently meant to be humorous. . . . For the life of us we fail to see where the fun comes in, though no doubt this strenuous facetiousness has its admirers.

What Maisie Knew is of a quality incredible in a writer whose work has heretofore been, morally, beyond reproach. In what it says, still more in what it suggests, it ranks, except for a terrible underlying dullness, with the worst schools of French fiction. Maisie is a little child, not more than five or six years old, when her parents obtain a mutual divorce with an agreement that she shall divide her year equally between them. In the six months spent with her worthless father she hears her mother's name daily mentioned with oaths and foulest reproach. Going thence to an equally worthless mother, she learns, in language only less profane and foul, that her father is a profligate wretch. Neither spares one detail of course objurgation for pity at her helpless babyhood. Presently the pretty governess, hired by the mother, follows Maisie to the home of the father and becomes that father's mistress. A little later the mother makes a second marriage. Husband No. 2, a good-natured person, as weak and dissipated as, but less violent than, his predecessor, takes a fancy to the little girl, and she learns to adore him. She also adores the ex-governess, her father's mistress and later his wife. When, therefore, father No. 1 deserts wife No. 2, and goes to live with (and on) a third lady, and mother No. 1, having tried a variety of lovers (all with Maisie's knowledge and connivance), elopes with the latest, and father No. 2 and mother No. 2 form a connection, Maisie by this time nine years old or so, sees no harm in the arrangement. She talks the situation over with her governess, and is prepared to except it happily.

Such a plot seems inconceivable. Its author exhibits not one ray of pity or dismay at this spectacle of a child with the pure current of its life thus poisoned at its source. To him she is merely the *raison d'être* of a curiously complicated situation, which he can twist and untwist for purposes of fiction. One feels in the reading that every manly feeling, every possibility of generous sympathy, every comprehension of the higher standards, has become atrophied in Mr. James's nature from long disuse, and that all relation between him and his kind has perished except to serve him coldly by way of 'material.'

It goes without saying that the style of the book is jerkily incoherent.

The characters, Maisie included, converse in vague innuendoes, and, as no answer is promised 'in the next number,' the readers of the story— may they be few—will probably never understand exactly what any one concerned said or did or meant. This is just as well, for what little one is able to understand is alike repellent to taste and feeling, to law and gospel.

IN THE CAGE

1898

and THE TWO MAGICS

1898

123. From an unsigned review, *Athenaeum*

October 1898, 3704, 564-5

It has become almost hackneyed to talk of Mr. Henry James's subtlety; but there is no other word which so adequately expresses a constant quality in his work, and his use of this common quality in the two volumes before us illustrates better than anything else their real diversity. *In the Cage* is an account of a telegraph girl's interest in two people's love story, which she guesses at from the telegrams she has to dispatch for them; she naturally falls half in love with the hero of the episode, but nothing comes of that except a charming conversation on a seat in Hyde Park. But the girl has to use the most extraordinary ingenuity to discover whatever she does of the story, and in her efforts she almost gets to talk and split logic as if she were the author himself. The fault of the story is that there is no adequate return for all the torturings of inquiry and expectation in it. The girl herself is charming; the greatest admiration is due to the author for the accumulation of delicate touches by which he shows her hunger for romance, her delight in knowledge, her perfect natural good taste joined to certain slight faults in breeding due to her surroundings, and her rigid command over her self-respect, even when venturing on a certain extravagance of conduct. But admitting all the charm of her character, one is inclined to think her too good to be squandered on the subtleties of a mystery which is never really cleared up. The whole story is set out with too vast an appendage of nods and hints and things kept back;

274

and it ends in fizzle. . . . The fact is that in such stories as these Mr. Henry James takes himself much too seriously. . . . It is like using a steam-hammer to crack a nut. The very style reflects the difficulty; all through the book the phrases are tortured and obscure, parentheses abound, and it almost looks as if an attempt were being made to conceal the poverty of the idea in vast swaddling-clothes of verbiage. Take this sentence, from the very first page:

That made it an emotion the more lively—though singularly rare and always, even then, with opportunity very much smothered—to see any one come in whom she knew, as she called it, outside, and who could add something to the poor identity of her function.

The idea intended to be conveyed is not particularly elaborate; but it would be hard to imagine a more involved and unemphatic way of conveying it.

But *The Two Magics* is a very different sort of book. The first tale, 'The Turn of the Screw,' is one of the most engrossing and terrifying ghost stories we have ever read. . . . Here the author makes triumphant use of his subtlety; instead of obscuring, he only adds to the horror of his conception by occasionally withholding the actual facts and just indicating them without unnecessarily ample details. A touch where a coarser hand would write a full-page description, a hint at unknown terrors where another would talk of bloody hands or dreadful crimes, and the impression is heightened in a way which would have made even Hawthorne envious on his own ground. And here, too, the style —braced up, as it were, to the task of not missing a detail of the author's effects—loses its flabbiness and indistinctness, and only gains in stimulating power where a curious turn of phrase is substituted for a more hackneyed expression.

124. From an unsigned review, *Critic*

December 1898, xxxiii, 523–4

Of late Mr. James produces on his readers the effect of one experimenting, for his own sole joy rather than for their edification, with all kinds of intricate problems, but chiefly with that of mastering and presenting situations so super-subtle as to be practically impalpable.

The two new books of his . . . contain striking examples of this kind of literary rarefaction. *In the Cage* is a romance in the thousandth dilution. . . .

The book is in no sense an agreeable one. The pleasure to be had from reading it comes solely from the reader's apprehension that here is a marvellous piece of work which does to an unprecedented extent a novel thing. That is, it puts intuitions into the place of facts; it makes the perceptions of the sub-conscious self the subject of perfectly definite and not undramatic fiction. It forces the things that usually linger in the antechamber of the mind to come forward and reveal themselves boldly. These impressions in which we all believe sneakingly, though we seldom affirm or deny them, are first assumed to represent fact and then proved to do so, and this high-handed method has a charm of its own which makes one willing to forget that the theme is dreary.

But if *In the Cage* convinces us that Mr. James deals as confidently and realistically with 'thoughts before thinking,' as a grocer deals with pounds of sugar or bars of soap, what is there left to say about 'The Turn of the Screw'? . . . The subject matter . . . is also made up of feminine intuitions, but the heroine—this time a governess—has nothing in the least substantial upon which to base her deep and startling cognitions. She perceives what is beyond all perception, and the reader who begins by questioning whether she is supposed to be sane ends by accepting her conclusions and thrilling over the horrors they involve. . . . It is the most monstrous and incredible ghost-story that ever was written. At the same times it grasps the imagination in a vise. The reader is bound to the end by the spell, and if, when the lids of the book are closed, he is not convinced as to the possibility of such horrors, he is at least sure that Mr. James has produced an imaginative masterpiece.

'THE TURN OF THE SCREW'

1898

---

125. Oscar Wilde to Robert Ross

1899

The Letters of Oscar Wilde, ed. R. Hart-Davis, 1962, 776.

I think it is a most wonderful, lurid, poisonous little tale, like an Elizabethan tragedy. I am greatly impressed by it. James is developing, but he will never arrive at passion, I fear.

126. Henry Harland on James's wonderful temperament

1898

Henry Harland, from an article, *Academy*, November 1898, lv, 339–40.
Harland (1861–1905) was an expatriate American writer, and the editor of the *Yellow Book*. This article, from which I print only the peroration, is one of the first whole-hearted 'cult' productions. Earlier in the year HJ had contributed a most charming and sympathetic review of Harland's volume of stories, *Comedies and Errors*, to the *Fortnightly* (April, lxix, 650–4).

An intenser, finer insight, served by a technique nearer to perfection, a freer, firmer, more accomplished hand, and guided, restrained, by a more exacting, a more sensitive literary conscience—that is the word one first feels impelled to speak, when asked to speak a word about Mr. Henry James. It is by no means the only word, it is by no means the last word. The last word of all, in speaking of any artist, must of course be *temperament*. But the temperament, golden and generous, human and sympathetic, exalted, fastidious, chivalrous, that glows through every page of Mr. James's writing, that warms every sentence, that gives to every syllable the ring of the living voice—that would be the theme for another and a far more ambitious study than the present.

127. Joseph Conrad's defence of James as the most civilized of writers

1899

Conrad to John Galsworthy, February 1899 (G. Jean Aubry, *Joseph Conrad, Life and Letters*, i, 270–1).
Evidently Galsworthy had passed on some criticisms of HJ (by his cousin) for Conrad's opinion. 'R.T.' is 'The Real Thing'.

Yes, it is good criticism. Only I think that to say Henry James does not write from the heart is maybe hasty. He is cosmopolitan, civilized, very much *homme du monde* and the acquired (educated if you like) side of his temperament,—that is,—restraints, the instinctive, the nurtured, fostered, cherished side is always presented to the reader first. To me even the R. T. seems to flow from the heart because and only because the work, approaching so near perfection, yet does not strike cold. Technical perfection, unless there is some real glow to illumine and warm it from within, must necessarily be cold. I argue that in H. J. there is such a glow and not a dim one either, but to us used, absolutely accustomed, to unartistic expression of fine, headlong, honest (or dishonest) sentiments the art of H. J. does appear heartless. The outlines are so clear, the figures so finished, chiselled, carved and brought out that we exclaim,—we, used to the shades of the contemporary fiction, to the more or less malformed shades,—we exclaim,—stone! Not at all. I say flesh and blood,—very perfectly presented,—perhaps with too much perfection of *method*.

The volume of short stories entitled, I think, *The Lesson of the Master* contains a tale called 'The Pupil,' if I remember rightly, where the underlying feeling of the man,—his really wide sympathy,—is seen nearer the surface. Of course he does not deal in primitive emotions. I maintain he is the most civilized of modern writers. He is also an idealizer. His heart shows itself in the delicacy of his handling. Things like 'The Middle Years' and 'The Altar of the Dead' in the vol. entitled *Terminations* would illustrate my meaning. Moreover, your cousin

CONRAD'S DEFENCE OF JAMES

admits the element of pathos. Mere technique won't give the elements of pathos. I admit he is not *forcible*,—or let us say, the only forcible thing in his work is his technique. Now a literary intelligence would be naturally struck by the wonderful technique, and that is so wonderful in its way that it dominates the bare expression. The more so that the expression is only of delicate shades. He is never in deep gloom or in violent sunshine. But he feels deeply and vividly every delicate shade. We cannot ask for more. Not everyone is a Turgeniev. Moreover Turgeniev is not civilized (therein much of his charm for us) in the sense H. J. is civilized. *Satis.* Please convey my defence of the *Master* with my compliments.

128. James on his detachment from the public

1899

HJ to Howard Sturgis, May 1899 (LJ, i, 325–6).
The book referred to is *The Awkward Age*. Sturgis (1855–1920)
was a wealthy and aristocratic American writer and host, bred in
England, who is best remembered for his novel *Belchamber* (1904).

That's right—*be* one of the few! I greatly applaud the tact with which
you tell me that scarce a human being will understand a word, or an
intention, or an artistic element or glimmer of any sort, of my book.
I tell *myself*—and the 'reviews' tell me—such truths in much cruder
fashion. But it's an old, old story—and if I 'minded' now as much as
I once did, I should be well beneath the sod. Face to face I should be
able to say a bit how I saw—and why I *so* saw—my subject. But that
will keep.

THE AWKWARD AGE

1899

129. From an unsigned review, *Spectator*

May 1899, lxxxii, 647

Arthur Morrison (1863–1945) was a novelist, dramatist, and expert on oriental art, whose first works were 'naturalist' in tendency, e.g. *Tales of Mean Streets* (1894).

We deeply regret to find Mr. Henry James in *The Awkward Age* once more carrying into practice that misguided opinion, by which so many modern writers of fiction are obviously actuated, that normal and wholesome themes being exhausted, a novelist can only display originality or achieve artistic results in the delineation of the detestable. It is needless to observe that in the execution of this aim Mr. James refrains from employing the methods in vogue amongst the naturalistic realists. He never calls a spade a spade, or a 'd—d shovel'; he does not visit 'mean streets,' or minutely describe the symptoms of epilepsy, or deal in physical or physiological horrors. His characters all belong to 'the classes'; they are clothed sumptuously, they live in luxury, and sedulously eschew violence in speech or action. And yet, in spite of this external suavity, the atmosphere of mental and moral squalor in which they move is far more oppressive than that into which we are transplanted by Mr. Morrison or any of the slum realists. The dialogue of *The Awkward Age*, with its scrupulous avoidance of candour, its wealth of sinister suggestiveness, is a marvel of enigmatic insinuation. The splendid phrase of Longinus, who defines sublimity as 'the echo of a noble mind,' moves one to describe this strange romance as a whispering-gallery of ignoble souls. All the resources of Mr. James's subtle analysis and ingeniously elaborate style are lavished on the portrayal of a set of smart degenerates, whose very nicknames—*e.g.*, 'Mitchy' and 'Tishy'—enhance their odiousness.

May 1899, iv, 475–6

Those of Mr. Henry James' readers who believed and perhaps hoped that *The Other House*, and still more *The Two Magics*, might be taken as marking the definitive adoption by him of a new and a broader and bolder artistic method than that of his earlier works will be, if not disappointed, at any rate undeceived by his latest novel. *The Awkward Age* is, from the point of view of manner, a most pronounced 'reversion to type.' It is Mr. James at his most subtly psychological, at his most overwhelmingly copious, at his most exasperatingly deliberate. As regards subject its affinities are more recent. It shows us again the Mr. James of *What Maisie Knew*, and, later still, of *In the Cage*, the minute and patient, and, if the truth must be told, the too often wearisome student of that curiously corrupt and frivolous section of contemporary society to which he has latterly devoted so much of his attention. Here he is at his acutest as an analyst, and as a storyteller at his slowest and his most difficult. The length of *The Awkward Age* is inordinate, and though the delicacy and fineness of the literary workmanship are, as usual, admirable, the reader's interest in the fortunes of its characters is in danger of waning to extinction before its close. This, too, is the more to be regretted because the main motive of the story—an exhibition of the contrast between the manners and sentiments of the 'old school,' as represented in the elderly Mr. Longdon, who has lived for some twenty or thirty years out of the world, and those of the newest new, as personified by Mrs. Brookenham and her daughter, Mr. Vanderbank, Mr. Mitchett, the Duchess, and the rest of the fashionable triflers and *intrigantes*, among whom he finds himself—is one which no living writer is capable of presenting with that half-humorous, half-tragic truth which so impresses one in all Mr. James' work on these particular lines.

Considered apart as character sketches, the various figures that flit through this long but almost eventless society drama are, many of them, individually excellent. Mrs. Brookenham, the attractive, witty, absolutely 'unmoral' woman of the world, with her modern, precocious, and too knowing, but frank, downright, and in many ways loveable, eighteen-year-old daughter, are both drawn with singular skill; and the way in which the elderly Mr. Longdon, who has cherished a hopeless attachment for the girl's grandmother, gradually overcomes the shock of the contrast between the faded romances of the past and the rather slangy prose of the present—a recovery which becomes at last so complete that he makes Nanda his wife—is made credible and, even in a suppressed sort of way, touching. The colourless husband of Mrs. Brookenham, and the 'decadent' son Harold, with his cynical vivacity of talk and his habit of helping himself to money from his mother's bureau and of borrowing casual five-pound notes from after-noon callers—these, too, slight as they are, are well realized portraits. . . .

But no skill of portraiture, no inventiveness in dialogue, will fully compensate a reader for the relentless *longueurs* of *The Awkward Age*, the intolerable thinness to which the material is beaten out, and the indescribable slowness with which the author conducts us to his con-clusion. It is only an apparent paradox to add that the journey is the more fatiguing because his face and ours are set steadily in the direction of the goal, and we advance towards it without halt or divagation. A frankly discursive book offers continual reliefs; but we feel here that nothing is purely episodical, that every chapter is conscientiously designed to bring the *dénouement* infinitesimally nearer—and it is this feeling which makes impatience ungovernable, just as to creep along a high road, 'unhasting but unresting,' at the rate of a mile an hour would tire one more than any number of rambles over the adjoining fields. In the avowedly 'short story' Mr. James can often be concise enough: if he would only learn to cultivate that art of compression and apply it in those longer works of his which need not be as long as they are, it would be much to the advantage of his art.

131. Unsigned review, *Saturday*

May 1899, lxxxvii, 598

Mr. James will imperil his vogue if he is not careful. We have grown to look upon him as a dainty, dapper, well-groomed author, who, despite some Transatlantic eccentricities, could be introduced to our friends of both sexes. But every year he grows more careless of his literary person, his epigrams are more flashy, his innuendoes are less clean-shaven, until in his present presentation he may almost be denied admittance as shabby-genteel. Were this his first appearance, we would dismiss him as an American intent upon a very serious attempt to depict English society, but possessed of no materials other than those reposing in his inner consciousness. His men, though represented as belonging to a smart set, are neither English nor gentlemen. They exclaim 'See here' upon the slightest provocation; we hear of 'the perfection of their evening dress and the special smartness of their sleeveless overcoats;' and their behaviour always recalls that of a strolling mummer, who mistakes insolence for ease and rudeness for wit. The ladies are mere caricatures of new women, and the children, of 'awkward age,' parody the precocity of the most unnatural French creations. Nine-tenths of the book are conversation, and consist of tedious, vain repetition. And yet we feel that the characters are alive, though we can never conjure up any interest in them or come to desire their better acquaintance. The coherence of the style may best be gauged by an extract: 'Lord Petherton, a man of five-and-thirty, whose robust but symmetrical proportions gave to his dark-blue double-breasted coat an air of tightness that just failed of compromising his tailor, had for his main facial sign a certain pleasant brutality, the effect partly of a bold, handsome parade of carnivorous teeth, partly of an expression of nose suggesting that this feature had paid a little, in the heat of youth, for some aggression at the time admired and even publicly commemorated.' Was there ever such a sentence outside a shilling shocker? As for the story, Mr. James has no more to tell than the needy knife-grinder, and equally little right to an expectation of our sixpences.

132. Unsigned review, *Academy*

May 1899, lvi, 532–3

Sir Francis Jeune (1843–1905) was one of the greatest of Victorian ecclesiastical lawyers. I guess that the reviewer is referring to his successful defence of the Bishop of Lincoln, Edward King, in the illegal ritual case of 1889–90. King was extremely High Church, and taught a doctrine of the 'real objective presence'.

Mr. Henry James is the wonderful artistic outcome of our national habit of repression. He has learned how to make repression a factor of art instead of an impediment. To all real things, even those over whose discomforture Sir Francis Jeune presides, belongs an infinite variety of words and gestures whose presence in a publication 'there's none to dispute.' But they are legible, and, emanating from the things themselves, they witness uncompromisingly to their existence. For the art of Mr. James such words and gestures are enough. Nay, holding aloof as he does, yet without affection of prudery, from the frank image of an act-in-itself, and dwelling with the thought behind it, he presents a more significant idea of both thinker and doer than were otherwise to be obtained. *The Awkward Age* is a complex illustration of his method. It is an urban drama of that fast life which, perhaps as a result of its 'fastness,' produces an atrophying cleverness that has learned to anticipate naïf opinion of its depravity. The members of the little West-end circle, on whose affinity with US Mr. James seems with astonishing affability to calculate, vie with one another in their appreciation of the old-world chivalrous gentleman who sits like a bewildered stranger at their feasts. They have arrived at the point when everything exists as it is conceived to exist. It is not with the eyes of backbiters, but of psychologists, for instance, that they read elopement in Lady Fanny's eyes. In the anticipatory relish of what, for convenience, we will call 'sins' they are such epicures that the sin itself, the act-in-being, would be anti-climax. So we ourselves thought as we read through what the plain but polite Briton will consider a masterpiece of ambiguity. We did not want to know if Lady Fanny eloped with her Captain, or if Vanderbank committed adultery with Mrs. Brookenham. The malaria of their atmosphere was accounted for by that delay in accomplishment which means the incessant re-creation of the same fact on the mental plane. The author gains his effect with the minimum of the kind of information which furnishes a newspaper. He knows it is not necessary for things to happen in the sense of making a noise or a rustle.

The story is a sad one, for it traces the gradual development of a tragic sense of the atrophy of which we spoke in two of the only three generous natures with whom it deals. Mr. Longdon, seeing in Nanda the outward counterpart of the woman he had loved in his youth, would have done anything to unite her with the man she loved. But the latter, Vanderbank—he is a portrait worthy to stand by Sir Claude in *What Maisie Knew*—is incapable of the sacrifice which a combination of futures demands. He has lights and stirrings, he knows what it is to be dissatisfied, but he is too clever to be mastered by impulse. Moreover, he owes allegiance to the girl's mother—that allegiance which may or may not be prejudicial to Mr. Brookenham. With one of those splendid feats of audacity by which Mr. James turns a sudden glare on the lurking badness which he plays the showman to so debonnairely, he makes Nanda beseech Vanderbank not to desert her mother.

Do stick to her. . . . I don't believe you thoroughly know how awfully she likes you. . . . I suppose it *would* be immodest if I were to say that I verily believe she's in love with you. Not, for that matter, that father would mind. . . That's the only thing I want. When I think of her downstairs there so often nowadays, practically alone, I feel as if I could scarcely bear it. She's so fearfully young.

There are few who dare write such a passage, or venture a pathos so supreme bordering on a vulgarity so abject. In achieving Nanda Mr. James has given us a veritable child of the age. But the 'awkward age'? It is not very easy to see where that comes in, except that it was awkward for Mrs. Brookenham to own in public a child of nineteen. As for Mrs. Brookenham she is marvellous; her talk radiates the subtlest shafts of femininity. Not less, however, does she emanate a deadliness to which even the lightest of us may accord a shudder, and incline to accept the last irony which leaves no shelter for Nanda from the miasm of polite corruption, save with one who had loved her grandmother and would fain have married her to another man. Let it be added that the style of this study of life is delicate and incisive as of old. The words are picked, but not with gloves: they hold the distinctive nuances which the refusal to use slang confers on words of ancestry on the lips of ladies and gentlemen. Here and there a wonderful bluntness is allowed. One feels it was heard in the soul—is authentic. Charming bits of landscape, alluring glimpses of a sweeter life, occur as occasion arises. Yes, the book is another 'Henry James.' Let us thank the proprieties, the conventions of this land, the genius of repression, which have created that need for a new realism, delicate as a silver-point, to which his works make so satisfying a response.

133. From an unsigned review, *Athenaeum*

May 1899, 3735, 651–2

The sort of people presented in Mr. Henry James's new novel are not met every day. Still, there are factors in them that must be reckoned with, and they have their prototypes in a certain small section of society. The smallness of that section and some other reasons make it improbable that they will appeal very strongly to the sympathy, or perhaps to the understanding, of the majority of readers. Interest they will evoke in a few, but even these will scarcely accord anything in the shape of liking or esteem except to one or two. The real amateur of Mr. James is, however, more concerned with his view and treatment of people than with the people themselves—with his consummate mastery of any material he chooses to work in than with the moral or other aspect of the subject. *The Awkward Age* is just another concrete expression of his keen observation of social tendencies and phases, and his truly remarkable power of selecting a difficult or uncommon situation or environment and making it his own. He can also make it the reader's, provided the reader be of the right sort—one who knows how to follow his intricate involutions of idea and phrasing. The amount of cleverness dispersed through these pages is amazing, though not amazing in the sense of being unexpected. . . . He is most truly at home in the chiaroscuro of faintly lit drawing-rooms, when talk is at its subtlest and veiled emotions are exchanged or suggested. There have been interludes when he has attempted life at high tide, or striven to penetrate the dubious regions of the supernatural. The strongly dramatic outlook and action in *The Other House*, and the strange horizons opened up in *The Two Magics*, are cases in point. But *The Awkward Age* again brings him back to more familiar ground. Needless to say, it is a place where strong incident and violent outbursts are excluded. . . .

To guard against giving the story away (the real difficulty would be the converse, since there is no story), reference need not be made to the few events that do occur. Very little of an external kind happens. The action passes for the most part in the brain-cells of a small group of intriguers and observers. Yet we find a life or two unobtrusively blighted by the schemers. The aim—and who shall say it is unsuccessful?—is to set in movement a train of carefully repressed emotions, a bewildering criss-cross of motives and interests (more or less intangible and ephemeral) that make the daily life of a few intensely sophisticated men and women. This extreme sophistication, mingled with not a little bad breeding, is perhaps somewhat forced. The elemental passions, the love of lovers, parents, children, have been so worn down by constant analysis and introspection as to be non-existent. The atmosphere has become so artificial, partaking so little of the quality of real air, that natural healthy breathing seems almost impossible. No outdoor being could thrive where these strange people live and expand. One is conscious of the sense of oppression that broods over the fitful brilliance of the picture. . . . It is by talk alone that the book advances: talk or significant silence broken by meaning gestures, marked emphasis, ejaculations, pauses, and a hundred devices of which Mr. James is master. Sometimes the conversation is a verbal fencing match in which thrusts, retorts, and parryings have to be closely watched. A charm, sometimes a snare, of Mr. James's method is that no such thing as explanation is ever vouchsafed either by himself or his characters. You overhear and interpret as you can, but nothing is said for your benefit. Therefore the need for an intelligent attention to every shade and half-shade in intonation and manner. If you have to strain an ear for what is said, you must do it still more for what is only implied. Many people will think that for all this trouble they get no adequate return—that so much careful and long-winded suggestion overbalances the thing suggested. This feeling condemns them as those for whom Mr. James spreads the net of conversational delicacy in vain. Yet with all respect for the sustained ability, adroitness, and suppleness of diction, moments of weariness and a sense as of ineffectual striving with shadows do overcome one. The artificiality—even triviality—of some of the issues at stake strike one, more especially when the coterie plume themselves on their superior smartness and entire absence of all prejudice. So much rarefied psychology, paralysis of will, and general bloodlessness has, after a time, a stultifying effect on the mind.

134. William Morton Payne, review, *Dial*

July 1899, xxvii, 21

For Payne see above, No. 61.

If drawing-rooms were the world, and those who have their being in them the whole of mankind, one could have no reasonable ground for dissatisfaction with the novels of Mr. Henry James. We certainly do get from his books about everything, in the way of both conversation and action, that a decorous drawing-room can shelter, and we get it in such delicate forms of artistic presentation that no pretext is left us for adverse criticism. In *The Awkward Age*, for example, than which even Mr. James has produced no better book, there are nearly five hundred pages of drawing-room talk and incident, all delightfully finished and subtle, all displaying workmanship of the highest cherry-stone order, and yet we are inexpressibly wearied by it, because it has so little to do with anything that makes life really worth having, and we worry through it from a sense of duty rather than for satisfaction with its message. The outcome is naught, as far as we are able to discern, and not one acquaintance has been made with whom we would desire further commerce.

135. Unsigned review, *Bookman* (America)

July 1899, ix, 472–3

The honest reader in search of a story will stare dazedly through perhaps a third of Mr. James's new book, and then shut it with a snort. Serious readers in search of a problem will go along the road a little farther, but if they continue too long their wrath at the end will surely consume the writer. Students of character may complain that too great a burden is put on them. Indeed, every one has excellent grounds of complaint against *The Awkward Age*. The book is extraordinarily clever. Such as have some time on their hands, who are well saturated with Mr. James's later style, and have no particular expectations to be cruelly disappointed, will enjoy a large portion of it, will marvel and chuckle over many pages, and yet think after all it was hardly worth the trouble of writing. In *What Maisie Knew* he suggested the tragic circumstances surrounding a young life, with a delicacy and a restrained pathos that were admirable. In *The Two Magics* he cast off restraint and revealed depths of horror lurking under the fairest surface. His new book is also to some extent a study of degeneration, but the question is dealt with so lightly and so politely, that you are convicted of priggery if you take it seriously at all. He introduces us to a London set, lively, graceful, perfect in their wordly rôle. It would be the worst of manners to inquire whether at bottom they are very good or very bad. They talk a great deal in a language of their own that has grown out of their constant intercourse with each other. An outsider must listen hard and guess a great deal. The set contains two girls. One of them has been guarded from its influence, the other has sucked in all it had to give, and judged the result, while she was still in pinafores. If you have leisure to study the members of the set in Mr. James's fashion, helped by the example of that other outsider, Mr. Longdon—a gentleman of the old school, who comes back to London after thirty years of retirement, to watch and wonder painfully—you will own that some of them, Mitchy, the Duchess, Mrs. Brookenham, and Nanda, are marvellously worked out. But you must take time and trouble. There is no other living writer who could have written the book, who could so patiently and delicately labour to make a fine point, who could deal so sensitively with fine shades, who could analyse the slight so subtly, so wittily. There is infinite grace in the detail; and there is genuine fun in the observation. But taken as a whole, the effect is clumsy and even wearisome. There is ten times too much good stuff. He works a delicate thing to death.

136. Unsigned review, *Literary World*

July 1899, xxx, 227

Four hundred and fifty-seven pages of Henry James's analysis, intricacy, dry cleverness, and disheartening suggestiveness make a pretty big dose for one time. Such is *The Awkward Age*. To add further weight to the volume, its contents are divided into ten books and each book-dose must be swallowed conscientiously; and you will taste it all the way down. Somehow, we think that a simple, fairly tender chapter from the Bible would make the best 'chaser.'

In *The Awkward Age* we have a thoroughly disagreeable study of English society and manners; a study whose detail will occupy many, many hours of careful reading. The plot itself, a mere thread of a story, deals with a so-called love affair between a middle-aged man and the granddaughter of his early love. This elderly hero is really the only comfortable person in the book. The rest of the volume is given over to the worldliness, the selfishness, the scandals, and gossip of the numerous people who make up its world. It seems as though no word or look or act in their lives had escaped the author's attention. The critical exactness is marvelous. His observation and knowledge seem to grow keener with each new novel. But where will they end, that observation and knowledge? Will they swamp themselves finally in pessimism and unpleasantness and horrors?

Oh, Mr. Henry James, why do you write like that? You do not always put sin into life, but you drain all the blood and warmth and goodness out of people, and leave them just with their sins, their wizened skin-and-bone sins. And dry sins are such awful things. Your people are dull or evilly clever, or common, or gross, or bad. But they are not big bad. They have no irresistible impetus of temperament. They have no fanatical or even childish enthusiasms. Their sins, their faults, their mistakes imply some ghastly mental element that suggests disease rather than passion. There are exceptions to this? Yes, surely. But the exceptions have not made your style or your reputation. Is this really the way you see life?

137. From an unsigned review, *Critic*

August 1899, xxxv, 754–6

As Mr. Henry James has no rivals in his own field to overcome, he continues to surpass himself with regularity and ease. *The Awkward Age* is ahead of anything he has yet produced, for subtlety and acute insight. What Mr. James will do next is beyond conjecture, for certainly it would seem that in this particular direction he has reached the utmost limit. The book is a study of certain phases of London society to which other novelists of late years have borne awkward and incomplete testimony. What they have intimated shamefacedly, Mr. James has set forth with his customary lucidity and exhaustiveness. . . .

Given such a society as this, what part in it must the young person play? This is the question which the book proposes. Mrs. Brookenham, the daughter of a lady of the old school of so fine a type that her memory is still an inspiration to the man who had loved her in his youth, has herself a daughter, Nanda, who reproduces the wonderful grandmother, Lady Julia, exactly in her physical aspect, but, greatly to her own regret and that of Mr. Longdon, the delightful elderly gentleman who had loved Lady Julia, it is out of her power to reproduce the mind and manners of that gentlewoman. For Nanda cannot be said to have led the sheltered life. In such a house as her mother's she has been 'exposed' to all kinds of information. Although Mrs. Brookenham complains that when Nanda arrives at the age where she must positively sit in the drawing-room and meet people, the tone of the circle is thereby altered to such an extent that its converse is flat and unprofitable, none the less Nanda arrives speedily at a state of enlightenment concerning the miasms of life which is undesirable for the unformed mind. Vanderbank, whom Nanda attracts, and whom Nanda in her turn loves, considers this illumination so undesirable that he makes it the ground of declining her hand when it is offered him by Mr. Longdon, who proposes to dower the girl generously if his young friend will marry her and remove her from her mother's sphere of influence.

Nanda, who knows everything, knows this, too, and her behavior under the circumstances is so wonderful and so exquisite, yet so simple and natural, that the reader's emotions are uncomfortably stirred in her behalf. Nanda is, in fact, Mr. James's supreme creation. He has always been interested in the niceness of the nice girl, and has believed in and set forth, at great length and in many ways, her essential nobility and high-mindedness. Daisy Miller was one illustration of this, and Isabel Archer another. Fleda Vetch demonstrated the same qualities in a different way, and Maisie,—poor little Maisie,—who clung by instinct to conventions and proprieties which she had known only in their overthrow, seemed, until Nanda appeared, the most convincing proof a novelist could devise of the elemental fineness of girl-nature. But Nanda is a piece of even more absolute, more beautiful evidence. Moreover, she fixes a type and points out the course evolution must needs pursue. She, in fact, supplies the ideal of the form the Nice Girl must take in the next century if society continues to grow more lax in its manners and morals. There always have been nice girls; there will continue to be nice girls, although they may have to develop under circumstances which have hitherto been considered prohibitive. Nanda is prophecy.

On the other hand, Mr. Longdon is history. He is the best of the old school of manners as Nanda is the best of the new, and his sufferings in modern London make very clear the difference between the atmosphere of forty years ago and that of to-day. The fact that it is possible for the polite world as he knew it to have evolved into the contemporary polite world sets him doubting the foundation of things: —'The more one thinks of it,' he bemoans himself, 'the more one seems to see that society—for we're *in* society, aren't we, and that our horizon? —can never have been anything but increasingly vulgar. The point is that in the twilight of time—and I belong you see, to the twilight—it had made out much less how vulgar it *could* be. It did its best, very probably, but there were too many superstitions it had to get rid of. It has been throwing them overboard, one by one, so that now the ship sails uncommonly light. That's the way'—and the old man with his eyes on the golden distance ingeniously followed it out—'I come to feel so the lurching and pitching.'

Another question which the book raises is, What part can any distinguished soul play in such a society? There seems to be no room in it for goodness, no formula nor convention to govern the instincts of those who happen by nature to be righteous or refined. It does not provide for such freaks. The adorable Mitchy, little as he looks it, is a distinguished soul, and at the end the reader, like Mr. Longdon and

Nanda, is 'anxious about Mitchy.' He is not provided for in the scheme of things, and, when this is the case, it is only the strongest who can provide for themselves.

Mitchy, Mr. Longdon, and Nanda are delightful acquaintances, but the reader has to pay a high price for meeting them, since to do so he must also meet Mrs. Brookenham, the Duchess, Lord Petherton, Mr. Cashmore, and other odious people. There is a certain satisfaction in observing that even Mr. James's art has a limitation. Although he writes, with equal sympathy, of the righteous and the unrighteous, he simply cannot achieve a fellow-feeling for the people who ought to have right feelings, and do not. This limitation is curiously illustrated by the fact that 'Mrs. Brook' and Vanderbank are the only characters in the book which do not impress the reader as they seemed to impress their associates. Their vaunted charm is invisible. Vanderbank strikes us as a superior variety of cad, and Mrs. Brookenham's grace is never realized, and her intelligence becomes unspeakably tiresome, as misapplied intelligence usually does. There is nothing quite so stupid as cleverness gone wrong.

138. From an unsigned review, *Nation*

August 1899, lxix, 155

For a good many years Mr. James has been disembarrassing himself of the serious view, and avoiding the representation of people whose force has a physical basis sufficient to support explosive passions, violent prejudices, or moral earnestness either in the practice or the criticism of life. He has now arrived at a point of intellectual remoteness from the flesh where he regards men and women with almost as slight reference to their bodies as if he were a philosopher contending that nothing is real except what cannot be perceived by the senses. If this attitude towards his creations were only a literary device, none could be cleverer or more discreet for an author embarking on the delineation of such a coterie as that which surrounds Mrs. Brookenham. To think of these frankly inquiring minds and untrammelled spirits united with bodies would be to picture to ourselves an uncommonly bad lot, much worse than we have any right to suppose Mr. James has ever wished to introduce. Readers will so think about them in proportion to their limitations or inability to be quite content with fiction that is no grosser than psychology. . . .

As a literary performance, *The Awkward Age* is very brilliant and fascinating. All the author's seriousness is devoted to the art of expression, the perfecting of method, form, and phrase. Yet he has his defects. The people who talk so well in the free-and-easy vernacular of the English 'classes' talk too much; they have too many catch phrases, such as, 'She is of a charm,' 'You are of a splendour,' which are not English at all; frequently, in their eager chase after the real meaning of things, they become Delphic, and break into ejaculations which, however expressive to the author, leave the reader in the lurch. These defects are trifling, yet peculiarly irritating, because they show how easy it is, while polishing a manner for perfection, to get quite adrift from nature and lapse into the most artificial mannerism.

139. From an unsigned review, *Sewanee Review*

January 1900, viii, 112–3

Mr. Henry James's latest novel . . . is a striking illustration of the danger a brilliant writer runs in giving himself up too exclusively to a particular method of composition. Mr. James's fortes are psychological analysis of character and brilliant management of conversation. These are two of the prime requisites of successful modern fiction, but even modern fiction requires fair narrative ability at the hands of its writers, and Mr. James in the overcultivation of his own special gifts seems to have lost whatever gift of narrative he may have once possessed. . . . We frankly confess that the Brookenham set is too clever for us. If, to be a really fine art, conversation has to be unintelligible to an ordinary mind, and if psychological analysis has to be carried to a point of subtlety considerably beyond any attempted by Shakspere or Balzac, and if conversations and character analysis are the two poles around which the ellipse of modern fiction is to be drawn—we are willing to commend the novels of to-day to the careful attention of students of advanced mathematics, and shall content ourselves hereafter with the simple old novelists who were unsophisticated enough to write straightforward stories.

140. Desmond MacCarthy on James's isolation

[1931]

Desmond MacCarthy, from 'Henry James' in *Portraits*, 1931, 151–2 and 154.

MacCarthy (1877–1952) was a literary critic and conversationalist, especially associated with the Bloomsbury Group, and (latterly) with the *Sunday Times*. These extracts start with his first meeting with HJ.

He went on to speak of *The Awkward Age*. 'Flat' was, it appeared, too mild an expression to describe its reception, 'My books make no more sound or ripple now than if I dropped them one after the other into mud.' . . .

Hastily and emphatically I assured him that where I came from, at Cambridge, his books were very far from making no ripple in people's minds. At this he showed some pleasure; but I noticed then, as often afterwards, that he was on his guard against being gratified by appreciation from any quarter. He liked it—everybody does, but he was exceedingly sceptical about its value. I doubt if he believed that anybody thoroughly understood what, as an artist, he was after, or how skilfully he had manipulated his themes; and speaking with some confidence for the majority of his enthusiastic readers at that time, I may say he was right. . . .

But an incident comes back to me which struck me as revealing something much deeper in him than this characteristic. It occurred after a luncheon party of which he had been, as they say, 'the life.' We happened to be drinking our coffee together while the rest of the party had moved on to the verandah. 'What a charming picture they make,' he said, with his great head aslant, 'the women there with their embroidery, the . . .' There was nothing in his words, anybody might have spoken them; but in his attitude, in his voice, in his whole being at that moment, I divined such complete detachment, that I was startled into speaking out of myself: 'I can't bear to look at life like that,' I blurted out, 'I want to be in everything. Perhaps that is why I cannot *write*, it makes me feel absolutely alone. . . .' The effect of this confession upon him was instantaneous and surprising. He leant forward and grasped my arm excitedly: 'Yes, it is solitude. If it runs after you and catches you, well and good. But for heaven's sake don't run after *it*. It is absolute solitude.' And he got up hurriedly and joined the others.

141. Edmund Gosse on *The Awkward Age* and the emergence of James's 'little clan'

[1922]

Edmund Gosse, from *Aspects and Impressions*, 1922, 43–4. Gosse (1849–1928) was a friend of HJ, and an influential critic and man of letters, whose most famous work is the account of his childhood in *Father and Son* (1907). This extract is only a tiny part of a long and important reminiscence of HJ.

He came back to England and to Lamb House at the end of June, to find that his novel of *The Awkward Age*, which was just published, was being received with a little more intelligence and sympathetic comprehension than had been the habit of greeting his productions, what he haughtily, but quite justly, called 'the lurid asininity' of the Press in his regard now beginning to be sensibly affected by the loyalty of the little clan of those who saw what he was 'driving at' in the new romances, and who valued it as a pearl of price. Nevertheless, there was still enough thick-witted denunciation of his novels to fill his own 'clan' with anger, while some even of those who loved him best admitted themselves bewildered by *The Awkward Age*.

142. A. C. Benson on James's pessimistic view of English Art

[1926]

A. C. Benson, from *The Diary of Arthur Christopher Benson*, ed. Percy Lubbock, 1926, 47.

The entry is for January 1900. Benson (1862–1925) was a teacher and man of letters who, after some years at Eton became Master of Magdalene College, Cambridge in 1915. The extract is from his account of his first visit to HJ at Rye, as a young admirer.

He was full of talk, though he looked weary, often passing his hand over his eyes; but he refined and defined, was intricate, magniloquent, rhetorical, humorous, not so much like a talker, but like a writer repeating his technical processes aloud—like a savant working out a problem. He told me a long story about————, and spoke with hatred of business and the monetary side of art. He evidently thinks that art is nearly dead among English writers—no criticism, no instinct for what is good.

143. James on the condition of criticism and his own style

January 1900

HJ to Sidney Colvin, January 1900 (E. V. Lucas, op. cit., 279).
Colvin (see No. 65) had written praising HJ's article on R. L.
Stevenson in the *North American*.

. . . I left unsaid all the really critical (I mean closely analytic) things
about his talent, manner, literary idiosyncrasies, views &c.—the
things one would have liked most to say. But the conditions of space,
attention, in which any literary criticism that is not the basest hand to
mouth journalism can get itself uttered at all now, are too beggarly
for one's courage. You are quite right—wholly—about my being in
places too entortillé. I am *always* in places too entortillé— & the effort
of my scant remaining years is to make the places fewer.

144. William Rothenstein on James as Grand Old Man

[1932]

William Rothenstein, from *Men and Memories 11*, 1932, 173. The period referred to is around 1900. Rothenstein (1872–1945) was a well-known painter who became Principal of the Royal College of Art.

Henry James, massive in face and figure, slow and impressive in speech, had now become one of the great pundits, to whom ladies sat listening in adoration; pilgrimages were made to his house at Rye; his dicta, elaborate, wise and tortuous, were repeated in clubs and drawing rooms. A man must have great gifts to become a national figure; but above all others—the gift of years. If he but live long enough, bright fame will come to him, position, honours and authority. Until his sixties war may be waged against a writer or painter; once on his way to the seventies the silver trumpet sounds, and all is peace and kindness.

THE SACRED FOUNT

1901

145. From an unsigned review, *Spectator*

March 1901, lxxxvi, 318–9

Whatever view may be taken of the ethical tendency of Mr. Henry James's recent works, they are at least entitled to attention as one of the most remarkable and significant literary products of the times. In no other author of the day is there such an extraordinary disproportion between the intellectual equipment of the writer and the moral futility of the characters he undertakes to dissect or interpret. . . . Wars may come and go, new stars swim into our ken, science unfold undreamt of wonders, Socialism, industrialism, capitalism assume new and alarming aspects, but Mr. Henry James, with imperturbable aloofness, continues, with unimpaired industry and unflagging interest, to apply his microscope to the sophisticated emotions of corrupt and luxurious idlers. In the volume before us, *The Sacred Fount*, the narrator finds himself confronted, during a visit to a superbly appointed country house, with a mysterious problem. . . . The ingenuity displayed by Mr. James in pursuing this strange investigation is at times positively fabulous, but in the end it carries one no 'forrarder' than the speculations of the schoolmen as to how many angels could dance on the point of a pin. We can only express our profound regret that Mr. Henry James should continue to squander his immense talent on the study of malarial psychology.

146. Cornelia Atwood Pratt, from a review, *Critic*

April 1901, xxxviii, 368–70

The Sacred Fount is sublimated gossip. The experienced reader does not need to be told that gossip plus Henry James changes its substance and becomes incorporeal, dazzling, and, to the vulgar, impossible. Doubtless Beyond, man will gossip thus. . . .

We have all had flashes of intuition and had them confirmed by our own interpretation of subsequent events; this gives us the basis for appreciating the constructive joy of the 'conscientiously infernal' narrator who adds one subtle sign to another and 'makes out' otherwise unattested marvels with unholy glee. He is conscious by flashes, this over-curious mind, that he is something of a cad, even if his prying is on the psychical and not the material plane; he has his reluctances, his intervals of sanity, when he feels that his complicated perceptions are extravagant, that his whole idea is a ridiculous obsession, but most of the time his plunges of insight so exhilarate him as to leave no room for misgiving. He feels 'the joy of the intellectual mastery of things unamenable, the joy of determining, almost of creating, results.'

The reader too, has an obsession. It is to keep up with the storyteller, to 'make out,' to take it all in, to believe in the brain-bubble. At first this is easy and delightful, but before the end it becomes almost a nightmare. He hypnotizes himself into holding the mood of acceptance while the book lasts, but when Mrs. Brissenden says to the psychological detective on the last page, 'My poor dear, you *are* crazy!' the reader breathes a sigh of relief. He is not sure he agrees with her, but even the possibility is refreshing!

In other words, to keep up with Mr. James in this story strains even a willing intelligence to the breaking point. This is, perhaps, because the book has none of those intimate relations with the world of ethics which usually enrich by implication this writer's art. Usually he holds up the torch and illuminates the dark places of life and thought in one way or another, but *The Sacred Fount* is a pure *tour de force*. It takes away our breath with astonishment and gives us nothing in return. It is wonderful, but is it worth while?

147. Harry Thurston Peck, from a review, *Bookman* (America)

July 1901, xiii, 442

Peck (1856–1914) was the editor of this periodical and noted as a classical philologist.

Henry James is beyond all question in a bad way. He became morbid and somewhat decadent several years ago, when he wrote *What Maizie Knew* and *In the Cage;* but even so, he was interesting, and one could read him through. When he wrote *The Awkward Age* we thought that it was only a temporary lapse; but now that he has produced *The Sacred Fount* he really seems to be sinking into a chronic state of periphrastic perversity.

148. Owen Seaman's parody of *The Sacred Fount*

1902

Owen Seaman, from *Borrowed Plumes*, 1902, 133–49. This parody is one of a series on a number of subjects. Seaman (1861–1936) was a poet and Professor of English at Newcastle, who became editor of *Punch*.

It superficially might have seemed that to answer Lady Cheveley's invitation to her daughter's wedding was a matter that would put no intolerable strain upon the faculties of discriminative volition. Yet the accident of foreign travel had brought about that this formal invitation, found on my return, consituted my first advertisement of even so much as Vivien Cheveley's engagement to M. le Comte Richard Sansjambes. The original question, simplified as it was by public knowledge of the fact that I regard all ceremonial functions with a polite abhorrence, had, accordingly, taken on a new complexity, involving considerations of a high sociologic interest; as, notably, whether and, if at all, in what form, I should offer the lady my felicitations.

My obsession by these problems over a space of four-and-twenty hours was only partially relieved by contact with the *divertissements* of Piccadilly as I drove to the Prytaneum Club. To my hansom's temporary arrest, however, attributable to the stream of vehicles converging in a transverse sense at the corner of St. James's Street, I owed an interval of recrudescent deliberation. During that so tense period I conscientiously—such is the force of confirmed habit—reviewed all the permissible methods—and scarce fewer than a round dozen of variants lay at that moment in my right breast-pocket—of addressing a woman-friend on the occasion of her betrothal. Always the equivocal detachment of an unrejected bachelor had for me the air of imparting to these crises, poignant enough in themselves, a touch of invidious dilemma. The delicate question why the felicitator himself—to hypothecate his eligibility—had not been a candidate for the lady's heart, a question answerable, on the lips of her friends, by a theory of self-depreciation, and, on those of her enemies, by one of indifference, remained—unless he chose, as one says, to 'give himself away'—incapable of adequate solution.

For myself, it is true, by way of a passable solace in this cornucopious predicament, there was my known prejudice, amounting almost, I am told, to a confessed morbidity, in favour of the celibate state. It was still, however, open to the contention of malice that I, nevertheless, conceivably might have—whereas, in fact I had *not* submitted—to the lady's charms, had they—as they apparently had *not*—been of a sufficiently overwhelming nature. But this, relatively, was, after all, a trivial embarrassment, mastered, on more occasions, already, than one, by a delicate subtlety of diction, in which I permit myself to take a pardonable pride.

'My dear Miss Vivien,' I, recalling the terms of a parallel correspondence, had written, 'what brings to you, for whom I entertain a so profound regard, brings, to me also, an exquisite joy.' And, again, alternatively, and in a phraseology more instinct with poetry and pith— 'I, in your gladness, am myself glad.' And, once more, with, I confess, a greater aloofness, yet at the same time, positing, by implication, a plurality of suitors to select from:—'Quite indubitably enviable is the man on whom your choice has fallen.'

But what complicated the situation and left me hesitant between these and, roughly, some nine other openings, was the reflection that, in point of fact, I had never set eyes on the Count, not yet even heard— and with this my long absence from England must be charged—the lightest tale of him. Mightn't it be, after all, a marriage, purely, I asked myself, of convenience?—wealth, possibly, a title, certainly, exchanged for the asset of youthful bloom? Mightn't it be—and there was recorded precedent for this—that the man, being French, as one gathered, and calling himself by a foreign title—a pretension, commonly, that invited scepticism—had exerted over her some Magic, or even, taking into account both his foreignness and his Counthood, as much as Two Magics? Or, again, most deplorable of all, mightn't he have acquired a hold upon her by secret knowledge of some skeleton, as the phrase is, in her private cupboard; an intrigue, let us daringly say, with a former butler, banished for that delinquency and harbouring vengeance against her house by the revelation of her complicity?

But here I subconsciously reminded myself that the nicest adepts in abstract psychology may, if they do but sufficiently long address themselves to problems abnormally occult, become the prey of a diseased imagination. And by great good luck the forward movement of my hansom, now disembroiled from the traffic, which had thrown off something of its congestion, caused a current of air which allowed me, the glass being up, a saner purview of the question. 'When I reach the Prytaneum, I'll,' I said, 'look the gentleman up in the *Almanach de Gotha*.' This, in fact, had been among the motives, had been, I might even say, the dominating motive, of my visit to the Club.

That atmosphere of considered serenity which meets one at the very portals of the Prytaneum, and is of an efficacy so paramount for the allaying of neurotic disorders, had already relieved the tension of my introspective mood by the time that I had entered the *fumoir* and rung for cigarettes and mineral water. The greeting, familiarly curt, that reached me from an armchair near the fire, was traceable, it appeared, to Guy Mallaby. Here, I was glad to think, I had found a living supplement to the *Almanach*, for I remembered him to have been a friend, some had even said a blighted admirer, of Vivien Cheveley. He had married, whether for consolation or from pique, his cook; and I now noticed, in a glance that embraced him cursorily, that his girth had, since his marriage, increased by some four to six inches.

It could scarce be more than a rude estimate, viewing the fact that I had no tape-measure about me, an adjunct that I from time to time have found serviceable in cases that, apparently, called for mere psychologic diagnosis; nor, had I so had, am I convinced that I should, in this instance, have allowed myself the application of it. Simply I moved towards him, and, at the same time, yielding to the usage which a twelve-months absence requires, held out my hand. He took it with, as I thought, a certain surprise, quickly dissembled, but not, as I repeat, before I'd mentally remarked it.

At any other juncture I should have been closely tempted to pursue the train of inference suggested by this phenomenon; but just then, for the moment, I was preoccupied. Besides, anyhow, his initial observation proved his astonishment to be derived from a quite transparent, if not altogether venial, cause. 'Been out of town,' he asked, 'for Christmas?' I confess that, though I had the good breeding not to betray it, this speech, the tone of which, under ordinary conditions, would not have affected me to the point of regarding it as a truancy beyond the prescribed bounds of gentlemanly casualness, caused me, having regard to the circumstance of my long absence a, calculable pain in my *amour propre*. Never so vividly had not merely the complexity, almost cosmic, of life in the Metropolis, its multiform interests and issues so exigently

The Sacred Fount

absorbing, but also the inconspicuousness of the vacuum created by the withdrawal of any single—in this case my own—personality, been forced upon my attention.

Here, again, at any other time, I should have found abundant matter for analysis; but the entrance of the waiter with my cigarettes and mineral water, one of the former of which I deliberately lighted, recalled me from this inviting diversion. By a natural process of reaction I become cognisant of the necessity, every moment more pressing, of composing an answer to Mallaby's question.

Scarce anything could have been easier than so to impregnate my reply with the truth, whole and unadulterated, as to compel, on his side, an embarrassment which I, for one, should have viewed, in the retrospect, as regrettable. Yet, for a full three-quarters of a minute, towards the latter half of which period it was evident that Mallaby conceived my memory to have strangely lapsed, the temptation possessed me to follow the course I have just indicated. But, in the issue—whether more from a desire to spare his feelings, or, at least as much, because the practice of *finesse*, even in conjunctions of negligible import, has had for me always a conquering fascination, I cannot determine—I, with a terseness sufficiently antiphonal to his own, replied:—'Yes. Monte Carlo.'

Then, from an apprehension that he might follow up his enquiries—for my travels had, in actual fact, been confined to Central Asia and the transit there and in an opposite sense—or invite a reciprocal curiosity, on my part, in regard to *his* Christmas, 'By the way,' I, as if by a natural continuity of thought, added, 'who is this Count Richard Sansjambes that is to marry Miss Cheveley?' At the same time, not to appear too intrigued by the matter in question, I withdrew my cigarette from my mouth, flicked it lightly in air, and then abstractedly replaced it, less the ash.

I'd scarce done asking myself whether I'd formulated my enquiry into the identity of this Sansjambes with an air of sufficient detachment, or, in default of this, had so clearly underlined the suggestion of indifference by my manner of manipulating my cigarette as to assure myself against the possible suspicion, easily avoidable, I had hoped, of a too immediately concerned curiosity, when 'Ah! the fellow without legs!' replied Mallaby, with, as it, perhaps unwarrantably, seemed to me, a levity so flippant that it might have appalled a controversialist less seasoned by practice than I'd the permissible satisfaction of crediting myself with the reputation of being.

'But you have not then lost it?' I threw off, on a note of implicit irony.

'Lost what?' he asked.

'Your old facility, of course, in *jeux d'esprit*,' I explained.

'On the contrary,' he replied, 'my translation of Sansjambes is not more literal than the facts themselves!'

His answer was so quite what I had not foreseen, that I was surprised, as by a sudden reflex jerk of the muscles, into an unwonted lucidity of diction.

'How did he lose them?' I asked.

'He didn't; he never had any to lose!' Mallaby, with unnecessary brutality, replied.

'An early ancestor lost *his* under the walls of Acre. Pre-natal influences affected his first-born, and ever since then the family has had no legs in the direct line.'

'But the title?'—I was still too altogether the sport of surexcitation nicely to weigh my words.

'The gallant ancestor's own choice—prior, naturally, to the birth of his heir—to perpetuate the deed of prowess that won it. And his descendants take it on as a matter of pride.'

By this I'd sufficiently recovered my habitual *aplomb* to be in a position, while reserving my perfected conclusions for a less disturbing occasion, to collate, as I sipped my drink, a few notes on the comparative periods of sustained effervescence in the cases, respectively, of Seltzer and Salutaris.

'And the cause you assign to this projected marriage?' I then, less with a desire for enlightenment, asked, than, my own judgment being made up to the point of finality, to seem to flatter him by an appeal to *his*.

'Oh, there's money, of course,' he answered. 'But that isn't all. It's the old tale—Eve, apple, curiosity, with a touch of the brute thrown in!'

You could have knocked me down, in the vulgar phrase, with a feather. Here was Guy Mallaby, immeasurably my unequal in fineness of spirit, laying his fat finger plumb on the open offence, while I was still complacently nosing it on a false scent of Womanly Pity. True, he had enjoyed a three-months start of me in the running down of a mystery that doubled too distractingly on its traces for that instinctive *flair* to which I hitherto had urged a predominant claim; or was it the cook-wife that had piqued, through the stomach's Sacred Fount, his intellectual appetite? Gratuitiously to admit him my superior on the strength of a forestalled judgment was the last of a quite surprising number of alternatives that just then occurred to me.

'I'm going to look in on Lady Jane,' I made evasion.

'She'll, if she's honest, endorse my conjecture; she's a woman!' he, without hesitation, observed.

More interestingly stimulated than I could, at the moment, remember to have been by any previous visit to the Prytaneum, I made my way westward down the Mall of St. James's Park, taking the broad boulevard on the left. In the particular atmosphere of exaltation by which I perceived myself to be environed, it was easy to image these widowed avenues in their midsummer fulness, to revive their inarticulate romance, to restore, in the grand style, the pomp of their verdurous pageantry. Oh, there was quite enough of analogy to reclothe a whole Arden of *As you like it*! It was really portentous on what a vista of alluring speculations I'd all but originally stumbled; virgin forest, in fact, before the temerity of just one pioneer, and that a woman, had stripped it this very summer so pitilessly bare. With how fine an abstraction from the moralities I'd, in the way of pure analysis, have probed its fungus-roots, have dissected its saffron-bellied toads, have sampled its ambiguous spices. And to have utilised a legless abortion for the genius of its undergrowths!

But I soon became aware of an appreciable recoil from the initial acerbity of my self-reproach at being anticipated by the author of *Sir Richard Calmady*, when, upon a more meticulous reflection—for, by this time, I'd arrived opposite the footpath leading over the bridge that commands the lake and its collection, recognisably unique, of water-fowl—I'd convinced myself how little of consonance was to be found between this theme and the general trend of my predilections. About the loves of a so ineffable prodigy—and to differentiate them as lawful or lawless didn't, for me, modify the fact of their uniform repulsiveness—I detected a quality something too preposterously flagrant, an element *un peu trop criant* of pungent indelicacy. It needed only this flash of recognition at once to disabuse me of all regret for having been forestalled in the treatment of a subject of which the narrow scope if offered for the play of hypersensitised subtlety remained the incurably fatal defect.

So immediate, indeed, and so absolute was my mental recovery that I had scarce cleared the façade of Buckingham Palace and addressed myself to what I have, from time to time, regarded as the almost contemptibly easy ascent of Constitution Hill, before I had in mind to rush to the opposite extreme, totally, in fact, to disregard the relation of legs to the question at issue. I won't I said, allow the hereditary absence of this feature from the Count's *ensemble* to prejudice, one way or another, the solution, which I hope ultimately to achieve, of the original problem, namely, should I, or shouldn't I, offer my congratulations to Vivien Cheveley? and that second problem, subordinately associated with the first, namely, what form, if any, should those congratulations assume?

But I was instantly to perceive the superprecipitancy of my revulsion. It imposed itself, and with a clarity past all possible ignoring, that in this matter of the Count's legs the introduction of a new element—or, to be accurate, the withdrawal of an old one so usual as to have been carelessly assumed—was bound, whatever dissimulation was attempted, to command notice. The gentleman's lower limbs were, to an undeniably overwhelming degree, conspicuous, as the phrase runs, by their absence. A fresh condition, as unique as it was unforeseen, had, with a disturbing vitality, invaded what had given promise, in the now remote outset, of being an argument on merely abstract and impersonal lines. For, even if one postulated in the bride the delicatest of motives, a passion, let us assume, to repair a defect of Nature, as much as to say, figuratively, 'You that are blind shall see through my eyes,' or, more literally, 'You having no legs to speak of, are to find in me a vicarious locomotion,' even so a sensitive creature might wince at the suspicion that the language of congratulation was but a stammering tribute to the quality, in *her*, of inscrutable heroism.

And there was still an equal apprehension to deplore, should it appear that it was to an artistic faculty, on the lady's part, capable, imaginatively, of reconstructing, from the fragmentary outlines of his descendant, the originally unimpaired completeness of the gallant ancestor—much as the old moon shows dimly perfect in the hollow of the young crescent—that the Count owed his acceptability in her eyes.

'There it is!' I said, and at the same moment inadvertently grasped the extended hand of a constable at the corner of Hamilton Place; 'there's no escaping from the obsession of this inexorable fact. It colours the whole abstract problem only a little less irritatingly than, I can well believe, it has coloured the poor Count's existence.' And I'd scarce so much as *begun* to exhaust the possible bearings of the case in their absorbing relation to simply *me*, as distinct from the parties more deeply committed and so, presumably, exposed to the impact of yet other considerations.

For, what lent a further complexity to the situation was that, even to suppose me arrived at the conclusion, effectively supported, that *her* motive for this so painfully truncated alliance was commendable, it still left her the liberty, accentuated by the conditions at which I have glanced, to misinterpret *mine* in congratulating her upon it. And if, on the other hand, her engagement were attributable to unworthy or frivolous causes, wouldn't the consciousness of this, on *her* side, give even stronger countenance to a suspicion of mere impertinence on *mine*?

That her motive indeed had been no better than one of curiosity— mother Eve's, in fact, for exploring the apple-tree—was the contention of Mallaby, and by him expressed with so resolved an assurance that it had, as I only now remembered, won me over, at the time, by its convincing probability. Hadn't his confidence even gone the length of claiming Lady Jane as of the same camp? And this recalled for me, what I had temporarily ignored in the so conflicting rush of ideas, the primary objective of my present discursion. I'd overlooked the bifurcation of ways where the traverse to South Audley Street leads in the direction of Lady Jane's house; and now was poising irresolutely before crossing at the convergence of Upper Brook Street and Park Lane.

But after all, I asked myself, was a woman's final word really just the thing I stood in dearest need of in so nice a hesitancy? If *I* was conscious of a certain strain in seeking to confine this incident of freakish abbreviation to its properly obscure place in the picture, would not *she*, with all her sex's reluctance to attack any question from an abstract standpoint, experience an insuperable difficulty in assigning to the Count's deficiency its relative 'value'? And mightn't I, in a moment of unguarded gallantry, of simulated deference, let me put it, to her (Lady Jane's) assumption of a larger knowledge of women, or, say, simply a more profound intimacy with the particular woman, be carried away, against what I foresaw, even at this incipient stage of my reflections, would, in the event, turn out to be my better judgment, on a veritable whirl of grossly material considerations? At worst, after all, there's still, I said, the last resort of an answer in the third person, declining the wedding invitation on a plea, strictly untrue, of an earlier engagement. Meantime, while so many hitherto unregarded aspects of the matter called on my intelligence for their dues, the fabric of my problem was, I told myself, of a delicacy too exquisite for——

[*Left reflecting on kerbstone.*

THE WINGS OF THE DOVE

1902

149. William James on the perverse success of *The Wings of the Dove*

WJ to HJ, October 1902 (JF, 338).

I have read *The Wings of the Dove* (for which all thanks!) but what shall I say of a book constructed on a method which so belies everything that *I* acknowledge as law? You've reversed every traditional canon of story-telling (especially the fundamental one of *telling* the story, which you carefully avoid) and have created a new *genre littéraire* which I can't help thinking perverse, but in which you nevertheless *succeed* for I read with interest to the end (many pages, and innumerable sentences twice over to see what the dickens they could possibly mean) and all with unflagging curiosity to know what the upshot might become. It's very *distingué* in its way, there are touches unique and inimitable, but it's a 'rum' way; and the worst of it is that I don't know whether it's fatal and inevitable with you, or deliberate and possible to put off and on. At any rate it is your own, and no one can drive you out or supplant you, so pray send along everything else you do, whether in this line or not, and it will add great solace to our lives.

'In its way' the book is most *beautiful*—the great thing is the way —I went fizzling about concerning it, and expressing my wonder all the while I was reading it.

150. James on the inevitability of his later style

1902

HJ to WJ, November 1902 (JF, 338). A reply to No. 149.

Your reflections on *The Wings of the Dove* greatly interest me. Yet, after all, I don't know that I can very explicitly *meet* them. Or rather, really, there is too much to say. One writes as one *can*—and also as one sees, judges, feels, thinks, and I feel and think so much on the ignoble state to which in this age of every cheapness I see the novel as a form, reduced, that there is doubtless greatly, with me, the element of what I would as well as of what I 'can'. At any rate my stuff, such as it is, is inevitable for me. Of that there is no doubt. But I should think you might well fail of joy in it—for I certainly feel that it is, in its way, more and more positive. Don't despair, however, even yet, for I feel that in its way, as I say, there may be still other variations of way that will more or less *donner le change*.

151. Unsigned review,
Times Literary Supplement

September 1902, 263

'H. Seton Merriman' was the pseudonym of Hugh Stowell Scott
(1862–1903), a popular novelist of adventure. Hall Caine (1853–
1931) and 'Marie Corelli' (pseudonym of Mary Mackay 1855–
1924) were also, of course, among the best-selling novelists of
their day.

Mr. Henry James is to be congratulated. It is a long time since modern
English fiction has presented us with a book which is so essentially a
book; a thing, conceived, and carried on, and finished in one pre-
meditated strain; with unbroken literary purpose and serious, unflagging
literary skill. *The Wings of the Dove* is an extraordinarily interesting
performance. We know nothing of Mr. James's to compare with it in
fulness of intention, and close, rich, elaborate workmanship but the
Tragic Muse and, possibly, *Roderick Hudson*; and in neither of these
works do we find the same element of grave and penetrating tenderness.
Mr. James's methods of minute, qualifying, cumulative detail have not
altered; but he has added to them. There is a new, a humanizing, note
in his long portrait–study of Milly Theale, the stricken little 'princess'
from New York, 'with her frankness, sweetness, sadness, brightness, her
disconcerting poetry.' 'For Milly was indeed a dove . . . with that
element of wealth in her which was a power, which was a great power,
and which was dove-like only so far as one remembered that doves
have wings and wondrous flights, have them as well as tender tints
and soft sounds.'
　　This is, we repeat, an extraordinarily interesting performance, but
it is not an easy book to read. It will not do for short railway journeys
or for drowsy hammocks, or even to amuse sporting men and the
active Young Person. The dense, fine quality of its pages—and there
are 576—will always presuppose a certain effort of attention on the
part of the reader; who must, indeed, be prepared to forgo many of his
customary titillations and bribes. Mr. James's novels are often accused

of lacking the supreme authority of an overwhelming emotion. But they are not alone in that. And what the average reader misses in them is far more a familiarity, a sense of good-fellowship, and a common attitude towards life. For Mr. James, so to speak, never button-holes his public; he does not even take it by the arm. There is something of the classic in his sense of aloofness, his detachment from his reader; and the pampered modern reader is apt to call the attitude inhuman. As a matter of fact it is not the illusion of Life, it is the illusion of Art which Mr. James sets before us. And that is why a book like *The Wings of the Dove* does not make so much for obvious pleasure as for a sort of deep and increasing satisfaction in its admirable workmanship; in its sense of atmosphere, its sense of character, its humour, its ingenuity of epithet, its untiring discriminating curiosity about life. From first to last every impression, even the facts about the 'situations,' reach us by a series of reflections and complicated counter-reflections a set of polished mirrors, as it were, reflecting other mirrors. The *scènes à faire* take place off the stage; and it is by reverberation, by allusion, by inference, that we are gradually drawn into the circle of what is, first and last, an elaborated work of art.

It is idle—it shows stupidity—to resent any artistic method which ultimately reaches its goal; and to enjoy Mr. James the reader must quite simply be ready to meet him half-way; to place himself at the writer's point of view, and frankly to accept his stipulations. As a matter of fact, this is the essential condition which every literary artist exacts. It is only the journalist who yields everything; who makes things easy, and amuses and excites us with an acute eye for ever fixed upon our line of least resistance. And it is precisely the contrast between this friendly familiar aspect of the mass of modern fiction (since the journalistic attitude of mind, after all, does not necessarily imply the newspaper)—it is the sharp contrast between this and Mr. James's habitual air of making no personal claim, of leaving the subject under discussion to the reader's intelligence without disconcerting appeals to his emotion—which makes a novel like *The Wings of the Dove* so significant and so distinct.

Take, for an example—and we select it at random—these few lines from a popular new book (which we notice below):

A muddy sea and a dirty grey sky, a cold rain and a moaning wind. Short capped waves breaking to leeward in a little hiss of spray. The water itself sandy and discoloured. Far away to east, where the green-grey and the dirty grey merge into one, a windmill spinning in the breeze; Holland.

That is Mr. Seton Merriman; and no one can deny that the impression is vivid and just; the words effective in their deliberate baldness. Then compare this description of a Venetian palace, where

The warmth of the southern summer was still in the high, florid rooms, palatial chambers where hard, cool pavements took reflections in their lifelong polish, and where the sun on the stirred sea-water, flickering up through open windows, played over the painted 'subjects' in the splendid ceilings—medallions of purple and brown, of brave, old, melancholy colour, medals as of old reddened gold, embossed and beribboned, all toned with time and all flourished and scolloped and gilded about, set in their great moulded and figured concavity (a nest of white cherubs, friendly creatures of the air) . . . which did everything to make of the place an apartment of state.

Each of these descriptions is the description of a realist—and they seem extreme examples of two opposing schools. But the truth is, one represents the realism of impression and the other the realism of association. They stand to each other as a cleverly chosen photograph to the precise and suggestive line-drawing of an old Master—and indeed the multitudinous careful outlines of figures and places in *The Wings of the Dove* often remind us of a collection of such drawings. We imagine a whole series of them, spread out before us, under glass, in the clear tempered light of some Italian gallery. Here is no popular urgency of colour; the work only charms and rewards the trained and loving eye. It is hardly a place for the crowd—who while we are about it may well be imagined as gathered together in the courtyard below shouting to the inspiriting strains of Mr. Hall Caine's vigorous brass band, or listening to Miss Corelli's surprising soprano up-raised in modern oratorio—the place is not perhaps crowded, but surely it is one of the qualities of all finer work that it can afford to be itself and wait.

152. From an unsigned review, *Saturday*

January 1903, xcv, 79–80

. . . after grappling—we venture to say sturdily—with Kate, Milly,
Susan, Mrs. Lowder, Densher and the rest, we confess our utter failure
to hold them, with any interest, for five consecutive minutes. George
Meredith at his most perverse is not more difficult to read. These
people are not merely colourless, nerveless and will-less, allowing themselves to be swayed in the most arbitrary manner by a perpetual rippling
stream of inconsequential and trifling feelings that it is inconceivable
should affect for a moment any human being—they are something more
and less than that: they are abstractions of abstractions, shadows of
shadows. No motive seems adequately to account for their actions; so
intangible are they that, to speak paradoxically, no motive could
possibly account for their actions. We say 'to speak paradoxically'
because of course it is the weakness of the motives that makes the people
intangible and their alleged actions so arbitrary, haphazard. Their
speech makes them no more solid. . . . The book consists of 576
closely printed pages. We were curious to know the average number of
dashes, commas and semi-colons on a page; and we found the calculation entirely beyond our powers. Suffice it to say it is enormous; and
most of these interruptions serve no purpose save that of making the
reading more difficult. The effect is irritating: what might have been
clean prose is broken, finicked, piffled away. Yet we see plainly enough
that such lame writing is essential to the effect Mr. James wished to get.
He wanted to make us feel all those artificial, subtle, trifling or meaningless changes of mood; and the more he makes us feel them the more
artificial, trifling, meaningless we find them, and the less inclined we are
to read on. We even suggest that the achievement of such a prose has
become with Mr. James somewhat of an end in itself. The incessant 'perhaps'-es, and 'consciousnesses of something deeper still', and
'clearly, as yet, seeing nothing'—these not only give that effect of
blurred vision and lack of definite intention, but weave into a word-
tissue which Mr. James seems to like and which we heartily dislike. It
is a word-tissue that hides the author's thought—that gives one a sense
of his reserve, aloofness. There is no energy, passion, colour, and

because there is no motion, there is no rhythm in this prose. The prose becomes as trivial as the trivial moods aroused by trivial middle-class things it is meant to express; and not from Mr. Henry James nor another do we require 576 pages of such prose fine-spun out with such an object.

After all, this kind of writing, crabbed, finicking, tedious in its struggle to be exact, intolerable when it tries, so to say, to be exact about nothing, marks a strong reaction against the kind that prevailed until twenty years ago or even later.

153. James on Howells's praise for *The Wings of the Dove*, on his indifference to the public, and on *The Sacred Fount*

1902

HJ to Howells, December 1902 (LJ, i, 415-7).
Unfortunately Howells's letter does not, so far as I know, survive.

Nothing more delightful, or that has touched me more closely even to the spring of tears, has befallen me for years, literally, than to receive your beautiful letter of Nov. 30th, so largely and liberally anent *The W. of the D.* Every word of it goes to my heart and to 'thank' you for it seems a mere grimace. The same post brought me a letter from dear John Hay, so that my measure has been full. I haven't known anything about the American 'notices,' heaven save the mark! any more than about those here (which I am told, however, have been remarkably genial;) so that I have *not* had the sense of confrontation with a public more than usually childish—I mean had it in any special way. I confess, however, that that is my chronic sense—the more than usual childishness of publics: and it is (has been,) in my mind, long since discounted, and my work definitely insists upon being independent of such phantasms and on unfolding itself wholly from its own 'innards.' Of course, in our conditions, doing anything decent is pure disinterested, unsupported, unrewarded heroism; but that's the day's work. The *faculty of attention* has utterly vanished from the general anglo-saxon mind, extinguished at its source by the big blatant *Bayadère* of Journalism, of the newspaper and the *picture* (above all) magazine; who keeps screaming 'Look at *me. I* am the thing, and I only, the thing that will keep you in relation with me *all the time* without your having to attend *one minute* of the time.' If you are moved to write anything anywhere about the *W. of the D.* do say something of that—it so awfully wants saying. But we live in a lovely age for literature or for any art but the mere visual. Illustrations, loud simplifications and *grossissements*, the big building . . . the 'mounted' play, the prose that is careful to be in the tone of, and with the distinction of, a newspaper or bill-poster advertisement—these, and these only, meseems, 'stand a chance.' But why do I talk of such chances? I am melted at your reading *en famille* *The Sacred Fount*, which you will, I fear, have found chaff in the mouth and which is one of several things of mine, in these last years, that have paid the penalty of having been conceived only as the 'short story' that (alone, apparently) I could hope to work off somewhere (which I mainly failed of,) and then *grew* by a rank force of its own into something of which the idea had, modestly, never been to be a book. That is essentially the case with the *S.F.*, planned, like *The Spoils of Poynton*, *What Maisie Knew*, 'The Turn of the Screw', and various others, as a story of the '8 to 10 thousand words'!! and then having accepted its bookish necessity or destiny in consequence of becoming already, at the start, 20,000, accepted it ruefully and blushingly, moreover, since, *given the tenuity of the idea*, the larger quantity of treatment hadn't been aimed at. I remember how I would have 'chucked' *The Sacred Fount* at the 15th thousand word, if in the first place I could have afforded to 'waste' 15,000, and if in the second I were not always ridden by a superstitious terror of not finishing, for finishing's and for the precedent's sake, what I have begun. I am a fair coward about *dropping*, and the book in question, I fear, is, more than anything else, a monument to that superstition.

154. J. P. Mowbray on *The Wings of the Dove*, and James's effeminacy

1902

J. P. Mowbray, from 'The Apotheosis of Henry James', *Critic*, November 1902, xli, 409–14.

Mr. Henry James's latest book may easily wear the distinction of being more so than any that preceded it. We adjudge it to be the logical ultimate of that specialization of talent to which he has so persistently devoted himself. In this sense if in no other it is consistent and is obedient to the laws of development. To have written any other kind of book would have disturbed our faith in the inevitableness of evolution. It may therefore be said that in *The Wings of the Dove* Mr. James, without allowing anybody else to arrive, has come to his own, and those of us who for years watched him with genuine admiration, must concede that in loyal obedience to an early determination of talents he has now successfully lost himself in the ultimate azure of himself.

We recall with a pensive memory that in every new flight he required of us larger instruments of observation, not that the field of vision grew larger, but that the terrestrial light grew less. We were not so ill-advised in sidereal remoteness as not to know that the blazing sun which, in its recessions, takes on to our vision the diminished importance of an asteroid, may still be a blazing sun to other systems. What chiefly concerned us was the growing unimportance of it to our system.

The orbit of Mr. James's endowment always promised an occultation. It was from the start predicable that if he held blazingly to his course the early light would get beyond even the reach of the Lick Observatory.

Out of sincere respect for receding if not for departed worth we have called this an apotheosis. We hold resolutely to the belief that there are systems somewhere to which Mr. James is an undiminished sun. But they are not ours.

If this similitude appears to be forced, in view of the fact that Mr. James had less to do with the starry realities of an upper world than any writer of the Victorian age, we may be permitted to drop the figure of a flight and come squarely down to a fashioning. If Mr. James has achieved indefiniteness it is not owing to the square of the distance but to the yards of fine-spun literary integument with which he has enswathed himself.

What criticism has to say of him, when it applies the comparative method, must be more or less deferential and acknowledge at once that there is not less imagination in his last book than in his first—indeed, it goes without saying that there could not be less—but there is more of Mr. Henry James, which, perhaps, is equivalent to saying that the feat of writing the last book—to use one of his own felicities —'throws a harmonizing blur' over the inadequacy of that which is written about.

Time was when this gifted author was content to keep his rare personality in leash while his personages were talking. With a young discretion which he has now outgrown, he suffered himself at times to peep and mutter most charmingly, always intimating that there were other depths that he could let us into were he so inclined, and as he was not wholly inclined, we forgave him. But now we must confess to some astonishment at a finite omnipresence that insists upon filling the stage, and not only pouring its asides into every ear but demands that every mortal soul of them shall use his patois and adopt his idiosyncrasies and carry his broken candy in its mouth not only to the utter discomfiture of differences but to the unique accomplishment of an edulcorated uniformity.

We enter upon what purports to be an ideal path, only to meet the accomplished fixity of Mr. James. We cannot well get on for the cunning barricades of him. When we would saunter through his meads of asphodel they are tunnelled with subways of Mr. James. He is continually present suggesting deeper and more perplexing chasms of Henry James. It does not seem to occur to him that in an urgent hour like this there is a much more expeditious and merciful way of accomplishing his purpose than in writing a two-volume novel,—and it is to present his photographs to the ravening multitude and let them figure out the two volumes for themselves and go their ways.

If we look back to the earlier and deeper impressions which Mr. Henry James made upon us when he had not wholly lost the naïveté of objective existence, we shall, perhaps, find lurking there a slightly grave fear that Mr. Henry James stood in some danger of mistaking Mr. Henry James for Life itself and was in a fair way of falling into the belief that saying things out of himself must in time, by mere nimbleness of utterance, come to take the place of things themselves.

One, of course, dislikes to refer to this now, because it gives one a rather preposterous air of prophecy, seeing that *The Wings of the Dove* are spread before us, and yet, here is Mr. Henry James taking 768 pages to say things and provoking his admirers to ask—not indeed if it were worth while to take two volumes to say these things—but was it worth while to say them at all. As persistent admirers, clinging still to him through all the progressive convolutions of his introspective genius, we cannot help feeling that it is somewhat unkind to sweat our appreciation to the utmost and tax our endurance on his decorated treadmill because he insists that it is a chariot.

In *The Wings of the Dove* a story is assumed, but the assumption requires a strong effort of faith. The ordinary and necessitous ongoing of events and the unfolding of character in action which we naturally include in the invitation of the book, meet continually with the obstructing laboratory of the chemical Mr. James, joyously intent not on getting on, but on demonstrating to us the infinite divisibility of literary matter. We cling resolutely to the faith that there *is* a story stalled somewhere in the labyrinth of Mr. James's bottles and pumps, and that it would lumber on somehow if he would only consent to stop pumping and move a little out of the way. But that he never does. How indeed can he, when he is himself the story and has come to believe that the constructive or co-ordinating ability to deal with material is of less account than the exhibition of a superb dexterity in keeping the material in the air. . . .

It is not within our jurisdiction to shut Mr. James out of the domain of Art, for there is an art of carving cherry-stones and making a pudding in a hat, no less than an art which 'carries on the dream of God' and breathes the breath of life into the dust of romance so that the children of the parturient imagination live and move and have their being among the populations of the finite mind as the sons of men have inhabited the zones of the earth. But it does seem to be within our privilege to say that the perfection to which Mr. James has now brought his method is beyond all endurance wearisome to the ordinary sanity of serious minds which have by actual contact with life itself learned humbly to estimate its invincible scale of values, and such a result presents a question of the kind of art and the use that is made of it. It is not its deficiency, but its superabundance that weighs upon us. To go no deeper than this the reader of *The Wings of the Dove* will, we think, suffer from a surfeit of Mr. James.

That he was free to detach himself from the complex which we call life and make a domain of his own and live and breathe in it, no one can dispute, but when he asks us to follow him, the question of art must give way to one of oxygen. We are quite willing to admit that it is a remarkable feat of disembodiment to live and flourish in so thin an atmosphere, but when it comes to living in it ourselves, art will not take the place of lungs.

To have lived with him even for twenty-four hours as we have done, not from any irresistible impulse of our own, but in obedience to the request of the editor of this magazine, invests us with a duty if not with a distinction that is unique. There are few persons, we cannot help feeling, who will undertake the flight without the extra wings which the editor has furnished, and coming back to the objective world, we shall be pardoned if we feel like the resuscitated man who, after being rolled on a barrel, is expected to reveal something of the mysterious midway between this and another state of existence. Nor is the analogy extravagant, for we have lived during those twenty-four hours in a domain peopled only by shades and ruffled only by the see-saw of Mr. James's subtlety. What they were all up to we could by no means make out. They seemed to be mainly intent on analyzing each other. Existence, such as our environment had emphasized it, had ceased. All the larger springs of action; those grandiose rhythms of propulsion and attraction; the centrifugal and centripetal swing of primal forces; the majestic tropical movements of passion; the pressure of inheritance and of duty—all were stopped in a pallid inquisitorial equilibrium.

And all this is very unlike that equally mysterious and far more beautiful borderland which, thanks to the creative imagination of literature, we always have with us. In this field of life, vexed with storm as well as garlanded with beauty, genius has most triumphantly walked in imitation of the archaic Father Who took the cool of the day for it and Who, seeing that His work, once having the inspiration, moved and acted and aspired and struggled—pronounced it good.

To that old legend the finite creations of imitative man are arbitrarily and benignly held. He must inspire the dust of his material and the inbreathing of the procreant flame must people the pages. No device of art can make a continual outpulling serve as a substitute.

In any examination of genius itself that is dealing potentially with the elements of humanity, it seems in its best estate to have moments when it is no longer compelling, but is compelled. The mute stuff of story, co-ordinated after the fashion of the divine original, but with much travail, must somewhere in the awakening take on the free will of finite creatures and begin to move with the impulses or the projection of its inheritance, its appetences, and its destiny. How else can it be life than by carrying in some measure in its system the energizing predisposition and the divine restrictions which turn life into stress and both punish and crown it?

This is the true test of Mr. James's progeny. Do they indeed live and move and have their being? Nothing can be more beautiful or more wondrous in the experience of literary genius than that first throb of independence in his assembled vessels of clay. They begin to palpitate and assert themselves in obedience to the foreordained canons of creation which he has summoned. After that, development takes the place of fiat. He can no longer ordain, only gently guide, and the great masters of literature have thus been surprised in their work by the fact so beautifully expressed long ago, that a little child shall lead them.

The free movement of duly commissioned human souls is no longer enjoyable in the personages who try to people Mr. James's pages. We miss not only the complexity but the determinism of actual existence—two essentials which invariably furnish for us in all romantic literature the conflict and the web of interest. So completely are results submerged in processes that we are sensible of a continual protest that this is not life but a hypothesis of life formulated and worked independently of the thing itself to no end, so that what should be vitality is content to be vivisection and a continual flourish of tools.

That which assumes to be psychologic wears a phraseologic stress. Its constant dependence upon arbitrary forms robs it of that naïve honesty which is always its own best simplicity. Nor is the shade of thought when finally balanced adverbially between colons, determinative of character or indicative of purpose. It seems always to accomplish its end in behavior.

Our author has thus reached a perfection of diction which exacts something of his own athleticism from the reader, who is compelled to leap the five-barred gates of his parentheses at every turn if he would keep him in sight. And yet, notwithstanding all this show of dexterity in arbitrary appliances, so averse is the author to action in what after all should be the real movement of things, that the predicates of his sentences hang fire as if ashamed of themselves, and conclusions run up against dashes and breaks as if our perplexity could by any means take the place of his deliverance. His generous belief that his reader is gifted not only with his agility but with a supernatural acumen to discover what he means without his saying it, is not as preposterous as his confidence that the reader will understand it when he does say it, and both these amiable qualities of the author sink into insignificance by the side of the superhuman faith that the reader will think it worth saying when he has said it. He is so apprehensive when dealing with one shade of thought or emotion that there may be other subshades that he will miss and that he must clutch as he passes, that he frequently produces the effect of a painting niggled and teased out of all frankness by manipulation, and this, as we have already said, belongs as a method rather to chemistry than to art and takes us back as far as Hahnemann, who, if we mistake not, had a theory that there was potency in pounding. But it must be said at the same time that Mr. James's style is in great measure the result of his indiscreet admirers' praise, for they have held him and incited him to a purely decorative endeavor, applying constantly to his work the criteria by which they judged work in another field of art, thus convincing him that the meaning is of less account in literature as well as in painting than the treatment. Here we suspect is to be found the determining mistake of Mr. James. It is that he is trying to make articulate speech, which deals primarily with ideas, follow the æsthetic laws of beauty in the treatment of tone and color, which do not and cannot deal with definite concepts at all. . . .

In trying to form anything like a comprehensive estimate of Mr. James's mature work, the effeminacy of it has to be counted with. One cannot call it virile, and—with the best examples still with us—hardly Saxon. In the selection of theme he appears to turn instinctively to the boudoir side of life, and to give himself, with a perspicacity and a zest that have been held to be characteristic of the other sex, to the intricacies of match-making and the silken embroideries of scheming dowagers and tender protégés. If there is any finesse or delicacy in the treatment, the merit we suspect is owing to the indisposition of a mind to contemplate more rugged aspects of humanity and content to loiter with a strange industry amid the foibles and fashions of mere intellectual coquetry.

Harriet Waters Preston, from an article, *Atlantic*, January 1903,
xci, 77–82.
Harriet Waters Preston (1836–1911) was noted as a translator of
Roman and Provençal poetry, and had reviewed HJ over some
years. Her disillusioned article is about Howells's *The Kentons* as
well as *The Wings of the Dove*.

Time was when to receive a package containing new books both by
William Dean Howells and Henry James would have been a delightful
and even exciting event. Such time was in the last century and ominously near a generation ago. It was in the eighteen-seventies that we
had *A Foregone Conclusion* from Mr. Howells's pen, and *Roderick
Hudson* and *The American* from that of Mr. James. These tales mark the
highest achievement in fiction of both writers; while their later imaginative work has been both so large in quantity, and, upon the whole, so
even in quality, that it may very well be considered collectively. . . .
I do not see how any one can think that Mr. James was ever very successful in the novel of English manners. He is hampered in his judgment,
and misled even in his observations, by the influence of a temperament
as un-English as it is possible to conceive; by his mystical inheritance,
his inveterate habit of minute analysis, and last, though not least, by his
inborn, though so deeply overlaid Puritanism. He knows his English
men and women of the privileged classes well,—at least he has had great
opportunities for knowing them, but he cannot, for his life, take them,
in the easy, unquestioning, matter of fact way in which they take one
another, and, undoubtedly, prefer to be taken. . . . Mr. James is complex, introspective, shrinking painfully in his fastidiousness from the
loud laugh that attends the too outspoken jest, *maladif* if not morbid.
The Trollopes and Austens love air and exercise (at the least of it, in a
'barouche-landau,' like Mrs. Elton), clear utterance, and the broad

light of common day. Mr. James must have his tapestries of the thickest, his curtains closely drawn, his artificial light doubly and trebly tempered by tinted *abats-jour*. . . .

But never, surely, in English drawing-rooms or anywhere else, please God! did living beings actually converse after the manner of Mr. James's characters. His people never say anything outright, but carry on their 'subtle' communion by means of whispered hints, remote suggestions, and the finely broken and shyly presented fragments of quite unspeakable epigram. They seldom complete even their own cryptic remarks, but start back as if scared by the sound of their own voices, and the possible dazzle of their own wit; while they shy, like frightened horses, from the faintest adumbration of a serious meaning.

Now this method is a peculiarly unfortunate one, in that it conveys, whether purposely or unconsciously, an impression of perpetual innuendo, and casts upon an entire class a slur which I believe to be quite unwarranted, save in the case of one little clique. . . . The fact is that all hush-hush and fie-fie methods are alien to the true English temper. But there are certain of Mr. James's later and more elaborate novels of English life, like *The Awkward Age*, and *What Marie Knew*, that are as full of the covert suggestion of foulness as the worst French novel of the last forty years. And there is one short story of his, 'The Turn of the Screw', which is a sheer moral horror, like the evil dream of a man under the spell of a deadly drug.

In his last book, *The Wings of the Dove*, Mr. James makes a palpable effort to shake off the nightmare of his uglier fancies and return to a less dubious method. . . . The book . . . has a plot, and not exactly a common one; though the difficulty of disengaging it from the clouds of refined and enigmatical verbiage in which it is all but smothered by the narrator comes near to being insuperable. . . . But it seems unlikely that the most conscientious reader will ever go entirely through the seven hundred odd pages which Mr. James takes to explain, in his own suave and studied diction, the very peculiar relations of his characters. He has to do almost all the talking in his own person, for they themselves rarely speak. Apparently the creatures of his brain have relinquished, once for all, the futile attempt to interpret one another's far-fetched allusions and recondite verbal riddles. Milly is the Dove of course, and there are faint iridescent gleams of something mild, alluring, and truly dovelike about her. The rather clumsy title of the tale is further explained by the fact that, before she flew quite away from an ungrateful earth, she spread her white wings in such a manner as to include in a double blessing the two persons who had most atrociously wronged her. In Kate, also, there is at times a touch of ardor and abandonment beyond what we have learned to look for in Mr. James's bloodless heroines. But for Merton Densher's fascination we have only the author's rather anxiously reiterated word. In all the two bulky volumes the hero neither says nor does anything in character which would in the least explain why one woman should have been ready to sacrifice her life for him, and the other, to all appearances, her honor.

156. F. M. Colby on James's bloodless perversity

1902

Frank Moore Colby, 'The Queerness of Henry James', *Bookman* (America), June 1902, xv, 396–7.
This, together with the next item, was reprinted in revised form in *Imaginary Obligations*, 1904, and again in Dupee's *The Question of Henry James*. I have thought it worthwhile to give the two essays in their original and separate form, and to follow them up with Edith Wharton's famous reminiscences of HJ in the late period on which they seem to me to throw considerable light. The 'passages' quoted from *The Awkward Age* are disjointed and misquoted. Colby (1865–1925) was an editor and essayist on various subjects.

A year ago, when Henry James wrote an essay on women that brought to our cheek the hot, rebellious blush, we said nothing about it, thinking that perhaps, after all, the man's style was his sufficient fig-leaf, and that few would see how shocking he really was. And, indeed, it has been a long time since the public knew what Henry James was up to behind that verbal hedge of his, though half-suspecting that he meant no good, because a style like that seemed just the place for guilty secrets. But those of us who formed the habit of him early can make him out even now, our eyes having grown so used to the deepening shadows of his later language that they can see in the dark, as you might say. We say this not to brag of it, but merely to show that there are people who partly understand him even in *The Sacred Fount*, and he is clearer in his essays, especially in this last wicked one on 'George Sand: The New Life,' published in the April *North American*.

Here he is as bold as brass, telling women to go ahead and do and dare, and praising the fine old hearty goings-on at the court of Augustus the Strong, and showing how they can be brought back again if women will only try. His impunity is due to the sheer laziness of the expurgators. They will not read him, and they do not believe anybody else can. They justify themselves, perhaps, by recalling passages like these in the *Awkward Age*:

335

What did this feeling wonderfully appear unless strangely irrelevant.

But she fixed him with her weary penetration.

He jumped up at this, as if he couldn't bear it, presenting as he walked across the room a large, foolish, fugitive back, on which her eyes rested as on a proof of her penetration.

'My poor child, you're of a profundity.'

He spoke almost uneasily, but she was not too much alarmed to continue lucid.

'You're of a limpidity, dear man!'

'Don't you think that's rather a back seat for one's best?'

'A back seat?' she wondered, with a purity.

'Your aunt didn't leave me with you to teach you the slang of the day.'

'The slang?' she spotlessly speculated.

Arguing from this that he was bent more on eluding pursuit than on making converts, they have let things pass that in other writers would have been immediately rebuked. He has, in fact, written furiously against the proprieties for several years. 'There is only one propriety,' he says, 'that the painter of life can ask of a subject: Does it or does it not belong to life?' He has charged our Anglo-Saxon writers with 'a conspiracy of silence,' and taunted them with the fact that the women are more improper than the men. 'Emancipations are in the air,' says he, 'but it is to women writers that we owe them.' The men are cowards, rarely venturing a single coarse expression, but already in England there are pages upon pages of women's work so strong and rich and horrifying and free that a man can hardly read them. Halcyon days, they seem to him, and woman the harbinger of a powerful Babylonish time when the improprieties shall sing together like the morning stars. Not an enthusiastic person generally, he always warms to this particular theme with generous emotion.

His latest essay, discussing what he calls the 'new life,' cites the heart history of George Sand as 'having given her sex for its new evolution and transformation the real standard and measure of change.' It is all recorded in Mme. Karénine's biography, and Mme. Karénine, being a Russian with an 'admirable Slav superiority to prejudice,' is able to treat the matter in a 'large, free way.' A life so amorously profuse is sure to set an encouraging example, he thinks. Her heart was like an hotel, occupied, he says, by 'many more or less greasy males' in quick succession. He hopes the time will come when other women's hearts will be as miscellaneous:

In this direction their aim has been, as yet, comparatively modest and their emulation low; the challenge they have hitherto picked up is but the challenge of the average male. The approximation of the extraordinary woman has been, practically, in other words, to the ordinary man. Madame Sand's service is that she planted the flag much higher; her own approximation, at least, was to the extraordinary. She reached him, she surpassed him, and she showed how, with native dispositions, the thing could be done. These new records will live as the precious text-book, so far as we have got, of the business.

This is plain enough. Any other man would be suppressed. In a literature so well policed as ours, the position of Henry James is anomalous. He is the only writer of the day whose moral notions do not seem to matter. His dissolute and complicated Muse may say just what she chooses. This may be because it would be so difficult to expose him. Never did so much vice go with such sheltering vagueness. Whatever else may be said of James, he is no tempter, and though his later novels deal only with unlawful passions, they make but chilly reading on the whole. It is a land where the vices have no bodies and the passions no blood, where nobody sins because nobody has anything to sin with. Why should we worry when a spook goes wrong? For years James has not made one shadow-casting character. His love affairs, illicit though they be, are so stripped to their motives that they seem no more enticing than a diagram. A wraith proves faithless to her marriage vow, elopes with a bogie in a cloud of words. Six phantoms meet and dine, three male, three female, with two thoughts apiece, and, after elaborate geometry of the heart, adultery follows like a Q. E. D. Shocking it ought to be, but yet it is not. Ghastly, tantalising, queer, but never near enough human to be either good or bad. To be a sinner, even in the books you need some carnal attributes—lungs, liver, tastes, at least a pair of legs. Even the fiends have palpable tails; wise men have so depicted them. No flesh, no frailty; that may be why our sternest moralists have licensed Henry James to write his wickedest. Whatever the moral purport of these books, they may be left wide open in the nursery.

To those who never liked him he is the same in his later writings as in his earlier. There were always mannerisms in his work, and his hunt for the distinguished phrase was always evident. His characters never would do enough things, and he was too apt to make them stand stock-still while he chopped them up. He was too apt, also, to think that when he had made a motive he had made a man. And there were many then, as now, who loathed his little cobweb plots and finical analyses. He often hovered very near the outer boundary of common sense, and it was a wonder sometimes how he escaped burlesque; but, still, he did it. His world was small, but it was credible—humanity run through a sieve, but still humanity. Since then his interests have dropped off one by one, leaving him shut in with his single theme—the rag, the bone and the hank of hair, the discreditable amours of skeletons. They call it his later manner, but the truth is, it is a change in the man himself. He sees fewer things in this spacious world than he used to see, and the people are growing more meagre and queer and monotonous, and it is harder and harder to break away from the stump his fancy is tied to.

157. F. M. Colby on James's slight improvement in *The Wings of the Dove*

1902

F. M. Colby, 'In Darkest James', *Bookman* (America), November 1902, xvi, 259–60.

In Henry James's latest book, the two-volume novel, *The Wings of the Dove*, there are signs of a partial recovery. There are people who will see no difference between it and *The Sacred Fount* or *The Awkward Age*, but they are no friends of his. By what vice of introspection he got himself lashed to that fixed idea we cannot say, but it was clear that neither of those books was the work of a mind entirely free. In one aspect it was ridiculous; but if one laughed, it was with compunctions, for in another aspect it was exceedingly painful. This only from the point of view of his admirers. It is not forgotten that there is the larger class (for whom this world in the main was made) to whom he is merely ridiculous. They do not see why thoughts so unwilling to come out need be extracted.

In *The Wings of the Dove* there is the same absorption in the machinery of motive and in mental processes the most minute. Through page after page he surveys a mind as a sick man looks at his counterpane, busy with little ridges and grooves and undulations. There are chapters like wonderful games of solitaire, broken by no human sound save his own chuckle when he takes some mysterious trick or makes a move that he says is 'beautiful.' He has a way of saying 'There you are' that is most exasperating, for it is always at the precise moment at which you know you have utterly lost yourself. There is no doubt that James's style is often too puffed up with its secrets. Despite its air of immense significance, the dark, unfathomed caves of his ocean contain sometimes only the same sort of gravel you could have picked up on the shore. We have that from thinkers who have been down him. But though this unsociable way of writing continues through *The Wings of the Dove*, it comes nearer than any other of his recent novels

339

to the quality of his earlier work. It deals with conditions as well as with people. Instead of merely souls anywhere, we have men and women living in describable homes. It would be hard to find in those other novels anything in the spirit of the following passage, which is fairly typical of much in this:

> It was after the children's dinner . . . and the two young women were still in the presence of the crumpled tablecloth, the dispersed pinafores, the scraped dishes, the lingering odour of boiled food. Kate had asked, with ceremony, if she might put up a window a little, and Mrs. Condrip had replied, without it, that she might do as she liked. She often received such inquiries as if they reflected in a manner on the pure essence of her little ones. . . . Their mother had become for Kate—who took it just for the effect of being their mother—quite a different thing from the mild Marian of the past: Mr. Condrip's widow expansively obscured that image. She was little more than a ragged relic, a plain prosaic result of him, as if she had somehow been pulled through him as though an obstinate funnel, only to be left crumpled and useless and with nothing in her but what he accounted for.

Not that the passage shows him at his best, but it shows him as at least concerned with the setting of his characters.

It is not worth while to attempt an outline of the story. Those who have done so have disagreed in essentials. It is impossible to hit off in a few words characters that James has picked out for their very complexity; and the story counts for little with him as against the business of recording the play of mind. One does not take a watch to pieces merely to tell the time of day; and with James analysis is the end in itself. His characters rarely do things; and though in this book one dies and leaves her fortune to the man she loves, and though there is a rich aunt who interferes with her niece's love affairs, no description of the people or the part they play could give the slightest clue to the interest of the book. By indefinable means, and in spite of the most wearisome prolixity, he often succeeds in producing a very strange and powerful effect. It is a lucky man who can find a word for it. Things you had supposed incommunicable certainly come your way. These are the times we are almost grateful to him for pottering in his nebulous workshop among the things that are hard to express.

If the obscurity of the language were due to the idea itself, and if while he tugs at an obstinate thought you could be sure it was worth the trouble, there would be no fault to find, but to him one thing seems as good as another when he is mousing around in a mind. It is a form of self-indulgence. He is as pleased with the motives that lead nowhere as with anything else. It is his even emphasis that most misleads. He writes a staccato chronicle of things both great and small, like a constitutional history half made up of the measures that never passed. And in one respect he does not play fairly. He makes his characters read each other's minds from clues that he keeps to himself. To invent an irreverent instance, suppose we were a distinguished author with a psychological bent and wished to represent two young people as preternaturally acute. We might place them alone together and make them talk like this:

'If'——she sparkled.
'If?' he asked. He had lurched from the meaning for a moment.
'I might'——she replied abundantly.
His eye had eaten the meaning—'Me!' he gloriously burst.
'Precisely,' she thrilled. 'How splendidly you *do* understand.'

We, the distinguished author, versed in our own psychology—the springs of our own marionettes—we understand it perfectly. For us there are words a-plenty. But is it fair to you, the reader?

158. Edith Wharton on the later James and his sensitivity

[1934]

Edith Wharton, from *A Backward Glance*, New York, 1934, 189–92.
Mrs. Wharton (1862–1937) was, as well as a very fine novelist, a New York aristocrat and an extremely wealthy woman. She was also a devoted friend of HJ, if occasionally oppressive in her general magnificence. But, in spite of being a rather unwilling 'disciple', she disliked the late novels and, in view of what Colby actually wrote, I wonder if her account should be quite so much admired as it commonly is. For Howard Sturgis see No. 128.

A similar perturbation could be produced (I later learned, to my cost) by asking him to explain any phrase in his books that did not seem quite clear, or any situation of which the motive was not adequately developed; and still more disastrous was the effect of letting him know that any of his writings had been parodied. I had always regarded the fact of being parodied as one of the surest evidences of fame, and once, when he was staying with us in New York, I brought him with glee a deliciously droll article on his novels by poor Frank Colby, the author of *Imaginary Obligations*. The effect was disastrous. I shall never forget the misery, the mortification even, which tried to conceal itself behind an air of offended dignity. His ever-bubbling sense of fun failed him completely on such occasions; as it did also (I was afterward to find) when one questioned him, in a way that even remotely implied criticism, on any point in the novels. It was in England, I think—when he and I, and a party of intimate friends, were staying together at Howard Sturgis's—that I brought him, in all innocence, a passage from one of his books which, after repeated readings, I still found unintelligible. He took the book from me, read over the passage to himself, and handed it back with a lame attempt at a joke; but I saw—we all saw—

that even this slight, and quite involuntary, criticism, had wounded his morbidly delicate sensibility.

Once again—and again unintentionally—I was guilty of a similar blunder. I was naturally much interested in James's technical theories and experiments, though I thought, and still think, that he tended to sacrifice to them that spontaneity which is the life of fiction. Everything, in the latest novels, had to be fitted into a predestined design, and design, in his strict geometrical sense, is to me one of the least important things in fiction. Therefore, though I greatly admired some of the principles he had formulated, such as that of always letting the tale, as it unfolded, be seen through the mind most capable of reaching to its periphery, I thought it was paying too dear even for such a principle to subordinate to it the irregular and irrelevant movements of life. And one result of the application of his theories puzzled and troubled me. His latest novels, for all their profound moral beauty, seemed to me more and more lacking in atmosphere, more and more severed from that thick nourishing human air in which we all live and move. The characters in *The Wings of the Dove* and *The Golden Bowl* seem isolated in a Crookes tube for our inspection: his stage was cleared like that of the Théâtre Français in the good old days when no chair or table was introduced that was not *relevant to the action* (a good rule for the stage, but an unnecessary embarrassment to fiction). Preoccupied by this, I one day said to him: 'What was your idea in suspending the four principal characters in *The Golden Bowl* in the void? What sort of life did they lead when they were not watching each other, and fencing with each other? Why have you stripped them of all the *human fringes* we necessarily trail after us through life?'

He looked at me in surprise, and I saw at once that the surprise was painful, and wished I had not spoken. I had assumed that his system was a deliberate one, carefully thought out, and had been genuinely anxious to hear his reasons. But after a pause of reflection he answered in a disturbed voice: 'My dear—I didn't know I had!' and I saw that my question, instead of starting one of our absorbing literary discussions, had only turned his startled attention on a peculiarity of which he had been completely unconscious.

This sensitiveness to criticism or comment of any sort had nothing to do with vanity; it was caused by the great artist's deep consciousness of his powers, combined with a bitter, a life-long disappointment at his lack of popular recognition. I am not sure that Henry James had not secretly dreamed of being a 'best seller' in the days when that odd form of literary fame was at its height; at any rate he certainly suffered all his life—and more and more as time went on—from the lack of recognition among the very readers who had most warmly welcomed his early novels. He could not understand why the success achieved by *Daisy Miller* and *The Portrait of a Lady* should be denied to the great novels of his maturity: and the sense of protracted failure made him miserably alive to the least hint of criticism, even from those who most completely understood, and sympathized with, his later experiments in technique and style.

159. The *Edinburgh Review* on James's achievement

1903

Unsigned article, *Edinburgh Review*, January 1903, cxcvii, 59–85. I have represented this long article by only a few extracts because it does not contain much interesting criticism; it is, as the author says, a 'mere descriptive bibliography'. Nevertheless, conventional or not, so sympathetic a treatment in the *Edinburgh* was bound to be of importance. It was a kind of accolade of respectability, confirming the relatively new view of HJ as an established celebrity (it was itself noticed in a number of periodicals—e.g. in the *Saturday* review of *The Wings of the Dove*, No. 152). The extracts start as the author moves on from the 'middle period' to the later (*c.* 1890).

In the period which one is leaving lies the greater part of the labour by which Mr. Henry James is popularly known, if, indeed, one may without suspicion of irony use such a description. It contains nine of his novels and some twenty-seven tales, and only in some of the slighter of these could the casual consumer of fiction pretend to discover any esoteric intention or other obstacle to the enjoyment of an easily exhausted mind. They have just that unreality which the public desires, the note of romance; sentiment and character are fitted with that consistency which gives the novel such an advantage over life; opinions are held with a clarity, and expressed with an accuracy which are of so great assistance in the development of character; and the dialogue has just that appositeness and cohesion which our ears are so accustomed not to hear. In short they have all the qualities that should commend them to a public which is very ignorant and very incurious of life, and one would have expected for them a far greater success even than they commanded. The chief preventive to such a popularity is a delicate and exquisite style which, because it tried to achieve an actuality to which they were unaccustomed, the critics called artificial. Style in every

345

country of the world warns off the 'stupid,' but it seems to possess a particular irritation for English and American readers. . . . But in addition to the wilful offence of their style, one must admit, as an unconscious one, that the author is always free from moral prejudice or intention. He only aims at giving a direct impression of life without preconception as to its purpose. Nowhere does he come forward with explanation and reproof; nowhere does he attempt any re-arrangement of the elements of life, to enforce a lesson or illustrate a theme. He tries seriously, strenuously, to produce the illusion of being, and he is well content to succeed in performing that part of his business. His seriousness lives, indeed, beyond reproof. That *is* his moral purpose. . . . And this detachment from his subject is, of course, against him with a British audience which, inveterately commercial, craves to derive profit from the occupation of its leisure, and is always suspicious of amusement which has no secondary aim. . . .

In 1890 the publication of *The Tragic Muse* inaugurated the new era. The inauguration possibly will not be apparent to many, for the book is certainly not a whit 'freer' than any of its predecessors; but it is strikingly nearer the ideal of 'an immense and exquisite correspondence with life.' There is a beautiful looseness, and inexpectancy in the handling. The story wavers, advances, retreats, and ceases in the very fashion of life itself. Its cohesion suffers naturally in consequence. It reads, indeed, in places like a very splendid first attempt. The author seems to be trying to write it in spite of his art, to be aiming at a simplicity, a closeness to life, which is being continually clouded by the charm of form and phrase which he is as yet unable wholly to transfuse with his new intention. . . . In 1899 appeared what is probably his most distinctive effort, *The Awkward Age*. As a novel it lacks the delicate freshness of *The Spoils of Poynton* and the dramatic distinctness of *The Other House*, but as a study of life, which it almost professedly is, it surpasses, by its completeness, its sympathetic intrusion, its fine impartiality, anything that Mr. James has done. The life it deals with, the life of Mrs. Brookenham's circle, is as limited as, despite its limits, it is minutely complex. It lacks virility; it is, saving appearances, indifferent to virtue; it affects rather an easy accommodation than good manners; but its quick intelligence, its very detachment from the strenuous effort of life make it worth study. Mr. James has provided a touchstone for its vulgarities, its indifferences, its freedoms, in the shape of Mr. Longdon, the remnant of an older generation; but he views the contrast thus afforded with impartial eyes, for if he treats the younger without extenuation, he makes of Nanda, its representative, the most charming portrait in the book. And the book is confessedly a portrait gallery. Its ten parts are each labelled, like picture frames, with the name of a person, and Mr. James brings to the filling of each the ultimate development of the art of vision. . . .

The range in his portraits of women is so wonderfully wide that it seems almost querulous to be conscious of what it does not include. And yet their very number and inclusiveness make more remarkable what has been left out. Besides Rose Armiger, there is among all his women not one who, save incidentally and retrospectively, found her heart too strong for her; and no study, even, of any profound strife between the passions and the will. His good women seem to win their triumphs too easily, the bad to accept too complacently their defeat. In the great matters of conduct our interest is scarcely ever enlisted by either, we know too well what each will do. And our knowledge comes, not from an appreciation of their moral qualities, but from a sense of their subjection or of their indifference to the social code. For the shadow of convention lies somewhat heavily on Mr. James's women; it usurps oppressively the offices of virtue and of duty. His Puritans retain the beauty, the freedom even, of an accusing conscience, but it is rather respectability than responsibility which seems to regulate the actions of the rest. It is true that in giving so large a place to so low a motive, Mr. James can plead to have but followed the proportion of things as they are; yet to have followed them so constantly, to have found so little attraction in the exceptional, to have celebrated so seldom the great conflicts of the soul, must indubitably influence one's estimate of his achievement.

How great that achievement is, one is profoundly conscious after traversing, for such an article as this, the entire spread of it without any sense of satiety or of iteration. There is no more genuine proof of power, of originality, of imagination, than this unfading freshness, delicacy, and variety in remembered work, and against all that has been written of those qualities in these pages, one can but set a disinclination, perhaps a disability to handle the naked issues of emotion, and too frequent a tendency to immerse his drama in a saturated atmosphere of convention. That, however, is a defect of his qualities, a determination to contrive 'an immense correspondence with life,' and he has so completely succeeded as to have added a new conception of reality to the art of fiction. If he has dropped a line but rarely into the deep waters of life, his soundings have so added to our knowledge of its shallows that no student of existence can afford to ignore his charts. He has lived, as it were, in the chains with the 'lead' in his hands, intent on definite knowledge of the channels and shoals of the human heart, where so many another pilot has been content to steer by the mere appearance of the surface water. And to the pleasure he has given us by his sketches of the beauty and variety of that enchanting coast must be added gratitude for such a diversity of enlightenment on its perilous approaches as he alone, of those who have studied it, seems able to supply.

160. Oliver Elton on *The Wings of the Dove* and the greatness of James

1903

Oliver Elton, from 'The Novels of Mr. Henry James', *Quarterly*, October 1903, cxcviii, 358–79 (reprinted in *Modern Studies*, 1907). This is in a way a complement to No. 159 in being a long and comprehensive article in one of the grand nineteenth century periodicals. But, unlike its predecessor, it is by one of the new enthusiasts for HJ, and significantly centres its interest on the later work. I have therefore reprinted entire the fine impassioned treatment of *The Wings of the Dove* which, despite the title of the article, constitutes the major part (the extracts start on p. 361). Elton (1861–1945) was Professor of English at Liverpool from 1901 to 1925, and one of the most prominent of academics in the first part of this century.

If Mr. Henry James had ceased to write about 1890, he might have been remembered for his choice of this fresh, distinct plot of ground, for his happy and varied cultivation of it. The flowers were a little 'pale,' but full of tender, clear colour, unlike any others. There was humour; and the pages were full of a softly stinging wit. The English was that of the easy classical tradition, a little chequered, as befitted the scene, with the French and American tongues. It was careful; it flowed and did not stick; it did not first of all try to express embroiled feeling or imperceptible changes of temperature. In a few pieces, like 'The Aspern Papers' (1888), the style might have seemed more tense, and the subject bizarre and a little ghostly. But few would have forecast this as the future field of the novelist. *The Princess Casamassima*, with its wonderful opening scene of tragic rage, wandered into some extravagance. These were experiments; the account might seem to have been closed.

But the century wore out, and over our fiction there came the breath of a stranger temper, different from that of the gallant Victorian crusaders. . . .

Each of the larger novels published since 1895, *The Other House*, *The Spoils of Poynton*, and *The Awkward Age*, would be worthy of studious review. It is curious how the passion for the scenery of the English country house and 'grounds' recurs in them, as in the delightful 'Covering End.' But the fresh gifts, the motives, the newly-modulated style that they reveal are all more perfectly apparent in *The Wings of the Dove*, the most remarkable book that Mr. James has written. It has been relatively little noticed amid the mart of dreadfully competent fiction. But, wherever it has penetrated, it is likely, after the manner of certain plays of Ibsen, to leave a long wake of disputation, partly over the question as to what actually happens in the story, and partly about the rights and wrongs of the solution. Hence a fuller analysis may be pardoned; for the book resumes so much that went before in the author's production, and intensifies so sharply the changes in his temper, that to know *The Wings of the Dove* is to know much of Mr. Henry James. He has gone back to his old topic of the rich American in Europe; and the contending parties have, in a sense, the same symbolism as before. The world and the spirit are afresh in conflict on the trodden battle-ground. But the arts of war, offensive and defensive, have been transformed in the interval; there are forces in the air that were unknown to the Osmonds and Madame Merles of an earlier day. And—chief alteration of all—the sympathies are entangled with both sides. The puritan dualism, so to call it, of the older books is greatly blunted; and the artist, borne along by his own discoveries, comes to bend his intensest and finest light upon the arch-conspirator, who nearly supplants her intended victim in tragic and intellectual interest. Moreover, there is no sharp solution by the sword of justice, moral or poetical. It belongs, also, to the movement of our time—which, as Matthew Arnold well said, is a 'lay' one—that nothing could be more wholly of this life, without hint or doctrine of a second world, than the tales of Mr. James. Very seldom, with a still questioning irony, something else seems to be indicated. The dove-like heroine dies, and the event is canvassed by a worldly old lady and the man who might have been her husband.

'Our dear dove, then, as Kate calls her, has folded her wonderful wings.'
'Yes—folded them.'
It rather racked him, but he tried to receive it as she intended, and she evidently took his formal ascent for self-control. 'Unless it's more true,' she accordingly added, 'that she has spread them the wider.'
He again but formally assented, though, strangely enough, the words

fitted an image deep in his own consciousness. 'Rather, yes—spread them the wider.'

'For a flight, I trust, to some happiness greater——'

'Exactly. Greater,' Densher broke in; but now with a look, he feared, that did, a little, warn her off.

But this is to forestall the history itself, which tells of a fray unprecedented enough.

The world first! The tale opens in the back, shady regions—surely on the south side of the Thames. . . . In a small room in 'Chirk Street,' Kate Croy awaits her impossible, jaunty father who has done something which reticence cannot specify, but who is 'all pink and silver,' with 'kind, safe eyes,' and an inimitable manner, and 'indescribable arts that quite turned the tables.' Here Kate tastes 'the faint, flat emanation of things, the failure of fortune and of honour.' The interview is a triumph of acrid comedy; the talk of Croy fully bears out his inventory. This nameless parent (her mother has died of her troubles) stands aside from the story, but is necessary in order to explain Kate. He is that from which she flies; yet she has sprung from him. She flies, by instinct, upwards in society, on the wings of the hawk, not of the dove; no mere kite, but a predatory creature of a larger sweep, with nobilities, with weaknesses after all. She flies to the only life in which she can imagine herself—where there is room for her will, room for her beauty—chances for her marriage, chances for winning money, and station, and love as well, and not merely one of these things without the rest. When she leaves the house we know something of Kate; her exhalation of silent power, her disregard of all cost to herself in pursuit of her quest, her mysterious, undeniable nobleness of stamp, which we must reconcile as best we can with her later piracies and perversities. Already she has got away from her father and her weariful widowed sister, whom, by the way, she supports with her own inheritance. Her aunt in Lancaster Gate, Mrs. Lowder, the 'Aunt Maud' of the story, has seen the value of Kate. She is a girl who might, and must, marry a 'great man,' and so satisfy the dowager affections and long-delayed ambitions of her aunt. Thus they would both escape from the amphibious society in which they move, into that region of the London world which is really 'great.' Fielding would have rejoiced in this view of 'greatness.' Their ambition, at bottom vulgar, is embraced by them with a religious gravity. The author himself almost seems to take it too seriously, at moments.

Kate, in her revulsion from Chirk Street, is ready enough for this programme, but for one obstacle. She loves a man who can never be great at all. He is merely a journalist of some parts, with a foreign education, Merton Densher, who from the standpoint of Mrs. Lowder is inadmissible. It would seem that Kate must either resign Densher or her expectations. She is weak; she cannot give up her expectations. But she is also strong; for she is prepared to play high, and to wait for an opportunity of winning both, should such present itself. It does present itself; there is the story, but there also is the tragedy. Meantime let her have her precarious, whole-hearted, stolen happiness, walking pledged in Kensington Gardens.

The difficulties sharpen. Densher is visiting on terms of sufferance, which are dissected to the thinnest point, at the house in Lancaster Gate, where the hostess accepts him because she feels she can crush him at any time, and positively likes him all the while. A certain 'Lord Mark' who is asserted rather than proved to be uncannily clever, but who is wanted for the conduct of the tragedy, is on the watch; and in any case Kate must tarry for the great man who is not yet forthcoming. At this point Densher is sent by his newspaper office to America to make articles. Kate's opportunity for high play is not ripe till his return. Unaware she waits the coming of the 'Dove.'

Milly Theale, strangely and richly left, the dying flower of an old wild family, carrying in herself, too, the seeds of an undefined malady, and, further, the memory of three calls paid to her in New York by a young Englishman, Densher—Milly Theale is found in Europe, whither she has restlessly fled with a lady escort, a simple, but not foolish, little New Englander, by profession a furnisher of novels. Fled, from what? and whither? From the fear and from the memory, which accompany her nevertheless. The method of reticence, of dumb actions and silences, is here followed worthily. The reader, as well as Milly's companion, Mrs. Stringham, are cunningly let into the secret, which is stoically kept. It comes out by degrees, on a wooded pass, in the little parlours of the inns; and before England is reached the charm is felt by the reader, who knows the pale face, coppery hair, and the radiation, strong, soft, and beneficent, of the lonely, wealthy woman, who 'thinks,' when congratulated, that she has *not* 'really everything.' To England they go; Mrs. Stringham remembers an old friend, Mrs. Lowder, now high in the world; and with her the Americans are next found in company, without it being at first known that Densher is a common acquaintance.

The Dove has to face fresh waters, that welcome her, unsparing as they may prove later, more than graciously at first. The opening dinner-

party is described, from the point of view of Milly, with Richard-
sonian prolixity; the dinner itself could hardly take longer. But this is
Mr. Henry James's way of enhancing his illusion. The persons move,
through a strange, turbid medium, towards a dramatic comprehension
of one another. We hear slowly—but we do not wish the tale shorter—
how the two girls, Kate Croy and Milly, become intimate; how they
discover, without words, that both know and think of Densher; how
Milly betrays her passion to the 'onyx-eyed Aunt Maud'; how Densher
returns, visits the National Gallery as a rendezvous with Kate, and is
thus beheld by Milly as she sits there forlornly 'counting the Americans.'
In one scene, which precedes this incident, the doom of Milly is fore-
shadowed. Milly is taken by Lord Mark, who is trying to wrap invisible
nets round the heiress, to a great house, in order that she may be seen
in his company. He brings her up to an old picture, 'by Bronzino,' of a
fair, dead lady to whom she has a surprising chance likeness.

She found herself, for the first moment, looking at the mysterious portrait
through tears. Perhaps it was her tears that made it just then so strange and fair
—as wonderful as he had said: the face of a young woman, all magnificently
drawn, down to the hands, and magnificently dressed; a face almost livid in
hue, yet handsome in sadness and crowned with a mass of hair, rolled back and
high, that must, before fading with time, have had a family resemblance to her
own. The lady in question, at all events, with her slightly Michaelangelesque
squareness, her eyes of other days, her full lips, her long neck, her recorded
jewels, her brocaded and wasted reds, was a very great personage, only unaccompanied by a joy. And she was dead, dead, dead. Milly recognised her
exactly in words that had nothing to do with her. 'I shall never be better than
this.'

This is but one of many passages that show how Mr. James has
shared in the special impulse towards beauty which distinguishes the
new generation. Such an American as Milly Theale becomes, by her
rich ancestry, by her affinity of type to the master-painting, herself a
member of an old world, no longer merely simple-minded and delightfully puritan, but with all kinds of complicated stirrings and concessions
that might surprise her countrywomen. And the style of Mr. James
gathers, itself, the dignity of an old master's as it rises to the expression
of these deeper and more dramatic things. It has become more and more
charged with beauty; it marches with slow, intricately measured paces,
as in a dream; and, in this book, even the harsher incidents and cruelties
of the story do not prove too much for the style. It would be idle to
credit younger Belgian or Celtic symbolists with a definite influence in

any direction upon Mr. James. This kind of enchantment is now in the air of literature; and Mr. Henry James, in the fullness of his powers, has returned spell for spell.

Soon Milly knows how she stands. A big, clear-witted physician, Sir Luke Strett, with his 'fine, closed face,' comes into her life. It is implied that she will die, or die the sooner, unless she has the happiness, the marriage that she needs. The doctor tells her, significantly, to 'live'; and that she wishes to do. The scenes in his consulting-room form one of the many accessory perfections of the book. Soon Sir Luke sees that Densher is the man. Soon they all see, they all crowd round from different sides. Mrs. Lowder is willing he should be tempted away, so that Kate may be free for greatness. Kate herself has to act, and the critical episodes begin. Mr. James has tried hard to render probable the bold and ugly scheme which she devises on behalf of herself and her lover. May it be conjectured that, having first thought of this central motive, he proceeded to invent backwards explanatory antecedents for Kate Croy, which should leave her capable of a crime even against her own passion; that he made her, nevertheless, a woman of large build, of sympathy, full of heart and pieties of her own kind; and that when the moment came for unscrupulous action, behold, she was too good for the work? So Chaucer, when his authorities tell him that the time is due for Cressida to be false to Troilus, has himself spent too much kindness on her to believe it, and refers, somewhat shamefacedly, to the 'books' to prove the fact. Kate goes wrong, but not in Cressida's way. At this point there is a change in the method of painting her, which serves to cover any violence in the transition. We are never again in her confidence as before, the curtain is dropped, and the story becomes a diary not of her feelings, but of the feelings of Densher. Thus any struggle in the mind of Kate is unknown. The second great difficulty of the author is to make Densher her accomplice, and to incline him to acquiesce in the false report that, while he is desperate for Kate, Kate is averse from him. On this footing of a person to be pitied he drifts, by delicate degrees, into the position of an intimate with Milly, whom she is ready to console.

The plan is virtually a kind of dubious, low insurance job; Mr. Henry James has never invented anything so extraordinary. Densher, while privately pledged to Kate, is to 'make up to a sick girl' who wishes to gain him, but who may die, after not too long an interval, leaving him well endowed and free to marry Kate. He is to pay certain premiums, for a term, in the way of simulated love; but he pays them on a 'bad life'; when that life 'determines' (these images are not used in the book) he is to receive the millions for which the policy has been taken out. The full position only comes home to him slowly; by the time he realises it the action is ready for the most startling turn of all. Man, woman, and fate conspire at first for the success of the plot, and the scene shifts to Venice, which 'plashed and chimed and called again' in sympathy, until cold and wicked weather, also in sympathy with events, sets in. Every one is present. For their beauty and strange grace these Venetian chapters, let us prophesy frankly, may come to be thought a classic in their kind. For the Dove, as her frail body fades in her palace, begins, in ways unforeseen, to prevail, though she seems to be deceived, and for a while is deceived, with the hope of 'living.' It is on Densher that the strain works. He knows what manner of man he is, when Milly, 'in all the candour of her smile, the lustre of her pearls, the value of her life, the essence of her wealth,' looks across her own hall at himself and Kate as they are furtively discussing the consequences her death may bring to themselves. Densher is not easy in mind, and his next act makes the knot insoluble indeed.

He cannot go on with his part in the game without realities. There, in the palace of Milly, he tells Kate what encouragement she must give him. She has ruled his action thus far; it is now the turn of the male. He has a lodging, a little dim old place, on one of the canals. If she comes to him, he will be immutably forced to go through with their programme. Kate sees, and blenches; but consents, and goes. This, by a deep but sound paradox, is the first sign that Densher is shaken by the influence of the Dove. For anything like this conception, and the way it is faced, we must go back to the freedoms of Jacobean tragedy.

The visit of Kate to the lodging is not narrated, though some inferior authors would have felt bound on theory to narrate it. Economy is in its place here. Tolstoi would have forborne to tell it, but might, as in *Anna Karénina*, instantly have informed us that there was an aftertaste of sick humiliation. But there was not. Nothing is told us but the preliminary compact, and then the man's aftertaste, in the lonely lodging, of glory and absorption. At this point we remember that psychology is in the blood of Mr. Henry James. The present, in such a case, is scientifically indescribable; it is an illusion, indeed it is *nil* if abstracted from its sequel; its life is in hopes and memories; their faintness, their vividness renewed in rhythmical fashion, their sudden chasing away by a new, black train of associations. Densher is left alone in Venice to carry out his agreement, and another chapter follows of equal power, showing the heavy cruelty of the new situation for all parties.

The Dove, now dying, and waiting vainly for her hopes, acts upon Densher in another paradoxical but natural way. The pursuit of her, after what has passed, seems to him more than ever necessary, if he is not utterly to cheat Kate, but less than ever possible, the Dove being the noble person that she is. After a little the very possibility is denied him. 'Susan Shepherd,' Mrs Stringham, who has followed everything silently, like some clairvoyant animal, comes to give him a last chance; she will accept anything, that her friend's last ray of happiness may be made possible. Densher is kept back from going through with his bond by a host of little cords of conscience and distaste, and soon it is too late. He has a final, astonishing interview with the dying lady, in which she receives him with invincible style, in full dress, refusing 'to smell of drugs, to taste of medicine.' What passed no others know: the interview is only mentioned in a later conversation with Kate; and Kate is not the person to hear its details—does not wish to hear them. But we gather that Milly, while knowing much, and divining we know not how much more—knowing certainly, since a malicious, finally killing revelation by Lord Mark, that she had been lied to, and that Kate had really cared for Densher throughout—Milly *pardons*. This divine impression is left on Densher: her last words

Enforce attention, like deep harmony.

Thus Milly prevails. Having lost all, she regains everything—not practically, but in the sphere of love, soul, and devotion, in which she moves, and in which Densher must henceforth be said to live a kind of absolved existence. Even practically, as the sequel shows, she exerts a decisive influence.

For the memory of her is now fixed in Densher. His experience of power and craft, of passion secular and unshrinking, is overborne by an experience yet stronger. The waft of the Dove's wings as she fled has altered him. He has, in a sense, killed her; he would not have her; now she, and not Kate, is mistress of *him*. By the same token, he is false to Kate. Where, then, is there an issue?

Nothing so vulgar is suggested as that possession had cooled Densher towards Kate: that is not the point at all. But another power, 'through creeks and inlets making,' controls him. He comes home to England, and the final act is played. All that went before is really nothing as compared with his present complication with Kate. And the last beneficent action of the Dove adds another coil to the tangle. He resumes, with a difference, his old wanderings with Kate; the change is best expressed in his phrase that they are 'damned civil' to each other. Kate is strong still, strong to the last. Though Densher has not married Milly, she guesses that she has gained her end nevertheless—without, for that matter, having had to pay the expected price of seeing him Milly's husband for a time. So far she has guessed right. Milly has left him a great fortune. Her last letter comes, in which he would have seen, had he read it, the wonderful and gracious turn she would have given to her bequest. Kate burns the unopened letter, when he offers it to her, under the sway of a wholly new feeling, which is out of her usual reckoning altogether—jealousy of the dead. This is one of the many profundities of the tale. Kate could bear to see her lover marry Milly without love; she cannot bear to see him in love with Milly dead. But she sees that the centres of his life have shifted; he is all with the dead, with the letter that is ashes. But he is still true in act to Kate. The business letter announcing the fortune comes from America; he sends this letter to her to 'test' her; she is positive-minded, she does not understand the 'test,' and she reads it. Densher refuses to read it, and the final crisis comes. He pursues his last sad advantage with Kate. He will not touch the money for himself. There must be a kind of expiation. Either she must marry him poor, as he was of old: or, he will make over the money to her; but in that case he will not marry her. Such at least seems to be the meaning of the latter pages. Thus the spirit of the Dove penetrates material life, as the ether penetrates the most stubborn substances of the earth. The strong, consistent person is at the disadvantage; the half-baked man, who has a conscience, but had not nerve enough to carry the policy through, is, in his converted state, the dominant partner. In the last sentences of the book Kate challenges him with being in love with the dead. He makes no answer, but says:

'I'll marry you, mind you, in an hour.'
'As we were?'
'As we were.'
But she turned to the door, and her headshake was now the end.
'We shall never be again as we were!'

So the tale ends. It is easy to ask the wrong question, to ask, What happens? Do they marry, or does she take the money? Probably she marries Lord Mark. But it does not matter. What matters is that it is the end of two personalities, the final unsoldering of the alliance so exquisitely sealed in Kensington Gardens. The irruption of forces from another world has done this. Other questions, equally hard but more profitable, we are forced to ask. What has the Dove accomplished by her high generosity? Spoilt, if we look into the matter, what she wished to mend. She had made the bequest in order that the two might be free as they desired. But they have no use for freedom. With whom does the sympathy finally remain? With the man, who through his very weakness, his two-sidedness, has been in a sense regenerate? Or with the partner, proud, strong, and true to her strange self, who has given herself unflinchingly, and is now dispossessed of her reward? Let us say that our sympathy is with her, as it would never have been had she simply succeeded.

We can put such questions without end. The book is not like a great tragedy of the older kind, which ends in some ennobling resolution of errors through death. It ends in a deep, resonant discord. But such a discord equally has its place in art, for it might actually close just such a passage of significant, tumultuous life. The conflict between the world and the spirit, with which we started, has ended drawn; the spirit has conquered in its own sphere; the world has been disconcerted and baffled. But Kate, the embodiment of the world, is not wholly eclipsed. She remains pathetic, dignified even after her failure, and above all strong. The last word is hers. The interest, almost the benediction of the author, goes with her. That marks, like much else, the long slow change in his way of facing life. The victims in his earlier novels were the clear-souled and innocent. Milly Theale is such a victim, certainly; but the sufferer, the protagonist, foiled by forces beyond her scope, yet holding firm, and remaining, in her own style, noble, is Kate, the daughter of Lionel Croy. Thus the interest and even the beauty begin to gather at last to the side of the will, craft and, energy that have failed in part and are now thrown back with little but themselves to live upon. In affairs and political theories the cult of these things is just now evident; and art also is touched by it—more legitimately. In this way, with his share in the specialist's temper, and his love for 'strangeness in beauty', Mr. Henry James, aloof as he appears, is trebly representative—one of the finer voices that may be heard telling the future for what sort of things our time cared.

THE AMBASSADORS

1903

---

161. Frederick Taber Cooper, from a review, *Bookman* (America)

January 1904, xviii, 532–4

Frederick Taber Cooper (1864–1937) was an editor, critic, and Professor of Classics. For further comment on *The Ambassadors* see below, Nos. 165, 186, and 189.

A great deal has been written, and with justice, about the obscurity of Mr. James, his bewildering mannerisms, his maze of qualifying words and phrases, in which a reader wanders, as through a verbal mist, to end hopelessly in a blind alley of inexplicable syntax. But what has not been generally recognised is that the obscurity and the queerness lie, not so much in Mr. James's manner of telling a tale as in the tale itself that he has to tell. He is not stating a clear story in a hopelessly involved manner; he is giving as clear a statement as he can of a much befogged condition of facts—and that is a radically different matter. . . .

In many ways, *The Ambassadors* will prove to be easier reading than the last three or four volumes by Mr. James have been. To begin with, he has obviously had, aside from the particular set of characters that he undertakes to study, a very definite central thought, a thought which his careful labours upon the biography of the sculptor Storey has naturally kept uppermost in his mind,—namely, the influence of Europe, its older culture, its radically different standards, upon the American temperament. Perhaps the best brief definition of *The Ambassadors* which can be given is, A study of the New England conscience, subjected to the hot-house atmosphere of the Parisian *Vie de Bohême*. And secondly the characters are chiefly American characters, deliciously, refreshingly American—yet the sort of Americans that you usually have to go to Europe to discover. To give a straightforward analysis of *The Ambassadors* would be to do violence to Mr. James's literary creed. He himself never gives you straightforward facts, but merely a series of impressions. And these you have to take as he gives them and let them accumulate and sink in, until their ultimate significance gradually dawns upon you. You do not need to wait long for an impression of Mr. Strethers; you get him in the opening page—a tall, thin, overworked man of letters, something better, yet not much better than a hack-writer, who has suddenly had the unexpected boon of a vacation, a private embassy to Paris, which may lengthen out for weeks and months. . . . Now just what Chad Newsome's life in Paris has been through all these years, and just what there is for Mr. Strethers to investigate, matters very little. What does concern us is to know what Mr. Strethers thinks that he finds out, the series of impressions which he receives. Somehow the atmosphere and traditions of the Latin Quarter, the laughter and the light and the gaiety of Paris gradually filter into Strethers's blood; the men he meets, and more especially the women, are all so different from what he had pictured them from the vantage-ground of far-away provincial Woolett, that his standards of morality undergo a curious and interesting readjustment. And acting according to this new light, he gives Chad some surprising advice, calculated permanently to wreck his own chances of ever filling the offices of the defunct Mr. Newsome. And yet throughout more than five hundred pages, Mr. Strethers has been wandering in a mental haze. He has not really known the simple basic fact that has kept Chad Newsome all these years in Paris. He has seen Chad and Mme. Vionnet in each other's company day after day; he has talked with them, singly and together, until he thinks there is nothing left for him to know. And yet the simple, elemental truth about them does not dawn upon him until the morning that he wanders alone out to the rural districts beyond Rennes, and there in one of those idyllic spots dear to artists, sees a rowboat containing a man who held the paddles, and a lady in the stern, with a pink parasol—saw them, recognised them, and suddenly awakened to a knowledge of infinite and undreamed possibilites. A book with all the tantalising vagueness of real life, and one which surely no one other than Henry James could have written.

162. Gertrude Atherton on discovering later James

[1932]

Gertrude Atherton, from *Adventures of a Novelist*, 363-5.
Mrs. Atherton (see No. 63) was by now (1904) an established
novelist, living away from America. For her story see No. 163. For
Edmund Gosse see No. 141. The *'sic'* is in the original text.

Until this visit to London I had not read Henry James for years. I
didn't like the books of his second period: his *Princess Casamassima*,
Spoils of Poynton, *The Tragic Muse*, *The Sacred Fount*; I had been unable
to read any of them through. They were dull; he had lost his light touch.
. . . I expressed this opinion to Edmund Gosse and he replied peremp-
torily; 'Oh, but you must read his later novels. He has entered upon his
period of real greatness. *The Ambassadors* is his last. Get it to-morrow
and read it.'

I did, and then I read all the others: *What Maisie Knew*, *The Other
House*, *The Two Magics* (surely 'The Turn of the Screw' is the most
horrifying ghost story ever written!), *The Golden Bowl*, *The Wings of
the Dove*—which still seems to me one of the greatest novels in the
history of fiction.

I had arranged with Macmillan & Company, my current publishers,
to bring out a volume of short stories in the following year; it was to
include those I had written some years before and published in *Vanity
Fair*, 'The Striding Place', one laid in Pont Aven, the tale that had appeared in *The Anglo-Saxon Review*, and several others.

A day or two after the luncheon at Sidney Lee's I wrote Henry
James asking if I might dedicate that book to him. Of course I expressed
my unbounded admiration for his work, and told him also that I had
been much under his influence when I began to write but had withdrawn
not only because I didn't care to imitate anyone but because I had come
to realize that it was a sort of theft and cheapened the idol's glory rather
than enhanced it.

361

His reply was rather pathetic, none too well expressed, and written in a hand that caused me hours of agony.

> Reform Club,
> Pall Mall, S.W.
> April 25th, 1904

Dear Mrs. Atherton:

It would give me great pleasure that you should dedicate a book to me—if you should see your way, in your own 'interest,' to doing anything so inauspicious as to invoke my presence in respect to the popularity of the outcome. May my name, I mean, contribute to bring your work better fortune than it usually contributes to bring mine. I am greatly obliged to you at any rate for your so friendly appreciation of my good influence, or [illegible] I may call it in the past. Such assurances give one a lift, send back echoes of one's voice, and make me feel at all events,

> Yours most truly,
> Henry James.

He had lost his large public during his second phase and was little read now save by intellectuals, who never supported anybody. Fortunately he had a private income.

I never could understand the point of that witticism (*sic*) apropos his three manners: James the First, James the Second, and James the Pretender. In his first period he showed a distinguished talent; in the second aridity descended upon him; but in the third he surely gave the world the genius that was in him. And who are his rivals? The Pretenders are those that try to imitate him. Really great critics like Edmund Gosse have set their seal upon him, and if there are any thinking critics to-day comparable with that distinguished galaxy of the late nineteenth and early twentieth centuries, and not wholly warped by middle-class ideology, they hardly can fail to agree with them.

In the course of the year I wrote a long short story of which Henry James was the hero and called it 'The Bell in the Fog'; and this title I gave to the volume of short stories I had asked permission to dedicate to him.

163. Gertrude Atherton's fictional tribute in 'The Bell in the Fog'

1904

Gertrude Atherton, from *The Bell in the Fog*, 1904, 4–6. I quote here the opening sketch of the Jamesian hero which is the most interesting part from the present point of view. The story continues in a fanciful and rather morbid vein, involving Orth's obsession with an ancient portrait of a little girl which he discovers in his newly acquired Tudor country house, and its remarkable resemblance to a little American girl he finds on the estate—etc.

Orth had left the United States soon after his first successes, and, his art being too great to be confounded with locality, he had long since ceased to be spoken of as an American author. All civilised Europe furnished stages for his puppets, and, if never picturesque nor impassioned, his originality was as overwhelming as his style. His subtleties might not always be understood—indeed, as a rule, they were not—but the musical mystery of his language and the penetrating charm of his lofty and cultivated mind induced raptures in the initiated, forever denied to those who failed to appreciate him.

His following was not a large one, but it was very distinguished. The aristocracies of the earth gave to it; and not to understand and admire Ralph Orth was deliberately to relegate one's self to the ranks. But the elect are few, and they frequently subscribe to the circulating libraries; on the Continent, they buy the Tauchnitz edition; and had not Mr. Orth inherited a sufficiency of ancestral dollars to enable him to keep rooms in Jermyn Street, and the wardrobe of an Englishman of leisure, he might have been forced to consider the tastes of the middle-class at a desk in Hampstead. But, as it mercifully was, the fashionable and exclusive sets of London knew and sought him. He was too wary to become a fad, and too sophisticated to grate or bore; consequently, his popularity continued evenly from year to year, and long since he had come to be regarded as one of them. He was not keenly addicted to sport, but he could handle a gun, and all men respected his dignity and breeding. They cared less for his books than women did, perhaps because patience is not a characteristic of their sex. I am alluding, however, in this instance, to men-of-the-world. A group of young literary men—and one or two women—put him on a pedestal and kissed the earth before it. Naturally, they imitated him, and as this flattered him, and he had a kindly heart deep among the cerecloths of his formalities, he sooner or later wrote 'appreciations' of them all, which nobody living could understand, but which owing to the sub-title and signature answered every purpose.

164. Sydney Waterlow on James as the subtlest and strongest modern writer

1904

Sydney Waterlow, 'The work of Mr. Henry James', *Independent Review*, November 1904, iv, 236–43.

The *Independent* was at this time the organ of the younger intelligentsia of Bloomsbury and Cambridge, and it is entirely appropriate that this advocacy of HJ's later work should have appeared in it. The reader will perhaps see it as an extension of the line taken by Oliver Elton in No. 160. Both articles are superior products of HJ's new small circle of admirers, and both untypical of the general level of understanding. Waterlow (1878–1944) was a diplomat and scholar. He later lost some of his enthusiasm for HJ's work, as is shown by an article in the *New Statesman*, February 1926, xxvi, 514–5, where he says, for example, that:

. . . there is something neuter and sterile about Henry James's art, a kind of mule quality. But the ivory tower of his self-imprisonment was built of a far more precious substance than verbal felicities. He was never in bondage to mere words; on the contrary, he wielded over them a steeled and disciplined mastery, a conscious control inspired by a central purpose. His achievement has the inevitability that nothing but an authentic individual vision can give, and in this respect, as in the integrity of the vision itself, he has nothing to fear from comparison with any true poet. The failure lies, if anywhere, in the scope and quality of his vision, not in a lack of intensity, nor yet in the absence of a relation to life, but in a certain etherealised poverty which it is no easy problem to define.

'Monsieur Bergeret' is the chief character—a provincial humanist Professor—of Anatole France's series of satirical novels, the *Histoire Contemporaine* (1896–1901).

The characteristic which is so prominent as to distinguish Mr. James from all other imaginative writers is his steady effort to give a picture of things as they are— to have done with conventional shams and expedients, and honestly to describe the complex emotions of a complex world. Even without *William Wetmore Story and his Friends*, this aim was to be gathered from the long progression of his novels; but it emerges beyond doubt in this recent biography, where the American artist, whether in Rome or Boston or London, gives occasion to evoke the shapes of actual people. The people evoked appear to us, players on the great international stage, each involved in the web of circumstance, in precisely the same light as do the people of the novels—clear evidence of the artist's seriousness, since he uses in this analysis of historical persons no other method than in that of the creatures of his fancy. By themselves, however, the novels were proof enough. They culminate in *What Maisie Knew*, *The Awkward Age*, *The Sacred Fount*, *The Wings of the Dove*, *The Better Sort*, *The Ambassadors*—books which enshrine in careful workmanship the rich results of his riper vision. The earlier books were often mistakes and experiments. He had to discover that it was not his vocation to kill Roderick Hudson over an Alpine precipice, nor to toil through the Dickens-like labyrinth of *Princess Casamassima*. But each experiment was an advance; each stage was marked by some new rejection of the extraneous and the irrelevant; until he attained sure knowledge of what he desired to represent, and perfect command of the means of representation. The result of the whole process is a description, unrivalled for completeness and detail, of those mental movements which underlie all outward manifestations of civilised life—no mere indication that beneath the surface even of ordinary people a mind is moving, but an account of exactly how it moves. Nor is it an artificial, mechanical dissection, such as the French practise; but rather an inspired pursuit of 'suggestion to her inmost cell,' only successful by reason of the exact and delicate instrument which language has become in his hands.

Mr. James's complexity and difficulty follow from this very devotion to reality. Although we all in practice confess the complexity of life, yet the theory that it is a struggle of majestically simple emotions seems to retain a curious power of warping the judgment. Nothing is commoner than the prejudice which confuses what is with what ought to be: and of this fallacy the view of Mr. James's complexity, as something perverse and malicious, is a typical instance. It *ought* perhaps to be true that things move towards satisfying ends on clear and simple lines. But nothing compels us to suppose that it *is* true; and there is no reason to dismiss as unreal the writer who dwells on the difficulty, the delicacy, the danger of everyday life. Reason there might be, if his vision were distorted, if he saw things which really do not exist, if he were a 'later Alexandrian' seeking refuge from the world in shadowy fancies. As it is, however, the attempt to give an impression of that ceaseless play of mind which takes place among human beings and is only half expressed in their actual utterance, constitutes no sin against reality; and, on the other hand, few have had a keener eye for the things which everybody can easily see—scenes and places, cities and quiet country, works of art, all the appurtenances of civilisation, down to cookery and furniture. He differs, in a word, from the mass, not by ignoring what they see, but by absorbing it and seeing more besides. If he is obscure, it is not from any pursuit of 'mystic wrynesses,' but because the subject however, clearly conceived and expressed, remains genuinely difficult. The difficulty, for instance, of such a book as *The Sacred Fount* arises, not from lack of reality so much as from its unusual nature, 'Life,' the author might be figured as saying, 'is complicated and puzzling; if you have any sense of the puzzle, I will try and explain it to you, not by expounding any General Law, but by giving you a clear and clever picture which you may behold with delight. Thus we will enquire—as do you not continually in actual life? —into the true posture of certain souls. We must not hope for any final understanding of their relations to one another; but hypotheses will be thrown out, partly verified, partly discarded—the whole process conducted by flashes of intuition, for which gross speech will not be the only nor the best medium, in drawing-rooms and gardens, in places of "noble freedom" and "over-arching ease" '. If we are deaf to the appeal, and are merely left with the impression of a baffling game of cross-purposes, the fault is not the author's; the blame lies rather with the traditional view of life which, by the common fallacy, prevents us from seeing that certain processes and states of mind may be real and even usual, although repugnant to our theory of what is desirable. At every turn, indeed, the fallacy meets us. Thus, because we think that we *ought* to be active, we easily imagine that we *are* active, and so can persist in blindness to our own likeness in these books, where action is conspicuously absent, and there is practically no medium through which the characters can make themselves known, except the author's description and their own spoken words. Again, Mr. James accords with experience in the method by which he produces his effects superimposing minute touches until the characters are gradually felt in their entirety. We would, no doubt, like to be able to hit off our friends in half-a-dozen broad strokes; but Carlyle's method, however amusing and convenient, is not a good engine of truth, and may easily become fatal to honest insight. Mr. James is a far truer mirror of our actual knowledge of one another—knowledge which, where it is most ample, passes into a sensation, quite definite indeed, but inexpressible, because of the multitude of touches which compose it.

'But,' says the objector, 'even when the truth of what he gives us is granted, all is spoiled by unreality of manner. People are not engaged in such a jargon of perpetual dialogue; and, what is more, the tone of talk never changes; whatever the circumstances, whoever the actors, nothing breaks the monotony.'

Now, as to the reproach that the characters use in whatever circumstances one and all the same language, two observations are in place. First, it is a salient trait of civilised life, and a peculiarity not without charm and excitement, that the actors do in fact use the same manner of speech on the most weighty as on the most trivial occasions. Even when the air is thick with passion, the departure from our commonplace, even our vulgar vocabulary, is small; and to have given expression in art to the fact that common words often go charged with shades of deep meaning, is among the greatest triumphs of fiction. Secondly, uniformity of speech became inevitable the moment the author refrained from treating widely different types and classes. The talk of most civilised people is in essentials so similar, that the artist has little to gain by dwelling on the differences. Differences of course exist; but that they are vastly significant there is no reason to suppose. The style of conversation of a society matron is not precisely the same as that of a lonely old maid; but to him whom life interests in proportion as it can be made to reveal the workings of the soul, the difference is so small as to seem irrelevant, and rightly to be neglected. And, finally, this fact—that the object of the talk is to reveal the workings of the soul—saves the talk from being a jargon. A novelist is not a phonograph, that he should record the exact words which fall from human lips. Not verbal accuracy, but skilful selection from the mass of talk heard and imagined, is necessary to the accuracy of his presentation. We can convince ourselves how wide are the limits of probability prescribed by common sense, by reflecting on the reason why we should be shocked were the dialogue of a novel occasionally to lapse into blank verse: evidently blank verse would offend, not because conversations are not in fact carried on in it, but simply because it would be inappropriate to the literary form. Under some conditions, blank verse may be a legitimate form into which to cast dialogue, because, as famous examples prove, the intercourse of human minds may be

faithfully reproduced in that metre. And, similarly, Mr. James's conversations, provided they reproduce the spirit, could not be justly
attacked as unreal, even were they far less real than is actually the case.
As it is, the careful reader cannot fail to discover, that the talk of the
persons glasses forth their minds from as true a surface as artist ever
polished, wrought with matchless skill and humour to arrest and
preserve whatever is of importance in the substance of our mental
life.

I now come to the question of moral values. In real life we, roughly
speaking, think it good to love good men and to hate bad; and, what is
more, we generally judge that man who strongly loves good and hates
evil, to be better both than one who loves evil and hates good, and
than one who is little affected by either. Hence, as it is the business of
novelists, and that of Mr. James in a unique degree, to give pictures of
real life, it seems plausible to suppose that the merit of the pictures will,
at any rate to some extent, depend on the emotions excited being such
as we can approve; *i.e.*, not only must what is presented as hateful or
admirable be hateful or admirable in point of fact, but also the feeling
displayed should be enthusiastic. No novel, it can safely be said, will
be of the highest excellence, which does not distinguish between good
and evil, passionately as well as accurately. Now, as regards accuracy
of discrimination, Mr. James leaves no opening for criticism. In the
consistent and reasonable judgment of right and wrong, he succeeds
where almost all other novelists fail at one time or another, Charlotte
Brontë and George Meredith being alone his peers in this respect.
Thackeray, for instance, has a sadly uncertain touch for this, which is,
after all, his main theme; we never know exactly what it is that Thackeray approves, and we always suspect that it was not so very admirable.
Dickens, again, says of Mr. Dick and Dr. Strong pacing before the
schoolroom windows: 'I feel as if they might go walking to and fro
for ever and the world might somehow be the better for it'—the one
being a harmless lunatic and the other a scholar whom we are asked to
love for his futility. This vice, the sentimentalism for over-praising what
deserves little or no praise, re-appears in an aggravated form in Mr.
Kipling, who stirs up yet greater admiration for yet worse things; and
in all its forms it is remote from Mr. James. Nor do we find in him
any trace of that more fashionable sentimentalism, which, as typified
by Monsieur Bergeret poring over his *Vergilius nauticus*, pretends that
the world is a cage of monkeys where everything is of small and equal
value. On the contrary, that some things are of very high value and

others of very low, is the conviction, not openly announced, yet implied, in every line of Mr. James's writing. Unwavering in this conviction, he never prostitutes his tremendous powers of analysis; he neither seeks for excuses, as does the fond moralist, for stupid, disingenuous, vulgar, and self-interested people, nor does he, like the cynic, depreciate those possessed of the contrary qualities.

Finally, the passionate love for one another of the people whose good qualities he thus acutely discriminates, is the dominant note of Mr. James's best work. The development of plot and the depiction of character are determined, down to the smallest details, by the emotion which conceived this love as the best thing in the world, the one end as means or hindrance to which all else is justified or condemned. Many, I know, do not feel the presence of this great emotional quality, and deny genuine passion to him, mainly on the ground that he shrinks from great issues, and attends too much to certain minor and abnormal aspects of humanity. He does not discourse of Life and Death and Fate in words which might be quoted; so that little can be done to show that he is as humanly passionate as Tolstoy, for instance, though more reticent, beyond pointing out how easily the passion may be present in his case and yet ignored. His reticence has, in fact, a definite reason, which, when understood, may make us pause before pronouncing him frigid; and that reason is his attitude towards questions of right and wrong action. He is gifted, as we have seen, with an acute and restless sense both of the intricacy and of the value of human relations. Their intricacy is so deeply felt, that he rarely, at least in his later books, finds it possible to say of a person, who took a particular course of action, that he did right or that he ought to have acted otherwise; and, so keen is his sense of their value, that he is equally unable to be sanguine in any given case as to the good results of forcible action. I am not concerned either to attack or to defend this position. I only mention it in order to suggest that, as it pervades Mr. James's novels, it may account for their being thought inhuman. For it is certainly an irritating position; by not meting out praise and blame to his character's actions, by leaving doubtful, for instance, the morality of what Kate Croy did, he inevitably makes on many an impression of indifference and pessimism; although obviously the position is not incompatible with passion, and he who doubts whether anything can be done to remedy a bad state of affairs need not be regarded as a trifler and a barren analyst.

To contend that some such irrelevant irritation obscures the passion of his novels, is, of course, a purely negative argument—it can not show the passion to be there; but, such as it is, it finds some support in the exactly converse case of Tolstoy. Beyond doubt, part of Tolstoy's popularity springs from the fervour with which he holds what Mr. James's work denies: to wit, that right action is simple. He gains admirers, that is, not only by his skill in representing people and situations; but also by arousing sympathy with his theory that the individual can make an immense difference for the better by doing something definite. For Tolstoy, the blaze of his conviction illumines life; in its light he approaches and can dare to portray the tragic moments directly —birth, death, the meeting and parting of men and women; and we must be stocks not to feel the intensity and genuineness of the passion in these pictures. At the same time, his assault on our emotions would not be so over-whelming, were it not that his belief in the effectiveness of the individual will sorts with what all desire to believe; if he did not hold this belief so strongly, we might conceivably think his passion less. And, just so, if Mr. James did not dash our spirits by scepticism about the individual will, we might conceivably think his passion greater.

Such negative arguments can do no more than pave the way for sympathy by removing prejudices. In the long run, nothing but sympathetic insight can decide whether or not Mr. James's sense of the nobility of noble things and the vileness of vile is genuinely emotional. But, if the last resort must be to the responsive thrill of feeling, we need not therefore reject the help of our reasoning faculties. Indeed, we are bound to employ them. The passion of his characters lurks in their mental developments, and is never fully exposed, either in words or action; so that we must spare no pains to follow these mental developments, if we would appreciate the significance of those half-smothered ambiguous cries which are the only outlets of the struggling soul. If his actors seem stunted, warped, and repressed, it is because their creator, filled with the sense of complexity, and intent on displaying the truth, shows us men and women, thwarted and hampered by circumstances as they in fact are, yet preserving, amidst evil, much that is good and beautiful. To the discovery of this goodness and beauty, surviving here and there in the machinery of modern life, he addresses himself with as much emotion as insight, and, in disentangling the good from the evil, suddenly brings us, for all his gentleness and urbanity, upon tragedy of the highest order. The gentleness and urbanity, the kind humour which makes the best of a faulty world—these flow naturally from his view of things as complex. The results of action being incalculable, and society a fabric of springs and checks and counter-checks, the wise man cannot but walk delicately. And again, this very view of complexity combines with the passion for goodness and beauty to draw about his creations an atmosphere of wistfulness, a sigh, as it were, for what they might have been, has the world been other than it is. Older novelists were content to portray men and women much as they were seen by the average man. Mr. James penetrates to their essence, sympathises with their inmost perplexities, and contemplates them in the mild light of eternity.

165. Arnold Bennett on not finishing *The Ambassadors*

1905

Arnold Bennett, from his Journal, January 1905 (*The Journals of Arnold Bennett*, ed. Newman Flower, 1932, i, 206).

On Wells's recommendation I have been reading Henry James's *The Ambassadors*. I have read 150 pages out of 450, and I have given it up. It certainly does contain, as Wells said, some wonderful little pictures of Paris, and the Anglo-Saxon colonies there. The writing, though difficult, is amazingly adequate. It is merely perfect. But I found the plot clumsily managed, and a very considerable absence of passionate feeling. I came to the conclusion that the book was not *quite* worth the great trouble of reading it.

THE GOLDEN BOWL

1904

166. From an unsigned review,
Times Literary Supplement

February 1905, 47

These remarks are preceded by a summary of *The Golden Bowl* up to Maggie's discovery of the adultery.

An artist is not most wisely praised by censure of his inferiors; but it is impossible not to glance aside from Mr. James to the common run of modern fiction. The situation we have reached in the story of the Prince and Princess is a situation to which any novelist could have led up, and it is easy to imagine how, each striving to be as like the other as possible till their very violence became commonplace, they would have forced from it scenes and explosions. The situation itself is one which we are tempted to call more human, at any rate plainer and more obvious, than those usual of late with Mr. James. It would lend itself to scenes and explosions. As it is, the only person who comes near to making a scene, in that sense, is Mrs. Assingham, who at most had shuffled and dealt the cards, and had no hand in the square game played with them. A game it was, a contest of wit and character. Each of the four players was asking himself or another—What cards do the rest hold, and what knowledge of the lie of the pack have they? In particular, what does Adam Verver hold and know? The reader—the spectator of the game—knows nothing of any hand except what he can gather from the fall of the cards. Mr. James is not going to tell him. If he misses or forgets a single card, the game is likely to mean nothing to him; but if he is patient, very patient, observant, and thoughtful, he will be rewarded by a fine high-comedy game, exceedingly well played. Adam Verver, the inscrutable, plays in masterly fashion, but he is playing, and knows it, for a loss; his partner, Charlotte, holds the worst cards, perhaps, and certainly plays the worst game of all; the Prince is little more than dummy to the Princess, and it is Maggie, the quiet, mouse-like little Maggie (she reminds us a little of Minnie Theale), who, by daring and endurance, by *finesse*, and by an astonishing inversion of 'bluff,' comes out triumphantly the victor. Well, there are spectators who like to be told beforehand where the cards are, and prefer to meet nothing in the play so deep as to call for thought. *The Golden Bowl* is not for them. There are others who find that, however patiently and alertly they may watch, the games that our author arranges for them are not played according to any rules they know, that none of the players seem to mean anything by their play, and that sometimes that no one seems to win in the end. To these we commend *The Golden Bowl*. Patience and attention are, of course, necessary; there must be a conscious surrender and a conscious effort, for Mr. James, artist though he is, is not one of the very great who, while they demand that you shall see things only as they see them, make it impossible, by their very force, that you shall see them otherwise. But at least he is great enough to be worthy of the effort he demands.

167. From an unsigned review, *Academy*

February 1905, lxviii, 128-9

The plot is cunningly contrived, artfully interwoven. Perhaps for 'plot' we should say 'situation,' since (as in all James novels) it is the evolution of character under the development of a situation rather than plot in the usual sense, which is the groundwork of the story. A James situation is always subtle; but this is intricately subtle—so intricate in its subtlety as to intimidate any attempt at brief description or analysis. . . . The emotion, the tragedy, though keen, is never violent, never full-blooded. Mr. James knows that modern domesticity is a thing of half-tints, even in its suffering: it bleeds, but it does not bleed red. The *Golden Bowl* is a crystal vessel cased in gold, which plays a part in the tale with somewhat Ibsen-like symbolism; a crystal vessel with a secret flaw, which finally shatters—allegorising the character and fate of the Italian Prince. Not only in length and elaboration is this a novel which claims attention, even among Mr. Henry James's work. As the plot, so is the execution, subtly intricate. Often, alas! but too much so! Mr. James's later work has frequently carried his peculiar qualities to a baffling extreme, and much of this book has the defect of those qualities harassingly in evidence. The intellectuality overpowers the sensuous and objective traits proper to a novel, until one has the impression of reading an abstruse treatise of psychology rather than a tale. . . . We know that in life people often answer to each other's meaning rather than to the thing actually spoken; that you may have passages of dialogue wherein the actual words are but signposts pointing to the intended significance. . . . But in this book it is at times pushed to a nebulousness, a tenuity, which gives one the feeling of walking on tight-ropes. Moreover, people, after all, talk in this way but at moments, under stress of some withheld emotion, impelled by some particular motive. But here people often propound enigmas to each other for page after page, till the wearied reader rebels. Then, too, Mr. James's extraordinary gift in detecting and expressing the most evanescent complexities of psychological feeling, subconscious or unconscious thought, has seemingly become such a passion that he cannot for an instant disembarrass himself of it. It overpowers his instinct of proportion: he must analyse everything, important or trivial, with like minuteness and like prolixity. Thus you have page upon page in which the game is beautifully played, but the game was really not worth the candle. . . .

But it fairly ranks as a master-work—if a master-work flawed by some of his obscurest later mannerisms. It is not built for popularity; but no lover of Mr. Henry James can neglect it without loss. It is a last word of subtlety, marred at times by subtlety out of place.

168. Unsigned review, *Illustrated London News*

February 1905, cxxvi, 268

Some philosophers hold it to be an error for races to intermarry. It is especially dangerous for a Latin to wed a Teuton, and awful warnings have been launched even against the marriage of Englishmen with Irish ladies. American women are said to be more than usually rash when they espouse Italian noblemen; and Mr. Henry James may have had this in his mind as a theme for his new book. An Italian Prince takes to wife the daughter of an American millionaire. More than that, he has an affair with another American lady, even when she becomes his step-mother-in-law. The social complication is what Mr. James, who is fond of an occasional lapse into slang, might call 'a little bit thick.' But when you reach the end of the story you see that he does not attribute to his nobleman any especially Italian characteristic, unless it be a capacity to love two women at once. What is really striking in the nobleman is his resignation to the stroke of destiny which deprives him of one of them. Luckily it is the stepmother-in-law; and she is barely out of sight when he displays the most sincere emotion in the discovery that he really loves his wife above all other women. It will be disputed by moralists whether a man who acts like Prince Amerigo could be capable of any sincere attachment. But Mr. James believes him capable, and somehow we have an implicit trust in Mr. James's observation of human nature, an observation which may be unduly minute, but is seldom astray. Minute it is in this book to an astonishing degree, astonishing even for Mr. James. He is not content with an infinite dissection of the principal characters; he treats us to a separate dissection by two onlookers, who commend their views to each other at great length. When Colonel Assingham, after listening for pages to his wife, exclaims, 'Oh, Lordy, Lordy!' we are grateful to him for the expression of our sentiments. But the book, despite this amplification of Mr. James's most divergent manner, has a very remarkable delicacy and charm—qualities that grow rarer in what is too often, by a stretch of courtesy, still called the art of fiction.

169. From an unsigned review, *Graphic*

March 1905, lxxi, 264

A new novel by Mr. Henry James excites in the mind of its unfortunate reviewer very mingled feelings, and the foremost of these is regret—regret that a writer who can analyse character in so masterly a manner should think fit to express himself in a manner which must prevent scores and hundreds of people from appreciating his great qualities. One of the tragedies of possessing and handling a manner, style, or method of expression which is peculiarly your own is that in process of time the method which has been your slave becomes your master. . . . And so it comes about that clever though *The Golden Bowl* may be, one thinks regretfully of *Daisy Miller* and the days when Mr. James was not apparently convinced that the essence of art was prolixity. Of the two schools of writers who analyse character and try to place living revealed people before us, we must admit to preferring the school which holds that art is suggestion rather than minute explanation, and not one of these characters lives as vividly in one's mind, even after plodding through 550 pages, as do a score of other fictional characters sketched by other writers in that number of words. And yet the story itself is a comparatively simple one. . . . This tale is told with wonderful insight into the springs of conduct, and with marvellous analysis of shades of feeling and of emotions hardly born; but the old saying about not being able to see the forest for the trees is always at the back of one's head when reading such passages as this:

It may be mentioned, also, that he always figured other persons—such was the law of his nature—as a numerous array, and that, though conscious of but a single near tie, one affection, one duty deepest rooted in his life, it had never, for many minutes together, been his portion not to feel himself surrounded and committed, never quite been his refreshment to make out where the many-coloured human appeal, represented by gradations of tint, diminishing concentric zones of intensity, of importunity, really faded to the blessed impersonal whiteness for which his vision sometimes ached.

After many hundred pages in this style one yearns for some simplicity. In brief, Mr. James is an acquired taste, and he should be left to the select circle.

170. From an unsigned review, *Athenaeum*

March 1905, 4038, 332

Here we are shown not the human heart under a microscope, as with the ordinary analytical novelist, but the soul developing itself from within, finding in other persons, circumstances, and happenings nothing but the matter of its thought. It is objected that Mr. James is super-subtle, and trails an idea through far too many windings, sets it in too many lights, refines and explains and exiguates, so to say, *ad nauseam*. This book will awaken this objection more than ever. But let any one reflect on his thought upon any matter that concerns him personally; let him take only half-an-hour of it, and try to retrace all its involutions, and he will find himself ten times as full of distractions, of strange backward twists, of hesitations, of reasons and imaginings, as any of Mr. James's characters. The fact is brought out in this new book, for none of the *dramatis personæ* is at all extraordinary. . . . Indeed, the lack of greatness in his characters—their essential littleness—while it may enhance the realism of Mr. James's work, strikes us as one of its serious defects as great art. . . .

The method, in spite of its 'inwardness,' is detached, cold, and, if the word is possible, a little cruel. But its mental agility, its likeliness, its atmosphere, are perfect. Why Mr. James should require so very disagreeable a situation to develop his study we cannot understand, but that he has elaborated it as no one else could, we are sure; indeed, we should have liked two more books in the novel, one giving the story as it affects the mind of Charlotte, the brilliant, hard, repulsive woman, and the other showing it in the mind of the millionaire, strange compound of shrewdness and simplicity, inexorable decision and inexhaustible kindliness. Mr. James can hardly achieve a greater success than that of making even one of his readers desire that the book were double its length.

March 1905, xcix, 383–4

The years are past when one's interest, one's concern, in opening a new book by Mr. Henry James was to discover how far he had retained or by how much he had modified his wonderful manner, which, first revealed to us in *The Tragic Muse*, seemed to attain completeness in *The Spoils of Poynton*. That manner, which has, as it were, shut a water-tight door on Mr. James's admirers, and made them feel themselves, unfortunately, but inevitably, a little community of the elect, is now as surely a part of his speech as a tone of voice or an alien accent, and one's preoccupation, with each fresh presentment, has been transferred to the material on which it is to be used. And for this reason. Wonderful as the manner is, intrinsically subtle, hyperæsthetically discreet, it is exposed alike by its subtlety and its discretion to a too easy satisfaction in its sources of interest. With existence so absorbingly perplexed, so prismatically trans-figured, the subject matter of romance becomes of a quite serious un-importance to the adroit manipulator; indeed, as his sense of the magic colour in every part of its web grows insistently acute, he is even led to avoid those parts of it which are impressed with the big dramatic patterns, lest these should divert attention from the exquisite intricacy of texture on which his thoughts are set. Such a danger confronts every writer who is primarily interested in what is to his public of only secondary account, and it is the greater danger to Mr. James, since his genius is essentially dramatic and, lacking the saliencies of drama, as high mountain peaks, to lead him from one wide outlook to another, is apt to keep us too long wandering in valleys beneath mountain mists of hypothesis and speculation.

The dramatic quality of Mr. James's work may not be obvious to readers who measure dramatic force rather by its disturbance than its significance. The stage, always eager for the obvious, has publicly affianced drama to a fury of gesture and a high voice, preferring its spent forces to its springs; but to productive intensity, the pregnancy of action is of more importance than its barren effect, however astounding; and thus putting a knife into one's pocket may have in it more of drama than putting it into a man. It is by the exhibition of what one may call deferred action that Mr. James achieves his dramatic effects, and by it he practically tells the whole story.

This is why the success of his method depends on the significance and variety and, one might add, the humanity of the dramatic moments arising naturally from his theme, and why, too, being such a perilous and impossible author to 'skip', he is represented so often by professional skippers as an extremely involved and difficult writer. Yet, with the exception of an occasional sentence which has been asked to carry more than it conveniently can, Mr. James is, considering all he has to say, very easily followed by those who read him.

But he is so exact, so continuous in his presentation of ideas, that often the omission of a single sentence may confuse the purpose of a page, and the omission of a page render unintelligible the dramatic moment—even if that be not missed too—on which an interpretive interest in the tale depends. For though these moments are few, they are tremendously led up to. Between the curtain's rising on each fresh tableau there is an intricate and indefatigable training of our perception to obtain the full effect of it. Without such training, indeed, the tableaux would not count for much; for pregnant as they are with action, they are themselves often so still, so slight, so dependent on, perhaps, the lifting of an eyebrow, or the length of a glance, that unless announced in Mr. James's deliberative way, one might scarcely notice them. Take the first meeting of Charlotte Stant and the Prince—the first, that is, of which we are spectators. As she enters the room, 'she could have looked at her hostess with such straightness and brightness only from knowing that the Prince was also there'. Such a regard may not seem much of a clue; yet to the Prince 'that immediate exclusive address to their friend was like a lamp she was holding aloft for his benefit and for his pleasure. It showed him everything'. It is to show us everything too, though we have never seen before and scarcely heard of Charlotte, and have spent a short half-hour with the Prince; everything, even to her having once so loved him that 'she might have been anything she liked —except his wife'. The peculiar significance of Charlotte's address is not a fair example of the author's wonderful manner, since it occurs at the opening of the story, and our intelligence, instead of being prepared, has to be coaxed back to appreciate it; but it quite fairly represents the claim he makes on our attention, and the delicacy and energy of suggestion he obtains from his effects.

The most revealing and dramatic moment of the book is a woman's mere leaning out of a window. 'Something in her long look at him now

out of the old grey window'—it is again Charlotte and the Prince—
'something in the very poise of her hat, the colour of her necktie, the
prolonged stillness of her smile, touched into sudden light for him all the
wealth of the fact that he could count on her'. And it does, yes, just as
wonderfully, touch into sudden light the fact for us as well, so that the
rosebud she throws down to him has, by comparison with her appearance, no meaning at all. Hence it is that one has come to measure Mr.
James's success by the amount and intensity of dramatic action which a
theme will yield him. It is rather curious, perhaps no more than a
coincidence, but the change in his manner, his substitution of implicit
for explicit action, dates from days when he was a good deal occupied
with that school of action, the stage. One would like to think that hours
one so intensely grudged to that occupation have yielded so unlooked
for a reward. Be that as it may, the somewhat surprising fact remains
that the basis of Mr. James's later manner is dramatic, not didactic; and
its drama is always, at its best, of a high and simple human interest.

It is true that the drama is often hid, like some secret queen, at the
centre of a maze, a maze of fine shades and ultra-sensitive perceptions,
which one might almost fancy to be here put half-humorously before
us in the involutions of Mrs. Assingham. 'She was a person for whom
life was multitudinous detail, detail that left her, as it at any moment
found her, unappalled and unwearied.' 'My first impulse', she declared,
'is always to behave, about everything, as if I fear complications. But I
don't fear them. I really like them. They're quite my element'. They are
also, unquestionably, quite the element of Mr. James. It is almost impossible to conceive him placing a fact before us without its attach-
ments. His vision of the social mechanism is so discriminating and so
tenacious that one occasionally follows its amazing flights, as Bob
Assingham did those of his wife's intelligence, 'very much as he had
sometimes watched, at the Aquarium, the celebrated lady who, in a
slight, though tight, bathing suit, turned somersaults and did tricks in a
tank of water which looked so cold and uncomfortable to the non-
amphibious', and feel, as Mr. Verver felt when dealing with that same
intelligence, 'never quite sure of the ground anything covered'. But
that insecurity is, for some of us, one of the author's most seductive
charms, even though he not infrequently seems to resemble the Prince
'in liking explanations, liking them almost as if he collected them' and
with the Prince also to share an 'inability, in any matter in which he was
concerned, to conclude'. The book itself is evidence of that inability, for
one sees, without wishing a word of it away, what its story might

occasionally gain by a somewhat closer handling. Even to hint at that story would spoil the pleasure of the fortunate ones who have yet to follow its unfolding, for though Mr. James's dramatic effectiveness depends so largely on an historic vividness of emotion, it is in the exquisite flower-like opening of the fine petals of human feeling to the light, and in the atmosphere often so oppressively intense which he distils from character that his art displays its most essential quality.

172. Unsigned review, *Nation*

January 1905, lxxx, 74

The story contained in the two volumes entitled *The Golden Bowl* is elaborately concealed. It is involved, swathed, smothered in many obscurities, obscurities inseparable from the author's method of presenting an inside and outside and all-round view; obscurities arising from excessive use of extended metaphor, from saying too much and saying too little, even from sentences too complex and too elliptical, too long and too short. To get the story you must pay the price, must attack and overcome the obscurities; and whether this be done in a spirit of happy satisfaction of delight in the obscurities for their own sake, or of irritation, or of mere plodding determination to stick and pull through, in the end you have your reward—a story, a situation, which, as you think about it, pierces the obscurities and strikes you in the eyes, like the low red autumn sun pushing out of a mass of black clouds.

It is a short story and bitter. No one except Mr. James could tell it in English without grossness or vulgarity, without challenging our prejudices and prepossessions, without making us all out to be, in his estimation, no better than the French—a state of things we should hate to have forced upon our notice. And he doesn't literally tell the story; he only examines witnesses, comments on testimony, infers and speculates prodigiously, leaving us free to make what we can of the case, to grasp or miss its facts and its wide significance, according to our capacity for independent mental operations. To rehearse the facts is perhaps the most useful part that a reviewer can play between Mr. James and the public. Such preliminary knowledge doesn't impair interest which really lies in beating the bush with the author, sharing breathless moments when it seems that the game is about to break for the open, and long periods of doubt whether it hasn't, after all, tucked itself up and gone to sleep in perfect security. The facts at the bottom of *The Golden Bowl* glare when you have found them.

Mr. Verver, a person so rich that his nationality may be taken for granted, buys for his daughter Maggie a husband, a Roman Prince, with whom she has fallen in love because he is beautiful and charming and because the history of his ancestors' follies and crimes is recorded in many volumes neatly ranged on a shelf in the British Museum. The Prince assumes responsibilities in good faith. He means to use the Verver money as his own, to be an agreeable husband, and perhaps, according to his subdued lights, a faithful one. Just before the marriage, appears in London Miss Charlotte Stant, a dear friend of Maggie's, an old love of the Prince's, a lady of great beauty, courage, and resource. She has left her own vast and uninteresting continent and crossed the Atlantic ostensibly to buy a wedding present for Maggie. Her real purpose is more sinister. The Prince, bound to secrecy, is obliged to assist in the hunt for a present, and when an apparently suitable one, a golden bowl, is found, it appears that the offering is intended for him, not for Maggie. The Prince refuses the bowl, making a pretext of a crack and a super-stition about cracks. He is, indeed, as adamantine as a Prince may be to a fair woman with a past between them.

Charlotte, baffled, disappears, only to descend two years later upon an ideally happy home consisting of Mr. Verver, the Prince, the Princess and the Principino. The Prince, not yet sated with the sensation of roll-ing in money, finds the moment opportune for retiring with his Princess to one of his Italian hill places, leaving Charlotte to console Mr. Verver at 'Fawns,' another of his splendid acquisitions. When Mr. Verver buys Charlotte for a wife, the fat is conspicuously in the fire. At the end of the first volume the Princess wakes from bliss to perceive that her stepmother is also her husband's mistress. The Golden Bowl is sharply cracked, and the spectacle of the second volume is the struggle of all concerned to prevent the crack becoming a fissure so wide and deep that neither love nor cunning may avail to preserve an illusion of soundness.

Essentially a hideous struggle, it is difficult to accept all of Mr. James's embroidery of it in representation. The Prince's behavior is perfectly in character. As soon as he knows his wife's suspicions, he is on the defence. He initiates nothing; he waits for tips. He emphatically means in the last resort to abandon nothing for Charlotte, to 'stay bought.' He has, by nature, handed down through generations as surely as his title and his manners, a familiarity with unspeakable situa-tions, a facility for handling them with what his wife called high decency. The phrase sounds his deepest moral note. Experience of life's shady ways has fitted Charlotte to play pretty well up to her noble partner; and when, in an agony of conscious loss, she shifts the burden of wrong from herself to the Princess, she really earns the epithet 'splendid' so lavishly bestowed on her. In the prolonged game of bluff, it is the unsophisticated Ververs who strike us as inhumanly deep. Why, if Mr. Verver could suspect, should he have let things go so far? How, if he had not suspected long and shrewdly, could he have solved the situation by carrying Charlotte off to America, meaning that she should stay there eternally—a proceeding equivalent to declaring: 'I know all about this rotten business. I've been waiting to see what my daughter really wants. She wants to have her Prince at any price. She shall have him. Trust me now to keep Charlotte muzzled.'

There is a Mrs. Assingham who flits about the Verver establishments, always in the thick of things, useful in explaining to the Prince the strange race with which he has allied himself; useful also to the reader as a fairly correct indicator of the true state of affairs. She is very positive that Maggie knows no evil, is of a delicate stuff born not to know evil. Such is the impression of Maggie distinctly made up to the moment of the crisis. It is almost incredible that, suddenly confronted with evil which might have made a hardened sinner scream with a sense of insult and disgust, she could meet it with stoical reticence, set herself to compromise, to minimize, to hush up things with the patience and wariness of a practised diplomatist. The assumed motive is her love for her father; and underneath that, of course, is the personal power of the charming Prince. But recognition of the mutual affection of father and daughter and of their horror of 'hurting' each other does not suffice to make us believe either that Verver kept on smiling at the Prince through thick and thin, or that Maggie let Charlotte go off scot free with her head high. It is certain that Maggie meant to keep the Prince, but one is constantly sceptical of her ability to conduct the campaign for possession of his person with such consummate repression of natural instincts. Of course, Verver, at least, was supported through the ordeal by confidence in what his money could do. It had bought the Prince, it had bought Charlotte; why should it not keep the one where Maggie wanted him, beside her in England, and the other where Maggie wanted *her*, beside him, Verver, wandering vaguely in America, yet held in leash?

The appalling power for moral disintegration, if not corruption, implied in the possession of immense wealth could hardly be more impressively illustrated than it is in *The Golden Bowl*. Lest any reader should miss the persistent undercurrent, we quote a passage near the end. The Ververs have come to take formal farewell of the Prince and Princess. Father and daughter are looking about the drawing-room at the beautiful things which their money had bought:

Their eyes moved together from piece to piece, taking in the whole noble-ness—quite as if for him to measure the wisdom of old ideas. The two noble persons seated in conversation at tea fell thus into the splendid effect and the general harmony; Mrs. Verver and the Prince fairly 'placed' themselves, how-ever unwittingly, as high expressions of the kind of human furniture required æsthetically by such a scene. The fusion of their presence with the decorative elements, their contribution to the triumph of selection, was complete and admirable; though to a lingering view, a view more penetrating than the occa-sion really demanded, they also might have figured as a concrete attestation of the rare power of purchase. There was much, indeed, in the tone in which Adam Verner spoke again, and who shall say where his thought stopped? '*Le compte y est*. You've got some good things.'

173. Claude Bragdon, from a review, *Critic*

January 1905, xlvi, 20–2

Bragdon (1866–1946) was an architect, stage designer, and painter, and the author of numerous works on art and metaphysics.

Like some microscopist whose instrument, focussed on a pellucid drop of water, reveals within its depths horrible monsters feeding on one another, Mr. James shows forth the baffled passion, fear, jealousy, and wounded pride, the high courage and self-sacrifice which may lurk beneath the fair and shining surface of modern life in its finest and most finished manifestations. . . .

'Fanny Assingham had at this moment the sense of a large heaped dish presented to her intelligence and inviting it to a feast.'

It is thus that I would express my own feeling about this remarkable novel: there are so many things in it—the obscure workings of hereditary traits, the seduction exercised by Europe on the American imagination, the regenerative power of married love, the differences in the 'moral paste' of individuals—that like her I feel that to help myself too freely, to attempt to deal, in other words, with all these aspects in the space assigned me, would 'tend to jostle the ministering hand, confound the array, and, more vulgarly speaking, make a mess,' and so, like Mrs. Assingham again, I pick out for the reader's consideration 'a solitary plum.'

If it be true, as Schopenhauer affirms, that a novel will be of a high and noble order the more it represents of inner, and the less it represents of outer, life, this latest novel of Henry James must be given a high place. Throughout it is the inner life, the life of the passions, the emotions, the affections of four people which is presented,—their souls' history, in other words, with only just enough of time and place and circumstance to give it verisimilitude, to make all vivid and real. The chronicle is accomplished with an art beyond all praise: by formulating the questions which the soul asks but which the lips fail to utter, by happy figures and comparisons which fall thick and golden like ripe fruit, by making all the characters impossibly articulate and lucid,—able 'to discuss in novel phrases their complicated state of mind.'

Those who lament the forsaking by Mr. James of his earlier themes, and the abandonment of his more direct and objective manner, perhaps betray the limit of their own interests and perceptions. Like all men of original genius arrived at maturity, the outward aspects of the world—manners, places, customs—no longer interest him exclusively. Little by little he has come to look for and to present the reality behind the seeming,—not circumstance, but the spiritual reaction of circumstance. Thus the Swedenborgianism of his father, like some pure, pale flower plucked from a cold Norwegian precipice, transplanted thence to a New England garden, blooms now in an English hothouse,—a thing to marvel at, a thing to be grateful for.

174. From an unsigned review, *Bookman* (America)

January 1905, xx, 418–9

For quotations from further American comment on *The Golden Bowl* see No. 180.

Except for the story, never of any importance in his books, he has not swerved a hair's breadth from the route he took in *The Wings of a Dove*. He continues, as one reviewer has said, to bestow on all his characters his own form of speech down to the disposal of the adverb. All are little faithful copies of their author, madly absorbed in introspection even in the crises of their lives. . . .

But his mannerisms and what the reviewers call his 'subtlety' do not account for the lack of contrast and variety in his characters. That follows rather from his method and his range of interest. There are one or two simple characters even here, and he would like to have them seem so, but by describing little thought processes that other people take for granted he gives the impression of difficulty. Seeing him so busy, we infer that there is a lot to do, and we often credit him with going in deep, merely because he takes so long to extricate himself. Flattened like a wood-tick against the tissues of a tinker he can tell us very little about the tinker's general architecture. He is interested in mental processes that are common to all kinds of minds. If the simplest of us could keep an accurate thought diary for half an hour it would be a fearful and intricate narrative. . . . Fully half of *The Golden Bowl* consists of notes which he ought in conscience to have destroyed, and of details the bare mention of which misleads by a sense of their importance.

175. William James on the perverse success of *The Golden Bowl* and the desirability of an easier 'fourth manner'

1905

WJ to HJ, October 1905 (JF, 339).

It put me, as most of your recenter long stories have put me, in a very puzzled state of mind. I don't enjoy the kind of 'problem,' especially when, as in this case, it is treated as problematic (*viz.*, the adulterous relations between Charlotte and the Prince), and the method of narration by interminable elaboration of suggestive reference (I don't know what to call it, but you know what I mean) goes agin the grain of all my own impulses in writing; and yet in spite of it all, there is a brilliancy and cleanness of effect, and in this book especially a high-toned social atmosphere that are unique and extraordinary. Your methods and my ideals seem the reverse, the one of the other—and yet I have to admit your extreme success in this book. But why won't you, just to please Brother, sit down and write a new book, with no twilight or mustiness in the plot, with great vigor and decisiveness in the action, no fencing in the dialogue, no psychological commentaries, and absolute straightness in the style? Publish it in my name, I will acknowledge it, and give you half the proceeds. Seriously, I wish you *would*, for you *can*; and I should think it would tempt you, to embark on a 'fourth manner.' You of course know these feelings of mine without my writing them down, but I'm 'nothing if not' outspoken. Meanwhile you can despise me and fall back on such opposite emotions as Howells's, who seems to admire you without restriction, as well as on the records of the sale of the book.

176. James on his intellectual separation from his brother, and the latter's crudity as a literary critic

1905

HJ to WJ, November 1905 (LJ, ii, 44–5).
A reply to No. 175. The relaxed tone of this reply is surely significant. It shows HJ at last able, late in his career, to calmly and affectionately dispense with his brother's support—not only not to rely on it any more, but to be essentially undisturbed by its failure.

I mean (in response to what you write me of your having read the *Golden B.*) to try to produce some uncanny form of thing, in fiction, that will gratify you, as Brother—but let me say, dear William, that I shall greatly be humiliated if you *do* like it, and thereby lump it, in your affection, with things, of the current age, that I have heard you express admiration for and that I would sooner descend to a dishonoured grave than have written. Still I *will* write you your book, on that two-and-two-make-four system on which all the awful truck that surrounds us is produced, and *then* descend to my dishonoured grave—taking up the art of the slate pencil instead of, longer, the art of the brush (vide my lecture on Balzac.) But it is, seriously, too late at night, and I am too tired, for me to express myself on this question—beyond saying that I'm always sorry when I hear of your reading anything of mine, and always hope you won't—you seem to me so constitutionally unable to 'enjoy' it, and so condemned to look at it from a point of view remotely alien to mine in writing it, and to the conditions out of which, *as* mine, it has inevitably sprung—so that all the intentions that have been its main reason for being (with *me*) appear never to have reached you at all —and you appear even to assume that the life, the elements forming its subject-matter, deviate from felicity in not having an impossible analogy with the life of Cambridge. I see nowhere about me done or dreamed of the things that alone for me constitute the *interest* of the

393

doing of the novel—and yet it is in a sacrifice of them on their very own ground that the thing you suggest to me evidently consists. It shows how far apart and to what different ends we have had to work out (very naturally and properly!) our respective intellectual lives.

177. W. C. Brownell on James's position in literature

1905

W. C. Brownell, 'Henry James', *Atlantic*, April 1905, xcv, 496–519.

Brownell (1851–1928) was a leading American critic, and for many years the literary editor for Charles Scribner's sons (he later saw HJ's New York edition through the presses). He was a friend of Mrs. Wharton, whose unfavourable opinion of the later HJ he shared, and she in turn was (privately) delighted with this article (see, for a penetrating account of their relationship, Millicent Bell's *Edith Wharton and Henry James: The Story of their Friendship*, 1966). I have reprinted the whole of this long essay because it pursues a coherent argument which would be damaged by cuts. It is therefore unusual in HJ's reception. In a sense it is the American counterpart of the earlier *Edinburgh* article (No. 159) in being a would-be definitive estimate in the most respected of periodicals. But, while it is extremely critical, it is of a quite different order of intelligence: it makes one regret that something as thoughtful had not appeared earlier in HJ's career. For criticism of it by another American see No. 180. Brownell later reprinted it in *American Prose Masters*, New York, 1909.

I

If any career can be called happy before it is closed, that of Mr. Henry James may certainly be so called. It has been a long one—much longer already than the space of time allotted to a generation. It has been quite free from any kind of mistake: there is probably nothing in it he would change if he could—for though he has more or less slightly revised two or three of his early books, the need of doing so would not have occurred to any one whose record was not so satisfactory on the whole as to make it seem to him worth while to add a touch or two and make it quite as he would have it. It has been, in a very special way and to a very marked degree, an honorable career. He has scrupulously followed his ideal. Neither necessity nor opportunity has prevented him from doing, apparently, just what he wanted. He has never, at any rate, yielded to the temptation to give the public what it wanted. The rewards of so doing are very great. Most writers in belittling them would be justly suspected of affectation. They include, for example, the pleasure of being read, and this is a pleasure usually so difficult to forego when it is attainable that Mr. James's indifference to it is striking. And—what is still more striking—he has never, as he himself expresses it somewhere in characterization of some other writer,—who must, however, have been his own inferior in this respect,—he has never 'saved for his next book.' Of his special order of talent fecundity is not what one would naturally have predicted, and though he has abundantly demonstrated his possession of it, he must have long given us his best before he could have been at all sure that he could count on matching his best indefinitely. Into the frame of every book he packed, not only the substance called for by the subject, but a substance as remarkable for containing all he could himself bring to it, as for compression. At least, if his substance has sometimes been thin, it has always been considered; however fine-spun its texture, it has always been composed of thought. And his expression, tenuous as it may sometimes appear, is (especially, indeed, when its tenuity is greatest) so often dependent for its comprehension on what it suggests rather than on what it states as to compel the inference that it is incomplete expression, after all, of the amount of thought behind it.

So that he never leaves the impression of superficiality. His material, even his result, may be as slight as his own insistent predetermination can make it; it is impossible not to feel that it is the work of an artist who is not only serious, but profound. Behind his sketch you feel the careful and elaborate preliminary study; back of his triviality you feel the man of reflection. And this is not at all because his triviality—to call it such—is significant in itself. It often is, and the trifling feature, incident, movement, or phrase, often has a typical value that makes it in effect but the expression of a larger thing than it embodies. But often, on the other hand, it is difficult to assign any strikingly interpretative or illustrative value to the insubstantial phenomena that he is at the pains of observing so narrowly and recording so copiously. And yet it can occur to no sensitive and candid intelligence to refer to the capacity of the recorder this flimsiness of the record. One has the sense in the treatment, the technic, of a firm and vigorous hand—such as is, in general, perhaps, needed for the carving of 'émaux et camées.' And still more in the substance one perceives, as well as argues, the solidity and dignity underlying the superficial and insignificant details with which 'wonderfully' —to use a favorite word of Mr. James—they are occupied. The sense of contrast is indeed often piquant. Cuvier lecturing on a single bone and reconstructing the entire skeleton from it is naturally impressive, but Mr. James often presents the spectacle of a Cuvier absorbed in the positive fascinations of the single bone itself,—yet plainly preserving the effect of a Cuvier the while. If, in a word, his work sometimes seems superficial, it never seems the work of a superficial personality; and the exasperation of some of his unfriendly critics proceeds from wondering, not so much how a writer who has produced such substantial, can also produce such trifling, work, as how the writer whose very treatment of triviality shows him to be serious can be so interested in the superficial.

The explanation, I think, is that to Mr. James himself life, considered as artistic material, is so serious and so significant that nothing it contains seems trivial to him. And as artistic material is, in fact, the only way in which he appears to consider it at all. In spite of his prolixity on occasion, there is no padding in his books, no filling in of general ideas or other interesting distention. His parentheses are, it is true, apt to be cognate digressions rather than nuances of the matter in hand. But that is a question of style, and in any case addiction to parentheses is apt to proceed from an unwillingness to stray very far from the matter in hand, to let go one's hold of it. And save for his parentheses, Mr. James holds his reader to the matter—or rather the absence of matter—in hand rather remorselessly. One would like more space, more air.

His copiousness, too, is the result of his seriousness. If he eschews the foreign, he revels in the pertinent; and, pertinence being his sole standard of exclusion, he is bound to include much that is trivial. We have the paradox of an art attitude that is immaculate with an art product that is ineffective. It is as crowded with detail and as tight as a pre-Raphaelite picture, because there are no salutary sacrifices. It is not because he is a man, but because he is an artist, that nothing human is foreign to him. No rectitude was ever less partial or more passionless. No novelist ever evinced more profound respect for his material *as* material, or conformed his art more rigorously to its characteristic expression. Thus it is due to his seriousness that a good deal of his substance seems less significant to his readers than to him, both in itself and because (out of his own deep respect for it, doubtless) he does little or nothing to enhance its interest and importance. It is not commonly appreciated that his work is, after all, the quintessence of realism.

II

The successive three 'manners' of the painters have been found in it. Mr. James has had, at any rate, two. There is a noteworthy difference between his earlier and his later fiction, though the period of transition between them is not very definite as a period. Perhaps *The Tragic Muse* comprises it. He has, however, thrown himself so devotedly into his latest phase as to make everything preceding it appear as the stages of an evolution. Tendencies, nevertheless, in his earlier work, marked enough to individualize it sharply, have developed until they have subdued all other characteristics, and have made of him perhaps the most individual novelist of his day, who at the same time is also in the current of its tendency,—Mr. Meredith standing quite apart from this in eminent isolation. It is through these tendencies, developed as they have been, that in virtue of originality as well as of excellence he has won his particular place in the hierarchy of fiction. He has created a *genre* of his own. He has the distinction that makes the scientist a savant; he has contributed something to the sum, the common stock. His distinction has really a scientific aspect, independent, that is to say, of quality, of intrinsic merit. If it should be asserted that Mr. Meredith has done the same thing,—in a way, too, not so very differently,—it can be replied that he has done so by weakening the correspondence of fiction to life, whereas Mr. James has striven hard for its intensification; it is not the construction of the scientific toy, however interesting it may be, and however much science there may be in it, that makes the savant. This flowering of Mr. James's tendencies has, in fact, been precisely what he conceives to be the achievement of a more and more intimate and exquisite correspondence with life in his art. This at least has been his conscious, his professed aim. His observation, always his master faculty, has grown more and more acute, his concentration upon the apprehensible phenomena of the actual world of men and women—and children —closer, his interest in producing his illusion by reproducing these in as nearly as possible their actual essence and actual relations, far more absorbing and complete. Indeed, he has been so interested in producing his illusion in precisely this way, that he has decidedly compromised, I think, the certainty of producing it at all.

He has parted, then, with his past,—the past, let us say, of *The Portrait of a Lady*,—in the pursuit of a more complete illusion of nature than he could feel that he achieved on his old lines,—the old lines, let us add, observed in the masterpieces of fiction hitherto. It is true that his observation has been from the first so clearly his distinguishing faculty that his present practice may superficially seem to differ from his former merely in degree. But a little more closely considered, it is a matter rather of development than of augmentation. In the course of its exercise his talent has been transformed. He has reversed the relation between his observation and his imagination, and instead of using the former to supply material for the latter, has enlisted the latter very expressly—oh! sometimes, indeed, worked it very hard—in the service of his observation. Of what he might have achieved by pursuing a different course, I cannot myself think without regret. But instead of seeking that equilibrium of one's powers which seems particularly pertinent to the expression of precisely such an organization as his,—instead of, to that end, curbing his curiosity and cultivating his constructive, his reflective, his imaginative side, the one being already markedly preponderant and the other comparatively slender,—he has followed the path of temperamental preference and developed his natural bent. The result is his present eminence, which is, in consequence, incontestably more nearly unique, but which is not for that reason necessarily more distinguished. His art has thus become, one is inclined to say, the ordered exploitation of his experiences. The change from his earlier manner is so great that it constitutes, as I say, a transformation. It is somewhat as if a transcendentalist philosopher should become so enamoured of truth as, finding it inexhaustibly manifested in everything, to fall in love with phenomena and gradually acquire an absolutely *a posteriori* point of view. Like Lessing, Mr. James has 'bowed humbly to the left hand,' and, saying to the Almighty, 'pure truth is for Thee alone,' has renounced the vision for the pursuit.

The most delicate, the most refined and elegant of contemporary romancers has thus become the most thorough-going realist of even current fiction. It is but a popular error to confound realism with grossness, and it is his complete exclusion of idealism and preoccupation with the objective that I have in mind in speaking of his realism as so marked; though of recent years he has annexed the field of grossness also,— cultivating it, of course, with particular circumspection,—and thus rounded out his domain. It must be granted that his realism does not leave a very vivid impression of reality, on the one hand, and that, on

the other, it does not always produce the effect of a very close correspondence to actual life and character. *The Spoils of Poynton*, with its inadequate motive and aspiration after the tragic; *The Other House*, with
its attempt to domesticate melodrama; *In the Cage*, with its exclusion of
all the surrounding data, needed to give authenticity to an even robuster
theme; *The Awkward Age*, with its impossible cleverness of stupid
people, are, as pictures of life, neither very lifelike nor very much alive.
But that is a matter of art. The *attitude* of the artist is plainly, uncompromisingly realistic. It is the real with which his fancy, his imaginative-
ness, is exclusively preoccupied. To discover new and unsuspected
phenomena in its psychology is the aim of his divination as well as of his
scrutiny. The ideal counterpart of the real and the actual which even
such realists as Thackeray and George Eliot have constantly, however
subconsciously, in mind, and the image of which, whether or no as
universal as the Platonic philosophy pretends, is at least part of the
material of the imaginative artist,—furnishing more or less vaguely the
standard by which he admeasures both his own creation and its model,
when he has one,—this ideal counterpart, so to speak, is curiously absent
from Mr. James's contemplation. Given a character with certain traits,
suggested, no doubt, by certain specific experiences, its action is not
deduced by ideal logic, but arrived at through induction from the
artist's entire stock of pertinent general experience, and modeled by its
insistent pressure. 'What conduct does my—rather unusual—experience
lead me to expect of a personage constituted thus and so, in such and
such circumstances?'—one may imagine Mr. James reflecting.

Categories like realism and idealism are but convenient, and not
exact, and in the practice of any artist both inspirations must be alternately present in the execution of detail, though one of them is surely apt
to preponderate in the general conception and in the artist's attitude.
But it is certainly true that what may be called the ideal of realism has
never been held more devoutly—not even by Zola—than it is by Mr.
James. All his subtlety, his refinement, his extreme plasticity, his acquaintance with the academic as well as the actual, are at the service of
truth, and that order of truth which is to be discovered rather than
divined. Long ago, in speaking of George Sand's idealism, which he
admitted to be 'very beautiful,' he observed: 'Something even better in
a novelist is that tender appreciation of actuality which makes even the
application of a single coat of rose-color seem an act of violence.' The
inspiration is a little different from Thackeray's 'If truth is not always
pleasant, at least it is best.' It is more 'artistic,' perhaps, certainly more

disinterested. And at the present day Mr. James would no doubt go farther, omit the word 'tender,' and for 'rose-color' substitute simply 'any color at all.' It is an unselfish creed, one may remark in passing. Color is a variety of form, and it is a commonplace that form is the only passport to posterity. Moreover, as Mr. James concedes, even idealism at times is 'very beautiful,' and to be compelled to forego beauty in 'appreciation of the actual' (for its actuality, that is to say, rather than its beauty) must for an artist be a rigorous renunciation.

Mr. James has renounced it for the most part with admirable consistency, and his latest works are, in effort and inspiration at least, the very apotheosis of the actual—however their absence of color or other elements of form and the encumbrances of their style (the distinction is his own) may fail to secure the desired effect of actuality for them. What Maisie knew, for example, may seem to have been learned by a preternaturally precocious child, so that her actuality has not, perhaps, the relief desired by her author. But she can have no other *raison d'etre*—for the supposition that even incidentally she is designed to illustrate the charm of the flower on the dunghill can be at best but a mere guess, so colorlessly is the assumed actuality of her precocity and extraordinary situation exhibited. The book, indeed, in this respect is a masterpiece of reserve. It is conspicuously free from any taint of rose-color. And in its suppression of the superfluous—such as even the remotest recognition of the pathos of Maisie's situation—it is an excellent illustration of an order of art that *must* be radically theoretic, since it could not be the instinctive and spontaneous expression of a normally humane motive.

III

The truth is that our fiction is in a period of transition, which perhaps is necessarily hostile to spontaneity and favorable to the artificial. We speculate so much as to whether fiction is 'a finer art' as practised by the little, than it was in the day of the great, masters, that the present time may fairly be called the reign of theory in fiction—as indeed it is in art of any kind. And Mr. James's art is in nothing more modern than in being theoretic. Whatever it is or is not, it is that. Difficult as, in many respects, it is to characterize, it is plainly what it is by precise intention, by system. Difficult as his theory is to define, it is perfectly clear that his art is the product of it. It is, in a word, a critical product. And it is so because his temperament is the critical temperament. Now, whatever may be said of the compatibility or incompatibility of the critical and the creative temperaments, in the matter of creating fiction it is evident that the critical genius will be a different kind of a practitioner from the creative genius. The latter may be considered to produce the 'criticism of life,' but the former will be likely to produce such criticism at one remove—with, in a word, *theory* interposed. Even supposing the creator to be also a critic, if his creative imagination preponderates, his theory will be a theory of life, whereas the theory of the writer in whom the critical bent preponderates will be a theory of art. We are said to suffer nowadays from a dearth of the creative imagination. Science, the great, the most nearly universal of the interests of the present time, is perhaps thought to be hostile to its entertainment, its development. But science with its own speedy determination toward specialism is probably less fatal to the imagination than is generally presumed. On the contrary, within its own range, its many ranges, it doubtless stimulates and fosters it. The decline of the creative imagination in literature, in poetry, and in fiction, is far more distinctly traceable to the spread of culture, with the consequent unexampled development of the philosophic and critical spirit and its inevitable invasion of the field of creative activity, the field, that is to say, of art. The contemporary artist, if he thinks at all, is compelled to think critically, to philosophize more expressly and specifically than the classic artist was. Consequently, even the creative imagination pure and simple is nowadays more rarely to be encountered than this imagination in combination with critical reflection.

But with Mr. James the case is far simpler. It would be idle to deny to the author of a shelf-full of novels and a thousand or two characters the possession of the creative imagination, however concentrated upon actuality and inspired by experience. Yet it is particularly true of him among the writers of even our own time that his critical faculty is eminently preponderant; that he has, as I say, essentially the critical *temperament*. He has never devoted himself very formally to criticism, never squared his elbows and settled down to the business of it. It has always been somewhat incidental and secondary with him. His essays have been limited to *belles lettres* in range, and they have not been the rounded, complete, and final characterization of the subject from a central point of view, such as the essays of Arnold, of Carlyle, or of Lowell. They have been instead rather agglutinate than synthetic, one may say,—not very attentively distributed or organized. But they have more than eschewed pedantry—they have been felicity itself; each a series of penetrating remarks, an agglomeration of light but telling touches, immensely discriminating, and absolutely free from traditional or temperamental deflection, marked by a taste at once fastidiously academic, and at the same time sensitively impressionable. The two volumes *French Poets and Novelists* and *Partial Portraits* stand at the head of American literary criticism. The *Life of Hawthorne* is, as a piece of criticism, altogether unrivaled in the voluminous English Men of Letters series to which all the eminent English critics have contributed. One may feel that his view of the general is, in this work, too elevated to permit him always correctly to judge the specific—leads him to characterize, for instance, Hawthorne's environment as a handicap to him, whereas it was an opportunity. But to this same broad and academic view, which measures the individual by the standard of the type (and how few there are to whom this standard does not equitably apply!), we owe the most searching thing ever said about Hawthorne: 'Man's conscience was his theme, but he saw it in the light of a creative fancy which added out of its own substance an interest, and I may almost say, an importance.' The genius itself of criticism is in the application to Tennyson's

> It is better to have loved and lost
> Than never to have loved at all,

of the epithets 'curt' and 'reserved' by comparison with Musset's *Letter to Lamartine*. The essay on Maupassant is an unsurpassed critical performance. In *Daniel Deronda: a Conversation*, there are more penetrating things said about George Eliot, one is tempted to say, than in all else that has been written about her. And Mr. James's penetration is uniformly based on good sense. It is—perhaps ominously—never fanciful. He writes of Musset and George Sand, of Balzac and Trollope, with a disinterested discrimination absolutely judicial. His fondness for Daudet, for Turgénieff, for Stevenson, is nothing in comparison with his interest in the art they practise, the art of which he is apt to consider all its practitioners somewhat too exclusively merely as its exponents. If he has a passion, it is for the art of fiction itself.

This is the theme, indeed, on which his criticism has centred, and the fact is extremely significant. It is almost exact to say that he has no other. He is vaguely preoccupied by it, even in the composition of his own fictions. That is what I mean by calling his art theoretic. It carefully, explicitly, with conviction, illustrates his theory. He has an essay expressly devoted to the topic, but he has almost none in which it is not more or less incidentally considered. In 'The Art of Fiction' he says, 'It is an incident for a woman to stand up with her hand resting on a table and

look out at you in a certain way,' and that 'the degree of interest' such
an incident has 'will depend upon the skill of the painter,' meaning the
author. In his essay on Daudet he says: 'The appearance of things is
constantly more complicated as the world grows older, and it needs a
more and more patient art, a closer notation, to divide it into its parts;'
'Life is, immensely, a matter of surface, and if our emotions in general
are interesting, the *form* of those emotions has the merit of being the
most definite thing about them;' 'Putting people into books is what the
novelist lives on;' 'It is the real—the transmuted real—that he gives us
best; the fruit of a process that adds to observation what a kiss adds to a
greeting. The joy, the excitement of recognition, are keen, even when
the object recognized is dismal.'

Each of these sentences—and many more might be cited—is a key to
his own fiction. The last is particularly indicative. The joy of recognition is what apparently he aims at exciting in his readers; what certainly
he often succeeds in exciting to the exclusion of other emotions, though
the kiss he adds to his greeting—to adopt his charming figure—is often-
est, perhaps, an extremely chaste salute. Of course, in a sense, the word
recognition defines the Platonic explanation of all appreciation of
phenomena, but it is needless to say that Mr. James does not use the
word in this sense, but refers to recognition of what we have already
encountered in this life. And it must be admitted that the pleasure we
take in his characters largely depends on whether or no we have so encountered them. If we have not, we are sometimes a little at sea as to the
source of even his own interest in them, which, though certainly never
profoundly personal, is often extremely prolonged. If we have, we
experience the delight of the *aficionado* in the virtuosity with which
what is already more or less vaguely familiar is unfolded to our recognition. But even in this case the recognition is something quite different
from that with which we realize the actuality of a largely imaginative
character. We recognize Daisy Miller, for example, differently from
Becky Sharp.

For one thing, we are not so anxious to meet her again. I know of
nothing that attests so plainly the preponderance of virtuosity in Mr.
James's art as the indisposition of his readers to re-read his books. This
would not be so true if this element of his work frankly appeared. If he
himself accepted it as such, he would make more of it in the traditional
way, give it more form, express it more attentively, harmonize its
character and statement more explicitly. There is no difficulty in re-
reading Anatole France. But Mr. James's virtuosity is not a matter of

treatment, of expression, of 'process,' as he would say. It is an integral part of the very fabric of his conception. It is engaged and involved in the substance of his works. The substance suffers accordingly. Instead of 'a closer and more intimate correspondence with life,' the result of his critical theorizing about the what and the how of fiction is a confusion of life and art, which are actually as distinct as subject and statement. Virtuosity of technic is legitimate enough, but virtuosity of vision is quite another thing. And it is to this that Mr. James's study and practice of the art for which he has quite as much of a passion as a *penchant* have finally brought him. *The Sacred Fount*, 'The Turn of the Screw', are marked instances of it. But all the later books show the tendency, a tendency all the more marked for the virility and elevation with which it is accompanied, and perhaps inevitable in the product of an over-mastering critical faculty exercised in philosophizing about, even in the process of practising, an eminently constructive art.

IV

When we predicate elusiveness of Mr. James's fiction we mean much more than that his meaning is occasionally obscure. We mean that he himself always eludes us. The completeness with which he does so, it is perhaps possible to consider the measure of his success. The famous theory that prescribes disinterestedness in art may be invoked in favor of this view. Every one is familiar with this theory, so brilliantly ex-pounded by Taine, so cordially approved by Maupassant, so favorably viewed by Mr. James himself. Any one to whom Aristotle's dictum that virtue resides in a mean seems especially applicable to art theories, must find it difficult to accept this prescription even in theory. Even in theory it seems possible to have too little as well as too much of the artist him-self in any work of art. The presence of the personality of the artist, indeed, may be called the constituting element of a work of art. It is even the element that makes one scientific demonstration what the scientists themselves call more 'beautiful' than another. But in practice one may surely say that in some instances or on some occasions we do not feel the artist enough in his work. Just as on others we are altogether too conscious of him.

It is the latter difficulty that has been the more frequent in fiction up to the present age, perhaps, and in English fiction perhaps up to the present moment. And very likely it is this circumstance that has led to the generalization, and the present popularity of the generalization, which insists on the attitude of disinterested curiosity as the only properly artistic attitude. Even in criticism, so much had been endured from the other attitude, Arnold—whose practice, to be sure, was quite different—observed that the great art was 'to get oneself out of the way and let humanity judge.' We have had so much partisanship that we have proscribed personality.

Disinterested curiosity is, however, itself a very personal matter. Carried to the extent to which it is carried by Mr. James, at least, it becomes very sensible, a very appreciable element of a work of art. It is forced upon one's notice as much as an aggressive and intrusive personal element could be. To say that if you set the pieces of a work of art in a certain relative position they will automatically, as it were, generate the effect to be produced is to be tremendously sanguine of their intrinsic interest and force. Even then the artist's presence is only minimized, not excluded, one may logically observe; the pieces must be set together in a certain way, and this way will depend on the idiosyncrasy of the artist and not upon the inherent affinity of the pieces. They may have a law of combination, but to prepare them for its operation the law must be perceived by the artist as a force to illustrate rather than merely to 'notate,' if the result is to have an artistic rather than a scientific interest. As Mr. James himself has aptly said, 'Art is merely a point of view, and genius mainly a way of looking at things.' And specifically as to fiction M. Bourget reports him as agreeing with him that the truest definition of a novel is 'a personal view of life.' How is the 'point of view,' above all the 'personal' point of view, to be perceived, if the artist himself eludes us completely? What is it we are looking at—the phenomena he is recording, or his view of the phenomena? But the phenomena should of themselves show his view, it may be contended. If they do, there is nothing to be said. The question at bottom is, do they?

The old practice gave us the point of view by stating it; nor could its statement even then always be called an artistic intrusion, a false note, a disillusion. It was not always imposed on the phenomena by main strength. When Thackeray was reproached with marrying Henry Esmond to Lady Castlewood, he replied, 'I didn't do it; they did it themselves.' Some such artistic rectitude as that, recognizing the law of his own creations, is certainly to be required of the artist. But if his devotion is so thorough-going as to involve complete self-effacement, the practical result will be the disappearance, or at least the obscuration, of his point of view. That, I think, is the peril which Mr. James's theory and practice of art have not sufficiently recognized. Disinterested curiosity may have much of the value that has been claimed for it. It may have been too much neglected in the past. And to point out its logical self-contradiction as an absolute prescription may be conceded to savor of hair-splitting. It is, nevertheless, only valuable as a means, as an agent. When it is worked so hard as itself to become a part of the effect, its value ceases. And in Mr. James's later work what we get, what we see, what impresses us, is not the point of view, it is his own disinterested curiosity. It counts as part, as a main part, of the spectacle he provides for us. We see him busily getting out of the way, visibly withdrawing behind the screen of his story, illustrating his theory by palpably withholding from us the expected, the needful, exposition and explanation, making of his work, in fine, a kind of elaborate and complicated fortification between us and his personality.

One notable effect of this detachment in the novelist is that his characters do not seem to be his characters. Being the results of his observation, the fruit of his experiences, they do not count as his creations. We meet Mr. James's in life,—or we do not meet them,—as it happens; but they do not figure importantly for us in the world of art. American travelers who drift about Europe—doubtless American residents of London—encounter their counterparts from time to time, and note with a pleasure that is always more acute than permanent how cleverly, how searchingly, Mr. James has caught an individual or fixed a type. Necessarily, however, a museum thus collected has rather an anthropological than an artistic interest. The novelist's personages are not sufficiently unified by his own *penchant*, preference, personality, to constitute a society of varied individuals viewed and portrayed from one definite and particular point of view—as the characters of the great novelists do. There is not enough of their creator in them to constitute them a particular society. The society is simply differentiated by the variety and circumscribed by the limits of Mr. James's experience (and, of course, its suggestions to an extremely sensitive and speculative mind); it is not coordinated, and, as it were, organized into an ideal correlation of the actual world as conceived by a novelist of imagination,—imagination not only such as Thackeray's and George Eliot's, but such as Trollope's, even.

V

It is, however, not precise enough to say that Mr. James's mind is essentially critical, and that therefore his attitude is essentially detached. There are two sufficiently distinct varieties of the critical mind, the philosophical and the scientific. Mr. James's is the latter. And when that portion of literature which includes the works of the imagination is conceived as a criticism of life, it is so conceived in virtue of its illustrating the former—the philosophical spirit. So far as fiction is a criticism of life, it is so because it exhibits a philosophy of life, in general or in some particular. It is far more the scientific habit of viewing life and its phenomena that Mr. James illustrates. His characteristic attitude is that of scrutiny. His inspiration is curiosity. Certainly to affirm of so mature so thoughtful, and so penetratingly observant a writer, that he has no philosophy of life would, aside from its impertinence, be quite unwarrantable. It is impossible not to feel in his fiction that he has made his own synthesis of 'all this unintelligible world.' However, impersonal and objective his art, it cannot conceal this. It is enough to be felt to give weight to his utterances, to furnish credentials for the larger correspondences and comparisons of his pictures to their moral analogies in life, to add authoritativeness to his expositions, and exorcise suspicion of their ephemeralness and superficiality. What I mean is that even in such a work as *The Sacred Fount* is to be discerned the man who has reflected on the traits and currents of existence, on their character and their implications, as well as the writer who notes the phenomena, without correlating them through the principles, of human life.

But what this philosophy is, it is idle to speculate. It is doubtless profound enough, and though one does not argue introspection of Mr. James's temperament,—unless, indeed, his work betray an effort to escape it, as the nuisance it may easily become,—he could doubtless sketch it for us if inclined, and very eloquently and even elaborately draw out for us its principles and positions. But he has no interest whatever in doing so—no interest in giving us even a hint of it. One may infer that taste plays a large part in it, the taste that some philosophers have made the foundation and standard of morals,—the taste, perhaps, that prevents him from disclosing it. He has the air of assuming its universality, as if, indeed, it were a matter of breeding, a mere preference for 'the best' in life as in art, a system, in a word, whose sanctions are instinctive, and so not strongly enough or consciously enough felt to call for emphasis or exposition. No manifestation or quality or incarnation of 'the best' evokes his enthusiasm. That it 'may prevail' is the youngest of his cares. His philosophy appears in the penumbra of his performance as a cultivated indifference, or at most a subconscious basis of moral fastidiousness on which the superstructure that monopolizes his interest is erected.

There are two sufficiently obvious results. In the first place, his work has less importance as literature, because it has significance only as art. In the next place, his individuality is not accented, his books are not unified. If they were pervaded by, or even tinctured with, some general philosophic character, they would count in the mass for far more,—his *œuvre*, as the French say, would have more relief, his position in literature would be better defined and more important. As it is, for the lack of some unifying philosophy, each one is an independent illustration of some particular exercise of his talent, and his personality is dissipated by being thus disseminated.

What is it to have a philosophy of life? In any sense in which it may be legitimately required of the artist, even of the artist who deals expressly with life,—of the poet, the dramatist, or the writer of fiction, —to have a philosophy of life certainly does not demand the possession of a body of doctrine 'based on inter-dependent, subordinate, and coherent principles,' as has been prescribed by pedantry for criticism. It is simply to be profoundly impressed by certain truths. These truths need not be recondite, but they must be deeply felt. They need be in no degree original. The writer's originality will have abundant scope in their expression. Goethe, it is true, replied to a perhaps not wholly pedantic criticism of *Wilhelm Meister:* 'I should think a rich, manifold life brought close to our eyes would be enough in itself without any express tendency.' And Goethe is probably the greatest example of the artist and the philosopher combined. This observation, however, is confined to a single work; it is impossible to think of the author of *Wilhelm Meister* as the author only of it and of works of like aim and scope. And furthermore, the life which Mr. James's books bring close to our eyes, though manifold, is not rich. It is remarkably multifarious, but 'rich' is precisely the last epithet that could properly be applied to it.

It is, nevertheless, the result of observation of the most highly developed material, and if it lack vitality, it is not because it is commonplace or rudimentary. The converse is so pointedly the case as to constitute Mr. James's chief excellence. It has been said of him that he has not sounded the depths, but 'charted the shallows' of life. But to say this is quite to miss the point about him. Occupy himself with the shallows he certainly often does, though quite without any attempt to chart them, any attempt at completeness. It is evident that he is not concerned to show them *as* shallows, with the inference that they compose a far larger part of life than is apprehended by current mechanical optimism. He does not deal with them in any such philosophical spirit.

His scientific curiosity does not distinguish between the phenomena, all of which seem inexhaustibly interesting to him. Except certain coarsenesses, which probably seem almost pathologic to him, or at any rate too ordinary and commonplace for treatment, nothing is to him, as I have said, too insignificant to be interesting, considered as material for artistic treatment. The treatment is to dignify the theme always. And in this attitude no one can fail to see, if not a deeper interest in art than in life, at least an interest in life so impartial and inclusive as to approach aridity so far as feeling is concerned. To take an interest in making interesting what is in itself perfectly colorless is, one must admit, almost to avow a fondness for the *tour de force* dear to the dilettante. Still it would be misleading to insist on this, because Mr. James's intention is, on the whole, to indicate the significance of the apparently trifling, and not to protest that an artistic effect can be got out of next to nothing. It betrays the interest of the naturalist asseverating that nothing is really trifling, since it exists.

It is easy to lose one's way in endeavoring to follow the clue of Mr. James's preoccupation, but with due attention I think it may be done. And his interest in making interesting the pose and gesture of a lady standing by a table, let me recapitulate, is not, or is only a little, to produce an artistic effect with a minimum of means; nor is it to show that of such trifles human life is largely composed; it is to show that in life itself such things are interesting not only because everything is, but also because, though slight, they are subtle and certain indications of the *character* to which they belong. In this way he can find something recondite in what is superficially very simple. And I should say that it is, in a word, to the pursuit of the recondite in life that he has come more and more to consecrate his extraordinary powers. He sees it in everything, in the shallows as well as in the depths. That is all one can truthfully say, perhaps, though of course in seeking it in the familiar and the commonplace it is difficult to avoid the semblance of mystification.

The pursuit of the recondite, however, is quite inconsistent with much dwelling on the meaning of life as a whole. And it is owing to his taking this so much for granted as so largely to exclude it from his fiction, that the life which Mr. James 'brings close' to us should lack the 'richness' that Goethe claimed for *Wilhelm Meister*. If he conceived the shallows *as* shallows and the depths *as* depths, he could hardly avoid taking a less arid view of them, and the astonishing variety of the phenomena that entertain and even absorb him would be grouped in some synthetic way around centres of coordinating feeling, instead of unrolled like a panorama of trifles hitherto unconsidered and tragedies hitherto unsuspected—exhibited like a naturalist's collection made in a country accessible to all, but heretofore unvisited by the scientist with the seeing eye.

Hence, I think, the lack of large vitality in his books, of a sensibly noble and moving effect. The search for the recondite involves the absence of direct dealing with the elemental. The passions are perforce minimized, from being treated in their differentiation rather than in their universality, as well as from being so swamped in minutiæ as largely to lose their energy. His books are not moral theses, but psychological themes, studies not of forces, but of manifestations. The latter are related as cause and effect, perhaps, but not combined in far-reaching suggestiveness. The theme has weight at times, morally considered, but it is not rendered typical, as in George Eliot, for example. It is never either ominous or reassuring. It is never brought close, in Goethe's words, to the reader. It makes him reflect, but speculatively; reason, but academically. It is an unfolding, a laying bare, but not a putting together. The imagination to which it is due is too tinctured with curiosity to be truly constructive. It has the disadvantage of never taking possession of the theme and conducting it masterfully. It is not *a priori* enough. It is held in the leash of observation and fettered by its voluntary submission to the material, to exhibit rather than to arrange which is its specific ambition. The work as a whole is thus necessarily coldly conceived. The heat is in the narration of detail. And thus the reader is impressed far more by the detail than by either the grand construction or by the general design. Above all, the characters, the portraiture of human nature, upon which the vitality of fiction depends, suffer from the recondite quality, which wars with the elemental and thus tends to eliminate the typical, the representative, which constitutes the basis of both effective illusion and significant truth. But of course all that makes types interesting is the possession of a philosophy of life. They imply classification, which is the last thing to be looked for in the *espièglerie* of the most precocious conceivable child among us merely occupied in taking notes.

VI

After all, the supreme test of a novelist's abiding interest is the humanity of his characters. This is so true that Mr. James himself professes a preference for *The House of the Seven Gables* over the other romances of

Hawthorne because it seems to him more of a novel. Hawthorne, however, was not a novelist, and *The House of the Seven Gables*, though no
doubt his best novel, is the least characteristic of his larger productions.
Actual life was not his theme. As Mr. James himself has pointed out, his
characters, save for the Donatello of *The Marble Faun*, include no types.
The same might be said of the personages of later and far less romantic
writers. The type in fiction has become a little old-fashioned—at least
the labeled and easily recognized type has. It is relegated to the stage,
where, apparently, it will continue, from the limitations of the histrionic
art, to be a necessity. In the novel it has largely succumbed to the conquering force of psychology, which in creating an individual and to that
end emphasizing his idiosyncrasies has, almost proportionally, robbed
him of his typical interest. And this is a loss for which absolutely nothing
can atone in the work of the realistic novelist whose theme is actual life.

The list of Mr. James's novels is a long one, and his short stories are
very numerous; and among them all there is not one with a perfunctory
or desultory inspiration. Why is it that they in no sense constitute a
comédie humaine? They are very populous; why is it that the characters
that people them have so little relief? Taken together they constitute the
least successful element of his fiction. Partly this is because, as I say, they
possess so little typical quality. But why also do they possess so little
personal interest? They have, seemingly, astonishingly little, even for
their creator. So far from knowing the sound of their voices, as Thackeray said of his, he is apparently less preoccupied with them than about
the situation—the 'predicament,' he would aptly say—in which he
places them. Apparently he is chiefly concerned with what they are to
do when confronted with the complications his ingeniuty devises for
them,—how they are to 'pull it off.' These complications are sometimes
very slight, in order to show what trifles control destinies; sometimes
they are very grave, and designed to show the conflict of the soul with
warring desires and distracting perplexities. And they are never commonplace—any more than the characters themselves, each one of which
is intimately observed and thoroughly respected as an individuality.
But their situation rather than themselves is what constitutes the claim,
the *raison d'etre*, of the book in which they figure. The interest in the
book, accordingly, becomes analogous to that of a game in which the
outcome rather than the pieces monopolizes the attention. It cannot be
said that the pieces are not attentively described,—some of them, indeed,
are very artistically and even beautifully carved,—but it is the moves
that count most of all. Will Densher give a plausible solution to the

recondite problem of how to combine the qualities of a cad and of a gentleman? Will Maisie decide for or against Sir Claude? What decision will Sir Claude himself make? Has Vanderbank ideality enough to marry Nanda? The game is very well, often exquisitely, played; and the result, which, nevertheless, from all we know of the characters, we can rarely foresee, wears—when we argue it out in retrospect as the author clearly has done in advance—the proper artistic aspect of a foregone conclusion. Mr. James rarely seems to impose it himself; except on the few occasions when, as in *The Princess Casamassima* or *The Other House*, he deals in melodrama, in which he almost never succeeds in being convincing, his rectitude is so strong a reliance as to exclude all impression of perversity or willfulness and convey the agreeable sense of sufficiently fatalistic predestination. Meantime you find out about the characters from the result. Since it has turned out in this way, they must have been such and such persons. In other words, they have not been characterized very vividly, have not been presented very completely as human beings.

At least they do not people one's memory, I think, as the personages of many inferior artists do. When one thinks of the number of characters that Mr. James has created, each, as I have said, carefully individualized, and none of them replicas,—an amazing world they certainly compose in their originality and variety,—it is odd what an effort it is to recall even their names. The immortal Daisy Miller, the sensitive and highly organized Ralph Touchett, the robust and throughly national Christopher Newman, the gentle Miss Pynsent, and a number of others that do remain in one's memory, mainly belong to the earlier novels and form but a small proportion of the great number of their author's creations. Different readers, however, would no doubt answer this rather crude test differently, and in any case it is not because they fail in precision that Mr. James's personages lose distinctness as their story, like all stories, fades from the recollection. They have a sharp enough outline, but they are not completely enough characterized.

Why? Why is it that when the American heroine of one of his stories, beautifully elaborated in detail, a perfect specimen of Dutch *intarsia* kills herself because her English husband publishes a savage book about her country, we find ourselves perfectly unprepared for this *dénouement*? Why is it that with all the pains expended on the portrait of the extraordinary Mrs. Headway of 'The Siege of London', we never quite get *his* point of view, but are kept considering the social duty of the prig who passes his valuable time in observing her attempts at rehabilitation and—no doubt most justly—exposes her in the end? There is nothing to complain of in the result, the problem is worked out satisfactorily enough, but Mrs. Headway herself does not count for us, does not hang together, in the way in which Augier's *L'Aventurière* does, or even Dumas's *Baronne d'Ange*. It would be difficult, for example, and for this reason, to make a play of 'The Siege of London'.

The answer to this query, the explanation of this incompleteness of characterization in Mr. James's nevertheless very precise personages, consists, I think, in the fact that he rather pointedly neglects the province of the heart. This has been from the first the natural peril of the psychological novelist, the neglect of what in the Scripture view constitutes 'the whole man,' just as the neglect of the mind—which discriminates and defines personalities once constituted—was the defect of the psychological novelist's predecessor. But for Mr. James this peril has manifestly no terrors. The province of the heart seems to him, perhaps, so much to be taken for granted as to be on the whole rather negligible, so far as romantic exploitation is concerned.

Incidentally, one may ask, if all the finest things in the world are to be assumed, what is there left for exploitation? Matter for curiosity mainly—the curiosity which in Mr. James is so sharp and so fruitful. The realm of the affections is that which—*ex vi termini*, one may say— most engages and attaches. Are we to be interested in fiction without liking it? And are we to savor art without experiencing emotion? The fact that no one re-reads Mr. James means that his form, however adequate and effective, is not in itself agreeable. But it means still more that his 'content' is not attaching. When Lockhart once made some remark to Scott about poets and novelists looking at life as mere material for art, the 'veteran Chief of Letters' observed: 'I fear you have some very young ideas in your head. We shall never learn to feel and respect our real calling, unless we have taught ourselves to consider everything as moonshine compared with the education of the heart.' Is it possible that Mr. James's controlling idea is a 'young one'? Is his undoubted originality, after all, the exploitation of what seemed to so wide a practitioner as Scott, 'moonshine'? That would account, perhaps, for the pallid light that often fills his canvas when his characters are grouped in a scene where 'the human heart'—insight into which used to be deemed the standard of the novelist's excellence—has a part of any prominence to play. The voluntary abandonment by the novelist of such a field of interest as the province of the heart is witness, at all events, of an asceticism whose compensations ought in prudence to be thoroughly assured. Implied, understood—this domain! Very well, one may reply, but what a field of universal interest you neglect, what a rigorously puritanic sacrifice you make!

Thus to neglect the general field which the historic poets and romancers have so fruitfully cultivated results, however, in only a negative disadvantage, it may be contended, and Mr. James's psychology may be thought by many readers a fair compensation. It is certainly prodigiously well done. A writer with nothing more and nothing better to his credit than the group of stories assembled under the title *The Better Sort* has an indisputable claim to be considered a master, whatever one may think of the tenuity of his themes and the disproportionate attentiveness of their treatment. 'It is *proprement dit*, but it is pale,' he makes a supposititious Frenchman say of his romance, in his clever and suggestive *The Point of View;* and he frankly records his failure to interest Turgénieff in the fictions he used to send him from time to time. All the same, a new *genre* is a new *genre*, and as such it is idle to belittle Mr. James's, as readers too dull to sieze its qualities sometimes impertinently and impatiently do. But specifically and positively a novelist's neglect of the province of the heart involves the disadvantage of necessarily incomplete portraiture.

A picture of human life without reference to the passions, the depiction of human character minus this preponderating constituent element of it, cannot but be limited and defective. The view that half-consciously regards the passions as either titanic or vulgar, and therefore only pertinent as artistic material to either tragedy or journalism, is a curiously superficial one. The most controlled and systematized life, provided it illustrate any ideality, is inspired by them as fully as the least directed and most irregular. The diminution of demonstrativeness under the influence of civilization is no measure of the diminution of feeling; and even if we feel less than our forefathers, our feeling is still the dominant element in us. Every one's consciousness attests this, that of the ascetic as well as that of the epicurean, that of the patrician and the brahmin as well as that of the peasant and the clown. Whether the drama of human life is of the soul or of the senses, it is equally real, universal, and the resultant of the passions. To assume that the modern man, whatever the degree of his complicated differentiation, is any more destitute of them than his autochthonous ancestor, is to leave out of consideration the controlling constituent of his nature and the mainspring of his action. All of these personages that people Mr. James's extraordinarily varied world must have them, and the circumstance that he rarely, if ever, tells us what they are, makes us feel our acquaintance with his personages to be partial and superficial. At times we can infer them, it is true. But every art, certainly not excepting the novelist's, needs all the aid it can get to make itself effective, and reliance on inference instead of statement results here in a very shadowy kind of substance.

Is it because of a certain coolness in Mr. James's own temperament that his report of human nature is thus incomplete? Does he make us weep—or laugh—so little because he is so unmoved himself, because he illustrates so imperturbably and fastidiously the converse of the Horatian maxim? Candidly speaking, perhaps we have no business to inquire. Whether it is due to his theory or to the temperament responsible for his theory, perhaps it is both pertinent and proper to rest in the indisputable fact that he does leave us unmoved. After all, the main question is, does the fact have for us the compensations that evidently it has for him? Say that he deals so little with the emotions because preoccupation with them deflects and distracts from the business of presenting in all its force of singularization and relief, at whatever cost of completeness, the truths and traits of human nature that most interest him, that interest him so intensely. Say even, in other words, that to feel an emotional interest in his personages is for an author to incur the risk of a partiality inconsistent with artistic rectitude. Certainly it is impossible to be blind to this controlling rectitude in Mr. James, impossible to avoid recognizing—however easy we may suspect nature has made it for him—his unalterable fidelity to his main purpose in his fictions, which is to clothe and depict the idea he wishes to illustrate, whatever becomes of his people in the process. Say, too, that though sometimes, in consequence, these remain very much on the hither side of realization; though sometimes they are subjected to remorseless procrustean treatment; and though they never take possession of the scene themselves and tell or enact their own story, without, at any rate, our feeling that they rely largely on the subtlest of prompters, they nevertheless always strictly subserve the larger design of their creator. Grant all this. The salient fact remains that their creator is too much concerned with the laws of his universe, apparently, to assign them other than vicarious functions, or to take other than what is called an 'intellectual' interest in them.

And this is an interest extremely difficult for an author to make his readers share. The reader is much more readily interested through his sympathies, and cannot be relied upon to attach to phenomena which exclude these the same importance which the writer who is exploiting them does. He will readily respond to the author who illustrates 'What a piece of work is man!' and at the same time imperfectly echo the enthusiasm of the artist who exclaims, 'How beautiful a thing is this perspective!' Mr. James's enthusiasm, one may fancifully say, is for the perspective rather than for the substance of human nature, and even this, of course, in taking it from him, we are obliged to enjoy at one remove; so that, even supposing our pure curiosity to equal his, we can hardly be counted on to feel the same amount for his report of life as he feels for life itself. We need something of *him* to compensate for the inevitable loss of heat involved in the process of translation. And this he is extremely chary of giving us. What chiefly we perceive is his own curiosity.

Of this, indeed, we get, I think, a surfeit. Without more warmth than he either feels or will suffer himself to exhibit, it is difficult for him to communicate the zest he plainly takes in the particular material he in general exploits. It is too special, too occasional, too recondite, at times certainly too trivial, to stand on its own merits, aided merely by extraordinary but wholly unemotional cleverness of presentation. In fact, I think one may excusably go so far as to confess a certain antipathy to the degree in which the author exhibits this curiosity. Scrutiny so searching seems to exclude chivalry. *In the Cage*, for instance, is a wonderful study, but so persistent and penetrating as to appear positively pitiless. How many years ago was it that Arnold complained that curiosity, which had a good sense in French, had a bad one in English? For Mr. James it is not only not a defect, and not merely a quality, but a cardinal virtue. Balzac was certainly not a sentimentalist, yet Taine ascribes what he considers the superiority of Valérie Marneffe to Rebecca Sharp to the fact that Balzac 'aime sa Valérie.' Would it ever occur to any one to suspect that Mr. James 'loved' any of his characters? Ralph Touchett, perhaps; but surely the extraordinary attention that almost all his later personages receive from him is not an affectionate interest, and, as I say, I think the result is less completeness of presentment, less vigor of portraiture.

Perhaps his frequent practice of identifying himself with one of his characters by making him narrate the tale is in part responsible for this impression of extreme coolness in the narrator that we get from the book and unconsciously refer to the author. There are a number of his stories in which the fictitious narrator exhibits his cold-blooded curiosity with a naïve single-mindedness that awakens positive distaste. One winces at the scrutiny of defenseless personages practised by the narrators of 'The Pension Beaurepas',—a delightful sketch; of 'Four Meetings',— a masterpiece of satire and of pathos; of a dozen other tales in which some inhuman naturalist studies his spitted specimens. The most conspicuous instance of this is undoubtedly *The Sacred Fount*, which for this reason is a disagreeable as well as a mystifying book. The amount of prying, eavesdropping, 'snooping,' in that exasperating performance is prodigious, and the unconsciousness of indiscretion combined with its outrageousness gives one a very uncomfortable feeling,—a feeling, too, whose discomfort is aggravated by the insipidity of the fanciful phenomena which evoke in the narrator such a disproportionate interest. Perhaps this nosing curiosity is itself a trait of the 'week-end' in England, and designed to be pilloried as such. No one can know. But in this case one may wish the point had been made plainer, even in a book where it is apparently the author's intention to make everything obscure.

There are, moreover, many stories by Mr. James in which this pathologic curiosity is manifested, not by the narrator,—for whom there is some artistic excuse,—but by one or more of the characters. 'The Siege of London' is an example. From this story one might infer that the close observation of a squirming and suffering though doubtless highly reprehensible woman could really occupy the leisure of a scrupulous gentleman. Is it true that curiosity is a 'passion' of our attenuated modern life,—curiosity of this kind, I mean; the curiosity that feeds on the conduct and motives of one's fellows in whom one feels no other interest? It is at all events true that it is the one 'passion' celebrated with any ample cordiality by Mr. James, whether or no to inquire if he shares it be to inquire 'too curiously.' He himself—whom nothing escapes that he does not exclude, one is sometimes tempted to think—has noted the characteristic. I wish I could put my hand on the passage—I am confident it is in one of his earlier works—in which he speaks of a certain indiscreet closeness of observation as a disagreeable trait of a certain order of Frenchman! But surely no French writer of distinction has ever shown it in such inadvertent profusion as Mr. James. Mr. James has carried the famous watchword, 'disinterested curiosity' so far, in a word, that his curiosity is not merely impartial, but excessive. It is 'disinterested' enough in the sense hitherto intended by the epithet, but in its own exercise it is ferociously egoistic. He is not merely detached; his detachment is enthusiastic. One may say he is ardently frigid. The result, I think, is the detachment of his readers; certainly the elimination from the field of interest of those characters and that part of every character which, too fundamental and general to reward mere curiosity, nevertheless constitute the most real, the most attaching, and the most substantial elements of human life.

VII

It is possibly owing in some degree to his dispassionateness that Mr. James passes popularly for preëminently the novelist of culture. A writer so refined and so detached is inferentially the product of letters as well as of life. Less than any other would it seem congruous to associate with him the notion of crudity in any of its aspects or degrees, the notion of non-conformity to the canon, recalcitrancy to the received. And certainly he has neglected nothing of the best that has been thought and said in the world so far as his own art is concerned. He does not look at life through books; far from it. But with the books that illustrate the problem of how art should look at life he is thoroughly familiar. On the art and in the province of latter-day fiction, at any rate, there is certainly nothing he has not read—and perfectly assimilated. No writer in any department of literature can more distinctly leave the impression of acquaintance with the modern classics of his chosen field in all languages, and with all the commentaries on them. There is, besides, in his moral attitude, his turn of phrase, his absence of emphasis, his esoteric diction, his carelessness of communication, even, his air of *noblesse oblige*, his patrician fastidiousness and manifest contentment with justification by his own standards, in the wide range of his exclusions, and—above all—in his preference for dealing with high differentiation instead of the elementary and universal,—in all this there is clearly manifest the aristocratic conformity to the conclusions of culture and of the good taste which culture alone—even if only—can supply.

There is, however, this peculiarity about his culture, considered as an element of his equipment. It is very far from being with him, as it is sometimes assumed to be in the case of the literary or other artist, a handicap on his energy, his originality—an emasculating rather than an invigorating force. It has, on the contrary, been a stimulant as well as a guiding agent in his activity. But its singularity consists in the circumstance that, though unmistakably culture, it is culture of a highly specialized kind. Prominent as Mr. James's culture is, in a word, it is precisely the lack of background, the background that it is eminently the province of culture to supply, that is the conspicuous lack in his work considered as a whole, considered with reference to its permanent appeal, considered, in brief, as a contribution to literature. Is there any other writer whose work, taken in the mass, is so considerable and marked by such extreme cleverness, so much insight, and so much real power, which is also so extremely dependent upon its own qualities and character and so little upon its relations and correspondences? It is so altogether of the present time, of the moment, that it seems almost an analogue of the current instantaneous photography. Behind it one feels the writer interested, not in Molière, but in Daudet, not in Fielding, but in Trollope, not in Dante, but in Théophile Gautier. He writes about 'Le Capitaine Fracasse,' not about 'Don Quixote,' about the 'Comédie Humaine,' not about the world of Shakespeare. This is treading on delicate ground, and where the end of culture is in any wise so conspicuously achieved as it is in Mr. James, it is perhaps impertinent to inquire as to his use of the means. But where a writer's work is so voluminous as his, as well as of such a high order, it is in the interest of definition to inquire why his evident culture betrays so little evidence of interest in the classics of literature or the course of history. It is very likely true that for the writer of modern fiction an acquaintance with *Salammbo* is of more instant pertinence than saturation with the *Divine Comedy*, that such an essay as Mr. James's on Maupassant—a very nearly perfect masterpiece—is more apposite than Lowell's—rather inadequate —paper on *Don Quixote*. I only point out that from the point of view of culture, his preoccupation with Du Maurier and Reinhart and Abbey and Stevenson and Miss Woolson indicates culture of an unusually contemporary kind. In mere point of time Mme. de Sabran is as far back as I remember his going. How exquisite his treatment of these more or less current themes has occasionally been I do not need to say, or repeat. If in the last analysis there is a tincture of 'journalism' in this, it is journalism of a very high class, and perhaps anything nowadays without a trace of journalism is justly to be suspected of pedantry and pretension, qualities absolutely foreign to Mr. James's genius. They are wholly absent, too, in such 'journalism' as his books of travel,—the *Little Tour in France*, which is curiously dependent upon 'the excellent Mr. Murray' and derives from the 'red-book' rather than from the library; and the *Portraits of Places* which, however abounding in penetration and *justesse*,—I recall some remarkable pages about Tintoretto, for example,—is too enamoured of the actual to think twice about its origins. But for a literary figure that seems and really is the antipodes of some of the prominent and by no means negligible apostles of crudity of the present day, it is plain that his rather exclusive interest in the literature of the present day is a peculiarity worth remark. The man is always more than the special province in which his talent is exercised, and Mr. James's culture is such that one does not associate him with such writers of fiction as Wilkie Collins, say, so much as with Arnold and Lowell and Browning and Tennyson and Thackeray and George Eliot and Bulwer. But beside any one of these, his culture seems quite modern and current in its substance and preoccupations.

It is not, however, merely paradoxical, and therefore noteworthy, that his culture should be at once so conspicuous and so apparently partial. The circumstance is particularly significant because it is particularly disadvantageous to his impressiveness as a writer of fiction. 'L'artiste moderne,' says Paul Bourget, 'lequel se double toujours d'un critique et d'un érudit.' The critic is conspicuous enough in Mr. James, but one cannot help thinking that precisely his kind of fiction would be more effective if he were more evidently *érudit*. For example, a writer interested in the *Antigone*, and imbued with the spirit of its succession, would naturally and instinctively be less absorbed in what Maisie knew, —to mention what is certainly a very remarkable, but what is also, by the very perfection of its execution, shown to be a fantastic book, except on the supposition that whatever is, is important. Saturation with contemporary *belles lettres* will no doubt suffice an artist whose talent, like that of Mr. James, is of the first class, for the production of delightful works, but to produce works for the pantheon of the world's masterpieces without a more or less constant—even if subconscious— reference to the figures already on their august pedestals, fringes the chimerical. One could wish the representative American novelist to be less interested in inventing a new game of fiction than in figuring as the 'heir of all the ages.' For lovers of 'the last new book,' Mr. James's is no doubt the most important. But why should it not be an 'event'—such as one of Thackeray's or George Eliot's used to be? It is certainly not because his talent is inferior; is it because his culture is limited, as well as because, as I have already said, his art is as theoretic as his philosophy of life is obscure?

To take the particular instance of *The Awkward Age*, which may be called Mr. James's masterpiece,—at least among the later novels. I cannot better explain what I have in mind in speaking of his peculiar kind of culture than by saying that *The Awkward Age* strikes one as a little like Lilliput without Gulliver. One has only to imagine what Swift's picture of that interesting kingdom would be if the figure that lends it its significance were left out of it. Its significance, of course, depends wholly on the sense of contrast, the play of proportion. So does the significance of the corresponding Brobdingnag. And not at all exclusively in an artistic sense, it is to be borne in mind, but in a literary and human one. If the futilities and *niaiseries* of *The Awkward Age*, instead of being idealized by the main strength of imputed importance, were depicted from a standpoint perhaps even less artistically detached, but more removed in spirit by knowledge of and interest in the sociology of the human species previous to its latest illustration by a wretched little clique of negligible Londoners, the negligibility of these *dramatis personæ* would be far more forcefully felt. It would constitute a thesis. As it is, the thesis apparently of an extraordinary number of pages is that a girl freely brought up may turn out a better girl than one claustrally reared. Of course this is not really all. There is a corollary—a coda: the former does not get married and the latter does. And there is a still further moral to be drawn by those expert in nuances of the kind. But one feels like asking brutally, in the name of literature, if this order of it is worth while, is worth the lavish expenditure of the best literary talent we have. If it is, there is nothing more to be said. But it can only be considered worth while by the amateur of novelty, and must seem attenuated from the standpoint of culture.

It is not a matter of realism. Fielding was a realist, if ever there was one. But is it likely that without his classical culture such a realist as Fielding, even, would have depicted figures of such commanding importance and universal interest as those with which his novels are peopled? Can one fancy Gibbon praising with the same elaborate enthusiasm that he expressed for *Tom Jones* the 'exquisite picture of human life and manners' provided by *The Awkward Age* or *The Other House*,—supremely clever as is the art of these books and their fellows? Nor is it a question of art. Mr. Meredith, for example, is not a realist like Mr. James, but his art constantly suggests that of the younger writer. Yet it differs from Mr. James's not more in its preoccupations—with the fanciful, that is to say, rather than the real—than in its whole attitude, which, in spite of its absence of pedantry and close correspondence to the matter in hand, is obviously, markedly, the attitude of culture, the attitude of not being absorbed by, swamped in, the importance of the matter in hand, but of treating it at least enough at arm's length to avoid exaggerating its importance. He leaves the impression of a certain lack of seriousness. He has the air of the dilettante; which, to my sense, Mr. James never has. But he also leaves the impression, and has the air inseparably connected with what is understood by culture. In art of any kind at the present time, it is well known that culture is not overvalued. It is quite generally imagined that we should gain rather than lose, for instance, by having Raphael without the Church and Rembrandt without the Bible. But the special art of fiction has not yet been emancipated to this implied extent, because the general life of humanity, of which this art is *ex hypothesi* a picture, is felt to have a unity superior in interest and importance to any of its variations.

Too great an interest in the history, as well as in the present status, of mankind, therefore, can hardly be exacted of the creator of a mimic world, I will not say of Mr. James's pretensions, for he makes none, but of his powers, of which in justice too much cannot be exacted. A novelist in whom the historic sense is lacking is, one would say, particularly liable to lack also that sense of proportion which alone can secure the right emphasis and accent in his pictures of contemporary life—if they are to have any reach and compass of significance, if they are to rise very far above the plane of art for art's sake. From the point of view of culture as a factor in a novelist's production, it may be said, surely, that no one knows his own time who knows only it. Any conspectus of the sociology of the present day, in other words, that neglects its aspect as an evolution, neglects also its meaning. The life of the present day can no more be satisfactorily represented and interpreted in isolation in fiction than in history or sociology. To record its facts, even its subtlest and most recondite facts, those that have hitherto been neglected by more cursory observers, without at the same time admeasuring them, in however indirect and unconscious fashion, by reference to previous stages of the evolution, or at least the succession, to which the life of the present day belongs is, measurably, to lose sight of their meaning, of the reason for recording them. As Buckle said, very acutely, any one who thinks a fact valuable in itself may be a good judge of facts, but cannot be of value. And it is hardly too much to say that this is how Mr. James impresses us in his recent studies of English society, the studies that, taken in the mass, constitute the bulk, as in some respects they do the flower, of his work. He is an excellent judge of the phenomena—the sharp-eyed and penetrating critic for whom, in a sense, perhaps, this extraordinary and extraordinarily inept society has in fancied security unwittingly been waiting. But of their value he seems to be no judge at all. If his culture included such development of the historic sense as would present to his indirect vision the analogues of other civilizations, other societies, other *milieux*, he could hardly avoid placing as well as fixing his phenomena. And this would, I think, give an altogether different aspect and value to his work.

In illustration, I may refer to a portion—the most interesting, and, I am inclined to think, the most important though not perhaps the most 'wonderful' portion—of this work itself. There was a time when Mr.

James did things with obvious zest, with a freedom that excluded the notion of the theoretic; when he communicated pleasure by first feeling it himself; when, therefore, there was a strong personal note in what he wrote, and he did not alienate by his aloofness; when, indeed, one could perceive and enjoy a strain of positive gayety in his compositions. Has any reader of his, I wonder, any doubt as to the period I have in mind? I refer to the period of his studies in contemporary sociology, so to speak, the years when the contrast between America and Europe pre-occupied him so delightfully. Then he produced 'documents' of real value and of striking vitality. He had the field all to himself, and worked it to his own distinct profit and that of his readers. Then he portrayed types and drew out their suggestiveness. His characters were not only real, but representative. He provided material not only for the keenest enjoyment, but for reflection. His scientific curiosity resulted in some-thing eminently worth while, something in which he excelled so not-ably as virtually to seem, if indeed he was not literally, the originator of a new and most engaging *genre* of romance,—to be, one may say, the Bopp of the comparative method as applied to fiction.

The literature that he produced at this period owes its superiority to his current product in general import and interest, I think, precisely to this factor of culture on which he now places so little reliance. It was inspired and penetrated with the spirit of cosmopolitanism, that is to say, culture in which the contemporary is substituted for the more universal element, and, if it does not quite make up in vividness for what it lacks in breadth, certainly performs the similar inestimable service of providing a standard that establishes the relative value and interest of the material directly dealt with. Out of his familiarity with contemporary society in America, England, France, and Italy, grew a series of novels and tales that were full of vigor, piquancy, truth, and significance. The play of the characters against contrasting backgrounds was most varied and interesting. The contrasts of points of view, of conventions and ideas, of customs and traditions, gave a richness of texture to the web of his fiction which, since it has lacked these, it has disadvantageously lost. His return to the cosmopolitan *motif* in *The Ambassadors* and (measur-ably) in *The Golden Bowl* is accordingly a welcome one, and would be still more welcome if the development of this *motif* were not now incrusted and obscured with mannerisms of presentation accreted in the pursuit of what no doubt seems to the author a 'closer correspondence with life,' but what certainly seems to the reader a more restricted order of art,—an art, at any rate, so largely dependent on scrutiny as perforce to dispense with the significance to be expected only of the culture it suggests, but does not illustrate. It is a part of Mr. James's distinction that he gives us so much as to make us wish for more, that he entertains us on so high a plane that we ask to be conducted still higher, and that his penetration reveals to us such wonders in the particular *locale*, that we call upon him to show us 'the kingdoms of the earth.'

VIII

We could readily forego anything that he lacks, however, if he would demolish for us the *chevaux-de-frise* of his later style. In early days his style was eminently clear, and at the same time wholly adequate, but in the course of years it has become an exceedingly complicated vehicle. Its complexity is probably quite voluntary. Indeed, like his whole attitude, it is even theoretic. It images, no doubt, the multifariousness of its substance, of which it follows the nuances and subtleties, and with its parentheses and afterthoughts and qualifications, its hints and hesitations, its indirection and innuendo, pursues the devious and haphazard development of the drama of life itself. It is thoroughly alive and sincere. It has mannerisms, but no affectations. One gets tired of the frequent recurrence of certain favorite words and locutions, but the author's fondness for them is always genuine. Least of all are they perfunctory, any more than is any other manifestation of Mr. James's intellectual activity. His vocabulary is remarkable, both in range and in intimate felicity; and it is the academic vocabulary, rendered vigorous by accents of raciness now and then, the acme of literary breeding, without, however, a trace of bookish aridity. He is less desultory than almost any writer of anything like his voluminousness. His scrupulous care involves often quite needless precautions, as if the reader were watching for a slip,—'like a terrier at a rat-hole,' a sufferer from his superfluous concessions once impatiently observed. But his precision involves no strain. His style in general shows no effort, though it ought to be said that, on the other hand, it also shows no restraint. It is tremendously personal in its pointed neglect of conformity to any ideal of what, as style, it should be. It avoids thus most conspicuously the hackneyed traits of rhetorical excellence. And certainly the pursuit of technical perfection may easily be too explicit, too systematic. Correctness is perhaps the stupidest way of achieving artificiality. But a writer of Mr. James's rhetorical fertility, combined with his distinction in the matter of taste, need have no fear of incurring artificiality in deferring to the more elementary requirements of the rhetorical canon.

He has, however, chosen to be an original writer in a way that precludes him from being, as a writer, a great one. Just as his theory of art prevents his more important fiction from being a rounded and synthetic image of life seen from a certain centralizing point of view, and makes of it an essay at conveying the sense and illusion of life by following, instead of focusing, its phenomena, so his theory of style prevents him from creating a texture of expression with any independent interest of its own. The interest of his expression consists solely in its correspondence to the character of what it endeavors to express. So concentrated upon this end is he that he very rarely gives scope to the talent for beautiful and effective expression which occasional lapses from his rigorous practice show him to possess in a distinguished degree. There are entire volumes of his writings that do not contain a sentence like, for example, this from a brief essay on Hawthorne: 'His beautiful and light imagination is the wing that on the autumn evening just brushes the dusky pane.' Of a writer who has this touch, this capacity, in his equipment, it is justifiable to lament that his theory of art has so largely prevented his exercise of it. The fact that his practice has not atrophied the faculty—clear enough from a rare but perfect exhibition of it from time to time—only increases our regret. We do not ask of Mr. James's fastidiousness the purple patch of poetic prose, any more than we expect from him any kind of mediocrity whatever. But when a writer, who shows us unmistakably now and then that he could give us frequent equivalents of such episodes as the death of Ralph Touchett, rigorously refrains through a long series of admirable books from producing anything of greater extent than a sentence or a paragraph that can be called classic, that has the classic 'note,' we may, I think, legitimately complain that his theory of art is exasperatingly exacting.

And of what may be called the strategy, in distinction from the tactics, of style he is quite as pointedly negligent. The elements of combination, distribution, climax, the whole larger organization and articulation of literary presentment, are dissembled, if not disdained. Even if it be possible to secure a greater sense of life by eliminating the sense of art in the general treatment of a fiction,—which is certainly carrying the theory of *ars celare artem* very far (the first word in the aphorism having hitherto stood for 'art,' and the last for 'artifice'),—even if in attitude and construction, that is to say, the amount of life in Mr. James's books atones for the absence of the visible, sensible, satisfying element of art as art, it is nevertheless clear that in style as such there is nothing whatever that can atone for the absence of art. Skill is an insufficient substitute; it is science, not art, that is the adaptation of means to ends. And upon skill Mr. James places his whole reliance.

He is, of course, supremely skillful. His invention, for example, which has almost the force and value of the creative imagination, appears in particularly exhaustless variety in the introductions of his short stories. Each one is a study in exordiums, as skillful as Cicero's. And the way in which the narrative proceeds, the characters are introduced, and the incidents succeed one another, is most attentively considered. But no amount of skill and care compensate for the loss of integumental interest in the handling, the technic, the style, that is involved in a subordination of style to content so complete as positively to seem designed to flout the traditional convention which makes the interpenetration of the two the ideal. Such an ideal is perhaps a little too obvious for Mr. James, who is as uninterested in 'the obvious' as he is unconcerned about 'the sublime,' of which, according to a time-honored theory, the obvious is a necessary constituent.

The loss of interest involved in obscurity is, to begin with, enormous. Such elaborate care as that of Mr. James should at least secure clearness. But with all his scrupulousness, clearness never seems to be an object of his care. At least, this is true of his later work. In his earlier, his clearness was so conspicuous as almost to suggest limitation. There are extremely flat-footed things to be encountered in it now and then—as, for example, his reprehension of the trivial in Hawthorne, the 'parochial' in Thoreau. But since his later, his preponderant, and what we must consider his true, manner has been established, no one needs to be reminded that obscurity has been one of its main traits. His concern is to be precise, not to be clear. He follows his thought with the most intimate exactness—no doubt—in its subtile sinuosities, into its complicated connotations, unto its utmost attenuations; but it is often so elusive, so *insaisissable*—by others than himself—that he may perfectly express without in the least communicating it. Yet the very texture of his obscurity is composed of incontestable evidences that he is a master of expression. The reader's pleasure becomes a task, and his task the torture of Tantalus.

It is simply marvelous that such copiousness can be so elliptical. It is usually in greater condensation—such as Emerson's—that we miss the connectives. The fact attests the remarkable fullness of his intellectual operations, but such plenitude imposes the necessity of restraint in direct proportion to the unusual extent and complexity of its material.

'Simplification' is a favorite word with Mr. James, but he himself never simplifies for our benefit. Beyond question, he does for his own. He has clearly preliminarily mastered his complicated theme in its centrality; he indisputably sits in the centre of the web in whose fine-spun meshes his readers are entangled. If in reading one of his fictions you are conscious of being in a maze, you know that there is an issue if you are but clever enough to find it. Mr. James gives you no help. He flatters you by assuming that you are sufficiently clever. His work, he seems to say, is done when he has constructed his labyrinth in emulating correspondence with the complexity of his model life, and at the same time furnished a potentially discoverable clue to it. There are readers who find the clue, it is not to be doubted, and follow it in all its serpentine wanderings, though they seem to do so in virtue of a special sense—the sense, it might be called, of understandingly savoring Mr. Henry James. But its possessors are marked individuals in every one's acquaintance; and it need not be said that they are exceptionally clever people. There are others, the mystically inclined, and therefore perhaps more numerous, who divine the significance that is hidden from the wise and prudent. But to the majority of intelligent and cultivated readers, whose appreciation constitutes fame, the great mass of his later writing is of a difficulty to conquer which requires an amount of effort disproportionate to the sense of assured reward.

Are the masterpieces of the future to be written in this fashion? If they are, they will differ signally from the masterpieces of the past in the substitution of a highly idiosyncratic *manner* for the hitherto essential element of *style*; and in consequence they will require a second reading, not, as heretofore, for the discovery of 'new beauties,' or the savoring again of old ones, but to be understood at all. In which case, one may surmise, they will have to be very well worth while. It can hardly be hoped that they will be as well worth while as those of Mr. James, and the chances are, accordingly, that he will occupy the very nearly unique niche in the history of fiction—hard by that of Mr. Meredith, perhaps— of being the last as well as the first of his line. He has a host of imitators, it is true; he has, in a way, founded a school, but as yet certainly this has produced no masterpieces. Has he himself? If so, they are, at all events, not unmistakably of the scale and on the plane suggested by his unmistakable powers,—powers that make it impossible to measure him otherwise than by the standards of the really great novelists and of the masters of English prose.

178. Sir Almeric Fitzroy on the hermit of Rye

1906

Almeric Fitzroy, from his diary, January 1906 (*Memoirs of Sir Almeric Fitzroy*, 1925, 278).
Fitzroy (1851–1935) was an aristocrat and historian, and Clerk of the Privy Council.

We had tea with Henry James, anchorite and novelist, who has a hermitage at Rye, and there nurses in spacious reverie his spiritual enchantments, not seldom the fruit of sheer loneliness of soul.

179. William James on the greatness of *The American Scene,* and the rumness of the late style

1907

WJ to HJ, May 1907 (JF, 341–2).

I've been so overwhelmed with work, and the mountain of the *Unread* has piled up so, that only in these days . . . have I been able to settle down to your *American Scene*, which in its peculiar way seems to me *supremely great*. You know how opposed your whole 'third manner' of execution is to the literary ideals which animate my crude and Orson-like breast, mine being to say a thing in one sentence as straight and explicit as it can be made, and then to drop it forever; yours being to avoid naming it straight, but by dint of breathing and sighing all round and round it, to arouse in the reader who may have had a similar perception already (Heaven help him if he hasn't!) the illusion of a solid object, made (like the 'ghost' at the Polytechnic) wholly out of impalpable materials, air, and the prismatic interferences of light, ingeniously focused by mirrors upon empty space. But you *do* it, that's the queerness! And the complication of innuendo and associative reference on the enormous scale to which you give way to it does so *build out* the matter for the reader that the result is to solidify, by the mere bulk of the process, the like perception from which *he* has to start. As air, by dint of its volume, will weigh like a corporeal body; so his own poor little initial perception, swathed in this gigantic envelopment of suggestive atmosphere, grows like a germ into something vastly bigger and more substantial. But it's the rummest method for one to employ systematically as you do nowadays; and you employ it at your peril. In this crowded and hurried reading age, pages that require such close attention remain unread and neglected. You can't skip a word if you are to get the effect, and 19 out of 20 worthy readers grow intolerant. The method seems perverse: 'Say it *out*, for God's sake,' they cry, 'and have done with it.' And so I say now, give us *one* thing in your older directer manner, just to show that, in spite of your paradoxical success in this unheard-of method, you *can* still write according to accepted canons. Give us that interlude; and then continue like the 'curiosity of literature' which you have become. For gleams and innuendoes and felicitous verbal insinuations you are unapproachable, but the *core* of literature is solid. Give it to us *once* again! The bare perfume of things will not support existence, and the effect of solidity you reach is but perfume and simulacrum.

180. H. G. Dwight on American hostility to James, and its probable causes

1907

H. G. Dwight, from 'Henry James—"in his own country"',
Putnam's Monthly, May and July 1907, ii, 164–70 and 433–42.
This admirable article documents and criticizes HJ's American
reception in a very economical fashion. Inconclusive as it is, it is
almost unique in the novelist's lifetime because it recognizes, and
tries to analyse at length, the central anomaly of his public career
which the majority of critics either did not notice or did not care
about. Dwight (1875–1959) was a diplomat, journalist, and story
writer. From 1903 to 1906 he was Curator of the New York
Author's Club. Dr. Hugo Munsterberg (1863–1916) was a
German psychologist who had moved to Harvard in 1892, and
who was known as the author of sympathetic critiques of
American society.

I

The biographer of Henry James will doubtless find one of his most telling chapters in that return to America, after an absence of twenty years,
of which the echoes have scarce yet died away. Latest among them, and
not least suggestive, is the admirable Bibliography of Mr. Le Roy
Phillips. Commemorating as it does the interest roused by Mr. James's
visit, it puts into the hands of readers for the first time a guide to their
author's complete work.

In general, however, the echoes in question were of no such sonority
as has sometimes been recorded in the annals of creative art. There was
neither firing of cannon nor ringing of bells on the late summer day of
1904 when a certain passenger stepped from his steamer at New York.
Youths did not unharness his horses and drag him triumphally between
gala brown-stone fronts. Virgins did not bestrew the asphalt with roses,
nor herald his progress with welcoming hymns. Nor did burghers of the
diamond stud and the flowing redingote advance, with top-hat in one

hand and gold box in the other, to offer him, in accents Hibernian or Teutonic, the freedom of the city of his birth. On the contrary, there was little in the event to bring it to the eye of the man in the street. Indeed, large numbers of the best-informed citizens might be discovered to have remained pacifically oblivious to any unusual occurrence in their midst; or, when apprised of the facts, might even confess themselves unmoved by the revelation. And if there were paragraphs in newspapers and sober appreciative dinners—to say nothing of fluttering feminine receptions not a few—there was also, on the part of those excluded from such functions as on that of the young gentlemen detailed to report the same, more persiflage than praise.

The event, nevertheless, for those whom it happened to concern— and they constituted, after all, quite an army—was sufficiently telling. The protagonist, for his part, signalized it by some of his most characteristic work. *The Golden Bowl*, the latest and in many ways the most striking of his novels, was completed in this country and was published during its author's sojourn in our tents. He also delivered in several cities a lecture on 'The Lesson of Balzac,' which had for many the more immediate interest of the lesson of James. And directer results of his American experiences were contained in the address on 'The Question of our Speech,' before the graduating class of Bryn Mawr and in the various 'Impressions' of *Harper's* and the *North American Review*.

But what marked the event even more conspicuously was the manner in which these productions, and the author of them, were received by a long-unvisited public. Rarely indeed has any single occasion in the life of a literary man—save that of his death—availed to call forth such a flood of remark as the return of Henry James. The generation which had grown up without him seized with one accord so inviting an opportunity to vent its opinion,—which proved to be almost as notable for unanimity as for volume. The event was therefore telling, if only because so much comment could be expended upon a person whose cryptic utterances and incomprehensible exile so little deserved the precious boon of publicity. And if there were who found in that exile something to remind them of Byron and Shelley and Browning, or whom the cryptic utterances happened to strike as being of a high order of significance, the event was for them only the more telling—as throwing into singular relief the position which a novelist at the height of his powers, after forty years of serious artistic work and after winning the highest recognition in other lands, may sometimes hold in the hearts of his countrymen.

433

This somewhat anomalous situation is not without an interest of its own for those who happen to be curious in literary matters. There is for them a certain interest in following the most desultory currents of criticism. And in this instance the current is so strong, and the occasion of it so much more salient than most incidents of the literary stream, that the spectator finds more to reward his observation than is often his fortune. In fact the matter really constitutes what Mr. James himself would call a 'case.' 'A man too great to be ignored, he is yet too ignored to be great, for his appeal is, and ever must be, to what Stevenson calls "a parlor audience".' That snapshot of popular criticism (by Claude Bragdon, in the *Critic* for February, 1904) is but the mildest of statements. For the event of which we speak served to precipitate a feeling which has long been gathering in solution, and which if negative in its actual critical residue was positive enough in its emphasis.

There have not lacked signs, in the process of years, that the generation did not take its Henry James quite as it took others of its spokesmen. It would be hard, for instance, to conceive that a chance illness of Mr. James in his native land could have called forth such demonstrations of popular sympathy as were evoked a few years ago by the illness, at a New York hotel, of Mr. Kipling. To what a degree, however, our own countryman seems to possess the power of arousing our combative instincts might not be apparent to those who had not taken the trouble to follow the matter. The present scribe, for his part, makes no claim to acquaintance with the entire body of utterance called forth by the event in question. It was only after the general tone of such remark as he encountered began to attract his attention that it occurred to him, as much for his own amusement as for a study in contemporary taste, to keep watch of such comment as might chance his way. And being by no means an omnivorous reader of the periodical press, he gathered his impressions from a limited range of publications, chiefly of New York.

Yet it is something to say that among a considerable number of reviews formal and informal, and of those letters from readers which are so interesting to a student of manners, the scribe happened to encounter only four notices which were completely favorable to the subject of this paper. These were an essay by Elisabeth Luther Cary in *Scribner's* (October, 1904), an 'Appreciation' by Joseph Conrad in the *North American Review* (January, 1905), and two letters from readers—one of them indeed wrote again—in a Saturday supplement of the New York *Times* (April 22, 1905). If one added to this list an admirably impersonal interview by Witter Bynner in the *Critic* (February, 1905), one should perhaps subtract from it Miss Cary's essay. For, besides intimating an inability to swallow *The Sacred Fount*, she confessed to a fear that Mr. James's later style might threaten his future! It is only fair to add, however, that this sympathetic paper has since been expanded to a volume (*The Novels of Henry James* G. P. Putnam's Sons, 1905), which furthermore contains an approximately complete bibliography of our author.

On the other side the list reached proportions far more imposing. It included, to be sure, a body of readers who had been faithful to Mr. James until the days—say—of *What Maisie Knew* (1897), but who since then have found themselves plunged into constantly deeper bewilderment. The larger number, however, seemed to be of the reigning generation, whose aloofness ranged from solemn perplexity to open ridicule. Their utterances, as was natural, were for the most part called forth by those of Mr. James himself. Although his approach and arrival had been duly reported by the literary scouts, it was not until the appearance of the *The Golden Bowl* (October, 1904) that the game really began. Then readers all over the country filled the papers with denunciation of this book—its undermining of the public morals ('decadence' was the favorite word), its general darkness and unintelligibility. Indeed, it quite enjoyed a *succès de scandale*, and performed for its author the unwonted feat of going into two or three editions in as many months. 'No other writer,' said Mr. Frederick Taber Cooper in *The Bookman* (December, 1904), 'has ever so far presumed upon the fact that the public will accept many revolting things if they are not put into plain words. Mr. James's books are a sort of verbal hide-and-seek. He never gives us any tangible facts, but always an endless chain of suggested improprieties. *The Golden Bowl* is, superficially, a shimmering mist of verbal cleverness, but the plot, if it has any meaning at all, is a tissue of hideous, nameless complications. And yet, instead of charging Mr. James with impropriety, you catch yourself wondering whether, as a matter of fact, he can possibly have meant anything half so unsavory as he suggests; whether in short you ought not to be very much ashamed of yourself for letting your imagination take such license.' Yet that even doctors will disagree was proven by another of our younger critics, Mr. Henry W. Boynton, who wrote in the Saturday supplement of the *Times* (November 26, 1904):

It is patent that the boundaries of Mr. James's audience were fixed long ago. Certainly nothing could be less likely to extend them than a book like this. It quite lacks, indeed, a property which has undoubtedly done something toward attracting a grosser audience for some of his other books. *The Golden Bowl* makes no delicate overtures to pruriency; its most dubious passages suggest nothing more than the most ordinary improprieties.' And we may add what he goes on to say, for its more general application: 'In other ways it seems to me to present Mr. James at his worst, as its predecessor, *The Better Sort*, presented him at his best. . . . In *The Golden Bowl* we find, standing for subtelty, a kind of restless finicking inquisitiveness, a flutter of aimless conjecture, such as might fall to a village spinster in a 'department store' . . . The situation, in fact, could only exist in that land of dubiety which Mr. James himself has peopled. The dwellers in that land are clever enough, intricate enough, psychological enough; they merely lack common sense.

By the time 'The Lesson of Balzac' began to be heard, so much had already been said that the lecture called forth comment less formal and less voluble. Its sentences, however, and those—generally of the fair sex —who flocked to hear them, afforded the newspapers an excellent opportunity to make merry at Mr. James's expense. But in order to avoid repetition, and because we shall use later on a certain familiar signature, we must content ourselves with a notice of the small book which afterwards contained this address and the one delivered at Bryn Mawr. The latter, it may be said in passing, aroused more remark than perhaps any other of Mr. James's public utterances. Even the 'Impressions' (*North American Review*, April, 1905, *et seq.*) did not stir up so much heat. If their alleged lack of patriotism was resented, their manner permitted the reviewer to dip his pen into that lightsome satire so copiously manufactured in this country. But in the question of our speech it was possible to divine the speaker's meaning, and it did not appear to be of a nature to undermine the morals of the young. On the contrary, it was visibly aimed at the uplifting of the young. The young, however, in our land above all others, are a powerfully organized body, and they, thanks to an age of reason and of discipline by love, are by no means accustomed to admonition so pointed. Accordingly the intimation that their use and pronunciation of words occasionally left something to be desired was met by the decisive retort that, if anything were to be said on the subject, Mr. Henry James, of Rye, Sussex, England, was hardly the man to say it. There was, in general, an airy superiority to the dangers apprehended by that gentleman, of which the following, from the literary columns of the New York *Sun* (October 21, 1905), is not an unfair example:

While Mr. Howells was enjoying himself in London, Mr. James was having nearly as good a time in the country of his birth. He was cooing to female audiences in the subdued tones that mark British good breeding and kindly pointing out to them the horrors of the language they spoke. Two of his lectures, 'The Question of our Speech' and 'The Lesson of Balzac,' are published in a thin volume by Houghton, Mifflin & Co. We can picture to ourselves the high glee with which Mr. James tangled himself up in his own sentences to mystify the Bryn Mawr girls. He is good enough to call it 'our speech,' but it is really the language of Mr. James in its most mischievous and perplexing confusion. We wonder that he never heard the faults of utterances he dislikes in the land where he resides. His eulogy of Balzac deserves far more attention; it is a pity that the great French novelist could not have been set forth in clearer and less affected English, such as Mr. James at one time was not ashamed to write.

The point of view of commentators of this order was rather strikingly set before the present writer in a conversation for whose veracity he can give only his own word. It occurred in a private place, and the second party to it probably had no idea that any use could be made of his remarks. One may at least say, however, that he belonged to the staff of a New York paper which devotes particular attention to literary matters. And that part of his discourse which has pertinence for us relates to an interview he had had with Mr. James. Having formed the project of making a 'feature' of this gentleman for a Sunday edition, the reporter had introduced himself to the novelist under a social guise and then had thrown off the mask. Mr. James, it appeared, objected to this not-unheard-of manœuvre, saying that he was more used to life in England, where a gentleman's privacy was not intruded upon. The interviewer, according to his own account, then proceeded to 'talk to' Mr. James 'like a Dutch uncle,' plainly informing him that such an attitude was un-American; that in this country people wanted to know the jockey on the racer, the man behind the gun (I speak by the card), and that if they were so obliging as to buy and read your books it was only fair to humor their harmless inquisitiveness; that, moreover, it helped along your own affairs—to put it crudely, it advertised you. After which account of the lesson he had administered to the celebrated novelist, the interviewer confessed himself incapable of reading the celebrated novels, or to understand why they should be so highly considered in the capital of our speech—as he was informed on the most credible authority (that, namely, of a popular 'lady novelist' just back from the other side), they were. And, to be candid, I quite believed him. There was nothing in his conversation to betray that he had ever read a word of the books whose author he had intended to honor. The only reason, he explained, why Mr. James should be made a 'feature' of at all, was that he undoubtedly afforded subjects of conversation to the 'ultra-intellectual' and to women. The novelist was, in fact, a woman's writer; no man was able to read him.

It is sufficiently notorious, of course, that these views are of no especial rarity. But since we are interested not so much in proving as in recording, let us, before going on to another part of our paper, quote from two critics who expressed in more permanent form opinions not altogether dissimilar to the preceding. In the case of the first of these the name of the writer is of less moment than, for instance, his address. He comes from Brooklyn, and as that progressive borough is rather in the way of being a larger and more unlicked Boston, such a letter as the following is of special significance. It speaks—and with what clearness we shall see—for a considerable element among those of our citizens who, without specific lesiure or enlightenment, go to make up, in their earnest appreciation of the printed word, the body of the reading public. The writer says (in the Saturday supplement of the *Times*, March 18, 1905):

During the past five years it has been one of my duties to cater for a reading club of about 100 members. All of the novels of Henry James have been given to the club with other current publications, and I find by reference to the charge book that not more than three of the hundred ever take out one of the James novels. Popularity may be a crude test of genius; nevertheless it is a test that has been applied with pretty uniform results to all great reputations in fiction. Poets and reformers sometimes write for posterity and, like Milton, content themselves with a 'fit audience, though few.' But the novelist who does not reach a large audience in his own day and generation will not have a large place in the history of literature, and it is no contradiction or exception to this natural law of literature that a very small novel frequently gains a very large audience and presently sinks into the oblivion of the commonplace.

It is suggested, however, that Henry James writes neither for fame nor for money; that with a high-minded and spacious renunciation he flings to the winds his opportunity to achieve greatness in the vulgar sense, in order to devote his genius to the development of certain principles of esoteric literary expression, a kind of twentieth-century Della Cruscan preciosity, that to the properly refined literary exquisite is—the real thing. Some such matter as this seems to underlie the reiterated declaration of Mr. Howells that Henry James is the greatest writer of English in modern times, though one is inclined to suspect that—with his constitutional tendency to humor—Mr. Howells is imposing upon the credulity and critical ignorance of his readers. But here again the test of popularity is fatal, for every really great work in English literature has proved its greatness through intelligible English expression. A piece of literature that requires a special preparation of the intellect to read it is not likely to achieve greatness or have greatness thrust upon it by the writer's friends.

So the problem of James's greatness remains a problem, for there certainly is a kind of vague conviction, or current literary superstition, that James is indeed great. It is perhaps a case not so much of the eccentricity of genius as one of the obliquity of genius, and—when one has spent a few hours with some of his favorite characters, one might call it the moral obliquity of genius. George Eliot once said that the test of greatness is a writer's 'contribution to the spiritual wealth of mankind'. Suppose we were to apply this test to the works of Henry James?

The interrogation point with which this letter ends is perhaps the characteristic note of the entire discussion. While readers expressed in general the most varied degrees of bewilderment, exasperation, or ridicule, their most frequent point of agreement was that of uncertainty as to what, after all, to make of Mr. James. One critic, however, and the most seasoned of them all, proposed to himself to answer the elusive question. And more than one eager commentator went so far as to call Mr. Brownell's essay in the *Atlantic Monthly* (April, 1905) the definitive essay on Henry James. There is something to be said of definitive essays, in a world where even such a question as that of perpetual motion occasionally proves itself unclosed! This particular definitive essay, at all events, dealt at far greater length, far more analytically, and offered more indications of acquaintance with the works it criticised, than any other notice, sympathetic or otherwise, which the present writer happened to see. For this reason, and because Mr. Brownell made articulate the vague impressions of a multitude, one would like to quote him more fully. But when we have said that, after appreciating Mr. James's possession of great powers, his sincerity of motive, and his incorruptibility of purpose, he went on to make reservations which left the paper a negative effect, we can allow ourselves space for only one or two of its more general statements.

[quotes Brownell on HJ's unfortunate tendency to reverse 'the relation between his observation and his imagination' (a remark taken up in various senses by many later critics), and on the later style in general.]

It is, of course, too easy, by that unconscious process of selection which goes on in the mind of one who has become interested in a given subject, to ignore such relations of that subject as do not happen to serve his immediate purpose. But in the present instance there is probably no need of proving the divided nature of the allegiance—to speak in euphemistic terms—inspired by Mr. James. And we have already pointed out that in transcribing the above more or less representative opinions we were recording, as a matter of critical curiosity, the case of a novelist well known in the world, who returned in the fulness of his days to his own people and found them neither willing to aclaim him nor able to ignore him. If a future generation should reverse the verdict of our own, the case would take on an added curiosity.

And yet, for persons like the present scribe, there is not quite an end of the matter. While not of those who find it natural to introduce monotheism into the literary world, with a single supreme figure and descending hierarchies of genius, he has come to regard Henry James as one of the few speakers of the day worth listening to. The spectacle of a talent so high and yet—in certain quarters—so far from recognition, is therefore extremely curious to him. And, while wondering whether there may not be others after his own mind—there are at least Mr. Conrad, Miss Cary, and two gentlemen who write to the New York *Times*!— it is natural for such a person to account to himself for the reasons which, in this particular case, make it possible for a prophet to be not without honor save in his own country and in his own house. Color for which impulse, if the mere instinct of fair play were not enough to justify it, might be found in Mr. Brownell's classification of those who are able to read Mr. James. Embarrassing as may be one's personal dilemma—of being either 'mysteriously inclined' and 'able to divine the significance that is hidden from the wise and prudent,' or a 'marked' person, not 'exceptionally clever,' endowed with the 'special sense' of 'understandingly savoring Mr. Henry James'—one may venture to hope that some account of one's symptoms will have at least a psychopathic interest.

II

The most obvious reason, to the mind of a friendly critic, why Mr. James is so slow to come into his own, is the impossibility of making anything like a final estimate of his work. While it is highly doubtful whether such a thing as a 'definitive essay' ever was or ever will be written in this world, it certainly can not be done during the life of a writer so voluminous, so varied, and so novel as Henry James. The more so as the remarkable development which has taken place in his work has so far cut him off from his first audience that he is forced to gain a second at a time when most men of his calibre are reaping their successes.

For him, therefore, the period through which great talents often pass, between their first vogue and their final acceptance, is doubly discomfiting. And, in the meantime, those who still feel disposed to make his acquaintance find small encouragement. No publisher has yet hazarded a collected edition of his fifty or sixty books, nor does it occur to librarians to repair the deficiency. At all events no public library in New York, where if anywhere one might expect to find the documents to one's hand, can afford a complete set of the writings of this not unknown New Yorker. To attempt to consider his published work as a whole is accordingly a formidable task. Yet it is only in that light that something of the import of the man begins to become apparent.

Curious indeed seem the freaks of fame when we consider that on one of the earliest and slightest of his novels, *Daisy Miller*, does Mr. James's reputation in America largely hang. It is, however, in the character of a novelist that he has most frequently appeared. Some twenty-five, or nearly half, of his books have been novels—a number which would be considered a very fair output for a man who had done nothing else. And whatever may have been brought against him, no one has ever accused Mr. James of being slipshod in his work. Yet he has made his mark in no less definite a manner as a writer of short stories. If it appear to the lay mind that a man who can produce so many novels merely requires a little patience to sit down and produce twenty volumes of short stories, the instructed are only too sadly aware that not every talent can pursue those two arts with equal success. But it is not alone to the fictive branches of literature that Mr. James belongs. His work as a critic, in fact,—although the later results of it have yet to be put into attainable form,—has won recognition from many who are unable to read his fiction. If the life of Hawthorne, in the English Men of Letters Series, should be included among his half dozen books of this class, that of the sculptor Story occupies a place by itself in American biography. And then we have said nothing of the early descriptive essays—that go on the same shelf with Hawthorne's *Our Old Home* and Howells's *Venetian Life* and *London Films*—of the ten or more volumes translated or edited, and of the many stories and essays which have never been collected between separate covers. The fecundity of mind and constancy of purpose capable of producing so much work, of so high an artistic level, with so little encouragement, would argue in itself a personality not without interest—were that the point at issue. So various is the expression of this personality, so novel in manner and matter, and so widely related to things beyond our Anglo-Saxon ken, that our inability, after forty years, either to accept or to reject it is perhaps not to be wondered at.

Proceeding in this way the affair of the second manner becomes easier to handle. That there is a second manner it is hardly necessary, at this late day, to point out. It has been made sufficiently patent even to the reader least versed in the technicalities of the art of which accident makes him a critic. It has not been made sufficiently patent to him, however,—because no one has told him and because it is hard to find out for himself,—that there are several Jameses of whom he must take account, and not one. Not only does Mr. James assume in turn the roles of novelist, story-writer, critic, essayist, biographer, and editor, but each category of his work contains examples of his two manners. If, therefore, *The Sacred Fount* and 'The Papers' and the new American impressions are Henry James, so are *Roderick Hudson* and 'A Passionate Pilgrim' and *Transatlantic Sketches*. And it seems to one reader, at least, that the difficulties of the former, elevated as they have been to the dignity of a tradition, are absurdly exaggerated. It also seems to him that the extreme tendency of the moment to recommend the telegram as a literary model has a good deal to do with it.

Far be it from us, however, to assume any appearance of special pleading for the second manner at the expense of the first. Whatever our opinion of the former may be, there is much in it to repay the study of those who happen to be interested in the art of writing. And it is quite possible that the matter of its development may become in time an interesting point of literary history. The present scribe has often connected it in his own mind with a passage of Mr. James's second essay on Turguénieff, in *Partial Portraits*. In this passage—which in spite, or perhaps because, of the comfort it would seem to give to the enemy one is sorry not to quote in full—Mr. James tells with the candor that is the mark of his criticism how he used to send his books to the great Russian novelist, and how the great Russian novelist, to the best of his friend's belief, was unable to read them. This, Mr. James opines, was because 'the manner was more apparent than the matter; they were too *tara-biscoté*, as I once heard him say of the style of a book—had on the surface too many little flowers and knots of ribbon.' The reader is accordingly free to wonder if this experience would not naturally tend to have an influence upon what we might call, after Mr. James, the little knots of ribbon of his youth. So distinguished a stylist, and one so sensitive to the passing impression, cannot have failed to study his instrument—with a constancy of which our rough and ready writers can have no inkling—

in every reflected light. Though if this particular light revealed what its beneficiary regarded as an excessive finish, it would seem on the other hand that he was not too easily to be moved. For the essay was written nearly twenty-five years ago, about the time of 'The Siege of London' (1883), and before the celebrated second manner, which though less smooth could be called more *tarabiscoté* than the first, began to take its present form.

There is another passage in the essays of Mr. James which has a still greater significance with regard to the development of his style. This is in 'The Lesson of Balzac', where he draws the distinction between poet and novelist, between the impression of life and the image of life. In his own work, as it has grown more impersonal and more architectonic, it is easy to trace the gradual suppression of what he calls the lyric element. And, at the same time, one thinks of his essential modernity. This is an aspect of his critical work, in particular, to which Mr. Brownell, in the essay to which we have alluded, takes exception. Yet, from another side, the fact is significant not so much of the partiality of Mr. James's culture—it may well have seemed to him, in the days of Lowell and Arnold and Taine, that he had little to add to the commentaries of Dante and Shakespeare—as of his essential freedom from the academic, his so little noted relation to the men of his time, his outlook upon a time to come. Moreover if one were polemically inclined one might point out that not only does such criticism as his necessarily presuppose a background of academic culture, to be anything more than the merest beating of wings in the void; but that to discuss accepted traditions may conceivably require less keenness of eye and a less synthetic type of mind than to lay the foundations of tradition. At all events, that in Mr. James which leads him to criticise the men he has known rather than the men he has not known, to write of the society in which he moves instead of some society imagined or desired, to seize so infallibly the accent of the contemporary, must have led him more and more to conform his style to his idea of the real. . . .

The present writer has sometimes wondered if so small a matter as the habit of dictation might in the least be concerned in it; not at all for laxity, but for conscious approximation to the spoken word. The later manner of Mr. James is more than anything else a speaking manner. If it is not the manner of the barrel oration, nor yet of such picturesque varieties of oration as were first transcribed by Bret Harte and latterly by the young men in whom his influence mingles with that of Mr. Kipling, it even more sternly eschews what they would call fine writing.

So colloquial is it, indeed, that many a reader otherwise amiably disposed would prefer the little knots of ribbon of the earlier days to the *argot* of Mr. James's present circle. It is probably safe to say that no one else has ever gone so far toward reproducing the actual course of thought and speech—which is to be figured not so much by the solitary tidal wave rolling unimpeded to its shore, as by the breaking crests of a sea subject to cross currents and inconstant winds. The clauses, the parentheses, the intonations of daily life are of course familiar enough to our ears; but they still have a strangeness for eyes accustomed to the telegraphic brevity of the newspaper.

This stretch of realism puts Mr. James into a category so new that he will not fit into any of our comfortable old pigeon-holes. Which would of itself create uncertainties, and be in no small measure responsible for the resentment he seems so curiously capable of arousing, without a tone that is highly exasperating to certain types of mind. There is too often, for instance, an unmannerly levity about him, as of him who should go into great company whistling, with his hands in his pockets. We relish the grand air better, and a proper sense of one's responsibilities. Then he will not tell you whether he is Guelf or Ghibelline—though he will sometimes leave you a horrid suspicion that he is neither. In other words, he does not obviously give you, as Mr. Brownell puts it, a 'synthetic view of life seen from a certain centralizing point of view.' . . .

It is time to point out, however, that the novelty to which we bear witness is even less one of manner than of matter. We might learn to swallow Mr. James's split infinitives and the adverbs of his love. We might come to feel a degree of friendliness toward persons with invented names. We might—who knows?—discover a way through the multiplicity of commas so bewildering to an unpuctuated age. For mannerisms, after all, are a part of every artist's medium. And time might reconcile us to Mr. James's tone. But there would still be things to which custom alone could scarcely soften us. He demands, for example, more attention than many readers think a mere book deserves. He is concerned with the things of the mind, and he takes a corresponding concern for granted. More particularly, though, he is concerned with the things of what we call, for lack of a better word, the soul. Indeed this interest has gradually superseded others in him, making all his later work a series of studies in the dark drama of the inner life. This is the real difficulty of his books, rather than any external matter of style. Not only does he explore a field as yet almost unexplored, but he happens, curiously enough, to belong to a people the most objective of any, the least sensitive to the movements of the inner life. If, therefore, professional critics hint at a lack of common sense in him, and a tendency to reinforce his observation by his imagination, it is scarcely to be wondered at that a public without leisure, and as yet unaccustomed to find amusement in the province of the intellect, should be somewhat nonplussed by books which not only compel thought but record things scarcely observed before.

The individual quality of Mr. James's work is best brought out by contrast with that of such a man as Rudyard Kipling. No two writers could be more different—and nothing could be more characteristic of our age than their well-known interest in each other. Children both of a wandering blood, and born outside the fold of their race, each typifies a phase of that race's greatness. The one speaks for all in it that is the fruit of time, of consciousness, of civilization. The other, with that in his veins which civilization never yet has quenched, is more at home in the hinterlands of civilization, where adventure wears a more open face than in boulevards and ballrooms. And Mr. Kipling is likely to grow rather than to diminish. Even after we shall have lost the stimulus of his immediate presence, his art—that little contradiction in itself!— is too perfect, he falls in too completely with a certain saving restlessness of the spirit, for us to let him go. At the same time the preponderance of his influence over that of Mr. James has one very curious aspect. Nothing is more natural than that we in this country should have fallen so helplessly under his spell. The conditions of our life are very much the conditions of his. The more elemental qualities of man and the less tamed aspects of nature are those with which he, and we, are most familiar. But with the word civilization so often on our lips, and with the spectacle so portentously in our eyes of our effort to achieve it, there is some singularity in the fact that the civilized man should have for us so little interest. The pioneer, the soldier, the sailor, the artisan, the vagabond, the criminal, are evoked among us to satiety. But where is the literature of the civilized man? Mr. James has been writing it for a generation, and we fly from it as from something unknown and abhorrent! If the situation be one from which a cynic might draw conclusions after his own heart, it is also one for the old proverb *de gustibus*. That proverb, however, might well be quoted anew to those who happen so strongly to prefer the literature of colonization to the literature of civilization. Such a preference is hardly the best of grounds for denying existence to the latter. The civilized man after all exists, poor dear, quite as palpably as the pioneer or the soldier or the sailor or the artisan or the vagabond or the criminal. Why then is he not equally worthy of study? He is a human being like another. He has passions, ambitions, sensations like another. It is even probable that his veins would be discovered to contain 'red blood,' although it may not lead him to speak in strange idioms or to fire pistols at inadvertent moments. And if the narrative of his achievements does not happen to constitute the 'strong and snappy' story beloved of the magazines, it is not his fault. He is what we have labored with great industry, for many centuries, to make him. Desperate indeed is his case when we consider that after sailing seas and conquering continents to produce him we at last shrink in horror, like the creator of Frankenstein, from the work of our hands!

One should no more expect identities of taste among the experienced, of course, than among the inexperienced. But one might expect, in the case of the critics, a little more interest in phenomena as phenomena, irrespective of personal leanings. The declaration is not seldom made that while Mr. James may be clever enough in what he chooses to do, it is not worth doing. The present writer, for his part, has never been able to rid himself of a sense that either everything is worth doing or that nothing is worth doing. And surely Mr. James is not to blame, as he says in 'The Beldonald Holbein' (*The Better Sort*), if he is 'so put together as to find more life in situations obscure, and subject to interpretation, than in the gross rattle of the foreground.' One might expect, too, among critics, a little more alacrity in connecting certain signs of the times. A point not the least significant about the work of Mr. James is one that has been least dwelt upon. Different as he is from Ibsen, from Maeterlinck, from D'Annunzio, from Hauptmann and Sudermann, from Paul Bourget and Anatole France and the Russians, he is yet one with them, as they are one with each other, in a certain unmistakable trend of modern literature. Whereas the episode, and particularly the denouement, were long the main object of the writer's care, they had been strikingly affected by an awakening of interest in that which lies behind the episode and a growing sense of the continuity of things—a sense that nothing ever really begins or ends. Interest in the plot has therefore been steadily yielding to interest in the atmosphere of the plot. Indeed in some parts of the world the presentation of an atmosphere, entirely apart from any weaving of 'intrigue,' has become recognized as a legitimate end of creative art. And Mr. James is the first considerable English novelist—he has a slight advantage of years over Mr. George

Moore!—to feel and to reflect this tendency. The repression of action in his later novels, the tracing of action to its secret sources, which to a public schooled in the older tradition seems perverted or ridiculous, may be primarily a matter of constitution; but it has the closest possible relation to a movement in the wider world of letters. If there is anything at all in what we vaguely call the *Zeitgeist*, it would seem that as consciousness increases, as we become more trained to the consequence of much that we have regarded as inconsequent, books like *What Maisie Knew* and *The Sacred Fount* and *The Golden Bowl* will take on for us a new significance.

All this has a very intimate relation with another aspect of the work of Henry James, and of the disapproval with which his countrymen so frequently regard it. What has been noted of him with regard to his so marked interest in his own age is in fact worth noting. It has made him the first English writer to reflect certain tendencies of European art. It has also made him the first American man of letters to be a citizen of the world. . . . . Whereas others have seen the world as did those who made the grand tour in the good old times through the rattling windows and from the comfortable cushions of their own travelling coach, he has seen it as one who fares afoot and puts up at country inns and forms familiar ties with the people of the land. And it is the thing that his own people most lay up against him. They can forgive almost any of his shortcomings before they can forgive his exile.

Nothing could be more natural than such a feeling. It is the feeling always inspired by those who worship other gods than ours, who act from motives to which we do not hold the clue. Moreover it seems to include and express the disagreeable effect of Mr. James's other idiosyncrasies—the novelty of his subjects, the strangeness of his style, the minuteness of his analysis, the lightness with which he goes about serious things, the curiosity he displays toward things which it is our Anglo-Saxon instinct to avoid, his evasion of our attempts to lay a finger upon one or another of the philosophies we profess. And this feeling is intensified by the nature of our relation to the world at large. Not only are we peculiarly isolated from that world, but we have been so deeply concerned for the success of our national experiment that the matter of comparisons has always been our tenderest point. In no other country, perhaps, is there so quick a national jealousy. The defection of Mr. James therefore touches us much more nearly than would otherwise be the case. . . . the fact is that Mr. James is as truly and typically American as Hawthorne or Bret Harte or Walt

Whitman or the strenuous young men of the hour. That he happens to be of another type takes nothing away from his representative quality —or from our honor. No other country could have produced him. And he has revealed a side of American life that no one before him has touched. Expressive of our secret relation to the world from which we sprang, of that in us which reaches back after the things we have renounced, he has voiced the predicament of thousands of his countrymen that, as a literary property, is perhaps our most original contribution to letters. We are not, as some of us would like to think, a legendary race in its infancy face to face with the primal problems of man. Neither are we, as others of us would like to think, a historical race rich with the accumulations of ages. We are, rather, the younger sons of the ages, with a tradition and a country that do not match. Our feverish activity, our prodigious progress, are the haste of pioneers with civilization in their blood to create anew—and more perfectly!— the world from which they came. Our case therefore, as such things go, is something new under the sun. And Henry James, instead of blinking it or failing to perceive it, has discovered the dramatic possibilities of the case. The eager American, with slumbering things in his veins, trying to waken them in his own clear air or suddenly confronted by the embodiment of them in richer and headier airs—that picturesque contrast, with many of the variations of which it is susceptible, Mr. James has recorded with a consummate art.

The contrast is more than picturesque, however. For all in our life that is of the finer consciousness it has a stimulating critical value. And no other method could so bring out the distinctively American quality. A certain deep and delicate simplicity of it, for instance—as it were the wisdom of the ages filtered through the primitive condition—Mr. James has particularly dwelt upon. Madame de Mauves, Isabel Archer, Christopher Newman, Francie Dosson, Milly Theale, the unforgettable Strether, and Adam and Maggie Verver of *The Golden Bowl*, testify so strongly to it, are altogether a tribute to their country so much higher than any one else has paid, that they disprove more effectually than any argument the charges of injustice and lack of patriotism so often brought against their creator. But of course the comparative method, disinterestedly pursued, is bound to reveal the less flattering points of the picture with the more so. Thus it is that the lives of Hawthorne and Story, and the recent American papers, often offend our passionate national sensitiveness. They are, nevertheless, documents of a striking and important kind. Of the last in particular it can be said that nothing of the sort has been done, with the same degree of sympathetic penetration—unless by Dr. Hugo Münsterberg. As free on the one hand from the animus of most foreign critics as they are on the other from the fatuous complacency of the average native, they form a valuable commentary, social and æsthetic, on the democratic experiment. They supplement too, in a highly suggestive way, the studies which have latterly been making objective certain aspects of our industrial and political life. But Mr. James's experience has been fed from so many sources as yet closed to us that we can hardly be expected to see with his eyes. Only a later generation, rich in a thousand things which we to-day must go without, and able to look back upon our time as we look back upon the dark ages of the early nineteenth century, will be in a position to judge of his attitude.

So, for one who does not happen to agree with the majority of his countrymen on the subject of Henry James, is it possible to account for the so marked indifference revealed by his return. The various elements of novelty in his work, that in it which tends to grate upon tender sensibilities, and the absence—as yet—of a proper perspective from which to regard it, would seem to afford reason enough for discounting anything that may be said about present unpopularity or the lack of qualities needful to fame. It must remain for the future to decide whether a work so voluminous and so studied was merely the most portentous of mistakes. But in the meantime we may note two or three points which the event of history will not affect. Significant as it is of Mr. James, for instance, and of our country, that he should be so deeply concerned with the finer flowers of civilization, his significance does not reside in the fact that he has written of drawing-rooms and ancestral acres rather than of mining shacks and the untrodden wild. Others have gone farther afield and have brought home emptier wallets. He has taken a longer step than any of his contemporaries in relating the scene of every day to the background of mystery against which it moves. And at a time when the cheap and easy seem almost to be at a premium, he has afforded one of the few examples of a talent never contenting itself with the second best and never ceasing in its own line of development. Moreover, with reference to ourselves, it is not necessarily detrimental that upon our huge welter, of races and traditions, so largely unconscious and unguided, there should sometimes be cast a light from without. Nor is it any dishonor to us that one of our own countrymen should have been the first, in his generation, to open a door between English letters and the wider world.

181. W. A. Gill on James's similarity to Marivaux

1907

W. A. Gill, 'Henry James and his double', *Atlantic*, October 1907, c, 458–66, and reprinted in the *Fortnightly*, October 1909, xcii, 689–700.

This was the first article to appear on HJ in the *Fortnightly*, which regularly published treatments of contemporary authors (including, around that time, e.g. Hall Caine, Louise Chandler Moulton, Pinero, Mrs. Oliphant, Maurice Hewlett, Jean Ingelow, Ouida, etc.).

Pierre Carlet de Chamblain de Marivaux, novelist, essayist, and playwright, was born in 1687 and died in 1763. From our slight knowledge of his private life, it appears that he was a travelled child; that he had the opportunities of a liberal education; and that he began his independent career with fair private means. Settling in Paris about the time he came of age, he was admitted to its most fashionable literary society. In the salons of Madame de Trencin and others he showed so much liking for the companionship of intelligent women that he was accused later on of confining himself to 'female coteries.' Having once begun to write, he was unremittingly industrious, producing essays, sketches, plays, and novels in abundance, though he was always a fastidious craftsman. He was elected to the French Academy over Voltaire, and on that occasion the Archbishop of Sens, who delivered the speech of welcome, paid a remarkable tribute to his moral worth. 'Your writings,' said the Archbishop, 'are known to me only by hearsay. Those who have read them tell me that they have admirable qualities. But it is not so much to them as to our high esteem for your personal virtues that you owe your election.' Marivaux, always sensitive about criticism of his writings, could hardly be kept from openly refusing this ecclesiastical compliment on the spot. It bore testimony, however, to a fact recognised by all his contemporaries. He was noted for a standard of conduct which seemed to them even austere. In the scandalous period of the Regency it could be said of him that 'he had no adventures or scandals.'

Married before he was thirty, he lost his wife so soon that he was virtually a lifelong bachelor—a fact which some of his critics have regretted in such terms as these: 'Had he been a married man, a deeper source of knowledge would have been open to him. As it was, he knew nothing about the woman in the family. Woman was his chief theme, but he was acquainted with her only in society.'

During the last twenty of his eighty years he withdrew into a seclusion which he seldom broke except to attend meetings of the Academy.

He is best known to-day by his comedies, some of which are still acted in France. For their subtle and airy truth, these trifles about courtship have often been compared to the pictures of his contemporary, Watteau. But the more considerable part of his work, both in volume and in the influence it has had on posterity is to be found in his novels and essays. He has been called 'the father of the psychological novel,' not altogether unreasonably, for Diderot, Rousseau, Richardson, and Fielding were among his immediate pupils. 'There is no *roman de mœurs*,' says Brunetière broadly, 'in modern French or English literature without something of Marivaux at the bottom of it.'

His chief novels are *La Vie de Marianne* and *Le Paysan Parvenue*. The first narrates the career of a pretty girl who rises from a humble position, is sorely tempted on the way, but triumphs, like Pamela; the second, the adventures in society of a handsome peasant lad—an anticipation of Joseph Andrews.

The essays, which appeared in journals edited by himself on the model of Addison's *Spectator*, contain sketches from life, psychological studies, short stories, and philosophical reflections.

Between the work of this author and that of Henry James so many close resemblances exist that a reincarnation of Marivaux in our age is not an altogether improbable supposition. If 'reincarnation' be too strong a word for the case, it has at least the merit of excluding all thought of a likeness due to imitation. One might guess from the critical essays of James, who is so contemporaneous, in most respects, that he has never studied very seriously any authors outside of his own century. But such surmises are unnecessary. It was a first principle of Marivaux's art to be scrupulously himself and to copy no one, and anyone who should imitate Marivaux closely must for that very reason be fundamentally unlike him.

The recurrence in our times of Marivaux's artistic personality pre-supposes some recurrence of his environment.

There may seem to be some analogies, to begin with, between his private career, as sketched above, and that of James, but on both sides the personal *data* are so insufficient that a comparison in this direction must be largely guesswork.

As to the 'times,' or public surroundings of the two men, the first part of the eighteenth and the latter part of the nineteenth century are surely similar at least in having something of an autumnal quality—in being, comparatively speaking, periods of dissolution.

Marivaux was contemporary with the iconoclasts of the *ancien régime*. In literature he was their leader. While Voltaire was carrying the unbroken tradition of French prose to its climax, Marivaux was sharply denouncing submission to literary tradition. Voltaire attacked him for this as a 'néologue,' and Marivaux retorted, from a point of view hardly recovered till our own time, that the famous pioneer was 'un bel-esprit fieffé et la perfection des idées communes.' Elsewhere than in art the period surely vies with the close of the Victorian era as a quicksand of crumbling faiths and shifting centres of social gravity. The deluge impending in Marivaux's day seems to have become permanent in ours.

Further traces of identity of environment may be seen in the attitude of either author toward his near predecessors in literature. Would not this account of Marivaux's relation to Molière, for instance, serve as well to describe James's relation to the mid-Victorian novelists? 'As men's faiths became less robust, stage-characters grew slighter and more refined. The spirit of analysis sweeping all before it in Marivaux's time was opposed to the broad, downright conceptions of a Molière.' And James's ideal of the 'ultimate novelist' as one 'entirely purged of sarcasm,' and some other differences between him and Dickens and Thackeray may come to mind when one hears Brunetière contrasting Marivaux with Le Sage thus:

Le Sage certainly aimed at giving a faithful picture of life, but he was energetically bent also on getting his fun out of the spectacle. All through his work the comic author is apparent, whereas in Marivaux one finds the exact observer. The portraits in *Gil Blas* belong to the Molière school; their intention is satirical; they are vigorously brushed in, and appear stronger and bolder than nature. Marivaux, on the other hand, paints gradually with minute, careful finish and imperceptible touches. If we recognise in Le Sage's work an excess of incident, we may admit that Marivaux gives us too much psychology.

To come now to the personal equation, the main source of the resemblances between Marivaux and James seems to be the wonderfully subtle and discriminating quality of their intelligences. 'Marivaux,' says Sainte-Beuve, 'is a man of many subtle distinctions and endless *nuances*. He carries his discriminativeness to extremes and abounds in microscopic anatomy. He refines and divides everything to excess. When he looks at an object he splits it in two; then subdivides it *ad infinitum*. He loses himself in the process and exhausts his readers. He will not stop at the principal traits. He does not let them stand out. His method is the opposite of that of the classical masters, who confine themselves to *la grande ligne*.' Voltaire accused Marivaux of 'weighing flies' eggs in cobweb scales'; all critics have insisted on the same tendency, and Marivaux insists on it himself. He acknowledges describing 'shades of extreme refinement which very few people ever notice till they are pointed out to them'; and when his comedies of courtship were blamed for monotony of theme, he replied in astonishment, 'The subject is sometimes a love of which neither party is aware. Sometimes it is a conscious love which they wish to hide. Sometimes, a timid love which durst not show itself. Sometimes, a wavering, undecided love, half-fledged as it were, which they suspect without being quite sure of it, and at which they peep, in its nest inside themselves, before letting it flutter forth. In all this, where is there any sameness?'

The question reveals Marivaux, 'Where is there any sameness?' might stand as the motto of his whole work.

As for Henry James, he cannot be mentioned by critics without the words 'subtlety' and *nuances* coming in. And in both cases, by the bye, this quality has been attributed to a feminine infusion. Faguet nicknames Marivaux 'la baronne de Marivaux'; and who has not heard of the 'feminine fineness' and 'feline observation' of his counterpart?

A devotion to shades of difference is naturally accompanied by a distaste for whatever is abstract and general. Indeed, the one tendency is the obverse of the other, and to the whole the chief characteristics of both authors seem to be due.

Both, for instance, are extremely anxious to be just precisely themselves as artists, not merely by unconscious instinct, but by self-conscious reasoning. And it may be noted here that each has a distinct philosophical gift, which in James might be regarded as a family affair, and which was so marked in Marivaux that Sainte-Beuve calls him 'a forerunner of Saint Simon, Comte, and Littré.'

So, in an age of artistic tradition, Marivaux boasts of being 'his own son.' He complains: 'Few authors have left us an impression of their own particular way of seeing the world. Swayed by some convention of taste, they do not move with their own step, but with a borrowed gait.' He lays down as the golden rule: *abandonner son esprit à son geste naturel.* He advises the young writer to 'imitate no one—neither the ancients nor the moderns. The ancients had an entirely different universe from ours, and, besides, copying of any sort is bad; it can only make an ape of one.'

'Marivaux is extremely logical,' says Sainte-Beuve, 'and consistent with this self-conscious individualism in production is his code of criticism. He admits no valid standard of taste but the individual's likes and dislikes. Critics have no right to say, "This is good; that is bad"; but only "I like this; I dislike that".' And in the same spirit he condemns the habit of classifying authors under abstract *étiquettes*— 'this or that kind of a novel'—and of judging them according to these labels, instead of individually.

In James all this is repeated—some of it in almost the same words. He defines a novel as 'successful in proportion as it reveals a particular mind, different from others.' His essay on 'The Art of Fiction' is one long declaration of independence on behalf of the individual and a defiance of conventions and *étiquettes*. 'Traditions,' he says, for instance, 'as to what sort of affair the good novel will be, applied *a priori*, have already had much to answer for. The idea that the novel has to translate the things that surround us into conventional, traditional moulds condemns the art to an eternal repetition of a few familiar *clichés*.' He pleads urgently for 'liberty of interpretation,' and, being as logical as Marivaux, James, too, postulates a purely individual standard of criticism. 'Nothing, of course,' he declares, 'will ever take the place of the good old fashion of liking a work of art or disliking it. The most improved criticism will not abolish that primitive—that ultimate test.'

Clearly, this fastidious individualism is near akin to the subtle discriminativeness. In regard to their objects of study it is as true of James as of Marivaux that 'his special art consists in singling out the individual from the broadly human.' And that outward tendency reacts inwardly. They single out their own personalities also from the broadly human. They are keenly alive to their personal differentiations from other artists, and the paths of similarity they shun. Nor has their watchfulness gone unrewarded. 'Marivaux is unique. Whether they are masterpieces or not, his novels stand alone. And this very fact, which gives them their historical value, explains their never having reached the crowd.' So Brunetière; and so also Howells about James: 'His novels are really incomparable, not so much because there is nothing in contemporary fiction to equal them, as because there is nothing at all like them.'

That artists so personal, being also artists of force, should be innovators, is natural. The term is invariably applied to both. Nor is it surprising that they should be characterised by 'modernity.' Brunetière attributes this quality to Marivaux, as if it were almost an invention of his; and parts of James's work—some of his dialogues, for instance— are so strictly of the passing moment that a fear has been expressed of their becoming unintelligible to-morrow.

Again, the distaste for the general and abstract accords with the avoidance by both authors of set plots and *dénouements*. Marivaux did not even finish either of his masterpieces. He issued them in parts extending over a number of years, and left the last part of each unwritten. 'He enjoyed the road too much to trouble about the goal or conclusion,' says Sainte-Beuve. 'He does not care for plots arranged beforehand in the study, but prefers taking his subjects straight from life as opportunity offers them.' James shows the same preference, of course, and consequently insists on dropping a subject brusquely, just as life may seem to drop it. Indeed, what is a plot leading up to a prepared *dénouement* but an abstract frame, which requires a generalising re-arrangement of the material to be fitted into it?

It is natural, too, that such authors should eschew the censorial attitude. Moral judgments as such are, as Kant said, unconditional; they declare 'This is right, that is wrong,' without any regard to particular modifications or circumstances, and artists whose chief aim is to record particular modifications are not likely to devote much space to them.

On the other hand, they are likely to devote a great deal of space to psychology, for what else is psychology in a novel but the 'singling out of the individual from the broadly human'? When once the question is insisted upon, 'But what kind of man, exactly, is the hero?' one passes from the 'novel of adventure' to the 'psychological novel.' And the more fully the question is answered, the more psychological the novel must be.

For discriminators like Marivaux and James that question can never be answered fully enough. In the preface to the first part of his *Marianne*, Marivaux describes the novels the public has hitherto been accustomed to as 'adventures which are only adventures,' and expresses the hope that adventures which are also studies of character may now prove acceptable. 'A detailed portrait is for him an endless task,' quotes Sainte-Beuve. Indeed, the novels of both are chiefly galleries of portraits, and in several important respects their methods of portrayal are similar. The central figure in both is virtually autobiographical—a self-confessor—but the rest are indicated as far as possible from the outside, since the senses are usually the most personal avenues of knowledge. To go from sense to reasoning is often to quit the particular for the general point of view. So James is always in search of 'the *looks* of things which convey a meaning,' and it was in Marivaux that Sterne seems to have studied the art of revealing character through expression and gesture. Brunetière holds that no one has ever surpassed Marivaux in showing 'the possession, as it were, which our habits take of our faces.' As an achievement of this kind, his interpretative account of the plumpness of a certain prioress is classical in French literature; and he abounds in thumbnail sketches like this: 'Madame de Far was a little, dark, stout, ugly woman with a large, square face, and small black eyes, which were never still. They were always hunting about to find something amusing to occupy her lively mind with.' Or this: 'Monsieur de Climal'—one of the hypocrites Marivaux loved to depict, and whose tactics he used to contrast rather disdainfully with the cruder methods of Molière's *Tartuffe*—'had a gentle, serious face, and a penitential air which kept you from noticing how stout he really was.' To show all James's triumphs in this order one would have to quote a large part of his works.

Our authors are alike, too, in not confining their search for 'the looks which convey a meaning' to the human form. 'What are circumstances but that which befalls us,' asks James, 'and what is incident but the determination of character?' So 'character' becomes almost equivalent to 'circumstance,' and both in their psychological researches bear us far out on a sea of surroundings—not only immediate surroundings, such as 'the major's trousers and the particular "smart" tension of his wife's tight stays,' but furniture, houses, streets, gardens. Marivaux is famous for his 'interiors,' which have been described as 'veritable Chardins'; but he, like James, is also blamed for over-elaboration of these pictures.

In their passion for 'walking on eggs' the pair adopt similar methods of complicating the subtlety of the psychological case. Marivaux's main object, it has been said, is to show 'the refraction of a character through different media.' He carries his Marianne and Jacques through many environments, and their surfaces are chameleonic as they ascend through the strata of society. James, in his 'international' novels, 'goes one better' than this. Not content to show the individual's response to different surroundings in his own country, he conveys him abroad, and analyses the influence of a foreign atmosphere on the national particularisation of the individually particularised character. He must ascertain how the New Englander, Chad, has 'his features retouched, his eyes cleared, his colour settled, his fine square teeth polished; a form, a surface, almost a design given to him'—by the atmosphere of the French capital.

And how could these discriminators avoid the charge of prolixity in their analyses? One blushes to think of the insults offered James on this score; and as for Marivaux—'It is a trifle too much,' exclaimed the Abbé Desfontaines, when the sixth part of *Marianne* appeared, 'to devote a whole book to carrying the heroine from mid-day to six p.m. ! Heaven forbid that she should live to grow old, or our lives would not be long enough to read about hers!' Detailed portraits must indeed produce some sacrifice of movement—of movement, at least, toward a *dénouement*. But then, since neither Marivaux nor James provides any *dénouement*, is it fair to blame them for not moving toward a non-existent point?

Again, both writers are accused of omitting the 'great things' of life. 'Marivaux,' says Voltaire, 'knows all the little paths of the heart, but not the high road.' 'In every case,' says Sainte-Beuve, 'we find him preferring the *je ne sais quoi* to true beauty, cleverness to greatness, coquetry to tenderness.' Indeed, neither author deals much in what James calls 'rounded perfections.' But is not this an inevitable result of their devotion to the particular? Before condemning them for omitting the 'great things,' one should squarely meet the question, which both seem to imply, whether the 'great things,' in the ordinary sense, really exist—exist, that is, apart from abstracting imagination? In one of his essays Marivaux denies the existence of 'great men'—apart, at least, from abstracting imagination. And in that profound little study, 'The Story in It', James seems to offer an allegorical disquisition on the point. Two women and a man are talking together. One of the women is secretly in love with the man; he is, or should be, in love with the other. They are discussing ideal, romantic love. The woman with the secret maintains the possibility of it, and when the others argue against her, claims to know for certain of its existence. 'Where is it, then?' they ask. She lays her hand on her unspoken and unanswered heart. It exists in her dream; but does it exist anywhere else? We are left asking that question.

'All great artists impress us as having some kind of a philosophy,' says James. He and Marivaux surely impress us as teaching the far-reaching doctrine of the absoluteness of 'the particular, given case.' 'There is no such thing as an abstract adventure,' says James somewhere; 'there is only your adventure and mine.'

Nowhere, however, is this likeness more striking than in the matter of style. And here, as indeed elsewhere in this essay, reference is more specially made to James's later manner—to the manner he evolved toward the end of the Victorian era, and which has since then accentuated itself to the admiration of some and the despair of others.

It was a Frenchman who originated the formula, 'The style is the man,' and French critics of Marivaux have instinctively concentrated their attention on his style as the most indicative part.

From his own day onward Marivaux has been censured for his mannerisms, his verbosity, his abuse of comparisons, his spun-out metaphors, his involved obscurity, his colloquialism, and, oddly mixed with that, his preciosity. 'A jargon at once familiar and precious,' D'Alembert called his style in his *Eloge*; and how aptly the phrase hits off one aspect of James's style!

'Marivaux's art,' says Sainte-Beuve, 'is to imitate *le style parlé*. He copies it as closely as he can, with all its little carelessnesses, with the small words that constantly recur, and, as it were, the very gestures. *Cela* is always cropping up, and such phrases as *cet homme-là, ces traits de bonté-là.*'

And what else than *le style parlé* characterises such sentences as this from James—'One of the other impressions was, at the end of a few minutes, that she—oh, incontestably, yes, differed less; that is, scarcely at all—well, superficially speaking, from——'?

No English writer of rank is more conversational than James, with his 'don'ts' and 'aren'ts' and 'isn'ts' and 'that sort of'; with his constant use of inverted commas for stray words outside of set dialogue; with his abundant slang—'he was at least up to that,' and so on.

Yet beside this colloquialism how prominent is the 'precious' element in both! Preciosity has been on the whole the main charge against Marivaux; and in James how often do we find phrases suggestive of the least colloquial, the most 'æsthetic' and 'architectural' of stylists—of Pater, for instance? James's Gallicisms, natural enough considering the circumstances of his education, must come under this head. And in short, if one should compile a lexicon of his vocabulary, would it not resemble a Marivaux lexicon in being 'very rich in common, trivial, popular phrases, and yet no less rich in far-fetched ones'?

And then, what a thorough parallelism in their use of metaphor! It may as truly be said of James, as of Marivaux, that it is 'his constant practice to convey the nicest shades of sentiment by figures borrowed from the vulgarest usage.' And they vie with each other in elaborating metaphors very, very far. More sensitive than Anglo-Saxons about the niceties of metaphorical expression, the French are especially wroth with Marivaux for his 'mania of pushing similes *au bout.*' In reality, James pushes them a great deal further than Marivaux—as witness that 'tall tower of ivory in a garden,' to which Maggie's state of mind is likened through three pages.

The typical sentences of both are often as rambling or plotless as their novels; and for the same reason in either case. The preservation of 'the straight impression' requires unpremeditated expression. The impression must be allowed to transcribe itself freely; any verbal re-arrangement might lead to remodelling of the object. Apparent verbosity also is inevitable for both. And yet of either style—naturally enough, given its subtlety—reticence and omissions are found to be characteristic. 'Reticence envelops Marivaux's thought and veils it as with twilight,' says that fine critic, Paul de Saint Victor. 'Swedenborg tells us he perceived spirits conversing with one another by merely winking their eyelids. In Marivaux we get something of the mystery of those palpitating dialogues in the clouds.' 'James conveys these things,' says Elton, 'by the method of reticence, by omissions, pauses, and speaking silences.' 'James does not say,' observes Howells; 'he insinuates. It is what he does not tell that counts.'

One would have to quote a great deal to illustrate all these common tendencies clearly, but 'for Achilles' image stand his spear!' Here is an ordinary specimen from Marivaux. At the door of a theatre he is observing the faces of those who come out.

I examined all these wearers of faces. I tried to make out what each of them felt about his lot. For instance, if there was one who bore his lot patiently, because he could do nothing else. I did not find a single one whose face did not declare, 'I stick to it!' And yet, I saw some women's faces which had small reason to be contented, and which might well have complained of their portion, without being esteemed too captious. It even seemed to me that on meeting some face more generously favoured than their own they were afraid of being driven to depreciate theirs; their hearts were distressed; and, to be sure, they *were* in a warm corner! To have a face which you would not willingly exchange for any other, and yet to behold, right in front of you, some accursed visage coming to pick a quarrel with yours and upset your good opinion of it—coming boldly to challenge yours to mortal combat and throwing you for a moment into the sad confusion of doubting what the issue might be—accusing you, in short, of indulging in an illegitimate satisfaction in deeming your face without peer and without reproach—such moments are fraught with peril! I could read all the disturbance of the insulted face. The disturbance, however, was only momentary.

Sainte-Beuve blames this sportive passage for 'bad taste.' What would he have said, then, of scores of passages in James? Of this, for instance:

He had turned awkwardly, responsibly red, he knew, at her mention of Maria; Sarah Pocock's presence—that particular quality in it—had made this inevitable; and then he had grown still redder. . . . He felt indeed that he was showing much, as, uncomfortably and almost in pain, he offered up his redness to Waymarsh, who, strangely enough, seemed now to be looking at him with a certain explanatory yearning. Something deep—something built on their old, old relation—passed, in this complexity, between them; he got the side-wind of a loyalty that stood behind all actual questions. Waymarsh's dry, bare humour —as it gave itself to be taken—gloomed out to justify itself. 'Well, if you talk of her, I've my chance, too,' it seemed stiffly to nod; and it granted that it was giving him away, but struggled to say that it did so only to save him. The sombre glow stared at him till it fairly sounded out, 'To save you, poor old man, to save you!'

Or of this specimen: 'We remained on the surface, with the tenacity of shipwrecked persons clinging to a plank. Our plank was our concentrated gaze at Mrs. Bridgeman's mere present. We allowed her past to exist for us only in the form of the prettiness that she had gallantly rescued from it, and to which a few scraps of identity still adhered.'

Not that one would accuse James of 'marivaudage' in the most evil sense of that word—in which, to tell the truth, it is inapplicable to Marivaux. It was far more Marivaux's *epigoni* than himself who brought on this term the significance of simpering affectation and false graces. Even Sainte-Beuve, who is severe enough on Marivaux's style, admits, 'The word *marivaudage* has become established in our language to indicate a vice, but the man from whom the name is borrowed is superior to its current meaning.'

Most of this resemblance in style seems ascribable to causes already indicated. That both authors should imitate colloquial idiom, for instance, is imposed on them by their loyalty to the 'straight impression.'

Yet that they should also be precious and metaphorical follows from the out-of-the-way *nuances* which they are describing. As Brunetière, another sharp critic of the French classic, recognises, 'Unexpected collocations of words, unusual turns of expression, peculiar phrases, are in fact merely the faithful reflection of odd, unusual, unexpected objects of observation. And if sometimes many words are used for a small matter, one must remember that the reader would not believe in the reality of the strange discovery unless the explorer allowed him to retrace with him, step by step, the paths which had led him to it.'

Such is indeed the defence which Marivaux himself set up of his style. Several times he replied at length to the frequent contemporary attacks on this side of his work. He asserts that his style is not 'affected'— he takes 'precious' in that sense—but a simple and sincere reflection of his thought. And he denies that it can be called 'obscure,' unless it can be shown that his thought is obscure. If his language is unusual, he says, it is solely because his perceptions are so. People may say he has no business to see such out-of-the-way aspects of every-day affairs; but that is the way his mind is constituted. If he is to blame, it is not for his style, but for his mind, of which his style is a mere mirror.

To this apology, which coincides, one is tempted to suppose, with what James might say, Sainte-Beuve and Brunetière concede that the author's mind and not his style is in question. 'He was in fact himself,' says Sainte-Beuve, 'and quite legitimately he expresses his unusual perceptions in language that often has a piquant singularity.' But, they both assert, he goes too far. In reference, one may ask, to what standard? If his style faithfully reflects his mind, it cannot be called 'affected,' at least. What, then, is 'the proper limit' which they accuse him of overstepping?

At bottom, these two critics clash with Marivaux over his claim to entire individual liberty. They deny his right to be utterly himself. They say he goes too far in personality. They denounce his individualism as 'libertine'—in the name of tradition and of the example of 'the masters.'

Anglo-Saxons may perhaps reject this French devotion to classicism, and yet feel that James and his double do err, somehow, from the way. Can it be that, instead of being too much themselves, as the French critics declare, they are not sufficiently themselves?

'It is not so much your being right—it is your horrible, sharp eye for what makes you so,' complains one of James's characters of another. Substitute 'individual' for 'right,' and are not the words applicable to our authors?

Their 'horrible, sharp eye' for what differentiates them from others cuts them off like a knife, it seems, from their kind, and, in so doing, mutilates them. One cannot rebel against what Wilde calls 'the humiliating fact' of the brotherhood of men without penalties of circumscription. 'The childish horror of our set for the *banal*'—what an exact suggestion, by the way, James gives there of Marivaux's set at Madame de Tencin's—carries with it an avenging limitation. To be only that in which one is different from others is to be less than oneself, and it is this curtailment of their universal nature which earns for both, sometimes, the epithet of 'inhuman.'

And yet, both accomplish so much by their specialisation! 'It is so rare to be a pioneer and to discover anything new in this moral world, which has been so thoroughly explored! And Marivaux,' allows Sainte-Beuve, '*has* added to what was known before.' Most of Marivaux's additions may have been assimilated by now; but it will be many a year, one may conjecture, before all the new knowledge which our great Anglo-Saxon note-taker has gathered, passes into popular currency.

182. John Bailey on *The Portrait of a Lady*

1908

John Bailey from his diary, July 1908 (*John Bailey 1864–1931. Letters and Diaries Edited by his Wife*, 1935, 112).

Bailey (1864–1931) was a critic and essayist of conservative temper. He was acquainted with HJ.

Finished H. James's *Portrait of a Lady*. Its cleverness is of course amazing, and I like hearing his voice, as I often do. But I miss any sense of the really great issues of life—no one either thinks about or does anything great—and I don't like ending on a note of interrogation.

183. Hugh Walpole's fictional reminiscence of the later James and his reputation in 'Mr. Oddy'

[1933]

Hugh Walpole, 'Mr. Oddy' from *All Souls' Night*, 1933, 129–52. This story, which according to Rupert Hart-Davis Walpole later selected as his best, clearly draws considerably on his memories of HJ, of whom, from 1909 onwards, he had been a devoted young disciple and friend. Its testimony as to the reputation of the older novelist in smart literary circles in the years before his death is therefore of great interest.

This may seem to many people an old-fashioned story; it is perhaps for that reason that I tell it. I can recover here, it may be, for myself something of the world that is already romantic, already beyond one's reach, already precious for the things that one might have got out of it and didn't.

London of but a few years before the war! What a commonplace to point out its difference from the London of to-day and to emphasise the tiny period of time that made that difference!

We were all young and hopeful then, we could all live on a shilling a year and think ourselves well off, we could all sit in front of the lumbering horse 'buses and chat confidentially with the omniscient driver, we could all see Dan Leno in Pantomime and watch Farren dance at the Empire, we could all rummage among those cobwebby streets at the back of the Strand where Aldwych now flaunts her shining bosom and imagine Pendennis and Warrington, Copperfield and Traddles cheek by jowl with ourselves, we could all wait in the shilling queue for hours to see Ellen Terry in *Captain Brassbound* and Forbes-Robertson in *Hamlet*, we could all cross the street without fear of imminent death, and above all we could all sink ourselves into that untidy, higgledy-piggledy, smoky and beery and gas-lampy London gone utterly and for ever.

But I have no wish to be sentimental about it; there is a new London which is just as interesting to its new citizens as the old London was to myself. It is my age that is the matter; before the war one was so *very* young.

I like, though, to try and recapture that time, and so, as a simple way to do it, I seize upon a young man; Tommy Brown we will call him. I don't know where Tommy Brown may be now; that Tommy Brown who lived as I did in two very small rooms in Glebe Place, Chelsea, who enjoyed hugely the sparse but economical meals provided so elegantly by two charming ladies at 'The Good Intent' down by the river, that charming hostelry whence looking through the bow windows you could see the tubby barges go floating down the river, and the thin outline of Whistler's Battersea Bridge, and in the small room itself were surrounded by who knows what geniuses in the lump, geniuses of Art and Letters, of the Stage and of the Law.

For Tommy Brown in those days life was Paradisal.

He had come boldly from Cambridge to throw himself upon London's friendly bosom; despite all warnings to the contrary he was certain that it would be friendly; how could it be otherwise to so charming, so brilliant, so unusually attractive a young man? For Tommy was conceited beyond all that his youth warranted, conceited indeed without any reason at all.

He had, it is true, secured the post of reviewer to one of the London daily papers; this seemed to him when he looked back in later years a kind of miracle, but at the time no miracle at all, simply a just appreciation of his extraordinary talents. There was also reposing in one of the publishers' offices at that moment the manuscript of a novel, a novel that appeared to him of astonishing brilliance, written in the purest English, sparkling with wit, tense with drama.

These things were fine and reassuring enough, but there was more than that; he felt in himself the power to rise to the greatest heights; he could not see how anything could stop him, it was his destiny.

This pride of his might have suffered some severe shocks were it not that he spent all of his time with other young gentlemen quite as conceited as himself. I have heard talk of the present young generation and its agreeable consciousness of its own merits, but I doubt if it is anything in comparison with that little group of twenty-five years ago. After all, the war has intervened—however young we may be and however greatly we may pretend, this is an unstable world and for the moment heroics have departed from it. But for Tommy Brown and his friends the future was theirs and nobody could prevent it. Something pathetic in that as one looks back.

Tommy was not really so unpleasant a youth as I have described him —to his elders he must have appeared a baby, and his vitality at least they could envy. After all, why check his confidence? Life would do that heavily enough in its own good time.

Tommy, although he had no money and no prospects, was already engaged to a young woman, Miss Alice Smith. Alice Smith was an artist sharing with a girl friend a Chelsea studio, and she was as certain of her future as Tommy was of his.

They had met at a little Chelsea dance, and two days after the meeting they were engaged. She had no parents who mattered, and no money to speak of, so that the engagement was the easiest thing in the world.

Tommy, who had been in love before many times, was certain, as he told his friend Jack Robinson so often as to bore that gentleman severely, that this time at last he knew what love was. Alice ordered him about— with her at any rate his conceit fell away—she had read his novel and pronounced it old-fashioned, the severest criticism she could possibly have made, and she thought his reviews amateur. He suffered then a good deal in her company. When he was away from her he told himself and everybody else that her critical judgment was marvellous, her comprehension of all the Arts quite astounding, but he left her sometimes with a miserable suspicion that perhaps after all he was not going to do anything very wonderful and that he would have to work very hard indeed to rise to her astonishing standards.

It was in such a mood of wholesome depression that he came one beautiful April day from the A.B.C. shop where he had been giving his Alice luncheon, and found his way to an old bookshop on the riverside round the corner from Oakley Street. This shop was kept by a gentleman called Mr. Burdett Coutts, and the grand associations of his name gave him from the very first a sort of splendour.

It was one of those old shops of which there are, thank God, still many examples surviving in London, in which the room was so small and the books so many that to move a step was to imperil your safety. Books ran in thick, tight rows from floor to ceiling everywhere, were piled in stacks upon the ground and hung in perilous heaps over chairs and window ledges.

Mr. Burdett Coutts himself, a very stout and grizzled old man enveloped always in a grey shawl, crouched behind his spectacles in a far corner and took apparently no interest in anything save that he would snap the price at you if you brought him a volume and timorously enquired. He was not one of those old booksellers dear to the heart of Anatole France and other great men who would love to discourse to you of the beauties of *The Golden Ass*, the possibility of Homer being a lady, or the virtues of the second *Hyperion* over the first. Not at all; he ate biscuits which stuck in his grizzly beard, and wrote perpetually in a large worm-eaten ledger which was supposed by his customers to contain all the secrets of the universe.

It was just because Mr. Coutts never interfered with you that Tommy Brown loved his shop so dearly. If he had a true genuine passion that went far deeper than all his little superficial vanities and egotisms, it was his passion for books—books of any kind.

He had at this time no fine taste—all was fish that came to his net. The bundles of Thackeray and Dickens, parts tied up carelessly in coarse string, the old broken-backed volumes of Radcliffe and Barham and Galt, the red and gold Colburn's Novelists, all these were exciting to him, just as exciting as though they had been a first Gray's *Elegy* or an original *Robinson Crusoe*.

He had, too, a touching weakness for the piles of fresh and neglected modern novels that lay in their discarded heaps on the dusty floor; young though he was, he was old enough to realise the pathos of these so short a time ago fresh from the bursting presses, so eagerly cherished through months of anxious watching by their fond authors, so swiftly forgotten, dead almost before they were born.

So he browsed, moving like a panting puppy with inquisitive nose from stack to stack with a gesture of excitement, tumbling a whole racket of books about his head, looking then anxiously to see whether the old man would be angry with him, and realising for the thousandth time that the old man never was.

It was on this day, then, rather sore from the arrogancies of his Alice, that he tried to restore his confidence among these friendly volumes. With a little thrill of excited pleasure he had just discovered a number of the volumes born of those romantic and tragedy-haunted 'Nineties.' Here in little thin volumes were the stories of Crackanthorpe, the poems of Dowson, the *Keynotes* of George Egerton, *The Bishop's Dilemma* of Ella d'Arcy, *The Happy Hypocrite* of Max Beerbohm.

Had he only been wise enough to give there and then for that last whatever the old man had asked him for it he would have been fortunate indeed, but the pennies in his pocket were few—he was not yet a book collector, but rather that less expensive but more precious thing, a book adorer. He had the tiny volume in his hand, when he was aware that someone had entered the shop and was standing looking over his shoulder.

He turned slowly and saw someone who at first sight seemed vaguely familiar, so familiar that he was plunged into confusion at once by the sense that he ought to say 'How do you do?' but could not accurately place him. The gentleman also seemed to know him very well, for he said in a most friendly way, 'Ah, yes, the "Nineties," a very fruitful period.'

Tommy stammered something, put down the Max Beerbohm, moved a little, and pulled about him a sudden shower of volumes. The room was filled with the racket of their tumbling, and a cloud of dust thickened about them, creeping into eyes and mouth and nose.

'I'm terribly sorry,' Tommy stammered, and then, looking up, was sorry the more when he saw how extremely neat and tidy the gentleman was and how terribly the little accident must distress him.

Tommy's friend must have been between sixty and seventy years of age, nearer seventy perhaps than sixty, but his black hair was thick and strong and stood up *en brosse* from a magnificent broad forehead. Indeed, so fine was the forehead and the turn of the head that the face itself was a little disappointing, being so round and chubby and amiable as to be almost babyish. It was not a weak face, however, the eyes being large and fine and the chin strong and determined.

The figure of this gentleman was short and thick-set and inclined to stoutness; he had the body of a prize-fighter now resting on his laurels. He was very beautifully clothed in a black coat and waistcoat, pepper-and-salt trousers, and he stood leaning a little on a thick ebony cane, his legs planted apart, his whole attitude that of one who was accustomed to authority. He had the look of a magistrate, or even of a judge, and had his face been less kindly Tommy would have said good day, nodded to Mr. Burdett Coutts, and departed, but that was a smile difficult to resist.

'Dear me,' the gentleman said, 'this is a very dusty shop. I have never been here before, but I gather by the way that you knock the books about that it's an old friend of yours.'

Tommy giggled in a silly fashion, shifted from foot to foot, and then, desiring to seem very wise and learned, proved himself only very young and foolish.

'The "Nineties" are becoming quite romantic,' he said in his most authoritative voice, 'now that we're getting a good distance from them.'

'Ah, you think so!' said the gentleman courteously; 'that's interesting. I'm getting to an age now, I'm afraid, when nothing seems romantic but one's own youth and, ah, dear me! that was a very long time ago.'

This was exactly the way that kindly old gentlemen were supposed to talk, and Tommy listened with becoming attention.

'In my young day,' his friend continued, 'George Eliot seemed to everybody a magnificent writer: a little heavy in hand for these days, I'm afraid. Now who is the God of your generation, if it isn't impertinent to enquire?'

Tommy shifted again from foot to foot. Who was the God of his generation? If the truth must be told, in Tommy's set there were no Gods, only young men who might be Gods if they lived long enough.

'Well,' said Tommy awkwardly, 'Hardy, of course—er—it's difficult to say, isn't it?'

'Very difficult,' said the gentleman.

There was a pause then, which Tommy concluded by hinting that he was afraid that he must move forward to a very important engagement.

'May I walk with you a little way?' asked the gentleman very courteously. 'Such a very beautiful afternoon.'

Once outside in the beautiful afternoon air everything was much easier; Tommy regained his self-confidence, and soon was talking with his accustomed ease and freedom. There was nothing very alarming in his friend after all, he seemed so very eager to hear everything that Tommy had to say. He was strangely ignorant too; he seemed to be interested in the Arts, but to know very little about them; certain names that were to Tommy household words were to this gentleman quite unknown. Tommy began to be a little patronising. They parted at the top of Oakley Street.

'I wonder if you'd mind,' the gentleman said, 'our meeting again? The fact is, that I have very little opportunity of making friends with your generation. There are so many things that you could tell me. I am afraid it may be tiresome for you to spend an hour or two with so ancient a duffer as myself, but it would be very kind of you.'

Tommy was nothing if not generous; he said that he would enjoy another meeting very much. Of course he was very busy and his spare hours were not many, but a walk another afternoon could surely be managed. They made an appointment, they exchanged names; the gentleman's name was Mr. Alfred Oddy.

That evening, in the middle of a hilarious Chelsea party, Tommy suddenly discovered to his surprise that it would please him very much to see Mr. Oddy walk in through the door.

Although it was a hilarious party Tommy was not very happy; for one thing, Spencer Russell, the novelist, was there and showed quite clearly that he didn't think Tommy very interesting. Tommy had been led up and introduced to him, had said one or two things that seemed to himself very striking, but Spencer Russell had turned his back almost at once and entered into eager conversation with somebody else.

This wasn't very pleasant, and then his own beloved Alice was behaving strangely; she seemed to have no eyes nor ears for anyone in the room save Spencer Russell, and this was the stranger in that only a week or so before she had in public condemned Spencer Russell's novels, utterly and completely, stating that he was written out, had nothing to say, and was as good as dead. Tonight, however, he was not dead at all, and Tommy had the agony of observing her edge her way into the group surrounding him and then listen to him not only as though he were the fount of all wisdom, but an Adonis as well, which last was absurd seeing that he was fat and unwieldy and bald on the top of his head.

After a while Tommy came up to her and suggested that they should go, and received then the shock of his life when she told him that he could go if he liked, but that he was not to bother her. And she told him this in a voice so loud that everybody heard and many people tittered.

He left in a fury and spent then a night that he imagined to be sleepless, although in truth he slept during most of it.

It was with an eagerness that surprised himself that he met Mr. Oddy on the second occasion. He had not seen Alice for two days. He did not intend to be the one to apologise first; besides, he had nothing to apologise for; and yet during these two days there was scarcely a moment that he had not to restrain himself from running round to her studio and making it up.

When he met Mr. Oddy at the corner of Oakley Street he was a very miserable young man. He was so miserable that in five minutes he was pouring out all his woes.

He told Mr. Oddy everything, of his youth, his wonderful promise, and the extraordinary lack of appreciation shown to him by his relatives, of the historical novels that he had written at the age of anything from ten to sixteen and found only the cook for an audience, of his going to Cambridge, and his development there so that he became Editor of *The Lion*, that remarkable but very short-lived literary journal, and the President of 'The Bats,' the most extraordinary Essay Club that Cambridge had ever known; of how, alas, he took only a third in History owing to the perverseness of examiners; and so on and so on, until he arrived in full flood at the whole history of his love for Alice, of her remarkable talents and beauty, but of her strange temper and arrogance and general feminine queerness.

Mr. Oddy listened to it all in the kindest way. There's no knowing where they walked that afternoon; they crossed the bridge and adventured into Battersea Park, and finally had tea in a small shop smelling of stale buns and liquorice drops. It was only as they turned homewards that it occurred to Tommy that he had been talking during the whole afternoon. He had the grace to see that an apology was necessary.

'I beg your pardon, sir,' he said, flushing a little, 'I'm afraid I have bored you dreadfully. The fact is, that this last quarrel with Alice has upset me very badly. What would you do if you were in my position?'

Mr. Oddy sighed. 'The trouble is,' he said, 'that I realise only too clearly that I shall never be in your position again. My time for romance is over, or at least I get my romance now in other ways. It wasn't always so; there was a lady once beneath whose window I stood night after night merely for the pleasure of seeing her candle outlined behind the blind.'

'And did she love you,' Tommy asked, 'as much as you loved her?'

'Nobody, my dear boy,' Mr. Oddy replied, 'loves you as much as you love them; either they love you more or they love you less. The first of these is often boring, the second always tragic. In the present case I should go and make it up; after all, happiness is always worth having, even at the sacrifice of one's pride. She seems to me a very charming young lady.'

'Oh, she is,' Tommy answered eagerly. 'I'll take your advice, I'll go this very evening; in fact, if you don't mind, I think it would be rather a good time to find her in now.'

Mr. Oddy smiled and agreed; they parted to meet another day.

On the third occasion of their meeting, which was only two days after the second, Tommy cared for his companion enough to wish to find out something about him.

His scene of reconciliation with his beautiful Alice had not been as satisfactory as he had hoped; she had forgiven him indeed, but given him quite clearly to understand that she would stand none of his nonsense either now or hereafter. The satisfactory thing would have been for Tommy there and then to have left her, never to see her again;

he would thus have preserved both his pride and his independence; but, alas, he was in love, terribly in love, and her indignation made her appear only the more magnificent.

And so on this third meeting with his friend he was quite humble and longing for affection.

And then his curiosity was stirred. Who was this handsome old gentleman, with his touching desire for Tommy's companionship? There was an air about him that seemed to suggest that he was someone of importance in his own world; beyond this there was an odd sense that Tommy knew him in some way, had seen him somewhere; so on this third occasion Tommy came out with his questions.

Who was he? Was he married? What was his profession, or was he perhaps retired now? And another question that Tommy would have liked to have asked, and had not the impertinence, was as to why this so late interest in the Arts and combined with this interest this so complete ignorance.

Mr. Oddy seemed to know a great deal about everything else, but in this one direction his questions were childish. He seemed never to have heard of the great Spencer Russell at all (which secretly gave Tommy immense satisfaction), and as for geniuses like Mumpus and Peter Arrogance and Samuel Bird, even when Tommy explained how truly great these men were, Mr. Oddy appeared but little impressed.

'Well, at least,' Tommy burst out indignantly, 'I suppose you've read something by Henry Galleon? Of course he's a back number now, at least he is not modern if you know what I mean, but then he's been writing for centuries. Why, his first book came out when Trollope and George Eliot were still alive. Of course, between ourselves I think *The Roads*, for instance, a pretty fine book, but you should hear Spencer Russell go for it.'

No, Mr. Oddy had never heard of Henry Galleon.

But there followed a most enchanting description by Mr. Oddy of his life when he was a young man and how he once heard Dickens give a reading of *A Christmas Carol*, of how he saw an old lady in a sedan chair at Brighton (she was cracked, of course, and even then a hundred years after her time, but still he had seen it), of how London in his young day was as dark and dirty at night as it had been in Pepys' time, of how crinolines when he was young were so large that it was one of the sights to see a lady getting into a cab, of how in the music-halls there was a chairman who used to sit on the stage with a table in front of him, ring a bell and drink out of a mug of beer, of how he heard Jean de Reszke in *Siegfried* and Ternina in *Tristan*, and of how he had been at the first night when Ellen Terry and Irving had delighted the world with *The Vicar of Wakefield*.

Yes, not only had Mr. Oddy seen and done all these things, but he related the events in so enchanting a way, drew such odd little pictures of such unexpected things and made that old London live so vividly, that at last Tommy burst out in a volley of genuine enthusiasm: 'Why, you ought to be a writer yourself! Why don't you write your reminiscences?'

But Mr. Oddy shook his head gently: there were too many reminiscences, everyone was always reminiscing; who wanted to hear these old men talk?

At last when they parted Mr. Oddy had a request—one thing above all things that he would like would be to attend one of these evening gatherings with his young friend to hear these young men and women talk. He promised to sit very quietly in a corner—he wouldn't be in anybody's way.

Of course Tommy consented to take him; there would be one next week, a really good one; but in his heart of hearts he was a little shy. He was shy not only for himself but also for his friend.

During these weeks a strange and most unexpected affection had grown up in his heart for this old man; he really did like him immensely, he was so kind and gentle and considerate.

But he would be rather out of place with Spencer Russell and the others; he would probably say something foolish, and then the others would laugh. They were on the whole a rather ruthless set and were no respecters of persons.

However, the meeting was arranged; the evening came and with it Mr. Oddy, looking just as he always did, quiet and gentle but rather impressive in some way or another. Tommy introduced him to his hostess, Miss Thelma Bennet, that well-known futuristic artist, and then carefully settled him down in a corner with Miss Bennet's aunt, an old lady who appeared occasionally on her niece's horizon but gave no trouble because she was stone deaf and cared only for knitting.

It was a lively evening; several of the brighter spirits were there, and there was a great deal of excellent talk about literature. Every writer over thirty was completely condemned save for those few remaining who had passed eighty years of age and ceased to produce.

Spencer Russell especially was at his best; reputations went down before his vigorous fist like ninepins. He was so scornful that his

brilliance was, as Alice Smith everywhere proclaimed, 'simply wither-
ing.' Everyone came in for his lash, and especially Henry Galleon.
There had been some article in some ancient monthly written by some
ancient idiot suggesting that there was still something to be said for
Galleon and that he had rendered some service to English literature.
How Russell pulled that article to pieces! He even found a volume of
Galleon's among Miss Bennet's books, took it down from the shelf
and read extracts aloud to the laughing derision of the assembled
company.

Then an odd thing occurred. Tommy, who loved to be in the intellectual swim, nevertheless stood up and defended Galleon. He
defended him rather feebly, it is true, speaking of him as though he
were an old man ready for the alms-house who nevertheless deserved
a little consideration and pity. He flushed as he spoke, and the scorn
with which they greeted his defence altogether silenced him. It silenced
him the more because Alice Smith was the most scornful of them all;
she told him that he knew nothing and never would know anything,
and she imitated his piping excited treble, and then everyone joined in.

How he hated this to happen before Mr. Oddy! How humiliating
after all the things that he had told his friend, the implication that he
was generally considered to be one of England's most interesting young
men, the implication above all that although she might be a little rough
to him at times Alice really adored him, and was his warmest admirer.
She did not apparently adore him tonight, and when he went out at
last with Mr. Oddy into the wintry, rain-driven street it was all he
could do to keep back tears of rage and indignation.

Mr. Oddy had, however, apparently enjoyed himself. He put his
hand for a minute on the boy's shoulder.

'Good night, my dear boy,' he said. 'I thought it very gallant of you
to stand up for that older writer as you did: that needed courage. I
wonder,' he went on, 'whether you would allow me to come and take
tea with you one day—just our two selves. It would be a great pleasure
for me.'

And then, having received Tommy's invitation, he vanished into
the darkness.

On the day appointed, Mr. Oddy appeared punctually at Tommy's
rooms. That was not a very grand house in Glebe Place where Tommy
lived, and a very soiled and battered landlady let Mr. Oddy in. He
stumbled up the dark staircase that smelt of all the cabbage and all the
beef and all the mutton ever consumed by lodgers between these walls,

up again two flights of stairs, until at last there was the weather-beaten door with Tommy's visiting-card nailed upon it. Inside was Tommy, a plate with little cakes, raspberry jam, and some very black-looking toast.

Mr. Oddy, however, was appreciative of everything; especially he looked at the books. 'Why,' he said, 'you've got quite a number of the novels of that man you defended the other evening. I wonder you're not ashamed to have them if they're so out of date.'

'To tell you the truth,' said Tommy, speaking freely now that he was in his own castle, 'I like Henry Galleon awfully. I'm afraid I pose a good deal when I'm with those other men; perhaps you've noticed it yourself. Of course Galleon is the greatest novelist we've got, with Hardy and Meredith, only he's getting old, and everything that's old is out of favour with our set.'

'Naturally,' said Mr. Oddy, quite approving, 'of course it is.'

'I have got a photograph of Galleon,' said Tommy. 'I cut it out of a publisher's advertisement, but it was taken years ago.'

He went to his table, searched for a little and produced a small photograph of a very fierce-looking gentleman with a black beard.

'Dear me,' said Mr. Oddy, 'he does look alarming!'

'Oh, that's ever so old,' said Tommy. 'I expect he's mild and soft now, but he's a great man all the same; I'd like to see Spencer Russell write anything as fine as *The Roads* or *The Pattern in the Carpet*.'

They sat down to tea very happy and greatly pleased with one another.

'I do wish,' said Tommy, 'that you'd tell me something about yourself; we're such friends now, and I don't know anything about you at all.'

'I'd rather you didn't,' said Mr. Oddy. 'You'd find it so uninteresting if you did; mystery's a great thing.'

'Yes,' said Tommy, 'I don't want to seem impertinent, and of course if you don't want to tell me anything you needn't, but—I know it sounds silly, but, you see, I like you most awfully. I haven't liked anybody so much for ever so long, except Alice, of course. I don't feel as though you were of another generation or anything; it's just as though we were the same age!'

Mr. Oddy was enchanted. He put his hand on the boy's for a moment and was going to say something, when they were interrupted by a knock on the door, and the terrible-looking landlady appeared in the room. She apologised, but the afternoon post had come and she thought the young gentleman would like to see his letters. He took them, was about to put them down without opening them, when suddenly he blushed. 'Oh, from Alice,' he said. 'Will you forgive me a moment?'

'Of course,' said Mr. Oddy.

The boy opened the letter and read it. It fell from his hand on to the table. He got up gropingly as though he could not see his way, and went to the window and stood there with his back to the room. There was a long silence.

'Not bad news, I hope,' said Mr. Oddy at last.

Tommy turned round. His face was grey and he was biting his lips. 'Yes,' he answered, 'she's—gone off.'

'Gone off?' said Mr. Oddy, rising from the table.

'Yes,' said Tommy, 'with Russell. They were married at a register office this morning.'

He half turned round to the window, put out his hands as though he would shield himself from some blow, then crumpled up into a chair, his head falling between his arms on the table.

Mr. Oddy waited. At last he said: 'Oh, I'm sorry: that's dreadful for you!'

The boy struggled, trying to raise his head and speak, but the words would not come. Mr. Oddy went behind him and put his hands on his shoulders.

'You know,' he said, 'you mustn't mind me. Of course, I'll go if you like, but if you could think of me for a moment as your oldest friend, old enough to be your father, you know.'

Tommy clutched his sleeve, then, abandoning the struggle altogether, buried his head in Mr. Oddy's beautiful black waistcoat.

Later he poured his heart out. Alice was all that he had; he knew that he wasn't any good as a writer, he was a failure altogether; what he'd done he'd done for Alice, and now that she'd gone——

'Well, there's myself,' said Mr. Oddy. 'What I mean is that you're not without a friend; and as for writing, if you only write to please somebody else, that's no use; you've got to write because you can't help it. There are too many writers in the world already for you to dare to add to their number unless you're simply compelled to. But there— I'm preaching. If it's any comfort to you to know, I went through just this same experience myself once—the lady whose candle I watched behind the blind. If you cared to, would you come and have dinner with me to-night at my home? Only the two of us, you know; but don't if you'd rather be alone.'

476

Tommy, clutching Mr. Oddy's hand, said he would come.

About half-past seven that evening he had beaten up his pride. Even in the depth of his misery he saw that they would never have got on together, he and Alice. He was quickly working himself into a fine state of hatred of the whole female race, and this helped him—he would be a bachelor all his days, a woman-hater; he would preserve a glorious independence. How much better this freedom than a houseful of children and a bagful of debts.

Only, as he walked to the address that Mr. Oddy had given him he held sharply away from him the memory of those hours that he had spent with Alice, those hours of their early friendship when the world had been so wonderful a place that it had seemed to be made entirely of golden sunlight. He felt that he was an old man indeed as he mounted the steps of Mr. Oddy's house.

It was a big house in Eaton Square. Mr. Oddy must be rich. He rang the bell, and a door was opened by a footman. He asked for Mr. Oddy.

The footman hesitated a little, and then, smiling, said: 'Oh yes, sir, will you come in?'

He left his coat in the hall, mounted a broad staircase, and then was shown into the finest library that he had ever seen. Books! Shelf upon shelf of books, and glorious books, editions de luxe and, as he could see with half an eye, rare first editions and those lovely bindings in white parchment and vellum that he so longed one day himself to possess. On the broad writing-table there was a large photograph of Meredith; it was signed in sprawling letters, 'George Meredith, 1887.' What could this mean? Mr. Oddy, who knew nothing about literature, had been given a photograph by George Meredith and had this wonderful library! He stared bewildered about him.

A door at the far end of the library opened and an elegant young man appeared. 'Mr. Galleon,' he said, 'will be with you in a moment. Won't you sit down?'

184. W. D. Howells on the 'wonder' of *The Tragic Muse*

1909

Howells to HJ, December 1909 (LH, ii, 276–7).

We are reading aloud now every night your *Tragic Muse*—very small shreds of her; for my wife's nervous strength is so slight and her interest in the book so intense that she can seldom let me go beyond a dozen pages. She hates to have the story finished, for as she says in a justifiable panic, 'Where shall we find anything like it?' I have supposed some other story of yours, but she has no hopes of anything else so good, even by you. The other night she sighed over a certain tremendous complication of emotions and characters, and said, 'I don't believe *I* could do anything with it from this point.' . . . My wife no longer cares for many things that used to occupy her: hoheits of all nations, special characters in history, the genealogy of both our families. 'Well, what *do* you care for?' I asked, and I found her answer touching. 'Well, James, and his way of doing things—and you.' I must own to you a constantly mounting wonder in myself at your 'way,' and at the fullness, the closeness, the density of your work; my own seems so meager beside it.

185. W. D. Howells on the greatness of *The Bostonians*

1910

Howells to HJ, February 1910 (LH, ii, 279).
'Your collection' refers to the New York edition which had by then been published. In spite of this plea and others HJ did not add *The Bostonians*, largely because of pressure exerted against it on economic grounds by his publishers (c.f. Nos. 191 and 195—but the real difficulties of persuading him to look kindly on early work are better conveyed by his hurt protest in 1914 against the tactless proposal that 'The Romance of Certain Old Clothes', 1868, should be included as 'representative' in the *International Library of Famous Literature*—see 'Henry James on one of his Early Stories' by Raymond D. Havens, *American Literature*, March 1951, xxiii, 131–3).

You owe me two letters, but I make you my debtor for a third because I can't resist writing to you about *The Bostonians*, which I've been reading out to my family. I'm still reading it, for there are a hundred pages left, and I wish there were a thousand. I've the impression, the fear that you're not going to put it into your collection, and I think that would be the greatest blunder and the greatest pity. Do be persuaded that it's not only one of the greatest books you've written, but one of the masterpieces of all fiction. Closely woven, deep, subtle, reaching out into worlds that I did not imagine you knew, and avouching you citizen of the American Cosmos, it is such a novel as the like of hasn't been done in our time. Every character is managed with masterly clearness and power. Verena is something absolute in her tenderness and sweetness and loveliness, and Olive in her truth and precision; your New Yorkers are as good as your Bostonians; and I couldn't go beyond that. Both towns are wonderfully suggested; you go to the bottom of the half frozen Cambridge mud. A dear yet terrible time comes back to me in it all. I believe I have not been wanting in a sense of you from the first, but really I seem only to be realizing you now.

186. Vernon Lee on the handling of words in *The Ambassadors*

1910

Vernon Lee, from 'The handling of words: Meredith, Henry James', *English Review*, June 1910, v, 427–41.
This was later made part of a book, *The Handling of Words*, 1923, which, although parts of it were written in the 1890's, strikingly anticipates some modern critical and metacritical ideas. The description of words as 'signals' evoking responses obviously suggests the work of I. A. Richards and others, and, in the present instance, the verbal analysis of the paragraph from *The Ambassadors* bears a very strong resemblance to Professor Ian Watt's 'Explication' of the opening of the book in *Essays in Criticism*, July 1960, x, 250–74. More importantly, the very idea that the intensive study of short passages of *prose* could lead to valuable general conclusions about a writer's sensibility must have seemed at the time of extraordinary interest and originality. Emil Reich (1854–1910) was a Hungarian intellectual and ancient historian, settled in England, and known especially for his stress on the importance of geographical and economic factors in history.

Three or four years ago a letter of Mr. Emil Reich to the *Times* on Statistical Tests of Literature, suggested the examination of the various sorts of words contained in pages, taken at random, from different writers. Thus, having made three groups severally of nouns and pronouns, adjectives and adverbs, and verbs and participles, I proceeded to count the number of each on an average of five hundred words. In this manner I analysed, and got others to analyse, several passages from Defoe, Fielding, Stevenson, Pater, and other writers. Such work is intolerably wearisome; and its results depend upon an amount of repetition which this wearisomeness makes difficult. For the class of word employed naturally varies considerably with the subject-matter of each page; so that it becomes necessary to count a great number of pages before obtaining a real average for each individual writer. While accepting the importance of this method if applied on a sufficient scale, and recommending it very earnestly to all readers who may be in want of a useful, but tiresome, discipline and task, I have preferred to study the individual differences between writers in a manner more endurable to myself and yielding a more definite result on a lesser amount of material.

The counting of words had not told me much; the analysis of how each individual writer employs whatever words he does use has taught me considerably more. This method is, to begin with, discriminating, while the other is wholesale; it does not matter much how many verbs Kipling may employ in a page as compared with Henry James; it does matter enormously how he chooses and combines the tenses of those verbs, and whether those verbs are of a more or less concrete or more or less abstract nature. That is to say: what we want to know about a writer is not the rough material he uses, but *how* he uses it.

This analytic, as distinguished from the mere statistical, method, has, moreover, the advantage of showing us not only how the mind of a particular writer works—and the working of a mind depends quite as much on individual character as on the subject-matter under treatment —but, what is quite as important, how that particular mode of working of the writer's mind affects the mind of the reader. For style, like every other fine art, implies a certain pattern of activity communicated by the artist—by the writer as much as by the painter, architect, or musician— to the person who listens, or looks, or reads. And the psychology of the writer is, at the same time, the psychology of the reader.

Psychology; I have at last employed the word which defines my object in undertaking (and urging other, younger, people to undertake) these studies.

The knowledge how great artists work will never, I believe, increase the number of great artists, nor even diminish appreciably the number of bad ones. If anything comes out of the six analyses I have just completed it is surely that *le style, c'est l'homme*; that the way of writing, in so far as it is not due to tradition and fashion (all writers of a given time and country being grouped together by resemblances of subject and treatment, and all groups of writers being connected with each other by filiation or collateral influence), that the individual style, in short, is an expression of the individual's modes of feeling, of thinking, of living: some writers being braced, balanced, unified; others slack, full of jerks, surprises, or of what I may call air-tight compartments; let alone some being active and logical; others passive and diffluent in their manner of seeing, feeling, dividing, combining, accentuating, in short *thinking*, a subject.

I have wanted to find out something about the mechanism, so to speak, of the writer's mind, and of its action on the mind of the reader. Later, when sufficient facts have been accumulated, and put in order on this one point, it may become possible to connect this study of the mere treatment of words with the study of the treatment of a subject; to connect also the evidence contained in a man's style (as in his hand-writing) with the evidence contained in his life, his actions as a mere human being. And in this manner we may learn something of the constitution of Man, that proper study, as Pope says, of Mankind; meaning by *man* not the abstraction hitherto constructed and then dissected by moralists, but the varieties and classes of individuals, nay, the individuals themselves, our neighbours, parents, teachers, children, pupils, all we depend on and that depends on us; and what does both: ourselves.

Meanwhile, while prosecuting these studies of words and of those who act, and those who are acted on, through them, it has been something to feel one's own literary understanding sharpened, one's literary appreciation increased, oneself become, if not a less bad writer, at least a better reader. . . .

The Ambassadors, p. 127. Paragraph of 500 words taken at random, only choosing pages without much dialogue. Nouns and pronouns, 137; verbs, 71; adjectives and adverbs, 48.

Our friend had by this time so got into the vision that he almost gasped 'After all she has done for him.' Miss Gostrey gave him a look which broke the next moment into a wonderful smile: 'He is not so good as you think.' They remained with him, these words, promising him, in their character of warning, considerable help; but the support he tried to draw from them found itself, on each renewal of contact with Chad, defeated by something else. What could it be, this disconcerting force, he asked himself, but the sense, continually renewed, that Chad was—quite in fact insisted on being—as good as he thought? It seemed somehow as if he couldn't *but* be as good from the moment he wasn't as bad. There was a succession of days, at all events, when contact with him—and in its immediate effect as if it could produce no other—elbowed out of Strether's consciousness everything but itself. Little Bilham once more pervaded the scene, but little Bilham became, even in a higher degree than he had originally been, one of the numerous forms of the inclusive relation, a consequence promoted, to our friend's sense, by two or three incidents with which we have yet to make acquaintance. Waymarsh himself, for the occasion, was drawn into the eddy; it absolutely, though but temporarily, swallowed him down; and there were days when Strether seemed to bump against him as a sinking swimmer might brush against a submarine object. The fathomless medium held them—Chad's manner was the fathomless medium; and our friend felt as if they passed each other, in their deep immersion, with the round, impersonal eye of silent fish. It was practically produced between them that Waymarsh was giving him then his chance; and the shade of discomfort that Strether drew from the allowance, resembled not a little the embarrassment he had known, at school, as a boy, when members of his family had been present at exhibitions. He could perform before strangers, but relations were fatal; and it was now as if comparatively Waymarsh was a relative. He seemed to hear him say 'strike up then' and to enjoy a foretaste of conscientious domestic criticism. He had struck up, so far as he actually could; Chad knew by this time in profusion what he wanted; and what vulgar violence did his fellow pilgrim expect of him, when he had really emptied his mind? It went somehow to and fro that what poor Waymarsh meant was 'I told you so—that you'd lose your immortal soul!' But it was also fairly explicit that Strether had his own challenge, and that, since they must go to the bottom of things, he wasted no more virtue in watching Chad than Chad wasted in watching him. His dip for duty's sake, where was it worse than Waymarsh's own? For he needn't have stopped resisting and refusing; he needn't have parleyed, at that rate, with the foe.

I begin with the first sentence virtually not dialogue: 'They remained with him, these words, promising him, in their character of warning, considerable help; but the support he tried to draw from them found itself, on each renewal of contact with Chad, defeated by something else.' Here I find *they—these—their—them—him—him—he*—besides an *itself*. Surely an unusual dose of pronouns, that is to say of words decidedly *personal*. And here I ask myself why I have written this word *personal*? Am I under the suggestion of the fact of Henry James being 'a novelist of personality'? Perhaps. But also it seems to me, that pronouns, used like this, have something more personal than nouns: they become here a sort of personification. There is, at all events, an extraordinary circling round these pronouns. I feel that, had they been *nouns*, they would have undergone some transformation, not remained this selfsame something we circle about.

Circle about and among; for we penetrate between them (one almost forgets what *they* really are, feeling *them* merely as something with which one is playing some game—pawns? draughts? or rather adversaries?), finding them now as a nominative, now a possessive, now a dative. It is noteworthy that this shifting of the *case* of these pronouns gives the sentence an air of movement, more than would be given by the presence of verbs. In the two next sentences I have again the impression of an unusual abundance of pronouns, perhaps because of the two its: 'What could *it* be, he asked himself,' &c. and '*It* seemed somehow,' &c. Evidently the use of pronouns implies a demand on the reader's attention; he must remember what the pronoun stands for, or rather (for no one will consent to such repeated effort where only amusement is at stake) the reader will have to be, spontaneously, at full cock of attention, a person accustomed to bear things in mind, to carry on a meaning from sentence to sentence, to think in abbreviations; in other words he will have to be an intellectual as distinguished from an impulsive or image-full person. In this sentence we get the equivalent as subject-matter, of this singular intellectuality and judicialism of form: 'What could it be, . . . but the *sense* that Chad was . . . as good *as he thought.*' What I mean is that the thing we are watching, almost hunting, with Strether is not a human being nor an animal, neither is it a locality we are trying to discover; not even a concrete peculiarity we want to run to ground; it is the most elusive of psychological abstractions: a *force*, a *sense*, in other words an intellectual residuum of experience, which, being defined, involves a comparison. The question is not: Did Chad do this or that? but: Did Chad come up to a conception which Strether had formed? Remark also the logical form (*by elimination*) of 'what could it but be,' &c.

In the next sentence we again have a comparison of degrees; and an affirmation of logical necessity—'it seemed *somehow* as if he couldn't but be as good from the moment he wasn't as bad.' I have underlined the *somehow*. For it denotes a scientific habit, accepting a fact with the reservation that at some future time an obscure part of it will be understood; it is a sign of careful classing of known and unknown.

In the next sentence we have an acknowledged parenthesis, a forestating of a logical objection or question: 'There was a succession of days, at all events, when contact with him—and in its immediate effect, as if it could produce no other—elbowed out of Strether's consciousness everything but itself.' Indeed the parenthesis is a double one, for inside the fact of being told that it was the immediate effect of the contact we are also assured (lest we should stray off to other possibilities) that 'it could produce no other'. Nay, in the beginning of the sentence there is another clause: 'at all events'.

Let me stop to say that I quite understand that such qualifying sentences may, at the first critical glance, seem padding, like the 'he said'—'says I'—of uneducated people; mere attempts to gain time to deal with disorderly thought. But I believe that they here betoken, and provoke, a subdivision of meaning, an act of intellectual care and prudence. Similarly, take note of the expression '*succession of days*': a less analysing and classifying writer would have been satisfied with 'there were days.' In the next sentence after that we have 'Little Bilham pervaded the scene,' Little Bilham being thereby volatilised into a thin essence; the elision meaning 'the fact or existence or idea of Little Bilham pervaded,' &c. With, however, a proviso '*but* Little Bilham became,' &c. Is this proviso going to restore to Little Bilham any of his forfeited concreteness? You little know Henry James if you think that! For the proviso proceeds to make Little Bilham into 'one of the numerous forms of the inclusive relation'; nay, he grows into a complex abstraction 'in a higher degree than he had originally been.' What nouns we have here! *Form, Relation, Degree!* And for adjectives and adverbs, *numerous, higher* (meaning more intense) and *originally*. And if we go on to the full stop we add 'a consequence promoted, to our friends' sense, by two or three incidents with which we have yet to make acquaintance.' In all this sentence only two words 'Little Bilham' have a concrete meaning, give a visual image; and even Strether becomes 'our friend,' that is to say gets considered not as anything tangible or visible, but as a relationship. Meanwhile we have added to the nouns of the first half-sentence '*consequence, friend, sense, incidents,* and *acquaintance*,' to the adjectives nothing! And to the verbs *promoted* and *make*, which merely represent alterations of intensity and valuation in these abstract nouns. I almost believe that my analysis is less abstract than this sentence out of a novel! But now comes a change. The next sentence is not only concrete but picturesque: 'Waymarsh himself, for the occasion, was drawn into the eddy; it absolutely, though but temporarily, swallowed him down; and there were days when Strether seemed to bump against him as a sinking swimmer might brush against a submarine object.' Here we have an *eddy*; the eddy *swallows* Waymarsh; and he and Strether are *sinking swimmers*, bumping against *submarine objects*. But even this is qualified with abstractions; it is 'for the occasion' and 'absolutely though but temporarily,' and it is governed, if not grammatically, at least in intention, by the verb *seem*. For in the next sentence, 'The fathomless medium held them,' &c., we learn that 'Chad's manner was the fathomless medium'—sufficiently abstract!

There is once more a curious concreteness in the continued metaphor: 'they passed each other in their deep immersion with the round, impersonal eye of silent fish.' Of course it only *felt* like this to Strether. But it feels like this to the reader; and this thoroughly carried out picture is probably what enables the reader to live on through more abstraction. If I may talk in an Irish manner, we seem to take a provision of breath in that concrete metaphorical world (even though a submarine one) sufficient for a continued walk in the rarefied atmosphere of the real story. This metaphor is a master-stroke. But this metaphor has awakened a sense of the concrete, and he caps it with a comparison, that of the exhibition at school 'and the shade of discomfort . . . resembled not a little the embarrassment he had known, at school, when members of his family had been present at exhibitions. He could perform before strangers, but relations were fatal,' &c.—actually rising to the dramatic point where Waymarsh, transformed into the schoolboy's relative, seems to cry 'Strike up!' The tendency to concrete thought continues: 'He had struck up, so far as he actually could; Chad knew by this time in profusion what he wanted; and what vulgar violence did his fellow pilgrim expect of him when he had really emptied his mind?' Not only a repetition of the *striking up* which is now metaphorically done by Strether; but we get 'profusion,' an expression singularly referable to concrete things; then 'vulgar violence,' then 'fellow pilgrims,' then 'emptied his mind'.

In the next sentences we get 'bottom of things,' 'wasting virtue'— 'dip' (in the sense of dipping in water), and finally so definite an image as 'parleying with the foe'. But all this concrete metaphor does not prevent our having had, in these hundred words or so—'so far as he actually could'—'wanted'—'expect'—'really'—'somehow'—'fairly explicit'—'at that rate'. And it is quite proper that the most conspicuous sentence of these hundred words should be 'I told you that you'd lose your immortal soul,' for the whole business is one of souls.

What the people do has no importance save as indicating what motives and what spiritual manners they have, and how these affect the consciousness of their neighbours. And, in these five hundred words, a considerable amount of extremely vivid feeling of concrete things becomes merely so much metaphor, illustrating surely subjective relations.

'Alles Tangible,' one might say, paraphrasing *Faust*, 'ist nur ein Gleichniss'.

Let us now examine the subtle working of these five hundred words.

How is it that all this is not vague, *swimmy*, and merely wearisome? How is it that we have not to clutch on to the meaning as on to that of a metaphysical treatise?

Because, I think, of the splendid variety, co-ordination, and activity of the verbal tenses.

In the first sentence, 'They remained with him, these words, promising him, in their character of warning, considerable help'; there is the passage from one real nominative (*these words*) to another (*their character*), through the 'promising him,' followed immediately by a change of active into passive, 'but the support he tried to draw from them found itself . . . defeated by,' &c. Then the sudden interrogation—'What could it be,' &c.—and the concatenation of parenthetically placed verbs, pressing on each other, 'but the sense, constantly renewed, that Chad *was*—quite in fact insisted on being—' &c. Here the parenthetical holding back merely hurls the meaning along with accumulated force. The immediately following sentences, 'It seemed somehow as if he couldn't but be,' &c., 'There was a succession of days,' &c., 'Little Bilham, once more,' &c., seem to me perfect models of clearness and cogency. The sense is abstract, far-fetched; but how the fine ordering of the verbs forces us to go right through, with no gaping or wondering, no shirking of any part of the meaning. It is useless to go through the whole five hundred words because the remark would always be the same. With what definiteness this man sees his way through the vagueness of personal motives and opinions, and with what directness and vigour he forces our thought along with him! This is activity, movement of the finest sort, although confined to purely psychological items. And it is in virtue of this strong, varied, co-ordinated activity forced on to our mind that we fail to feel the otherwise degrading effect of what is, after all, mere gossip.

These are storms in tea-cups; but under the microscope of this wonderful writer, what gales, currents, eddies, whirlpools, Scylla's sea-dogs ready to tear, and Charybdis yawning! We may wind up by repeating that we, like Strether, 'waste no virtue in watching Chad.'

THE FINER GRAIN

1910

187. Arnold Bennett on James's tedious perfection

1910

Arnold Bennett, under the pseudonym 'Jacob Tonson', review,
New Age, October 1910, NS vii, 614–5.
The writer Bennett prefers to HJ, Stephen Reynolds (1881–1919),
was an expert on fisheries and on social questions from the working man's point of view. Although he was a highly educated man
he chose, after 1903, to work for a Sidmouth fisherman.

At the beginning of this particularly active book season, reviewing the
publishers' announcements, I wrote: 'There are one or two promising
items, including a novel by Henry James. And yet, honestly, am I likely
at this time of day to be excited by a novel by Henry James? Shall I even
read it? I know that I shall not. Still, I shall put in on my shelves, and
tell my juniors what a miracle it is.' Well, I have been surprised by the
amount of resentment and anger which this honesty of mine has called
forth. One of the politest of my correspondents, dating his letter from a
city on the Rhine, says: 'For myself, it's really a rotten shame; every
week since "Books and Persons" started have I hoped you would make
some elucidating remarks on this wonderful writer's work, and now
you don't even state why you propose not reading him!' And so on,
with the result that when *The Finer Grain* came along, I put my
pride in my pocket, and read it. (By the way, it is not a novel but a
collection of short stories, and I am pleased to see that it is candidly
advertised as such.) I have never been an enthusiast for Henry James,
and probably I have not read more than 25 per cent. of his entire output. The latest novel of his which I read was *The Ambassadors*, and upon
that I took oath I would never try another. I remember that I enjoyed
The Other House; and that *In the Cage*, a short novel about a post-office

girl, delighted me. A few short stories have much pleased me. Beyond this, my memories of his work are vague. My estimate of Henry James might have been summed up thus: On the credit side: He is a truly marvellous craftsman. By which I mean that he constructs with exquisite never-failing skill, and that he writes like an angel. Even at his most mannered and his most exasperating, he conveys his meaning with more precision and clarity than perhaps any other living writer. He is never, never clumsy, nor dubious, even in the minutest details. You would never catch him, for example, beginning a sentence as the *Westminster Gazette* began one the other day, thus: 'Further, the Duke of Albany's only and posthumous son by a family arrangement'! Also he is a fine critic, of impeccable taste. Also he savours life with eagerness, sniffing the breeze of it like a hound . . . But on the debit side:— He is tremendously lacking in emotional power. Also his sense of beauty is over-sophisticated and wants originality. Also his attitude towards the spectacle of life is at bottom conventional, timid, and undecided. Also he seldom chooses themes of first-class importance, and when he does choose such a theme he never fairly bites it and makes it bleed. Also his curiosity is limited. It seems to me to have been specially created to be admired by super-dilettanti. (I do not say that to admire him is a proof of dilettantism.) What it all comes to is merely that his subject-matter does not as a rule interest me. I simply state my personal view, and I expressly assert my admiration for the craftsman in him and for the magnificent and consistent rectitude of his long artistic career. Further I will not go, though I know that bombs will now be laid at my front-door by the furious faithful. As for *The Finer Grain*, it leaves me as I was—cold. It is an uneven collection, and the stories probably belong to different periods. The first, 'The Velvet Glove', strikes me as conventional and without conviction. I should not call it subtle, but rather obvious. I should call it finicking. In the sentence-structure mannerism is pushed to excess. All the other stories are better. 'Crafty Cornelia', for instance, is an exceedingly brilliant exercise in the art of making stone-soup. But then? I know I am in a minority among persons of taste. Some of the very best literary criticism of recent years has been aroused by admiration for Henry James. There is a man on the *Times Literary Supplement* who, whenever he writes about Henry James, makes me feel that I have mistaken my vocation and ought to have entered the Indian Civil Service, or been a cattle-drover. However, I can't help it. And I give notice that I will not reply to scurrilous letters.

*　　*　　*

A book which fills me with sensations quite the opposite of those caused by my perusals of Henry James is Stephen Reynolds's new volume of sketches, *Along-shore: where man and the sea face one another.* I am in no sort of doubt about this book. There is only one adjective for it—it is a ripping book. It is a book which has my enthusiasm and my almost unqualified regard. I read it with acute pleasure.

188. Clara F. McIntyre on James's late style in the light of his revisions for the New York edition

1912

Clara F. McIntyre, 'The Later Manner of Mr. Henry James', *Publications of the Modern Language Association of America*, 1912, xxvii, 354–71.

Those who have doubts as to how far Mr. James has travelled from his earlier style will find interesting testimony in a bit of early criticism. Writing of *The Passionate Pilgrim* and *Transatlantic Sketches* J. C. Heywood [1877] says, 'Ambiguities and obscurities, as well as inadequacies of expression, are so uncommon in these books that those which appear are all the more displeasing and inexcusable, since the writer has plainly shown that they might have been avoided.'

Even the most ardent admirers of Mr. James to-day will, I think, admit that they have to work at times to grasp his meaning. To most of us, the fact that it should ever have been possible to speak of ambiguities and obscurities as 'uncommon' with him, comes with a little shock of surprise. The object of this paper will be, not to show that his style *has* become more involved and less clear; for it seems to me that the attitude of the present-day public and critics, as compared with the earlier critic just quoted, sufficiently establishes this; but to discover, if possible, some of the causes for this loss of clearness, and to decide whether there is any compensating gain.

Mr. James has made a comparison of his earlier and later ways of doing things rather easier by bringing out, recently, a complete revised edition of his works. In order to get at the subject as definitely as possible, I have selected three or four representative books, and read them side by side in the two editions, noting any changes which seemed to me significant. I shall give the result of this examination first, before discussing in a more general way the development of his style judged from his work as a whole.

I took first *Roderick Hudson*, which Mr. James speaks of in his introduction to the new edition as his first attempt at a real novel, a long and sustained piece of work. He looks at it, apparently, with a sort of pity and patronage, as filled with crudities which he regrets, and yet with fondness, too, as one of his earliest inspirations. To the average reader, unlearned in the James cult, the book would perhaps appeal more than any of his others. The story is simple and direct; there is plenty of action —not merely talk about states of consciousness—and the problem is not too deep for a mind untrained in psychology to grapple with. Mr. James says that Roderick's disintegration is too rapid, but I cannot feel that he is right. An 'artistic temperament' of that sort, as it goes up with a leap, comes down with a rush; and the very essence of Roderick's character is his incapacity to realize any other point of view than that of his own capricious mood, his utter lack of any impulse to pull himself together. The other characters, even those lightly sketched, interest us. Perhaps Mr. James has never created a more fascinating woman than Christina Light. Her indifference, her beauty, her cleverness masking as *naïveté*, all tantalize the reader as they did her fellow-personages in the story. We are not merely told of her power; we feel it. As for the style of the earlier edition, if we were asked to judge it, not knowing the author, we should probably say that it had no very marked peculiarities. It is straightforward, without excessive use of figures, but rich in apt and expressive phrases. It does not thrust itself upon our notice; our attention is held by the events and emotions portrayed, not by the medium of portrayal. In reading the later version, on the contrary, I found myself, after some sentence which meant nothing to me, turning back to the earlier text to find out what the author really intended to say. The clean, clear-cut lines have been blurred in the revising; the apt word has been replaced by a roundabout phrase which may be to Mr. James himself more accurate expression, but which often seems to be used only because it is less natural. He has tried to amplify, but one feels often that he has succeeded only in diluting.

One of the changes which strike us as showing a lapse of vigor, as well as, frequently, a loss of clearness, is the substitution of a general word or phrase for a particular. This is still more common in the later work, but it is noticeable even in this revision. For instance, the earlier text has 'It would have made him almost sick, however, to think that on the whole Roderick was not a generous fellow.' In revising, Mr. James makes this 'It would have made him quite sick, however, to think that on the whole the values in such a spirit were not much larger than the voids.' 'A transparent brown eye' becomes 'a transparent brown regard'. Where in the first book we are told that Roderick 'looked at the straining oarsmen and the swaying crowd with the eye of a sculptor,' the second version has him look 'with the eye of an artist and of the lover of displayed life'. This last phrase is vague enough to make one ponder a bit; at all events, it does not express with finality what the author apparently wanted to say—that Roderick saw everything in relation to the plastic art.

Another form of change is the substitution, for the natural and ordinary word, of one which is commonly used in a rather different sense, as 'I shall be better *beguiled*' for 'I shall be better entertained'. I must confess that on reading 'She had already had a long colloquy with the French chambermaid, who had published her views on the Roman question,' I was dense enough to feel for a moment slightly bewildered at the learning of French chambermaids, and was relieved, on referring to the other book, to find that she merely 'expounded' her views.

We find some of Mr. James's later favorites of expression creeping in. For 'another man admired her,' he puts 'another man is in a state about her'; and instead of 'she went on with soft earnestness' we have 'she wonderfully kept it up.' Just how we should classify these phrases, it is hard to say. 'In a state' might be looked upon as another example of the general for the particular, and as for *wonderfully* and *beautifully*, Mr. James seems to keep them ready to put in whenever some other adverb is not absolutely demanded.

He makes a considerable point of inversion in sentence structure, having the theory, evidently, that to put a word out of its natural place is to call attention to it. This, of course, is an obvious fact, but in some cases there seems to be no particular reason for such emphasis. For instance, 'she said dryly' conveys just about the same degree of meaning as 'she dryly said.' In conversation, especially, the inversion strikes one as decidedly unnatural. 'Go and get me a piece of bread' certainly has the ring of colloquialism more than 'get me somewhere a piece of bread'.

The mention of colloquialism brings us to a rather notable phase of Mr. James's later manner, his seeming attempt to approach the forms of conversational English. This is shown in the increased use of abbreviations,—'he's,' instead of *he is*, 'haven't,' for *have not*, and so forth—and in the frequency of parentheses. This parenthetical construction is certainly not a step in the direction of clearness, especially since a good deal of unrelated matter is often packed into the parentheses. The colloquial aim is displayed in the bits of slang which we find introduced, not always with entire appropriateness. Christina, instead of 'Do you think he's going to be a great man?' says in the second version, 'Do you think he's going to be a real swell, a big celebrity?' We find 'How could I ever meet her again if at the end of it all she should be unhappy?' replaced by 'if at the end of it all she should find herself short?'

The question of foreign influence on Mr. James interests me, much. We know his admiration of Balzac, and his fondness for Continental settings. I seem to have found several instances where the French idiom has impressed itself upon his construction. In the early text he has 'It is still lotus-eating; only you sit down at a table, and the lotuses are served up on rococo china.' The later has 'always' in place of *still*—a clear reminiscence, it would seem, of the French *toujours*. Christina says, 'She's capable of thinking that, mamma,' using *mamma* not as a noun of address, but as a Frenchman would say, 'Elle est capable de penser cela, la mère!' For 'paying, to Rowland's knowledge, his first compliment,' we have later, 'acquitting himself, to Rowland's knowledge, of his first public madrigal.' This is not the ordinary English use of the word *acquit*; it is, exactly, the use of the French *s'acquitter de*. In 'It won't be a tragedy, simply because I sha'n't assist at it,' where *assist at* replaces 'I sha'n't survive it,' 'assist' is used as the French use *assister*, in the sense of witnessing, being present.

The actual use of foreign words and phrases is much more frequent in the later text. We have Christina called a *brava ragazza* instead of a 'good girl'. Where, in the early version, 'Roman princes come and bow to her,' in the later, '*les grands de la terre* come and do her homage'. 'He examined the new statue, said it was very promising,' becomes 'Pronounced it tremendously *trouvé*'. Exclamations like, 'Dieu sait pourquoi!' and 'Che vuole?' are fairly abundant. It is strange that a writer like Mr. James, who seeks not vulgar popularity but the following of a cultivated few, should have fallen into a practice which the cheaper class of novelists has always delighted in. It is true that his French and Italian words are correct in form and aptly used; it is true, also, that there are cases when only a French or an Italian word will express the shade of meaning he is attempting to give. But there are many cases where the foreign word is absolutely unnecessary, and only serves to confuse a reader who is not familiar with the language. There surely was no excuse for changing the statement that Roderick had no fixed day to 'no fixed *jour*'.

There are some cases where the English idiom is faulty. We should naturally say *get to work*, when Mr. James says 'get *at work*,' and one would hardly understand the question, 'Are they already *giving on* his nerves?' if it were not for the earlier form, 'Is he already tired of them?'

Frequently we find examples of what I have called 'dilution,' where the author, in his desire, apparently, to explain fully and precisely every turn of his thought, has weakened the effect by putting in too much. When Roderick, in an argument about his work, says, 'My America shall answer you,' there is a certain nobility in his self-assurance. But when Mr. James writes, 'My colossal "America" shall answer you,' he spoils it by trying to put into black and white the bigness of Roderick's conception. At the very last of the book, in the description of Rowland's relations with Mary, we have in the first edition an admirable directness: 'During the dreary journey back to America, made, of course, with his assistance, there was a great frankness in her gratitude, a great gratitude in her frankness.' In the second, the description finishes, more vaguely, with 'she had used him, with the last rigour of consistency, as a character definitely appointed to her use'.

One very noticeable thing in the later books of Mr. James is that all his people talk alike. There is almost no attempt at differentiation through characteristic talk. Naturally, then, in the revision, we find speeches changed to more typical 'James dialect,' regardless of the speaker. This is especially true in the case of Roderick's mother. A timid, elderly lady from a little New England town, thoroughly refined, thoroughly innocent, thoroughly provincial, she remarks in the early text, naturally and characteristically, 'But we are very easy now, are we not, Mary?' The corrected form, 'Now, however, we are quite ourselves, and Mary, I think, is really enjoying the revulsion' does not belong to Mrs. Hudson at all, but to some lofty lady in perfect control of her situation. She would never have thought of saying, 'No wonder he found Northampton mild'; but the first form, 'No wonder he found Northampton dull,' might easily have suggested itself to her. When we come to changing 'To think of her being a foreigner! She speaks so beautifully' into 'She speaks the language as if she were driving her own carriage—and with her whip well up in her hand, don't you think?' we have something hopelessly out of character. This is not Mrs. Hudson, or anybody else, except Mr. James.

Roderick, looking at his own work, says, 'I think it is curiously bad,' and this amount of detachment, in the mood he is in, is not unnatural. But he would not have said, 'I think it curiously, almost interestingly bad'—he was too excited to weigh his words so carefully. The omission of the verb, too, is hardly colloquial.

There are some passages in which no definite fault can be found with the new form of expression except perhaps some slight awkwardness or vagueness that makes it less effective than the old. So, 'Her daughter had come lawfully by her loveliness,' in the old—'Her young companion was therefore accountably fair,' in the new. 'Let me model you, and he who can may marry you' loses in becoming 'Let me be your modeller, and he who can may be your husband'. 'You almost come up to one of my dreams' is weaker than 'You almost satisfy my conception of the beautiful'.

Roderick Hudson was written in 1874. We could find many imperfections in it, no doubt, but I must confess that I cannot see where the revision of 1908 has improved the original. In almost every case, where I have compared the two versions, I have preferred the earlier form.

The Portrait of a Lady is to me one of the finest of modern novels. For its sake, I can forgive Mr. James much:—I can even, temporarily, forget the perplexity and irritation he frequently causes me. I could not have forgiven him, had he laid very violent hands upon it. But he himself has evidently realized the power of his early work, and has tampered comparatively little with the expression. In the introduction he calls the book 'a structure reared with an "architectural competence" as Turgénieff would have said, that makes it, to the author's own sense, the most proportioned of his works after *The Ambassadors*,—which was to follow it so many years later, and which has, no doubt, a superior roundness'. He accounts for this successful building of the story by the fact that he has placed the center of the subject in the young woman's own consciousness. Certainly Isabel is, throughout, the center of interest, and we get into her personality, have a more human approach to her than to most of Mr. James's people.

There are comparatively few foreign words in the story, though so much of the action takes place in Italy. We have *simpatico* instead of nice; *carrière* for career; 'You wouldn't at all have the *tenue*,' replacing 'You would make a very poor butler'. 'He's Mr. Osborne who lives in Italy' is enlarged by foreign phrasing to 'who lives *tout bêtement* in Italy'. The influence of this last idiom is seen in English, when we have 'the letter that she carried in her pocket all sufficiently reminded her,'—the first expression having merely *sufficiently*.

One or two new tendencies can be noticed in this revision. Mr. James has a way of piling up adverbs, regardless of sound—'At present, obviously, nevertheless'. The earlier construction, 'But at present, obviously,' is superior both in clearness and in harmony. He is inclined to use unusual, if not entirely original compounds, as, 'he had no intention of disamericanizing,' for 'he had no intention of turning Englishman'. Figures are used more freely, and they are often rather far-fetched; we feel that the author must have strained his imagination to see a comparison. For example, the statement, 'She was much excited, but she wished to resist her excitement,' becomes 'She found herself now humming like a smitten harp. She only asked, however, to put on the cover, to case herself again in brown holland'. The elaboration of detail here gives a rather ludicrous effect. Again, 'every now and then Isabel heard the Countess say something extravagant' is expanded into 'heard the Countess, at something said by her companion, plunge into the latter's lucidity as a poodle splashes after a thrown stick'. 'A certain fund of indolence that he possessed' is elaborated by the addition of what seems an utterly unrelated figure, 'a secret hoard of indifference—like a thick cake a fond old nurse might have slipped into his first school outfit'.

There is the same substitution of the general for the particular which we have observed in *Roderick Hudson*. Sometimes it seems to be done with some intention of humor, as 'Miss Stackpole's ocular surfaces unwinkingly caught the sun,' for 'Miss Stackpole's brilliant eyes expanded still further,'—but the humor is certainly not very apparent. It is hard to see how anyone could have changed 'shaking his hunting-whip with little quick strokes' into 'still agitating, in his mastered emotion, his implement of the chase'. And it is simply inconceivable how a man of artistic power could substitute for the simple directness of the first passage following, the vague wanderings of the second. 'To see a strong man in pain had something terrible for her, and she immediately felt very sorry for her visitor'. 'This immediately had a value—classic, romantic, redeeming, what did she know?—for her, "the strong man in pain" was one of the categories of the human appeal, little charm as he might exert in the given case.'

Speaking of Rome, Isabel asks, in the first version, with perfect naturalness, 'Ought I to dislike it, because it's spoiled?' In the second, her question, 'Ought I to dislike it because, poor old dear—the Niobe of Nations, you know—it has been spoiled?' gives us the idea of a person who is tucking in scraps of learning to make an impression—an idea which is not at all the conception Isabel's creator wants us to have of her.

Since I remarked on the first appearance of favorite words and phrases in the other book, perhaps comment should be made on the expression, 'she vaguely wailed,' which is used here in place of 'she murmured to herself,' and which occurs rather frequently in the later books, sometimes in connection with situations that would seem to give no real cause for wailing. Mr. James seems to develop a fondness for adverbs. His description of Isabel as 'thin and light, and middling tall' becomes 'she was undeniably spare, and ponderably light, and proverbially tall'. The adverbs here have an argumentative tone which seems a trifle unnecessary.

On the whole, *The Portrait of a Lady*, begun in the spring of 1879, shows a decided advance in structure and in finish over *Roderick Hudson*, of some five years before. This is probably the reason why Mr. James looked at it in a less critical mood, and made fewer changes, though it is not much nearer than the earlier book to the complication of his later style.

When we turn to *The Awkward Age*, which Mr. Brownell has pronounced 'the technical masterpiece among the later works,' we make a jump of some twenty years, as this book was not published till 1899. The comparative lateness of the work is very evident when we see how closely the original and the revised edition keep to each other. Only a trifling change, here and there, is to be noted. The figures are somewhat more elaborated, and usually less effective, in the later version. 'She shows things, don't you see? as some great massive wall shows placards and posters'—loses much of its force when it is changed to 'as some fine tourist region shows the placards in the fields and the posters on the rocks'. There is the tendency noted before, to destroy the aptness of the figure by adding too much incongruous detail. We find foreign idiom, as in 'I see you coming,' meaning 'I see what you're driving at'. There is still less attempt than in the first edition to suit the speech to the character. Mr. Longdon, a gentleman of the old school, would be far more likely to say, 'Kindly give me some light then on the condition into which he has plunged you,' than 'Kindly give me a lead then as to what it is he has done to you'. When Mr. James tells us that 'Mr. Cashmore soundlessly glared his amusement,' he seems to have tried desperately hard to find a roundabout way of saying, 'Mr. Cashmore stared'.

The book, in the 1899 edition, shows all the characteristics of what we have been calling Mr. James's 'later manner'. We have, every few pages, such expressions as, 'of a strangeness,' 'of a profundity.' These, by the way, are themselves French idioms, and so give evidence of the foreign influence already mentioned. The author's fondness for unusual adverbs, and his habit of putting them before the verb, are very noticeable,—for instance, 'he robustly reflected'. The book is full of parentheses, not merely in the talk of the characters, but in the author's comment, and he is constantly throwing in interjectional phrases like, 'don't you know?', 'don't you see?', and his much-worked expression, 'There you are'. There is an increasing use of the pronoun 'one'—for *you* or for the definite pronoun of the third person.

The Golden Bowl, published in 1904, is so near the time of the revision, that it is hardly worth while to compare the two versions. It will be more to the point to look for developments in this as compared with the earlier work.

We find several new examples of foreign idioms. 'Before twelve assistants only' has the French meaning of *assistants*, as spectators. In 'But from the moment you didn't do it for the complications, why shouldn't you have rendered them?'—'from the moment' is evidently used with the meaning of *since*, in exact equivalent of the French *du moment que*. We have the *toujours* again in 'she always confessed,' 'she always went on,' referring not to an habitual action but to one continued. 'I see them never come back. But *never*—simply.' Here 'but' is used as the French would say *mais jamais*.

The piling up of adverbs becomes more marked still. 'She couldn't of course however be at the best as much in love with his discovery.' Not merely adverbial phrases are treated in this way, but we find sentences made up of a string of loose words and phrases. 'They didn't, indeed, poor dears, know what, in that line—the line of futility—the real thing meant.' There seems to be some intention here of reproducing the natural rambling of conversation, the tacking on of thoughts as they develop, but it seems to me that Mr. James's parenthetical structure does not really reproduce conversation. We do string our thoughts together in a more or less rambling fashion, but most of us talk in loose sentences instead of periodic.

In this book we find grammatical peculiarities which sometimes amount to positive incorrectness. One thing is the use of the double negative, as in 'She did it ever, inevitably, infallibly—she couldn't possibly not do it'. I suppose this is, according to strict logic, correct, although it is a trifle confusing, and to most of us it would be more natural to say, 'she couldn't help doing it'. The same thing is seen in 'I can't not ask myself; I can't not ask you,' and in 'he hadn't for a good while done anything more conscious and intentional than not quickly to take leave'.

But such a sentence as 'with the sense moreover of what he saw her see he had the sense of what she saw him' is not only hopelessly obscure; it seems grammatically incomplete. So in 'She admitted accordingly that

she was educative—which Maggie was so aware that she herself inevitably wasn't,'—the relative refers, incorrectly, to an adjective. 'Each
appears, under our last possible analysis, to have wished to make the
other feel that they were' is a slip that Mr. James should not have been
guilty of; and 'Their lips sought their lips,' referring to two people, is
hardly accurate. There are several cases of the adjective used like an
adverb, to modify another adjective, as, 'modest scattered,' 'slim
sinuous and strong'.

The book throughout is vague in expression. We feel as if we were
groping in a fog, and a bit of Mr. James's typically sketchy conversation
sums up our sensations at the end:

'Then do you yourself know?'
'How much?—'
'How much.'
'How far?—'
'How far.'

Fanny had appeared to wish to make sure, but there was something she
remembered in time, and even with a smile. 'I've told you before that I know
absolutely nothing.'
'Well—that's what *I* know,' said the Princess.

This elliptical style of conversation is of course meant to be suggestive, and it sometimes fulfills its purpose admirably, but often it irritates
us by completely failing to suggest. We feel like echoing the remark of
one of the characters, 'Everything's remarkably pleasant, isn't it?—but
where for it after all are we?'

Mr. Howells, unwaveringly loyal to the novelist who in an earlier
time was so often classed with him, asserts that though he sometimes
cannot understand, he trusts Mr. James, and feels that he will write
nothing which is not worth understanding. I should not wish to be less
modest than Mr. Howells, but I would humbly protest that, if I can read
Balzac, whom Mr. James owns as his master, with a fair degree of
comprehension, Mr. James ought to be able to make me understand at
least as well, writing in my native tongue. I had thought at first that the
same thing might be true of Mr. James's later work that the critics have
found in Shakespeare's later plays—he might have had too much
thought for his expression, have tried to pack too much in a single
sentence. But, as we have seen from the investigation, he has more
frequently *thinned* a passage than enriched it; he has packed in more
expression rather than more thought.

Part of the vagueness of the style undoubtedly comes from the detachment which Mr. Brownell speaks of as characteristic of Mr. James, his habit of 'passing the story to the reader through the mind of one of the personages in it'. Mr. James himself, in one of his introductions, speaks of presenting the story 'not as my own impersonal account of the affair in hand, but as my account of somebody's impression of it'. Again, in 'The Figure in the Carpet', he says, 'Literature was a game of skill, and skill meant courage, and courage meant honour, and honour meant passion, meant life'. This deliberate reasoning seems to show once more a certain aloofness of attitude. With the very greatest writers, do we not feel that there are fewer removals, that literature means, quite directly, life?

And yet, in spite of this device of making some character the spokesman, although, as Mr. Brownell says, 'we see him busily getting out of the way, visibly withdrawing behind the screen of the story . . . making of his work, in fine, a kind of elaborate and complicated fortification between us and his personality,' we are left at the end thinking not of what the people in the story have said or done, but of how Mr. Henry James has expressed himself. It may be that his mannerisms have grown up in an honest attempt to communicate subtle shades of thought; but it certainly seems, often, that when two forms of expression are possible, he deliberately chooses the less natural and the more awkward. Mr. Howells speaks of 'that wonderful way of Mr. James by which he imparts a fact without stating it, approaching it again and again, without actually coming into contact with it'. This is pretty good description, only most of us feel that there are many times when he approaches a fact again and again but does not impart it.

Mr. Brownell says, 'Cuvier lecturing on a single bone and reconstructing the entire skeleton from it is naturally impressive, but Mr. James often presents the spectacle of a Cuvier absorbed in the positive fascinations of the single bone itself,—yet plainly preserving the effect of a Cuvier the while'. This phrases very satisfactorily to me the feeling I had in reading *The Ambassadors*. There was so much talk about so little; the people and the situation had so little appeal to one's sympathy; the language, at times, was so hesitating and elusive; and yet, somehow, the whole thing was masterly. We can only regretfully wonder what the world of literature might have gained if Mr. James had kept along the road to which *The Portrait of a Lady* pointed, instead of turning off into the manneristic byways that have led to *The Sacred Fount* and *The Golden Bowl*.

I said in the beginning that we should ask the question whether there has been any gain to make up for the loss of clearness that we have traced in Mr. James's work.

Stevenson says, 'That style is the most perfect, not, as fools say, which is most natural, for the most natural is the disjointed babble of the chronicler; but which attains the highest degree of elegant and pregnant implication unobtrusively, or, if obtrusively, then with the greatest gain to sense and vigor'. Mr. James's style—that is, the later style—is certainly not unobtrusive; and I think only the most extreme of his supporters would affirm that the increase in obtrusiveness has meant a gain in sense and vigor. If, as some of them seem to think, he *must* write in this way to express the windings of his thought, it would seem to the uninitiated that there must be something wrong with the thought. In any case, the question may well arise whether a mode of writing which so constantly distracts attention from the substance to the form of expression is still to be called *style*. Certainly not according to Goethe's definition, which Mr. Brownell seems to have had in mind when he said: 'Are the masterpieces of the future to be written in this fashion? If they are, they will differ from the masterpieces of the past in the substitution of a highly idiosyncratic *manner* for the hitherto essential element of *style*, and in consequence they will require a second reading, not as heretofore, for the discovery of new beauties or the savoring again of old ones, but to be understood at all.'

189. M. Sturge Gretton on James's later development in the light of the Prefaces to the New York edition

1912

M. Sturge Gretton, from 'Mr. Henry James and his Prefaces', *Contemporary*, January 1912, ci, 69–78, and reprinted in the *Living Age*, February 1912, cclxxii, 287–95.

This article seems to me to propose one of the very few fresh approaches to HJ in the later years. Again, it is untypical. I regret having been unable to find out more about Gretton; but the reader might like to compare his implied estimate of the established success of the New York edition with HJ's gloomy letter to Gosse in 1915 (No. 195).

Few literary careers can compare with Mr. Henry James's in achievement. He has been publishing for almost half a century, his aims from the first have been distinctive and uninfluenced by any popular demand, he chose his own methods and brought them well-nigh to perfection. He is a theorist, and his theories have been enunciated in a long series of critical essays. But what amazes us is the consistency with which they have been illustrated in his work. It is this very coherence which makes his work in its totality so difficult to estimate. It is easy enough to point out certain of his books which we like or dislike, but the mass, the momentum almost, of the solid block he fills in our shelves is hard to appraise. We gaze at the backs of Mr. James's volumes to feel them individually perhaps less vivid and significant than those of any equally great writer, but their weight, their space, the gap they make between our days and days the other side of them, that is immense. And lately he has increased our debt to him by a generosity new in its form. The essays, one of which precedes each volume of the tales in the New York Edition, enable the reader in a unique degree to compare an author's performance with his theory. A great artist puts himself before us, not as a magician producing mysterious, spontaneous results, but as a craftsman revealing the nature of his methods and avowing his invariable habit of experimentation. It was twenty-seven years ago, when writing his 'Art of Fiction', in reply to Sir Walter Besant, that Mr. James first ran atilt at the novelist's ordinary conventions and formulated his creed. 'A novel,' he said, 'is in its broadest definition a personal, a direct, impression of life'; 'the characters, the situations that strike one as real will be those that touch and interest one most'; 'experience is an immense sensibility, a kind of huge spider-web of the finest silken threads suspended in the chamber of consciousness and catching every air-borne particle in its tissue'; 'what is incident but the illustration of character? It is an incident for a woman to stand up with her hand resting on a table and look out at you in a certain way.' In regard to these statements, and others like them scattered throughout Mr. James's critical essays, the prefaces find little to add or to alter.

But if on the level of the theorist the prefaces add very little, on a secondary plane they are altogether invaluable. They establish much that must otherwise have been only surmise; they give the conditions and places in which the novels were written, the nature and order in which themes suggested themselves. It has always been impossible to miss the fact that Mr. James's gifts had their root in 'internationalism,' yet only amid the circumstantial details now afforded us does the truth become fully apparent. To think of Mr. James's vision as a cosmopolitan product we do not, of course, need to be reminded of Mr. Beerbohm's delightful caricature. Mr. James exclaiming on revisiting America, 'I might, in regarding and, as it somewhat were, over-seeing, *à l'œil de voyageur*, these dear good people find hard to swallow, or even to take by subconscious injection, the great idea that I am—oh! ever so indigenously—one of them'. Paris, London, Rome, the subtlety and brilliancy of each capital, have heightened his power of refraction; but his lenses themselves remain more trans-Atlantic than many of his readers are apt to suppose. Never, perhaps, will there be a more satisfying presentation of the old country as seen through the eyes of the new, than was given in 'A Passionate Pilgrim'. It is not the smallest of Mr. James's contributions to knowledge that he has revealed how much Europe stood in need of American eyes to intellectualise, if not actually discover, her beauties. London he has seen as no Englishman could have seen it, from the days when as a child in New York he pored over pictures in *Punch*, down to the time of the broad-washed, essential portrayal in which Kate Croy has her being. 'There is an emotion,' he tells us in writing of Hampton Court, 'familiar to every intelligent traveller, in which the mind seems to swallow the sum total of its impressions at a gulp, to take in the whole place whatever it be.' 'A Passionate Pilgrim' appeared in 1871, *Roderick Hudson* in 1875, *The American* in 1877, *Daisy Miller* in 1878, *The Portrait of a Lady* in 1880, *The Reverberator* in 1888, and all these, with a score of shorter stories, presented American characters on a European background. So constant, in fact, up to about 1890, was Mr. James's attention to this theme that it has become customary to divide his work into two periods— the earlier portion respecting 'the adventures of the rich Americans in our corrupt old Europe'; while the latter contains simply those works which have been published since 1892. To extol Mr. James's success in the earlier of these periods would be an impertinence. What he accomplished is without parallel; he invented a *genre* of his own. . . .

Later, since 1890 or thereabouts, Mr. James has abandoned this specialised interest, this particular angle, for a cosmopolitan temper. He has shared, say his exponents, in a general European tendency towards the recondite rather than the rare, the kind of obscurity offered only by over-ripe civilisations. And here in this region of non-moral, at times almost pathological, interests, his genius has found its true scope. Whether this verdict is just, time only can tell. To find any of the myriad whisperings and beckonings which solicit our hyper-sensibility tabulated for us is a boon we may over-estimate easily. However that may be, I cannot but think that in the employment of his methods upon English themes Mr. James has exposed an essentially un-English mind. '*The Golden Bowl*,' he tells us, 'is not "international," the subject could have been perfectly expressed had all the persons concerned been only American, or only English, or only Roman.' Now even to Mr. James's most unquestioning admirers this must come as a hard saying. If Maggie Verver is not to be seen as American, some of us will not be able to see her at all. She is lovely, with a loveliness no one may gainsay; but is she not what she is because she belongs with Newman and Francie? She is the rarest of the bunch, but she belongs to them, and it is that fact, surely, that gives us our grip of her. Manners and morals in her are the result of uniquely American conditions. The equivalently well-bred Englishwoman in similar circumstances would have been neither so lovely nor so unintuitive. European good breeding consists of personal simplicity made possible by what has come to be effortless responsiveness to complexities. Such simplicity as Maggie Verver's differs essentially from that of, say, a home-staying duchess. English readers are apt to lose sight of the difference, from their consciousness of the taste and wealth by which Maggie is surrounded. But, for good or for evil, these are no part of her; she is sprung neither of generations having them, nor of generations not having, and craving them. She is what she is because she has escaped the moulding of either initiation. The equivalent Englishwoman is, perhaps, more independent of the things themselves; but she is in no way independent of the processes they represent. Her great grandmother built certain conditions into life and her successor responds to them intuitively. Mr. James seems altogether to have missed a fact, which is really the central fact about an Englishman or Englishwoman of good breeding, that their past is actually made present, summed up, in a certain refusal to analyse. And what this failure of perception may amount to, *The Sacred Fount* and 'The Siege of London' have exposed. Call us a nation of hypocrites if you like, but if you come to describe us you will be quickly aware that the whitening is part of our sepulchres. The separate constituents of *The Sacred Fount* may exist, but the totality of English country-house life it portrays is simply incredible. The atmosphere, the medium suggested could not exist for a day unless the house were given up to detectives. Conventions are, after all, Society's tribute to decency, and incidents such as those of *The Sacred Fount*, portrayed without their corresponding conventions, result merely in nightmare. The actions described may be those of Englishmen, but outside kitchens, through the length and breadth of the land, no collection of men and women would be found to share in what are represented as their actor's habitual reflections upon them. Mr. James's scientific search for phenomena has led him astray. Interested only in discovery, in tracking down, he has missed truth that should have been perceived intuitively. He has analysed individuals and placed them together without a co-ordinating atmosphere. And in England—in Europe—their atmosphere is so much more than themselves. This failure is most markedly present in certain scenes in *The Ambassadors*. Mr. James sets forth to satiety in the prefaces his theory that everything in the tale must be seen through the mind of some actor in the drama. Essentially this is, after all, Wilkie Collins's method, and, however widely different the material it is employed on, is likely to retain some of the dangers of the detective story—dangers which, where delicate themes are involved, wrest certain actors to 'impossible' actions and speeches because such and such things must be brought into the story. But, however we should explain it, perhaps the most astounding example of unreality of situation, and character destroyed for want of its atmosphere, is to be found in *The Ambassadors*.

All the growing discomfort the reader may have experienced as to Madame de Vionnet's not being a consistent really-drawn character comes to a climax in the incident of her call on Sarah Pocock. No woman of the world could have imposed that call. Considered on the lowest, the most obvious ground, it is not the way to propitiate the 'Sarah Pococks' of life to cheapen oneself to them. Even if we suppose the call to be paid, Madame de Vionnet's talk is incredible. Surely it is diametrically opposed to all we have been told of her that she should again and again place Strether in predicaments which even Waymarsh perceives and struggles to rescue him from. Then the taste of her talk, her 'Strethers,' her chaffing about 'dear old Maria,' her insistence on her daughter's being permitted to see Mamie, her proprietorship of Chad—justifying Sarah's 'I'm much obliged to you, I'm sure, for asking me to his rooms'—and, finally incredible, her inquiry of Sarah, 'Do you know dear old Maria?' which compels Strether to turn to Sarah with 'Your mother knows everything'—the author cannot really have attempted to imagine this scene. Exactly the same kind of failure of imagination is to be found in some of Maggie Verver's speeches, but here it is very much worse because there is no loophole for defence. Madame de Vionnet is supposed to stand for just the opposite of *naïveté*, for polished and perfected sophistification. There is no opening to argue, as it is just possible to do in Maggie's case, that a crystalline ultra-simplicity may be some part of the author's conception. Madame de Vionnet is pre-eminently a social being. Yet throughout this scene she ignores the primary law of society—mutuality of intercourse—the agreement that no individual shall make social advances, except on a common profession of feeling. The author's intention, of course, is that we shall think of Madame de Vionnet as suffering and distracted. But we are shown the condition of mind at the price of the crumbling of the character. Does not the difference between one social level and another lie just in the manner in which such nervousness betrays itself, the expression it takes? The nervousness of the woman who makes this *faux pas* would have introduced into her relations with Chad all the elements that our whole conception of Madame de Vionnet rests upon her not introducing. Of Mr. James's heroine (who earlier in the book has been so alluringly, so consummately, ours also) in this chapter and others that follow, we find ourselves exclaiming in the author's words from elsewhere: 'On the basis of so great a weakness, where was your idea of the interest? On the basis of so great an interest, where was the provision for so much weakness?'

And if Mr. James fails in penetrating a certain temper of mind in European society—and how, after all, could it be otherwise when to the alien in him we owe so much in so many directions?—there is, I believe, an element of our life in regard to which his nationality operates even more deeply. In the Preface to Volume XVII. Mr. James tells us that he has placed together a group of his compositions concerning the side of life to which he has felt himself most susceptible. 'The fairy tale side of life,' he says, 'has used for the tug at my sensibility a cord all its own. . . . The ghost story, as we may for convenience call it, has ever been for me the most possible form of the fairy tale.' Now a number of the tales in this volume are among Mr. James's most oustanding successes. But these, such as *The Beast in the Jungle*, *Owen Wingrave*, and *The Birthplace*, are not really concerned with the 'supernatural' at all. They are brilliant presentations of rare and delicate but 'natural' psychological experiences. If this point needed proof it has surely been attested sufficiently by the degree in which perhaps the best of these tales, *Owen Wingrave*, was ruined in effect by its recent dramatisation. It was by the strangest of ironies, surely, that an incident Mr. James had so consummately balanced upon the tight-rope between temperament and phenomena should have been reduced to the level of a stage 'apparition'. It had been part of the adroitness and perfect taste of the story that the catastrophe—confined to thirty lines in fifty pages—was only narrated through a third person, and could not be conceived of as having an eye-witness. In the tale, too, Owen Wingrave was justified in not fleeing from the haunted room at the last by the fact that his cousin had turned the key in the door. In the play, as given at the Little Theatre recently under the title of *The Saloon*, half the audience was left, at the fall of the curtain, in the belief that the sensitive and delicately-minded Owen had committed suicide in the presence of the girl he adored. And, for all its ugliness, this idea, after all, is not one atom more nonsensical than that he should have died from nervous terror while in her company. There was not the smallest need to determine in regard to the story whether the ghost was of an objective or a subjective kind, but it must have been obvious to every reader that it was of the kind that cannot appear when we are not alone.

In view of the very recent performance of *The Saloon* this digression, to speak of *Owen Wingrave*, has seemed pardonable. But the point we are really dealing with is that neither that tale nor the best-known tales in the volume are concerned with the supernatural. The first of those that are, and the first in the book, is *The Altar of the Dead*. And this is a

story so finished and delicately adroit in all its secondary considerations
—the level of ideas within the range of direct analysis where Mr. James's
powers are unrivalled—that readers are apt to overlook the blind spot
at its centre. Its skill is so great that they may well be decoyed: yet in
regard to matters of taste a danger signal hangs out in the earliest pages,
when Stransom, the hero of the tale, gazing in a jeweller's window,
sore for the forgotten and innumerable dead, is spoken of as 'lingering
long enough to suspend in a vision a string of pearls about the white
neck of his own vanished love'! Intercepted in this occupation by an
old friend, Creston, who is accompanied by his second wife, Stransom's
nerves are immediately on edge for the first and deceased Mrs. Creston,
a woman, who, in common with many of Mr. James's rarest relegated
heroines, has died at child-birth. This final contact with the temporal
drives Stransom back on a long latent thought. He enters 'a high doorway'. We are told 'it was a temple of the old persuasion, and there had
evidently been a function, perhaps a service for the dead; the high altar
was still a blaze of candles'. This means, we suppose, that it was a
Roman Catholic Church and that a Mass had been sung, though it was
afternoon. The moment, the author suggests, is for Stransom one of
superlative insight: 'more than it had ever yet come home to him it
struck him as good there should be churches'. He gazes at the lighted
altar; he sets to work to name and group the candles after his departed
friends. His feeling intensifies: 'he almost caught himself wishing that
certain of his friends would now die that he might establish with them,
in this manner, a connection more charmingly'. For whom? With
Chapter Five, the tale, entering on the definitely restricted personal
region, concerning only Stransom and the living woman who shares
the altar he has bought, moves with admirable security. From here to
the end it is singularly perfect. But, when we consider the theme that
is chosen, is it not more than strange that this should be the only part
that is spiritual? Presenting Stransom to us in churches and before
altars, the author has given us no atmosphere. For artistic purposes, he
might as well have been set in a parlour. That which to the most
everyday minds a church in some degree stands for has been unfelt.
In so far as the story is vital, it is concerned with the living and not, as
its author means it to be and says that it is, with the dead. And our
dissatisfaction, under this heading, must deepen immensely when we
learn of the story's genesis—the funeral on its way to Kensal Green and
Mr. James's friend who cried out 'Mourir à Londres, c'est être bien
mort'. Mr. James thinks of himself as placing self-imposed limits on his

use of the supernatural. But, as a matter of fact, does he share in susceptibility to 'spiritual' atmospheres to the degree of an ordinary Englishman? Happily to most of us, however unorthodox, to buy up an altar would not be to 'raise' or consecrate one, but to commit a sacrilege, to destroy a bridge with the unseen. Stransom's vision of purchasing the altar as a private preserve is no subtlety and illumination, but a blunted and inartistic idea. For normal minds, apart from and outside theologies, envisage a church as a community—a way of escape by communion. In thinking over these points we find our minds casting back to New England. From stock of the Pilgrim Fathers there rises, after two and a half centuries, a past-master of subtleties, but of subtleties only convincing considered apart from communities, restricted to individuals outside societies—the kind left to the Puritan when he broke with tradition and deified personal conscience. Centres of interest have shifted of course. The problems now offered us have respect rather to questions of taste than what our forefathers thought of as matters of conscience. But the dislocation—the segmentation—of vision is surely akin?

Among the most moving scenes in all fiction is that in which Milly Theale, mortally stricken but superb in her beauty, is piloted by Lord Mark in the low afternoon sunlight past 'patches of colour,' behind layer and layer of paintings, and curios, and tapestries, to discover her likeness in the Bronzino deep in the heart of the burnished old house:

She found herself for the first moment, looking at the portrait through tears. Perhaps it was her tears that made it just then so strange and fair—as wonderful as he had said; the face of a young woman all splendidly drawn, down to the hands, and splendidly dressed; a face almost livid in hue, yet handsome in sadness, and crowned with a mass of hair rolled back and high, that must, before fading with time, have had a family resemblance to her own. The lady in question, at all events, with her slightly Michaelangelesque squareness, her eyes of other days, her full lips, her long neck, her recorded jewels, her brocaded and wasted reds, was a very great personage—only unaccompanied by a joy. And she was *dead, dead, dead*! Milly recognised her exactly in words that had nothing to do with her. 'I shall never be better than this'.

Lord Mark does not understand—it is part of the rare weaving of this tapestry-like picture that the Englishman should offer perfected adroitness to mate with her feeling. He protects without understanding, and the two pass on through an assembly whose personages gaze 'as if Milly had been the Bronzino and the Bronzino only Milly,' and murmur,

' "Superb".' It would be absurd to pretend that Mr. James in his earlier writings gave us anything quite so rare—so dim and deep in colour and texture—as this. It is the greatest scene in the whole of his work. Yet *The Wings of a Dove* has other pictures, in Venice, worthy at least of such company. And almost, if not quite, on a par with them is that cameo in *The Golden Bowl*; Charlotte acting as cicerone at Fawns—the clear-lighted gallery, the grey-blue tones of the tapestry, the austere high voice which Maggie and Adam hear going on and on with its exposition from tension too great to allow it to stop or to quaver. Before passages such as these all criticism is silent, enthralled. In them, the deeper, the more turbid the stirring of human emotions, the better the 'spider's web' catches its 'particles' and sets them to gleam in its mesh.

But why, we presently find ourselves asking, are the parts so often greater than the whole, passages and incidents surpassingly thrilling with comparative flatness in the whole they should subserve? It is part of Mr. James's theory that no material is unworthy of treatment, and may be dignified by use. Speaking of his search for illustrations, he says: 'Both our limits and the very extent of our occasion lay in the fact that, unlike wanton designers, we had not to create, but simply to recognise—recognise, that is, with the very last fineness.' Such an attitude has obvious dangers. Phenomena in life are grouped about centres of feeling. Incidents lie scattered like beads, but ourselves are the string; and, strung on ourselves, they show larger and smaller. Shallows no doubt have their recondite qualities, but to chart these too intricately may be to fill up the space for the channels between them; and in reading Mr. James's later novels one cannot but be impressed by want of perspective. Every successive mood of his characters is moulded and crystallised into sharp and resonant images. These images have in themselves extraordinary beauty and appositeness, but the employment of them, normally, in transitional passages, puts the very greatest demands on the subject. A reviewer of Mr. James's last book has just said: 'It shows again Mr. James's marvellous faculty for making people do blunt things with infinite finesse, and not very beautiful things beautifully. His world is his own, and he raises it to his own power.' That is an admirable saying. It is possible, however, to endorse it with a qualification. Mr. James does indeed quicken 'his world'— all the accoutrements, so to speak, of human existence—to an extraordinary poignancy. His intricate furnishings—the tapestries and paintings, dim deep old colours, curious outlines of features, thoughts about thought—lend their living completeness to characters which in themselves are incomplete, and we forget through what peep-holes and slits we look on to life.

The question about the later novels is not whether they are astoundingly brilliant—on that score there is no room for differing opinions—but whether their centres are living enough to carry the complexity their author lays on them. In this matter a comparison with Meredith might be instructive. In his essay on George Sand (1877), Mr. James wrote: 'Something even better in a novelist (than idealism) is that tender appreciation of actuality which makes even the application of a single coat of rose-colour seem a violence.' Here, idea and epithet alike recall passages of Meredith. But iconoclast as Mr. Meredith was, and curiously lacking in part of Mr. James's equipment, 'the rose-pink of sentiment' was in his creed eschewed for a fiction 'fortified with philosophy'. He was, of course, only too apt to detract from his work by a didactic element, lumps of unkindled philosophy, but none the less it was his poet's vision that gave the necessary impetus—the unifying passion in short—to his novels. Had that been less vital and glowing the impedimenta of his tales must have submerged them. More even than Mr. Meredith, though in a much more sublimated fashion, Mr. James in his later novels 'rubs all the old lamps—metaphor, simile, analysis'—to afford us 'a glimpse of the fray'. The method is heavily freighted. Have the stories sufficient human impulsion to carry it? Is their 'stuff,' 'a soul's epic encounter between nature and circumstance'?—an *epic* encounter; that seems the test.

190. Muriel Draper on James's cultured admirers

[1929]

Muriel Draper, from *Music at Midnight*, 1929, 86–7 and 95–6. Mrs. Draper was the sister-in-law of Ruth Draper (the celebrated exponent of the dramatic monologue and a fellow admirer of HJ—a poem by her in his honour is to be found in Morton Dauwen Zabel's 'Memoir' in *The Art of Ruth Draper*, 1960, 46). These are two separate extracts, the first from an American childhood, and the second, as will become obvious, an episode at a very distinguished musical gathering at Edith Grove, the Drapers' London house. Montague Vert Chester was a music impresario.

Since a day when, as a small child, I sat unnoticed in a room in which a great woman, Elizabeth Cummings, was reading aloud to my mother, I had wanted to meet Henry James. The book was *What Maisie Knew* (didn't I say I was unnoticed?) and after a particularly dazzling passage Elizabeth Cummings had paused. My mother looked up from her sewing and exclaimed, 'How does he manage to bring about such a thing!' and Elizabeth Cummings answered, 'He doesn't manage, my dear Susan; he is a genius'. The functionings of genius presented a problem beyond my power to solve, but the effect the word had on me was magical. I rose from the corner where I had been sitting in guilty quiet, and asked, 'Is he alive?' Disturbed by my presence, Elizabeth Cummings put the book down; alarmed by my voice, my mother said 'Yes'. After a nervous pause I was sent from the room on some needless errand, bearing within me a firm resolve, which was that if there was one genius still alive (at that age, one always thinks of them as dead—indeed it is a delusion from which many people never recover), I must somehow manage to see him.

*   *   *

He took in the fragile, minute and blonde delicacy of Mme. Thibaud as she sat in timorous sprightliness in an enveloping armchair of exaggerated dimensions, under a vase of heavily blossoming, formally petalled pink and white camellias, gleamily bending through glossy dark green leaves. He did not neglect Mme. Suggia, the gifted cello-playing friend of Casals before he married Susan Metcalf, who sat in swarthy gold, white, and black of dress and skin and hair on a small upright Chinese Chippendale chair in the spectral shadow of paling almond flowers. He saw the sensitive aloof protection which Karol Sczymanowski threw about himself and the life-defying speed with which Arthur Rubinstein managed to stand still. To all this he gave the steady orderliness of his observation. Toward the end of the octet, Montague Vert Chester, in a new pair of white gloves, came into the room. As was the unvarying custom at Edith Grove he crept into the nearest seat he could find without even a whisper of greeting, and listened with the rest. It happened to be a seat on the other side of James, and when the music was over, I presented him. 'Chester, this is Mr. James.' Chester, with a scant nod, for he had no social grace, said, 'Good evening, Mr. James,' and began to talk across him to me. Knowing that Chester admired his works with an enthusiasm that he rarely accorded anything other than music, my son and pink food, I added, 'Mr. Henry James, Chester'. He bounded up from his seat and shouted with excitement:

'What, not *the* Mr. James? Not the great Henry James?' offering his white-gloved hand in clumsy respect, eyes popping from his head.

From under benevolent eyebrows *the* Mr. James looked up and said soothingly, 'Take it gently, my good man, take it gently'.

Chester sat down.

191. Theodora Bosanquet on James and his readers

[1924]

Theodora Bosanquet, from *Henry James at Work*, 1924, 13–4 and 25–6.
These are two short passages from the famous Hogarth pamphlet by HJ's amanuensis. In the first she is discussing his preparation of the New York edition, and using a metaphor taken from the family.

. . . whatever the reason, their author certainly found it necessary to spend a good deal of time working on the earlier tales before he considered them fit for appearance in the company of those composed later. Some members of the elder family he entirely cast off, not counting them worth the expense of completely new clothes. Others he left in their place more from a necessary, though deprecated, respect for the declared taste of the reading public than because he loved them for their own sake. It would, for instance, have been difficult to exclude *Daisy Miller* from any representative collection of his work, yet the popularity of the tale had become almost a grievance. To be acclaimed as the author of *Daisy Miller* by persons blandly unconscious of *The Wings of the Dove* or *The Golden Bowl* was a reason among many for Henry James's despair of intelligent comprehension. Confronted repeatedly with *Daisy*, he felt himself rather in the position of some *grande dame* who, with a jewel-case of sparkling diamonds, is constrained by her admirers always to appear in the simple string of moonstones worn at her first dance.

* * *

Henry James was a voluminous letter-writer and exhaustively communicative in his talk upon every subject but one, his own work, which was his own real life. It was not because he was indifferent to what people thought of his books that he evaded discussion about them. He was always touched and pleased by any evidence that he had been intelligently read, but he never went a step out of his way to seek this assurance. He found it safest to assume that nobody read him, and he liked his friends none the worse for their incapacity. Meanwhile, the volumes of his published works—visible, palpable, readable proof of that unceasing travail of the creative spirit which was always labouring behind the barrier of his silence—piled themselves up year after year, to be dropped on to the tables of booksellers and pushed on to the shelves of libraries, to be bought and cherished by the faithful, ignored by the multitude, and treated as a test of mental endurance by the kind of person who organised the Browning Society. Fortunately for literature, Henry James did not lend himself to exploitation by any Jacobean Society. Instead of inventing riddles for prize students, he scattered about his pages a number of pregnant passages containing all the clues that are needed for keeping up with him. It was his theory that if readers didn't keep up with him—as they admittedly didn't always—the fault was entirely in their failure of attention. There are revelations in his books, just as he declared them to be in the works of Neil Paraday. 'Extract the opinion, disengage the answer—these are the real acts of homage.'

192. H. G. Wells's attack and parody in *Boon*

1915

H. G. Wells, from *Boon, The Mind of the Race, The Wild Asses of the Devil, and The Last Trump*, 1915, 101–28.

This book is supposed to consist of the papers of the late 'George Boon' edited by 'Reginald Bliss'; in fact it is a collection of Wells's views on all kinds of subjects in semi-conversational form. This extract is part of a chapter, 'Of Art, of Literature, of Mr Henry James' which was a late addition to the book, and is partly a response to HJ's articles on 'The Younger Generation' in *The Times Literary Supplement* (March and April 1914). The original text is diversified by some sketches of Mr. Blandish and Mutimer, and the dots indicating ellipsis are Wells's (or Bliss's) own. Readers of this collection may find it difficult to think that Wells had any freshly felt sense of cramping inadequacies in HJ—the most original thing about his criticism and parody being its quite extraordinarily bland lack of delicacy or consideration.

'. . . James has never discovered that a novel isn't a picture. . . . That life isn't a studio. . . .

'He wants a novel to be simply and completely *done*. He wants it to have a unity, he demands homogeneity. . . . Why *should* a book have that? For a picture it's reasonable, because you have to see it all at once. But there's no need to see a book all at once. It's like wanting to have a whole county done in one style and period of architecture. It's like insisting that a walking tour must stick to one valley. . . .

'But James *begins* by taking it for granted that a novel is a work of art that must be judged by its oneness. Judged first by its oneness. Some one gave him that idea in the beginning of things and he has never found it out. He doesn't find things out. He doesn't even seem to want to find things out. You can see that in him; he is eager to accept things—elaborately. You can see from his books that he accepts etiquettes, precedences, associations, claims. That is his peculiarity. He accepts very readily and then—elaborates. He has, I am convinced, one of the strongest, most abundant minds alive in the whole world, and he has the smallest penetration. Indeed, he has no penetration. He is the culmination of the Superficial type. Or else he would have gone into philosophy and been greater even than his wonderful brother. . . . But here he is, spinning about, like the most tremendous of water-boatmen—you know those insects?—kept up by surface tension. As if, when once he pierced the surface, he would drown. It's incredible. A water-boatman as big as an elephant. I was reading him only yesterday *The Golden Bowl*; it's dazzling how never for a moment does he go through.'

'Recently he's been explaining himself,' said Dodd.

'His "Notes on Novelists." It's one sustained demand for the picture effect. Which is the denial of the sweet complexity of life, of the pointing this way and that, of the spider on the throne. Philosophy aims at a unity and never gets there. . . . That true unity which we all suspect, and which no one attains, if it is to be got at all it is to be got by penetrating, penetrating down and through. The picture, on the other hand, is forced to a unity because it can see only one aspect at a time. I am doubtful even about that. Think of Hogarth or Carpaccio. But if the novel is to follow life it must be various and discursive. Life is diversity and entertainment, not completeness and satisfaction. All actions are half-hearted, shot delightfully with wandering thoughts— about something else. All true stories are a felt of irrelevances. But James sets out to make his novels with the presupposition that they can be made continuously relevant. And perceiving the discordant things, he tries to get rid of them. He sets himself to pick the straws out of the hair of Life before he paints her. But without the straws she is no longer the mad woman we love. He talks of "selection," and of making all of a novel definitely *about* a theme. He objects to a "saturation" that isn't oriented. And he objects, if you go into it, for no clear reason at all. Following up his conception of selection, see what in his own practice he omits. In practice James's selection becomes just omission and nothing more. He omits everything that demands digressive treatment or collateral statement. For example, he omits opinions. In all his novels you will find no people with defined political opinions, no people with religious opinions, none with clear partisanships or with lusts or whims, none definitely up to any specific impersonal thing. There are no poor people dominated by the imperatives of Saturday night and Monday morning, no dreaming types—and don't we all more or less live dream-ing? And none are ever decently forgetful. All that much of humanity he clears out before he begins his story. It's like cleaning rabbits for the table.

'But you see how relentlessly it follows from the supposition that the novel is a work of art aiming at pictorial unities!

'All art too acutely self-centred comes to this sort of thing. James's denatured people are only the equivalent in fiction of those egg-faced, black-haired ladies, who sit and sit, in the Japanese colour-prints, the unresisting stuff for an arrangement of blacks. . . .

'Then with the eviscerated people he has invented he begins to make up stories. What stories they are! Concentrated on suspicion, on a gift, on possessing a "piece" of old furniture, on what a little girl may or may not have noted in an emotional situation. These people cleared for artistic treatment never make lusty love, never go to angry war, never shout at an election or perspire at poker; never in any way *date*. . . . And upon the petty residuum of human interest left to them they focus minds of a Jamesian calibre. . . .

'The only living human motives left in the novels of Henry James are a certain avidity and an entirely superficial curiosity. Even when relations are irregular or when sins are hinted at, you feel that these are merely attitudes taken up, gambits before the game of attainment and over-perception begins. . . . His people nose out suspicions, hint by hint, link by link. Have you ever known living human beings do that? The thing his novel is *about* is always there. It is like a church lit but without a congregation to distract you, with every light and line focused on the high altar. And on the altar, very reverently placed, intensely there, is a dead kitten, an egg-shell, a bit of string. . . . Like his "Altar of the Dead," with nothing to the dead at all. . . . For if there was they couldn't all be candles and the effect would vanish. . . . And the elaborate, copious emptiness of the whole Henry James exploit is only redeemed and made endurable by the elaborate, copious wit. Upon the desert his selection has made Henry James erects palatial metaphors. . . . The chief fun, the only exercise, in reading Henry James is this clambering over vast metaphors. . . .

'Having first made sure that he has scarcely anything left to express, he then sets to work to express it, with an industry, a wealth of intel-lectual stuff that dwarfs Newton. He spares no resource in the telling of his dead inventions. He brings up every device of language to state and define. Bare verbs he rarely tolerates. He splits his infinitives and

fills them up with adverbial stuffing. He presses the passing colloquialism into his service. His vast paragraphs sweat and struggle; they
could not sweat and elbow and struggle more if God Himself was the
processional meaning to which they sought to come. And all for
tales of nothingness. . . . It is leviathan retrieving pebbles. It is a
magnificent but painful hippopotamus resolved at any cost, even at the
cost of its dignity, upon picking up a pea which has got into a corner of
its den. Most things, it insists, are beyond it, but it can, at any rate,
modestly, and with an artistic singleness of mind, pick up that pea. . . .'
[New Section]
'A little while ago,' said Boon, suddenly struggling with his trouser
pocket and producing some pieces of paper, 'I sketched out a novel,
and as it was rather in the manner of Henry James I think perhaps you
might be interested by it now. So much, that is, as there is of it. It is to
be called *The Spoils of Mr. Blandish*, and it is all about this particular
business of the selective life. Mr. Blandish, as I saw him, was pretty
completely taken from the James ideal. . . . He was a man with an
exquisite apprehension of particulars, with just that sense of there being
a rightness attainable, a fitness, a charm, a finish. . . . In any little
affair. . . . He believed that in speech and still more that in writing
there was an inevitable right word, in actions great and small a mel-
lowed etiquette, in everything a possible perfection. He was, in fact,
the very soul of Henry James—as I understand it. . . .

'He didn't marry, he didn't go upon adventures; lust, avarice,
ambition, all these things that as Milton says are to be got "not without
dust and heat," were not for him. Blood and dust and heat—he ruled
them out. But he had independent means, he could live freely and
delicately and charmingly, he could travel and meet and be delighted
by all the best sorts of people in the best sorts of places. So for years he
enriched his resonances, as an admirable violin grows richer with every
note it sounds. He went about elaborately, avoiding ugliness, death,
suffering, industrialism, politics, sport, the thought of war, the red blaze
of passion. He travelled widely in the more settled parts of the world.
Chiefly he visited interesting and ancient places, putting his ever more
exquisite sensorium at them, consciously taking delicate impressions
upon the refined wax of his being. In a manner most carefully
occasional, he wrote. Always of faded places. His *Ypres* was wonderful.
His *Bruges* and his *Hour of Van Eyk*. . . .

'Such,' said Boon, 'is the hero. The story begins, oh! quite in the
James manner with——' He read—

' "At times it seemed inaccessible, a thing beyond hope, beyond imagining, and then at times it became so concrete an imagination, a desire so specific, so nearly expressed, as to grow if not to the exact particulars of longitude and latitude, yet at any rate so far as county and district and atmosphere were concerned, so far indeed as an intuition of proximity was concerned, an intimation that made it seem at last at certain moments as if it could not possibly be very much farther than just round the corner or over the crest. . . ."

'But I've left a good bit of that to write up. In the book there will be pages and sheets of that sentence. The gist is that Mr. Blandish wants a house to live in and that he has an idea of the kind of house he wants. And the chapter, the long, unresting, progressing chapter, expands and expands; it never jumps you forward, it never lets you off, you can't skip and you can't escape, until there comes at last a culminating distension of statement in which you realize more and more clearly, until you realize it with the unforgettable certainty of a thing long fought for and won at last, that Mr. Blandish has actually come upon the house and with a vigour of decision as vivid as a flash of lightning in a wilderness of troubled clouds, as vivid indeed as the loud, sonorous bursting of a long blown bladder, has said "*This is it!*" On that "*This is it*" my chapter ends, with an effect of enormous relief, with something of the beautiful serenity that follows a difficult parturition.

'The story is born.

'And then we leap forward to possession.

' "And here he was, in the warmest reality, in the very heart of the materialization of his dream——" He has, in fact, got the house. For a year or so from its first accidental discovery he had done nothing but just covet the house; too fearful of an overwhelming disappointment even to make a definite inquiry as to its accessibility. But he has, you will gather, taken apartments in the neighbourhood, thither he visits frequently, and almost every day when he walks abroad the coveted house draws him. It is in a little seaside place on the east coast, and the only available walks are along the shore or inland across the golf-links. Either path offers tempting digressions towards *it*. He comes to know it from a hundred aspects and under a thousand conditions of light and atmosphere. . . . And while still in the early stage he began a curious and delicious secret practice in relationship. You have heard of the Spaniard in love, in love with a woman he had seen but once, whom he might never see again, a princess, etiquette-defended, a goddess, and who yet, seeing a necklace that became her, bought it for the joy of owning something that was at least by fitness hers. Even so did Mr. Blandish begin to buy first one little article and then, the fancy growing upon him more and more, things, "pieces" they call them, that were in the vein of Samphire House. And then came the day, the wonderful day, when as he took his afternoon feast of the eye, the door opened, some one came out towards him. . . .

'It was incredible. They were giving him tea with hot, inadvisable scones—but their hotness, their close heaviness, he accepted with a ready devotion, would have accepted had they been ten times as hot and close and heavy, not heedlessly, indeed, but gratefully, willingly paying his price for these astonishing revelations that without an effort, serenely, calmly, dropped in between her gentle demands whether he would have milk and her mild inquiries as to the exact quantity of sugar his habits and hygienic outlook demanded, that his hostess so casually made. These generous, heedless people were talking of departures, of abandonments, of, so they put it, selling the dear old place, if indeed any one could be found to buy a place so old and so remote and— she pointed her intention with a laugh—so very, very dear. Repletion of scones were a small price to pay for such a glowing, such an incredible gift of opportunity, thrust thus straight into the willing, amazed hands. . . .

'He gets the house. He has it done up. He furnishes it, and every article of furniture seems a stroke of luck too good to be true. And to crown it all I am going to write one of those long crescendo passages that James loves, a sentence, pages of it, of happy event linking to happy event until at last the incredible completion, a butler, unquestion-ably Early Georgian, respectability, competence equally unquestionable, a wife who could cook, and cook well, no children, no thought or possibility of children, and to crown all, the perfect name—Mutimer!

'All this you must understand is told retrospectively as Blandish installs himself in Samphire House. It is told to the refrain, "Still, fresh every morning, came the persuasion 'This is too good to be true'." And as it is told, something else, by the most imperceptible degrees, by a gathering up of hints and allusions and pointing details, gets itself told too, and that is the growing realization in the mind of Blandish of a something extra, of something not quite bargained for,—the hoard and the haunting. About the house hangs a presence. . . .

'He had taken it at first as a mere picturesque accessory to the whole picturesque and delightful wreathing of association and tradition about the place, that there should be this ancient flavour of the cutlass and the keg, this faint aroma of buried doubloons and Stevensonian experiences. He had assumed, etc. . . . He had gathered, etc. . . . And it was in the most imperceptible manner that beyond his sense of these takings and assumptions and gatherings there grew his perception that the delicate quiver of appreciation, at first his utmost tribute to these illegal and adventurous and sanguinary associations, was broadening and strengthening, was, one hardly knew whether to say developing or degenerating, into a nervous reaction, more spinal and less equivocally agreeable, into the question, sensed rather than actually thought or asked, whether in fact the place didn't in certain lights and certain aspects and at certain unfavourable moments come near to evoking the ghost— if such sorites are permissible in the world of delicate shades—of the ghost, of the ghost of a shiver—of *aversion*. . . .

'And so at page a hundred and fifty or thereabouts we begin to get into the story,' said Boon.

'You wade through endless marshes of subtle intimation, to a sense of a Presence in Samphire House. For a number of pages you are quite unable to tell whether this is a ghost or a legend or a foreboding or simply old-fashioned dreams that are being allusively placed before you. But there is an effect piled up very wonderfully, of Mr. Blandish, obsessed, uneasy, watching furtively and steadfastly his guests, his callers, his domestics, continually asking himself, "Do they note it? Are they feeling it?"

'We break at last into incidents. A young friend of the impossible name of Deshman helps evolve the story; he comes to stay; he seems to feel the influence from the outset, he cannot sleep, he wanders about the house. . . . Do others know? *Others?* . . . The gardener takes to revisiting the gardens after nightfall. He is met in the shrubbery with an unaccountable spade in his hand and answers huskily. Why should a gardener carry a spade? Why should he answer huskily? Why should the presence, the doubt, the sense of something else elusively in the air about them, become intensified at the encounter? Oh! conceivably of course in many places, but just *there*! As some sort of protection, it may be. . . . Then suddenly as Mr. Blandish sits at his lonely but beautifully served dinner he becomes aware for the first time of a change in Mutimer.

'Something told him in that instant that Mutimer also *knew*. . . .

'Deshman comes again with a new and disconcerting habit of tapping the panelling and measuring the thickness of the walls when he thinks no one is looking, and then a sister of Mr. Blandish and a friend, a woman, yet not so much a woman as a disembodied intelligence in a feminine costume with one of those impalpable relationships with Deshman that people have with one another in the world of Henry James, an association of shadows, an atmospheric liaison. Follow some almost sentenceless conversations. Mr. Blandish walks about the shrubbery with the friend, elaborately getting at it—whatever it is—and in front of them, now hidden by the yew hedges, now fully in view, walks Deshman with the married and settled sister of Mr. Blandish. . . .

'"So," said Mr. Blandish, pressing the point down towards the newly discovered sensitiveness, "where we feel, he it seems *knows*."

'She seemed to consider.

'"He doesn't know completely," was her qualification.

'"But he has something—something tangible."

'"If he can make it tangible."

'On that the mind of Mr. Blandish played for a time.

'"Then it isn't altogether tangible yet?"

'"It isn't tangible enough for him to go upon."

'"Definitely something."

'Her assent was mutely concise.

'"That we on our part——?"

'The *we* seemed to trouble her.

'"He knows more than you do," she yielded.

'The gesture, the half turn, the momentary halt in the paces of Mr. Blandish, plied her further.

'"More, I think, than he has admitted—to any one."

'"Even to you?"

'He perceived an interesting wave of irritation. "Even to me," he had wrung from her, but at the price of all further discussion.

'Putting the thing crassly,' said Boon, 'Deshman has got wind of a hoard, of a treasure, of something—Heaven as yet only knows what something—buried, imbedded, in some as yet unexplained way incorporated with Samphire House. On the whole the stress lies rather on treasure, the treasure of smuggling, of longshore practices, of illegality on the high seas. And still clearer is it that the amiable Deshman wants to get at it without the participation of Mr. Blandish. Until the very end you are never quite satisfied why Deshman wants to get at it in so private a fashion. As the plot thickens you are played about between the conviction that Deshman wants the stuff for himself and the firm belief of the lady that against the possible intervention of the Treasury, he wants to secure it for Mr. Blandish, to secure it at least generously if nefariously, lest perhaps it should fall under the accepted definition and all the consequent confiscations of treasure trove. And there are further beautiful subtleties as to whether she really believes in this more kindly interpretation of the refined but dubitable Deshman. . . . A friend of Deshman's, shameless under the incredible name of Mimbleton, becomes entangled in this thick, sweet flow of narrative—the James method of introducing a character always reminds me of going round with the lantern when one is treacling for moths. Mimbleton has energy. He presses. Under a summer dawn of delicious sweetness Mimbleton is found insensible on the croquet lawn by Mr. Blandish, who, like most of the characters in the narrative from first to last, has been unable to sleep. And at the near corner of the house, close to a never before remarked ventilator, is a hastily and inaccurately refilled excavation. . . .

'Then events come hurrying in a sort of tangled haste—making sibyl-like gestures.

'At the doorway Mutimer appears—swaying with some profound emotion. He is still in his evening attire. He has not yet gone to bed. In spite of the dawn he carried a burning candle—obliquely. At the sight of his master he withdraws—backwards and with difficulty. . . .

'Then,' said Boon, 'I get my crowning chapter: the breakfast, a peculiar *something*, something almost palpable in the atmosphere—Deshman hoarse and a little talkative, Mimbleton with a possibly nervous headache, husky also and demanding tea in a thick voice, Mutimer waiting uneasily, and Mr. Blandish, outwardly calm, yet noting every particular, thinking meanings into every word and movement, and growing more and more clear in his conviction that *Mutimer knows— knows everything*. . . .

'Book two opens with Mr. Blandish practically in possession of the facts. Putting the thing coarsely, the treasure is—1813 brandy, in considerable quantities bricked up in a disused cellar of Samphire House. Samphire House, instead of being the fine claret of a refuge Mr. Blandish supposed, is a loaded port. But of course in the novel we shall not put things coarsely, and for a long time you will be by no means clear what the "spirit" is that Mr. Blandish is now resolved to exorcise. He is, in fact, engaged in trying to get that brandy away, trying to de-alcoholize his existence, trying—if one must put the thing in all the concrete crudity of his fundamental intention—to sell the stuff. . . .

'Now in real life you would just go and sell it. But people in the novels of Henry James do not do things in the inattentive, offhand, rather confused, and partial way of reality: they bring enormous brains to bear upon the minutest particulars of existence. Mr. Blandish, following the laws of that world, has not simply to sell his brandy: he has to sell it subtly, intricately, interminably, with a delicacy, with a dignity....

'He consults friends—impalpable, intricate, inexhaustible friends.

'There are misunderstandings. One old and trusted intimate concludes rather hastily that Mr. Blandish is confessing that he has written a poem, another that he is making a proposal of marriage, another that he wishes an introduction to the secretary of the Psychical Research Society. . . . All this,' said Boon, 'remains, perhaps, indefinitely to be worked out. Only the end, the end, comes with a rush. Deshman has found for him—one never gets nearer to it than the "real right people". The real right people send their agent down, a curious blend of gentleman and commercial person he is, to investigate, to verify, to estimate quantities. Ultimately he will—shall we say it?—make an offer. With a sense of immense culmination the reader at last approaches the hoard. . . .

'You are never told the thing exactly. It is by indefinable suggestions, by exquisite approaches and startings back, by circumlocution the most delicate, that your mind at last shapes its realization, that—the last drop of the last barrel has gone and that Mutimer, the butler, lies dead or at least helpless—in the inner cellar. And a beautiful flavour, ripe and yet rare, rich without opulence, hangs—*diminuendo morendo*—in the air. . . .'

193. James on *Boon*

1915

HJ to Wells, July 1915 (LJ, ii, 503–5).
A reply to Wells's gift of a copy of *Boon*.

I was given yesterday at a club your volume *Boon, etc.*, from a loose leaf in which I learn that you kindly sent it me and which yet appears to have lurked there for a considerable time undelivered. I have just been reading, to acknowledge it intelligently, a considerable number of its pages—though not all; for, to be perfectly frank, I have been in that respect beaten for the first time—or rather for the first time but one— by a book of yours; I haven't found the current of it draw me on and on this time—as, unfailingly and irresistibly, before (which I have repeatedly let you know.) However, I shall try again—I hate to lose any scrap of you that *may* make for light or pleasure; and meanwhile I have more or less mastered your appreciation of H. J., which I have found very curious and interesting after a fashion—though it has naturally not filled me with a fond elation. It is difficult of course for a writer to put himself *fully* in the place of another writer who finds him extraordinarily futile and void, and who is moved to publish that to the world—and I think the case isn't easier when he happens to have enjoyed the other writer enormously from far back; because there has then grown up the habit of taking some common meeting-ground between them for granted, and the falling away of this is like the collapse of a bridge which made communication possible. But I am by nature more in dread of any fool's paradise, or at least of any bad misguidedness, than in love with the idea of a security proved, and the fact that a mind as brilliant as yours *can* resolve me into such an unmitigated mistake, can't enjoy me in anything like the degree in which I like to think I may be enjoyed, makes me greatly want to fix myself, for as long as my nerves will stand it, with such a pair of eyes. I am aware of certain things I have, and not less conscious, I believe, of various others that I am simply reduced to wish I did or could have; so I try, for possible light, to enter into the feelings of a critic for whom the deficiencies so

527

preponderate. The difficulty about that effort, however, is that one can't keep it up—one *has* to fall back on one's sense of one's good parts— one's own sense; and I at least should have to do that, I think, even if your picture were painted with a more searching brush. For I should otherwise seem to forget what it is that my poetic and my appeal to experience rest upon. They rest upon *my* measure of fulness—fulness of life and of the projection of it, which seems to you such an emptiness of both. I don't mean to say I don't wish I could do twenty things I can't— many of which you do so livingly; but I confess I ask myself what would become in that case of some of those to which I am most addicted and by which interest seems to me most beautifully producible. I hold that interest may be, *must* be, exquisitely made and created, and that if we don't make it, we who undertake to, nobody and nothing will make it for us; though nothing is more possible, nothing may even be more certain, that that my quest of it, my constant wish to run it to earth, may entail the sacrifice of certain things that are not on the straight line of it. However, there are too many things to say, and I don't think your chapter is really inquiring enough to entitle you to expect all of them. The fine thing about the fictional form to me is that it opens such widely different windows of attention; but that is just why I like the window so to frame the play and the process!

194. James on Wells's apology for *Boon*

1915

HJ to Wells, July 1915 (LJ, ii, 506–8).
A reply to Wells's letter of explanation (which, together with the material reprinted here, may be found in *Henry James and H. G. Wells. A Record of their Friendship, their Debate on the Art of Fiction, and their Quarrel*, ed. Leon Edel and Gordon N. Ray, 1958).

I am bound to tell you that I don't think your letter makes out any sort of case for the bad manners of *Boon*, as far as your indulgence in them at the expense of your poor old H. J. is concerned—I say 'your' simply because he has *been* yours, in the most liberal, continual, sacrificial, the most admiring and abounding critical way, ever since he began to know your writings: as to which you have had copious testimony. Your comparison of the book to a waste-basket strikes me as the reverse of felicitous, for what one throws into that receptacle is exactly what one doesn't commit to publicity and make the affirmation of one's estimate of one's contemporaries by. I should liken it much rather to the preservative portfolio or drawer in which what is withheld from the basket is savingly laid away. Nor do I feel it anywhere evident that my 'view of life and literature,' or what you impute to me as such, is carrying everything before it and becoming a public menace—so unaware do I seem, on the contrary, that my products constitute an example in any measurable degree followed or a cause in any degree successfully pleaded: I can't but think that if this were the case I should find it somewhat attested in their circulation—which, alas, I have reached a very advanced age in the entirely defeated hope of. But I *have* no view of life and literature, I maintain, other than that our form of the latter in especial is admirable exactly by its range and variety, its plasticity and liberality, its fairly living on the sincere and shifting experience of the individual practitioner. That is why I have always so admired your so free and strong application of it, the particular rich receptacle of intelligences and impressions emptied out with an energy of its own, that your genius constitutes; and *that* is in particular why, in my letter of two or three days since, I pronounced it curious and interesting that you should find the case I constitute myself only ridiculous and vacuous to the extent of your having to proclaim your sense of it. The curiosity and the interest, however, in this latter connection are of course for my mind those of the break of perception (perception of the veracity of *my* variety) on the part of a talent so generally inquiring and apprehensive as yours. Of course for myself I live, live intensely and am fed by life, and my value, whatever it be, is in my own kind of expression of that. Therefore I am pulled up to wonder by the fact that for you my kind (my sort of sense of expression and sort of sense of life alike) doesn't exist; and that wonder is, I admit, a disconcerting comment on my idea of the various appreciability of our addiction to the novel and of all the personal and intellectual history, sympathy and curiosity, behind the given example of it. It is when that history and curiosity have been determined in the way most different from my own that I want to get at them—precisely *for* the extension of life, which is the novel's best gift. But that is another matter. Meanwhile I absolutely dissent from the claim that there are any differences whatever in the amenability to art of forms of literature aesthetically determined, and hold your distinction between a form that is (like) painting and a form that is (like) architecture for wholly null and void. There is no sense in which architecture is aesthetically 'for use' that doesn't leave any other art whatever exactly as much so; and so far from that of literature being irrelevant to the literary report upon life, and to its being made as interesting as possible, I regard it as relevant in a degree that leaves everything else behind. It is art that *makes* life, makes interest, makes importance, for our consideration and application of these things, and I know of no substitute whatever for the force and beauty of its process. If I were Boon I should say that any pretence of such a substitute is helpless and hopeless humbug; but I wouldn't be Boon for the world, and am only yours faithfully . . .

195. James on the New York edition, on *The Bostonians*, and on the destruction of the 'plates' of his novels

1915

HJ to Edmund Goose, August 1915 (LJ, ii, 514–6).
Gosse had written praising *The Bostonians* and urging its inclusion in the New York edition (c.f. No. 185); HJ's reply is vital in assessing the final effects of his reception.

I am really more overcome than I can say by your having been able to indulge in such freedom of mind and grace of speculation, during these dark days, on behalf of my poor old rather truncated edition, in fact entirely frustrated one—which has the grotesque likeness for me of a sort of miniature Ozymandias of Egypt ('look on my *works*, ye mighty, and despair!')—round which the lone and level sands stretch further away than ever. It *is* indeed consenting to be waved aside a little into what was once blest literature to so much as answer the question you are so handsomely impelled to make—but my very statement about the matter can only be, alas, a melancholy, a blighted confusion. That Edition has been, from the point of view of profit either to the publishers or to myself, practically a complete failure; vaguely speaking, it doesn't sell—that is, my annual report of what it does—the whole 24 vols.—in this country amounts to about £25 from the Macmillans; and the ditto from the Scribners in the U.S. to very little more. I am past all praying for anywhere; I remain at my age (which you know,) and after my long career, utterly, insurmountably, unsaleable. And the original preparation of that collective and selective series involved really the extremity of labour—all my 'earlier' things—of which the *Bostonians* would have been, if included, one—were so intimately and interestingly revised. The edition is from that point of view really a monument (like Ozymandias) which has never had the least intelligent critical justice done it—or any sort of critical attention at all paid it—and the artistic problem involved in my scheme was a deep and exquisite one, and moreover was, as I held, very effectively solved. Only it took such time—*and* such taste—in other words such aesthetic light. No more commercially thankless job of the literary order was (Prefaces and all —*they* of a thanklessness!) accordingly ever achieved. The immediate inclusion of the *Bostonians* was rather deprecated by the publishers (the Scribners, who were very generally and in a high degree appreciative: I make no complaint of them at all!)—and there were reasons for which I also wanted to wait: we always meant that that work should eventually come in. Revision of it loomed peculiarly formidable and time-consuming (for intrinsic reasons,) and as other things were more pressing and more promptly feasible I allowed it to stand over—with the best intentions, and also in company with a small number more of provisional omissions. But by the time it *had* stood over, disappointment had set in; the undertaking had begun to announce itself as a virtual failure, and we stopped short where we were—that is when a couple of dozen volumes were out. From that moment, some seven or eight years ago, nothing whatever has been added to the series—and there is little enough appearance now that there will ever. Your good impression of the *Bostonians* greatly moves me—the thing was no success whatever on publication in the Century (where it came out,) and the late R. W. Gilder, of that periodical, wrote me at the time that they had never published anything that appeared so little to interest their readers. I felt about it myself then that it was probably rather a remarkable feat of objectivity—but I never was very thoroughly happy about it, and seem to recall that I found the subject and the material, after I had got launched in it, under some illusion, less interesting and repaying than I had assumed it to be. All the same I *should* have liked to review it for the Edition—it would have come out a much truer and more curious thing (it was meant to be curious from the first;) but there can be no question of that, or of the proportionate Preface to have been written with it, at present—or probably ever within my span of life. Apropos of which matters I at this moment hear from Heinemann that four or five of my books that he has have quite (entirely) ceased to sell and that he must break up the plates. Of course he must; I have nothing to say against it; and the things in question are mostly all in the Edition. But such is 'success'! I should have liked to write that Preface to the *Bostonians*—which will never be written now. But think of noting now that *that* is a thing that has perished!

196. Anthony Hope on James as man and writer

1916

Anthony Hope from his diary, February 1916 (Sir Charles Mallet, *Anthony Hope and his Books*, 1935, 230).

Anthony Hope Hawkins (1863–1933) (the Christian names were used as a *nom de plume*) was, of course, the popular novelist of Ruritania.

This morning news of Henry James's death, a dear old fellow, a great gentleman, kindly, modest, always seeming a little upset by the noise of this world. . . . The critics call him a 'great novelist': I can't think that. He had *a great subtlety*, but in the end, I think, fell a victim to it in thought as well as in language. I believe his fate is to be not a possession but a hobby. However, it's something to be that. *Moriturus te non omnino moriturum saluto*—with real affection and respect.

197. Mrs. Humphry Ward on James as a great man and a great master

1918

Mrs. Humphry Ward, from *A Writer's Recollections*, 1918, 332–6. Mrs. Ward (1851–1920) was a novelist and social worker of distinction, now best remembered for *Robert Elsmere* (1888). The extract begins with her recollection of hearing the news of HJ's death, and with a quotation from 'The Youth of Nature' by her uncle, Matthew Arnold.

Yes!—

> . . . He was a priest to us all
> Of the wonder and bloom of the world,
> Which we saw with his eyes and were glad.

For that was indeed true of Henry James, as of Wordsworth. The 'wonder and bloom,' no less than the ugly or heart-breaking things, which like the disfiguring rags of old Laertes, hide them from us—he could weave them all, with an untiring hand, into the many-coloured web of his art. Olive Chancellor, Madame Mauve, Milly, in *The Wings of a Dove*—the most exquisite in some ways of all his women—Roderick Hudson, St. George, the woman doctor in the *Bostonians*, the French family in the *Reverberation*, Brooksmith—and innumerable others:—it was the wealth and facility of it all that was so amazing! There is enough observation of character in a chapter of the *Bostonians*, a story he thought little of, and did not include in his collected edition, to shame a Wells novel of the newer sort, with its floods of clever half-considered journalism in the guise of conversation, hiding an essential poverty of creation. *Ann Veronica* and the *New Machiavelli*, and several other tales by the same writer, set practically the same scene, and handle the same characters under different names. Of an art so false and confused, Henry James could never have been capable. His people, his situations, have the sharp separateness—and something of the inexhaustibleness—of nature, which does not mix her moulds.

534

As to method, naturally I often discussed with him some of the difficult problems of presentation. The posthumous sketches of work in progress, published since his death, show how he delighted in these problems, in their very difficulties, in their endless opportunities. As he often said to me, he could never read a novel that interested him without taking it mentally to pieces, and re-writing it in his own way. Some of his letters to me are brilliant examples of this habit of his. Technique—presentation—were then immensely important to him; important as they never could have been to Tolstoy, who probably thought very little consciously about them. Mr. James, as we all know, thought a great deal about them, sometimes, I venture to think, too much. In *The Wings of a Dove*, for instance, a subject full of beauty and tragedy is almost spoilt by an artificial technique, which is responsible for a scene on which, as it seems to me, the whole illusion of the book is shattered. The conversation in the Venice apartment where the two *fiancés*—one of whom at least, the man, is commended to our sympathy as a decent and probable human being—make their cynical bargain in the very presence of the dying Milly, for whose money they are plotting, is in some ways a *tour de force* of construction. It is the central point on which many threads converge, and from which many depart. But to my mind, as I have said, it invalidates the story. Mr. James is here writing as a *virtuoso*, and not as the great artist we know him to be. And the same, I think, is true of *The Golden Bowl*. That again is a wonderful exercise in virtuosity; but a score of his slighter sketches seem to me infinitely nearer to the truth and vitality of great art. The book, in which perhaps technique and life are most perfectly blended —at any rate among the later novels—is *The Ambassador*. There, the skill with which a deeply interesting subject is focussed from many points of view, but always with the fascinating unity given to it, both by the personality of the 'Ambassador', and by the mystery to which every character in the book is related, is kept in its place, the servant, not the master, of the theme. And the climax—which is the river scene, when the 'Ambassador' penetrates at last the long kept secret of the lovers—is as right as it is surprising, and sinks away through admirable modulations to the necessary close. And what beautiful things in the course of the handling!—the old French Academician and his garden, on the *rive gauche*, for example; or the summer afternoon on the upper Seine, with its pleasure-boats, and the red parasol which finally tells all—a picture drawn with the sparkle and truth of a Daubigny, only the better to bring out the unwelcome fact which is its centre. *The Ambassador* is the

535

master-piece of Mr. James's later work and manner, just as *The Portrait of a Lady* is the masterpiece of the earlier.

And the whole?—his final place?—when the stars of his generation rise into their place above the spent field? I, at least, have no doubt whatever about his security of fame; though very possibly he may be no more generally read in the time to come than are most of the other great masters of literature. Personally, I regret that, from *What Maisie Knew* onwards, he adopted the method of dictation. A mind so teeming, and an art so flexible, were surely the better for the slight curb imposed by the physical toil of writing. I remember how and when we first discussed the *pros* and *cons* of dictation, on the fell above Cartmel Chapel, when he was with us at Levens in 1887. He was then enchanted by the endless vistas of work and achievement which the new method seemed to open out. And indeed it is plain that he produced more with it than he could have produced without it. Also, that in the use of dictation as in everything else, he showed himself the extraordinary craftsman that he was, to whom all difficulty was a challenge, and the conquest of it a delight. Still, the diffuseness and over-elaboration which were the natural snares of his astonishing gifts were encouraged rather than checked by the new method; and one is jealous of anything whatever that may tend to stand between him and the unstinted pleasure of those to come after.

But when these small cavils are done, one returns in delight and wonder to the accomplished work. To the *wealth* of it above all—the deep draughts from human life that it represents. It is true indeed that there are large tracts of modern existence which Mr. James scarcely touches, the peasant life, the industrial life, the small trading life, the political life; though it is clear that he divined them all, enough at least for his purposes. But in his vast, indeterminate range of busy or leisured folk, men and women with breeding and without it, backed with ancestors or merely the active 'sons of their works,' young girls and youths and children, he is a master indeed, and there is scarcely anything in human feeling, normal or strange, that he cannot describe or suggest. If he is without passion, as some are ready to declare, so are Stendhal and Turguéniev, and half the great masters of the novel; and if he seems sometimes to evade the tragic or rapturous moments, it is perhaps only that he may make his reader his co-partner, that he may evoke from us that heat of sympathy and intelligence which supplies the necessary atmosphere for the subtler and greater kinds of art.

And all through, the dominating fact is that it is 'Henry James' speaking—Henry James, with whose delicate, ironic mind and most human heart we are in contact. There is much that can be *learnt* in fiction; the resources of mere imitation, which we are pleased to call realism, are endless; we see them in scores of modern books. But at the root of every book is the personality of the man who wrote it. And in the end, that decides.

198. Henry Newbolt on James's amusing lack of talent

1920

Henry Newbolt to Lady Hylton, April 1920 (*The Later Life and Letters of Sir Henry Newbolt*, ed. Margaret Newbolt, 1942, 270). Newbolt (1862–1938) was a patriotic and Christian poet, and an expert on naval affairs. For the de la Mare article see *Times Literary Supplement*, April 1920, 951, 217–8.

I suppose you've read de la Mare in the *Lit. Supp.* on Henry James? Quite good, I thought, and it interests me to see that he makes a great man of Henry not exactly on the littery side but on the *moral*—a 'dark splendour' of expressed *goodness* seems to be the idea. I daresay that's all right, but it doesn't exactly explain to me *my* puzzle—the great attractiveness of Henry in life and to some extent on paper, combined so incredibly with a lack of all the possible artistic gifts. . . . He had an *idea*—the idea of extending the boundaries of the novelist—but it was a purely intellectual idea and when he called on his aesthetic self to put it into an artistic product the response was muddled and sapless. He believed in method as much as any German: I mean he believed you can make Ersatz intuitions out of thought and industry: a blasphemous notion. But what fun it was to see him trying to milk his own mind while the company stood by holding out their caps for the drink—the fun really compensated us for the good stuff which was always coming and never came.

199. W. D. Howells on American unkindness to James

1920

Howells, from an essay he was working on just before his death, May 1920 (LH, ii, 396–7).
His remarks were prompted by Percy Lubbock's edition of HJ's *Letters* (LJ).

He ignores the cause of James's going to live abroad which was that he was a sick man who was less of a sufferer in Europe than in America. . . . The climate was kinder to him than ours, and the life was kinder than his native life, and his native land. In fact America was never kind to James. It was rude and harsh, unworthily and stupidly so, as we must more and more own, if we would be true to ourselves. We ought to be ashamed of our part in this; the nearest of his friends in Boston would say they liked him, but they could not bear his fiction; and from the people, conscious of culture, throughout New England, especially the women, he had sometimes outright insult. At the same time his work unanimously found favour with editors who eagerly sought it in all the leading periodicals. The case was not very different in England when he went to live there except that the popular rejection and contumely which met it were neither so vicious nor so general. But a public grew up in Europe such as never grew up in America, and made England more like home to him.

The following is a list of the critical and other documents that are important to an understanding of James's reception and his response to it, but which have not been reprinted above (see Introduction, Section 1).

I. WORKS

James's fiction contains the most eloquent and comprehensive evidence of his view of his situation as a writer. It also dramatizes his feelings and insights, generated by that situation, concerning the ideal and actual relations of artists to their publics. I find it unique, inside or outside of fiction, for the sustained generosity and intelligence of its treatment of this subject, in spite of the fact that it was increasingly coloured by a reaction to the deficiencies of his own reception. The following works seem to me the most illustrative.

Novels: Roderick Hudson (1875), *The Tragic Muse* (1890); *Stories* 'The Madonna of the Future' (1873), 'Benvolio' (1875), 'The Author of "Beltraffio" ' (1884), 'The Lesson of the Master' (1888), 'Nona Vincent' (1892), 'The Private Life' (1892), 'The Real Thing' (1892), 'Greville Fane' (1892), 'The Middle Years' (1893), 'The Death of the Lion' (1894), 'The Coxon Fund' (1894), 'The Next Time' (1895), 'The Figure in the Carpet' (1896), 'John Delavoy' (1898), 'The Great Good Place' (1900), 'The Tree of Knowledge' (1900), 'Broken Wings' (1900), 'The Birthplace' (1903). Even the dates of these acquire significance when compared with the external facts of James's reception (the intense concentration on the subject in the early 1890's, the mellower, but still bitter, revival about 1900 after the poor English reception and tiny sale of *The Awkward Age*). In particular it is not always fully recognized that he was led to formulate some really radical ideas, as a way, presumably, of accounting to himself for the unsatisfactoriness of his position. Consider, for example, the tendency in the stories from 'The Lesson of the Master' onwards to suggest a straightforward negative equation between real artistic distinction discernible to the few, and conventional and financial success. In the late stories the two simply cannot go together, as is exemplified in the almost mechanical symmetry of the plot of 'The Next Time'. Or again, there is a complete reversal of accepted attitudes in the greatest of his fictions on this subject, *The Tragic Muse*. Here the conflict is explicitly 'between art and "the world" '. The artist of integrity has become something of a modern hero, but we should recall that the traditional dilemma—and the traditional duty—are almost the reverse of Nick Dormer's. Noble sacrifices are conventionally made in favour of Love or Public Affairs or perhaps Family—or at least the tension depends on the interrelations of these. But Nick sacrifices them all for art. Normally it is Peter Sherringham's refusal to give up his career for the life of 'art' with Miriam which would be seen as strength. But it is seen as a rather shameful compromise, which is all the more striking in view of the dubious nature of the artistic life renounced. James's treatment is a drastic variation on the classic pattern.

2. PERSONAL DOCUMENTS

There are various personal documents of obvious importance, which I have used sparingly, if at all, in the collection. The chief sources are:

The Letters of Henry James, ed. Percy Lubbock, 1920.

The James Family, F. O. Matthiessen, New York, 1947.

The Notebooks of Henry James, ed. F. O. Matthiessen and K. B. Murdock, New York, 1947.

Henry James and Robert Louis Stevenson: a Record of Friendship and Criticism, ed. Janet Adam Smith, 1948.

Thomas Sergeant Perry, Virginia Harlow, Durham N.C., 1950.

Selected Letters of Henry James, ed. Leon Edel, 1956.

There are, of course, many other minor sources. I would particularly recommend that the reader should follow up the fascinating relationship between William and Henry James which is documented in *The James Family*. And he might also consider the evidence of many passages in the *Notebooks* which more and more resemble, as the years advance, a kind of internal dialogue, creating an intelligent listener in default of any other.

3. JAMES'S CRITICISM

James's criticism is also very illuminating. The main, and most personal, source for his pessimistic view of his own readers (but also a soon frustrated act of faith in his having some) are the prefaces to the New York edition, collected as *The Art of the Novel* (a misleading title) by R. P. Blackmur, New York, 1934. But many earlier essays are just as valuable, in particular 'The Art of Fiction' (1884) and 'Criticism' (1891).

Both of these are reprinted in Morris Shapira's useful *Henry James. Selected Literary Criticism*, 1963. And there are a number of other collections.

4. OTHER CRITICISM

Of the criticism of contemporaries perhaps the greatest single omission is Ezra Pound's essay 'Henry James' which appeared in the *Little Review* for August 1918 and is reprinted in *Literary Essays of Ezra Pound*, ed. T. S. Eliot, 1954. I find many of Pound's particular judgements highly questionable, but in the context of a mass of pious and uninteresting obituary his protest against the current view of James does the highest honour to his concern for literature:

I am tired of hearing pettiness talked about Henry James's style. . . . I have heard no word of the major James, of the hater of tyranny [of] the passion of it, the continual passion of it in this man who, fools said, didn't 'feel'. . . . His art was a great art as opposed to over-elaborate or over-refined art by virtue of the major conflicts he portrays.

5. Other contemporary or near contemporary criticisms of varied interests are reprinted in F. W. Dupee's *The Question of Henry James*, New York, 1945:

T. W. Higginson, 'Henry James, Junior' in *Short Studies of American Authors*, Boston, 1880.

W. D. Howells, 'Mr. Henry James's Later Work', *North American Review*, January 1903, clxxvi, 125–37.

Herbert Croly, 'Henry James and His Countrymen', *Lamp*, February 1904, xxviii, 47–53.

Joseph Conrad, 'Henry James: An Appreciation', *North American Review*, January 1905, clxxx, 102–8. (Dupee has abridged this, but it is also currently available in Conrad's *Notes on Life and Letters*, 1921. It is mainly valuable for being a sincere compliment *inter pares*.)

T. S. Eliot, 'On Henry James', *Little Review*, August 1918.

6. An essay by J. C. Powys in *Suspended Judgements*, New York, 1916, is interesting because of its source. But I doubt whether many readers will find it useful as criticism:

People do not and perhaps never will—even in archetypal Platonic drawing-rooms—converse with one another quite so goldenly; or tell the amber-coloured beads of their secret psychology with quite so felicitous an unction. What matter? It is the prerogative of fine and great art to create, by its shaping and formative imagination, new and impossible worlds for our enjoyment.

And the world created by Henry James is like some classic Arcadia of psychological beauty—some universal Garden of Versailles unprofaned by the noises of the crowd—where among the terraces and fountains delicate Watteau-like figures move and whisper and make love in a soft artificial fairy moonlight dimmed and misty with the rain of tender regrets; human figures without name or place. For who remembers the names of these sweet phantoms or the titles of their 'great good places' in this hospitable fairy-land of the harassed sensitive ones of the earth; where courtesy is the only law of existence and good taste the only moral code?

A whole book might be written about why (apart from emulating Pater) intelligent people wanted to talk in this way, even during a war, and why we now find it so very inadequate.

7. Three critical books on James were published before, or around the time of, his death:

(a) Elizabeth Luther Cary, *Henry James*, New York, 1905. The chief virtue of this is in appearing when it did. It is a slight work of 188 small pages, written in a style of cultured and unconcentrated appreciation consonant with the picture of James—an 'art' novelist of the period —which it presents.

(b) Ford Madox Hueffer, *Henry James: A Critical Study*, 1913. This starts magnificently: 'Mr James is the greatest of living writers and in consequence, for me, the greatest of living men. . .' . But the rest of it is, unfortunately, quite fairly described by two contemporary reviewers—'Garrulous, slap-dash, untidy . . . worthy of neither of the eminent names its cover bears' (Dixon Scott in the *Bookman*); 'Blank carelessness, tedious verbosity, incompetence . . . the slap dash comments of an incorrigible egoist' (W.R.L. in the *Academy*). It is indeed a most unsatisfactory performance from so distinguished a writer, full of self-advertisement and based on the most elementary idea that art is either 'moral' in the very crudest sense, or morally indifferent. Hueffer's main thesis is reasonable: that James is both an unprecedented 'artist' of the novel in England, and an unparalleled recorder of contemporary social reality. But in the erratic pursuit of this he makes some amazing judgements. 'Compassion or any trace of a desire to be helpful are in fact almost entirely wanting in the works of this impersonal writer'— for example 'Maisie for him is just a child in a basement'. *The Spoils of Poynton* is James's 'greatest book'. The whole of the English novel before James—Scott, Dickens, and George Eliot, but with the honourable exception of Trollope—is botched and amateurish. The climax of James's career, after which he fell into a decline, was his association with *The Yellow Book*, 'technically a high water mark of English achievement in the Arts' (actually James disliked the magazine and published little there). His 'final note is despair' and a stress on 'the essential dirtiness of human nature' (a conclusion largely based on the quotation, out of context, of 'cats and monkeys' etc. from 'The Madonna of the Future'). Hueffer's book is also full of suggestive inaccuracies like 'Milly Strether'.

(*c*) Rebecca West, *Henry James*, 1916. This is a very bright but also intelligent study, with a suffragette bias.

8. In 1906 LeRoy Phillips commenced James Studies with 250 copies of his *A Bibliography of Henry James*, New York.

9. Two prominent articles omitted from this collection solely for reasons of space are:

(*a*) Arthur Tilley, 'The New School of Fiction', *National Review*, April 1883, i, 257–68. This is an enlightened and moderate response to Howells's crusading Century article (No. 51 above) and the *Quarterly's* furious rejoinder to that (No. 52).

(*b*) Morton Fullerton, 'The Art of Henry James', *Quarterly Review*, April 1910, ccxii, 393–408, and *Living Age*, June 1910, cclxv, 643–52. This is a 'disciple's' essay, mainly on James's later work, which complements those by Oliver Elton and Sydney Waterlow (Nos. 160 and 164 above). Edith Wharton may have had a 'hand—or at least a small finger' in it—in a loyal attempt to cheer James after the failure of the New York edition.

10. Frank Harris's reminiscences are too amusing to miss, although too long to print. They are a fine example of unconscious comedy, and appear in his *My Life and Loves*, London 1964, elsewhere 1925, which is available at all kinds of bookshops.

11. Besides the parodies of James printed above there are Max Beerbohm's well-known 'labours of love'. 'The Mote in the Middle Distance' is reprinted in *The Question of Henry James* (see section 5 above); 'The Guerdon' in *Parodies*, ed. Dwight Macdonald, 1961.

12. Lastly I should mention two enthusiastic compilations which appeared in James's lifetime, but which do not invite reprinting. *The Henry James Yearbook*, selected and arranged by Miss E. G. Smalley (published in Boston in 1911 and—850 copies—in England in 1912) consists of extracts from James—sumptuously got up—for every day of the year, like a calendar. The self-explanatory *Pictures and Other Passages from Henry James* was issued in both England and America in 1916, and contains an account by Ruth Head, the editress, of having been a lone admirer of James in the 1880's ('not one of my contemporaries shared my enthusiasm') but of having now found 'co-religionists'. Both print notes of approval from James.

I

The records of the sales of James's books are fairly complete, those of his profits very fragmentary. What there is of both gives an unusually concrete picture of the fluctuations of his reputation. And this, especially in comparison with the sales and profits of other authors, also provides an interesting parallel to our analysis of the quality of response to his work. The following is offered as a summary of the subject. I have omitted much minor detail (e.g. of colonial issues); have dealt only with James's fictional work (and not quite all of this); and have for the most part only been concerned with book, as opposed to magazine serial, publication. Nevertheless I believe the picture to be complete in essentials, and of considerable corroboratory interest.

Some preliminary observations are necessary:

(a) In BHJ—to which I am much indebted in this respect and a reading of which can fill in a great deal of detail for the specialist —Edel and Laurence give the numbers printed of most works, as well as full bibliographical description, but do not always specify up to what date the figures go. I have therefore checked with Macmillan for the later history up to 1916 of the English and (1886–90) American editions of books published by them—i.e. almost all before 1893, and a few afterwards. Heinemann and Methuen, the main English publishers of the late books, have been unable to supply new information, as have those of James's American publishers still in business. As it turns out the only useful result of this check has been negative: to show that James's novels were, on the whole, simply not reprinted after the first year or two. But this, of course, has its own importance. The sole significant positive result is in the case of *Roderick Hudson* where Edel and Laurence record 'two batches of 250' sheets imported from Macmillan in 1882 by Houghton, Mifflin in America, but do not mention a further 2,250 copies (all in batches of 250) imported between 1902 and 1915. (There were also three later printings of *French Poets and Novelists*—January 1893, March 1904, and August 1908—and three of *Partial Portraits*—June 1899, December 1905, and February 1911— which are not mentioned, but these have little importance here.)

I am reasonably satisfied that the figures quoted below for most of the English publications are complete up to 1916. Those for the American ones are far less so—but it seems unlikely that there would be important reprintings there when there were none in England. I have indicated in the appropriate places where the figures are incomplete.

(*b*) There is little account of payments to James in BHJ. The second two volumes of Edel's *Life of Henry James* (1953–) contain some scattered information. The Macmillan records up to 1896 (i.e. over the important period) have been destroyed; but they have allowed me access to those after that year, and these are some help. Much of an author's income in this period in any case derived from magazine serialization rather than book publication, and I have relied for facts about this (as well as for other odd pieces of information about the sales and profits of James and his contemporaries) on letters, memoirs, biographies, trade journals etc.

(*c*) Profits from fiction did not, of course, provide the whole of James's income. He had some private means (although an interesting passage in Edel's introduction to SL, 16–17, points out that for most of his life he did not rely on these), and he seems sometimes to have made more from his criticism, travel sketches, etc. in magazines than he did from the stories and novels—e.g. at least $1,600 in 1877 as against $1,350 for the serialization of *The American* (in May 1880 the exchange rate was $4.85 to the pound). I shall not include further details of these payments, but it is possible that a disparity of reward may have had, if anything, a depressing effect on James.

(*d*) It can be assumed that all but the last printing of a book equates roughly with sales. But this printing, especially in the case of the later works (when larger and cheaper first editions became the rule) was often also the first with James, and was by no means always sold out. Sheets of the one printing of *The Sacred Fount* (1901) for example, were still at the publishers (to be bound in hope of a sale after the relative success of *The Outcry*) in 1911—and even then were not all sent out (BHJ, 119). When the Times Book Club was formed in 1905 James became their largest author because of the ease with which remainder sheets of works from all parts of his career could be bought from publishers (BHJ, 386–7).

(*e*) Besides the regular publishers Tauchnitz published a lot of early James on the continent (but after 1885 there was a gap until *The Finer Grain* in 1910). The Baron, although not obliged to do so, paid royalties to his authors.

(*f*) A glance at the serializations of James's books throughout his career can give an indication of the fluctuations of his popularity, at least among the magazine reading public. This could be worked out in detail according to the type and circulation of the magazines etc., but here a simple sketch will suffice. All the novels from *Watch and Ward* (1871) up to *Confidence* (1879-80) were serialized only in America; *Washington Square* and *The Portrait of a Lady* (1881) in England and America; all up to *The Spoils of Poynton* (1896) in one country *or* the other; *What Maisie Knew* (1897) in both countries; *The Awkward Age* (1898-9) in America; and all the rest with the exception of *The Ambassadors* (America in 1903) not at all. It is not my impression that novels in general were being serialized less than before in the later period—rather the contrary. So the development tends to confirm the supposition that James's elevation as the 'Master' did not result in his being read any more widely.

(*g*) Small sales of first editions in this period were, no doubt, partly due to their enormous price in England up to *c*. 1895 (31*s* 6*d* in 1880 would equal at least £5 5*s* 0*d* today). However cheaper reprints quickly followed in most cases. In America prices were never so high ($2.00 or $1.50 usually—roughly equivalent to 8*s* or 6*s* at the time). It should also be remembered that in England booksellers usually sold at a price lower than the 'official' one, and that many readers would not buy books which they had already read in magazines (and occasionally newspapers). This latter has a slight bearing on our view of the sales of those of James's books which were not serialized. And all these conditions apply equally to the sales of James's contemporaries.

(*h*) James was never popular enough to suffer much from 'pirating'. But the first English edition of *The American* was published unauthorized by Ward, Lock and Co. in 1877 (with a rather lurid cover reproduced in BHJ), the authorized Macmillan edition not appearing until 1879; *Daisy Miller* was 'promptly' reprinted in two American magazines in 1879 without payment ('a sweet tribute I hadn't yet received and was never again to know' as James called it in his later Preface); and 'A Bundle of Letters' appeared unauthorized in both countries in 1880. In his *American Literature in Nineteenth Century England*, New York, 1944, Clarence Gohdes says that Chatto and Windus pirated the English edition of *Confidence* in 1879, but actually this was an authorized publication.

(*i*) All the figures given below exclude the very small sales of the New York edition of 1907-9, which are dealt with separately.

II

Roderick Hudson

In America Osgood published 1,500 copies at $2.00 in November 1875. Some of these were sent to England in 1876. Apart from later imports from England (see Section I (*a*) above) there was no further issue in America. The growth of James's reputation is better shown by the English printings. 500 copies came out in June 1879 at 31*s* 6*d*, 1,500 in May 1880 at 6*s*, and 2,000 in June 1888 at 2*s*. In 1883 Macmillan published 5,000 copies of a 'Collective Edition' of James in 14 volumes at 1*s* or 1*s* 6*d* (which illustrates James's relative popularity at the time, and also incidentally supplies some indication of which of the early books were liked best—Macmillan did a large number of 2*s* reprintings in ordinary, Yellow Back, editions in 1888–9, which were presumably needed to replace copies sold out in the Edition: *Roderick Hudson, Daisy Miller, The Madonna of the Future*, and *Washington Square* were reprinted; *The Portrait of a Lady, The American*, and *The Europeans* were not). Thus the novel sold approximately 10,500 in both countries in James's lifetime.

What were contemporary conditions? Among authors of comparable appeal Howells's *The Undiscovered Country* reached 11,000 in America in its first year, 1880; Mrs. Craik's *The Ogilvies*, which was 'originally published elsewhere' sold 11,000 from Macmillan in England 1875–8 and went on reprinting; and Mrs. Oliphant's *He That Will Not When He May* sold 10,500, 1880–92. Great popular successes are very much less relevant (here or elsewhere), but it is interesting to note how far these sales were from those of e.g. Mark Twain's works—*The Innocents Abroad* sold 67,000 in America in its first year, 1869; *Roughing It* 30,000 in two months of 1872; and *A Tramp Abroad* 100,000 in America and Canada in nine months of 1880.

Such comparisons can be misleading—they do not account for example for the sales of Mrs. Craik and Mrs. Oliphant in America, or for those of Howells and Mark Twain in England, and they ignore the extent to which some of these authors had already established reputations. But they do establish fairly conclusively—especially if we bear in mind the time given in each case—that *Roderick Hudson* sold rather less than averagely well, even though, as will appear, it fared better than most of its successors.

The American

Publishing evidence on this novel is rather conflicting. James had received $1,200 (*c.* £240) for the serialization of *Roderick Hudson*. On the basis of a rising interest in his work he demanded $1,350 for *The American*. The *Galaxy* refused this demand, but Howells, for the *Atlantic*, accepted it. Against this, however, must be put the remarkable fact that when James asked Macmillan to publish the novel (it had already been pirated in 1877) the reader, Grove, 'broke down in his attempt to read it'. This perhaps accounts for its late appearance in February 1879, when 1,250 copies were printed. The only subsequent authorized printing in England was the 5,000 of the Collective Edition. But the pirating of unspecified numbers in 1877, 1888 or 1889, and 1894 makes calculation of the total sale impossible. In America Osgood's first printing (the only one recorded in BHJ) was 1,000 at $2.00 in May 1877—and some of these were sent to England.

The Europeans

In England there was an edition of 250 copies at 21*s* in September 1878. The small initial printing suggests that Frederick Macmillan, who was always a warm friend to James, did not share the latter's confidence in the growth of his reputation in this period—later he wrote that 'certainly the money result (for 1878) was not very encouraging'. But the novel was quickly reprinted in batches of the same number in October and November; a second edition of 1,000 at 6*s* came out in April 1879; and it was included in the Collective Edition. In America Houghton, Osgood & Co. published 1,500 copies at $1.50 in October 1878 (the only printing recorded). A total sale of 8,250 confirms the impression given by later silence: that this novel was quickly forgotten, in spite of relatively favourable reviews.

Daisy Miller, etc.

This is generally considered by scholars to have been James's winner in the mass market: 'the greatest popular success he was ever to know' (Michael Swan); 'widely read and admired' (Janet Adam Smith); 'one of the best sellers James ever wrote' (R. N. Foley); 'an international triumph . . . became a best-seller overnight' (Leon Edel); etc. I doubt that the evidence quite warrants such enthusiasm. It is true that when James told Howells that he had made only '$200 by the whole American career of D.M.' he had mainly, as he suggests, publishing conditions to complain of: the story sold 20,000 in weeks, but in Harper's 20 or 35 cent pamphlets on which royalties were negligible. But in England it was clearly more discussed than bought and read. It was published (after serialization in the *Cornhill*) with 'An International Episode' and 'Four Meetings' in an edition of 250 at 21*s* in February 1879. This was repeated in March. In November Macmillan mentioned to James that the volume had sold 285 copies. A second edition of 500 at 6s was printed in August, and another 1,000 in December. The 5,000 of the Collective Edition was followed by a further 2,000 at 2s in January 1888—9,000 in all, the same as for *Roderick Hudson* in England. Thus comparison with figures already quoted for other authors would suggest that James's big success was somewhat *d'estime*; and how far it was from a true best-seller appears when its initial printing of 250 (or even the American cheap sale) is put against the 30,000 prepared before the publication of *Huckleberry Finn* in 1885, or its total sale against the 'at least half a million' (in America) of Bill Nye's comic *History of the United States*.

Confidence

James received $1,500 for serialization ($150 more than for *The American*), and the novel was published in December 1879 by Chatto and Windus in an edition of 500 at 21s. In October 1880 2,500 were issued at 3s 6d, and in September 1882 a further 500. In America Houghton, Osgood published 1,500 at $1.50 in February 1880, and reprinted an unspecified number in 1891 at 50 cents. The novel was included in the Macmillan Collective Edition. Thus sales confirm the impression given by reviews—that there were few discriminations made between this and the more important works of the period.

Washington Square

This was the first of James's novels to be serialized on both sides of the Atlantic. Subsequently Macmillan printed 500 at 21s in January 1881 (the increase on the initial printing of *The Europeans* suggests that *Daisy Miller*—and perhaps a reasonably successful *Madonna of the Future* volume not included here—had had some effect). By March 430 of these had been sold, which Macmillan considered a great success, and so a further 250 were printed. There was a second edition of 500 at 6s in August. The Collective Edition was followed by a further 2,000 at 2s in January 1889. A good average sale (for James) of 8,250 in his lifetime in England (although less than that of *Confidence*). No figures are available for America.

The Portrait of a Lady

Despite the more interesting reviews of this book, and although James received far more than before for serialization ($2,500 from the *Atlantic* and £250 from *Macmillan's*), there was a slight drop in his English sales.

Macmillan printed 750 at 31s 6d in November 1881, and another 250 in January 1882. There was a 6s edition of 1,000 in June 1882. With the Collective Edition, a total of only 7,000. But in America, where the novel was brought out by Houghton, Mifflin in November 1881 in 1,500 copies at $2.00, there were five further impressions by August 1882, making a total of 6,500. This high overall figure perhaps helps to explain the expansive element in James's mood of the next few years.

SHORT STORIES OF THE EARLY 1880'S

In this period James perhaps came nearer to notoriety than ever before or afterwards. Two of his stories, 'Pandora' and 'Georgina's Reasons' appeared—'a prix d'or' as he put it—in the New York Sunday Sun; and the latter penetrated even further and was printed in the Cincinnati Enquirer under the headline 'Georgina's Reasons: Henry James's Latest Story: A Woman Who Commits Bigamy And Enforces Silence On Her Husband'. But it is doubtful whether James profited in any serious way from being a sensational writer. In England his volumes of short stories sold as sluggishly as the few and dull reviews would suggest. Tales of Three Cities was published in October 1884 in an edition of 1,500 at 4s 6d and never reprinted. In America Osgood brought out the same number in the same month at $1.50 (the only recorded printing). Stories Revived had two editions (in England only), of 500 (in 3 volumes) at 31s 6d in May 1885, and of 1,000 (in 2 volumes) at 6s in November. Most of the stories in the latter had been printed before in books, but none duplicated the Collective Edition. The two collections thus together sold less than half as many as The Portrait of a Lady in England—itself a decline on Washington Square.

The Bostonians

James's later memory of the ill success of this novel in serialization (No. 195 above) is corroborated by his earnings from it. Partly owing to the failure of Osgood in America he received only £492 from both markets *and* serialization. And this is considerably less than half of what he had asked for the more or less concurrent serialization of The Princess Casamassima (see below). We might compare this with an average novel of the time, Mrs. Oliphant's The Perpetual Curate, which fetched £1,500 for book publication alone.

Reflecting the decline of the 'three-decker' novel The Bostonians was printed by Macmillan in two editions: 500 at 31s 6d in February 1886, and 5,000 at 6s in May. The latter supplied the American market as well (Macmillan having taken over Osgood's rights). 100 more of the expensive edition were brought out in March. This—5,600—was all in either country until the two or three thousand of Percy Lubbock's 'Complete Edition' of 1923.

The Princess Casamassima

The element of confidence in James's mood in the early 1880's is reflected in his correspondence with T. B. Aldrich of the *Atlantic* over the serialization of this novel. He demanded (in the tone of an established master) $500 for each of 12 instalments—$6,000 compared with the American fee of $2,500 received for *The Portrait of a Lady*. And indeed, as might be expected from reviews, the book sales were an improvement of those of *The Bostonians*. In October 1886 Macmillan published 750 at 31s 6d and 3,000 at 6s. Again a part of the cheap edition sufficed for America. Two printings of 2,000 at 2s followed in May and December 1888. But 7,750, by far the highest sale of the late 1880's, was still far below the average for the earlier novels. Like *The Bostonians* the book failed to earn what Macmillan advanced for it (£550 for both England and America). We can compare the fantastic success of another novel which, like the *Princess*, attracted by its subject: Mrs. Humphry Ward's *Robert Elsmere*. This is reputed to have sold well over a million in England in 1888, and, according to its author, over half a million in America. Issued in a cheap edition more than twenty years later it sold 50,000 in two weeks. But perhaps even more instructive is the completely unsensational sale, in England alone, of Hardy's *The Woodlanders*. This was published in March 1887, and, initially about as successful as James (only 3,000 in the first year), went on reprinting in steady batches of 2,000 of the 6s edition, until by 1912 it had sold 15,000. From then, as Hardy became the patriarch of English letters, there were another 11 printings up to 1923 totalling 22,500—making 37,500 in England before the author's death. Whereas, as usual, James's book dropped dead two years after publication. He had during his lifetime neither the benefits of the serious best-seller nor those of the steadily emerging classic.

SHORT NOVELS AND STORIES OF THE LATE 1880'S

It is reported—by about treble hearsay—that James had been offered for one of his books of the late 1880's 'only £50 for the copyright by one of the leading publishers'. That this is not incredible will be seen when we come to the case of *The Tragic Muse*, but meanwhile sales, although very low, kept steady. *The Reverberator* came out in an edition of 500 in England at 12s, and 3,000 in America at $1.25 in June 1888, and was reprinted in England only—1,000 at 6s in August. *The Aspern Papers etc.* was issued in September with 650 at 12s in England and (in November) 2,000 at $1.50 in America, and a further 2,000 in England in October 1890. *A London Life etc.* had an almost identical history with 500 at 12s in England and 2,000 at $1.50 in America in April 1889, and 2,000 at 3s 6d in England in May.

The Tragic Muse

In SL Edel prints a letter from James to Macmillan in which he declines an offer of £70 for this novel. This minute sum compares directly with the £550 received for *The Princess Casamassima*, and tells its own story. But Macmillan (who did, after all, publish it) seems to have been right— the book reached a new low point in sales for a novel. It came out in June 1890 in 500 at 31s 6d, and was reprinted once, in January 1891, in 2,000 at 3s 6d. In America Houghton, Mifflin published 1,000 at $2.50 in June 1890 (the only printing recorded).

SHORT STORIES OF THE EARLY 1890'S

James published six collections while engaged with the theatre. Macmillan printed 2,900 of *The Lesson of the Master* for both countries in February 1892, at $1.00 and 6s; and 1,500 of *The Real Thing* in March 1893, at the same prices. *The Private Life* and *The Wheel of Time* were published in America by Harper's in August and September and for these no figures are available; but *The Private Life* was issued in England by Osgood, McIlvaine in June 1893 in just one edition of 1,000 at 5s. Heinemann printed 1,000 of *Terminations* in May 1895 at 6s, and a further 500 in July. Again there are no figures for the Harper's publica- tion (June) in America. *Embarrassments* was also published by Heine- mann, with 1,250 in June 1896 at 6s, and a further 250 in February 1897. The sole printing in America was one of 1,600 at $1.50 by Mac- millan in June. These figures—never as high even as those for *The Tragic Muse* (although collections of stories always tended to sell less than novels)—only confirm the impression of James's rapid develop- ment into the writer of a small minority.

THREE SHORT NOVELS OF THE LATE 1890'S

Soon after giving up the theatre James produced a batch of short novels. The least of these, *The Other House*, sold the best—but even so, and in spite of its reviews, not very well. Heinemann issued two editions: 1,000 at 10s in October 1896, and 1,500 at 6s in July 1897. In America Macmillan published 2,150 at $1.50 in October 1896 (the only printing).

But 4,650 copies was not really a demonstration of popularity—and *The Spoils of Poynton* confirms that the new tendency of reviewers to be at least respectful to James were not as yet felt in terms of sales. There was one Heinemann edition of 2,000 at 6s in February 1897, and two by Houghton, Mifflin in America in February and March 1897 of 1,500 and 500 respectively (the only ones recorded). No figures are available for *What Maisie Knew* in America. In England only the first Heinemann printing of 2,000 at 6s in September 1897 is recorded, but it seems likely that there were further impressions soon afterwards.

A more definite indication of James's position is given by his correspondence with Clement Shorter of the *Illustrated London News* over the serialization of *The Other House* (printed by Edel in SL). This illustrates the doggedness of his desire to be read, and his determination to write something with a wide appeal. It also shows him sticking out for £300, Shorter having offered 'a great deal less' than he was wont to receive. It is difficult to say how this fee compares with those of other writers, but it is a considerable decline on the *c.* £1,200 demanded for the (admittedly much longer) *Princess Casamassima*—especially if we consider the popular character of the *Illustrated London News*—and a return after twenty years to earlier figures like those for *Roderick Hudson* and *The American*.

But an author's income does not derive solely from current work. The Macmillan records show, after 1896, exactly how well James's novels continued to sell—how well the new public respect revived interest in his earlier work. The average annual payment until 1909 (when the records stop) was £12 4s 9d, the total payment £171 6s 8d.

In the Cage and *The Two Magics*
There are no figures available for the sale of *In the Cage* in America. It was first published there in 1898 by Herbert S. Stone and Co., and reprinted in 1906 by Fox Duffield and Co. The English edition, published by Duckworth in August 1898 at 3s 6d had only one printing of 1,500. *The Two Magics* was issued by Heinemann in England in October 1898 in 1,500 copies at 6s and by Macmillan in America with 2,250 at $1.50. No subsequent printings are recorded.

The Awkward Age
In his later preface to this novel James reports his publisher as saying 'the book has done nothing to speak of; I've never in all my experience seen one treated with more general and complete disrespect'. The remark seems justified by the sales. The sole printing in England was of 2,000

by Heinemann in April 1899 at 6s, and the first in America of 1,000 by Harper's in May at $1.50 (there may have been another a little later). In England this compares with the 22,000 printed by Macmillan of *The Benefactress* by Countess von Arnim in 1901–2, or the 14,500 of Maurice Hewlett's *Richard Yea and Nay*, 1900–2; and F. M. Crawford, often spoken of in this period as America's greatest living novelist, sold 35,000 of his *Marietta* in England in 1901.

The Soft Side and *The Sacred Fount*

After 1900 the generally accepted view of James as a fine old master, with his small but exquisite niche in literature, seems to have had a slight, but favourable, effect on his sales. *The Soft Side* was published by Methuen in England in August 1900 in a first (and perhaps not only) printing of 3,000 at 6s, and by Macmillan in America in September in only one printing of 2,800 at $1.50. Unlikely as it might have seemed *The Sacred Fount*, the quintessence of all that might be thought obscure, trivial, or dubious in the later James, had more copies printed (though not all of them sold—see Section I (*d*) above). In America Scribner printed 3,000 at $1.50 (the only one recorded) in February 1901, and in England Methuen printed 3,500 at 6s a little later in the month.

THE MAJOR WORKS OF THE EARLY 1900'S

The Wings of the Dove was published in August 1902 by Constable in England in one printing of 4,000 at 6s, and by Scribner in America in a first (and only recorded) printing of 3,000 at $2.50. *The Better Sort* was published by Methuen in England in February 1903 in one printing of 3,500 at 6s, and in America by Scribner (no figures available). The English edition was probably remaindered later. *The Ambassadors* followed in September with the same publisher, numbers, and price in England. Of these 3,110 were sold and 341 remaindered, and the edition went out of print in 1909. In America Harper's printed 4,000 at $2.00 in November, and some of this may have been sold in England. It was remaindered about 1906. *The Golden Bowl* was published by Scribner in November 1904 in America in a printing (the only one recorded) of 2,000 at $2.50, and by Methuen in England in a printing of 3,000 at 6s. Most of the later figures for England include colonial issues.

These figures are, however, rather misleading. *The Ambassadors* sold poorly, and the initially small printings of *The Golden Bowl* reflect this. But of the latter James (in America) wrote in 1905 that 'the thing has done much less ill here than anything I have ever produced' (the phrasing is characteristic), and a little later that '*The Golden Bowl* is in its *fourth* edition—unprecedented'. In England there were, over some years, two further impressions (of unspecified numbers)—making three in fact. The upward swing in reviews is interestingly reflected in these sales, and one wonders what might have happened had James soon produced another major novel—though it should be remembered that by his own account *The Golden Bowl* owed much of its relative success to the curiosity aroused in America by his visit. In any case a few comparisons with other serious writers should prevent any great sense of James's new well-being. In 1905 alone Macmillan printed two batches of 7,500 of Wells's *Kipps*. In the same year he published 6,000 of Edith Wharton's *The House of Mirth*, and followed with another 5,000 early in 1906. In 1904 Maurice Hewlett's *The Queen's Quair* came out in a first edition of 22,500. And all these figures are for England alone.

THE NEW YORK EDITION

With this background the fate of the New York edition—elaborate and expensive—is no great surprise. But it was a bitter disappointment to James. The edition was published by Scribner in America from December 1907 to July 1909. There was a limited special issue of 156 copies, and a first printing of 1,500 for the first 10 volumes, and of 1,000 for the remaining 14 (there were probably subsequent printings, but these must have been very small). This served England as well. BHJ states that by Macmillan 'One hundred sets of sheets of the original twenty-four volumes were imported. The publisher reports that only a fraction of these were bound, the balance being used as package wrapping during the Second World War . . . '—although this was informally denied upon my request for confirmation. The greater part (Vols. 1–6 and 13–24) of the English edition is dated 1908, and the rest was issued the following year. I have seen a set issued by Macmillan in 1913. But it seems likely that a payment to J. B. Pinker (James's agent) on 30th June 1909 'By H. J. Edn. de Luxe £84 17s 0d' (the only payment for the edition extant in Macmillan's records) represents most of what James received from the immediate English sale. In 1915 he told Gosse that his annual profit from it had been about £25 in England, and 'very little more' in America (No. 195 above). And this would explain the bitterness of many of his references to it.

LAST YEARS

The figures for James's subsequent publications of fiction are not very interesting: in September 1909 Harper's printed 4,000 copies of a slim volume of *Julia Bride* for both countries; in October 1910 Scribner published *The Finer Grain* in America (no figures available) and Methuen followed in England with an edition of 1,500 at 6s. *The Outcry* (which James tried, and failed, to get serialized in America) was issued in October 1911 by the same two publishers—the English first printing consisting of 2,000 copies—and was apparently something of a success (possibly another instance of the appeal of topical subject matter). James, calling it a 'commonplace triviality' and an 'inferior little product' told Edith Wharton that it was 'I blush to say . . . on its way to a fifth edition (in these few weeks)'—though in fact it never reached this. Finally, shortly before his death James sanctioned a Uniform edition of his tales by Secker, which started to appear in April 1915 in England in editions of 1,000 or 1,500 copies, and in America in September 1917 in editions of 200 or 400.

Index

Bold figures indicate quotations

Academy, The, 9, **45–6**, **54–5**, **201–2**, **266**, **269**, **278**, **286–8**, **376–7**
Acton, Lord, 8
Adam Bede, 56
Adams, Henry, **120**
Adams, Mrs. Henry, **120**
All Souls' Night, 464
'Altar of the Dead, The', 279, **508–10**
Ambassadors, The, 359–60, 361, 366, 373, 424, 457, 480–7, **482–3**, 488, 496, 506–7, 535–6, 547; sales, 555
American, The, 4, 43–8, 57, 63, 65, 72, 73, 75, 78, 101, 115, 122, 129, 130, 136, 144, 185, 222, 227, 253, 332, 505, 546, 547; dramatized, 13; sales, 548–9, 550, 554
American Literature, 479
American Scene, The, 430–1, 448–9
Anglo-Saxon Review, The, 361
Anna Karenina, 355
Antigone, 421
Appleton's Journal, **63–4**
Archer, William, 13, 187
Arnold, Matthew, 56, 87, 187, 263, 350, 402, 417, 443; on Wordsworth, **534**
'Art of Fiction, The', 10, **11**, 149, 184, 403–4, 454, 504
Art of the Novel, The, 541
Aspern Papers, The, 227, 349; sales, 553
Athenaeum, The, **53**, **97**, **195–6**, **274–5**, **289–90**, **380**
Atherton, Gertrude, on the Henry James craze, **155**; on James's later works, **361–2**; fictional tribute of, **363–4**
Atlantic Monthly, 3, 9, 24, 26, **31–4**, **35–8**, 44, **66–9**, **71–3**, **92**, **109–10**, 127, 128, 133, 140, 165, **166–8**, 207, 209, **213–17**, **332–4**, **395–428**, 439, **450–62**
Aubrey, G. Jean, 279
Augier, Emile, 414

Auld Lang Syne, 70
Austen, Jane, 6, 205, 332
Author of 'Beltraffio', The, 154, 227
Awkward Age, The, 2, 15, 281, 282–302, 308, 333, 335–6, 339, 346, 350, 366, 400, 421–2, 498–9, 547; sales, 544–5

Bailey, John, **463**
Balzac, Honoré de, 24, 57, 125, 170, 226, 251, 299, 393, 403, 417, 429, 433, 436–7, 500
Barham, R. H., 467
'Beast in the Jungle, The', 508
Beerbohm, Max, 3, 245, 467–8, 504, 544
'Beldonald Holbein, The', 446
Bell, Millicent, 395
Bell in the Fog, The, 362, **363–4**
Bennett, Arnold, 15; on reading *The Ambassadors*, **373**; on *The Finer Grain*, **488–91**
Benson, A. C., on James's view of English Art, **303**
'Benvolio', 227
Besant, Sir Walter, 504
Better Sort, The, 366, 415, 436, 446; sales, 555
Bibliography of Henry James, A, (Edel and Lawrence), 19, 545ff.
Bibliography of Henry James, A, (Phillips), 544
'Birthplace, The', 508
Blackwood's Magazine, 8, **80–2**, **101–4**
Blake, William, 125
Blithedale Romance, The, 167
Bookman, **267**; (USA), **292–3**, **308**, **335–41**, **359–60**, **391**, 435
Boon . . . . , 15, **517–26**, 527–30
Bosanquet, Theodora, on James and his readers, **515–16**
Bostonians, The, 11–12, 156, 158–69, 182–3, 209, 227, 230, 231, 479, 531–2, 534; sales, 551–2; serialization, 552

Bourget, Paul, 187, 406, 421, 446
Boynton, H. W., on James, **435–6**
Bragdon, Claude, **389–90, 434**
British Quarterly Review, **78**
Brontë, Charlotte, 53, 234, 369
Brooke, Stopford, on James's style, **263**
Brownell, W. C., 15, 498, 501–2; on James's position in literature, **395–428**; essay on James criticized, 439, 443
Browning, Robert, 125, 421, 433
Brunetière, Ferdinand, on Marivaux, **451ff**
Buchanan, Robert, 190; on James as a critic, **187–9**
Bulwer-Lytton, Sir Edward, 179, 421
'Bundle of Letters, A', 88, 122, 132, 547
Burnett, Mrs. Hodgson, 56, 135
Bynner, Witter, 434
Byron, Lord, 433

Cable, George, 135
Caine, Hall, 319, 321, 450
Carlyle, Thomas, 113, 367–8, 402
Cary, Elizabeth Luther, 434–5, 440, 543
Century Magazine, 10, **126–34**, 152, 532
Chester, M. V., 513; and James, 514
Clarissa Harlowe, 126, 234
Colby, F. M., on James's bloodless perversity, **335–8**; on *The Wings of the Dove*, **339–41,** 342
Collins, Wilkie, 420, 506
Colvin, Sidney, 1, 157, 304
Comédie Humaine, 420
Confessions of a Young Man, The, **170–2**
Confidence, 79, 83–6, 547; sales, 550
Conrad, Joseph, 434, 440, 542; on *The Spoils of Poynton*, **268;** defends James's writing, **279–80**
Contemporary Review, **173–4, 503–12**
Cooper, F. T., **359–60**, 435
Corelli, Marie, 319, 321
Crackanthorpe, H., 467
Craik, Mrs., 548
'Crapy Cornelia', 489
Crawford, F. Marion, 166, 555
Critic, The, **107–8, 154,** 179, 207, 263, **276, 295–7,** 307, **326–31, 389–90,** 434

'Criticism' (James), 1, 541
Cruse, Amy, 268
Cummings, Elizabeth, 513

Daisy Miller, 5, 14, 54, 59, 61, 115, 126, 128–9, 130, 132, 135–6, 140, 203, 222, 227, 245, 253, 344, 379, 441, 505, 515, 547; scandal, 74; skit on, 234–6; sales, 549–50
Daniel Deronda, 67, 102–3
'*Daniel Deronda*: a Conversation,' 403
D'Annunzio, Gabriele, 446
Dante, 420, 443
d'Arcy, Ella, 467
Daudet, Alphonse, 133, 142, 187, 188, 403, 404, 420
Defoe, Daniel, 105, 467, 480
De la Mare, Walter, **17,** 538
Dennett, 29
Dial, The, **111–12, 153, 209, 291**
Dickens, Charles, 126, 132, 138, 264, 366, 369, 452, 467, 472
Diderot, Denis, 451
Divine Comedy, The, 420
Don Quixote, 420
Dowson, Ernest, 467
Draper, Muriel, on James's cultured admirers, **513–14**
Draper, Ruth, 513
Dr. Breen's Practice, 109
Dublin Review, 206
Dumas, Alexandre, 414
Du Maurier, George, 188, 251, 420
Dupee, F. W., 335, 542
Dwight, H. G., 15; on U.S. hostility to James, **432–49**

Eclectic Magazine, **65**
Edel, Leon, 9, 19, 529, 541, 545, 546, 549
Edinburgh Review, 15, 395; on James's achievement, **345–8**
Egerton, George, 467
Eliot, George, 16, 67, 68–9, 99, 105, 109, 113, 116, 124, 125, 130, 133, 136, 156, 188, 190, 400, 403, 407, 411, 421, 439, 469
Elton, Oliver, 15, 365, 459, 544; on James's greatness, **349–58**

Embarrassments, 259–60; sales, 553

Emerson, R. W., 113, 247, 253, 427

English Review, The, **480–7**

Essays in London and Elsewhere, 243, 246

Eugénie Grandet, 226

Europeans, The, 2, 5, 6–7, 9, 16, 49–73, 75, 122, 125, 132, 222, 227; sales, 549

'Extraordinary Case, An', 26

Fawcett, Edgar, 10, **144–7**

Fielding, Henry, 114, 126, 132, 174, 191, 234, 420, 422, 451, 480

'Figure in the Carpet, The', 259, 501, 540

Finer Grain, The, 15, 488–90, 546; sales, 557

Fitzroy, Sir Almeric, on James at Rye, **429**

Flaubert, Gustave, 8, 188, 243, 251, 420

'Fleshly School of Poetry, The', 187

Ford, F. M., see under 'Hueffer'

Ford, G. H., **1**

Ford, W. C., 120

Foregone Conclusion, A, 332

Foreign Parts, 221

Fortnightly Review, The, 245, 278, 450

'Four Meetings', 227, 230, 417, 549

France, Anatole, 365, 369, 404, 467

French Poets and Novelists, 54, 403; sales, 545

Fullerton, Morton, 544

Galaxy, The, 3, 57, 128

Galsworthy, John, 279

Galt, John, 467

Garnett, Edward, 268

Gaskell, Charles Milnes, 120

Gautier, Theophile, 249, 420

'George Sand: The New Life', 335

'Georgina's Reasons', 154, 551

Gibson, W. M., 156

Gilder, R. W., 532

Gill, W. A., 15; compares James with Marivaux, **450–62**

Gladstone, W. E., 8, 190

Godkin, E. L., **5**

Goethe, Johann Wolfgang von, 409, 410, 411, 486, 502

Gohdes, Clarence, 547

Golden Bowl, The, 2, 15, 17, 254, 343, 361, 374–92, 393, 422, 433, 435–6, 447, 448, 499–501, 505, 511, 515, 518; sales, 555–6

Goncourt, Edmond de, 142, 251

Gosse, Edmund, **13**, 18, 361–2, 503, 531; on James's 'little clan', **302**

Graphic, The, 9, **200, 379**

Gretton, M. Sturge, on James's later development, **503–12**

'Guest's Confession', 28, 33

Guy Domville, 13

Handling of Words, The, 480

Hapgood, Norman, on James, **246–53**

Hardy, Thomas, 114, 270, 552; on James, **15, 186**

Harland, H., on James's temperament, **278**

Harlow, Virginia, 19

Harper's Magazine, **70,** 91, 128, 182, **210–12,** 433

Harris, Frank, 544; on James, **245**

Hart-Davis, Rupert, 14, 277, 464

Harte, Bret, 135, 443

Hauptmann, Gerhart, 446

Havens, R. D., 479

Hawthorne, Julian, 125; on James, **140–1**

Hawthorne, Nathaniel, 35, 40, 124, 125, 133, 140, 156, 158, 167, 193, 403, 411–12, 426, 427, 441, 447

Hawthorne (James), 87, 403, 441, 448–9

Hay, John, 324; on James and patriotism, **139**

Head, Ruth, 544

Henley, W. E., 9; on James, **54–5**

Henry James (Hueffer), 543–4; (West), 544

Henry James: Selected Literary Criticism, 542

Henry James Yearbook, The, 544

Hewlett, Maurice, 450

Heywood, J. C., 491

Histoire Contemporaine, 365

Hope, Anthony, on James, **533**

House of the Seven Gables, The, 124, 125, 411–12

Howells, Mildred, 19

Howells, W. D., 5, 10, 17, **21**, **29**, 31, 43, 60, **74**, 109, 113–14, **126–34**, 135–8, 139, 140, 141, 142, **148**, 155, 156, 166, 169, 171–2, 182, 190, 199, **210–12**, 220, 324, 436, 441, **455**, **459**, **478**, **479**, 500, **539**, 548

Hueffer, F. M., on James, 543–4

Huntington, H. A., **111–12**

Hutton, R. H., **49–52**, **75–7**, **88–90**, **93–6**, **162–3**, **175–8**, **185–6**

Huxley, T. H., 8

Hylton, Lady, 538

Ibsen, H. J., 8, 446

Illustrated London News, 14, **378**

'Impressions of a Cousin', 150

In the Cage, 274–6, 283, 308, 400, 417, 488–9; sales, 554

Independent Review, The, **365–72**

Ingelow, Jean, 450

International Episode, An, 75, 80–2, 222, 549

International Library of Famous Literature, 479

Is He Popenjoy?, 56

Jacks, L. P., 263

Jane Eyre, 56, 234

Jeune, Sir Francis, 286

James Family, The, 19, and *passim*

James, Henry, see under titles of individual works

James, William, 9, 17, 19, 27, 158, 161, 194, 318, 393; on the early stories, **24–6**; on James's early style, **28**; on *The Bostonians,* **159–60**; on *The Tragic Muse,* **193**; and Vernon Lee, 238; on success of *The Wings of the Dove,* **317**; on *The Golden Bowl,* **392**; on James's late style, **430–1**

John Inglesant, 8

Johnson, Samuel, 111

Joie de Vivre, La, 143

Joyce, James, 17

Jude the Obscure, 270

Julia Bride, sales, 556–7

Karénina, Mme., 336

Kemble, Mrs. Fanny, 43

Kipling, Rudyard, 264, 369, 443, 445, 481

'Lady Barbarina', 150, 153

Lady of Launay, The, 59–60

Lady of the Aroostook, The, 60

'Lady Tal', 3, **238–42**

Landon Deecroft, 173, 174

'Landscape Painter, A', 4

Lang, Andrew, 10, 170, 171, 184; skit on *Daisy Miller,* **234–6**

'Last of the Valerii, The', 47

Lathrop, G. P., 35

Laurence, Dan H., 19

Lawrence, D. H., on James, **15**

Lee, Sidney, 361

Lee, Vernon, 3, **238–42**; on *The Ambassadors,* **480–7**

Lemuel Barker, 169

Le Sage, Alain René, 452

Lessing, G. E., 399

'Lesson of Balzac, The', 433, 436–7, 443

Lesson of the Master, The, 237, 258, 279, 540; sales, 553

Letters of Henry James, The, 19, and *passim*

Life in Letters of William Dean Howells, 19, and *passim*

Lippincott's Magazine, **10–11**, **118–19**, 128

Literary World, The, **91**, **105–6**, **121–3**, **150–1**, **165**, 208, **272–3**, 294

Literature, **246**, 283–4

Little Tour in France, A, 221, 420

Living Age, The, 503

London Films, 441

London Life, A, 192, 553

Longman's Magazine, 149

Lowell, J. R., 74, 207, 402, 420, 421, 443

Lubbock, P., 19, 539

Lucas, E. V., 157, 304

MacCarthy, Desmond, on James's isolation, **300–1**

Macdonald, Dwight, 544

McIntyre, Clara F., 15; on James's late style, **491–502**

'Madame de Mauves', 33–4, 47, 57, 225–6, 534

'Madonna of the Future, The', 29, 47, 130, 140, 227, 230, 544

Maeterlinck, Count Maurice, 446

Mallet, Sir Charles, 533

Mallock, W. H., 71, 173

Marble Faun, The, 412

Marivaux, Pierre Carlet de Chamblain de, 15, 201; compared with James, 450–62

Martin Chuzzlewit, 126

Matthiessen, F. O., 19, 24, 158

Maupassant, Guy de, 187, 405, 420

Meredith, George, 16, 202, 322, 369, 398, 422, 428, 480, 512

Mérimée, Prosper, 247

Merriman, H. Seton, 319, **321**

'Middle Years, The', 279

Middlemarch, 116

Milman, Lena, on James, **256–7**

Moore, George, 187, 446–7; on James, **15;** on James's limitations, **170–2;** on Howells, **171–2**

Mordell, Albert, 140

Morrison, Arthur, 282

Moulton, Louise Chandler, 450

Mowbray, J. P., **16;** on James, **326–31**

'Mr Oddy', 14, **464–77**

Münsterberg, Dr Hugo, 432, 449

Murray, D. C., on James, **264–5**

Murray's Magazine, 12, **203, 221–33**

Musset, Alfred de, 403

My Life and Loves, 544

Nation, The, **4,** 15, 21, 25, 28, 29, **113–17,** 133, 140, **152, 164,** 165, **180–1, 218–19, 237, 243–4, 298, 385–8**

National Review, The, **190–1**, 544

New Age, The, **488–90**

'New England Winter, A', 142, 148, 150–1

New Statesman, The, **365**

New York edition, 491–512, 531–2; sales, 556

New York Sun, on James's lectures, **436–7**

New York Times, 434, **435–6, 438–9,** 440

Newbolt, Margaret, 538

Newbolt, Sir Henry, on James, **538**

Newcomes, The, 45, 126

'Next Time, The', 261, 540

Nichol, John, on James, **124–5;** 126

North American Review, **6, 39–42, 56–61,** 304, 335, 433, 434, 542

Northanger Abbey, 234

Norton, C. E., 21, 30

Oliphant, Mrs, 270, 450, 548, 551

Other House, The, 261–3, 283, 289, 346, 350, 361, 400, 413, 422, 488; serialization of, 14; sales, 553–4

Ouida, 234, 450

Our Old Home, 441

Outcry, The, 254, 546; sales, 557

'Owen Wingrave', 508

Pall Mall Gazette, 10, 121

Parker, Gilbert, 270

Partial Portraits, 66, 403, 442; sales, 545

Passionate Pilgrim and Other Tales, A, 4, 31–4, 47, 129, 130, 144, 442, 491, 504, 505

Paston, George, 270

Pater, Walter, 458, 480, 543

Payne, W. M., **153, 291**

Paysan Parvenue, Le, 451

Peabody, Miss, 158

Peck, H. T., on James's morbidity, **308**

'Pension Beaurepas, The', 88, 122, 129, 132, 227, 230, 417

Perry, T. S., 9, 22, 35, 45, 79, 87, 135, 149

Phillips, LeRoy, 3, 432, 544

Pictures and Other Passages from Henry James, 544

Pinero, Sir Arthur Wing, 450

'Point of View, The', 139, 415

'Poor Richard', 21, 24–5, 33, 127

Portrait of a Lady, The, 2, 5, 8, 9, 10–11, 93–120, 122–3, 125, 126, 127, 129,

136–8, 144–7, 170, 179, 203, 209, 227, 232, 344, 399, 463, 501, 505, 536, 547; serialization, 547; revision, 496–8; sales, 548, 550–1, 552
Portraits of Places, 221, 420
Pound, Ezra, on James, **542**
Powys, J. C., on James, **542–3**
Pratt, Cornelia Attwood, **307**
Prefaces to N.Y. edition, 502–12
Preston, Harriet Waters, **332–4**
Princess Casamassima, The, 11–12, 157, 158, 159, 173–83, 209, 227–8, 230, 253, 349, 361, 366, 413; sales, 551–2, 553, 554
Princeton Review, 10, **140–1**, **144–7**
Private Life, The, 243–4, 540; sales, 553
Publications of the M.L.A. of America, 15, **491–502**
Punch, 188, 249, 309, 504
'Pupil, The', 237, 279
Putnam's Monthly, **432–49**

Quarterly Review, The, 10, **135–8, 349–58**
'Question of Our Speech, The', 433, 436–7

Radcliffe, Mrs Ann, 467
Rambler, The, 111
Ramsey, Laon, 173, 174
Ray, Gordon N., 529
Robert Elsmere, 8, 534
Robinson, E. A., on James's genius, **258**
Reade, Charles, 66, 133
Real Thing, The, 540; sales, 553
Reich, Emil, 480
Reverberator, The, 185–6, 227, 505; sales, 552–3
Reynolds, Stephen, 488, 490
Richards, I. A., 480
Richardson, Lyon N., 121
Richardson, Samuel, 126, 132, 234, 451
Rise of Silas Lapham, The, 166
Roderick Hudson, 4, 35–42, 47, 65, 114, 126, 130, 144, 155, 230, 247, 319, 332, 366, 367, 442, 505; English edition, 75–8; revision, 491–8; sales, 545, 548, 550, 554

'Romance of Certain Old Clothes, The', 24–5, 31, 479
Romola, 124, 125
Ross, Robert, 277
Rothenstein, William, on James as G.O.M., **305**
Rousseau, Jean-Jacques, 451

Sacred Fount, The, 15, 254, 306–16, 325, 335, 339, 361, 366, 367–8, 405, 408, 418, 435, 442, 447, 501, 506; parody of, **309–16;** sales, 546, 555
Sainte-Beuve, C. A., 22–3, 223; on Marivaux, 453ff
Saintsbury, George, **45–6, 201–2**
Salammbo, 420
Sales of James, 545–57; compared with other authors' sales, 548, 550, 551, 552, 555, 556
Saloon, The, 508
Sand, George, 335, 336–7, 400, 403, 512
Saturday Review, The, **98–100, 197, 261–2, 285, 322–3,** 345, **381–4**
Scott, Sir Walter, 105, 120, 136, 414
Scots Observer, **198–9**
Scribner's Monthly, **47–8, 62,** 79, 126
Scribner's Magazine, 434
Scudder, H. E., **109–10, 166–8**
Seaman, Owen, parody of *The Sacred Fount*, **309–16**
Selected Letters of Henry James, 9, 19, 546, and *passim*
Serialization, 547
Sewanee Review, **299**
Shakespeare, William, 56, 85, 170, 228, 299, 314, 420, 443, 500
Shapira, Morris, 542
Shaw, G. B., 245
Shelley, P. B., 433
Shorter, Clement, 554
Shorthouse, J. H., 8, 173
Sidgwick, H., on Howells and James, **169**
'Siege of London, The', 227, 413–14, 418, 443, 506
Sir Percival, 173
Smalley, Miss E. G., 544

Smith, Harry de Forest, 258

Smith, H. N., 156

Smith, Janet Adam, 184, 541

Soft Side, The, sales, 555

'Solution, The', 227

Spectator, 5, **12**, 15, **49–52, 75–7, 83–6, 88–90, 93–6, 162–3, 175–8, 185–6, 192, 204–5, 259–60, 270–1, 282, 306**

Spoils of Poynton, The, 266–8, 325, 346, 350, 361, 381, 400, 543, 547; sales, 554

Stedman, E. C., 21

Sterne, Laurence, 456

Stevenson, Mrs. R. L., on James, **157**

Stevenson, R. L., 9, 149, 184, 188, 218, 304, 403, 420, 434, 480; on style, **502**

Stockton, F., 165

'Story in It, The', 457

'Story of a Masterpiece, The', 24–5

'Story of a Year, The', 127

Sturgis, Howard, 281, 342

Sudermann, Hermann, 446

Sunday Times, 300

Swift, Johathan, 421

Swinburne, A. C., 245

Taine, H. A., 405, 417, 443

Tales of Three Cities, 150–3; sales, 551

Tauchnitz, Baron, 546

Tener, Robert H., 49

Tennyson, Alfred, Lord, 7, 403, 421

Terminations, 279; sales, 553

Thackeray, W. M., 39, 45, 109, 114, 124, 132, 136, 138, 369, 400, 406, 407, 412, 421, 452

That Lass o' Lowries, 56

Thayer, W. R., 139

Thomas Sergeant Perry, 19, and *passim*

Thoron, Ward, 120

Tilley, Arthur, 135, 544

Times Book Club, 546

Times Literary Supplement, The, **319–21, 374–5,** 489, 538

Tolstoy, Leo, 355, 370, 535

Tom Jones, 114, 126, 174, 191, 234, 422

'Tragedy of Error, A', 3

Tragic Muse, The, 2, 3, 12, 184, 193–220, 227, 228, 229, 250, 253, 319, 346, 361, 381, 478; sales, 552–3

Transatlantic Sketches, 442, 491

Trollope, Anthony, 56, 59–60, 124, 133, 332, 403, 407, 420

Tupper, Martin, 245

Turgenev, Ivan, 40, 54, 68, 84, 114, 125, 140–1, 170, 171, 187, 188, 247, 248, 280, 403, 415, 442

'Turn of the Screw, The', 245, 275, 276, 277, 325, 333, 361, 405

Twain, Mark, 245, 548, 550; on *The Bostonians,* **156**

Two Magics, The, 275–6, 283, 289, 292, 361; sales, 554

Universal Review, The, **187–9**

Vanitas, **238–42**

'Velvet Glove, The', 489

Venetian Life, 441

Vicar of Wakefield, The, 211

Vie de Marianne La, 451, 455–6, 457

Von Arnim, Countess, 555

Wagner, Richard, 7

Walpole, Hugh, 14; fictional reminiscence of James, **464–77**

Ward, Mrs Humphry, 8, 253; on James, **534–7**

Washington Square, 5, 88–92, 225, 226, 547; sales, 550, 551

Waterlow, Sydney, 15, 544; on James as a modern writer, **365–72**

Watch and Ward, 547

Watson, William, on James, **190–1**

Watt, Ian, 480

Wedgewood, Julia, **173–4**

Wells, H. G., 15, 373, 527–30, 534; attack on and parody of James, **517–26**

West, Rebecca, 544

Wharton, Edith, 14, 335, 395, 544, 557; on James's sensitivity, **342–4**

What Maisie Knew, 269–73, 283, 287, 292, 308, 325, 333, 361, 366, 401, 421, 435, 447, 513, 536, 547; sales, 554

Wheel of Time, The, 243–4

Whistler, James Abbott McNeill, 204

White, Richard Grant, 6, 7, 9, 16, **56–61**

Whitman, Walt, 447–8

Wilde, Oscar, 462; on 'The Turn of the Screw', **277**

Wilhelm Meister, 409

William Wetmore Story and His Friends, 366, 441, 448

Wings of the Dove, The, 16, 254, 317–34, 339–41, 343, 345, 349, 350–8, 361, 366, 391, 511, 515, 534, 535; revision, 515; sales, 555

Woolson, Constance F., **66–9**, 142, 143, 420

Wreck of the Grosvenor, The, 70

Yellow Book, The, **256–7**, 278, 543

Zabel, Morton Dauwen, 513

Zola, Emile, 8, 133, 142, 143, 400

10